Contemporary Models
of Psychotherapy

Contemporary Models of Psychotherapy

A Comparative Analysis

SECOND EDITION

by

Donald H. Ford

Hugh B. Urban

John Wiley & Sons Inc.

New York • Chichester • Weinheim • Brisbane • Singapore • Toronto

This text is printed on acid-free paper.

Copyright © 1998 by John Wiley & Sons, Inc.

This publication is designed to provide accurate and authoritative information in regard to the subject matter covered. It is sold with the understanding that the publisher is not engaged in rendering professional services. If legal, accounting, medical, psychological, or any other advice or other expert assistance is required, the services of a competent professional person should be sought.

Library of Congress Cataloging-in-Publication Data:

Ford, Donald Herbert, 1921–
    Contemporary models of psychotherapy : a comparative analysis / by Donald H. Ford, Hugh B. Urban.—2nd ed.
        p.   cm.
    Rev. ed. of: Systems of psychotherapy. 1963.
    Includes bibliographical references (p.   ) and indexes.
    ISBN 0-471-59638-8 (hardcover : alk. paper)
    1. Psychotherapy.   I. Urban, Hugh B., 1926–   .   II. Ford, Donald Herbert, 1921– Systems of psychotherapy.   III. Title.
    RC480.F62 1998
    616.89'14—dc21   97-28994
                                                                                        CIP

Printed in the United States of America

10 9 8 7 6 5 4 3 2 1

To Carol and Natalie for putting up with us all these years

Contents

Preface

THIS BOOK IS about theories of psychotherapy. Its purpose is not to describe how to do psychotherapy but rather to compare the different theories that guide it—their guiding assumptions, concepts, and propositions about the nature of normal and dysfunctional human development, and their strategies and tactics for facilitating change. We believe that each of the hundreds of therapies in existence must share some similarities because they all deal with the same basic phenomena—the nature of humans' being and becoming in natural, designed, social, and cultural contexts. This book identifies families of approaches that differ in guiding assumptions and intervention strategies; it analyzes exemplars of each family in terms of their conceptual, propositional, and procedural models so as to identify and compare similarities and differences in contemporary psychotherapy approaches. Ideas of over 300 different psychotherapy theorists are considered, with several dozen examined in detail.

Contemporary Models of Psychotherapy has three sections. Section I describes a framework for comparing approaches. Section II defines families of approaches and analyzes contemporary exemplars of each family. Section III examines similarities and differences among the families in their conceptual, propositional, and procedural models and discusses implications of the findings.

This book should be useful to all therapists; however, we believe it will be particularly useful to beginners or those early in their careers, because they will be the primary source of future advances. To that end, we begin by examining the nature of theory and theory construction to help them become better theorists in their own right, and to provide a historical perspective for understanding the development of psychotherapy approaches. Experienced therapists typically have implicitly or explicitly developed a guiding model and strong habits of practice related to it. This book can help them make their own approaches more explicit to themselves, and help them elaborate and polish their preferred approaches in service to their clients. Others who have a general interest in normal development, psychopathology and psychotherapy will find this book a useful, less technical summary and comparison of existing theories and change strategies.

The book can be used as a text for graduate level courses in clinical psychology, counseling professions, social work, psychiatry, psychoanalysis, and psychiatric nursing to show similarities and differences among psychotherapy approaches. Students can be asked to apply the comparative analysis method used in the book to approaches not covered here and to do their own comparative analyses of these therapy approaches as another way of helping them develop skill as theorists and in analyzing and understanding therapy approaches. *Contemporary Models of Psychotherapy* can also be used by psychiatrists and clinical psychologists to prepare for various kinds of licensure, board, and certification examinations. It can also serve as a text for advanced undergraduate courses surveying psychotherapy or counseling approaches.

We thank Wiley's associate managing editor Joseph Mills and the Wiley copy editors for their efforts to help produce a first rate book. We express our gratitude to the many clients and colleagues who have shared their meanings and lives with us and have helped to deepen our understanding of human nature over the past half century. It is they, and our loving, supportive spouses—Carol and Natalie—who have motivated us and given us the courage to attempt this daunting task. The ideas in this book are not ours, but those of thousands of creative psychotherapists and scientists. We have sought to assemble those ideas in integrated form to make them more accessible to others. Our contribution lies not so much in their content as in their organization.

DONALD H. FORD
HUGH B. URBAN

Prologue
Psychotherapy Approaches: Past and Present

THIRTY-FIVE YEARS AGO we conducted a comparative analysis of 10 major approaches to psychotherapy (Ford & Urban, 1963). That effort was motivated by our own continuous involvement in psychotherapy and by questions raised by clinical psychology doctoral students, such as "How can I decide whether a psychoanalytic or a client-centered approach is more effective?" "How do Sullivanian, Freudian, or Adlerian approaches differ?" "Should I use the same approach with every client, or would one approach be better for one type of client and a different approach better for another?" "Would it be possible and effective to mix different approaches?" "Are there any guiding principles for understanding how different therapy techniques produce changes?" "Is there any way to apply the knowledge-being generated in scientific Psychology about perception, cognition, emotions, personality and learning to psychotherapy theory and practice?" "How can I determine when and under what conditions a therapy intervention is effective?"

CURRENT CHARACTERISTICS OF PSYCHOTHERAPY

The way in which psychotherapy has expanded since 1963 is extraordinary. Change is apparent in virtually every aspect. The history of advances in the field has been admirably summarized in Freedheim's recent *History of Psychotherapy* (1992).

DIVERSITY OF PSYCHOTHERAPIES

There has been a remarkable proliferation in the variety of psychotherapeutic approaches. Instead of sculpting and refining the seminal therapy systems created by 1960, practitioners have increased them. As of 1986, the number of different approaches had grown to over 400 (Karasu, 1986). Many variants of each major approach have been developed. An array of other intervention methods has been added to traditional interview methods, significantly broadening the definition of psychotherapy. For students and professionals, this explosion has magnified the problem of deciding what approaches to use, with what clients, when, and how to evaluate their efficacy.

PSYCHOTHERAPY PROVIDERS AND SETTINGS

Mirroring the expansion in therapeutic approaches is the number and diversity of professionals engaged in psychotherapy. Nonmedically trained psychotherapists now provide the majority of services. These practitioners are legitimized by accreditation and continuing professional education requirements, authorized by state licensure laws, and sanctioned by third-party payers. Cushman (1992) reports that in 1990 there were approximately 10,000 psychologists, 6,500 psychiatrists, 11,000 clinical social workers, and 19,000 marriage, family, and child therapists in the state of California alone! By some estimates, at least 100,000 fully qualified, highly trained psychotherapists are in current practice throughout the United States, and this number rises to roughly 250,000 when broader definitions of competence are employed (Vandenbos, Cummings, & Deleon, 1992).

Public knowledge, acceptance, and use of psychotherapeutic services has also grown. By 1990, at least one-third of the U.S. population had used psychotherapy at some point in their lives (Vandenbos et al., 1992). Psychotherapeutic settings have also become more numerous and diverse. Facilities such as marital and family services, day care centers, partial hospitalization programs, supervised community residences, rehabilitation services, and drug treatment programs have been added to the traditional inpatient units, outpatient clinics, and private consulting offices that predominated in 1963.

PSYCHOTHERAPY CLIENTS

Accompanying increased numbers has been diversification in the clientele utilizing psychotherapy. In 1963, psychotherapy was not widely available, was fairly expensive, and carried some stigma for users. Typical clients were white, Anglo-Saxon, middle-aged or young adults from advantaged backgrounds. Most were suffering from neuroses or problems of living. U.S. government initiatives and the health insurance industry's inclusion of psychotherapy as a health benefit in recent years has helped stimulate service to new client populations and promote greater public acceptance of such services.

Treatment methods were adapted and extended for use with clients previously underserved, such as adolescents and small children as well as the elderly. Other adaptations were created to recognize gender differences; to meet the needs of a multicultural population, including African Americans, Hispanics, and Native Americans; and to serve clients from less advantaged socioeconomic groups. The methods were also adjusted to address a much more extensive range of problems. Psychotherapy is now applied to a broad array of physiological, psychological, behavioral, and interpersonal difficulties.

ECONOMIC AND SOCIAL CONSEQUENCES

This broad pattern of treatments and their use by large numbers of people indicates that the field of psychotherapy is now a well-established and economically profitable health-service industry. With psychotherapy becoming legitimized as a treatment, people have demanded equal access to service; this demand has led to problems in equitable distribution and funding. Psychotherapy has thus experienced the same cost escalation as health services generally. The problem of cost containment is particularly difficult, as psychotherapy has been traditionally reimbursed in terms of time spent rather than procedures used, as is the case in most other health services. The combination of increased demand and steadily increasing costs has led to growing pressures for accountability in psychotherapy as in other health services.

As a result, the practice of psychotherapy is being subjected to evaluative criteria similar to those that Americans characteristically apply to any product or service industry. Purchasers of the service expect increasing levels of effectiveness, defined as maximal beneficial effects at minimal cost. These pressures are forcing providers to get their houses in better order—both conceptually and procedurally—to meet society's demands.

The demands themselves have assumed a variety of forms. Mechanisms were initially directed toward attaining greater efficiency through cost-containment practices, such as benefit limitations, utilization reviews, and discounted reimbursement rates. Recently, expectations have moved toward accountability with respect to effects—documenting not only the nature of treatments used but also the extent of beneficial outcomes. Together these have accelerated the search for high-effect, low-cost procedures. Brief psychotherapy sufficient to ameliorate the presenting problem and targeted, problem-focused treatments capable of generating definable and observable outcomes are being favored over longer-term approaches (Vandenbos et al., 1992). Additionally, a growing tendency is to emulate medicine by pursuing a different approach to the treatment of different problems occurring in differing persons functioning under different conditions. Recognition of this trend appears in recent professional literature organized around the specification of problematic conditions and their treatment, in the practice guidelines being developed by various entities and in the trend toward managed care delivery systems (e.g., Newman, 1993). There are now guidelines defining contemporary professional standards for treating specified conditions, such as Major Depressive, Bipolar, Schizophrenic, or Panic Disorders. Also, the U.S. Department of Health and Human Services issued clinical practice guidelines in March 1992 recommending behavior therapy as the first-line approach to treating urinary incontinence in adults. Funding for research on patient-treatment matching is another indicator of this trend.

Despite the consternation these developments have produced in some professionals, they hold considerable merit, pressing the field in the direction recognized as being needed some 30 years ago (Ford & Urban, 1963). The move is toward the creation and validation of systematic procedures to specify with precision *what* needs to be changed, *how* it needs to be changed, *which* procedures can systematically effect those changes, and *how* one can determine whether the desired outcomes have been attained. The idea that one type of treatment serves all is no longer tenable.

The human sciences have made major strides in addressing many of the issues about human nature identified as important to psychotherapists in our 1963 analysis, and which the human sciences had been largely ignoring (e.g., see D. Ford, 1987, 1992). For example, there has been a massive expansion of theory and research in psychology concerning cognitive processes; attention and consciousness; and the nature, functioning, and learnability of different kinds of emotions. A growing literature identifies how personal goals, goal setting, and personal agency beliefs and emotions motivate and organize human behavior (M. Ford, 1992). Knowledge has developed concerning the ways in which genetic predispositions and biological processes can influence psychological and behavioral functioning and vice versa, leading to applications in health psychology and behavioral medicine. Much more is known about differences in developmental patterns across the life span (Ford & Lerner, 1992). Psychotherapists can no longer argue that little knowledge in the basic human sciences has potential relevance to psychotherapy. In fact, tapping into that growing knowledge base may be one of the quickest routes for psychotherapists to meet the increasing accountability demands of the society they serve. Integration and differentiation among therapy theories themselves is therefore insufficient; integration with the basic human sciences is likewise needed.

However, the human sciences have been slow to create unifying theories. These are theories that would combine basic knowledge about various parts of humans into broad representations of humans as complete entities. For example, psychology concentrates on organizing its empirical data with minitheories that represent some aspects of humans, but, none of these represents the whole person. This fragmentation has led some to call for a subdiscipline of theoretical psychology (Slife & Williams, 1997). Staats (1991), has observed, "We will never achieve a related, meaningful, coherent, compact, and parsimonious field of knowledge if we do not relate and organize the phenomena studied" (p. 905). Bevan (1991) expressed a similar view:

> My concern is, rather, that the character of psychology is increasingly manifest in the rapid proliferation of narrowly focused and compulsively insular camps, a proliferation that seemingly knows no limits. We persevere in looking at small questions instead of large ones and our view of the forest is forever obscured by the trees. Yet, specialized knowledge derives its meaning. . . . from the context of larger perspectives and questions. When it loses touch with that larger context, it loses its coherence and meaning." (Bevan, 1991, p. 475)

Minitheories are essential because they help to integrate empirical findings and explain component processes. Some say that fragmentation through specialization "is a perfectly natural outgrowth of the maturing of a science" (Bower, 1993, p. 905) and that the resulting diversity of specialized domains means that "there cannot be any kind of coherent discipline devoted to the empirical study of human beings" (Koch, 1993, p. 902). In psychotherapy, however, it is not wise to separate a part of a living person from the whole being. Humans always function as a person in a context as a result of the integrated behavior of their component structures and processes. Thus, an empirical science of humans may operate without integrative theories, but professionals who must deal with real people in real life contexts cannot do so. To be of utility to psychotherapists, comprehensive theories must combine minitheories to show the interrelatedness of a person's biological, psychological, behavioral, and environmental characteristics with which therapists must deal in their day to day work. Perhaps psychotherapy scholars can provide leadership in creating larger integrative frameworks within which the minitheories of basic discipline scientists can be related to one another and made useful to therapists and their clients.

Moreover, the continuing verification of therapy approaches needs to be seen as a form of applied research. Psychotherapists need to use the growing diversity and sophistication of research methods in the human sciences to meet society's increasing demands for accountability. Likewise, the human sciences can learn much from the kinds of methodological sophistication psychotherapists have developed with qualitative methods and as participant observers in the study of the nature and dynamics of complex human behavior during the psychotherapy process.

It is within this current cultural milieu that we have prepared this book. It responds to requests from our publisher and colleagues over the past 20 years to do a new analysis. Its objectives are to look beneath the surface diversity of current psychotherapies to identify basic similarities and differences, to facilitate theoretical and technical advances, and to facilitate linkage of advances in basic human sciences to advances in psychotherapy.

HUMANS AS COMPLEX SYSTEMS: A FRAMEWORK FOR COMPARING PSYCHOTHERAPIES

O NE IMPORTANT OBSTACLE to understanding and comparing different psychotherapy approaches is that psychotherapist scholars and psychological scientists have invented their own conceptual and propositional language jargon for their particular approaches, which makes it difficult to determine whether they are talking about different phenomena or whether they are simply using different words. Because they are all examining the same human phenomena—different aspects of humans as they develop, function, and change in varying contexts—there must be some shared meanings underlying their differences in technical terminology. If underlying similarities are identified in their ideas and methods, linkages might emerge among seemingly disparate approaches and potentially relevant knowledge bases. Similarly, when important differences are identified, they could be targeted for further investigation.

Now, however, direct comparison of different theorists' concepts and propositions is not possible because the same words might mean different things, and different words might mean the same things. For example, the word *anxiety* has been used to mean fear; a combination of distressing emotions such as anger, fear and depression; or certain patterns of evaluative thought. Therefore, some standard way is needed, to represent the *meanings* underlying each theorist's terminology so that ideas can be compared. For example, the height of things can be compared by using the same framework (e.g., measuring in inches). Different comparison frames are possible (e.g., inches or centimeters), but meaningful comparisons are possible as long as the same frame is used for all comparisons.

Section I summarizes a comparison framework for these analyses that represents a theory-based way to link the extensive knowledge bases of psychotherapy and basic human sciences. A more detailed presentation and justification of that framework can be found in *Humans as Self-Constructing Living Systems* by D. Ford (1987, 1994). Copies are available from IDEALS, INC., 130 Slab Cabin Lane, State College, PA 16801.

CHAPTER 1

Theories and Models: Tools for Simplifying Complexity

THE STREAM OF life is composed of a multitude of events and processes that occur in continually varying patterns. How can we comprehend and deal with this complexity? Without some simplifying strategy, we would be incapable of coping with the kaleidoscopic events that arise each day. This chapter describes how models can be used to simplify life's complexity and facilitate an effective understanding, and response to these events. Psychotherapy theories are a particular kind of model for describing the elaborate detail, varying organization, and flow of clients' lives and development, and for guiding psychotherapeutic interventions. A comparative analysis of psychotherapy theories requires a framework for comparison. The following brief review of the nature and functions of models provides a context for creating this framework.

THE NATURE AND FUNCTION OF MODELS

THE PROBLEM

As therapists try to understand clients, the clients are changing. People are bombarded with constantly changing situations every day. These multiple person and context variables are intricately related and interact in different ways and to different degrees. Moreover, these patterns change over time. It is impossible to represent the content and organization of this complex flow of events in all of its intricate detail in an understandable and useful form. Yet humans do effectively cope with varying complexity every day. How do we do it?

THE SOLUTION

Evolution has endowed us with capabilities for constructing simplified representations of our complex realities and for using them to organize and guide our thoughts and actions. For example, if we cannot simultaneously identify and comprehend every detail of a particular situation, our minds selectively focus on some aspects and ignore others. This leads us to construct generalized representations or models of consistent patterns and ignore the moment-to-moment variability. There are different types of models, and a *theory* will be described later as one particularly useful type of model—a *symbolic model.*

The meaning of new perceptions results when we combine current news about a situation with our previously constructed generalized representations. Therefore, whenever we use a model to understand and guide our behavior in a specific situation we must interpret it to fit the specifics of that situation. Because our perspectives are continually changing, we react differently to situations at different times, and our coping models may not be sufficiently equipped to respond. Thus, models must be modifiable by further experience. New representations can be constructed by disassembling, combining, and reassembling existing ones. This process may produce new representations that have no obvious relationship to any personal experience or observable reality and even of things that may not exist.

Humans build and use coping models throughout their lives. Every model has some similarities to the situation it represents, but a model selectively emphasizes and omits information to serve the purposes of the person constructing it. Such representations have been given various labels, (e.g., concepts, propositions, hypotheses, schemas, conceptual frameworks, theories and models). We will use the term model to encompass all forms of generalized, simplifying representations.

People often construct different models from the same set of situations or ideas. Using different models leads to different responses, which can result in misunderstandings and conflict among people. It is possible, through education and socialization, however, for people to share the same models. Shared models produce similarities in interpretations and behaviors among individuals, which provides the basis for social organization and group living.

A good model aids humans' attempts at understanding; themselves, others, and their environments; and predicting and influencing future events. It makes communication among people possible, and enables collective and individual action. Scientists use hypotheses and theories to construct and improve the soundness of models so that people have a sounder basis for accepting and using them as shared models.

It is generally accepted now that all observations and behavior is theory guided. For example, Popper (1963) states "The belief that we can start with pure observation alone, without anything in the nature of a theory is absurd. . . . observation is always selection." (p. 46) O'Donohue and Krasner (1995) state "Their significance is created through their relationships with other claims, particularly . . . theoretical claims." (p. 696)

THE UNIVERSALITY AND MAJOR TYPES OF MODELS

Everyone uses models. People typically are unaware of their reliance on models to organize and guide their behavior. However, they could not function or manage their affairs without relying on generalized representations of themselves, their world, and potential future events. Any set of phenomena can be represented with different types of models. Each type has different characteristics and logical properties. Different models have different relationships to each other and to what they are intended to represent; different advantages and disadvantages are associated with their use. Therefore, each has greater utility for some purposes than for others. A review of some of the different kinds of models that people typically use for personal, social, and professional purposes can illustrate their universality.

ICONIC MODELS

An *iconic model* is one of the most specific and concrete models. An icon is a two- or three-dimensional model that looks like what it represents. Photographs, paintings, and sculptures are iconic models, as are a toy automobile, a globe, perceptual images, and imagistic memories. In general, the properties of iconic models are isomorphic with the things being represented, so they are well-suited for representing characteristics of things as they exist at a particular moment. They can represent dynamic as well as static events (such as a motion picture) but are less useful as representations of dynamic processes.

Iconic models are often larger or smaller than what they represent. On a globe, for example, the size of the earth and its features are scaled down, but their relative shapes and sizes remain approximately correct. A model of an atom is scaled upward to make it more readily visible. Transformations of scale make these models easier to use. Human ingenuity has led to many elaborations of iconic models (e.g., holograms; virtual realities).

Analogue Models

An *analogue model* employs one set of properties to represent the actual set of properties of the idea or event using transformation rules. Maps are familiar examples. Unlike an iconic model, the representation is analogous to, rather than isomorphic with, the phenomena represented. However, the representations are selected to resemble in some respect certain aspects of the phenomena—the width of a line on the map is analogous to the width of a road.

Graphs are analogue models; they convert a mathematical relationship into a visual image. In a decision-chart, for example, boxes are used to represent functions to be performed, arrows indicate the sequence of actions to be carried out, and diamonds represent the decisions that need to be successively made.

Analogue models are easier to manipulate and modify than are iconic models because they are not isomorphic. For example, it is easier to change the contour lines on a two-dimensional map than to rebuild a three-dimensional iconic model. Analogue models, unlike iconic models, can be used to represent processes or successive changes. Another advantage is that an analogue model can be used to represent different processes of a similar type, so they are more generalizable; but to understand the meaning of an analogue model requires knowledge of its transformation rules. For example, a dream's symbolism may be an analogue model, but to understand its meaning, the interpreter must decode the dream imagery in terms of the dreamer's private meanings or transformation rules.

Symbolic Models

Symbolic models represent ideas, things, or events by using intrinsically meaningless symbols. Unlike iconic and analogue models, there is no similarity between the representation and what is represented. Verbal descriptions, mental models, scripts, and mathematical formulas are types of symbolic models. A set of transformation rules is required to map the meaning of the symbols onto the phenomena represented because their relationship is completely arbitrary. Linguistic representations follow the rules of the language used (e.g., word definitions and rules of grammar). Mathematical representations follow the rules of a particular mathematical system (e.g., algebra or geometry).

Scientists and professionals construct and use linguistic and mathematical symbolic models (theories) all the time. Scientists use them to simplify and explain empirical findings and to guide the design, execution, and interpretation of their research. Professionals use them to guide their professional plans and actions. For example, the *medical model* provides physicians with a generic framework within which the defining characteristics, causes, etiology, prognosis, and methods of treating any specific illness can be identified and applied. Diagnostic manuals such as the *Diagnostic and Statistical Manual of Mental Disorders* (DSM-IV) (American Psychiatric Association, 1994) describe symbolic models—prototypical representations of different kinds of psychiatric syndromes.

The methods that health professionals use are also symbolic models, frequently called *procedural models* or treatment protocols. Procedural models are prescriptive; they specify what ought to be done, when, and under what conditions to produce a particular outcome. B. F. Skinner's behavior modification strategy is a procedural model as are Freud's therapy strategy and experimental research designs.

Procedural models are typically linked to, or derived from, a rationale that explains why they work. This rationale, or symbolic model, is called a *propositional model or theory*. For example, Freud proposed that (1) three major sets of psychological phenomena—*id, ego,* and *superego*—interact to create personality and behavior patterns; and (2) several types of psychological/behavior patterns, which he called *defenses,* function to protect and maintain existing personality patterns. His theory led to a procedural model that included methods for overcoming resistances (e.g., free association) and methods (e.g., interpretations) for altering troublesome patterns. Scientists often use a procedural model called an experimental design that reflects a theory about the nature of causal relationships among things, events, or variables.

Propositional and procedural models have two types of origins. *Empirical propositional models or laws* summarize observed consistencies in sets of similar occurrences. Skinner's generalizations concerning schedules of reinforcement are examples. Psychotherapists trying to create treatment plans based solely on empirical evidence of effectiveness, or on clinical experience are using an empirical model. *Theoretical propositional models* utilize, but go beyond, existing empirical evidence. By combining creative thought and empirical evidence, they seek to explain why empirical regularities occur and to make it possible to anticipate or predict what may occur in a wider array of potential future occasions. For example, Einstein's theory of relativity not only explained existing empirical knowledge but also predicted new possibilities.

Methods created as an expression of a propositional model may work even though the theoretical explanation that led to their creation later turns out to be incorrect. Therapists seeking *theoretical integration* construct a broad theoretical propositional model that encompasses and explains the operation of methods of proven utility (i.e., diverse procedural models) regardless of their initial theoretical origins. Theoretical propositional models are the most powerful form of model because they enable humans to go beyond what we already know and can do and guide us in charting the unknown. For example, in a situation where empirical evidence for guiding action is inadequate or does not exist, a potentially applicable procedural model can be deduced from a relevant theory. Therapists refer to the "art" of psychotherapy when they make treatment decisions based on theory in the absence of adequate empirical evidence.

MIXED MODELS

A single model may suffice to represent a limited amount of information (e.g., a three-dimensional iconic model of a proposed new building), but to represent large and complex amounts of information, a combination of models is often more effective. For example, books, newspapers, and magazines combine linguistic and mathematical symbolic models with iconic (pictures) and analogue (tables and graphs) models. Each type of model presents certain kinds of information better than others, and combining them can create new models and facilitate communication. Psychotherapy approaches often combine procedural models. For example, when actors act out a scene they create an iconic model; when observed by a therapy client, this model may effect changes in the client's mental or symbolic model representing that kind of social interaction. The therapist's interpretations—a symbolic model—may be used to add to the influence.

LEVELS OF MODELS

Models also vary in the scope or range of phenomena they represent. The greater the number, variety, and organizational complexity of the phenomena or ideas a model encompasses, the more inclusive and removed it becomes from actual experience. For example, a model representing depressive states would be less inclusive than one intended to represent all types of dysfunctional states. Models can range from micromodels of specific and elementary levels of phenomena up to the most inclusive levels, called metamodels. Models are related to one another in hierarchical patterns, with micromodels representing components of more inclusive models, as illustrated in Table 1.1.

Each level of model requires analytic units appropriate to that level. For example, the levels and units of analysis that biologists use in their study of cells are different from those psychologists use in their study of human thoughts and actions, which in turn are different from the ones sociologists use in studying social institutions. Each scholar and each practitioner uses a pri-

Table 1.1.   An illustration of the way models may represent an embedded hierarchy of phenomena. Each level of model represents a level of analysis that requires its own units of analysis and may, to some extent, be studied separately from other levels. However, because each higher level is an organization of components represented in lower levels and is embedded in levels above it, knowledge of interrelationships between levels, particularly adjacent levels, is also important.

Levels of Representation	Content of Representation	Levels/Units of Analysis
Meta-Model	The Universe	nth order level of analysis
	Galaxies	|
		|
	The Biosphere	|
Macro-Models	Human Habitats	|
	Human Colonies	|
		|
	Human Organisms	|
Mid-Range Models	Human Organ Systems	|
	Human Organs	|
	Human Tissues	3rd order level of analysis
Micro-Models	Human Cells	2nd order level of analysis
	Organelles	1st order level of analysis

mary level of analysis, sometimes called the unit of reference. As models are human constructions, decisions about how to analyze phenomena are arbitrary, but not capricious. They must serve the purposes of the person constructing them and usefully represent some portion of reality. For example, a family therapist's primary level and unit of analysis is the family, whereas geneticists' primary level is the genetic material in a cell.

The strategy of analytic science is to take things apart to try to understand them; this is called *reductionism.* On the other hand, practitioners must be synthesizers. Use of these different strategies creates a schism between scientists and practitioners. The different levels are related to one another, and knowledge of how the levels are related is important; as a practical matter, however, developing models for understanding different levels can proceed independent of one another (e.g., Simon, 1992). For example, one can understand the content and logic of a computer program without understanding the electronic circuitry that makes its operation possible. Therefore, models useful to psychotherapists focused on person-level functioning need not encompass many other micro- or macro-level models (e.g., of individual cells or societies).

However, it is typically unwise to ignore all other levels. Adequate understanding of any level usually requires at least some understanding of how that level is related to levels immediately below and above it. Psychotherapy often requires knowledge of multilevel interactions. For example, when a client suffers from a depressive state, the procedural model should differ depending on whether the faulty pattern results from a brain tumor (the organ system level), chronic negative self-evaluative and anticipatory thoughts (the cognitive level), or rejecting behaviors of others (the social level). Sometimes levels beyond the next highest or lowest may be important. For example, current evidence indicates that neurotransmitter dysfunctions may influence depressive states.

Linking knowledge from different levels is difficult because different symbolic codes are used (e.g., biological; psychological; sociological), and few models exist that integrate these levels of influence. This lack of shared understanding between scientists and practitioners obstructs progress because there are no transformation rules for mapping the meanings of the symbolic jargon at one model level onto those at another level (e.g., relating neurochemical imbalances to psychological malfunctions).

VARIETIES OF MODELS

Because everyone constructs and uses models, there are potentially as many models as there are phenomena and people in the world. Multiple models exist at personal, social, and cultural levels, and people may use conflicting models both within and between levels.

Personal Models
All people construct and use their own personal models or theories about all sorts of things. These are often called personal constructs, mental models, schemas, or personal theories. We all, for example, have some personal model as to what we are like, what others around us are like, what our own sector of the world is about and how to behave in different settings. Models representing ourselves are called self-images, self-constructs, self-concepts, or just the self. Cognitive maps are mental models constructed to guide us through

spatial surroundings. Frequently used personal models become habitual and operate automatically outside of our awareness; this can be troublesome if they are faulty in any way. Each person's models have some distinctive and unique features, but no one's models can ever be entirely unique. If they were, communicative exchanges, collaborative actions, or cultural creations based on human experience would not be possible. Each person would have to reinvent the wheel.

Social-Level Models

When people have similar personal models, a social-level model exists. Being reared within the same culture, using the same language, being exposed to comparable educational programs, and living in a similar historical period all increase the likelihood that individuals' personal models are similar enough to enable them to function collaboratively as components in social groups. Schools and socialization practices are designed to create and maintain shared models. Shared models facilitate family cohesiveness.

Cultural Models

When a large group of people has a shared history, they produce a cultural model. These models become institutionalized in various cultural forms such as religion, law, literature, customs, and the arts. Scientific models are a type of cultural model. They are constructed and evaluated using special methods intended to limit the role of personal bias and idiosyncratic views in the choice of social and cultural models used by human societies.

Thus, everyone uses models, but people may differ in the form and substance of their models and the extent to which they are aware of them. The work of all psychotherapists is guided by some (at least implicit) conceptual, propositional, and procedural models representing the nature of humans and psychotherapeutic processes. Professional responsibility and client welfare require all psychotherapists to make their guiding models, assumptions, or beliefs as clear and explicit as possible—at least to themselves—because only then can they evaluate, modify, and improve them. Growing demands from society for accountability will increasingly require this.

MODELS CONCERNING THE NATURE OF HUMANS

Psychotherapy theories are models representing the nature of humans, including why and how they remain the same or change. Every theory is constructed within the framework of some starting assumptions or beliefs that are accepted as givens; these are often called metamodels, paradigms, or worldviews. Differences among theories and psychotherapy theorists often seem irreconcilable because they are based in different metamodels. The roots of contemporary psychotherapy metamodels go far back in history where the major alternatives for representing the nature of humans and reality were created. Interpersonal differences in the guiding assumptions of theorists, therapists, and clients are a frequent source of misunderstanding and conflict because they typically remain tacit and unstated.

Concern with metamodels is no idle academic exercise. People's worldviews selectively influence the ideas and actions they will accept and perform: What is normal or abnormal? How do people change? Different worldviews represent alternate answers to basic questions about reality (metaphysics) and how humans apprehend it (epistemology). Every therapy approach implies some metaphysical and epistemological assumptions that are seldom made an explicit part of its theory. They remain unexamined because intuitively they seem self-evident or true. However, what appears self-evident to one theorist may be suspect to another; allegiance to different guiding assumptions yields significant theoretical differences.

Another reason for examining a theory's starting assumptions is that if those assumptions are in error, all that logically derives from them is likely to be erroneous as well. This observation is often not appreciated by psychotherapists or behavioral scientists (Meehl, 1997; Mahoney, 1996). Moreover, it is incorrect on formal logical grounds to conclude that a true conclusion implies a true premise; because a therapy method works doesn't necessarily mean that the theory from which it was derived is true. That is why Popper (1972) argued that science cannot succeed in its search for answers if it takes its basic premises for granted, seeking only to gather confirmatory evidence in support of them. It must attempt disconfirmation instead. When a conclusion is demonstrated to be false, one can validly infer that the assumptions from which it is derived must also be false if the appropriate rules of reasoning have been followed.

Historically, several types of guiding assumptions have been developed that undergird contemporary therapy approaches. There may be as many as 400 different psychotherapy approaches (Beitman, Goldfried, & Norcross, 1989). But how different are they? Inspection of their underlying assumptions reveals that they can be classified as operating from a limited number of major metamodel alternatives. Therefore, they probably represent a limited number of general theoretic families. Throughout history, philosophers have devoted extensive, sophisticated thought to these metaphysical issues. A brief excursion into philosophy will help identify the alternative assumptions around which psychotherapy theories have coalesced. The sophisticated, highly technical treatments they have received in the philosophical literature cannot be summarized here (see Mahoney, 1988, 1991, and Davar and Bhat, 1995, for summaries relevant to psychotherapy and psychoanalysis, and Reese and Overton, 1970, Overton and Reese, 1973, for relevance to theories of development). However, a brief overview of principal options is useful. Later, families of psychotherapy theories are identified based on their allegiance to different metaphysical and epistemological assumptions.

THE METAPHYSICAL PROBLEM: WHAT IS REALITY?

The metaphysical question concerning the nature of reality has two parts: What is reality made of (ontology)? How is it organized (cosmology)?

The Ontological Question
Key components of every theory are its concepts, which specify the phenomena it seeks to explain; but selection of concepts implies some prior assumptions about the ontological question, "What is the substance of reality and of humans?" If one assumes that everything, including humans' experience, is composed of the same substance and it is materials, the resulting concepts will be different from those that emerge from assuming that there are different kinds of substances—material and immaterial; body and mind. A theory's *conceptual model* reflects and is constrained by its ontological assumptions.

The Cosmological Question
A theory also requires propositions about how the content of interest is organized and functions. However, selection of propositions implies prior assumptions about or answers to the cosmological question: "How is the world organized, and how does it operate and change?" Both regularities and variations exist, and different assumptions about their nature are possible, (such as gestalt and association assumptions in psychology), leading to different propositional formats. A key philosophical and scientific concern has been with questions of chance, causality, and personal agency as propositional forms. A theory's initial cosmological assumptions shape its *propositional model.*

THE EPISTEMOLOGICAL PROBLEM: HOW DO HUMANS KNOW REALITY AND CONSTRUCT KNOWLEDGE?

Any theory that addresses humans' relationships to their world and themselves requires some starting assumptions about the basic epistemological question: "What is the place of human subjectivity in nature, and how do humans apprehend, understand, and guide their interactions with themselves and their world?" These questions address the correspondence between objects and events in the world, humans' comprehension of them, and the relationship of that comprehension to the knowledge and actions that humans construct. Originally called the philosophy of mind, this is now called epistemology. A theory's guiding epistemological assumptions are manifest in its procedural model.

ALTERNATIVE ONTOLOGICAL ASSUMPTIONS: THE NATURE OF REALITY

The issues of metaphysics and epistemology are interrelated; a solution to one typically leads to a particular commitment regarding the other. Over the centuries, philosophers have proposed alternative guiding assumptions, and psychotherapy approaches probably differ in which ones they adopt. In examining these alternative views, we begin with the perspective of the ordinary person, often called the commonsense view.

THE COMMONSENSE VIEW

Ordinary people consider it obvious that two major types of phenomena make up their world: material objects—things that can be seen, touched, and manipulated, and that can move and change; and nonmaterial experience—sensations and perceptions, emotions, or thoughts. People ordinarily consider the latter to be every bit as real as the objects they encounter. Moreover, people consider themselves a combination of both material (bodily) and immaterial (mind, spirit) substances, each of which seems relatively independent of the other.

Typically, people easily distinguish between the two, although sometimes they find it difficult to determine whether something is physical, or just in their mind. For most people, their identity rests primarily on the content and organization of their immaterial aspects—skills, personality, values, hopes, loves, and fears. Their body is something they live in, and sometimes its frailties interfere with what they want to do; their immaterial essence exists in some form different from their body. Moreover, people ordinarily subdivide both material and immaterial phenomena into discrete subclasses and units: material as trees, light, body parts, or physical actions; immaterial as perceptions, thoughts, or affects. Material units are seen as physically arranged in three-dimensional space, and their interactions take place through time in accordance with natural laws. In contrast, people typically think of immaterial phenomena as existing and functioning according to principles different from the physical laws of nature; they transcend time and space.

Clients typically enter therapy with this commonsense model. If the therapist's guiding model is incompatible with this commonsense view, the therapist must either teach the client an alternate way of thinking or become adept at translating—that is, making analyses and decisions within one metamodel frame but rephrasing them when talking with the client to make them intelligible within the client's commonsense view.

The Dualist View

Many philosophers agreed with this commonsense view, formally called *dualism*, but they reached different conclusions on how best to account for this duality of reality. If people are assumed to be made up of two different kinds of being, both equally real—a body *(soma)*, and a mind *(psyche)*—then the relationship of these two must be considered. If both exist and are fundamental, how do they act upon, or relate to, one another? This is the classic mind-body problem. Moreover, if the environment is also composed of the material and immaterial (i.e., objects, events and other people's minds), then the question of how those aspects of reality interact with the person must also be considered. This is the classic person-context problem. For example, can people interact only physically or can they interact mentally as well?

Three different forms of dualism have been proposed: (1) *Psychophysical parallelism* proposes that material and immaterial, body and mind, operate in parallel streams, each with its own principles and rules and neither influencing the other. (2) *Psychophysical interactionism* argues that the two are related through interactional influence: biological functions influence the operation of the mind, or mental events influence the functioning of the body. Of course, choosing an interactionist position requires one to specify how such interactions take place. (3) *Epiphenomenalism* conceives both physical and mental events to be real, but considers mental events to be noninfluential by-products of the body's operation; they are epiphenomenal. Subjective experiences, such as emotions, thoughts, or consciousness, may occur, but they have no influence in determining what the person actually does. The world is considered to be governed by physical laws without any intrusion from an immaterial realm.

The Monist View

Some scholars have rejected dualism and argued that reality is made up of only one kind of substance, a view called *monism*. In Western thought, two principal forms of monism have been proposed: *materialism* and *idealism*.

Materialism

To the *materialist*, matter constitutes the only reality, with matter understood to be roughly the subject matter of the physical sciences. At least from the time of Democritus through Hobbes, to modern physics and some forms of behaviorism in psychology, materialism or physicalism has had its stout defenders. Advocates of materialism are persuaded that all things, forces, and events, including those that characterize humans, can be reduced to a core of elements from which the entire universe is created: the fundamental particles of physics. All manifestations of life and mind are said to arise, develop, and end by changes in the content and organization of matter. Mind in this instance is reducible to the physical properties and functioning of the nervous system—the biochemical/electrical neuronal processes. Changes result from material influences. If one asserts that *all* qualities of subjective experience are reducible to changes in matter without any remainder, one espouses what is called *reductive materialism*; all qualities of experience are illusory; the operation of the person is construed to be controlled by natural, universal physical laws. A softer materialist position can also be espoused. It accepts the idea that people have subjective experiences but argues that these are simply manifestations of the material organization and functioning of the body.

Some materialists distinguish between nonliving and living entities, proposing that the animate entities represent an organization of physical matter qualitatively different from that of inanimate objects. To the subject matter of physics and chemistry must be added that of the biological sciences, to accommodate the distinctive features of living entities, and humans are construed, along with other animate beings, to be a special kind of material entity, a *biological organism*. This is still a materialist position, but it assumes that additional principles or laws of material organization are necessary to understand living things. This materialist view is sometimes called *biological determinism*.

Idealism

Others reject a materialistic monism, arguing that the only reality humans know is their own experience. The existence of a material reality is simply an idea created by humans. Therefore, the mind or ideas can be considered the only reality on which humans can safely rely; *idealism* holds that the universe is the expression or embodiment of mind. Ideas, sometimes called archetypes, are said to exist prior to and independent of the world we experience on a daily basis. For example, specific objects that we call tables are embodiments or varied forms in which the idea of a table may be expressed. Extreme forms of phenomenology and radical constructivism are a version of the idealist metamodel.

Double Aspect Monism

Emerging from the cutting edges of philosophy and science is a form of monism that accepts the existence of the material-immaterial, or body-mind, but explains them as different manifestations of one underlying phenomenon, a view termed *double aspect monism*. Pribram (1986), who studied brain-mind relationships, argues that this dichotomy holds only for the ordinary world of appearances described by Euclidian geometry and Newtonian mechanics. He proposes a *neutral monism* in which brain-mind are considered realizations of "identical structures" derived from a more basic "existential given"; by *structure*, he means *organization*. In most psychological and psychotherapy theorizing, the word *structure* is used as a synonym for *organization*. Because structure connotes a *physical* existence, this usage tends to encourage a reification of nonmaterial patterns of organization, implying that mental structures and brain structures both have a physical existence.

Pribram (1986) points out that even physicists attempting to understand nature at both the microphysical quantum and nuclear level and the macrophysical universe level have concluded that different material forms are simply manifestations of different patterns of organization of a single phenomenon called energy. It is the configurations of energy rather than their raw amounts that are critical for the form that appears. Stated another way, he proposes that the principles and dynamics of organization are the basic phenomena whose operation results in the multiple material and immaterial forms manifest in the ordinary world of experience. To illustrate, the same pattern of organization can be retained although it may be transformed from one form (patterns of reflected light) to another (patterns of sensory stimulation). Pribram draws on theory and empirical evidence in the cognitive and brain sciences—neural dynamics and holographic representations—to illustrate the utility of such an ontology.

ALTERNATIVE COSMOLOGICAL ASSUMPTIONS: THE ORGANIZATION OF REALITY

Consideration of ideas about the organization of reality may focus on patterns of stability over time—statics—and/or how they may vary or change over time—dynamics. The cosmological assumptions to which a therapy approach is anchored will have an important influence on the selection and use of therapy interventions and how they are evaluated, as the purpose of interventions is to alter the content and organization of clients' unwanted states.

ASSUMPTIONS ABOUT PATTERNS OF CAUSE AND EFFECT

There is a commonsense view of this issue also. The ordinary person assumes that when something occurs or changes, it is because something was done, or happened, to produce the event or the change, sometimes called *generative causality.* In this view, a cause is anything that influences what happens or produces a result, and an effect is the outcome that follows the occurrence of a cause. The commonsense view assumes that each effect has a specific cause (e.g., some germ caused the illness), and that cause-effect relationships occur in linear chains. Successful identification of cause-effect sequences produces explanations of why things occur. Generalized versions of such explanations are often called principles or laws. Humans consider this kind of knowledge most valuable because its use enables them to predict and control events.

Philosophers have transformed this commonsense view into more sophisticated forms. The use of cause-effect analysis assumes two organizational properties: temporal contiguity or sequence, and regularity or contingency. *Temporal contiguity* or *sequence* means that events occur simultaneously and in succession during the passage of time; events occur before, concurrent with, or after one another. *Regularity* or *contingency* means that the same event pattern recurs from one occasion to another and that components of the pattern have relationships of influence. An event is judged the cause of another if it occurs first and the other is observed invariably to follow; the prior event is assumed to be a necessary and sufficient condition for the effect to occur. Multiple causality assumes that a causal event must be present, but the effect will not occur unless other conditions are also present; a single causal event may be a necessary but not sufficient condition for an effect to occur. The doctrine of *determinism* asserts that any occurrence can be fully explained by identifying all its causal antecedents.

Traditional Types of Causes

Centuries ago, Aristotle produced a detailed analysis of the idea of causality that revealed it to be considerably more intricate than the commonsense view. He argued that the explanation of a thing or event must answer all the queries included under the question, "Why is something as it is?" and proposed several types of causes that must be considered to answer that question.

1. The *material cause*—the substance of which a thing or event is made. For shoes, the material cause is what the shoes are made of: leather, glue, and thread; for people, it is their physical/biological characteristics.
2. The *efficient cause*—the agents or forces external to the thing or event by means of which its occurrence or change is produced. In shoemaking, the efficient causes are the actions of the shoemaker that transform the materials into a shoe; in people, the environment influences their development and functioning.
3. The *formal cause*—the particular organization, configuration, or form the material is to assume. In shoemaking, the formal cause is the design of the particular kind of shoe to be produced: boots or dress shoes; in people, it is the biological form of a mature adult or the pattern of skills a person is trying to learn.
4. The *final cause*—the purpose to be served by the result produced. In shoemaking, it is the objective of protecting and/or adorning the foot; in people, it is the goals they seek to accomplish, or survival and reproductive success in evolutionary theory.
5. The *incidental cause*—chance occurrences. In shoemaking, leather may stretch on a very hot day and accidentally alter a shoe's shape; in people, an accidental meeting may lead to love and marriage.

From such a multicausal perspective, events result from *multidetermination:* The explanation of any effect is multiple causes that combine to produce it, rather than a single cause. Thus, to explain what caused a person's cancer, one might consider whether (1) her genetic history was a predisposing factor (material cause), (2) she smoked (efficient cause), (3) her blood biochemistry matched a normative healthy pattern (formal cause), (4) she wanted to join a loved one who had died (final cause), or (5) she was accidentally exposed to polluted air (incidental cause).

Scholars and professionals differ about which Aristotelean causes they emphasize. The idea of efficient cause dominates the commonsense view and also has been most influential in the natural sciences. This is illustrated by the emphasis on experimental designs in which some independent variables are manipulated and the changes in or effects on dependent variables are observed. Most efforts to evaluate psychotherapy's effectiveness focus on efficient causes—for example, how therapists' methods influence client change. Rationales for matching treatments to client characteristics and problems represent a multicausal model. The idea of final cause has been most seriously challenged because it implies teleological explanations.

Lyddon (1995) links different types of causes to Pepper's (1942) "world hypotheses" or metamodels. *Formism* groups phenomena into categories or types by identifying similarities and differences. It assumes that phenomena have intrinsic, stable properties or essences that determine their functioning; this is the idea of material cause: a ball rolls because it is round. *Mechanism* links different phenomena into cause-effect relationships, so it combines the ideas of material and efficient causes: a ball rolls because it is round and is pushed. *Contextualism* assumes that events and their contexts occur in integrated patterns at each moment in time, but that no necessary relationship exists between the patterns at one moment and another; thus it emphasizes formal causation: a ball rolls as a result of the pattern of immediate relationships among its properties and its context. *Organicism* construes living entities as manifesting progressive qualitative transformations in the direction of increased complexity and integration, moving toward a final endpoint: maturity. This is the idea of final cause.

Delprato (1995) summarizes three stages in the evolution of ideas about causality and the organization of the world. The first assumed that natural events result from self-contained powers or properties (e.g., spirit) called *substance theory* (Einstein & Infeld, 1938). The second retained substances but described their relationships in terms of attractive and repulsive forces that link the occurrence of events here and now with conditions there and then, called the *mechanical view* (Einstein & Infeld, 1938). Modern physical sciences emphasize the third stage (Capra, 1977; Jantsch, 1980; Zukav, 1979), which uses the idea of event fields; any event is a function of the nature and organization of all conditions in which it is embedded, initially called *field theory* (Kantor, 1941; Lewin, 1951). *Self-organizing systems* is a more recent version. Certain similarities and differences underlie all the other models. Each therapy model relies primarily on one of these cosmological views.

MECHANISTIC MODELS

The cosmological view of *mechanism* is the model of organization that has dominated both science, including the discipline of psychology, and practical affairs; the reliance of modern technologies on machines illustrates its great utility. A mechanistic model of organization assumes that all complexities may be understood as a set of parts linked together in patterns of cause-effect relationships. Complex entities are constructed by successively linking together multiple parts. Such entities and their functioning can be fully understood in terms of these determinate causal relationships. Mechanistic or cause-effect processes follow fixed sequential pathways, so that any output (or final state) is fully determined by the initial conditions and process pathways. Parts and their interactions are not modified by their relationships or history. Mechanisms are reactive; they behave in predictable and controllable ways in reaction to influences on them according to the nature of their parts and causal connections (Deutsch, 1951). That is why humans create them. Doctrines of *reductionism, associationism,* and *determinism* reflect this model. The assumptions of linearity and additivity underlying the general linear model of statistics likewise reflect a mechanistic model.

CONTEXTUAL MODELS

Contextualism assumes the world is composed of a continuously changing combination of object arrangements and temporal events, none of which can ever recur (Capaldi & Proctor, 1994). Every event results from a unique combination of occurrences in its immediate context. Therefore, the meaning of all observations—scientific or professional—is restricted to the context in which they were made. Sometimes the uniqueness of context is small enough to be safely ignored. However, in human affairs, context-free generalizations are seldom sound because of the complex, variable nature of real-life conditions. Therefore, psychotherapy cannot be guided by propositions that apply regardless of context, or client and therapist characteristics (Deese, 1996). People's functioning can be understood only as resulting from person-in-context patterns.

ORGANISMIC MODELS AND LIVING ENTITIES

The mechanistic model of organization was criticized and rejected by scholars studying living entities. For them, embryological development convincingly demonstrates a different organizational model that was termed *organismic*. It reverses the relationship between parts and wholes proposed in the mechanistic model. The whole, or organism, exists from the beginning as a coherently organized entity. Parts come into existence through processes of differentiation and elaboration from the whole; parts are constructed from the whole rather than the whole being constructed by a linking together of parts.

Development proceeds from simple to complex organization under the primary influence of processes internal to the entity itself, predetermined by hereditary and maturational factors. Environment may speed up, slow down, or arrest some developmental patterns, but it does not cause them. Change often occurs in discontinuous patterns or stages resulting in emergent properties, and there is a final end state, maturity, toward which these intrinsic change processes move. In contrast to a mechanistic model in which entities are buffeted and shaped by their contexts, an organismic model sees entities shaped primarily by their own nature.

SELF-ORGANIZING OPEN SYSTEMS AS A DYNAMIC MODEL OF ORGANIZATION

The ideas summarized here represent only some of the diverse views that have been proposed about the idea of causality (e.g., White, 1990). Advances in natural sciences, such as quantum theory, nonlinear thermodynamics, chaos theory, and complex dynamic systems, have raised serious doubts about the adequacy of traditional cause-effect analyses. These advances have suggested a different view in which the traditional one is seen as a special case within a more general frame. Toffler (1984, pp. xiv–xv) states: "the old universal laws are not universal at all, but apply only to local regions of reality." The traditional view emphasizes "stability, order, uniformity, and equilibrium." He contrasts that with the emerging paradigm that shifts attention to "disorder, instability, diversity, disequilibrium, nonlinear relationships, . . . and temporality"—in open systems.

Koestler (1978) describes the essence of these emerging views: "What all of these theories have in common is that they regard . . . Nature's striving to create order out of disorder . . . as ultimate and irreducible principles beyond mechanical causation" (p. 270). Two basic ideas are combined: Humans are open systems whose existence and development require continual exchanges with their contexts of material/energy and information/meaning forms; and both stability and change result from the organization producing dynamics internal to the entity itself as it deals with perturbations of its existing states that result from its own functioning and transactions with its contexts. This idea has been labeled autopoiesis (Maturana, 1975), self-organization (Prigogine & Stengers, 1984), and self-organization and self-construction (Ford, 1987).

Complex, dynamic systems operate to create, maintain, and when disrupted, recreate coherent organization within themselves and in relationship to their contexts. In this view, events or forces do not directly cause a change. Rather, they perturb or disrupt existing states and the dynamics of the organization then operate to overcome the perturbation, or to change so as to accommodate it, within the possibilities and constraints provided by their current states and contexts. Moreover, if the organization is far from equilibrium, a small influence can produce a perturbation that can lead to major changes, sometimes called *sensitive dependence on initial conditions*. Thus, the same influence may have different effects depending on the state and dynamics of the entity at the time the influencing event occurs. For example, the impact of a psychotherapy intervention may differ depending on the state and dynamics of the person when the intervention occurs; thus the timing of an interpretation may be crucial.

Mutual causality means that a change in any part of a dynamic system, such as the habitual thoughts or emotions of a person, will be a function of the dynamic organization of the attributes of the system. This has been called a causal field to distinguish it from traditional linear causal analysis (Ford & Lerner, 1992). In this view, the apparent purposiveness of humans' behavior can be understood as a manifestation of the operation of the system's dynamics—the interaction of thoughts, emotions, actions, and biological states. As in an organismic model, development occurs through differentiation and elaboration of wholes; unlike that model, environmental influences play key roles in change processes. Unlike a mechanistic model, however, environmental influences are not automatic; system dynamics mediate and shape their influence. Near the end of his career, Pepper (1972) considered this a new root metaphor—a dynamic self-regulating system that was potentially "the most fruitful or even the correct one for a detailed synthetic comprehension of the structure of the universe" (p. 548).

ALTERNATIVE EPISTEMOLOGIES

Epistemology deals with assumptions about how humans comprehend the nature of their world and themselves, and how they can distinguish between sound knowledge and idiosyncratic opinion. The correspondence between reality and people's comprehension of it has been an issue for philosophy and science for centuries. Epistemologies differ in their emphases on and proposed relationships among three basic ideas: experience, knowledge or knowing, and reality. *Experience* refers to the subjective, conscious manifestations of a person's current varying states of biological, psychological, and behavioral activity. It results from what is traditionally called sensory/perceptual functioning and consciousness. *Knowledge* refers to the fund of generalized representations a person has constructed, such as the nature and meaning of experience, and *knowing* is the process of formulating knowledge. Psychologists typically call this the cognitive or information processing functioning. *Reality* refers to the nature of things and events within and outside people's bodies independent of their experience and knowledge of these events. Virtually all epistemologies agree that humans have subjective, conscious experience. They disagree on how such experience is related to knowledge development and to reality.

It is useful to group epistemologies into three broad classes: *empiricism, intuitionism,* and *rationalism.* Within each are various versions, and they differ as a function of their metaphysical assumptions. *Phenomena* are aspects of reality that may become manifest in *phenomenal experience*. We start with realism and end with idealism.

EMPIRICISM

Empiricism assumes a reality separate from humans' experience of it. Much knowledge has been accumulated based on an empirical epistemology. The methodologies of the natural sciences rely on it. So valuable have been its fruits that some have disparaged all other forms of knowing as suspect and unreliable. Subtypes differ in their assumptions about the relationships among reality, experience, and knowledge development. Two versions are described.

Realism or Presentationism

People typically assume that what they see, people they meet, and events represented in their experience are all what they appear to be. This assumption stems from a metaphysics of realism that argues that any object or event has properties that can directly affect other objects or events, such as humans' sensory structures. Therefore, phenomenal experience corresponds with the objects, people, and events the person encounters, and these encounters can yield *objective knowledge*. Modern ecological theories of perception—that perceptions directly and accurately correspond with reality—illustrate this epistemology.

One version of realism, *radical empiricism*, maintains that knowledge development requires the slow, laborious accumulation of observations by many different observers, which—once classified and arranged—would constitute the knowledge about any phenomena at any point in time. Proponents argue that as long as people confine their knowledge generation to their observations, they have a method of knowledge construction they can trust. Scientific laws are simply regularities represented in sets of observations. There is an attraction of simplicity to this epistemology. Detractors criticize it as simplistic and call it *naive realism.*

Representationism or Constructivism

Representationism accepts experience as a source of information but considers it insufficient by itself to explain reality for at least four reasons. First, phenomenal experience is continually varying and changing, manifesting the inevitable tendency of all things and events to come into being, to exist for a time, and to pass away, replaced by others. Each experience is discrete and specific to a particular time and place, never to recur, and no two experiences are ever identical. Perceptions can only yield fragments of knowledge. Therefore, representationists argue, if human knowledge rested solely on experience, humans would have an infinity of facts but would know nothing of how they might relate to one another. Second, humans' sensory/perceptual capabilities are limited. People directly observe only a limited portion of the events that go on around and within them; the existence of unobservable realities can only be imagined. For example, knowledge of gravity, electricity, X-rays, or human learning would never have developed had people relied solely on immediate experience for their understanding about reality.

Third, perception is always selective. People cannot observe everything going on simultaneously within and around them; they must attend to some things and ignore others. As a result, two people may select different aspects of the same event to observe, deriving different perceptions or experiences. Moreover, people often report their interpretations as if they were perceptions: they report seeing what they expect to see or what others say they ought to see. Therefore, relying solely on experience for understanding reality puts one in a vulnerable position, because the differences among multiple observers in the experiences produced by the same events requires one to choose which version of reality to accept—and such decisions must rely on criteria beyond the experiences themselves.

Fourth, presentationism does not allow for imaginative thought that produces knowledge about anything that has not yet been experienced. However, people create ideas about things they have not observed, such as germs or angels; they anticipate and predict future events that have not yet happened and therefore could not have been experienced.

Representationism combines realism and idealism, arguing that knowledge is constructed by mental processes that utilize but go beyond the fruits of direct experience. Once created, such mental constructions can exert selective influence on future experience, on what is perceived. Recently, this has also been called *constructivism.* Disagreements exist about how to verify or falsify mental constructions or even to know accurately what they are. Proponents vary in the extent to which they believe the processes of mental construction occur within or outside the contents of consciousness, but they usually assume that the processes are subject to conscious control, and that experience may provide links between cognitive constructions and reality. *Evolutionary epistemology* argues that the continuous interplay between experience and cognitive construction produces a diversification of ideas and representations about reality and humans' relationships to it, and like the evolution of other attributes, representations are selected in or out, depending on their adaptive utility or *viability,* on what works. Which is the correct representation of reality cannot be justified, falsified, or verified; some forms are more or less viable for different purposes in different contexts. Some are viable for people at one time and place, but may become less viable as their life proceeds.

INTUITIONISM

Intuitionism also proposes that knowledge is a mental construction, but how experience is linked to the construction process is unknown. Intuition was once considered the most valuable and significant source of knowledge available to humans. For some people, intuition is so compelling that it is synonymous with absolute certainty. Ordinary people are said to operate on the basis of intuitive understandings of themselves—that is, they consider themselves the same from day to day. Interpersonal relationships are said to rely heavily on intuitive processes, as in the exercise of empathic understanding. Consider the psychotherapist who is said to "listen with the third ear" and who creates a view of a client's basic difficulties without an explicit understanding of why it seems sound. Controversy has been not so much over whether intuitive understanding occurs as in how it takes place and whether it can serve as a reliable avenue to knowledge.

RATIONALISM

Rationalism limits the importance of experience in knowing, in contrast to empiricism's emphasis on its importance. Because the world as experienced is continually changing, rationalists proposed that only through reasoning, divorced from immediate and changing experience, could humans uncover the regularities and order presumed to lie behind continually changing experience. Such order and regularity is presumed to exist and to govern what takes place, but only by means of reason can that order be discovered and understood. Reason has been considered a means of knowing that can range far beyond and even function independently of experience. Rationalism requires a person to follow a set of rules in conducting consciously controlled, careful, and systematic thinking. The rules are collectively referred to as logic, and the form of thinking as logical thought. Different forms of logic exist, but if different people reason with the same rules, they should reach similar conclusions. Mathematics is one example of the power of reasoning within a formal set of rules.

Phenomenalism

An extreme version of a rational epistemology, called *phenomenalism*, deemphasizes the role of reality in knowledge creation and manifests metaphysical idealism in pure form. Phenomenalists do not presume the existence of a reality independent of human observers to apprehend it. Rather, they affirm that what is known directly is experience itself, and reality is whatever a person experiences or construes it to be. Objects and events external to the person viewing them have the appearance of substance, with qualities that seem inherent in them; but these appearances, which constitute the real world for the realist, and the real world to be approximated by representationists, are fictions to the phenomenalist. What is real, or at least existent, are the subjective experiences that occur; these in turn lead to the formation of our ideas, so *subjectivity* (rather than objectivity) becomes the emphasis.

Rationalistic epistemologies also have their critics. One can reason logically and still arrive at unsound conclusions. There is no way to evaluate the products of reason without any connection to experience and reality except by appeal to the rules that reasoning must follow. Critics also note that reasoning uses ideas that depend on knowledge about objects and events rather than ideas that are independent of things and happenings. If the assumptions with which a line of reasoning begins are somehow insufficient, misleading, or inaccurate, the thinking will turn out to have little utility, no matter how logical. The extreme idealism of some phenomenalists is equivalent to *solipsism*, which asserts that there is no basis for the human mind to believe in the reality of anything but itself and its own creations. If there is no external reality within which humans must live and against which their ideas can somehow be tested, then any belief must be considered as valid or useful as any other.

IMPLICATIONS FOR IDENTIFYING "FAMILIES" OF PSYCHOTHERAPY THEORY

All theories start with some metaphysical and epistemological assumptions. Therefore, we should expect that the therapy approaches examined later will differ in the underlying metamodels on which their origins are based. It is unlikely that any theory we examine will adhere to any of these basic assumptions in their pure form. However, we do expect them to differ in their relative emphasis on different assumptions—such as realism or idealism, empiricism or rationalism. Historically, metaphysical and epistemological positions have been pitted against each other, as realism versus idealism or empiricism versus rationalism. We think this is a misleading way of formulating the issues; combinations are possible. Each may have some merit. For example, one may be a realist with regard to perception and an idealist with regard to abstract thought. No single emphasis—sense experience, or intuition, or reason alone—may be sufficient; building a fund of useful knowledge probably requires the skillful art of combining these approaches, or what Pribram

(1986) calls an *epistemological pluralism.* Many therapy theorists are pursuing this more inclusive strategy because as practitioners, they find that all are operative in some way in humans' daily lives.

Not all of the hundreds of approaches to psychotherapy can be analyzed in this book; however, groups of them share similar perspectives. Children of the same parents display family resemblances because they share a gene pool, similar contexts, and common modes of thinking. Analogously, families or groups of psychotherapy approaches are based on similar metaphysical and epistemological assumptions about the nature of humans, how they change, and how they may be understood. Recognizing these commonalities, rather than focusing primarily on individual systems as we did in 1963, we have analyzed groups or families of approaches that have similar orientations.

DEFINITION OF PSYCHOTHERAPY.

Psychotherapy is a professional form of intervention focused primarily on alleviating psychological distress, psychological and behavioral dysfunctions, and problems of social living. It uses primarily psychological and behavioral means, mediated primarily by verbal methods and interpersonal interactions, conducted with individuals or small groups under relatively intimate, private conditions that facilitate clients' self-direction and self-regulation.

This approach differs from that of medical practice, which focuses on alleviating or preventing biological dysfunctions through the expertise and authority of the physician, using medical, surgical, and pharmacological interventions. No family of biological approaches is analyzed as biology is the primary domain of medicine. Psychotherapy, however, can be used to influence psychological and behavioral consequences of biological dysfunctions as well as to influence biological functioning indirectly. Moreover, therapists may use drugs as part of their interventions, but biological interventions are not their primary focus, just as effective physicians use interpersonal interactions and verbal methods in support of their primarily biologically focused strategies. Psychotherapy also differs from teaching and socialization traditions that focus on competence development and from the legal interventions emphasizing punishment and restitution.

DEFINITION OF FAMILIES OF PSYCHOTHERAPY

There is broad agreement on a general classification of therapy approaches manifest in the psychotherapy literature and in studies of the theoretical and methodological preferences of training programs and therapists (Jensen, Bergin, & Greaves, 1990; Nevid, Lavi, & Primavera, 1986; Norcross, Prochaska, & Gallagher, 1989; Smith, 1982; Zook & Walton, 1989). These consensus groupings include behavior and cognitive-behavior therapies, cognitive therapies, psychoanalytic and psychodynamic therapies, humanistic and experiential therapies, and eclectic and integrative therapies. However, the rationale for clustering over 400 approaches into these groupings is unclear. Is it based on similar ancestry? procedural similarities? professional affiliations? Without having criteria to define these groups, it is difficult to understand how they differ, or to identify the family to which any specific approach belongs.

The metaphysical and epistemological assumptions used by these approaches when they first began seem to provide the primary implicit criteria for these traditional groupings. Therefore, the family groups to be examined are defined in terms of their initial metaphysical and epistemological assumptions. Their metamodels are inferred from descriptions of theory and methods when they are not explicitly stated. Two points should be emphasized. First, we do not expect any psychotherapy approach to have adopted any of the alternatives described earlier in their pure form, so we have tried to identify each one's primary emphases. Second, we expect to find that the metamodel assumptions with which each family began may have become significantly modified as experience and research led to elaborations of their models. For example, behavior therapy has significantly influenced other approaches and has been influenced by them.

The historical development of therapy approaches suggests a pattern: The founders adopt a distinguishing set of starting assumptions; but as the approach is applied and evolves, it sprouts variations that may deviate from one or more of the starting assumptions. Therefore, each family has developed considerable diversity within it. Sometimes a founder of an approach expresses concern if its versions have deviated too far from the original assumptions. In our comparative study, we define the families of approaches in terms of what appears to be the framework of starting assumptions on which they were initially founded.

Behavior Therapies

Originators of the behavior therapies (BT) emphasized the importance of people's physical and communicative actions in relationship to their context; these proponents converted psychological experiences such as emotions into patterns of biological responses. This is an ontology of *materialism*. They emphasized material, efficient, and linear chains of cause-effect relationships, the linking together of stimuli and responses through learning to create complex patterns, and the automatic influence of environmental events on human learning and action. Behavior therapy was initially rooted in a cosmology of *mechanism*. The founders emphasized formal empirical research as the preferred way to identify cause-effect relationships and used careful, objective observation of people's behavior within contexts to produce accurate information. Nomethetic knowledge is assumed to be possible because all change or learning is the same for all people. Thus, BT was rooted in an *empirical epistemology* with a *realist (presentationist)* emphasis.

Cognitive Therapies
Early proponents of cognitive therapies (CT) considered thoughts to be the primary influence regulating what people do, how they feel, and what effects their contexts might have on them. They believed that thoughts can function as causes. This belief stems from an ontology of *idealism.* They also relied on notions of material, efficient, and linear cause-effect models, assuming that complex patterns result from learned associations among thoughts, affects, actions, and contexts, consistent with a *mechanistic* cosmology. General principles of learning were presumed to exist, and empirical research was emphasized as the preferred way of identifying cause-effect relationships. The originators assumed that people's reports of their thoughts accurately represent their cognitions. Objective observation of people's self-reports was considered the primary way to understand individuals and to construct nomethetic knowledge about people in general. These presuppositions derived from an empirical epistemology, using both *realist* (presentationist) and *representationist* (constructivist) versions.

Cognitive-Behavior and Skill Training Therapies
For the family of cognitive-behavior and skill training therapies (CBST), early advocates combined the assumptions underlying both behavior and cognitive therapies. Initially, they emphasized patterns of thoughts, actions, and contexts, consistent with an *interactive dualism* ontology. They also typically relied on a *mechanistic* cosmology, albeit a more complex version, and used a combined *empirical* epistemology similar to that of the cognitive therapies.

Behavioral Medicine/Health Therapies
The ontology, cosmology, and epistemology of the behavioral medicine/health therapies (BMHT) group are very similar to those of the CBST family. However, BMHT's ontology differed somewhat in placing more emphasis on the biological components of a person, and on reciprocal causal influences of psychological, behavioral, and biological factors on each other.

Humanist Therapies

Members of the humanist therapies (HT) family initially asserted that humans have qualities different from all other entities, so they must be understood and treated differently: Humans are proactive, not reactive. Their capacities for awareness; subjective (phenomenal) experience; self-reflection and self-knowledge; symbolization; complex affect; personally chosen values and meanings; and the use of foresight, choice, and intentionality in the pursuit of personal goals were considered to be distinguishing attributes of humans alone. This view is consistent with an *idealistic* ontology. As development was said to result from the organization, differentiation, and elaboration of phenomenal experiences, moving toward full realization of the person's potentials, an *organismic* cosmology was being used.

Because humans differ from objects, they cannot be understood with the same empirical methods. Direct access to phenomenal experiences is possible only by the person in whom these experiences occur, but that person can subjectively observe them and report them to others. Such reports must be relied on as the source of knowledge and understanding about them. They are accepted at face value because what matters is the person's subjective view, not whether that view may or may not correspond with a presumed reality. Clients' subjectivity must be relied on as the source of knowledge and understanding about these clients. Therapists can augment their understanding by using intuitive or empathic processes drawn from their own subjective experience. Each person is unique, so an idiographic understanding of each client must be developed. Therapy requires idiographic knowledge of a person, as people cannot be characterized in terms drawn from nomethetic knowledge. The epistemological assumptions on which these assertions are based are those of *rationalism* and *intuitionism*.

Traditional Psychoanalysis

Historically, the term *psychoanalysis* referred to variants of Freud's model of psychotherapy. Some who continue to label themselves psychoanalysts have created rather different approaches using different assumptions, so they are treated as part of an interpersonal family of approaches. Traditional psychoanalysis (PT) traditionally emphasized instinctual or biological influences on human functioning and the role of cognition in controlling and channeling these influences into behavioral forms adaptive in, and acceptable to people's sociocultural environment. This approach was psychobiological in contrast to the behavioral, psychological, or psychobehavioral emphases of other approaches. Because Freud considered instincts unmodifiable, interventions were focused on cognitive processes. Although materialist—biological and environmental—factors were acknowledged to exist, their influence on people was presumed to be mediated through cognitive processes and constructions. Although espousing an *interactive dualism*, Freud operated primarily from a form of *idealist* ontology.

Instinctual drives and cognitive processes were assumed to regulate human development and functioning, but a generic pattern of development was proposed, defined as a sequence of psychosexual stages. These ideas reflect a cosmology of *organicism*. Traditional psychoanalysts rely on careful observation of clients' verbal and nonverbal communications. These communications cannot be taken at face value, however, because the therapists assume that unconscious processes often find conscious symbolic expression in order to preserve the person's psychological dynamics and to be socially acceptable. Therapists have to interpret their observations to identify unconscious meanings underlying the clients' statements. Thus, traditional psychoanalysis adheres to an *empiricist* epistemology, using a combination of *realist* and *representationist* positions.

Interpersonal and Sociocultural Therapies

Influenced by the interpersonal and sociocultural emphases of the early neo-analysts (e.g., Adler, Horney, Sullivan), some psychoanalysts developed approaches called object relations or self-psychology, and some psychologists developed interpersonal psychotherapy. Emerging feminist and subculturally oriented therapies espouse somewhat similar views. A central theme of the interpersonal and sociocultural therapies (ISCT) is that humans are embedded in significant interpersonal relations throughout life. These in turn are embedded in sociocultural contexts within which language plays a fundamental role in linking interpersonal and sociocultural factors to individual development and functioning. The nature of a person's psychosocial transactions and contexts influences the kinds and organization of ideas they construct about themselves and their relationships. The organization of psychosocial and self-concepts plays the key role in providing coherence and continuity to both functioning and development. Biological factors set boundaries but do not function as primary determinants of development and functioning. The underlying ontology is an *interactive dualism* although the emphasis is clearly on the mental or *idealist* aspects of the duality.

A person's psychological patterns are described as dynamic and subject to continual change and elaboration. One's lifelong interpersonal and psychosocial embeddedness continually produces transactions that can either help to stabilize these patterns or prompt them to change. This view implies a cosmology of a *self-organizing open system*. To account for a person's behavior, one must understand the nature of the psychological patterns with which the person functions. This can be achieved by listening carefully to clients' self-reports and analyzing them for thematic content and organization. Traditional quantitative methods are considered inadequate for these purposes. Members of this family use somewhat different epistemologies. Some appear to be *empiricists* and *representationists,* with the addition of *evolutionary epistemology* assumptions. Others emphasize the primacy of cognition and the inability of humans to verify any reality other than their own, similar to the *rationalist* and *intuitionist* epistemology of the humanist therapies family.

Eclectic and Integrative Therapies

In the eclectic and integrative therapies (EIT), people are viewed as biopsychosocial entities embedded in and in continual transaction with dynamic environments. Therefore, all aspects of their lives are of potential importance. This ontology appears to be either a *psychophysical interactionism* or a *double aspect monism.* Eclectic versions tend to use antecedent-consequent models of causality, implying a *mechanistic* cosmology. However, all EIT approaches view humans as both proactive and reactive, having processes by which they create and maintain their functional patterns. Collectively, they use a *self-organizing open systems* cosmology with mechanistic components. Representatives of EIT capitalize on any empirically supported intervention. This characteristic suggests a *pluralistic epistemology,* which assumes that knowledge is advanced by the integration of information derived from everywhere.

RISKS AND FALLACIES IN THE USE OF MODELS

Although models are essential for organizing, guiding, and evaluating all human activity, they can be misused. Fallacies, which are false and misleading ways of thinking, may appear in client and/or therapist behavior during psychotherapy and may distort the therapy processes. Each involves a form of overgeneralization.

THE FALLACY OF REIFICATION

Reification attributes a real existence to some conceptual abstraction—interpreting some symbolic model as if it were a real thing. For example, a client may label a recurrent pattern of thoughts, feelings, and actions in some situations as incompetence—but, concepts like incompetence are ideas, not things. Reification leads a person to think of such patterns as always there and functioning (like a wart on the neck). Reification can lead to mistaken actions and can affect interpersonal relations. People may construct ideas about themselves and one another, and then behave as if people are what their idea of them depicts. Some uses of the concept of personality trait manifest this error.

THE NOMINAL FALLACY

Concepts represent sets of phenomena grouped together because they share one or more attributes—such as skin color or gender—and have been given a name—gay, black, woman. Models are more complex abstractions because they not only represent different concepts or kinds of things but also their interrelationships or propositions. The *nominal fallacy* occurs when a specific instance that has one attribute of a model is named as an example of that model, and is then assumed to have all the other attributes of the model as well. For example, a person who sometimes displays confused thinking may be labeled schizophrenic and then be assumed to have all the other attributes of that syndrome.

THE REDUCTIONIST FALLACY

Concepts and models are inherently selective and simplified representations. One can lapse into supposing that the facets one has chosen are the only ones that really matter. We recognize this fallacy in clients' characterizations of themselves as "nothing but" a loser, or of someone else as "nothing but" a pathological liar. Therapists may also make such errors. For example, in the past some have characterized many complex patterns of behavior as "subliminations" for socially unacceptable "wishes," thereby reducing something like knitting to "nothing but" a substitute for masturbation. Stereotyping illustrates the operation of nominal and *reductionistic fallacies*.

THE NUMERICAL FALLACY

The *numerical fallacy* holds that if something exists, it exists in some quantity and is therefore capable of being measured. Everything can be represented in a numerical model. What this fallacy ignores is that numbers can represent only quantitative attributes, not qualitative ones, such as differences in kind; numbers cannot show the organization of attributes, for example, that produce a car rather than a plane. Some hospitals, to remind physicians and nurses that measures reported on patients' medical charts do not represent all the patients' important aspects, display signs such as "Remember. The chart is NOT the patient!" Clients who interpret measures of their cholesterol or blood pressure to signify good or bad health lapse into this fallacy.

THE FALLACIES OF PRESUMPTIVE TRUTH, MISPLACED BELIEF AND IMPERIALISM

The fallacy of *presumptive truth* appears when people assert that their guiding model alone is right. Indeed, much therapy is often directed at dislodging the absolutist assertions clients frequently make about themselves, their experiences, and other people. Presumptive truth evolves into *misplaced belief* when people become fervently committed to their model; it ceases to be provisional and becomes doctrine or dogma instead. Certainty replaces possibility. The *imperialist fallacy* occurs when people insist that others should adopt their belief or model. The zeal with which some have promoted their approach and denigrated the beliefs of others has at times approached this extreme; consider the ejection of deviationists from Freud's original circle. Mishne (1993) stated that disputes among psychoanalysts "resemble religious wars over contradictory dogmas rather than scientific disagreements" (p. 377). Some early behaviorists were equally dogmatic.

CHOOSING AMONG ALTERNATIVE MODELS

Anyone can construct any kind of a model to represent anything: humans as robots, their minds as digital computers, or society as a jungle. However, people also have to make choices about which models to use. Scientists argue that such choices should be guided by epistemic criteria such as general utility, predictive accuracy, internal coherence, external consistency, fertility, and unifying power. However, other criteria often influence choices: The model feels right in light of one's personal experience (Cushman, 1992); its basic premises are more compatible with one's general philosophy; there is a fit between the therapist's personality and theory; a special teacher has been influential; or one's early experience or value system may be important (Freimuth, 1992). These other criteria may help to explain why therapists judge some theories to be more compelling than others and why such theories are persistently maintained, despite shortcomings with respect to epistemic criteria.

Remember that any model is a simplified representation of some set of phenomena or ideas and in that sense it will be limited or wrong to some degree. When people need to act, ideally they try to use a model that provides for the least expedient error (Vahinger, 1924), the one that produces a desired outcome with the least likelihood of mistakes. Thus, the ultimate test of any model is what it enables a person to do. Different models have different utility or viability, depending on the purposes they are intended to serve. No single model is likely to serve all purposes or encompass all empirical evidence equally well. All models have advantages and disadvantages. For example, physics has constructed both particle and wave theories to represent different aspects of the same set of phenomena. Hence, multiple models are often useful when dealing with complex sets of phenomena. However, as Table 1.1 implies, it is desirable to be able to relate models to one another. For example, one may have models of cognition, emotions, and the limbic system, but in psychotherapy it is essential to understand how these different aspects of humans interact.

A model or theory is not only a tool for understanding certain phenomena; it is also a tool for guiding actions. In this sense, models are embodiments of purpose and tools for carrying out such purposes. Using a model, one acts to make the future conform to some present idea of it; the model is prescriptive in the sense of guiding the courses of action (Wartofsky, 1979). Finally, because models are generalized representations constructed by humans, they are subject to error and should always be considered provisional, subject to change, improvement, and eventual replacement (Hebb, 1949; Popper, 1972). Recognition that currently preferred models are provisional and imperfect representations of the "truth," can lead people to be more tolerant of alternate truths represented in other people's models. It is through the creation, comparison, evaluation, and combination of alternate models that humans expand the accuracy of their understanding of themselves and their world, and their capability for effective action.

NEXT STEPS

The primary objective of this book is to present a comparative analysis of currently popular approaches to psychotherapy. However, approaches differ in their conceptual and propositional language. To compare them requires some way to identify and compare the meanings underlying their different terms or "jargon." Therefore, we need a very general comparative framework useful for that purpose. In Chapter 2, selection criteria for such a framework are discussed.

Design Criteria
for a Comprehensive
Comparative Framework

REQUIREMENTS FOR A
COMPREHENSIVE COMPARATIVE FRAMEWORK

What kind of approach would be useful for comparing diverse models of psychotherapy? All models have their own starting assumptions and conceptual and propositional language, so they cannot be directly compared using their specialized terminology. For example, how similar or different are the phenomena or meanings to which the terms *object relations, interpersonal relationships,* and *therapy relationships* refer. Some way is needed to compare the meanings represented by their idiosyncratic terminology. This chapter summarizes criteria that the comparative framework (CF) should meet.

Criteria are identified using a requirements analysis similar to the strategies used by professionals in design and engineering fields. They define in advance what the product must be capable of doing; then, they specify the attributes it should have and the constraints it should meet. The resulting criteria guide their design decisions and evaluations of the result. For example, before architects design a building they specify the activities it is to serve (teaching chemistry, building automobiles, playing basketball) and its basic attributes and constraints (location, cost limitations, size, and materials). This chapter summarizes a requirements analysis for a comparative framework comprehensive enough to be useful for a comparative analysis of diverse psychotherapy approaches.

FUNCTIONS TO BE SERVED BY THE COMPREHENSIVE COMPARATIVE FRAMEWORK

The comparative framework used in this book is not intended to be a comprehensive, integrative theory of psychotherapy, so it does not include a specific theory of psychopathology or a procedural model. The analyses are intended to clarify similarities and differences among diverse approaches and to help creative psychotherapists consolidate the confusing mass of current proposals. The framework should encompass all the characteristics that scientists and professionals collectively identify as manifest in the basic nature of humans and their processes of living and changing, although each scientist or professional typically emphasizes only a part of that totality. Therefore, the CF must serve two broad purposes.

COMPARING THEORIES OF PSYCHOTHERAPY

It must provide a context within which the meanings of the *concepts* and *propositions* used in various models of psychotherapy can be identified and compared in terms of the generic kinds and organization of phenomena they represent.

Concepts specify the what of a model. Because all psychotherapy approaches deal with humans, the concepts of these approaches must represent essentially the same kinds and attributes of biological, psychological, behavioral, and social phenomena, even though they may emphasize different aspects and patterns of those phenomena and may give them different names. The conceptual structure of a psychotherapy model is a guide for selecting the kinds of things that should be looked for and what may be less important, and in interpreting and dealing with what is observed. For example, an organic model for depressive states would lead to a selective focus on biological variables, whereas a psychosocial model would direct attention to interpersonal variables.

Propositions specify the how or dynamics of a model—the kinds of relationships, interactions, and influences considered important in organizing the phenomena specified by the theory's concepts. Descriptions such as "intrapsychic conflict" or "avoidance pattern" connote such relationships. We assume that there must be prototypical kinds of relationships among humans' characteristics and their contexts, and that the propositions of psychotherapy theories can be related to such generic dynamics. Propositions about why humans change or don't change are particularly important because they provide the rationale for the design and use of psychotherapy methods. Propositions direct attention toward the kinds of relationships among person and context variables considered important and away from those that are less relevant. For example, organic models proposing that psychological disorders are caused by biological disturbances imply the use of drug or surgical interventions. Psychodynamic models proposing that distressing ideas and emotions are the cause imply the use of reeducative or developmental interventions. Biopsychosocial models proposing mutual causality among multiple variables imply combinations of interventions.

The comparative framework should also make it easier to compare the ways that different models of psychotherapy combine their conceptual and propositional content into functional patterns. These patterns provide therapists with the following:

1. A way of understanding each client's current states and the nature of the dysfunctional aspects of those states that have brought the client to therapy. This includes identifying the eliciting and constraining conditions for the patterns of concern, such as the elicitors and terminators of anxiety attacks.
2. A way of identifying desirable states or conditions to be sought.
3. Strategies and methods capable of effecting changes in clients' troublesome states as well as criteria for selecting from among them the ones most relevant to producing changes from clients' current to their preferred states.
4. Guidance in evaluating the results.

LINKING PSYCHOTHERAPY THEORY AND HUMAN SCIENCES THEORY

Both psychotherapists and scholars in the human sciences deal with the basic nature of humans and their processes of living and changing. Collectively, they must be concerned with essentially the same fundamental kinds of human phenomena, although they may label these differently and selectively emphasize different attributes. It should be possible to enrich the work of each through knowledge of the other. Therefore, another function of the comparative framework is to help in relating psychotherapy concepts, propositions, and data with those of relevant human sciences, and vice versa. For example, scholars studying human emotions and psychotherapists dealing with humans' emotional problems surely can learn from one another; scientists studying developmental and learning processes and psychotherapists actively trying to facilitate human change could productively combine their knowledge. To do this requires mutual understanding of one another's ideas, and their specialized conceptual and propositional language makes communication difficult.

CHARACTERISTICS TO BE ENCOMPASSED BY A COMPREHENSIVE COMPARATIVE FRAMEWORK

The next step is to identify the types of issues that therapy models may address and on which they may differ. They are summarized in five categories:

1. They may differ in their guiding metaphysical and epistemological assumptions.
2. They may use different levels of analysis and primary units of reference.
3. Their concepts may emphasize any of the multiple aspects of humans and kinds of responses of which people are capable, and any of the diverse contexts in which people live and work.
4. Their propositions may include both stability-maintaining and change-producing dynamics.
5. They may use diverse units of analysis, ranging from micro to macro, to divide the flow of human behavior into meaningful and useful chunks.

Criteria for each of these categories are discussed next.

MULTIPLE EPISTEMOLOGIES AND METAPHYSICAL STARTING ASSUMPTIONS

Chapter 1 discussed different kinds of starting assumptions and epistemologies and the selective influence they exert on theorists' proposals about human nature and development; it also examined what is considered relevant for evaluating the truth, falsity, or utility of proposals. At one extreme is logical positivism. It starts with assumptions of realism and a radical empiricist epistemology. This leads to the selection of methods such as objective measurement for obtaining precise information that can be replicated both within and across persons. General knowledge represents consistencies among specific, discrete observations. A form of knowledge that cannot be anchored directly or indirectly to objective observations cannot be evaluated for truth, falsity, or utility. At the other extreme is phenomenalism, a view that begins with idealism and a rationalistic epistemology. All people can know is their own experience, so all knowledge represents personal constructions. Reality

is not something to be discovered; each person constructs his or he
sion. This view leads to methods for accessing people's phenomenc
subjective observation or empathy. Cosmological views range i
mechanistic models at one extreme to volitional models at the other.

Different starting assumptions are often presented as incompatible, ei-
ther/or alternatives. However, each may be appropriate for different levels
and units of analysis and aspects of humans. An adequate comparative framework should consider all these possibilities.

LEVELS OF ANALYSIS AND A PRIMARY UNIT OF REFERENCE

When a therapist first sees clients, they usually start by talking about specific
symptoms or characteristics of their lives that they find troublesome and unwanted, such as marital discord, anxiety or depressive states, or cognitive
confusion. Typically, they do not discuss their symptoms as isolated experiences. They also talk about patterns and circumstances in which their problems occur and the developmental sequence of these patterns. Moreover, they
talk about their concerns in terms of both their own attributes and their life
contexts. Analogously, when scientists study humans, they typically choose
specific variables to measure or observe, but they must also be concerned
with the person in whom those variables occur—the person's motivation to
participate in the research, her ability to fit it into her daily schedule; her understanding of what she is supposed to do. Moreover, scientists are always
collecting their data in a specific context, and variations in the context may affect the status of the variables they have chosen for study.

Thus, both therapists and scientists use multiple levels of analysis in their
work—from specific symptoms/characteristics or variables to the person-
hood of their clients or subjects to people's roles as parts of larger contexts or
environments. As discussed in Chapter 1, it is not necessary to deal with all
possible levels of analysis. Each theorist focuses on a level of primary interest but is likely to consider phenomena at least one level above and below the
primary level. Therefore, the comparative framework should encompass at
least three levels of analysis.

The Person as the Primary Reference Unit
It is inescapably a person—not just an idea, problem, symptom, or emotional
experience—with whom therapists must deal. As long as a person is alive, he
or she exists, functions, and develops as a structural/functional unit in a context—as a unitary organism. This *principle of unitary functioning* implies that
any change in any part of a person will be facilitated and constrained by its

relationships with other aspects of the person and his or her contexts, and may trigger accommodating changes in those other aspects. Therefore, the *person-in-context* must be the primary level of analysis or unit of reference to which therapy theories are anchored. It is with human *personality* (*-ality* means the quality of being human) in all its complexity and diversity that psychotherapy and psychotherapists must deal. However, effective psychotherapy requires attending to at least two other levels of analysis.

Components of Humans as a Level of Analysis
The concept of personality refers to the complex and dynamic organization of interrelated, specialized behavior subsystems that organize our functioning from infancy through old age. Therefore, the unitary functioning of humans cannot be satisfactorily understood or changed without an understanding of the specialized, qualitatively different structural and functional subsystems, and the dynamics of their organization and interactions. Our framework must provide for all the parts of humans that psychotherapy theories and the human sciences emphasize: the nervous system, cognition, emotions, actions, and so on. This is a level of analysis one step below the *person-in-context* level.

The Environment as Another Level of Analysis
People are simultaneously individual entities and components of social groups, communities, cultures, designed and natural environments. Their functioning as a person is facilitated and constrained by the nature of those environments. Because the role of environments in human functioning and development has been controversial in both the human sciences and psychotherapy theory, a brief discussion of alternate views is useful.

One old and still influential view asserts that behavior results from properties of the person. Aristotle argued that objects have properties and that any object's functioning may be understood in terms of its properties. For example, why does a ball roll? Because it is round. Its behavior—rolling—results from its inherent properties—roundness. Similarly, people's behavior results from their personal attributes—that is, $B=f(P)$. For example, why do only some people develop depressions? Because only some people have genes for depressive states. This Aristotelian mode of analysis underlies the influential tradition of trait psychology, which holds that people behave aggressively because they have an aggressive trait, instinct, motive, or gene.

The Italian physicist Galileo argued that Aristotle was only partly right; the behavior of any object is a function of both its properties and its interactions with its context. For example, a ball will not roll, despite its roundness, unless some force is applied and it is unimpeded by other forces. Extended to humans, this Galilean mode of analysis asserts that behavior results from the interaction of person and environmental attributes—that is, B=f(P,E). For example, why do some people develop depressions? Because they have genes that make them vulnerable *and* they experience environmental conditions that transform that vulnerability into a depressive state. Lewin (1931) gave many everyday examples of this view: seeing is not possible without light; walking involves both actions and gravity. Evolutionary theory is based on the interaction of organisms' attributes and their environmental niche. The suffix, *-ment,* in environment means "has an effect on."

Clients use both Aristotelian and Galilean explanations; they may blame themselves or their contexts for their difficulties. They describe both functioning differently in different contexts and generalized behavior patterns across contexts. Therefore, the comparative framework must encompass both.

What is the nature of those person-environment (P-E) interactions? Four types of answers have been proposed: action; action-reaction; interaction; transaction. The action view fits common sense ideas about causality. People act on their environment—for example, "I hit him"; "I ate the pie." Their environment acts on them— "My wound became infected"; "The medicine cured the infection." Thinking in terms of action-reaction sequences is a somewhat more elaborate version of the action view because it identifies one occurrence as a precursor or a prompt to another: "I hit him; he cried; Mother punished me." This is sometimes called the ABC view, as A(ntecedent events) elicit B(ehavior), which is followed by C(onsequences). One version of this view is called a mechanistic model. In it, a person's behavior is controlled by stimuli; people react to events; influence flows from E to P. It is sometimes called a robot model. In another version, the person is said to control his or her own destiny, sometimes called a pilot model. People use the environment to serve their own goals; influence flows from P to E. This linear causality view has been a source of controversy among psychologists. For example, are the effects of "reinforcement" automatic? Are teleological explanations useful? In the interaction view, people and their contexts continuously interact and simultaneously prompt and are prompted by one another.

These three views each have some utility, but none adequately captures the full nature and dynamics of the phenomena. The transactional view (the prefix *trans-* suggests a "change across" or a "cross-action" effect) says people don't just interact with their contexts; they are part of their contexts. People and their contexts simultaneously and reciprocally influence one another so that each is changed by the interaction, sometimes called circular or mutual causality. Examples abound. For example, when you breathe, the composition of oxygen changes in your lungs and throughout your cardiovascular system.

Simultaneously, you are changing the composition of the air around you, as people quickly discover in a crowded room. Intraperson patterns may also be viewed as transactional—for example, action patterns and cardiovascular functioning reciprocally influence one another; thoughts shape actions and vice versa.

One way humans influence their own development is through the design of environments intended to affect them beneficially (such as purifying water, creating communication and transportation systems). Environments must also be understood as dynamic organizations of things, events, or conditions external to a person but providing contexts in which people are embedded and with which they transact.

PSYCHOTHERAPY AS A MULTILEVEL PROCESS

We should expect that psychotherapy theories will emphasize some aspects of each of these three levels of analysis and their relationships. Therefore, the comparative framework must represent individuals as integrated units, composed of dynamic organizations of structural and functional components, and embedded in and in continual transaction with changing environments that themselves are complex, dynamic organizations of components. Of course, some psychotherapy theories may give attention to phenomena at other levels of analyses as well—such as genetic characteristics—and, if they do, that will be noted. Figure 2.1 represents a person as a contextually embedded, complexly organized, multilevel organization of structures and functions. Each component of Figure 2.1 is briefly discussed.

CONCEPTUAL CONTENT

Over the centuries, scientists and professionals studying or serving humans have evolved categories they have found useful for representing the generic characteristics of humans. Broad consensus exists about the usefulness of this classification system, illustrated by its use in scholarly, professional, and everyday discourse. Using the same classification system has the advantage of facilitating communication across professional and scientific boundaries. We require our comparative framework to encompass all aspects of that classification system. It is discussed in biological, psychological-behavioral, and environmental subsets.

Generic Biological Characteristics

Biological and biomedical sciences have agreed on and systematically use the same classification system for the biological structural and functional prop-

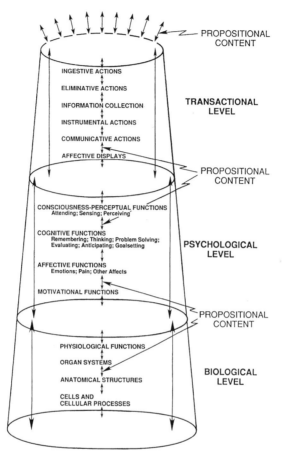

ENVIRONMENTAL CONTEXT
Natural-Designed-Interpersonal-Sociocultural

PROPOSITIONAL
CONTENT

INGESTIVE ACTIONS

ELIMINATIVE ACTIONS

INFORMATION COLLECTION

INSTRUMENTAL ACTIONS

COMMUNICATIVE ACTIONS

AFFECTIVE DISPLAYS

**TRANSACTIONAL
LEVEL**

PROPOSITIONAL
CONTENT

CONSCIOUSNESS-PERCEPTUAL FUNCTIONS
Attending; Sensing; Perceiving

COGNITIVE FUNCTIONS
Remembering; Thinking; Problem Solving;
Evaluating; Anticipating; Goalsetting

AFFECTIVE FUNCTIONS
Emotions; Pain; Other Affects

MOTIVATIONAL FUNCTIONS

**PSYCHOLOGICAL
LEVEL**

PROPOSITIONAL
CONTENT

PHYSIOLOGICAL FUNCTIONS

ORGAN SYSTEMS

ANATOMICAL STRUCTURES

CELLS AND
CELLULAR PROCESSES

**BIOLOGICAL
LEVEL**

Figure 2.1   A representation of a human being as an integrated, multilevel organization of physical structures and biological, psychological, and behavioral functions embedded in and in continual transaction with a dynamically organized, multilevel environment. The categories within each level represent the conceptual content of the model of a person. The arrows connecting categories and levels represent the propositional content of the model. This can also be understood as representing interrelated levels and units of analysis. Disciplines and professions differ in terms of the levels and units of analysis they choose to emphasize. A person is always functioning in some context, so the primary unit of analysis for psychotherapists is the person-in-context level.

erties of humans as well as common concept labels for each property and combinations thereof. This convention greatly facilitates communication among them, the integration of new and existing knowledge, and teaching the information to students. Morphology deals with structure and form; physiology focuses on biological functions and structural-functional systems. Cell biology focuses on the structure and function of different types of cells that compose different tissues, organs, and organ systems.

The human body is an embedded hierarchy of biological structures. Cells are organized into tissues and organs, which are organized into organ systems. Structurally a person may be represented as an organization of organ systems. Structural differences, deficiencies, or anomalies will alter functional and developmental possibilities. For example, being born without arms will directly and indirectly influence not only what a person can do but also what he or she may think, feel, and try to do, and how others may react to that person. A person who is seven feet tall may find it relatively easy to become a basketball star, but hard to find a bed that is large enough for comfort.

Humans' biological structures are constructed and maintained by biological functions carried out by different biochemical processes interacting in different ways. These biological processes also make possible generic psychological/behavioral functions but do not determine their content. Biological processes are also organized hierarchically, so that organ systems' physiological processes—such as respiration, digestion, and circulation—emerge from a complex of lower-level biological processes carried out at organ, tissue, and cellular levels. Some processes, such as cell metabolism, operate solely at one level whereas others, such as nervous system functioning, operate at more complex levels. Psychotherapists may confront psychological or behavioral consequences of dysfunction in any biological process in individual clients. For example, a hyper- or hypothyroid condition may alter mood and activity levels. Conversely, behavior patterns may alter biological processes—inadequate dietary habits may cause thyroid dysfunction.

A sophisticated knowledge of human biology requires understanding of each of the biological levels and their interrelationships, whereas most psychotherapy models will probably encompass only the biological organizations just below the person level of analysis. This might be called the physiological subsystem level. The functioning of all physiological subsystems must be continuously synchronized to produce unitary person-level functioning, so dysfunctions in any subsystem may trigger functional changes in other subsystems.

Generic Psychological and Behavioral Characteristics

Biological structures and functions make possible but do not strictly determine the different kinds of psychological and behavioral processes; the biological base provides necessary but not sufficient conditions for their development and functioning. There is a broad, widely used classification system for psychological and behavioral functions, but it is not so precisely defined nor subdivided into such clear subcategories as biological components. This lack of specificity makes more difficult the accumulation of knowledge, communication among scholars and professionals, and the teaching of students.

Selective sensory-perceptual processes produce subjective information about the content and flow of intraperson and person-context interactions. People create mental or psychological representations of many types. They manipulate these through cognitive processes to direct, organize, and evaluate different patterns of functioning in different contexts. These cognitive processes enable people to appraise themselves in the midst of action. They can transcend both space and time by exercising retrospective remembering and prospective foresight through expectations and anticipations. They can guide their current functioning by merging representations of past, present, and potential futures. People behave not only in terms of automated reflexes and habits, but also in terms of motivational processes that guide them through the opportunities and constraints provided by their contexts and biological states. They remain conscious and aware, exercising selective attention, producing thoughtful direction and control over what they do, who they are, and what they become through use of personal goals, values, personal agency beliefs, knowledge, and skills. People also experience qualitatively different states such as fatigue, pain, and emotions that influence the flow of their behavior.

Through motoric actions, people selectively ingest and eliminate materials into and from their bodies, move their bodies through space in various ways, physically relate to and manipulate objects and other organisms (including people), and modify their environments to serve their purposes. Through communicative actions, such as information collection, gestures, speech, and writing, people use information and meaning forms to influence the behavior of others and to create and operate social organizations and cultures.

Generic Environmental Characteristics

Humans cannot function or develop without exchanging materials and information with supportive environments. Environments, like individuals, must be understood as dynamic organizations of things and events. There are multiple environmental classification systems, but there is no consensus on which ones to use. Four broad categories appear to be widely useful and to encompass diverse disciplines studying environments. The *natural environment* encompasses all the physical properties of nature as studied by disciplines such as physics, chemistry, biology, geology, and the atmospheric sciences. It represents the ecological niche in which life evolved and provides materials essential for human life, such as food and oxygen, as well as materials and natural events that may endanger life, such as infectious diseases, predators, and natural disasters. Allergies are an example of the influence of the natural environment on human functioning. The *designed environment* includes all the material/energy forms humans have created to increase their adaptiveness and the quality of their lives, such as cars, radios, eyeglasses and wheelchairs. The boundary between natural and designed environments has become unclear as a result of humans' growing ability to genetically engineer modifications in various life forms.

Humans evolved as social entities and require intimate social relationships as well as larger instrumental ones to fulfill needs that are products of their evolutionary and sociocultural history. Humans are simultaneously separate units and components of social contexts. This Janus-faced duality (Koestler, 1978) often produces conflicting influences on people, sometimes facilitating and sometimes constraining their development and functioning. Two ways of categorizing human social environments have demonstrated utility. *Interpersonal contexts* are situations in which direct interactions among people are the critical factor such as friendships, families, and workmates. These are contexts studied in fields such as social psychology and family studies. Intimate interpersonal relationships provide a form of social nutriment that seems as important to human life as material nutriment and are essential for reproductive success and species survival. *Sociocultural environments* are a form of designed environments humans have created to facilitate social group living. They are manifested in cultural forms such as education, religion, government, languages, laws, and customs. These phenomena are studied in fields such as anthropology, economics, political science, and sociology. Humans' sociocultural contexts vary greatly from society to society, and from one historical period to another, but they are inevitably there in some form to provide critically important facilitating and constraining conditions within which each person is born, lives, develops, and dies.

Multidisciplinary-Multiprofessional Orientations Necessary
The biological, psychological, behavioral, and environmental characteristics represented in Figure 2.1 have been conceptualized as qualitatively distinct; however, they represent different aspects of a highly organized, complex sys-

tem that must operate as a team if people are to function as unified entities in varying contexts. This summary of the diversity of phenomena involved in understanding human living makes it clear that psychotherapists face a *multidisciplinary* and *multiprofessional* situation. Moreover, because knowledge is undergoing continual development, they must work to stay abreast of the expanding base of knowledge and methods being generated by a diversity of human sciences and professions. Effective utilization of such advances cannot result from simple, additive accretion; they must be combined in compatible ways if they are to contribute to an understanding of the person-in-context as a unified entity. Such integration depends significantly on the propositional content of the model used.

PROPOSITIONAL CONTENT

Humans must be understood as continuous and ongoing processes, as an existence rather than something fixed and static, as an essence, not just as an instance of being but as also engaged in a process of becoming something other than what they already are. Moreover, a life-span view is needed because those dynamics appear to operate throughout life.

Organization and Unitary Functioning

All of a person-in-context's specialized parts are simultaneously and continuously operative. The parts are not unrelated, specialized bits and pieces but are continuously and dynamically interrelated to produce unified intraperson and person-context patterns. This means that to produce such unity there must be organizing processes and functional dynamics within and between the specialized structures and functions symbolized by the vertical arrows in Figure 2.1. Processes of living involve continual activity, with every component in continuing flux, involved in a never-ending process of variation and change throughout life. Yet, life and personal identity require stability of pattern, so the propositional content of psychotherapy theories must account for dynamics that produce stable, unitary patterns of functioning and simultaneously permit and produce variability and change.

Propositions Concerning Stability of Pattern

One of the puzzling things about psychotherapy clients is that they maintain dysfunctional patterns despite the unhappiness, misery, and disruptions these patterns cause in daily life. One would think that if an existing pattern didn't work, a person would do something to fix it. Many people do. However, one characteristic of psychotherapy clients is that they have been unable to change their troublesome patterns on their own. That is why they have sought professional help. How does each psychotherapy theory explain the persistence of misery-producing, self-defeating patterns of functioning? What do they propose to be the dynamics that produce and maintain such stability?

More broadly, an efficiency of human functioning is that frequently performed behavior patterns can become automated so that we don't have to start from scratch and think carefully to deal with recurrent episodes of living. Such automation dynamics are a cornerstone of skill development. Therefore, development and maintenance of stable patterns is a key to humans' adaptive success. One of the difficult tasks for psychotherapists is that it is not enough to get an alternate, more satisfactory behavior pattern to occur; it is also necessary to cultivate it to the point that it replaces the troublesome pattern and becomes the person's dominant mode of functioning. In other words, the behavior must become habitual. What do psychotherapy theories propose to be the dynamics by which such automation of pattern occurs? Are such dynamics thought to be the same or different from those that maintain the stability of clients' troublesome behavior patterns? The comparative framework must provide a general context for comparing proposals about the dynamics by which stability of pattern is produced and maintained.

Propositions Concerning Variability and Change in Pattern
Continual variations are manifest at every organizational level of a person. Biologically, heart rate, blood pressure, and body temperature vary, but do so within some typical range; behaviorally, even when performing well-learned tasks for which they have constructed strong habits, people never behave exactly the same way twice. Variability of pattern does not necessarily mean that a person has changed. Stability in human life exists as bounded or limited patterns of variable functioning; but pervasive patterns of variability create conditions from which changes arise. A change may be temporary, to disappear later, like a bruised arm; it may endure over an extended period of time, such as a child's growth in height; it may be an elaboration of existing capabilities, as when a person learns new skills, or a decremental reduction of them, as suffering a memory loss. By what dynamics do these different kinds of changes occur? Some of them appear to occur through some kind of progressive elaboration of pattern, as when a child learns to walk. Others appear to occur rather suddenly through some kind of transformation of pattern, as with a stroke. By what propositions do psychotherapy theories explain processes of variation and change? What produces variability in pattern, and under what conditions does that lead to change? Are the dynamics of slow change the same as or different from those of sudden change?

It is important to recognize that any psychotherapy intervention is an intrusion into continuously operative client processes that may be functioning to maintain stability of pattern, to allow variability of functioning to meet new conditions, or to facilitate change to create new capabilities. Therefore, proposals about therapy methods to facilitate client change or produce preferred stable patterns must be linked to propositions about clients' natural stability-maintaining and change-producing processes. Of course, the objectives of treatment will be constrained by each client's developmental potential and what their contexts can be shaped to permit. Some changes may be more possible within certain clients and contexts than in others. Moreover, because people are multilevel, dynamic organizations, processes of variation and change may occur both within and between levels. The propositional content of psychotherapy theories must accommodate multilevel as well as multidimensional relationships.

Therapists face choices about where to target their interventions, and their propositions guide their thinking about the extent to which changes produced in one part of a person may lead to changes in other aspects. For example, correcting a person's thyroid deficiency may lead to changes in sleep and activity patterns and in school performance; changes in negative self-evaluations may lead to improved social relations, and reductions in emotional disturbances or distressing physical symptoms; changes in social skills may alter others' reactions, which in turn may lead to changes in one's thoughts and feelings. The comparative framework must be broad enough to facilitate comparison of diverse proposals about the dynamics of stability maintenance, variability, and change and about the procedures required to influence those processes.

UNITS OF ANALYSIS

The metaphor of a flowing stream is frequently used to characterize the continuous yet variable properties of human functioning. As Kelly (1955) observed years ago, people are not inert or static entities, in need of either a carrot or a stick to prompt behavior. Activity is an intrinsic and inherent property of life. Even structures that seem to be fixed and static undergo continual reconstruction. There is no point while a person is alive that activity ceases. A casual observer might suppose that it does—during states of sleep or comatose conditions, for example. However, a rich variety of activity is going on throughout such apparently inactive periods. It is simply a question of which events are occurring under what conditions. If behavior is always occurring, then the problem is not to account for why behavior occurs, but why one pattern occurs rather than another from one occasion to the next.

A continuous stream of behavior cannot be understood and managed in its entirety; it must be divided into meaningful chunks for both scholarly and practical purposes. It is possible to divide the behavioral stream into different units of analysis, and the units people choose are a function of their purposes, their preferred levels of analysis, and the model they are using to guide their work. The units chosen, however, constrain what one can learn about the stream of life; different units represent different ways of viewing that stream of events.

Units of Analysis as Organized Patterns
Human behavior inherently displays organization; different component behaviors are regularized and orderly with respect to one another, operating as a network of interdependent and coordinated parts that function as a whole, to produce harmonious and concerted action. The organization of the biological aspects of humans is widely understood. Less well understood are the dynamics of psychological and behavioral organization, manifested in driving a car, composing music, speaking, or making love. Units of analysis differ in the kinds, amount, and organization of behavior encompassed in the unit, ranging from small, simply organized kinds and amounts to large, elaborately organized kinds and amounts, illustrated by units named reflex, memory, habit, schema, attitude, experimental trial, phobia, and panic attack. Representing units of analysis in terms of both their content and organization reveals that modifying an existing unit may involve not only adding, subtracting, amplifying, or attenuating elements in the pattern, but also changing the organization of the pattern. Units may be defined by temporal, quantitative, and complex characteristics in addition to qualitative characteristics.

Temporal Characteristics of Units
One mode of analysis represents the flow of a person's behavior in relationship to time. Some responses may occur at the same time. For example, one method for identifying a person's emotional state is to observe the pattern of muscle activity in his or her face; one pattern produces a happy face and others an angry or sad face. These are sometimes referred to as *behavior patterns*, a unit of analysis that represents a set of responses or events occuring at the same time. Another mode of temporal analysis represents behaviors and events as occurring in a temporal sequence, often called *behavior sequences,* and sometimes referred to as the chaining of behavior. The frequently used A(ntecedent) ➤ B(ehavior) ➤ C(onsequent) analysis is illustrative. An exam-

ple of sequential description of a specific episode is "He entered the elevator, became frightened, and ran off." Specific episodes are typically relatively meaningless unless they exemplify a recurrent pattern, and sequential analysis can serve that purpose, as "Whenever he enters a small, enclosed space, he becomes frightened, and leaves." Sequential analysis can be elaborated to include multiple behaviors, antecedents, and consequences. *Path analysis* is a statistical method for performing sequential analyses. Neither pattern nor sequence analyses can represent the complexity of many human patterns. Therefore, the two are often combined to represent a more complex chunk of behavior as a *pattern sequence.* Often these more complex units of analysis are represented by a single concept label, such as claustrophobia or manic depressive.

Qualitative and Quantitative Characteristics of Units
Temporally defined units of analysis were used as the analytic framework in our earlier study of systems of psychotherapy (Ford & Urban, 1963), but we came to agree with critics of that approach, judging it to be too limited in scope. It is a form of *qualitative analysis.* This does not include information about quantitative aspects of human functioning: the intensity, frequency, latency, duration, and rate of different aspects of behavior and of their relationships. Quantitative attributes are often critical for understanding a person's behavior and for distinguishing between pathological and normal functioning. For example, fear is a normal, useful emotion, but excessive fear is maladaptive, as in a panic state. Such quantitative or dimensional analyses increase the completeness of descriptions of functional patterns.

Complexity Characteristics of Units
Even so, temporal, qualitative, and quantitative analyses are insufficient for representing the diversity and elaborateness of human behavior. They are not adequate for representing complex phasic or cyclical patterns, such as cyclical depressions, considered of fundamental importance by some theorists. Nor can discontinuities in functioning and development, or embedded hierarchies of behavioral organization be represented solely by such analyses. Some form of *complexity analysis* is needed. For example, picking up a pencil can be represented as a unit of behavior, but that action is typically a component of a larger behavioral unit, such as writing a letter or taking an examination. Discrete or small-scale units commonly play a role, contributing to more complex levels of behavioral functioning. Moreover, the same discrete unit is frequently found to participate in a variety of more complicated patterns. Psychotherapists who deal with people's seriously dysfunctional pat-

terns are likely to use such complex units. So our comparative framework must accommodate qualitative, temporal, quantitative, and complexity differences in units of analyses.

PROVIDING FOR TESTING, IMPROVING, OR REPLACING THE MODEL OF PSYCHOTHERAPY

All models or theories should be viewed as imperfect and therefore provisional, so it is important to construct them to be evaluated against growing bodies of knowledge. For psychotherapy theories, there are two sources of relevant knowledge. The first obvious source is knowledge derived from the practice of psychotherapy itself, arising from both naturalistic clinical observation and formal empirical study. This is a rich and fruitful source, but obligations to clients seriously limit the ideas that can be tested, or the ways in which they can be tested, and therefore the potential advances that might be made if it is the only source used. The second source is the human sciences—biology, psychology, sociology, and anthropology—where careful and creative theorizing and empirical research concerns the nature of many of the same phenomena that psychotherapists confront in their daily practice. After all, the nature of humans and the ways they may be influenced to change are the same whether they are observed as clients in psychotherapy or as subjects in a research project. The purposes of therapists and scientists may be different, but the raw material from which they construct their theories is the same. One clear implication of this criterion is that psychotherapy reflects a multidisciplinary base and that the most effective treatment strategies are apt to require multiprofessional interventions, such as individual therapy combined with medications, educative procedures, or environmental changes.

NEXT STEPS

The nature of models or theories and their utility for psychotherapy has been summarized, and design criteria have been specified for a framework to be used in comparing the propositional and procedural models of psychotherapy currently in use. The next step is to create a comparative framework that fulfills these design criteria. That is done in the next two chapters.

CHAPTER 3

Understanding Humans as Complex, Dynamic Systems: A Comparative Conceptual Framework

T HIS CHAPTER DESCRIBES a general propositional model for and summarizes the conceptual components of a comparative framework that fits the design criteria summarized in Chapter 2. Chapters 4 and 5 will elaborate on the propositional components of the framework introduced here.

To demonstrate how all the properties of living described in Chapter 2 are manifested in real-life contexts as well as in psychotherapy, the example of a troubled psychotherapy client, Mrs. K, is summarized. A comparative framework must encompass all the complex patterns experienced, described, and displayed by clients such as Mrs. K. Her problems are used to show how different aspects of clients' problems can be linked to various components of the comparative framework to be described. These illustrations should help readers link the broad, abstract concepts and propositions of the framework to their own knowledge and experience, and to the meanings and properties of human life that its components are intended to encompass.

Different models can be used to understand Mrs. K's difficulties, and various models emphasize different aspects of a person and point toward varying intervention strategies, as are illustrated. If we assume that each model is useful for some purposes, it follows that an adequate comparative framework must be inclusive enough to interpret them all—that is, it must be a *meta*model that can incorporate and reveal the relationships among more specific models. A framework representing people as complex, dynamic systems is shown as a combination of control system theory, which has demonstrated extensive utility in other fields, and emerging theories of complexity and non-linear dynamics, such as chaos theory. The remainder of the chapter applies that model to meet the design criteria summarized in Chapter 2.

THE CASE OF MRS. K

Mrs. K, a 45-year-old, married, Caucasian housewife, mother of three grown children, had earlier been employed as an elementary school teacher. The following summary represents her initial interview discussion of her persistent troublesome states. She was referred by her family physician for help with her depression and anxiety. Like most clients, she came because she had been unsuccessful in resolving her problems with her own resources and capabilities, and she hoped an "expert" could help her accomplish what she had been unable to do on her own.

BIOLOGICAL STATES

She reported a succession of physical problems that had occurred during the previous three years. First, she had had a total hysterectomy because of sizable ovarian cysts. Later, she developed head, neck, and back pains intense enough to impair her ability to function; these were diagnosed as resulting from a cervical spondylosis and degenerative arthritis in her spine. In her view, her depressive and anxious feelings had originally begun some two and one-half years earlier. Before that, she felt that she had pursued a normal and happy life. She traced the beginnings of her difficulties to the onset of urinary urgency and leakage following her operation. She didn't leave her house for months, afraid of being too far from a toilet and dreading the possibility of a urinary accident in public. Her eyes reddened as she stated that "the whole thing was simply more than I could cope with." Her urinary problem was eventually corrected by regulation of her estrogen replacement medication, but by then she had "lost my self-confidence and began to be afraid of everything."

With the development of headaches, pain, and stiffness in her neck, shoulders, back, arms, and hands, and her failure to gain satisfactory relief with analgesics and physical therapy, her discouragment increased in regard to her future. Her diagnosis suggested to her a condition of premature aging. She envisioned becoming progressively disabled, confined to her home and eventually a wheelchair, useless to herself and others, and ignored by people more actively engaged in life. At the same time, she admitted that such a state of affairs might be desirable; at least, she wouldn't have to struggle any longer and could rely on others to take care of things instead. Her appetite had become poor, and she suspected that she had lost weight.

EMOTIONAL/AFFECTIVE AND AROUSAL STATES

She described her typical mood throughout each day as despondency and sadness, punctuated at intervals with abrupt feelings of fear, bordering on panic, especially when faced with particularly challenging tasks. Her despondency, accompanied by frequent weeping, had become progressively intense over the past six months. Questioning revealed that her depressed mood was accompanied by pronounced feelings of fatigue, a sense of loss in her overall energy and stamina, a generalized loss of interest in her usual activities, and excessive feelings of anger and irritability. She could not anticipate when her feelings of intense fright might occur. They had happened at frequent and unexpected times. For example, while traveling a familiar route to visit her parents, she was overwhelmed with fear that something catastrophic would happen, and she was forced to abandon her trip. She feared she might lose her way or that she would have an accident and someone—herself or others—would be injured or killed. She experienced a sudden and inexplicable panic while singing a well-rehearsed alto part in her church choir; she remained frozen for the balance of the service, too embarassed to flee. She complained of restless sleep, with periodic bad dreams and occasional nightmares. She experienced muscle stiffness and soreness on waking that eased after several hours but never left her entirely free from pain.

COGNITIVE AND PERCEPTUAL STATES

She admitted a tendency to fret and stew throughout the course of each day, preoccupied with the decline in her health and with pessimistic foreboding about her future. She was disgusted with the kind of person she had become and critical of herself for having failed to work through her problems despite varied efforts. She found especially bewildering and frightening the succession of what she called evil thoughts that repeatedly intruded into her awareness; she had recurrent visions of falling down stairs or of being stabbed in the back with a knife. She found these notions abhorrent—bad enough when she imagined them happening to herself but a great deal worse when she pictured them happening to others.

BEHAVIORAL STATES

She had been unable to maintain a schedule of daily walking, becoming demoralized over the fatigue it generated and her lack of progress or improvement. She had tried to remain involved in group activities and to do all the things said to be helpful in combating a depressed mood, only to find her condition worsening.

INTERPERSONAL/ENVIRONMENTAL CONDITIONS

Mrs. K described her life situation as far from satisfactory. She had been happier before her children had left home; she had been absorbed in and content with her role as a mother and thought that doubtless part of her problem was coping with the empty nest. She had felt impelled to do something productive and had tried to carve out some useful role for herself. Several attempts had led to failure. For example, she tried returning to teaching but gave up the effort after discovering herself too emotionally perturbed and physically drained to continue as a substitute. She had emerged from such attempts feeling both inadequate and incompetent.

Mrs. K said her husband had become a difficult person with whom to live primarily because of his drinking. Promoted to a responsible, high-pressure position, he had begun drinking more heavily—cocktails after work, wine during dinner, and highballs during the evening hours, which he devoted to solitary activities, such as working on papers from the office, using his computer, or watching TV. He chose news and political panel programs, during which he angrily denounced much that was said. Mrs. K spent most evenings alone in her room. She and her husband slept in separate rooms because she could not tolerate his snoring, apparently worsened by his drinking. They had not been physically intimate for many years. She reported that her husband would permit no criticism of his behavior and was especially angry and caustic when she objected to his drinking. She could not remain entirely silent about it, however, because she found it so distasteful.

She could not comprehend the changes that had taken place over the years and why her husband had become increasingly intolerant and domineering. In her view, he had become disparaging of people in general and his wife in particular. Her ideas were now labeled as stupid and ill informed; her present handling of their children was misguided; she was incompetent in the management of funds. He reserved total control of the money to himself, taking pride in the detailed computerized records he maintained. She was relegated to the task of mailing out checks on designated days throughout the course of the month and subjected to scolding if she made a mistake. She was inclined to accept his judgment of her inadequacy, as she was unable to defend her views in the face of his apparent superiority in knowledge and intellect. She would end up feeling helpless, collapsing into tears, and fleeing to the quiet of her room. She interpreted the experience of a knotting in her stomach and the involuntary clenching of her teeth when they talked as evidence that she had become afraid of him. At the same time, she described her husband as more relaxed and more like his old self on weekends. She asked the therapist for some explanation of this.

A friend had suggested that she consider a separation or a divorce. Mrs. K ruled out both possibilities. Her husband was skeptical of the benefits of marital counseling and opposed to her consulting a "skull-candler," pointing out that in the case of another couple, the wife had been encouraged by her counselor to leave her husband. Her husband was also provoked over the accumulation of medical bills. She said, however, "I've got to do something, and I really think he knows it—anyway, he's paid all the bills so far."

ALTERNATE MODELS FOR UNDERSTANDING/INTERPRETING MRS. K'S CONDITION

The information provided by clients such as Mrs. K cannot be simply taken at face value. The situations and events are described as Mrs. K has construed them to be: They are a product of her customary ways of looking at, thinking about, and trying to make sense of the thoughts and actions of herself and others. They are also a product of her interactions with her therapist—what she considers appropriate to report and what the therapist is able to elicit from her. Some things are not discussed, such as conflicts with her children, relationships with friends, or financial problems. Does that mean they are not problematic? In short, her construction/interpretation of what has been happening is a product of her personal models for understanding and dealing with her world and the psychotherapy situation. Although her view of herself and her situation is plausible, it is deficient in at least two important respects: (1) It is incomplete because it fails to account for the ways all these happenings influence one another (Mrs. K acknowledges that she cannot understand what has been happening and why). (2) It has failed to suggest alternatives to her fruitless attempts to resolve her difficulties and create a better life for herself. She has sought the assistance of a therapist because of those deficiencies.

The views Mrs. K has developed cannot simply be declared wrong. They are one legitimate way to represent herself and her situation. The more compelling question is whether, and to what extent, her construction has been and will be useful in analyzing what has gone wrong and what might be done to correct it. Harry Stack Sullivan, a famous psychiatrist, often said that one must always address this question: Why has the person been unable to resolve the problem on her own—what's the matter with her way of understanding and dealing with the problem to be solved? Clearly, if the psychotherapist accepts and acts solely on Mrs. K's current personal models, their collaborative effort is likely to be no more successful than her individual model in coming up with useful solutions. An alternate model for construing what has been taking place and what might be done about it will be needed. But what kind of model should it be? A number of schemes are possible.

ORGANIC MODELS

One is that her primary difficulties are direct or indirect products of some biological dysfunction(s). Perhaps the depressive and anxious feelings (along with osteoporotic changes) are consequences of hormonal imbalances so common in women undergoing premature menopause, augmented perhaps by related neurochemical changes and by her exaggerated concerns of what they might mean. Was this the initial presumption of her physician, or did her doctor conclude that additional factors must be involved? Could there be some kind of incipient brain tumor or other type of neurological damage that is disrupting Mrs. K's psychological functioning? Is a consultation with her doctor indicated?

PSYCHODYNAMIC MODELS

Alternatively, would her situation be more usefully represented as a mental illness or as a psychological disorder, as many of her symptoms match diagnostic criteria for a Major Depressive Disorder of an agitated type? Because such conditions often seem stress related, she might have developed what Selye (1976) would term a "disease of adaptation" as a consequence of intense stress sustained over a lengthy period of time. Would this suggest combining antidepressant drugs to redress stress-induced imbalances in neurotransmitter functioning with psychotherapy to identify and alleviate the sources of stress? What does one make of her autochthonous thoughts and images or catastrophic visions? These are some of the events that appear to perturb her the most. Because apprehensive thoughts of impending doom (dying, loss of love object or sanity) are common components of an agitated depressive states, can they be expected to disappear following alleviation of her condition? Do they instead signify the presence of unacknowledged anger toward both herself and others? Is a view like psychoanalysis applicable here? Perhaps her apprehensions represent a compromise formation in relation to an underlying conflict. They may allow her to give some form of expression to her aggressive feelings without running the risk of actually putting them into action.

PSYCHOSOCIAL MODELS

Would such views adequately accommodate other relevant elements? There are some indications of difficulties linked to the loss of her maternal role and her inability to define another identity to give her life meaning and significance. Should feminist perspectives and therapy be applied? Alternatively, does Mrs. K's apparent pattern of self-criticism, helplessness, submissiveness, and acquiescence to her husband suggest a longer term dependency pattern, antecedent to the more recent difficulties and contributing to her present illness and her inability to cope? What about the marital difficulties that loom so prominently in her thinking? Apparently, Mrs. K. has been content to attribute these to changes having taken place in her husband, implying that his workaholic and alcoholic habits are jointly responsible. She fails to realize, however, that all relationships are transactional in character and that she must have been a participant, albeit unwittingly, in the development of difficulties between them. If so, what does this imply for further inquiry and treatment? Is an interpersonal or object relations framework of analysis needed, or should a model be drawn from the cognitive-behavioral or family systems literature?

MULTIVARIATE INTEGRATIVE MODELS

The foregoing discussion of alternate generic models emphasizes the wide variety of problems occurring simultaneously in Mrs. K's life. She has been undergoing physiological and biological changes and they have played some part in her overall condition; this cannot be ignored. Her habitual ways of perceiving and thinking and the emotional and psychological distress they seem to generate are also vital aspects of her life. Her customary patterns of interaction with others, particularly her husband, also appear to be important. A person functions as an integrated unit and the various components cannot occur independently from one another, so all facets of Mrs. K's life must somehow be interrelated. We call this the *principle of unitary functioning*. A physician or psychotherapist may choose to focus on some aspect of a person and neglect others, but to do so entails risks of faulty or partial understanding of clients' problems, of the use of ineffective or problem-producing interventions, of higher than necessary treatment costs, and of discrediting the utility of psychotherapy itself.

Even when a therapist ignores the operation of some parts of a person, this does not negate the reality that each is operative, influencing and being influenced by the larger pattern—the person—in which it is embedded. Therefore, to understand clients-in-context as the unit of concern, why they function as they do, and what activities might facilitate desired changes, a more integrative framework is necessary, one that can encompass the more specific, useful models of different aspects of people's lives. It must include both the kinds of phenomena (thoughts, feelings, actions, interpersonal relationships) that are important (the conceptual content), and ideas about how such phenomena interrelate with and influence one another (the propositional content). Proponents of integrative models assume that each type of psychotherapy that has been created and has persisted must have some kind of utility for some purposes; they suggest that integrative models would be useful in providing guidance in deciding why, when, and how the methods of each type of approach might be helpful with different clients and how they might be related.

Model Building by Analogy

Following publication of *Systems of Psychotherapy* (Ford & Urban, 1963), we began a search for a comprehensive model that could integrate the diverse facets of humans emphasized by different psychotherapy approaches and the human sciences so that the two might be better linked. A model is required that could represent all the content, organization, and dynamics of human functioning and change. We found no model in psychotherapy theory or psychological science that could fulfill most of these criteria. Psychological science is organized around specialized subsets of phenomena and has produced intriguing and useful theories about each, sometimes called *minitheories*. In a personal communication, one publisher stated that psychologists are "not interested in grand, integrative theorizing these days; they think only minitheories are scientifically useful."

Minitheories are essential because they help users understand component processes. In professional and personal life, however, as well as in research projects, it is never possible to deal with only one part of humans separate from other parts. To be of practical utility, comprehensive models must link the important knowledge foundations represented by the minitheories that have been constructed. Therefore, a metamodel representing a whole person could be considered an organization of compatible minitheories, each of which represents some aspects of a person; these minitheories would include theories of perception, emotion, cognition, action, and social behavior.

THE CONTROL SYSTEM MODEL

As no adequate metamodel existed, we adopted a strategy commonly used in scientific model building; we examined models of demonstrated utility in other domains to find one that might be transformed to serve our purposes. This is an age-old strategy. Hundreds of years ago the fundamental mechanism by which clocks operate was utilized as a model for trying to explain and demonstrate the organization and functioning of the solar system. A more generic version of this view, often called a *mechanistic model*, came to dominate thinking in the natural sciences for centuries—for example, Newtonian physics. The development of psychology as a science was heavily influenced by this generic model. Mechanistic models have produced much valuable scientific knowledge and have spawned many technologies of great human utility.

One special offspring of this mechanistic tradition, called a *control system model*, has had great impact on technological advances in the twentieth century. Automation, servomechanisms, and robotics illustrate products of the use of this model. It has also been useful in helping scientists understand and represent basic biological processes, such as homeostasis. Its special value results from a property termed *self-regulation*. It is called a *system* because it is an organization of component structures and processes designed to operate as a unit in a given environment. It can preserve and restore its basic configuration of structure and function against nondestructive perturbations (Weiss, 1971) by utilizing products of its own functioning to create and maintain (i.e., control) previously specified intrasystem and system-context states, so it is called a control system. Theory and research in domains termed *cybernetics*, and *systems science*, and *engineering* provide a solid foundation on which control system technologies have been built.

There are many examples of control systems in contemporary industrialized societies, such as controls that regulate the heating and air conditioning of our homes, the picture quality in our TV sets, the flight path of airplanes, the operation of modern automobile engines and military weapons, and the functioning of communication networks. The invention of computers has made possible much more complex versions of this model, illustrated by computer control of living environments on space ships and the development of unmanned space ships to explore the solar system.

Individuals function as units composed of component structures and processes, and self-regulation is a fundamental characteristic of humans' biological, psychological, and behavioral functioning. Therefore, the control system model so useful to engineers in designing technological self-regulating mechanisms might be a useful tool for understanding humans. In the decades following the end of World War II in 1945, scholars in the biological, psychological, and social sciences began seriously exploring that possibility. (See Miller, 1978, for discussion and bibliographies about these efforts, and Miller, Galanter, and Pribram, 1960, and Powers, 1973, for early efforts to use a control system model for representing human functioning.) Searching for a comprehensive model by which to understand human development, we carefully examined those efforts. Next, we describe the control system model's properties and summarize why we found it promising but inadequate for our purposes.

COMPONENTS OF THE CONTROL SYSTEM MODEL

Figure 3.1 summarizes key properties of a control system model. In the following paragraphs, the conceptual components—the boxes of Figure 3.1—are briefly explained. Then the propositional components—the arrows—that represent the dynamics of the model are discussed. Remember, however, that each part by itself is useless. It is the *organization* of the parts so that through their interactions they collectively operate as a self-regulating unit that makes it a control system.

The distinguishing feature of a control system is its *functional capabilities,* but there must always be some *physical structure* that makes possible that functional, self-regulating capability. One aspect of control system flexibility is that the *same* functional pattern can be realized through *different* physical structures. For example, the structures of an automated atomic power plant, of the guidance system that regulates the flight path of an airplane, and of the sensory-motor arrangements by which birds guide their flight are quite different. Yet, in one way or another, all make possible the same generic self-regulating functional pattern represented in Figure 3.1. All activity uses energy; therefore, there must be an *energizing function* or source. In most modern control systems that is some source of electricity, but it can be some other form of energy, such as mechanical or thermal. Living systems are unique in that they have built-in capabilities for generating the energy needed to fuel their activities.

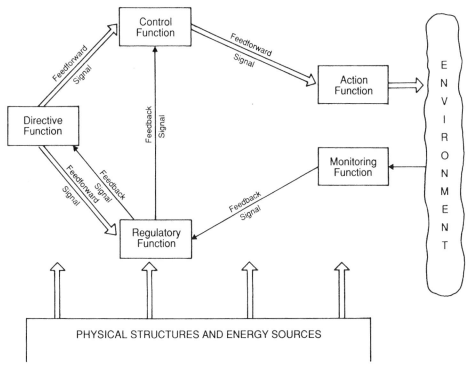

Figure 3.1 *A Prototypic Control System.* A representation of the functional organization of a self-regulating control system. A *directive function* specifies the state of specific variables to be achieved/maintained; a *monitoring function* collects information about the current state of the variables to be controlled; a *regulatory function* compares the current state with the desired state to detect any discrepancy that may exist; the *control function* organizes system activity to produce the necessary changes in the current state of the relevant variables; and an *action function* carries out the activity in relation to the system's environment. This pattern of functioning is continuous. There are always some requisite physical structures and energy sources to make this functional process possible. Wide arrows signify feedforward functions; narrow arrows signify feedback functions. All functions are continuously and simultaneously occurring, and the entire organization functions as a unit.

A self-regulating system is one whose functions collectively and cooperatively produce and maintain coherently organized states of specified variables by the following means:

1. A *directive function* that specifies the state to be produced or maintained, sometimes called the *set point* or *command function*

2. A *monitoring function* that continuously monitors the consequences of the system's functioning that are relevant to the states specified in item 1, sometimes called the *input* or *information collection* function

3. A *regulatory function* that evaluates the input provided by monitoring to identify any existing discrepancies between its current and specified, preferred state, sometimes called the *comparative* or *evaluative* function

4. A *control function* that coordinates and organizes system activity to reduce discrepancies between current and specified states, often called *throughput* functions

5. An *action function* that can implement activity to modify relevant conditions so as to reduce the discrepancy between current and desired states, sometimes called an *output* function

6. An *environment* within which the system's action capabilities can produce and maintain desired states.

Such arrangements are called control systems because they operate to control the status of specified variables against any influences that might disrupt or perturb the preferred states, such as the altitude, speed, and direction of flight controlled by a plane's automatic pilot. This is a particularly powerful and flexible arrangement because it does not require identification of the cause or source of the disruption; it must only recognize that a discrepancy exists and influence the relevant variables to produce the desired state, regardless of the nature or source of the disrupting influence.

DYNAMICS OF CONTROL SYSTEM MODELS

The arrows in Figure 3.1 represent signals or interactions by which each function may influence others, so they symbolize the dynamics, or propositional model, by which the system operates as a unified entity. The slim arrows are called *feedback signals* because they represent the current state of the variables to be controlled and the discrepancies that may exist between the specified and current states, i.e., they represent the current, relevant consequences of the system's ongoing activity. The wide arrows are called *feedforward signals* because they proactively organize system activity to try to produce the designated preferred state, within the constraints of the capabilities provided by the system's structure, its current state, and its environment. Each control system can only do certain kinds of things under its operating conditions.

The feedback and feedforward signals are typically represented as information flows: The system collects, evaluates, and uses information about itself, its environment, and the relevant consequences of functioning. That is why information sciences and computers have been so important in expanding the complexity of the kinds of conditions that control systems can regulate. However, if the arrows in Figure 3.1 are understood as representing modes of influence, then it becomes obvious that the influences could be accomplished through either informational or physical signals, or both. This is an important distinction for understanding humans. The biological processes are regulated primarily by physical signals, for example, biochemical compounds; psychological processes are regulated primarily by informational signals, such as perceptions or thoughts. Remember, the same prototypical functional pattern can be made possible by different physical arrangements.

A control system involves a pattern of *circular processes*; the consequences of the system's activity serve to modify its activity, so these processes are called *feedback loops*. Each component in Figure 3.1 must be present, functioning well, and appropriately connected with one another for the system to operate effectively. If any component is missing or performing inadequately, the system will be ineffective in regulating specified system states. When structural damage or functional disruptions occur, the system is said to be *malfunctioning* or *dysfunctional*. A dramatic, costly example occurred in 1993: Ground controllers lost contact with a space lab designed to explore Mars. Years of work and a billion dollar investment were lost because some components malfunctioned in that complex control system arrangement.

Note that all the functions in Figure 3.1 occur continuously. Visualize Figure 3.1 as flowing through time with the content of each function varying with time, including properties of the environment that may vary unpredictably and independently of the system's activities. The specific content at any moment is called a *system state*. As the content of any function can change from moment to moment, system states will vary. The pattern of variability among a sequence of system states reveals the dynamics of the system's functioning. Later we discuss the importance of this for studying and understanding humans.

The system is continuously comparing where it is with where it wants to be. That comparison could reveal two kinds of discrepancy patterns over time: They could decrease or increase. When the system is operating to *reduce the discrepancy* between current and specified states, the operation is called a *negative feedback process*. The content and context of system functions are always varying. Negative feedback processes operate to contain such fluctuations within preferred or permissible ranges of variation, as specified by the directive and regulatory functions. When they succeed in doing so, a sequence of system states displays a dynamic stability, typically called a *steady state*. For example, most healthy people's bodies maintain a normal or steady state body temperature that varies in a small range from hour to hour around a norm of 98.6 degrees Fahrenheit. Thus, negative feedback processes produce steady states; they are *stability-maintaining processes.*

However, it is possible for system activity to act on itself in such a way as to increase the discrepancy between current and specified states. Such a *deviation amplifying process* is called *a positive feedback process.* Obviously, this will produce the opposite effect of stability-maintaining processes. These processes are a potential source of change because they drive the system further and further away from its previous steady states. They have dangerous potential because if unchecked, these deviation-amplifying processes would eventually exhaust or destroy the system. For example, an atomic power plant's fission process operates by feeding on itself; unless the positive feedback process is limited, it will accelerate into an atomic explosion. Similarly, marital conflicts may accelerate over time into a marital breakup unless methods exist for resolving such disagreements before they become too divisive. Hence, the deviation-amplifying, change-producing influences of positive feedback processes are typically linked to the deviation-reducing, stability-maintaining influences of negative feedback processes. The negative feedback processes become operative when the consequences of positive feedback processes reach certain levels. Thus, control system dynamics can operate so that stability and variability can coexist in the interest of maintaining the integrity of the system.

The concepts of positive and negative feedback make intuitive sense, and the terms are now in wide general usage. Unfortunately, their popular usage is the opposite of the technical meaning, producing confusion about the nature of control system models. Popular use refers to the *content of the feedback signal* rather than to the *nature of the regulatory feedback process.* For example, "The boss just gave me some positive feedback!" refers to a *feedback signal* with positive content—a favorable appraisal by the boss. However, workers feel good about such appraisals because they operate as part of a *negative feedback process*—the workers want the boss to think well of them so the positive appraisal reduces the gap between what they want and what they are getting. On the other hand, "The boss gave me some negative feedback today!" is a negative appraisal or *feedback signal* that makes them feel bad because it is part of a *positive feedback process* and increases the gap between what they want and what they are getting.

ANALOGIES BETWEEN CONTROL SYSTEM COMPONENTS AND HUMAN CAPABILITIES

If a control system model is to be useful in representing humans, users must be able to map the basic human characteristics summarized in Chapter 2 and

Figure 2.1 onto the generic control system model summarized in Figure 3.1. As the reference level of analysis is the *person-in context,* that is the unit of analysis to which this discussion is directed. Similar analogies to Figure 3.1 could be considered for other levels of analysis, such as the cellular level.

Humans' biological characteristics are analogous to the physical structures of a control system: Humans' biological characteristics make possible their psychological and behavioral functions and provide a physical boundary separating the person's internal dynamics from those of their contexts. Humans' metabolic capabilities perform functions analogous to the energizing processes; cognitive processes provide capabilities analogous to the directive, regulatory, and control functions of a control system; action and communicative capabilities are analogous to the action functions; sensory/perceptual capabilities perform the monitoring functions; and natural, designed, interpersonal, and sociocultural contexts are analogous to the environment.

Humans' sensory/perceptual processes generate afferent information-based feedback signals the system can use to carry out its regulatory and self-organizing processes. Humans' cognitive processes generate efferent information-based feedforward signals that make possible anticipatory, future-oriented functioning to organize and coordinate action patterns. Humans' motoric and communicative actions can influence environmental conditions and their impact on the person. Finally, the model summarized in Figure 3.1 operates as a unit in a context, just as a person does, so it provides a framework for representing complex organization of behavior patterns or personality as system states. Thus, the components in Figure 3.1 can be reinterpreted to encompass many of the important human characteristics specified in Chapter 2.

LIMITATIONS OF CONTROL SYSTEM MODELS FOR REPRESENTING HUMANS

Because the control system did not encompass key features of humans, many thoughtful scholars rejected a control system as a model for understanding people. For example, where are the phenomena of attention and consciousness, memory and meaning construction, interpersonal communication, emotion, motivation or creative thought? The almost exclusive emphasis on negative feedback processes portrayed humans as reactive entities and failed to account adequately for the intentional, future-oriented, proactive aspects of human functioning that many psychotherapists consider important. Humans behave in terms of imagined, potential futures as well as current circumstances. Error-correcting feedback dynamics seemed inadequate for representing that property of human life.

Finally, the model did not seem to accommodate humans' capabilities for physical growth, for learning new behavior patterns, for creating new purposes to strive for and values to guide their striving, for creating new knowledge, for imaginative thought, and for development of self-defeating, self-destructive behaviors. In short, although it was reasonably adequate for representing the self-organizing characteristics of human functioning, it did not encompass the self-constructing properties of human life. Negative feedback processes of the typical control system model could represent *being* but not *becoming*.

In retrospect, this should have come as no surprise. After all, control system models are another type of machine designed by engineers. Like all machines, they can do only what they were built to do in the contexts within which they were designed to operate. Their designers do not want control systems to have a mind of their own. Their primary purpose is to exercise control over specific variables to produce stable patterns, such as a stable flight path of an airplane, therefore, it is not surprising that their negative feedback, stability maintaining functions, has been emphasized. Of course, some control systems can do pretty complicated things. For example, they can be made to mimic impressively some properties of human life when capabilities are designed in to let them operate under the simultaneous influence of multiple goals and evaluative rules. Some have large stores of information and can write "if-then" computer programs to use that memory; others have computer programs that let them construct new memories, as illustrated by computer chess playing programs that can now defeat most skilled chess players. However, they are still reactive entities. They cannot construct, repair, or alter their physical structure; they cannot imagine and construct completely new functional programs; they cannot have subjective experiences such as emotion and pain; they cannot love and procreate; they cannot imagine and create alternate futures. Humans can do all this, and more!

Even so, the control system was the most promising model available, so we asked, "Can it be elaborated or transformed to encompass these important human attributes?" We spent two decades trying to answer that question. During that period, new ideas relevant to our effort were being developed and applied in the natural sciences, particularly efforts focused on understanding complex, dynamic, nonlinear systems, such as chaos theory. The next section summarizes the way we have transformed the mechanical control system model into a model for representing living entities by merging it with these new ideas. We have called it the *Living Systems Framework (LSF)*.

To simplify the presentation, the thousands of sources from which the LSF was derived will not be cited. Extended discussion of the ideas to be presented and extensive relevant bibliographies may be found in D. Ford (1987; 1994), Ford and Ford (1987), Ford and Lerner (1992), M. Ford (1992), Urban (1978, 1987), Anokhin (1969), Arbib and Hesse (1986), Cambel (1993), Gallistel (1980), Gleick (1987), Jantsch (1980), Lewin (1992), Mahoney (1991), Maturana (1975), Miller (1978), Milsum (1968), Prigogene and Stengers (1984), Smith and Thelen (1993), Stelmach and Requin (1980), von Bertalanffy (1968), von Foerster and Zopf (1962), Weaver (1948), Wiener (1948), and Zeleny (1981).

HUMANS AS SELF-CONSTRUCTING LIVING SYSTEMS

Control systems have the important property of being *self-organizing*—that is, they can create and maintain relatively stable patterns of organization both within themselves and between themselves and their contexts; they can restore these patterns when they are disrupted, just as humans can. However, they lack the critical characteristic of being *self-constructing* that distinguishes living from nonliving entities. Humans are self-constructing in two senses: They grow and develop as biological organisms, and they learn and develop as psychosocial and behavioral persons. If a control system model is to be transformed to represent humans, properties must be added to make it both biologically and psychologically/behaviorally self-constructing. Moreover, it must display the combinations of unpredictable and predictable slow and sudden change patterns demonstrated in research on complex, dynamic systems. Biological self-construction results when humans ingest material-energy forms, and from biochemical functions by which those materials are taken apart, distributed throughout the body, and reassembled in new ways to create body structures and to make possible physiological functioning. Psychological/behavioral self-construction results when humans selectively collect, organize, and reorganize information about their contexts and their own activity, and from information processing functions that construct meanings and psychological/behavioral patterns to guide their current and future activities. These two types of self-construction and how they interrelate are discussed more fully in Chapters 4 and 5.

The Living Systems Framework (LSF):
A Transformed Control System Model

The rest of this chapter summarizes the general model and the conceptual components of the framework that is used for the comparative study of psy-

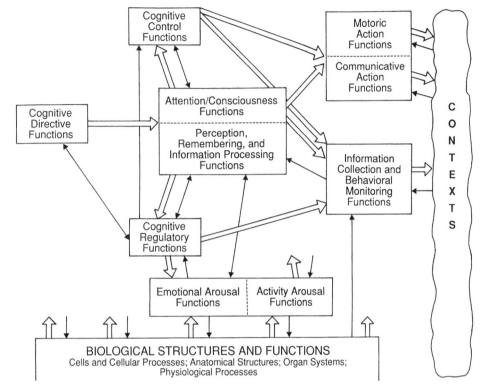

Figure 3.2 *The Person as a Living System.* A prototypic representation of a person as a self-organizing, self-constructing control system—as a living system. Basic attributes of humans are substituted for the prototypic control system functions depicted in Figure 3.1. To transform a mechanical control system into a living system, biologically based and information/ meaning-based self-constructing functions as well as attention/consciousness and emotional functions are added to the model. All functions are continuously and simultaneously occurring so that the person can function as a coherently organized unit in a context. Wide arrows signify feedforward functions; narrow arrows signify feedback functions.

chotherapy approaches in the remainder of this book. The living systems framework (LSF), represented by Figure 3.2, was constructed by elaborating the control system model in Figure 3.1. This was done by adding biologically based and information/meaning-based self-constructing processes as well as attention/ consciousness and emotional functioning. Then, the generic control system functions of Figure 3.1 were equated to human biological, psychological, and behavioral functions. Figure 3.2 may be considered an organization of domain-specific theories—for example, of sensory-perceptual, cognitive, emotional, and communicative functioning. Each component theory was derived from an intensive analysis of the scientific and professional literature about each response domain. A more detailed description and justification of this metamodel may be found in D. Ford (1987 or 1994), with elaborations and improvements in Ford and Ford (1987), Ford and Lerner (1992), and M. Ford (1992).

The components of Figure 3.2 are discussed separately, but remember that they do not function separately. They always operate continuously and collaboratively to produce a person-in-context as a structural-functional unit—to produce dynamic patterns of system states. Therefore, the theoretical model for each component function or minitheory must be formulated to fit with the minitheories representing other components. It is helpful to keep the total organization of Figure 3.2 in mind while reading the component descriptions, and to think of it as dynamic, flowing through time and contexts. A verbal representation of the effective operation of the model in Figure 3.2 is this: Effective behavior is the result of a biologically capable, motivated, skillful person guided by selectively collected, constructed, organized, and accurately interpreted relevant information, knowledge, and ideas, and interacting with a responsive environment (see M. Ford, 1992 for discussion of this definition and its relationship to the concept of competence).

The components of Figure 3.2 are discussed in three groupings. We start with material/energy-based structural and functional components, termed the *biological person*. We then consider information/meaning-based components, labeled as the *psychological person* and *action person*. (In our 1963 book we used the term *behavior* to refer to all functions including the biological ones. We still believe that is theoretically sound. However, it was confusing to some readers, so we have limited its meaning in this edition to a more typical usage.) For ease of reference, Figure 3.2 is repeated in each section; the components being discussed are highlighted.

THE BIOLOGICAL PERSON: LIFE MAINTAINING PROCESSES

First, there must be *biological life*. It results from material/energy-based processes or, more briefly, biological processes. Information/meaning-based psychological and behavioral processes are made possible and constrained by the conditions of biological life. Therefore, an adequate psychotherapy theory cannot ignore clients' current biological states. Typically, theorizing about psychotherapy focuses on psychological and behavioral processes with little consideration of biological processes. Neither the exercise of logic nor the accumulation of empirical evidence supports proceeding as if psychotherapy clients have intact and adequately functioning physiological subsystems, nor to conducting therapy as if clients' biological states are unrelated (and therefore irrelevant) to the rest of their life. Evidence about the diverse conditions with which psychotherapists deal—the schizophrenic, depressive, phobic, addictive, and other states—make it abundantly clear that people's biological capabilities and states are relevant to possibilities for psychological and behavioral changes through psychotherapy.

For example, some people are more genetically vulnerable than others to disorders such as alcoholism and depression. General states, such as being fatigued, sedated, or inadequately nourished, can influence what clients will do or say and how they interpret events. Chronic psychological states (e.g., high levels of emotion) may alter some steady state biological patterns (e.g., neurochemical, circulatory, gastrointestinal or immune system functioning) that then compound a client's problems. A person's interpretations of the potential meaning of his or her biological dysfunctions, deficiencies, or losses may significantly impact psychological and behavioral functioning.

For example, Mrs. K had a total hysterectomy three years before she entered therapy. Obviously, that operation changed her biological state, and medical treatment was used to help her establish a revised biological steady state. Her urinary incontinence was eventually solved, but she reports that it damaged her self-confidence and social behavior. Was that the only impact of her hysterectomy? Sometimes, when a woman loses her uterus, she interprets it as a loss of her female sexuality. Sometimes a husband may attribute such meaning to his wife's biological loss. Could such private interpretations be contributing to her difficulties with her husband? Perhaps sleeping in separate rooms is motivated by more than her husband's snoring.

The major characteristics of the human body are represented in empirically supported anatomic and physiological models summarized in standard texts of anatomy, cell biology, and human physiology, so only a brief overview of key characteristics placing them in a complex systems context is presented here. First, structural characteristics are noted, followed by consideration of biological functions. Relevant components are highlighted in Figure 3.2A.

STRUCTURAL ORGANIZATION OF THE HUMAN BODY

Anataomically, the body is an embedded hierarchy of biological structures. Cells, the basic structural unit, are themselves complex organizations of parts such as genes, organelles, and membranes. The nuclei of all of a person's cells contain the same genetic material. However, cell development creates different patterns of active and inactive genes that produce different types of cells

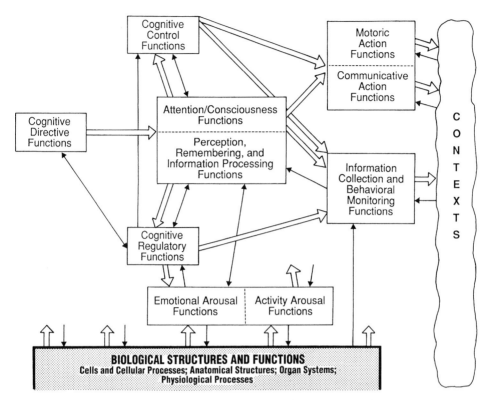

Figure 3.2A   *The Biological Person.* Material/energy-based processes construct and maintain the biological components of a person, organize and coordinate the functioning of all biological components, and generate energy to support all other functions. These life-maintaining processes both enable and simultaneously constrain the psychological and behavioral capabilities and performances of the person as a whole. They can in turn become modified to some degree by the operational effects of psychological and behavioral activities in which the person engages.

that elaborate into different types of tissues. Tissue subtypes then differentiate into different types of organs such as bones, heart, brain, and skin. Groups of organs are organized into organ systems, such as skeletal, nervous, and gastrointestinal systems. Organ systems are interrelated to produce a single structure that can operate as a unit—the human body.

Additional functional possibilities emerge at each higher level of organization, and higher levels of organization facilitate and constrain functional possibilities at lower levels. Different structural patterns create different functional possibilities. For example, the structure of neurons creates different functional possibilities from those created by the structure of muscle cells;

similarly, there are different functional possibilities created by the structure of the brain and the structure of a single neuron.

FUNCTIONAL ORGANIZATION OF THE HUMAN BODY

Physiologically, the body is an embedded hierarchy of biological functions. The basic functional component is cell metabolism, which refers to all the chemical processes that go on inside cells to accomplish three basic functions: (1) producing energy, (2) building cells' physical structures, and (3) decomposing, transforming, and synthesizing materials into forms needed for these functions as well as for regulating interactions with and among other cells. A cell's metabolism is controlled by its genes through the production of two types of proteins: (1) structural proteins that regulate the formation of cellular structures, and (2) enzymes that catalyze the different chemical reactions within the cell. The dynamics of these cellular processes operate through a complex network of positive and negative feedback and feedforward loops so the cell may function as a unit.

Every cell of a person has the same genetic material in its nucleus, and genes operate in organized patterns; single genes do not independently determine any specific human characteristic. It is now known that genetic influences are not static and fixed at birth as was once thought, but are dynamic and changeable. In each cell some genes are turned on and others are turned off. The pattern of active and inactive genes produces different kinds of cells, different patterns of cellular activity, and therefore different patterns of genetic influence on the development and functioning of the person. The pattern of active and inactive genes in any cell may change across the life span, depending on biochemical influences on or within the cell. For example, cells become cancerous and continually multiply in uncontrolled ways when genetic regulation of their reproductive capabilities is altered. The current development of genetic-based therapies involves the direct alteration of genetic patterns themselves.

Cells are open systems and therefore must carry out continual selective transactions with their contexts. The dynamics of cell metabolism are protected by the membrane that separates the cell from its context. The membrane selectively permits some materials to enter and leave the cell; in that way, each cell can selectively influence and be influenced by its environment and, through that, the functioning of the rest of the body. Thus, genes exert their influence on person-level development and functioning through their influence on cell metabolism and products produced and exported to other cells. Similarly, any substance can influence any cell only if it can pass through, or can influence what can pass through, the membrane into the cell.

For example, specific hormones may influence some cells and not others, depending on their state. Similarly, drugs can influence biological processes either by being transported into cells and affecting their metabolic activity, or by altering the membrane's permeability to other kinds of chemical compounds—for example, increasing or decreasing neuronal uptake of neurochemicals such as seratonin. The extensive use of drug therapies is one reason that psychotherapists need some basic understanding of how cells work, because of possible psychological/behavioral side effects. Therapists must know that medications work only if they can participate in these natural cellular processes. Medications don't cure people, they facilitate and supplement natural biological processes, thereby helping peoples' bodies to cure themselves.

Mrs. K's hysterectomy removed cells that influenced the production of chemical compounds important in regulating many biological processes in a woman's body. Such biochemical disruption can result in many types of dysfunctions. Mrs. K reported that in the two years following her surgery she developed (1) disabling head, neck, and back pains, (2) depressive and anxious feelings, (3) urinary urgency and leakage, and (4) a deteriorating marital relationship. To what extent might any of these have been influenced by that biochemical disruption or be consequences of her psychological reactions to it?

Additional functional possibilities emerge at each level of structural organization. The regulation of these multilevel activities is accomplished through self-organizing processes that utilize varied, interrelated feedback and feedforward loop-assemblages to produce two main results:

1. *Self-maintenance* through control of the subsystem components. This control allows successive adaptation to variable resources and demands from the system environment, ensuring that the variables of the system remain within preferred or permissible limits.
2. *Role fulfullment.* The parts of the structure perform specialized functions within the suprasystem of which they are a part.

As Mrs. K's symptom patterns illustrate, the dysfunctional biological patterns typically confronting psychotherapists operate at physiological subsystem levels. For example, digestion, absorption, and elimination are functions of the gastrointestinal subsystem; movement results from the operation of the skeletal-muscle subsystem; blood circulation is a function of the cardiovascular subsystem. Thus, Mrs. K's hysterectomy eliminated her reproductive functions; her head, neck, and back pains manifested dysfunctions in her skeletal-muscle subsystem; her urinary urgency and leakage were dysfunctions in her genitourinary subsystem.

Because a person's body must function as a unit, disruptions in any physiological subsystem will trigger activity to restore or maintain unitary functioning. Clients' biological symptoms are manifestations of such activity and may represent three types of processes: (1) physiological manifestations of the disruption itself, such as pain; (2) physiological processes operating to overcome the disruption through the body's well-known self-corrective capabilities, as when white blood cells increase and temperature rises to overcome an infection; and (3) physiological processes operating to accommodate the disruption, such as hypertension produced by chronic overarousal. Therefore, the prototypic pattern of signs and symptoms (called syndromes) for different kinds of recognized biological disorders invariably includes not only indicators of the disruption of normal functioning but also indicators of the body's efforts to overcome or adapt to the disruption. Distinguishing among these three types of symptoms is important for deciding on treatment approaches. For example, trying to alter the direct manifestations of disruptions is different from facilitating or interfering with the body's efforts to overcome the disruption.

Physiological integrity is facilitated by another capability. A person's body is capable of exercising a *priority interrupt* of the functioning of other more complex system operations in order to redirect the person's energies to deal with emergency states or conditions. For example, an infant would become so angry when thwarted he would hold his breath and seemed unable to renew breathing activity. After a brief period, his brain would be sufficiently deprived of oxygen that he would pass out, lower-level physiological processes would take over, and normal breathing behavior would begin again.

Integrative Physiological Subsystems
All physiological subsystems must operate in an integrated fashion to produce person-level functional unity. Both biological health and effective psychological and behavioral functioning depend on the intricate, continuous orchestration of these multiple, interdependent biological functions. A dysfunction in any single component will necessarily affect the operation of the other components with which it is interrelated. Moreover, because a person always must function as a unit in a context, a failure or disruption of any component function may have consequences for the entire system as a whole.

To coordinate a set of complex physiological subsystems to produce unitary functioning at the person level requires some kind of integrative structural-functional components. The human body has two. The first is the circulatory system. Biological components require a continual supply of materials with which to carry out and regulate their functions, some way of shipping their metabolic products to serve and influence one another, and some way of disposing of waste products generated by their activity. The circulatory system provides integrative functions for the material/energy-based operation of the body by serving as a distribution system for all biochemical compounds essential for the constructive, self-organizing, and defensive operations of the body. Through linkages to the circulatory system, every cell can potentially influence and be influenced by any substances that get into that system. It is not surprising then that one of the most valuable diagnostic procedures used by physicians to get clues about humans' biological functioning is to examine the properties of a person's blood, or fluids filtered from the blood and excreted as urine.

Information/meaning-based functioning is integrated by a second subsystem—the nervous system. Through the central nervous system branch (CNS), the sensory-perceptual, brain, and skeletal-muscle subsystems are linked, making it possible to combine self-generated (conceptual) and environmentally and biologically provided (perceptual) information to construct integrated behavior patterns. Through the autonomic nervous system branch (ANS), a person's physiological subsystems can be indirectly influenced by both conceptual and perceptual processes. The linkage of the CNS and ANS in a comprehensive nervous system makes it possible to tune physiological functioning to support the needs of the person's behavior patterns and vice versa. Emotional arousal patterns play a particularly important role in this linkage, primarily through limbic system structures in the brain. Of course, the nervous system is composed of cells, so its biological functioning can be influenced by the functioning of the circulatory system—as illustrated by a deficiency of oxygen supplies. It is not surprising that the most valuable diagnostic procedures used by psychotherapists assess perceptual, conceptual, affective, and motoric functioning, to make inferences about the state of the nervous system itself and about the operation of those particular functions.

Failure in either of these biological integrative subsystems results in death: nervous system failure results in brain death; circulatory system failure results in heart death. The systems are interdependent, so the failure of one leads to failure of the other.

IMPLICATIONS FOR PSYCHOTHERAPY

Each person functions as an integrated unit in a context. Therefore, psychotherapy theories should accommodate the properties of the biological person so as to articulate their relevance to and participation in the formation of clients' problems and the implementation of psychotherapy interventions.

Historically, many psychotherapists have implicitly assumed an ontology similar to parallel dualism, acting as if psychological and biological problems could be understood and treated separately. They have contented themselves with suggesting that their clients consult a physician for help with their biological complaints. Current knowledge contradicts the view that these component problems operate separately. As with Mrs. K, most persons who seek psychotherapy also have a medical problem. The illnesses as well as the drugs and other forms of medical treatment used may directly and adversely affect the clients' mental or emotional status and functioning. Moreover, clients' thoughts and feelings about their biological condition often generate psychological distress, which can influence their response to both psychotherapy and medical care. This sequence is especially so with more dramatic forms of illness, such as asthma, cancer, or AIDS.

Symptomatic complaints by clients about their thoughts, feelings, or actions can have either biological or psychological sources. When there is ambiguity in the symptoms, diagnostic errors and treatment failures can result—hypothyroidism can be mistaken for a depression; a drug-induced psychosis can be mistaken for a paranoid schizophrenia. Both medical and and psychotherapy practitioners must have some knowledge of both biological and psychological factors and their relationships. Even in conditions where no significant physiological or psychological/behavioral symptoms are apparent, this knowledge is still of great value because effective implementation of any therapy depends to some degree on relationships among component processes. For example, effective medical treatments require patient cooperation and compliance in the treatment process, and effective psychotherapy may require patients to understand how their emotional states may influence their physiological and behavioral functioning. Of course, each type of professional must have much more knowledge in depth about the domain of his or her specialty—physicians about the biological person, and psychotherapists about the psychological/behavioral person.

Evolutionary processes have produced a high degree of automation of physiological functioning. People don't need to think about or try to consciously control their physiological functions; these just happen. In fact, excessive self-conscious attention to physiological functions can interfere with their smooth and automatic functioning, as when anxious people begin to pay undue attention to their heartbeats. Current evidence indicates that by concentrating attention on a biological function, a person may be able to influence it, as in biofeedback. However, biological processes require a continual supply of materials they cannot obtain themselves. Humans' elaborate psychological and behavioral capabilities evolved to serve these and other adaptive needs, such as procreation.

Material/energy-based biological processes make psychological processes possible, but the psychological person operates through information/meaning-based processes. However, the basic dynamics are analogous. Just as biological processes require selective and continual inputs and outputs of relevant material/energy forms, so too does psychological functioning require selective and continual inputs and outputs of information/meaning-based forms. Moreover, just as biological processes disassemble material/energy forms and use them to construct new forms that are functionally valuable, so too do psychological processes disaggregate and recombine information/meaning forms to construct new and functionally valuable ideas, understandings, and behavior patterns. The characteristics called the psychological person are discussed next.

THE PSYCHOLOGICAL PERSON: INFORMATION/MEANING-BASED GOVERNANCE AND SELF-CONSTRUCTION

A tradition in personality theory and research has drawn sharp distinctions between the biological and the psychological aspects of people. It is a point of view ordinarily associated with humanistic, phenomenological, and existential theorists (e.g., Allport, Buhler, Maslow, Murray, Sartre, Adler, Binswanger, Frankl, May, Perls, Rogers). They propose that humans have certain properties and capabilities that distinguish them from other objects and organisms. People are understood to be conscious, experiencing, organized, and deliberative entities; they are seen as purposeful and intentional in orientation, capable of volition and decision, and guided by values and emotions; they are self-directing, self-regulating, and self-constructing in operation.

Historically, many theorists have considered impossible the integration of mechanistic and organismic models with humanistic or phenomenological ones. The living systems framework tries to bridge that gap by showing how material/energy-based (biological) and information/meaning-based (psychological and behavioral) functioning are qualitatively different, but interrelated, mutually influential functions. In discussing the components of the psychological person, the term *governance* is used to refer to the role played by human affective and cognitive directive, regulatory, and control functions. The term *psychological self-construction* is used to refer to an elaborated version of the central role played by what is typically called information processing functions in current psychological theorizing. The components of the psychological person are discussed in two groupings: arousal functions and cognitive functions. The relevant components of Figure 3.2, are highlighted in Figure 3.2B.

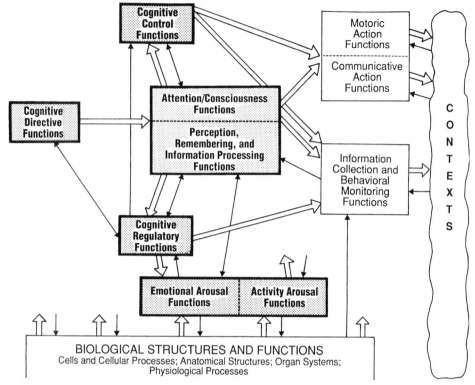

Figure 3.2B *The Psychological Person.* Information/meaning-based processes construct, maintain, and carry out psychological functions so as to selectively direct, organize, and evaluate the person's transactions with their environmental contexts. These psychological functions selectively facilitate and constrain a person's actions in both anticipatory and reactive ways. They also selectively influence a person's biological functioning.

HUMAN AROUSAL FUNCTIONS

A well-established principle in physics is that energy must be used if any activity, movement, or work is to occur. Activity of different kinds and amounts requires different and variable amounts of energy, and that energy may be manifested in different forms: mechanical, electrical, or thermal. Humans are always active but in continually varying patterns, so variable energy supplies must constantly be available to support life. Humans evolved with capabilities for generating and distributing variable amounts of energy as needed to fuel their diverse and highly variable functioning, which we have labeled *arousal functions*. Figure 3.2B shows two of three forms of arousal functions: activity arousal, consciousness-attention arousal, and emotional arousal. Each is briefly discussed.

Activity Arousal

All functions expend energy. Biological, psychological, and behavioral functions are all activity. Activity is fueled by the energy-producing capabilities of cell metabolism. Variations in activity patterns create variations in energy production demands on the tissues involved. For example, the energy production demands on muscle tissue created by running and sleeping are very different. Considering the variability in the amount of energy needed to support different kinds of activity, humans' ability to provide this selectively is remarkable. The human organism presents to right tissues at the right time, through circulatory processes, the raw materials needed for increased energy production—a truly astonishing capability.

These functions are highly automated and proceed without conscious thought or effort. However, anticipatory thoughts, through feedforward processes, can pretune energy producing functions in preparation for activity; this anticipation is called *preparatory set*. Some biological processes involved in activity patterns produce subjective experiences called *affective states*. These are useful feedback signals that people can consciously use in trying to regulate activity patterns. In addition to tissue specific information (signals of the need to urinate or defecate, variations in heart rate), there are five general affective states that signal different kinds of activity conditions: relaxed-contented-drowsy, alert-restless-energetic, sluggish-tired-fatigued, physical discomfort, and pain. Psychotherapy clients often report symptoms in these domains. For example, Mrs. K reported that she had pronounced feelings of fatigue and a sense of loss in her overall energy and stamina. Activity arousal represents the basic energizing capabilities of the body. The other two arousal functions are specialized expressions of this fundamental capability. The specialized arousal functions that support information/meaning-based functions are considered next.

Consciousness-Attention (CA) Arousal Functions

Radio or television sets can receive and process information signals only when they are turned on—their circuits are energized with electricity. Even then, they cannot process all available signals simultaneously; they require a tuner to make the set sensitive to one set of signals—one channel—and insensitive to others. The set can be adjusted to select different channels, but only one can be focused on at a time. Consciousness and attention perform analogous general and selective energizing functions for organizing humans' psychological and behavioral functioning. They do so by energizing different patterns of nervous system activity.

When humans are in a nonconscious state, automated biological processes continue to operate but people are unable to collect, interpret, or use information/meanings or to organize and implement action patterns, just as a TV set cannot produce pictures and sound when it is turned off. The psychological phenomenon of consciousness, of being awake and alert, is manifested when the nervous system is appropriately energized. We call this consciousness-attention (CA) arousal. It varies in amplitude, ranging from high levels of alertness, through marginal levels of consciousness (illustrated by rapid eye movement or REM sleep during which loosely organized information processing occurs in the form of dreams); it continues down to nonconscious states such as stage IV sleep, or coma. The degree of consciousness-attention arousal varies in a cyclical fashion, called the basic rest-activity cycle (BRAC), apparently influenced by the part of the brain called the reticular activating system (RAS). The level of consciousness-attention arousal can be influenced by other factors such as fatigue, illness, and substances ingested (alcohol, or anesthetics).

In the energized state of nervous system arousal termed consciousness, the system is prepared for activity utilizing information/meaning-based forms. Consciousness-attention arousal itself is content free, however. Some meditation practices try to generate and maintain such a content-free state of consciousness. Much of the literature about consciousness is confusing, as careful distinctions often are not made between the arousal functions of consciousness itself and the informational or conceptual contents of consciousness. If consciousness can be compared to a turned-on TV set, what determines which signals will occupy the contents of consciousness, analogous to the TV tuner selecting a particular program?

The answer is a function called *selective attention*. When people are conscious, their perceptual processes can continually and simultaneously monitor diverse internal and external sources of information and meaning. No one, however, could deal simultaneously with all the information such monitoring would produce; also, much of it is irrelevant to one's current concerns. To address this problem, a specialized subset of CA arousal functions, called *attention*, operates to select some information as relevant—selective attention—and to ignore other signals—selective inattention. Selective attention provides the contents of consciousness from moment to moment. Because attention is always functioning, there is always some conscious content. The sources and amount of information to which a person can attend at any moment—the channel capacity (and therefore be "conscious" of) are limited. If this were humans' only attentional capability, serious adaptive problems could result; a person inattentive to a pending attack by a predator could be killed. Two processes of selective attention deployment compensate for this limited capacity.

Most attention resources are selectively allocated to the information considered most relevant to the person's current concerns; this condition is focal attention or awareness. Sustained focal awareness on limited sources and limited categories of information is referred to as concentration. A small portion of the resource is allocated to superficial monitoring of other information sources with potential relevance, referred to as peripheral attention or awareness. This is analogous to modern TV sets in which a second channel may be monitored in a small box in the corner of the screen while the program of primary interest appears on the rest of the screen. Of course, focal and peripheral attention operate in conjunction with one another. For example, people can concentrate on reading, largely unaware of the sounds around them. If a scream suddenly intrudes, however, their focal attention will shift abruptly from their book to the source of the scream. Their *startle response* interrupts their attention patterns so their focal attention can be shifted to potentially important new information. The survival value of such safety interrupts is obvious.

Attention processes perform both selection and amplification functions. Information in focal attention has greater clarity and influence on consciousness; information in peripheral attention is more vague and has less immediate influence. This selective deployment of attention helps explain why two people in the same situation often fail to recall it in the same fashion; their attention is often deployed in different ways. The contents of consciousness result from these two modes of attentional monitoring.

A second strategy entails a shift of focal attention back and forth among different information sources. This can be very useful and adaptive because it enables a person to collect and utilize a greater diversity of information in any particular situation. Imagine a child who discovers some gift-wrapped packages. She may first look for a package with her name on it. She wants to know what is inside, but she doesn't dare unwrap it, so she explores different kinds of information about it. She may lift and squeeze the package; she may hold it next to her ear and shake it; she may smell it. By combining the visual, tactile, auditory, and olfactory information, she may be able to infer what lies inside.

Two kinds of factors influence the selective deployment of attention. The first stem from properties of information sources, called *stimulus-driven attentional capture*. For instance, an intense stimulus is more likely to be attended than a weaker one. Its size, the extent to which it stands out in contrast to its context, its newness or the degree to which it changes—intensity, color, or movement—are influential in attracting and holding a person's attention. Such factors are used by advertisers trying to attract the attention of potential customers and by designers of instrument displays for man-machine interfaces.

However, personal factors—a person's interests, values, and purposes, referred to as goal directed selection—typically exert more influence on attentional deployment, particularly for the kinds of behavior of concern to therapists. People usually attend to the information and meanings they see as relevant to their current concerns and goals. For example, Mrs. K reports her husband to be pervasively critical, intolerant, and domineering. Perhaps he is, but it is also possible that she is so selectively sensitive to those aspects of his behavior that she tends to ignore occasions when he behaves more positively toward her. Her report that he is "more like his old self" on weekends adds plausibility to such a possibility.

The range and variety of sources to which one's focal awareness can be deployed are very large. It can be directed toward obtaining current news from sources both outside and within one's body. It can pull information and meanings from prior experiences, previously constructed knowledge, or potential futures provided through remembering and thinking processes. People develop attentional habits. Some are so task oriented that they remain inattentive to body states such as fatigue; others maintain an exaggerated, hypochondriacal attention to their bodily functions due to excessive concern over their health. A person's attentional habits may take a particular focus, paying particular attention to the words and actions of others (extroversive orientation) or to one's own subjective experience (introversive orientation). Careful deliberation typically requires people to pay close attention to the structure and organization of their own thought processes. They may attend either to current events or to their reconstructions of past events. For example, it is not unusual for therapy clients to selectively seek evidence to support their negative self-beliefs and to selectively ignore potentially contradictory evidence.

In addition to selective focusing on information sources, attention may also be focused on the creation and execution of action patterns, sometimes called intention. When people's attention is concentrated on careful thinking and remembering, or on performing skilled actions, they can be only vaguely aware via peripheral attention of the current news provided by perception. Skilled athletes and musicians agree that concentration that blocks disruptive inputs of information is critical for skilled performances; scientists find uninterrupted work periods essential for creative scholarship.

The skilled performance of behavior patterns does not require the actors to focus attention on the details of its performance. Humans are capable of considerable automation in learning and performing repetitive behavior patterns.

By repetition and rehearsal, they can automate behavior patterns that initially required attentional effort; these can then be carried out in rote fashion, thereby freeing the limited attention capacity to deal with other matters. When this occurs, the behavior patterns themselves are no longer within focal awareness; people are only peripherally aware, or even unaware, of doing them. Ordinarily, however, they can focus attention on these behaviors and become conscious of their manner of operation when this is necessary.

Intense concentration of attention on one information source impedes information flows from other sources. This provides a basis for distinguishing between two concepts that have been a source of some confusion. The term *nonconscious* refers to a state in which no information/meaning-based functioning can occur, such as a coma. In contrast, the term *unconscious* refers to psychological or behavioral activity that occurs as part of a current pattern but which is not represented in the current contents of the person's consciousness (e.g., "tacit" knowledge). Ongoing behavior patterns are complex, and they also occur in complicated contexts. Consciousness-attention processes have limited capacity and some kinds of response processes cannot enter the contents of consciousness at all—such as feedforward signals for motor behavior. Therefore, only some aspects of an ongoing person-context behavior pattern can be in consciousness at any moment. Many aspects of a person's ongoing behavior will be unconscious in operation; therefore, unconscious processes are a normal part of everyday life. An ongoing behavior pattern is something like an iceberg. Only some is visible in the contents of consciousness, but because the total pattern functions as a unit, the unit can be influenced by manipulation of its conscious components.

For a person to learn something, it must be part of a current behavior pattern on which focal or peripheral attention is focused. The selection and amplification functions of attention influence what will be learned, and how well. States of intense arousal produce more intense learning. There is no initial learning without awareness. However, performance without awareness is possible. Once learning has created a habit, the learned behavior may be activated as part of a larger pattern and occur outside awareness, just as any habitual pattern may function. An example is the unconscious thought processes activated by perceptions or interpretations in a therapy interaction. It follows that to alter any behavior pattern, particularly automated ones, the person's attention must be focused on it.

Sometimes, constitutional or other factors can impair regulation of attention and the resulting contents of consciousness, illustrated by the symptoms of distractibility in Attention Deficit Disorders, or the attentional fixations encountered in some schizophrenias.

Psychotherapy clients often report problems related to control of attention and the contents of consciousness. Remember that Mrs. K was distressed by evil thoughts that repeatedly intruded into her awareness. Clients frequently misconstrue the nature of their difficulties because of habits of selective attention, which guard them from information/meanings that might disrupt their preferred modes of thought or activate emotional distress. The proposition that unconscious processes may be a source of difficulty implies that some cognitive/emotional elements may be operative in ongoing behavior patterns but that they are not presently accessible to the person's focal awareness, perhaps because of active prevention (e.g., defense mechanisms). To modify habitual patterns, the person must make unconscious processes part of the contents of consciousness through focal attention. Many therapy techniques selectively direct clients' attention to thoughts they habitually ignore to encourage awareness of them. For example, free association and stream of consciousness methods assume a person's psychological dynamics will bring to consciousness relevant thoughts and memories; reflections of feelings, or instructions and interpretations selectively direct client's attention to things therapists consider important.

Emotional Arousal and Affective Experience

The term *affect* refers to a consciously experienced/perceived manifestation of some biological and/or psychological state. Different states produce qualitatively different affective experiences (just as vision and audition produce qualitatively different perceptions) that provide one type of feedback signals about the person's functioning. Affects are of three types: (1) manifestations of body/tissue states, such as fatigue, pain, or relaxation; (2) manifestations of qualities of sensory-perceptual states, such as pleasant or noxious odors or tastes; and (3) manifestations of varied kinds of emotional states.

All affective experiences carry an evaluative valence; they are to some degree either positive or negative. In general, affects with a positive or pleasant valence signal attainment of or progress toward preferred states. They signal that something good is happening so they encourage exploratory/approach activity. Affects with a negative valence signal the presence of actual or probable pain or distress, or probable obstructions to the achievement of a preferred state (e.g., anticipatory fear or anger) probable failure (e.g., discouragement/depression). Something bad is happening or may happen. Negative affects encourage attack, avoidance/withdrawal, or giving-up behavior. Thus, affective experience directly regulates people's behavior and combines with evaluative thoughts in performing regulatory functions.

Affective experiences have a quality of immediacy and their regulatory influence an apparent automaticity. They are probably a more primitive process than cognitive regulation. In some circumstances, cognitive regulation apparently can modify or override the regulatory impact of affect, but when affects are intense, such cognitive control is difficult. For example, when pain is acute, hunger exceedingly strong, or anger intense, individuals may violate personal, ethical, or legal constraints they would ordinarily be inclined to follow. When a person's behavior is regulated by affects rather than thought, it is often termed irrational.

Key sources of affective experience are humans' emotional arousal patterns. Emotions have always been widely believed to be a significant aspect of human life, but understanding of them has been theoretically and empirically elusive. However, recent theory and research have converged on a shared view of the nature and functioning of emotions (e.g., Buck, 1984; deRivera, 1977; Ekman, 1982; Ekman & Davidson, 1994; Izard, 1991; Lazarus, 1991; Plutchik, 1980). This view considers emotions as systematic patterns of functioning rather than as a separate kind of response. Each emotional state is a pattern of biological, (e.g., hormonal; circulatory), psychological, (e.g., affective), and action (e.g., facial; gestural; vocal) components. Such integrated patterns are made possible by structural and functional linkages (e.g., feedback-feedforward loops) among the autonomic nervous system (ANS) that regulates physiological functions, the central nervous system (CNS) that organizes thought and behavior, and the hormonal regulation of the limbic system-linked hypothalamus-pituitary-adrenal (HPA) axis via the circulatory system. The experiential core of emotional states is a conscious manifestation of limbic system processes, supplemented by awareness of feedback from physiological, action and hormonal components of the pattern. It is the evaluative quality of emotions that exerts a psychological regulatory influence.

There is broad agreement that humans are equipped with a few inborn emotional arousal patterns that are qualitatively different from one another in their prototypic configuration of biological, psychological, and action components. Some disagreement exists as to which ones and how many. However, all lists include some emotions whose functional significance seems to be the facilitation and regulation of instrumental behavior episodes, such as fear, pleasure, discouragement and anger, and others whose special function seems to be the regulation of interpersonal relationships and social group living, such as love or sorrow. Unless people disguise their emotional states people across cultures recognize these by their prototypic facial, vocal, and motoric gestures. This communicative function of emotions exercises a regulatory effect on social relationships.

Each kind of emotional pattern is activated by perceptions and/or evaluative thoughts. Emotions occur in anticipation of, and in preparation for dealing with some kind of behavioral problem or impending consequence; they augment ongoing energizing or regulatory activity to facilitate people's capacity to cope with specific types of situations (see Lazarus, 1991, and Plutchik, 1980). Because the physiological components of emotional patterns involve temporary adjustments of metabolic, hormonal, neurochemical, and other biological processes, emotions are said to perform an energizing/arousal function. They are temporary in that a state of emotional arousal will usually subside in a relatively brief period of time—for example, hormonal blood concentrations return to their steady states in 15 to 20 minutes. Emotional arousal can be maintained for longer periods if the person repeatedly reactivates it with anticipatory evaluative thoughts.

In infancy, each emotional pattern can be aroused by perceptions of prototypic situations: obstruction of actions ➤ anger; loss of support ➤ fear. Infants differ in their emotional lability, from slow, low amplitude reactions to quick, intense ones, but inborn, reflex-like patterns are too inflexible to be adaptive in humans' diverse, highly variable living conditions. Evolution has provided a very adaptive alternative: Learning can modify the inborn patterns in four ways, but initial differences in emotional lability can influence the nature of that learning.

The first way elaborates the conditions that will elicit or terminate emotional arousal. Through learning, a person can see virtually any kind of experience as an elicitor or terminator. Phobias have their roots in this kind of emotional learning. Anticipatory or interpretive thoughts can also become learned elicitors or terminators. The fearful anticipation of possible or imagined events is often called anxiety. For example, the sight of spiders does not innately elicit fear, but a person may have developed fear-laden thoughts about insects, so that seeing a spider elicits intense anxiety. It is important to understand how behavior is regulated by combinations of evaluative thoughts and emotions because of the powerful motivational effects that result. The second way learning can change inborn patterns is to modify the configuration of elements that make up an emotional pattern. For example, people may learn to inhibit relevant actions, facial expressions, or their blood pressure when they are angry. Such learning results in individual variations of each emotional pattern; the version expressed will vary depending on the situation and each person's learning history. For example, a person may show one fear pattern variant when standing on a precipice and a different one in a school examination.

In a third way that learning effects change, steady states are altered to include emotional elements. Emotions are time-limited states. Like a flywheel, they decline and stop unless given another shove. People can continue to activate an emotional pattern so that it persists over an extended period of time.

Persistence of some emotion pattern elements that are typically temporary can result in their becoming a part of a habitual steady state. For example, some people create lifestyles in which anger states are persistently activated and maintained—Type A personality patterns. Over time, this can produce steady-state changes in some physiological functions such as hypertension.

A fourth way is to learn a mixed emotional pattern. Perhaps a child becomes angry when thwarted by her father. The father responds by beating her, which activates a fear pattern while the anger state still exists. As a result, she learns to react with fear when she becomes angry, producing a blend of anger and fear patterns: She simultaneously wants to attack and withdraw. Such learning renders human emotionality relatively complex and produces important individual differences in emotionality.

HUMAN COGNITIVE AND INFORMATION PROCESSING FUNCTIONS

In our living systems framework, person-level governing functions are carried out by information/meaning-based processes, typically called cognitive and information processing functions by cognitive scientists. There are five inter-related functions. Three of them are directly analogous to the directive, control, and regulatory functions of a control system (see Figures 3.1 and 3.2B). Diverse terms are used for these three aspects of cognitive functioning. Concepts such as needs, purposiveness, goal setting, personal agency, and intentional behavior refer to the directive function of cognition. Thinking, decision making, problem solving, and behavior coordination refer to the control function of cognition. Personal values, attitudes, self-efficacy beliefs, performance evaluation, moral reasoning, and evaluative thought represent the regulatory function of cognition.

All three require sources of information and meaning for their operation. There are two sources. The first is sensory-perceptual functions. These selectively monitor what is currently going on within and around a person and in the environmental transactions to provide useful feedback information. This perceptual current news about what's happening now is essential for effective governance of the system by cognitive functions. However, the adaptive utility of perception's current news is severely limited because perceptions represent only moment-to-moment, transient events. If people behaved solely in terms of their direct perceptions, their behavior would be stimulus controlled by here-and-now events; behavior could not be guided by past experience or future possibilities.

The second source is cognitively constructed representations and meanings. Humans are proactive, not just reactive, toward both themselves and their environments. Proactive behavior requires people to use representations of past experience and imaginatively constructed meanings, to interpret the significance of perceptions and to anticipate future possibilities. Such information and meaning-based self-construction requires a fourth cognitive capability, called cognitive information processing functions. Therefore, cognitive governance relies on the interpretation of current perceptions using representations of past experiences—realism—and generalized knowledge and personal meanings—idealism. The activation of such representations occurs through a fifth cognitive function called remembering.

Thus, the comparative framework adopts a realist metaphysics for perception and resulting imagistic memories, an idealist metaphysics for other cognitive constructions, synthesized through a constructivist epistemology. A summary of cognitive functions begins by discussing the forms of representation, or coding systems, used in cognitive constructions. Chapter 4 considers the dynamics of humans' information/meaning-based self-construction.

Construction of Information/Meaning Forms as a Cognitive Function
Infants function much like the control system mechanistic model: They react to events with inborn "scores" for a limited number of behavior patterns that become operative as they develop, such as sucking or urinating. If development stopped with inborn reflexive patterns, humans could not survive in their complex, variable environments. However, rather than developing prewiring of the diverse patterns valuable to humans in their environmental niche, people developed information/meaning-based self-construction capabilities that enable them to create whatever behavior patterns are useful to them, constrained only by the limits of their biological capabilities and their environments. What a creative solution to a very complicated adaptive problem!

Cognitive constructions are information/meaning-based models representing properties of people's experiences as well as their ideas and beliefs. In Chapter 1, three types of models were described that differed in terms of the coding systems used: iconic, analogue, and symbolic. Human cognitive constructions use all three of these codes plus an abstract code. Sensory-perceptual processes produce accurate feedback about what is going on within and around a person. Perceptions are conscious representations, perceptual images, of the properties and organization of things and events, like a picture resembles a person or a motion picture represents an action pattern. Perceptual images use different iconic or imagistic codes named for each of the senses. Humans function as an integrated unit, so different perceptions are combined psychologically to produce unified experiences: A baby experiences a ball as a yellow, round, smooth, warm, and tasteless object that makes a sound when squeezed. Perceptual images and the representations constructed from them are a form of iconic model providing a direct link between people's subjectivity and the reality in which they live.

A single perceptual image is fleeting, gone in a moment and replaced by another and then another, like a multimedia show. Thus, any percept by itself is adaptively useless beyond the moment in which it occurs. If the fruits of perceptual experiences are to be useful for future behavior, there must be some way to use them beyond the specific moment they occur. Humans' capabilities for constructing concepts and propositions produce representations with more lasting value than percepts. This construction process selectively emphasizes some aspects of perceptual experience and deemphasizes others, and individuals differ in what they emphasize. Therefore, there will be individual differences in cognitive constructions. However, similarities also result because their perceptual images represent the same realities.

Concepts and propositions can be represented in different levels of abstraction. The first level results from creating iconic/imagistic representations of consistencies in similar percepts. For example, from multiple experiences with the family pet, a child can construct an image of a gentle, black and white, furry and cuddly cat, named Whiskers. Such representations may be called first-order or imagistic concepts because they are generalized versions of a particular set of phenomena using the same iconic codes as the percepts they represent. However, there are consistencies in the functioning and interrelationships of objects and events. For example, a child can represent Whiskers as snarling when its tail is pulled or purring when it is petted. Such representations of consistencies in perceived patterns of action or interrelationships may be called first-order propositions. An imagistically coded representation of a specific event is called an episodic memory. Concepts and propositions at this level approximate the phenomena that produced the perceptions; they represent reality as experienced by the person.

First-order imagistically coded concepts and propositions are only the beginning, however. Children rapidly accumulate a large array of imagistically coded representations, some of which are similar. For example, a child not only repeatedly encounters Whiskers but also other cats both in real life and in pictures—a neighbor's cat, Scooter; a cousin's tabby, Pest; a cluster of barn cats at her grandfather's farm; and pictures of cats in books and on television. The same capabilities that enable people to construct first-order imagistic concepts and propositions from similarities in percepts also enable them to construct generalized versions of similar imagistic representations—that is, to construct second-order concepts and propositions. The child may construct the generalized concept of "cat" or "kitty," and generalized propositions such as "cats may scratch" or "cats and dogs fight." Moreover, similarities among sets of second-order concepts and propositions can provide the basis for constructing higher order abstractions. For example, the concepts of cat, dog, cow, and horse may all be represented by the concept of animal, and similar movement patterns may be represented by the proposition "animals run." Einstein's famous $E = MC^2$ illustrates the very high order abstractions that humans can construct.

Second- and higher order concepts and propositions cannot use iconic/imagistic codes because such generalized representations have no physical reality and therefore cannot be perceived. For example, no such thing as an animal exists. Only specific animals exist, such as the cat Whiskers. A different code must be used in constructing generalized representations—that is, an abstract code. Concepts and propositions are also referred to as ideas, and organizing and manipulating them to carry out other cognitive functions is called ideation or thinking. When thinking uses imagistically coded representations it is called imagistic thought; when it uses abstractly coded representations it is imageless or abstract thought. There is a problem hidden in this distinction. Only imagistically coded representations can enter consciousness; abstractly coded ones cannot. Therefore, abstract thought is unconscious thought. As most concepts and propositions are higher order abstractions, most thought necessarily occurs as an unconscious process; unconscious processes are a normal rather than pathological process (see D. Ford, 1987 or 1994, for supporting evidence). We will return to this issue later.

The process just described limits the ideas humans can construct to generalized versions of percepts, and all cognition would fit a realist metaphysics. However, cognitive construction can go beyond perceptually based knowledge. Just as biological processes take materials apart and reassemble them into completely different forms, so too can information processing functions take apart perceptually based concepts and propositions and reassemble their parts into different concepts and propositions. As a result, humans have imagined things and events that had not yet been perceived but later were, such as germs, or that did not exist but later were created, such as space stations, as well as things and events that can never exist, such as leprechauns. This kind of cognitive activity is often called creative thought or imagination because it represents cognitive creations not derived directly or indirectly from percepts. Human imagination knows no bounds; imaginative thought can bring people both pleasure and misery. Humanists have emphasized this form of cognitive construction, perhaps because it fits the ontology of idealism.

Once formed, generalized or abstract concepts and propositions will be activated when relevant to a new perception, providing an attribution of meaning to, or interpretation of, that perception. Thus, perceptual information and cognitively constructed meanings are merged to guide current behavior. People often use the term *perception* to refer to the interpretation resulting from such mergers—"I perceived he was mad." Carelessness in distinguishing percepts from their interpretation is a source of much intra- and interpersonal misunderstandings. Newborn infants immediately begin forming concepts and propositions from their percepts, and begin using them to make meaning attributions to their new perceptions.

Conscious Control of and Communication of Abstract Thought

Abstractly coded representations have no physical reality so they cannot be perceived. For example, you can never see a generalized dog; only specific dogs exist. The idea of dog exists only in a person's mind. This poses two problems: (1) How can people be aware of what they are thinking and consciously manipulate their thinking, if abstractly coded thinking is unconscious? (2) How can they communicate their abstractly coded thoughts to others if these thoughts aren't coded in a perceptible form?

Conscious control and communication of abstract thought is made possible by linking abstract codes to perceptible codes. People can then use perceptible surrogates for abstractly coded thoughts to control their unconscious abstract thoughts and to communicate them to others. This is analogous to the way people control a computer program they cannot see by manipulating visible instructions linked to the program. Imagistic thought can be conveyed to others iconically, as an architect conveys her mental image of a building in a drawing or three-dimensional model. Many ideas cannot be meaningfully linked to imagistic codes, so humans create other perceptible codes and use them to translate abstract ideas into conscious and communicable forms. These are the analogue and symbolic models or codes described in Chapter 1.

Recall that an analogy is a construction devised to convey the notion that two things appear to correspond with one another in certain respects, even though they are actually different in form and appearance. An analogue uses one imagistic code to represent the properties of something other than itself. In Chapter 1, a map was used as an example. The way the information in the analogue code is related to the actual information is specified by a set of transformation rules. Without knowing the transformation rules, a person will not understand the information or meaning being conveyed. Analogue codes may appear in psychotherapy sessions. For example, an analogue code may convert hand gestures into a way of conveying abstract meanings. Colors may be used to represent emotions: red for anger, blue for sadness. Interpreting dream symbolism involves cracking the analogue code to decipher the underlying meanings. For example, a dreamer was riding downhill on a bicycle built for two with an academic colleague; in real life they were partners in designing a new course. They met a llama, a snooty looking South American animal, walking uphill and getting in their way—they were being opposed in their course design by a snooty, academic colleague from a southern country who was having an uphill struggle with his career (Blackmore, 1981). Analogue codes may be culturally shared or idiosyncratic; many wouldn't know what a llama was, so they couldn't use it as dream symbolism.

Humans have an even more impressive capability; they create and use symbolic codes to control their thinking and to communicate with others. A symbol is anything that is used to stand for or represent something other than itself. Symbolic codes are human inventions and are completely arbitrary; the symbols used have no intrinsic meaning. In contrast to iconic and analogue codes, the imagistic or perceptible form of symbolic codes bears no resemblance to the phenomenon to which it refers. Therefore, whatever information or meaning a symbolic code represents must be completely specified in a set of transformation rules that accompany it. Dictionaries link verbal symbols to the meanings they represent. This gives symbols a unique value in that a simple symbol can be used not only to refer to complex phenomena in short-hand form but also to refer to them in their absence. Humans have constructed many symbolic codes such as mathematics and languages.

Verbal languages are a widespread form of symbolic code. Words are the symbolic elements; the rules of grammar and syntax govern the ways words can be organized to represent more complex and dynamic meanings. It is critical to remember that symbolic codes have no intrinsic meaning; they acquire meaning as a function of the imagistic and abstract representations to which they are linked. Therefore, learning a language requires learning it in relation to meanings provided by direct experience and other types of cognitive construction, such as culturally defined meanings.

Facility in the use of symbolic codes is a product of cultural transmission. Parents use words and language in their interactions with children from their birth onward, so children learn language as a way of communicating personally and culturally defined meanings as a natural part of their daily experience. Each person experiences a mixture of idiosyncratic and idiomatic terms, along with those in the modal cultural language, producing both culturally shared and individualistic representations. Because language refers to human experiences that are in continual flux and change, languages undergo steady modification with the passage of time. Further, in pluralistic cultures such as the United States, there is a steady borrowing of symbols across subcultural lines. Contemporary cultures strive to maintain language consistency through the use of various codifications (e.g., dictionaries), and use extended schooling to induce a degree of conformity in language usage. Moreover, there are also the specialized languages developed for specialized purposes such as the jargons of varied scientific and professional fields. Mathematics is a special kind of symbolic code designed solely to represent relationships among phenomena rather than their properties; it is a propositional language. For example, in the statement $X + Y = Z$, the transformation rules of mathematics specify the meaning of $+$ and $=$ but X, Y, and Z can symbolize anything a person chooses. People sometimes devise an unusual language linked to special experiences. An example is the language a psychotic person may create and use.

How do symbolic codes enable people to communicate their subjective experiences and abstract ideas? Symbolic communication requires that people share an understanding of the codes being used, but communication doesn't transfer meanings from one person's head to another's. Rather, words are used to try to activate in the receiver's mind the meanings they already possess that are similar to the meanings the communicator is trying to convey. Miscommunication results when incorrect meanings are activated. Then the communicator may try a different combination of words to try to activate the intended meaning.

The interconnection of symbols (e.g., words) with thoughts is of particular significance to psychotherapists. To understand clients' meanings, therapists must be knowledgeable about culturally based language differences and skillful in using language relevant to clients' language history and habits. People don't think with words; they think with abstract meanings. People can become conscious of what they are thinking only by representing it in some perceptible form that can appear in the contents of consciousness—in iconic, analogue, or symbolic images. Nonlinguistic codes are useful with people who have limited symbolic capabilities, as in art or play therapy with small children. This is the source of the adage, "You don't know what you are thinking unless you say it, write it down, draw it, or act it out." This is the way people can become aware of and consciously control the content and sequence of their abstract and unconscious thoughts. People learn new meanings by starting with meanings they already have.

There are limits, however, to the utility of symbolic representations. Some human experiences are ineffable; they are incapable of being expressed in words. This is a reason for creation of alternate modes of expressive communication, such as art, music, and dance. Further, the vast majority of what any given person may think and know remains tacit and unstated knowledge simply because several lifetimes would be needed to speak or write it all.

Therefore, a psychotherapist must abandon any attempt to elicit all of what a client may think and know, and focus selectively on what seems most relevant for the client.

These distinctions between symbols and what they represent are often lost in people's thinking. There is a tendency to elide the differences between words and things and words and thoughts. For example, *attitude* is a word representing the idea that a person displays certain psychological/behavioral consistencies, Too often people commit the error of reification and begin to think that an attitude is an entity existing in a person that causes the consistencies observed. Psychotherapy clients are often careless about these important distinctions.

Remembering as a Cognitive Function

Neither past nor potential future events can directly influence a person's current functioning, yet past experience and future possibilities do seem to exert an influence. How is that possible? The only way the past and future can affect present functioning is if some representations of them are active in the current episode of behavior. Similarly, the only way one's knowledge or ideas can influence present functioning is if they are currently operative. The process of activating previously constructed representations is called remembering, and the products are called memories. In ordinary conversation, the term *memory* is often restricted to remembrances of particular past experiences, often termed *episodic memories,* such as "I remember what we had for dinner." When some idea or piece of knowledge is activated and used in a current episode people typically don't think of that as remembering, but it results from that same process.

Several metaphors for understanding remembering and memories have been proposed (e.g., Roediger, 1980). The dominant one has been a storage and search metaphor. It represents the brain as a huge filing cabinet and remembering involves searching the files for desired records. Much empirical evidence invalidates this metaphor. Some version of a reconstruction metaphor is now believed to be more appropriate. Just as movement patterns are constructed or reconstructed as needed, so too are cognitive representations. Because they are reconstructions rather than file copies, the reproduction may vary from occasion to occasion, in part as a function of the motivational and environmental context in which the remembering occurs. This means, for example, that clients' reports of episodes experienced in the past will always be only approximations of what actually happened and may be completely manufactured products of their imagination. However, it is the nature of the current reconstruction that influences current behavior, rather than the actual past event, so the accuracy of the current remembrance is not crucial except for providing clues about the nature of troublesome, cognitive constructions and how they might be altered. The contents of the directive, control, and regulatory cognitions and action patterns at any moment in the flow of behavior are primarily the result of a reconstruction remembering process, supplemented with current perceptions and feedback from current activity.

Self-Direction as a Cognitive Function

There has been a growing realization among scholars studying human nature that people are inherently purposive in their activity. They function to imagine possible future states, and to try to create them. Such representations of future possibilities have been called purposes, objectives, intentions, and goals. A person's goals are called personal goals; goals shared by a group may be called social goals. Personal goals are cognitive representations of outcomes, called goal content; people consider these as desirable to produce, capable of being achieved, and worthy of pursuit. Earlier in this century scholars focused on trying to clarify and catalogue the content of human goals (e.g., Maslow, 1954; McClelland, 1961; McDougall, 1933; Murray, 1938). More recently, the tendency has been to limit attention to specific types of goal content—such as achievement motivation—perhaps because of the great diversity of outcome states for which people appear to strive. However, M. Ford (1992) has recently constructed a theoretically based taxonomy of goal content that appears useful. Goal content not only specifies outcomes a person wants to produce or maintain, but it also serves as the criterion against which the outcomes produced can be evaluated; it defines the conditions of satisfaction that must be met by the person's efforts to produce those outcomes.

Goal content operates through feedforward influences to facilitate certain behavior patterns and to constrain others; these are called goal processes. There is a rapidly growing body of literature about the influence of goal setting on subsequent behavior and task performance (see Locke & Latham, 1990). For example, when some goals become active in organizing a person's behavior in a particular context, they serve to potentiate a selected set of values and regulatory rules of utility in evaluating one's progress. The dominant goals also selectively potentiate relevant types of information, ideas, strategies, and skills of relevance for attaining the guiding goals.

A person's behavior on any occasion may be organized by only one goal, but usually multiple goals are simultaneously operative. People usually try to produce a variety of desired outcomes through a single strategy and behavior pattern; stated another way, they have more than one reason for engaging in a course of action. A common observation in psychotherapy is that a client's behavior appears to be determined by multiple influences. The simultaneous pursuit of multiple goals appears to generate a higher level of motivation. However, pursuit of multiple goals requires psychological organization so that the goals don't compete for behavioral control. One form of organization is a goal hierarchy, possible when some goals function as subgoals for attaining a larger goal. Focusing on short-term subgoals that are more readily achievable within one's current capabilities and context can help to maintain higher levels of motivation for two reasons. First, pursuing larger goals seen as very difficult to attain can lead to discouragement and abandonment of efforts. Second, accomplishing short-term goals produces a sense of accomplishment and progress that encourages one to persist in the larger effort.

Even though peoples' behavior is organized in relation to goals, they may not be aware of their goals; goals can be automatized and remain implicit, tacit, and unverbalized. The personal goals of effective, well-adjusted people often operate outside their awareness, but they can usually bring their goals to awareness and verbalize them to others, if necessary. People's goals may be vague, implicit, poorly interrelated, incompatible, or unrealistic. People may misunderstand or misrepresent the goals guiding their current activity. Faulty goal content, organization, or awareness is likely to lead to ineffective or self-defeating behavior, generating disappointment, distress, and self-denigration. Therapy clients often require help in recognizing and articulating their unacknowledged, implicit, or disowned goals; in clarifying ill-defined goals; in reconciling conflicting goals; and in selecting realistic and achievable goals. For example, Mrs. K's initial discussion with her therapist conveys little about why she behaves as she does, what she wants for her life, or what she wants out of psychotherapy.

Controlling the Design and Execution of Behavior as a Cognitive Function
Personal goals specify desired outcomes—the *what*—but they do not define *how* to achieve them. Other cognitive processes operate to devise, coordinate the execution of, and evaluate and revise the means by which goals can be achieved Reasoning, problem solving, and planning are the most frequently studied cognitive functions and the ones assessed by intelligence and ability tests. It is useful to divide the cognitive control functions used by people into three phases: (1) problem formulation, (2) problem solving and plan formulation, and (3) plan execution. These are not discrete, rigidly sequential phases; they overlap and interact—for example, difficulty in (2) may lead to reframing (1). Conceptually, the distinctions are useful, however. What is a *problem?* In its most generic sense, it means a discrepancy between what exists and what is wanted. Such discrepancies are resolved through problem-

solving behaviors. Other terms, such as *cognitive dissonance,* are used with similar meanings, but *problem* carries the broadest meaning and is more typically used by psychotherapists. Subtypes of problems are defined in clinical practice by the content involved, whether they are psychological, emotional, or behavioral problems.

The *problem formulation or framing the problem* phase begins when a person identifies a discrepancy between a current and preferred state, or creates one through goal setting: She feels chilly or apprehensive, or she decides she wants to go to a movie. This motivates the person to initiate activity designed to change the existing state (chilliness or apprehension) to a more desirable one (warmth or composure). It is also possible for the person to anticipate, based on prior learning, that the current state might degrade into something even less desirable—the apprehension may escalate into fear or panic. Then, the person may act to prevent the occurrence of an even less desirable state. Problem formulation defines the criteria for a problem solution and can be an iterative process. For example, difficulty in devising an effective approach may lead people to change their formulations, called reframing the problem. The problem formulation exerts a selective influence on the information, knowledge, and actions the person will consider for resolving the discrepancy. This involves understanding (1) the current state; (2) the nature of the future state to be produced, maintained, or forestalled; (3) the personal and environmental conditions under which it must be achieved; and (4) the criteria by which potential problem solutions can be evaluated.

People do not always effectively carry out these problem formulation functions and may not even recognize the tacit problem formulation on which their actions are based. Socialization agents, such as parents and teachers, may have failed to help them gain proficiency in problem formulation. Also, people often adopt habitual ways of framing their problems and are unaware of how that method biases and restricts the solutions they imagine and consider. Whenever people's formulation of their problems remains vague, poorly fashioned, incomplete, or inappropriate to their circumstances, they will have difficulty developing an effective course of action. Clients typically enter psychotherapy recognizing that their problem-solving attempts are unsuccessful and productive of misery and distress, but they are often unaware of deficiencies in the ways they define their problems. For example, Mrs. K. is unhappy with her marriage but seems to define the problems solely in terms of inadequacies in her husband's behavior and seems unaware of any ways in which she might be contributing to their problems. Often, one significant part of psychotherapy is helping clients reframe their problems, particularly in the early phases.

The *problem-solving and plan formulation* phase involves constructing and evaluating alternative solutions and implementation plans, and selecting one, a process called decision making. It entails selecting, organizing, interpreting, and integrating both perceptual and conceptual information construed to be relevant to the problem. It encompasses remembered information, strategies and skills in regard to comparable past situations, and perceptions of the current situation in which the problem solution must be executed. Components of this phase include (1) the generation of alternative approaches, called alternative thinking; (2) the delay of action until the potential utility of each option is evaluated, called consequential thinking; and (3) the formulation of a clear plan of action, called means-end thinking. The last step involves predictions about future possibilities rather than simply reactions to current events.

Each person's life is full of recurrent episodes of the same type, and individuals develop habitual approaches for addressing them, called problem-solving heuristics. This habit creates problems only when the habitual heuristics are inappropriately applied in new situations; some heuristics are more useful and effective than others for different types of problems. For example, one may interpret a current episode as familiar and use an approach that yielded past success but that may be inappropriate for the present circumstances. Moreover, some people rigidly adhere to familiar habits, without formulating and evaluating alternate options. In unfamiliar occasions others—particularly small children—implement the first option that occurs to them without delaying action to consider its utility or review other options. In some adults, such impulsive and unreflective tendencies have become an enduring behavioral style. They haven't learned to live by the adage, "Look before you leap!" Still others characteristically delay action so as to explore alternatives exhaustively; some may ruminate and remain indecisive for so long that the opportunity for effective action eludes them.

Therapy clients' problem-solving heuristics may be an important part of their difficulties. Mrs. K's habitual heuristic for dealing with marital conflicts appears to be to withdraw to her private room. Is that the only or best way for her to deal with such conflicts? Clients can be rigidly committed to their ways of dealing with life tasks, using them inefficiently, ineffectively, or inappropriately. They may be either impulsive or erratic in their selection of action patterns. They may have failed to acquire an adequate base of information on which to draw, or they may not utilize relevant information. They may never have learned effective heuristics for generating and evaluating alternatives. Thus, the acquisition of more effective problem-solving approaches may constitute a significant therapeutic task.

The *plan execution* phase involves organizing and coordinating implementation of activity designed to produce or maintain the preferred states. Also included are operations that monitor the flow of the behavior pattern in order to effect any midcourse revisions judged to be needed. This is an iterative process in which both feedback and feedforward information are used to maintain and modify the coordinated flow of behavior. Sometimes, conditions call for quick creation and implementation of different solutions, as in a fast-paced business meeting, a political debate, an athletic contest, or a group psychotherapy session. The ability to create alternate plans and modes of action rapidly has been called generative flexibility.

Psychotherapy clients display deficiencies in plan execution. For example, there are parents who seem capable of developing reasonable plans for dealing with their troublesome children and begin to implement them, but then display a lack of follow-through in carrying them to completion. Some clients can be inattentive to feedback signals indicating that their efforts are alienating others or otherwise producing unwanted results. Still others seem unable to modify or abandon an ineffective course of action and to try an alternative.

Regulating the Flow of Behavior Through Evaluative Cognitions
Directive cognitions specify desired outcomes, and control cognitions design and implement ways of producing them. Effective behavior requires evaluating alternatives to guide choices and to determine whether the plan implemented is working. That regulatory function is performed by evaluative cognitions that (1) prioritize goals and estimate the likelihood of achieving them, (2) evaluate the acceptability and probable effectiveness of alternate problem solutions, (3) evaluate one's own characteristics and capabilities, and (4) facilitate staying on track toward effective action in the face of obstacles, distractions, unsuccessful efforts, and other disrupting influences. Regulatory evaluative cognitions function not only reactively by evaluating what is happening but also in an anticipatory fashion by evaluating cognitive representations of what might happen (e.g., self-efficacy beliefs).

Regulatory cognitions coordinate and use both feedback and feedforward information from different sources, using different regulatory rules, values, or guidelines, to estimate how things are going now and how they might go in the future under different scenarios that the person can imagine. These regulatory cognitions can be subdivided into four types.

1. *Goal Evaluations.* People can imagine many goals they might pursue. They must make choices among them, and choices rest on evaluations of the goal's acceptability, importance, and relevance. One kind of evaluation is of

goal acceptability within the framework of personal values or broader social values. For example, killing a neighbor or burning down a store are unacceptable goals to a person or a society that believes the protection of life and property are essential. Because people construct multiple personal goals, and because new ones may be constructed or adopted at any time in life, they must have an evaluative process by which to determine the value of each goal, called goal importance: "How important is this goal to me? Is it still as important as it used to be?" Typically, people have many valued goals, and not all can be accomplished at the same time, so some form of trade-off is needed. This requires evaluations of relative goal value or importance. In addition, different circumstances make the pursuit of different goals more feasible or desirable, requiring an evaluation of goal relevance.

2. *Means Evaluations.* When people imagine alternatives for accomplishing a goal, they must have criteria for choosing among them. One criterion is feasibility within the constraints and opportunities of current conditions: "Will it cost too much; take too much time; be opposed by others?" A second is effectiveness, how likely the approach is to produce the desired results in the conditions under which it will operate, and what adverse side effects it might generate: "How well will it work, and will it cause me any other kinds of problems along with it?" A third is desirability, which is a judgment of the degree to which the proposed option conforms to the rules, norms, and standards—personal, ethical, social, legal—the person has adopted: "That would be against the law." "My parents wouldn't approve." "I don't believe that would be right." Such desirability evaluations are sometimes referred to as moral reasoning.

3. *Performance Evaluations.* To behave effectively, people must monitor and evaluate whether the approach they are implementing is producing the desired results: "How well is it working?" This requires performance standards or criteria for success that are used as rules in evaluating behavioral effectiveness: "I'll be satisfied with a C in this course."

4. *Personal Agency Evaluations.* People must make anticipatory evaluations of the likelihood that they can execute a course of action that will achieve a desired result. Two types of personal agency evaluations have demonstrated their importance. Capability beliefs, sometimes called self-efficacy beliefs, have to do with people's evaluations of their own competence for executing a particular activity and their likely persistence in such an effort. Self-judgments of inadequacy, inferiority, or incompetence in the face of a prospective undertaking may lead a person to forgo the effort: "Why try if you know that you will fail?" Context beliefs are anticipatory evaluations about whether the environment in which the behavior will occur will be responsive to the

person's efforts: "It doesn't make any difference what I do. They won't give me the job because I'm a woman [or black, or too old]."

Psychotherapy clients may have deficiencies in any of these types of cognitive regulation. For example, some clients adhere to unrealistically high standards of performance for themselves and others. Some have pervasively negative or grandiose evaluations of their own competence and capability. Others routinely anticipate critical and rejecting responses from other people. Some are driven by moral imperatives that imperil their or others' welfare, while others believe themselves compelled to abide by the values of others rather their own. Some have incompatible values, predisposing them to the stress of recurrent value conflict.

It is conceptually convenient to discuss psychological functions separately, but it is important to reemphasize that they do not operate separately; they function as a team. Remember that affects, particularly emotions, also perform regulatory functions. In fact, affectively based evaluations influence the construction of cognitive evaluations; humans' values often have deep emotional roots. As a result, cognitive and affective evaluations often operate as regulatory partners. When they do, their impact is powerful and they are more difficult to change, but they may also be competitors: "My heart says yes but my mind says no." The widely used concept of motivation represents one important pattern of psychological components.

MOTIVATIONAL PROCESSES

Many models of human behavior rely heavily on events postulated to impel the person to activity, such as underlying needs, drives, or motives. Despite the protracted absence of agreement among theorists regarding such notions, they were believed necessary to explain the instigation of activity in people who, it was assumed, would otherwise be inactive. However, activity is an inherent property of humans, continuing unceasingly in some form throughout life. Therefore, it is not necessary to postulate forces that impel people to activity. It is necessary, however, to account for variations in the content and direction of activity, the intensity and persistence with which it occurs, and why one pattern of activity ceases and another begins. The concept of motivation is useful for these purposes.

In Figure 3.2, motivation is construed not as a qualitatively different function (e.g., a biological drive) but as a pattern of affective and cognitive functioning. In the living systems framework, motivation is defined as a psychological process resulting from an organization of directive and regulatory functioning combining personal goals, emotions, and personal agency beliefs (see M. Ford, 1992, for extended discussion of this model of motivation, and how it synthesizes other theories of motivation). People's motivation will vary within and between behavior episodes, depending on the nature, strength, and interrelationships of the goals, emotions, and personal agency beliefs of the pattern. Each of the components is necessary, but none alone is sufficient to lead to a particular pattern of activity. Effective motivation requires that they function synergistically.

For example, a date with an attractive and popular girl might rank high in a schoolboy's hierarchy of personal goals, and thoughts of a date might engender pleasurable emotions. However, he might have negative personal agency beliefs, leading him to expect a refusal were he to ask, so he doesn't. Perhaps he is confident he could get a date if he asked, but he doesn't like the girl, so he doesn't ask. It is like a tricycle; if any wheel is defective the tricycle won't go anywhere.

Motivation is a key psychotherapy issue from the very outset, as a client's motivation to seek professional assistance and to persist in therapy will significantly influence how therapy turns out. Mrs. K initiated psychotherapy when her agitated and depressed state became unbearable (emotions), her aspiration to "become well again" became strong enough to seek psychotherapy (goals), she decided that it would be feasible and helpful (personal agency context beliefs), and that she might be able to do what the therapist asked of her (personal agency capability beliefs). Mrs. K's motivation contrasts with that of some clients remanded to treatment by court order. A judge may see that a defendant has an antisocial or substance abuse problem, the judge's recognition does not mean that the defendant's personal goals include adherence to social regulations and continuing abstinence from alcohol or drugs. With such clients, the therapist's first task is often to help construct a motivational pattern of personal goals, emotions, and personal agency beliefs that will lead to commitment to the psychotherapy process. Of course, motivational factors remain of importance throughout therapy, influencing what changes clients are willing to pursue, and the energy and persistence they will devote to the effort.

Psychoanalysis and psychotherapy use approaches directed primarily toward cognitive and affective functions, but people always function as a unit-in-a-context. A change in any part of that unit may initiate changes in other parts. Therefore, psychological problems might also be influenced indirectly by having the client focus on related action patterns and contexts. When people change they way they act, the resulting consequences may stimulate changes in the way they think and feel; if the context is changed, there may be changes in how they act, think, and feel. These behavioral components are discussed next.

THE BEHAVIORAL PERSON: PERSON-ENVIRONMENT TRANSACTIONAL FUNCTIONS

Humans are open systems. Their existence, capacity to change and develop, and ability to function effectively all require continual exchanges of matter, energy, information, and meanings with their environments. Any specific context provides opportunities for, and imposes constraints on, how people may effectively function within it. People's current functioning cannot be understood apart from the environments in which it occurs, and understanding this requires some way of conceptualizing human's environments. People can simultaneously influence and be influenced by their contexts through two types of transactional behaviors: physical actions and communicative actions. Person-environment transactions would be untargeted and ineffective unless guided by relevant information about the nature of their contexts and their mutually influential interactions. Therefore, this section considers ways of understanding humans' environments and then reviews the interrelated types of transactional capabilities that have evolved to enable people to exist and develop within their ecological niche as represented in Figure 3.2C.

HUMANS' ENVIRONMENTS: DYNAMIC NESTED SYSTEMS

All human functioning occurs in some specific place at some particular time. The impossibility of understanding a person's functioning without reference to the contexts in which it occurs was discussed in Chapter 2. Clarification of terms and consideration of various ways scholars have represented environments are added here.

What Is an Environment?

What is environment and what is not can be specified only in relation to an entity that is the focus of interest. Anything outside that entity's boundary is part of its environment. For example, if a cell is the focus, then everything outside its cell membrane is its environment. If a person is the focus, then the environment is everything outside her or his skin. If a social group such as the family is the entity of interest, then the contexts in which that group is embedded form its environment. Not all aspects of environments are of equal

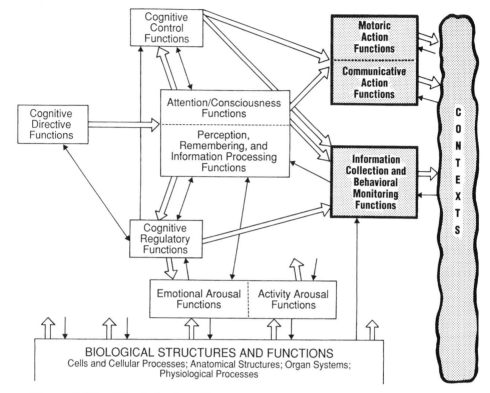

Figure 3.2C *The Behavioral Person.* A person's existence, functioning, and development require continual exchanges of material/energy and information/meanings with their environments. This is accomplished through three principal types of functions: instrumental, communicative, and information collection transactions. The content and organization of environmental contexts both facilitate and constrain behavioral possibilities. Behavioral functions affect biological functioning by utilizing resources, exercising biological components, and providing material/energy-based nutriment. They affect psychological-behavioral functioning by providing information/meaning-based nutriment to regulate ongoing behavior and to facilitate or constrain further psychological development.

significance for a person at each moment, as three hierarchically related concepts reveal.

- *Environs* are the totality of phenomena in which people are embedded, from their clothing, to their home, community, and nation. Different aspects of the environs have different potentials for affecting a person, depending on whether they are in close physical proximity or far away.

- *Environment* is the part of the environs that has the potential for directly affecting a person. For example, the north pole's weather will not directly affect you even though it is a part of your environs. People's environment varies both as they act on it and move around in it, and as influences within it and on it from its environs produce change.

- *Contexts* are parts of a person's environment that are organized so that they display structural and functional coherence and may exert their influence as an organized unit. Every environment provides multiple contexts. Because people can be in only one place at a time, they are always functioning in a particular context. Therefore, people's current functioning and the habitual patterns of functioning they develop are best understood in terms of the content, contingencies, and consequences of specific contexts. For example, their homes, cars, churches, families, or psychotherapy sessions are contexts.

Environments as Organizations of Things, Events, and Processes

Environments are not unorganized "heaps of stuff" like piles of dirty clothes in a child's bedroom. They are extensively organized, both within themselves and in relationship to people within them; that is the meaning of the concept of ecology. Therefore, understanding environments, the contexts within them, and the ways they may be involved in people's functioning requires ways of representing both their content and their organizational properties. Different ways of classifying environments give primary emphasis to different aspects of content and organization.

One content classification distinguishes between natural and constructed environments. Humans evolved in and depend on the natural ecology of their world—air, water, plants, animals, light, and gravity. Significant changes in natural environments can threaten human health and existence. Worries about allergies, infectious diseases, endangered species, and pollution reflect recognition of the importance of the natural environment to human life and of the potential damage humans' living patterns may inflict on the natural environment. One powerful product of humans' adaptive capabilities is their ability to transcend the constraints of their natural environment by constructing objects and contexts that make their lives easier. The designed environment includes tools and processes, such as drugs, eyeglasses, houses, cities, communication and transportation systems, clothing, and processed foods. Through breeding and genetic engineering strategies, humans can even redesign aspects of their natural environment. They construct social and cultural environments as well as physical ones. Humans live their daily lives in interpersonal environments they create among friends, family, neighbors, and co-workers; these environments serve a variety of life needs and objectives. These immediate, day-to-day interpersonal contexts are embedded in larger sociocultural environments constructed by humans to provide a framework of beliefs, languages, governments, and institutions essential for orderly and effective social group living.

Societies display wide individual differences in the nature of the natural and constructed environments within which people's lives are embedded: rural or urban, suburb or ghetto, work settings, and subcultures. These differences are important to psychotherapists, as the sources and meanings of clients' behavior patterns, as well as conditions that may help them alter troublesome patterns, will be significantly influenced by the specific contexts in which they developed and presently live.

Other classifications focus on environmental organization. One approach emphasizes spatial organization; *proximal* includes environments physically near a person; *distal* includes physically distant environments. For example, an elderly parent living with a client will have a different impact from that of one living a thousand miles away. One type of environment features hierarchical organization. For example, Bronfenbrenner's (1979) concepts of microsystems, mesosystems, exosystems, and macrosystems represent environments as embedded hierarchies that have organizational properties within as well as between levels. Another approach assumes that environments facilitate some types of behavior patterns and constrain others. It combines behavioral and environmental variables to specify contexts, called behavior settings; examples are church, school, hospital, theater, basketball court (Barker, 1968; Wicker, 1979). The discipline of psychology has given little rigorous attention to environments. The term *stimulus* is often used, but it is defined not by environmental attributes but by behavioral consequences. Psychotherapists have focused primarily on interpersonal and family contexts.

Because people's habits are constructed as behavior-context patterns, consistency in contexts helps to maintain consistency in behavior. However, contexts differ from one another in terms of their content, organization, and the ways in which they function. Therefore, behavior patterns that are useful in one context often prove to be inappropriate or ineffective in others. Each person must therefore become proficient in a wide variety of behavior patterns appropriate to a broad range of contexts or behavior settings. Major changes in context—going to college, changing jobs, marrying—produce changes in the opportunities and constraints in one's life and typically require changes in one's behavioral repertoire. Also, environments and contexts are dynamic systems of phenomena that exist in a continual state of flux and change. A person's customary behavior in a context may have been effective at one time but may have become inappropriate later because the context and the person have both changed. An example is adults who continue to behave toward parents in childlike ways. Such changes are inevitable, and people must adapt to them if their behavior is to be effective.

People may change by altering their own functioning within their existing contexts, by changing those contexts, or by moving to different contexts. A sophisticated understanding of person-context functioning is important to psychotherapy interventions in three fundamental ways. First, the content of each client's habitual patterns will vary with the contexts in which those patterns were constructed. Second, psychotherapy interventions involve designing special contextual conditions, represented by each psychotherapy session, to facilitate desired client changes. Functioning differently in therapy sessions is of little importance, however, unless it brings desired changes in clients' functioning in the significant contexts of their lives. Thus, facilitating generalization of within therapy changes to real-life environments and contexts is a third basic intervention task (Goldstein & Kanfer, 1979).

The influence of environments on people is not automatic. Contexts influence people as a function of the way people influence their contexts; people simultaneously influence and are influenced by those reciprocal exchanges. Contexts may change because of people's actions, and vice versa. People's instrumental actions are labeled transactional functions because they are the behaviors that provide both the inputs and the outputs essential for an open system, such as a person, to operate and develop as a dynamic, unified entity. These are considered next in three categories: sensory-perceptual monitoring or information collection functions, sensory-motor action functions, and communicative action functions.

SENSORY-PERCEPTUAL MONITORING: INFORMATION COLLECTION FUNCTIONS

Humans must collect and use nutritious materials and eliminate potentially disrupting surplus and noxious materials for their biological maintenance and development. They must also collect and use information nutrients for their psychological/behavioral functioning and development. Figure 3.2C reveals that the effectiveness of self-regulation depends on feedback signals that provide relevant information about current system states, the system's current context, and the current consequences of its functioning. In humans, these feedback signals are produced by a diversity of sensory-perceptual capabilities that can collect information both from internal and external sources. Information is conveyed by the organization of different kinds of material/energy carriers, and different kinds of information can be coded onto different kinds of carriers; therefore, a highly adaptive system requires a diversity of information and should be sensitive to a diversity of carriers and codes. It should also be able to combine information from different sources to be adequately informed.

Collecting Different Information from Different Carriers

Information collection is accomplished by a highly developed set of specialized sensors, called sensory receptors, each of which can be stimulated by different types of material/energy carriers, including electromagnetic, mechanical, chemical, and thermal. Sherrington's fourfold classification of these receptors relies on the relationship of the source of the stimulus and the location of the receptor. Teleceptors, located in the eyes, ears, and nose, provide information about environmental conditions at a distance from the person. Exteroceptors, located in body surface tissues, provide information about contextual conditions in direct contact with the body. Proprioceptors, found in muscles, tendons and joints, and in the labyrinth of the ear, provide information concerning body movements and positions in space. Interoceptors, located in the body's organs and tissues, provide information about internal body states. Another classification system relies on the kinds of carriers from which they can collect information. These include electromagnetic—vision; mechanical/air pressure waves—hearing; mechanical/contact—touch and pain; mechanical/movement—vestibular and kinesthetic; thermal—cold and warmth; and chemical—taste and smell.

Receptors are continually bathed with stimulation. If they collected and fed back all that diverse information, the person would be flooded and overwhelmed with excessive and redundant information: Try listening to ten people talking while you are playing the piano. This would not be adaptive. Fortunately, humans evolved with selective perception capabilities that collect only information relevant to current purposes and activities and filter out the rest. This is accomplished by selective attention feedforward processes (see the wide arrows in Figure 3.2C) directed by the operation of cognitive governing functions. These feedforward processes selectively tune the sensory-perceptual functions to be sensitive to certain aspects of the information flow and to ignore the rest. In addition, sensory receptors abstract and transmit to the brain only the consistencies in the variable flow of stimulation and cancel out the rest. People may concentrate so intensely on what they are reading that they will not hear someone speak to them. There is a built-in safety feature, however, a priority interrupt. Stimulus events that may be of personal significance—sudden loud sounds or bright lights—can override the feedforward control of perception.

These feedforward processes do not create the patterns of sensory stimulation: they only select from the pattern produced by contextual stimulation and their own functioning. Therefore, patterns of sensory stimulation and the resulting perceptions are direct manifestations of the content and organization of the reality around or within a person.

The Unity of Perceptual Experience

Even with these selection operations, the person's brain is still getting different messages from different sensory receptors. For example, one feeds back information that an object is red and round; another that it is smooth and flexible; another that it smells fishy; and another that it makes squealing sounds. If treated as separate pieces of information, they would be of little use. Fortunately, sensory-perceptual functions evolved so that the brain automatically integrates the separate messages into a unified experience. Instead of the fragments just listed a person perceives a cat's toy that is a red, round object that is smooth and flexible, smells fishy, and squeals when squeezed. A person can selectively attend to and perceive different attributes, and that is useful when detailed analysis of phenomena is desired. Thus, while sensory structures react to stimuli, information collection is a proactive process that organizes a selective search for relevant information and integrates the multiple messages collected from different carriers. The selective nature of sensory-perceptual functioning is often a source of difficulty and a barrier to change in psychotherapy clients because it enables clients to avoid dealing with information that might be distressing to them.

Sensations, Perceptions, and Meanings

What then is a perception? It is the conscious manifestation of information currently collected through multiple sensory modalities. Sensation and perception are simply two aspects of one process, so the term *sensory-perceptual functions* is used to convey their integrated nature. There has been considerable disagreement over what the term *perception* should mean. It has been construed by some to be an idea (interpretation) mentally constructed from sensations; perception is derivative or indirect. More recently, ecological models view perception as we defined it above; perception is both immediate and direct. The information represented by a perception is directly coded in the sensory pattern created by selective receptor functioning. No intervening act of mental construction is necessary to translate the sensory pattern into a conscious perception. The utility of sensory-perceptual functions, then, is to provide people with accurate information about current events within and around them. To this extent, the metaphysical assumption of realism is sound.

The adaptive utility of perceptions is seriously limited, however, because they only provide current news about what's happening in the here and now; that leaves unanswered the question of "what does it mean?" The meaning of perceptions results from relating them to representations constructed from previous relevant experiences, as well as cognitively created ideas; it results from the wedding of perceptions and conceptions. To this extent, the metaphysical assumption of idealism is sound.

The Utility of Distinguishing Perception from Conception
The value of the distinction between perceptions and conceptions is basic for both science and practice. Empirical science relies on the relationships between them as the cornerstone of the scientific method. In science, perceptions are called observations (measures are quantified observations). Scientific reports are expected to describe accurately and thoroughly the conditions under which the observations were made so that other scientists can precisely duplicate those conditions to see whether their observations match those reported by the first observer. The assumption is that two observers will experience essentially the same perceptions under the same observational conditions, and that the information in those perceptions accurately represents what actually occurred. The second step is called inference or interpretation. In it, the scientist relates the observations to previously constructed knowledge and theory and forms generalized conclusions about the meaning of the specific observations produced by their methods. Scientists may agree about the observations but disagree about their interpretations. Accurate observations represent facts; interpretations represent opinions that may vary depending on the framework of ideas, beliefs, and methods used for the interpretation. The ethics of science requires complete honesty in accurately reporting methods and observations, whether or not they support the beliefs that led to the study. Scientific fraud occurs when that ethical rule is ignored.

Conceptions do influence what is observed because, through feedforward processes, they selectively direct attention toward some phenomena and not others. That is the meaning of the saying, "All observation is theory guided." Although conceptions influence the selection of what is attended to, they do not determine the content of the perceptions that result. The content results from sensory-perceptual processes reflecting the phenomena observed. This means, of course, that perceptions may be biased in the sense that some important information was selectively ignored. Perceptions are not fictions, however; they represent some aspects of the real thing. Even so, people construct imagistically coded conceptions that represent perceptions. Under special conditions, these imagistic representations can be remembered without relevant sensory stimulation, called sensory-perceptual hallucinations.

We have discussed the nature of perception in some detail because of its importance for professional practice. Unfortunately, people often make the error of labeling their interpretations perceptions; "He was hostile toward me" should be stated as "I interpreted his actions as hostile." Adaptive problems can result. For example, a person's hostile intent and affective state are not directly observable. What can be observed are facial and hand gestures, vocalizations, statements, and movements observers might interpret as manifestations of a hostile attitude. Their interpretation may be wrong, however; other interpretations to explain the observed actions are always possible, e.g., the person is "kidding" or ill. One frequent task in psychotherapy is to help clients learn to be careful about distinguishing between what they observe and how they interpret their observations. When clients begin to realize that the facts provided by their perceptions are contradictory to their habitual interpretations and beliefs, they can explore the implications.

Therapists can also be limited by inadequate recognition of this distinction. Therapists committed to a particular theory will guide their therapy interactions with their psychotherapy model. In the extreme, this can lead therapists to pay attention only to phenomena that fit their model and to ignore those that don't, thus creating a self-fulfilling prophecy. It can also lead them to confine their interpretations of client behaviors to a particular framework of beliefs without testing the validity of that interpretation against alternate plausible ones. This issue is considered further in Chapter 4. Now we consider actions by which people can influence their environments and produce desired states for themselves.

ACTIONS AND SENSORY-MOTOR FUNCTIONS

Adaptively dealing with a variable environment requires movement that can vary in kind, intensity, rate, direction, and spatial-temporal organization. Human's skeletal-muscle and central nervous systems make possible a great diversity of movement patterns through which they can move around in, interact with, and manipulate their environments; these patterns include ingestive and eliminative actions, physical mobility, and object manipulation. Action is so important in our everyday existence that we have to lose only a small part of that capability through injury or disease to realize its value for our functioning and survival.

Assimilative and Eliminative Actions

Some material/energy exchange action patterns are highly automated as a result of evolutionary processes because of their importance to life: breathing, sweating, urination, and defecation. Through learning, some of these actions may come under some degree of intentional control, but their basic automaticity remains, as anyone experiencing an unexpected episode of diarrhea will attest. However, because of the highly variable and changeable nature of humans' environments, and because of humans' capabilities for manipulating and shaping their environments, most useful action patterns could not be automated through evolutionary processes. Instead, evolution led to self-construction capabilities for creating useful action patterns.

It is not possible to describe the great diversity of actions of which humans are capable. The same act may never be performed in precisely the same way because conditions are always somewhat different from occasion to occasion. Typically, people focus on how specific action patterns develop and operate, as in the design of man-machine systems, athletics, or musical performances.

Motor Skill Development and Maintenance
Acquisition of motor skills is important in infant, child, and adolescent development because people's ability to provide for themselves and to deal effectively with their contexts depend on those skills. Being accepted by and functioning effectively as a member of social groups is often a function of motor skills—as an example, participating in games with other children. Initially, simple patterns develop. These become subroutines of increasingly more complex motor patterns, thereby enabling the youngster to function within increasingly complex behavior settings. Motor skills tend to be acquired in a developmental sequence, which has been subdivided into phases: order and onset of an emerging skill; strategy and mastery of a developing skill; and control and upkeep of an established skill. The brain systems for acquiring a behavior appear to be different from those needed to sustain and maintain it, once acquired. For example, recent research on brain-damaged children indicates that skill acquisition and maintenance call on different localizations within each hemisphere of the brain, and even on different hemispheres.

Effective action cannot occur without sensory feedback. Proprioceptive components provide moment-to-moment information so as to set, adjust, align, regulate, synchronize, or track what the muscles are doing and thus enable a course of action to run smoothly through to completion. However, all the other receptors also become involved, particularly vision, depending on the nature of the task and the contexts in which it occurs. Therefore, these action functions are often termed sensory-motor processes to emphasize the necessary coordination of both.

Benefits and Limitations of Different Degrees of Motor Capabilities
High levels of motor skills provide a pathway to fame and fortune for some people, such as professional athletes, singers, and dancers. Deficiencies in

motor skills, whatever their cause, can impose serious constraints on people's living and development, and consequently on what they are able to do and how they view themselves. Limitations in motor capabilities constrain the kinds of personal goals, beliefs, and activity patterns people may construct as well as the kinds of contexts to which they will expose themselves and the reactions they receive from others. Rehabilitating action capabilities and designing more responsive environments may open pathways to future developmental possibilities for such people.

COMMUNICATIVE FUNCTIONS

There is a subset of motor actions that have a different and special significance in humans' individual and social functioning and development; these are called communicative actions. Because of their major importance in the conduct of human affairs, communicative capabilities have been extensively studied under the headings of gestural communication, verbal-symbolic behavior, and language acquisition and use.

How Do Communicative Actions Differ from Other Actions?

Actions in general are physical, energy-based processes that directly affect the environment or a person's physical relationship to it. Because actions are themselves organized patterns and organization conveys information, any action conveys information of some sort. Skilled therapists capitalize on this by paying attention to a client's physical postures and movements, often called body language, for clues about subjective states. Any action conveys information as a by-product, but such unintentional information conveying is not considered a communicative act.

A motoric act is a communicative act when its influence on the environment results primarily through the information intentionally coded on the act rather than through the physical nature of the act itself, such as asking for something to eat rather than taking it. The organization of the action deliberately conveys meaning to influence the environment. Any kind of action could be intentionally coded to communicate a message. Thus, one may intentionally communicate perplexity by shrugging one's shoulders, pleasure with a smile, anger with a fist, or a message of joy through dance. These kinds of nonlinguistic communicative acts are typically called gestural communication. However, the most powerful and widely used communicative codes are called languages, and they are typically coded onto motoric acts of speech and writing that can be perceived through hearing and vision. When hearing, vision, or speech capabilities are deficient, languages can be coded onto hand gestures (e.g., American sign language) or onto surface textures (e.g., Braille). The same meanings can be communicated with different languages or codes.

Communication refers to an exchange of information ideas, or meanings between two or more people. Such communicative transactions require (1) a communicator; (2) a meaningful message to be communicated; (3) a code used to convey the message; (4) a carrier or action pattern onto which the message can be coded; and (5) a receiver who can perceive the carrier, knows the code, and can correctly interpret it to abstract the meaning intended by the communicator. If any of these components are absent or malfunction, miscommunication or noncommunication will occur. For example, the communicator may use a carrier that receivers cannot perceive, such as speaking to a deaf person, or a code they don't know, such as speaking Spanish to a person who knows only English. The receiver may selectively focus on one part of the message and ignore other parts, or incorrectly interpret the intended meaning.

Strictly speaking, information is not transmitted from brain to brain. Symbols are intrinsically meaningless; their meaning is arbitrarily assigned by cultural agreement. Therefore, different symbols may stand for the same meanings or the same symbol may stand for different meanings. A communicator uses a shared symbol system to activate from among meanings receivers know the specific ones intended by the communicator. Receivers may construct new meanings by combining perceptual and symbolic meanings. For example, when a therapist makes an interpretation to a client, its communicative effectiveness depends on whether it activates the intended meanings from the client's existing store of meanings.

Different kinds of motor acts may be used as carriers on which messages can be coded, so it is possible to communicate the same message simultaneously in two different ways, or to send different messages at the same time. When simultaneous messages are contradictory, interpreting their meaning is difficult. A husband may say to his wife, "I am not angry!" At the same time, he displays an angry facial expression with a tense body and clenched fists.

Languages and their use are multifaceted phenomena. Each language is a complex network of interrelated components that require an intricate combination of biological capabilities for their learning and use. Contemporary analyses of languages have become correspondingly more intricate and detailed, subdivided into specialized but interrelated topics. A language is composed of symbols that are organized by grammatical rules, and expressed through some physical carrier. Its articulation (purpose) is to convey information and meaning (its semantics), to influence interpersonal and social contexts, it pragmatics.

Psychotherapy is accomplished primarily through shared meanings produced in communicative transactions between clients and therapists. The effectiveness of psychotherapy is a function of the meanings activated by the messages that are exchanged—their structure, relevance, intelligibility, and timeliness—and of the ways such exchanges benefit clients' functioning. With the exception of treatments directed toward brain-damaged children or adults, the domains of semantics (meaning) and pragmatics (influence) are likely to be of greatest value to psychotherapists; these include analyses of the social variations in language usage, and how conversations and narratives serve interpersonal communication and discourse functions. The information processing functions and operations of which humans are capable, and how they contribute to behavioral self-construction in humans are examined in Chapter 4.

NEXT STEPS

This brief summary of the major biological, psychological, action, and environmental component theories that compose the person-in-context unit represents the conceptual content of our comparative framework. Psychotherapy approaches will differ in the aspects of humans they emphasize, as a result of different metaphysical and epistemological emphases. We next examine the dynamics by which these components interrelate, symbolized by the arrows in Figure 3.2. Chapter 4 summarizes the propositional content of the model and presents proposals of how the dynamics of human functioning take place and generate complex, unified patterns of living.

CHAPTER 4

Dynamics of Functional and Dysfunctional Development: A Comparative Propositional Framework

C HAPTER 3 ADDRESSED ontological issues—the "what" of human nature—and summarized a conceptual model for the comparative framework. The "how" of human functioning must also be understood, including how it can go awry and produce undesirable, distressing outcomes. Chapters 4 and 5 focus on cosmological issues—the "how" of human development. They provide a general propositional framework for representing the processes by which the prototypical components of humans interact to produce structural-functional unity at the person-in-context level of analysis. Chapter 4 considers units of analysis, the dynamics of functional organization, and the nature of functional and dysfunctional patterns. The discussion utilizes eight key ideas: structure, function, process, dynamics, behavior episode, behavioral state, behavior episode schema, and dysfunction.

STRUCTURES, FUNCTIONS, PROCESSES, AND DYNAMICS

STRUCTURES AND FUNCTIONS

Evolutionary processes manifest a principle called the division of labor in economic theory; it holds that complex systems are organizations of parts or components, each of which specializes in doing something. Two benefits result from appropriately linking the activities and outputs of multiple specialists: A more complex unitary entity can exist and effectively function, and the needs of each part are served by the activity of the other specialists. The activity, product, or output of each specialist is its *function.* For example, the function of an air conditioning system thermostat is to regulate the temperature in a room by telling the system when to turn on and off. The entity's physical nature that makes possible a particular functional potential is called its *structure.*

The body is an organization of structural components. The normal and specific contribution of a body structure, or an organization of structures, to the economy of a person is called its function. The way its function facilitates or constrains other functions is called its functional utility. A function of the heart is to pump blood and maintain certain pressures. Combined with arteries, veins, and capillaries, it becomes a component of a larger structure, the circulatory system, whose function is to circulate blood. Its functional utility is to provide materials to and receive materials from every cell, tissue, and organ in the body. Physiology is the study of body structures and functional capabilities they make possible. Sometimes an entity's function is called its purpose, but purpose implies a goal that is intentionally and self-consciously sought. Instead, we use the term *function* because its broader meaning does not have such a teleological connotation and it can encompass the purposive qualities of human behavior.

PROCESSES AND DYNAMICS

A *process* is a series of activities or operations by which a particular kind of output or function is produced. For example, the cognitive functions of goal setting and problem solving are carried out by processes often termed *thinking* or *information processing.* However, process does not suggest a sequence that happens willy-nilly. It means a pattern of activities or operations organized and directed toward producing some outcome, such as the process of digesting food. Each *process* fulfills a *functional role.* If it operates effectively, it displays *functional utility.* In Chapter 3, prototypical human functions were identified, such as directive, regulatory, communicative, and biological functions. One could try to identify the processes by which each function is accomplished. For example, how do thought processes accomplish the directive and regulatory functions? How is the biological function of digestion accomplished? Understanding the processes by which a function is carried out is essential for designing effective intervention strategies for influencing a function.

Functions and processes are usually studied as separate elements, but no function operates in isolation; each participates in larger organizations of interdependent functions and their implementing processes. The production of unified, harmonious, and concerted activity is often called *system dynamics.* As an example, personality dynamics typically refers to the interaction of cognitive, emotional, and behavioral functions/processes to produce psychosocial outcomes. Psychotherapy interventions are attempts to influence the dynamics by which a set of functions—cognitions, emotions, actions—are currently interacting. Both machines and humans can be subjected to a functional analysis, and the dynamics by which their processes generate functional outcomes can be studied. However, living systems are fundamentally different from machines because they are capable of functions that machines cannot perform. We call them *self-constructing functions.* Other terms are also used, such as *autopoesis,* (Maturana, 1975; Zeleny, 1981).

HUMANS AS SELF-CONSTRUCTING SYSTEMS

Chapter 3 describes a variety of built-in human capabilities; some of these are self-directing, self-monitoring, self-regulating, and self-correcting in relation to their functional effectiveness. Machines have been created that can perform such functions to some degree. Therefore, if humans are more than a fancy machine, there must be some additional distinguishing functions.

What does it mean to say that humans are self-constructing? Their functional capabilities include processes that enable them to utilize matter and energy to construct, modify, and repair their biological characteristics, they can also utilize information and meanings to create, elaborate, and modify their psychological and behavioral characteristics. Humans are continuously constructing themselves; in basic ways they are architects of their own development. This is a jarring statement to those who construe people as passive recipients of whatever events and experiences come to them. The possibilities for self-construction are not unlimited, however. They are constrained and facilitated by the contexts, genetic histories, current personal states, and resources available to the person. However, multiple developmental pathways are always possible within such boundaries.

To use a computer analogy, humans construct and modify both their hardware and their software; machines cannot. Some computer programs can modify themselves in limited ways, but these are miniscule compared to the complex development of which humans are capable. Moreover, no one has been able to fashion a machine that can reproduce, elaborate, modify, or repair its own physical nature.

MATERIAL/ENERGY-BASED AND INFORMATION/MEANING-BASED
SELF-CONSTRUCTION FUNCTIONS

Centuries-old attempts to understand humans as seeming to manifest both material and nonmaterial natures were summarized in Chapter 1. If both are accepted as inherent properties of humans, one must specify the nature of each and their relationship. *Materialism* proposes to resolve this dilemma by asserting that material/energy forms and processes are all that exist. Phenomena such as thought, imagination, and memory are epiphenomena that can be explained in terms of material functions and processes—the biophysical and biochemical operations of people's body and brain. Biological determinism manifests this metaphysical assumption. Psychophysical interactionism proposes that people function as much in terms of meaning as of materials. It argues that material/energy-based biological functions and processes are necessary but not sufficient bases for representing psychological, behavioral, and social aspects of human life. Such nonmaterial functions and processes cannot be dismissed as merely epiphenomenal. Mrs. K's multiple difficulties cannot be explained solely in terms of her biological nature. There must have emerged in the evolution of life forms some new property that manifests another form of reality, but what could that nonmaterial reality be?

We propose that humans' self-constructing capabilities provide a basis for understanding their integrated yet dualistic nature and how body and mind interrelate. First, we briefly consider the nature of biological or material/energy-based self-construction, and then we present an approach to understanding nonmaterial-based self-construction.

BIOLOGICAL SELF-CONSTRUCTION

Compare the relatively simple and undifferentiated biological properties of a fertilized ovum with the exceedingly complex and highly differentiated characteristics of a mature person. How does one become the other? It does not occur by a process of manufacture in which parts are assembled in accordance with some blueprint, as machines are constructed. Rather, that fertilized cell elaborates, differentiates, and subsequently organizes diverse versions of itself through its own internal processes and the dynamics of interactions with its contexts, until the processes eventuate in the adult biological person. Through the selective ingestion and digestive disassembly of materials from their environment, and through their subsequent recombination and transformation into other material forms and configurations, these living cells progressively construct all the biological components and functions that make up the adult human. Throughout this lengthy process, the organism maintains both a structural and functional unity, despite the variety and complexity of the changes that take place. It is a self-organizing, self-regulating, and self-constructing entity—a living system.

Disciplines such as genetics, cell biology, embryology, and developmental biology and physiology have produced much information about the nature and sequence of these changes and the processes involved. Exactly how this astonishing biological development is actually orchestrated, however, remains a mystery. Genetic material plays a key role, but not in the form of instructions, or of some blueprint of a human that is sequentially followed. Rather, genetic materials seem to function, in transaction with their biochemical context, to generate patterns of complex nonlinear biochemical/biological dynamics that progressively converge on the biological form called a human (cf. Gleick, 1987; Lewin, 1992; Pool, 1989; Prigogene & Stengers, 1984; Schroots, 1988; Yates, 1988).

Humans do construct themselves, from a cell to a biological person, if their contexts provide the essential conditions for evolutionary based processes to operate effectively. Deviations in cells (e.g., missing or "lethal" genes), or adverse biochemical contexts (e.g., nutritional deficits; disrupting drugs), can alter the self-constructing dynamics and create deviations from the prototypic human form. Once a person is fully developed, biological dynamics operate to maintain, or to restore insofar as possible, that same form in spite of disruptions such as injury or infectious disease. Lifestyle can also alter these biological dynamics and outcomes.

The biological person constructed by these material/energy-based dynamics provides the conditions from which all psychological and behavioral functioning can emerge. Therefore, psychotherapists must always consider the possibility that dysfunctions in clients' psychological or behavioral functioning may, at least in part, result from disruptions of supportive biological processes. This means that paranoid ideation could be caused by biochemical imbalances induced by substance abuse; behavioral apathy could result from hypothyroidism rather than depression. Biological processes, however, do not operate as direct causes of psychological and behavioral functioning. They provide material resources and limits from which capabilities for psychological/behavioral modes of functioning emerge. They are necessary but not sufficient conditions for development of the psychological and behavioral person. The next section examines the nature of these nonmaterial-based self-constructing functions.

Information/Meaning-Based Self-Construction

Beginning in the 1940s, new ideas and discoveries began to explicate the importance and utility of a non-material phenomenon called information. It is a kind of phenomenon as fundamental as material and energy have been for understanding ourselves and our world (see D. Ford, 1987 or 1994, and Miller, 1978, for a fuller discussion).

Information and Organization

What is information if it is not material or energy? Zeman (in Miller, 1978) related information to basic physical concepts. "If mass is the measure of the effects of gravitation, and of the force of inertia, and energy the measure of movement, information is . . . the measure of the organization of the material object . . . Matter, space, time, movement, and organization are in mutual connection" (p. 42). Thus, information is not a material/energy form per se but rather a representation of the organization or patterning of such forms. Every object or array of objects, every person or set of persons, everything that objects and persons do, and every way they interact to influence one another, involves some patterning or arrangement, and therefore contains information.

Information and material/energy forms are necessarily linked. Because information is organization, no information exists unless there is some material/energy form that is organized, so conveying information can be accomplished only through organizing some material/energy medium. If that is the case, why do we say that information/organization is a phenomenon fundamentally different from material and energy? It is because the existence of information/organization is demonstrably independent of any particular material/energy form.

The same information can be conveyed with different material/energy forms. For example, "My name is Mary McGonnigal" can be conveyed through (1) organizing air pressure waves by speaking the words, (2) organizing patterns of reflected light by writing the words, or (3) organizing patterns of bumps and ridges on a sheet of paper—writing in Braille. The information conveyed is identical; the material/energy forms used are distinctly different. Also, information/organization can remain invariant as it is transformed from one material/energy form to another. A girl may say, "My name is Mary McGonnigal" into a telephone, thereby creating a distinct organization of air pressure waves. These waves go through the telephone microphone and become a pattern of vibrations of another material that is transformed into a pattern of electrical signals. The signals are transmitted to the phone of the other person where they are transformed into a pattern of vibrations in the phone's receiver; these produce a pattern of air pressure vibrations, which wiggle some structures in the ear, which activate a neural pattern, and the person hears "My name is Mary McGonnigal." Despite these multiple transformations from one material/energy medium to another, the information remains the same because the organization is invariant across all those material/energy transformations.

Codes, Messages, and Carriers
In information science, the information, or pattern of organization, is called the message, the rules of organization for creating messages are called the code, and the material/energy form on which it is conveyed is called the carrier. Engineers call mechanisms that convert information from one kind of carrier to another transducers. Many types of information transducers have evolved in humans (see Miller, 1978). For example the human ear can be understood as a complex transducer that, through a series of transformations, converts the specific pattern of organization of air pressure waves into an analogous pattern of organization of electrochemical neuronal activity.

Relationship Between Information and Meaning
The concept of meaning plays a key role in the conceptual models of many psychotherapy approaches, but it is never defined (e.g., Neimeyer & Mahoney, 1995). Meanings are described as being both personal and shared; they are represented as something more than or different from information. However, if concepts of information and meaning are not defined, their relationship cannot be specified. Information and meaning are related but different concepts. Information is a specific message. Meaning is a construction or interpretation of the significance attributed to information by relating it to other information and ideas, including ideas about potential future events. This distinction is of basic importance in understanding human behavior and psychotherapy processes. Sensory/perceptual functions are fundamentally information collection processes (see Chapter 3); cognitive activity is a meaning construction process, referred to as meaning making by psychotherapists. Sensory-perceptual processes fit an ontology of realism, whereas cognitive processes fit an ontology of idealism; perceptual processes yield information, and cognitive processes produce meanings. They function as a team in organizing behavior; adaptive functioning merges realism and idealism. We use the label *information/meaning-based* to convey the symbiotic relationship between them. The more complex the pattern of organization, the more information it contains, and the more potential meaning it may activate in others. People can communicate information to one another on any carrier—material/energy form—that both can perceive, and with any code—organizational format—that both understand. The degree of match between the person's intended meanings and the meanings activated in the receiver by the message produces shared understanding. Languages are shared codes that can be systematically used to construct messages to convey information and activate meanings, through transmission on multiple carriers (e.g., gestural, vocal, or written communication).

Information/Meaning-Based Anticipatory Nature of Human Functioning

All living forms have biological self-construction processes. Although animals use information to guide their functioning, humans evolved with elaborate information/meaning-based self-construction capabilities that enable them to be far less dependent on the here and now than other organisms. For people, past and present information/meaning-based constructions serve as tools for trying to create imagined and desired future states; people live their lives as much in terms of meanings and potential futures as materials and current conditions. Indeed, in human life such self-constructed meanings can override all other influences. For example, people risk or sacrifice their biological well-being for purposes they judge to hold greater meaning or significance; they commit suicide because of their negative interpretations of their current and potential future life.

The ability to create ideas about things and events in their absence contributes to a special capability of humans—that of anticipation or foresight—which has basic adaptive value. Each person is in a continual process of unending variability and change, and so are their environmental contexts. Not only are the contexts themselves made up of a continual flow of objects and events, but also people move through and affect those same contexts as their behavior unfolds. Mere reaction to such changes based solely on information would have limited adaptive value, as their actions must deal with the temporal flow of organizations of things and events.

The ability to imagine or anticipate events prior to their occurrence and to interpret the meaning of their perceptions to predict future possibilities enables people to be proactive as well as reactive. Anticipations serve as the basis for the formation of personal goals—an inventor's imagined new product or a student's imagined professional success as a surgeon. Most human behavior is organized and functions in relation to such anticipatory processes, and is therefore inherently predictive in character. For example, the successful batter must predict the trajectory of the baseball and start his swing before the ball gets to the plate. Similarly, when parents discipline a child, their actions are based on predictions as to how those measures are apt to influence the child's future behavior. Self-regulating system models represent anticipatory or predictive functioning as resulting from feedforward processes.

Forethought—the use of ideas to anticipate and predict events—requires the combined use of perceptual and conceptual functions which, though different, operate together to construct adaptive psychological/behavioral patterns (see Chapter 3). People guide their functioning by interpreting the meaning of current perceptions using previously constructed knowledge and generalized representations of previous experiences construed to be similar.

In the jargon of systems models, perceptual processes provide feedback signals, whereas cognitive processes carry out throughput functions and provide the feedforward signals necessary to organize behavior. In the jargon of science, perception provides observations or facts while cognition provides inferences, interpretations, and theories representing the meaning of observations or facts.

Implications of the Two Forms of Self-Construction

This model of humans' patterns of functioning and development as resulting from two qualitatively different forms of influence is of basic importance to psychotherapists. First, the model provides a solid theoretical base for trying to understand and deal with biological functioning as a manifestation of material/energy-based processes and psychological/behavioral functioning as a manifestation of information/meaning-based processes.

Second, the model provides a basis for understanding how the two processes interrelate, through the relationships between material/energy carriers and information/meaning codes and messages, to produce the integrated functioning that epitomizes people. The concepts of biobehavioral health and health psychology emphasize that health or illness must be understood as products of the mutually influential interactions of information/meaning-based and material/energy-based processes in individuals. For example, for people like Mrs. K., for whom a depressive pattern seems to be a part of her difficulties, material/energy-based interventions such as antidepressant drugs, may indirectly alter psychological/behavioral functioning by directly altering biological processes that serve as material carriers for information/meaning-based emotional arousal. Medication may facilitate changes in Mrs. K's mood, appetite, sleep patterns, and activity level, as well as in her cognitive processes such as self-evaluations, interests, and expectations of the future. Thus, directly altering a person's biological neurochemical substrate can create conditions that somehow facilitate altered information/meaning-based psychological and behavioral functioning.

Similarly, methods that help people alter information/meaning-based components of their problems (e.g., changes in Mrs. K's self-evaluations) can reduce stressful emotional demands on the body's resources, and facilitate changes in biologically based functions. Biobehavioral, cognitive, and neuroscientific efforts to expand the knowledge base about how these two processes interrelate is of great potential value to psychotherapists in improving their strategies and methods.

Third, this model reveals three basic avenues for modifying the functioning of a person like Mrs. K: (1) Material/energy-based interventions may be used to try to directly alter biological functioning (traditionally the primary domain of medicine), and thereby to indirectly facilitate psychological/behavioral changes. (2) Information/meaning-based methods may be used to try to directly alter psychological or behavioral functioning (traditionally the domain of psychotherapy) and thereby to indirectly facilitate changes in biological functioning. (3) Modifications may be made in relevant aspects of the person's environment to alter ways in which it facilitates and constrains different patterns of functioning (traditionally the domain of social work) and thus to indirectly facilitate changes in biological or psychological/behavioral functioning. Various combinations of these strategies may be useful in specific cases, suggesting the utility of a multiprofessional posture in the search for optimal treatments.

Fourth, this model underlines the crucial role of communicative exchanges between clients and psychotherapists to influence changes in personal meanings that may affect the psychological and behavioral changes sought. Fifth, these self-constructing capabilities are very important for all forms of educative, biomedical, or psychosocial treatment, including psychotherapy, pointing out that all modes of intervention are collaborative in nature. Agents of change cannot directly change other people. They can only ally themselves with the self-constructing, self-organizing properties of clients, participating in the processes through which people change themselves. For example, a surgeon may remove a tumor but the person must agree to permit and cooperate in the procedure, and her biological self-constructing processes must heal the wound. Psychotherapy methods work only when they collaborate with the information/meaning-based self-constructing capabilities of clients, limited of course by what the client's self-corrective capabilities happen to be. These points are elaborated at greater length in the next chapter.

THE PRINCIPLE OF UNITARY FUNCTIONING

Living is a continuous process, occurring within bounded environments from conception until death, often compared to a river. The flow of a stream is bounded by the land through which it flows, sometimes rushing through a narrow gorge, at others meandering across a fertile valley. Thus, the content and organization of a stream will vary as a function of its own activity, the characteristics of the contexts through which it flows, and its transactions with them. And so it is with a person's stream of life. At work or at play, in solitude or social interaction, healthy or ill, the flowing organization and functioning of lives always take place within the contexts of people's environments.

For example, a person may be quietly listening to members of her family converse; she may participate in the conversation; or she may go to her room and think about what was said. All three patterns involve her family's discussion, but the content differs: one is observational, another interactive, and the third ideational. Yet there is a common feature; all aspects of the person are operating in each episode. Sensory-perceptual processes are active, although focused on different kinds and sources of information; thoughts are occurring, but of differing content and patterns; affects are experienced, albeit different in intensity and type; motoric and communicative actions are occurring, although their type, organization, and amplitude vary. All these elements are interrelated so she can function as a unified person. This interaction is called the *principle of unitary functioning;* it emphasizes that while aspects of a person may be thought of separately, they do not operate separately. Behavior always occurs in and is functionally related to a specific context. Each episode cited occurred in a specific context, which influenced the episode in some way. An adequate model of human functioning must represent the person as an integrated unit in transaction with a succession of contexts. In the language of models, the unit of reference must be the *person-in-context.*

Therefore, researchers and psychotherapy practitioners cannot deal separately with the perceptions, thoughts, emotions, actions, or physiological processes taking place within their research subjects or clients because all these functions are always going on and the interplay among them significantly influences what takes place. A person's functioning will inevitably vary from one context to another. For example, the tendency of a child to behave aggressively will differ on the playground, at home, in church, or facing a school principal. Similarly, clients will behave differently in a psychotherapy session and in day-to-day life, from one therapy session to another, and from one psychotherapist to another. One may choose to focus on some person or contextual "parts" and ignore others, but doing so risks generating conclusions that are misleading. If a person tries to facilitate change in some part— such as actions, thoughts, emotions, or family context—he or she must recognize that other aspects of himself or herself and the context may also change, because all the parts are interrelated.

BEHAVIOR EPISODES AS NATURAL UNITS OF ANALYSIS

The flow of a person's life in continually changing contexts cannot be observed or comprehended in its entirety. Some way must be found to analyze the flow in subsidiary units that are both intelligible and of practical utility.

Many units have been suggested and tried—habits, reflexes, conditioned responses, attitudes, lifestyles. What is needed is a unit that reflects the principle of unitary functioning, one that represents coherently organized person-in-context patterns of component structures and processes over varying periods of time.

Imagine observing a person's activities for a day. When she awakes, she goes to the bathroom, showers, dresses and grooms herself, eats breakfast while reading the paper, gathers her things and drives to work, talks to a colleague on the way to her office, reads and responds to telephone messages, prepares for and attends a meeting, and so on. This sequence can be combined into larger descriptive functional units, such as preparing for work, going to work. The pieces can be grouped into more finely graded units, such as the sequence of actions involved in dressing and grooming herself. All these analyses differ in scope, but they involve the same basic components. They reflect a motivated person, interacting with different contexts, and integrating her biological, psychological, and behavioral capabilities to achieve an objective or a series of subgoals. Each segment can be recognized as an internally coherent event, occurring within and distinguishable from a larger framework, a part of a larger series, like a scene within a play (Kuo, 1967). Over several decades, many scholars have suggested that the flow of each person's behavior is organized in a succession of natural units that have been called action, transactive, or behavioral cycles, social episodes, or acts (Bruner, 1982; Forgas, 1979; Gibbs, 1979; Miller, Galanter & Pribram, 1960; Petrinovich, 1979; Tolman, 1932; Young, 1952). Here they are called behavior episodes (BE); the term *behavior* is used to encompass all biological, psychological, and behavioral aspects occurring as an organized pattern, and *episode* connotes a flow of events in a specific context, organized by an integrating theme, like an episode in a television series.

Definition of a Behavior Episode (BE)
Bruner (1982) described these natural units as action cycles:

> Most of what we speak of in common sense terms as human action is stirred by intentions . . . An intention is present when an individual operates persistently towards achieving an end state, chooses among alternative means . . . to achieve that end state, persists in deploying means and corrects the deployment of means to get closer to the end state, and finally ceases the line of activity when specifiable features of the end state are achieved. . . . . it is not necessary that, in such human action, the actor be able to account for or be conscious of the nature of his intentions. (pp. 313–314)

A behavior episode begins when a personal goal begins to organize a person's behavior in relation to a specific context—what Brunner called an intention. The opportunities and constraints provided by the person's current biological state and the person's current context create boundary conditions within which the episode is constructed. The activity unfolds over time; it is made of varied and interrelated thoughts, feelings, and actions, undergirded by biological functions that make them possible. Each behavior episode ends when any of three conditions occurs: (1) The outcome toward which the activities are directed is attained, or as much progress has been made as is feasible at the time. (2) The goal-directed sequence is interrupted by some set of events, preempting the person's attention and prompting the initiation of a different episode guided by different goals. (3) The goal is judged to be unattainable, and the episode is aborted, at least for the time being. One cannot render a person's behavior intelligible without a recognition of its organization into behavior episodes and a knowledge of the current personal goals, contexts, and biological states that frame the organization and dynamics of those episodes. Behavior episodes may vary in scope and duration, from those that are simple and brief to others that are elaborate and long.

Psychotherapists will recognize the similarity between the concept of behavior episode and the idea of a cycle, frequently used in therapy theory and practice. Some clients are described as displaying repetitive cycles of behavior. One with self-defeating properties is termed a vicious cycle, following this order: anticipation of rejection ➤ covert experiences of retaliatory anger ➤ self-criticality ➤ guilt over one's own hostility ➤ presumption that others would also be critical were they to discern such hostility ➤ fear of discovery with anticipation of rejection. Reverberating cycles may occur in clients suffering from severe disorders, manifesting as compulsions, for example. However, the concept of a cycle identifies a repetitive circular pattern without specifying the nature of its content. The concept of behavior episode cycles, derived from the model summarized in Figure 3.2, specifies both the generic content and dynamic organization of all behavior episodes. This makes it a particularly useful tool because it can be used to guide analyses of behavior cycles so that important components or interrelationships are not overlooked either in clinical practice or in research.

Organization of Behavior Episodes

Behavior episodes are unitary patterns of functioning, so typically only one episode can occur at a time. However, they follow one another in a continuous stream, analogous to the flow of stories on a television newscast that remains continuously on, 24 hours a day, seven days a week:

> One episode follows another, each one coherent in its own right. Some episodes are long; some are short; some are funny; some are sad; some are meaningful; and some are forgettable. Some episodes build upon one another to tell a larger

story. . . . Occasionally there are dramatic life events that receive a great deal of attention for a period of time . . ., but most behavior episodes, like most new stories, are pretty mundane, even repetitive. On the other hand, it is always possible to "preempt" such episodes when something important does happen (analogous to a news bulletin). (M. Ford, 1992, p. 24)

There is a good deal of organization within the flow of episodes. One pattern is hierarchical and serial in form. A larger episode, guided by a longer-term goal, is usually composed of several shorter-term episodes, each guided by interrelated subgoals. Successive accomplishment of the subgoals enables people to evaluate themselves as making progress toward the larger goal and leads to the eventual accomplishment of the longer term goal. Thus, a youth may entertain the long-term goal of obtaining a college degree. Pursuit of that goal requires the completion of subepisodes (semesters of study), which require successful completion of subsubepisodes (courses), which are composed of smaller episodes, such as quizzes and examinations. Progress through the series of assignments, courses, and semesters involves successfully completing a series of component episodes, which collectively achieve the larger goal of a degree. This form of organization can maintain motivation through a multiyear process, because each sub–behavior episode that is achieved yields satisfaction and moves the person toward the larger goal.

This form of behavior episode organization has another value. Pursuit of the larger goal can be temporarily suspended after completion of some lower level episodes, so that other episodes organized in relation to quite different goals can be pursued. Thus, students perform other behavior episodes between academic episodes—related to working, engaging in extracurricular activities, or dating. These additional episodes may significantly influence and even alter their pursuit of academic episodes. For example, students can become so absorbed in their nonacademic behavior that their grades suffer, jeopardizing their longer term goal of a degree.

Sometimes behavior episodes can be pursued in parallel: a person may converse with a friend while driving a car, or she may knit while reading a book. Such dual task patterns are possible only when a behavior has become habitual, when behaviors are not incompatible, and when neither requires undivided attention so that each may be attended to as necessary.

Psychotherapy can be construed as a large behavior episode—analogous to a student pursuing a degree—beginning with the first session and ending with the last. Each session is a subepisode within which there are smaller episodes. However, psychotherapy involves a multiperson system; client and therapist are individual units and simultaneously components of a larger social unit—the therapy relationship. This complicates things. While each is participating in the same behavior episode, each has his or her respective goals, regulatory criteria for judging progress, and ways of proceeding. If their efforts are to be synergistic rather than conflicting, they must function as a team guided by shared long-term goals, by agreement on subgoals for each session, on the roles of each, and on ways to pursue the goals and subgoals.

Therapy sessions are interspersed at infrequent, periodic intervals within the ongoing flow of other kinds of episodes that make up the client's daily life outside the therapy context. Of course, these real-life episodes impact on a treatment plan, sometimes deflecting or facilitating its course and sometimes forcing revisions to be made. This overwhelming dominance of nontherapy behavior episodes in clients' experience places a heavy burden on the specially designed but relatively infrequent therapy behavior episodes if they are to be successful in facilitating desired behavior changes. Most forms of psychotherapy probably use at least some of the clients' real-life episodes to facilitate change.

Types of Behavior Episodes
Given the versatility of humans, the diversity of behavior episodes each person can have is enormous. Conceptually, the episodes can be classified in different ways: types of goals served, such as leisure versus work goals; kinds of contexts in which they occur, such as church versus school. However, three very general types of episodes are prototypic of different patterns of psychological and behavioral organization. In *instrumental episodes,* all components are organized to produce some desired environmental consequence of value and utility to the person. They require motoric and communicative transactions with a context, because the episode's purpose is to impact the environment. In *observational episodes,* the focus is on information collection, so attempts to influence the environment through motoric and communicative actions are inhibited, as when someone is watching what others do. This is the basis of social modeling. In *ideational or thinking episodes,* all communicative, information collection, and action functions are inhibited and replaced by abstract thought, imagined perceptions, and actions. These are *simulated behavior episodes,* both because they involve imagining rather than acting out a possible course of action, and because of the diversity of covert, non-oral, skeletal-muscular activities that occur during such episodes (McGuigan, 1978). Larger episodes usually involve all three kinds as subepisodes—for example, a person may observe others do something, then think about how they might do it, and then try to do it.

Behavioral States and State Descriptions
For some kinds of behavioral analyses, the concept of a state is useful. In conventional systems analysis, a *state* is defined as the sum total of all the char-

acteristics of a system and their relationships at a given point in time and under a given set of conditions. The simultaneous pattern of thoughts, feelings, actions, and biological events taking place at any given moment can be construed as a person's *functional or behavioral state,* and a representation of such a pattern is called a *state description.* However, the states of systems beyond a minimal level of complexity cannot be represented in their entirety. For example, there is no feasible way to construct a complete description of the status of every aspect of a person's biological, psychological, behavioral, and environmental functioning at any moment. The only practical alternative is to create a state description of those particular characteristics of the person-in-context that are considered to be salient, significant, and useful for the purposes at hand. Thus, what one includes in a state description will vary depending on what one is concerned about or trying to accomplish. The state descriptions used by physicians typically emphasize biological structures and functions; psychologists ordinarily emphasize psychological/behavioral aspects of states.

There is always some form of behavior episode in operation, so any state description of a person constitutes a cross-sectional representation of what is taking place within a specific episode, a momentary slice of life. One state description is of limited usefulness because it is a *static representation;* in principle, it is obsolete the moment it is described because the person's flow of behavior has already created a somewhat different state. It contains no information about processes or dynamics. One can gain a *dynamic representation* of how people's behavior varies and changes only by tracking their behavior across time and occasions to produce and compare a succession of state descriptions at varying intervals. By identifying similarities and differences between successive descriptions, one can identify temporal consistencies, variations, and changes in them. For example, motion pictures are created by taking a series of still photographs and then displaying them in rapid succession to recreate the dynamics of movement.

Time intervals between state descriptions can vary in length. Different intervals produce different kinds of information and should be selected to serve particular purposes. The briefer the interval between state descriptions, the easier it is to identify processes generating change. The longer the interval, the less information about variations is provided. As an example, patients' vital signs may be continuously monitored to detect life-threatening change quickly, but measuring children's height once a year may suffice to track their growth. Therapists sometimes hospitalize a depressed, suicidal client so the person's state can be closely monitored to prevent a suicidal act. States are never identical; there are always variations. When several state descriptions are similar, they are called persistent or recurrent states, or *steady states* in systems theory. Habits are a behavioral form of steady states. A sequence of state descriptions can reveal an enduring shift from one pattern to a different one. Such shifts are referred to as *state transitions,* and focusing on state transitions is one way in which changes in functioning and the conditions under which they occur can be identified.

The utility of state descriptions is illustrated by their use in the diagnosis and treatment of illnesses. Clinical medicine typically focuses on undesirable recurrent or persistent states. A clinical *syndrome* is a prototypical pattern of signs and symptoms representing a persistent or recurrent state that manifests as a particular kind of illness. Many useful syndrome or state descriptions have been developed, such as those for diabetes mellitus or grand mal epilepsy. Evaluation of the developmental course of an illness focuses on state transitions, which questions such as "When did you first begin to notice the symptoms?" "Has the child's temperature gone down?" These queries seek to identify transitions between healthy and ill states.

Syndrome descriptions are starting points for analyzing the development of dysfunctional steady states. Construed as clinical states, they anchor the search for antecedent states from which the syndrome develops—its etiology—and for the consequent states or sequelae that may follow. This yields a dynamic description of the illness phases in the form of transitional states through which a dysfunctional state is likely to proceed if untreated; the description is called a *prognosis.*

State descriptions and analyses of state transitions are also useful in guiding medical interventions. By using a match/mismatch process, a practitioner can determine the extent to which a client's persistent state corresponds with any known prototypic syndrome. When a match is found, anything that is known about the condition in general can be usefully applied to the treatment of the specific client's state—which kinds of interventions have been effective, what sorts of precautions should be observed. They are used to compare the relative merits of different treatments.

Similarly, the effects of psychotherapy can be represented and evaluated in terms of persistent states and state transitions. For example, the nature of client states and state transitions manifested during each session and across sessions enables clients and therapists to identify consistencies and changes in relevant states during any phase of therapy. Comparing clients' initial, current, and preferred outcome states facilitates decisions about their overall progress and when to terminate therapy.

Behavior Episode Schemas (BES)

Behavior always occurs in the here and now—at a specific time in a specific context. Thus, although the flow of a person's behavior is organized in terms of behavior episodes and manifested in state sequences, these are fleeting phenomena, happening, then disappearing forever. No two behavior episodes are ever identical although they may have similarities. How, then, can people capitalize on past experience and use it to guide their coping with current and potential future events? What do they learn that generates recurrent, cyclical, or steady states?

The answer lies in the nature of humans' information/meaning-based self-construction capabilities. If generalized knowledge, ideas, and skills were initially constructed as a collection of separate pieces or fragments of experience, human memory would be like a library with its books randomly shelved; most knowledge and skills would be available, but access to them would be very difficult. Then, a complex act of accessing and combining relevant pieces for each new episode would be required; organized behavior patterns or wholes would be newly created each time by combining parts. Human evolution produced a different strategy. Generalized knowledge and skills are initially constructed as organized, unitary patterns; specific parts, such as concepts or propositions, are created by differentiation and elaboration from those wholes. This process is analogous to embryological development, wherein specific parts emerge from wholes—the embryo—through sequential differentiation and elaboration.

The study of human learning, problem solving, and memory has grown extensively in recent decades; several conclusions about how specific behavior episodes and self-constructing processes interact to produce generalized knowledge and competence appear to be emerging. Illustrations of current views and key ideas from that literature are summarized in Table 4.1. Theoretical and empirical support for these generalizations may be found in numerous sources (Arbib, 1989; Arbib & Hesse, 1986; Edelman, 1989; Ford, 1987; Ford 1994; Holyoak & Spellman, 1993; Horton & Mills, 1984; Johnson & Hasher, 1987; Newell, 1991; Squire, Knowlton, & Musen, 1993).

The ideas summarized in Table 4.1 show how behavior episodes serve as the tool for all learning, and how learned patterns function to organize selectively these episodes. If all human experience occurs within the framework of specific behavior episodes, and if humans always function as unitary entities, it follows that all remembrances are probably initially constructed as representations of unified experiences resulting from behavior episodes.

For example, when infants encounter a dog, they do so in some context—

Table 4.1

Generalizations about the Functions/Processes of Remembering and Utilizing Previously Learned or Experienced Ideas and Behavior.

1. The brain functions as a unitary organization of components, each of which plays a leading role in facilitating different kinds of learning, remembering, and performing. Complex behavior results from the coordinated operation of multiple components.

2. The remembrances that occur in any behavior episode are a function of its context and content, such as specific features of its context, the personal goals guiding the episode, and biological and affective states operative at the time. These features function as cues that activate or produce selective remembrance of previously constructed ideas, knowledge, habits, and skills. These remembered elements are potentially relevant to effective performance in the current episode. Different patterns of cues will activate different patterns of remembrances and meaning making. A remembrance includes not only cognitive components but other aspects such as affects and actions as well.

3. Remembrances are of two types: Some are generalized representations of very recent experiences that are retained for only brief periods of time (short-term memories, or STMs). Others are more enduring representations constructed from the person's history of experience or created from imaginative thinking (long-term memories, or LTMs).

4. Some remembrances are manifested as contents of current consciousness and may be described to others. Often called declarative memory, these include events and ideas. Others will be unconscious and cannot be described to others. Often called implicit memory, these include skills and habits.

5. In any episode, the declarative and implicit remembrances selectively activated are organized in relation to one another and to the content and context features of that episode. The term, *schema,* is often used to refer to that organization; its parts are often referred to as component schemas—cognitive, affective, or motor schemas.

6. Schemas are not mechanistic blueprints or programs for executing specific behavior patterns. They are generalized, dynamic organizations of information, ideas, and propositions or rules that both selectively constrain and facilitate the construction of a specific behavior pattern to fit a specific behavior episode. This organization makes possible generative flexibility in the construction and modification of specific behavior patterns to fit varying conditions, such as the potential construction of alternate behavior patterns to produce similar outcomes.

Table 4.1 *(continued)*

7. Specific experiences result in declarative or implicit memories, but the extent of these memories is dependent on several elements. One of these is the integrity and maturity of the person's brain structures—for example, infants and brain-damaged adults will display memory deficiencies. Another aspect is the part of the episode to which the person gave most attention—and as a result, remembers someone's face but not his or her name. A third aspect is a function of the content of the experience; as an example, muscle patterns underlying muscle skills cannot become conscious. Selective performance reveals implicit memories whereas declarative memories can be revealed by both selective performance and self-report.

8. Constructing implicit long-term memories is relatively effortless and automatic; constructing declarative long-term memories typically requires conscious effort. Propositional knowledge representing how things or events are related or influence one another is typically implicitly learned. However, a person can create a declarative memory if he or she selectively focuses attention on constructing conscious propositional representations.

9. Declarative memories are of two types: (a) Episodic memories are representations of specific behavior episodes experienced. When a long-term memory of a specific episode is activated and reported to others, it is not a carbon copy of the episode as originally perceived but a reconstructed version. In this version, a person may imaginatively fill in gaps to provide a coherently organized story; sometimes the reconstructed version may be largely imaginative. The nature of that reconstruction will be a function of the context and content characteristics of the episode activating the remembering. (b) Semantic memories are abstract, generalized representations of meanings constructed from multiple experiences and/or imaginative thought. These meanings may vary in their generality from specific concepts and propositions to generalized representations of complex patterns.

10. Remembrances are more difficult to activate if the content is not meaningfully organized: Remembering a list of nonsense words is more difficult than recalling the lyrics of a song. People tend to remember the meaning or gist of verbal descriptions rather than the specific words. People construct remembrances so that they are meaningfully organized.

outdoors, in the kitchen, or lying on a bed. Their experiences with dogs take place in the form of episodes in which they are watching dogs (observational behavior episodes), interacting with dogs (instrumental behavior episodes), or imagining dogs (simulated behavior episodes). In each episode, they do not merely perceive the dog as if it were a phenomenon presented to them from their context. Rather, they undergo a unified experience of themselves doing something, in relation to the dog, which is doing something, at a particular time, and under a particular set of conditions. They construct a representation of the behavior episode in which the dog is a component. Such constructions are called *episodic memories,* and serve as a starting point for further information-based self-construction.

No two episodes are ever exactly alike, so episodic memories are of limited utility for guiding one's behavior in future behavior episodes. Humans evolved with capabilities for solving this problem by automatically constructing more generalized versions to represent a set of similar episodes. We refer to these as *behavior episode schemas (BES)* to denote that they are an organization of component schemas, including all the subsidiary perceptual, cognitive, affective, and motoric schemas (see Arbib, 1989) involved in the person-in-context as the unit of analysis. Behavior episode schemas are generalized approaches for accomplishing certain kinds of goals in certain types of contexts.

The behavior episode similarities identified are a matter of the person's subjective interpretation, but they are typically based on the degree to which different behavior episodes involve the pursuit of similar goals in similar contexts. (Recall that contexts and goals are key constraining and facilitating conditions within which behavior episodes are organized.) The actions used need not be similar for episodes to be considered similar, and the evaluation of similarity does not need to be an intentional or conscious act.

The process of constructing and elaborating behavior episode schemas appears to work as follows. When a new behavior episode begins that is similar to an episodic memory, the cues in the new episode activate reconstruction of that episodic memory. Behavior in the second episode is then guided by a merger of two kinds of representations: perceptions of the current behavior episode, and the reconstructed episodic memory. This combination results in revision of the initial episodic memory through assimilation and accommodation. This process is repeated in each new behavior episode, resulting in a progressively revised and generalized version, a behavior episode schema, including the prototypical content and organization relevant to that type of episode. Strategy and skill components are often called *scripts.* Generalities are represented, and many of the details that vary from one episode to the next tend to drop out.

Different schemas are constructed for different types of episodes. They then function as tools for organizing behavior in new, similar episodes. Perceptions occurring during an episode are assigned meaning in accord with the meaning frames provided by the guiding schema. Perceptions for which no relevant schema exists are meaningless and useless. An example is listening to a foreign language that one has not learned. Developing a repertoire of schemas provides the person with a set of generalized approaches for accomplishing recurrent similar life episodes. Each functions as a kind of overall approach or strategy for constructing a behavior pattern for accomplishing one's goals in a specific context. Typically, a schema does not operate as a rigid and detailed script, which some concepts, such as habit, imply. Of course, tightly scripted behavior patterns such as a gymnast's highly practiced routines can be acquired by constructing a schema that narrowly constrains the content and range of behavior patterns that may be performed.

THE DEVELOPMENT OF BEHAVIOR EPISODE SCHEMAS

The day-to-day lives of small children are guided by a relatively limited number of goals pursued within a limited range of contexts. These generate a limited variety of behavior episodes, such as eating meals, taking a bath, playing with toys, going to church, or playing with friends. Children construct a schema for each type of behavior episode. Use of those schemas then brings past experiences to bear to guide their behavior in new episodes, which yield new information and result in elaboration of the guiding schema, enabling them to be prepared for a greater diversity of future possibilities. A repertoire of schemas is thereby constructed. When a new behavior episode is initiated, a schema similar to it will be reconstructed. A merger of behavior episode schemas may occur when more than one is activated. Performance in that episode is then guided by the potential schema through which the perceptual representations of the immediate situation are interpreted and utilized. Within a culture or subculture, there are many normative, culturally developed schemas that socialize children into constructing appropriate behavior patterns in different kinds of settings (e.g., Barker, 1968).

Obviously, the kinds of behavior episodes that are prominent within a person's repertoire undergo change over their lives. Preschool episodes give way to school-age ones, which are in turn supplanted by those that are related to work, marriage, parenting, retirement, and late life. The solitary play and close parental companionship of the toddler become supplemented by playtime with age-mates, relationships with co-workers, and interactions of courtship, marriage and parenting. People continue to elaborate and modify their repertoire of schemas through revision, elaboration, combination, and reconstruction of earlier ones in keeping with their changing purposes and contexts. They also construct new schemas as they encounter and deal with entirely novel sets of goals, conditions, and contexts.

Functional Autonomy of Concepts and Propositions and Creative Thought
Chapter 3 presented the construction of different concepts and propositions using different imagistic, analogue, and abstract codes. That raises the question of how construction and use of specific concepts and propositions is related to the construction and operation of behavior episode schemas. Although different types of schemas are developed for differing contexts and objectives, they may nonetheless contain common conceptual and propositional components. One component that remains common throughout is, of course, the person. Similarly, a child's parents are common to many types of episodes the child experiences. So are other elements, such as chairs and tables, telephones, bicycles and cars, dogs or other pets, and many, many more. In this way, a diversity of schemas may contain the same concept, such as self or Mommy, or the same proposition—hitting something may break it. Specific concepts, propositions, strategies, and skills useful in a variety of schemas acquire a property, termed *functional autonomy,* which means that a person can use them as building blocks for new cognitive constructions and for elaborating, revising, or constructing schemas without including all the other aspects of the original ones in which they were formed. The functional autonomy of concepts and propositions makes possible imaginative and creative thought free of any linkage to specific perceptual realities. People can cognitively dissect and recombine functionally autonomous ideas to create new ideas and beliefs about possibilities that have never been experienced and may not exist.

Formal education cultivates the functional autonomy of generalizable conceptual and propositional schema components by facilitating the acquisition of shared meanings and behavior patterns for symbolic codes, such as word definitions, and behavior settings of the culture. It can also help students acquire the propositions, rules, and strategies that enable them to construct heuristics for processing information, attributing meaning, and designing new forms of behavior.

Meaning Making and Behavior Episode Schemas

Although any component of a specific behavior episode state may stimulate the reconstruction of relevant schemas—the sight of a cat, the picture of a cat, the word cat, or an emotional reaction to cats—no component of a specific behavior episode state carries any direct personal meaning in and of itself. Personal meanings of current events are provided by interpreting them in the framework of past experience and previously constructed beliefs, and schemas provide that framework leading to two implications: (1) There will be a great deal of implicit knowledge influencing the meanings attributed to any behavior episode component that is involved in multiple behavior episode schemas. For example, the concept of *school* may activate multiple meanings, such as a place, a set of activities, certain rules of conduct, friendship experiences, and fearful anticipation. (2) The same concept or proposition may activate different personal meanings depending on which kinds of schemas are in operation at the time. Recall that the individual's personal goals, the nature of the context, and the affective and biological states operative in the current episode all exert a strong influence on which schema will become activated. Thus, when a teacher asks a child to define the word *father*, the kinds of meanings that become activated may be different from those prompted when her mother says to the same child, "Your father wants to talk to you, RIGHT NOW!"

SOME IMPLICATIONS FOR PSYCHOTHERAPY

The meanings activated by a behavior episode called a therapy session are a key issue in the conduct of psychotherapy. It is the behavior episode schemas clients have previously constructed that continually re-create inappropriate or unwanted patterns of functioning in their encounters with new and changing circumstances, such as generating intense and conflicting emotions of affection and hostility. Thus, it is the relevant schema that must be altered if the client's persistent or recurrent patterns of behavior are to change. A behavior episode schema cannot be modified, however, unless it is currently operative. Musicians and athletes, for example, know that repetitive reactivation of their schemas through rehearsal and practice is required if the behavior patterns are to be perfected. Therefore, all approaches to psychotherapy must include (1) strategies and tactics for ensuring that the schema containing the troublesome components or one containing preferred components becomes activated during the current therapy session; and (2) tactics and strategies for promoting desired changes in that schema, or uses of it, once the activation has taken place.

Much of the art of psychotherapy lies in the effective orchestration of and interplay between these two kinds of tactics. For example, there has been considerable discussion of the appropriate timing of the change tactic called interpretation. Presenting clients with an alternate way to construe their experience or beliefs is unproductive if it is premature, occurring apart from the activation of the behavior episode schema that is the target of change. Ill-timed interpretations may teach clients different ways of talking about their problems without actually altering the problematic schema; the alternate ideas are functionally autonomous from the troublesome schema. For example, Mrs. K's therapist might suggest that the experiences she labels fear or anxiety are really an anger pattern, but do so in a context in which it does not affect the troublesome schema.

The concepts of behavior episode and behavior episode schema provide a basis for understanding other aspects of psychotherapy, such as the generalization of changes within therapy sessions to relevant portions of clients' daily lives. Therapy sessions represent a special kind of recurrent behavior episode which are, by design, markedly different from what goes on in clients' actual lives. This difference makes it possible for a client to construct and implement a modified or new schema within the confines of therapy sessions, but it may not become operative under real-life conditions. For example, her therapist might help Mrs. K construct an improved representation of her inappropriate patterns of submissiveness during encounters with her husband and coach her in implementing more assertive patterns through in-session role-playing techniques. Even so, Mrs. K may revert to her former state of fright and consternation when later conversing with her husband in their home. Specific kinds of behavior episodes are typically required to facilitate the transfer of within-therapy schema changes to real-life behavior episodes (cf. Goldstein & Kanfer, 1979).

DYSFUNCTIONS IN THE OPERATION OF HUMAN SYSTEMS

The term *pathology* is typically used to refer to persistent states judged to be unwanted and undesirable. This is because they ordinarily result in pathos or suffering, not only for those in whom the state occurs but also for those concerned about their welfare. For example, Mrs. K's recurrent fears and tearful despondencies resulted in misery and suffering for her. Persistent distressing states are also termed *disease* or *disorder*. The prefix "dis-" means "away from"; hence, any state or condition that departs from a preferred condition of comfort (dis-ease) or from a preferred orderly arrangement (dis-order) is typically deemed by people to be unwanted and in need of change. The large body of knowledge accumulated about states of pathology, disease, or disorder, and the extent of efforts and resources devoted to changing them, testifies to their significance. Psychopathology refers to serious disorders in psychological/behavioral functioning.

THE CONCEPT OF DYSFUNCTION

How can pathological states be understood within this living systems framework? A *function* was earlier defined as a particular role, output, or product that an entitity, system, or system component is designed or organized to perform. A *process* was defined as an organized pattern of activities that operate to accomplish a function. The patterns of interaction of the processes of multiple functions that produce larger unified functional patterns was termed *system dynamics.* The ways in which and the effectiveness with which any function participates in system dynamics and contributes to accomplishing the functions of the larger entity is called its *functional utility.* Psychological and behavioral capabilities are different kinds of functions.

It follows from these definitions that patterns of system structures and processes whose operation detract from, interfere with, or are incompatible with effective accomplishment of system functions and the maintenance of their unified, dynamic organization may be considered dysfunctional patterns or states. Thus, conditions labeled pathological or a disease or disorder can be understood as different kinds of significant dysfunctional patterns or states. This formulation is similar to Wakefield's (1992a; 1992b) rationale of "harmful dysfunction" which has recently attracted considerable interest (Spitzer, 1977). The terms harmful or significant are important and need further definition in light of the tendency "to convert nearly all of life's stresses and bad habits into mental disorders." (Leo, 1997, p.20). The key ideas of function and organization are used later to formulate criteria for differentiating functional from dysfunctional states.

Dysfunctional Patterns as Subtypes of Functional Patterns
This rationale makes it clear that dysfunctional states are a version of functional states in general. A sharp separation has often been maintained between the natural and the unnatural, the normal and the abnormal, health and disease. Ideal states for human functioning and development that would naturally occur were assumed to exist unless some intrusion altered the expected course. Once such deviations took place, it was thought that a qualitatively different set of pathological processes came into play, requiring different explanatory principles and methods of study.

Such distinctions are inappropriate. The person is a complex unit equipped with the capability for a broad array of functions and supporting processes. The development of cancer or schizophrenia represents human possibilities, just as does the development of superior athletic or musical accomplishments. What humans have labeled dysfunctional patterns are simply a subset of outcomes generated by humans' basic functional capabilities, albeit outcomes with properties judged to be undesirable. As such, dysfunctional states do not call for a separate set of concepts or explanatory principles. This means that the view of psychopathology utilized by any approach to psychotherapy should be compatible with or derived from the theorists' view of normal, healthy development and functioning.

CRITERIA FOR IDENTIFYING DYSFUNCTIONAL STATES

Identifying something as dysfunctional requires a preestablished reference frame defining what is considered functional. Then, deviations from that reference frame that are great enough to be considered dysfunctional can be identified. A useful reference frame involving two kinds of criteria or norms can be derived from the concepts of function and organization in relation to the person-in-context as the unit of reference.

Specification of Normal, Typical, or Effective Functioning as a Criterion

All systems and their components develop because they can accomplish something; they can produce some type of consequence that can be regarded as the purpose or function of the system (Beer, 1964). Note that this concept of purpose is much broader than the narrower definition of purpose as a conscious human intention. Thus, a system can behave in a purposive fashion— operate to produce a particular kind of result—without simultaneously being aware of the results its processes are organized to produce. For example, a person's liver performs complex functions without the person or the liver being self-consciously aware of what these functions are.

In the case of extant systems, the identification of functional role or purpose is made by an observer outside the system itself. For example, a cat scratches at a door, the owner opens the door, and the cat enters the house. Although the scratching behavior was followed by the cat entering the house, to assert that entering was the purpose for which the scratching was performed is a matter of inference and is open to the possibility of error. Inferences about the purpose or function of any pattern of activity must be made carefully.

Once the prototypical nature of any function has been specified, it then becomes possible to identify deviations from the expected form and to evaluate their significance. In complex systems that are multilevel organizations of functions, such as humans, functional analyses may be conducted at any level from cells to organ systems to the person-in-context. For example, the heart's function is to pump blood; the function of the lungs is to exchange gases between the person's body and the environment; the function of the skeletal-muscle system is to accomplish movement and object manipulation; people function to carry out useful and effective transactions with their contexts. There is a range of variation in the performance of every function that is generally considered normal or typical, but when states exceed that range they are often evaluated as excessively deviant and undesirable. Table 4.2 summarizes several concepts, applicable at any level of analysis, often used to refer to such deviant functional states.

Specification of Normal, Typical, or Effective Organization *as a Criterion*
Because functions are interrelated in complex, open systems, each function must normally be able to vary its states in relation to other functions to ensure unitary, effective operation of the system as a whole. This makes difficult the judgment that any functional state is abnormal when the function is considered in isolation from its context, because almost any state of any function may be considered normal or desirable under some circumstances. For example, is a rapid heartbeat normal or abnormal? Under conditions of vigorous exercise, it would be considered typical, but it would be atypical when a

Table 4.2
Examples of Concept Labels for Significant Deviations from a
Norm of Functioning

1. *Atypical:* States appear unusual, different from expected patterns, perhaps benignly eccentric, perhaps idiosyncratic, perhaps bizarre, depending on the degree of deviation from accepted norms or standards.
2. *Abnormal:* States are judged to depart significantly or be discrepant from a hypothetic ideal or norm that specifies a prototypic preferred pattern under particular circumstances.
3. *Impaired:* The function is performed but in some partial or limited form in which some aspects of the function are diminished in quality, value, excellence, or strength.
4. *Malfunctioning:* The function fails to operate in a typical, appropriate, or effective fashion.
5. *Inactivated:* The function is absent or fails to occur in circumstances when it is expected to occur.

person was at rest. Is the experience of a visual image in the absence of appropriate visual stimuli normal or abnormal? If it occurred as part of a dream, it would be considered normal, but in a waking state, it would be considered abnormal—a hallucination. Is a person shooting a gun normal or abnormal? If the shooting occurred at a target range or deer hunting, it would be considered normal, but if the person were randomly shooting at other people on a train, it would be considered abnormal.

Identifying some functional pattern as abnormal/atypical also requires specifying its expected relationships to other functions in the context in which it is operating; there should be some norm or standard for appropriate organization of multiple functions. When people are the system of concern and the person-in-context is the reference unit, three organizational issues must be considered: (1) intraperson organization of functions, (2) organization of person-context interactions and relationships, and (3) temporal organization of the flow of functioning. Table 4.3 summarizes some of the concepts that represent dysfunctions as deviations from normal, expected patterns of organization in each of these three categories.

USE OF CRITERIA TO IDENTIFY DYSFUNCTIONAL STATES

In summary, people are considered *functionally effective* when they are capable of performing all human functions, when each function is in good working order and is occurring within normal boundaries of variability, and when all functions are appropriately organized in relation to one another and to the contexts in which they are occurring to serve the person's purposes. When any of those conditions is absent or deficient, the behavior pattern is considered *dysfunctional*, and the degree of dysfunctionality will vary with the extent to which the conditions are deficient. Remember that humans' functional capabilities are organized in a complex, hierarchical fashion, so it is possible for some form of dysfunction to occur at one level but not disrupt other patterns of functioning at higher levels. For example, a cell in a woman's breast may begin to malfunction and divide inappropriately, as in an incipient cancer. However, the impact of that dysfunction will be only local, at least for some period of time. Discovering how and under what conditions dysfunctions at one level produce dysfunctions at another level—interlevel influences—remains a challenge; for example, how do dysfunctions at a neural level produce dysfunctions at a cognitive level, and vice versa?

Because behavior is always organized in a flow of states within specific behavior episodes and because the conduct of different types of episodes is guided by relevant schemas, it follows that behavior may be dysfunctional in some

Table 4.3

Concepts Representing Different Kinds of Functional Disorganization within a Person, between Persons and Their Contexts, and in the Temporal Organization of the Flow of Their Functioning

Intraperson Functional Disorganization

1. *Autonomy:* Behavioral sequences are reported or observed to occur but to be taking place independent of the person's volition and beyond the person's capability for regulation and control (e.g., motoric tics or fugue states).
2. *Conflict (Cancellation):* Two or more sequences of behavior are activated, but they are mutually incompatible and cannot simultaneously occur; the result is performance of neither (e.g., ideational blocking or hysterical aphonia).
3. *Fragmentation:* A series of responses occurs in discontinuous and abortive fashion, in a previously well-integrated behavioral sequence (e.g., word salad or word hash).
4. *Incongruence:* Two or more behavior sequences are activated and occur simultaneously, but they are considered inappropriate and discordant with one another when they occur together (e.g., laughter in association with morbid thought content).
5. *Incoordination:* A response sequence of inappropriately related responses occurs, particularly in motoric movements, that serves to disrupt otherwise synchronous and synergic activity (synchrony = timing; synergy = functional coordination and integration). An example is stuttering.
6. *Inconsistency:* The response is reported to occur but judged to be inappropriately related to other aspects of the ongoing behavior sequence (e.g., parathesia, or visual illusions or distortions).
7. *Interpenetration:* A response (movement, thought, word) intrudes into an ongoing behavior sequence; it is not only judged to be inconsistent with that sequence but is also recognized as belonging to some other coordinated pattern. (An example is the autonomous production of unusual sounds, shouts, or swear words when making these sounds takes the patient by surprise.
8. *Interruption:* Ongoing behavior sequences suddenly stop and are not followed by resumption of the original sequence (e.g., caesuras—sudden gaps in speech or thought).
9. *Migration:* A response occurs but in inappropriate sense organs, or to inappropriate areas of the body (e.g., sexual sensations occurring in feet or nose).

Table 4.3 *(continued)*

Intraperson Functional Disorganization

10. *Nonintegrated (Disorganized) Responses:* Components of behavior patterns are inappropriately and inadequately linked to one another in both their simultaneous and sequential relationships (e.g., incoherent speech or cognitive disorientation and confusion).
11. *Oscillation (Vascillation):* Equal but inconsistent responses alternate in occurrence, with neither response tending to continue the sequence to its apparent terminus (e.g., uncontrolled alternating spells of weeping and laughing).
12. *Perseveration:* A response, or a response sequence, recurs repeatedly and does not continue the sequence to its apparent terminus (e.g., repetitive picking and plucking at oneself).
13. *Suppression (Inhibition):* Two oppositional and incompatible sequences of behavior are activated. One is dominant, but the second appears occasionally within the behavioral flow (e.g., aperiodic regression).

Person-Context Functional Disorganization

1. *Illegality:* The person's behavior is discrepant from patterns defined as acceptable by laws (e.g., pedophilia, or arson).
2. *Ineffectiveness:* Behavior patterns are judged to be inadequate, insufficient, inept, or inefficient for producing the consequences desired (e.g., delusions of identity or grandiose thinking).
3. *Irrelevance:* Behaviors occur that are judged to be inapplicable or inappropriate to the purposes and context under which they occur (e.g., tangential thought or speech).
4. *Maladaptiveness:* Person displays behaviors that are unsuited for producing outcomes he or she seeks and that may produce outcomes that endanger the person's current or future health, welfare, or success (e.g., suicidal ideation).
5. *Maladjustiveness:* Behaviors reflect a lack of harmony with actual demands of the context and may produce biological and psychological stress and distress (e.g., catastrophic or hypochondriacal thinking).
6. *Nonconformity:* Person's behavior may be legal and may serve the person's purposes, but may not be in accord with the modal patterns of behavior established and preferred by some social reference group; a person's behavior may be conventional with respect to one reference group and unconventional with respect to another (e.g., rebellious actions).

Table 4.3 *(continued)*

Person-Context Functional Disorganization

---

7. *Overexclusion:* The person performs appropriate behaviors, but only under an excessively restricted range of conditions; often the behaviors do not occur when expected, desired, or sought (e.g., forms of sexual frigidity and impotence).
8. *Overgeneralization:* The behavior, appropriate under certain types and ranges of situations, also occurs under extended and inappropriate varieties of conditions (e.g., feelings/ideas of reference, or feelings of being distanced from others.)
9. *Intensity:* The behavior is appropriate but occurs with an amplitude that is excessive or insufficient for the circumstances (e.g., bulimia or anorexia).

Temporal Disorganization of Behavioral Flow

---

1. *Duration:* The temporal interval over which a behavior pattern continues is judged to be inappropriately abbreviated or unduly prolonged (e.g., fascination; inability to free self from fixation on an object or a person).
2. *Latency:* The time interval between the cessation of the antecedent events and the initiation of a behavior pattern is judged to be excessively short (hyperreactivity) or unduly prolonged (hyporeactivity) (e.g., impulsivity or response delay).
3. *Rate:* The behavior occurs excessively fast (acceleration) or inappropriately slowly (retardation) (e.g., topical flight or thought deprivation).

---

kinds of behavior episodes and not others, and that some of a person's behavior episode schemas may contribute to dysfunctional behaviors whereas others do not. Moreover, it is clear that for any given purpose in any behavior episode, a variety of alternate functional patterns are possible, in principle. For example, there are a number of different ways to study for a test or to achieve sexual satisfaction. Not all ways, however, will have equal merit, because they will have different levels of utility in bringing about the effects being sought. Some may generate what is wanted in most relevant behavior episodes, others may produce only partial results. Moreover, as all processes result in some kinds of consequences, functional patterns with low probabilities of effectiveness may generate undesirable outcomes or dysfunctional properties instead.

The pattern that is functional for one set of purposes may prove to be dysfunctional for others. This is especially so in complex systems that operate with multiple purposes in relation to multiple system components at multiple levels; the greater the number of subsystems, the larger is the number of subordinate objectives for which provision must be made, and hence, the more complex are the selection processes that must occur. For example, drinking alcohol is a practice that has functional utility in that it can generate some desired effects, such as muscular relaxation or a reduction of sensations of fatigue. However, there are other short- and longer term impacts known to be potentially detrimental to other aspects of the person.

The same behavior can be functional in one context and dysfunctional in others. For example, humans are equipped with inborn patterns of fear that are appropriately elicited under certain conditions, such as escape from a burning house. However, a person may experience fear and flight in an encounter with harmless spiders; this behavior may be judged a form of phobia and categorized as dysfunctional. It is not feasible to remedy such a phobia by eliminating the built-in pattern of fear, so the relationship of that context to the fear pattern must be changed instead.

As a general rule, negative feedback over time will result in patterns being extinguished when they are consistently ineffective. Therefore, when dysfunctional behavior persists over a sustained period of time, regardless of how peculiar or self-defeating it appears to be, it must retain some functional utility for certain effects. Otherwise, the person would discontinue the behavior.

From this perspective, therapists would not address a major retarded depressive disorder solely as an undesirable—or pathological—state. They would also consider the possibility that it developed because it has some functional utility for the person expressing it; perhaps it helps that person avoid noxious life circumstances, even though it is also dysfunctional because it interferes with the simultaneous pursuit of other goals, such as work. Remedial treatment should consider not only modification of the depressive condition itself but also the possible functional utility of the depressive state. Similarly, rather than concluding that a person has done something for no reason at all a therapist should realize that the functional utility of the behavior has not yet been discerned.

Designating processes as demonstrating functional or dysfunctional properties depending on the purposes being sought and the contexts under which they are implemented is a generic approach, applicable across the entire spectrum of human activity. It can be used at any level of analysis and with any kind of problem, whether it is biological, psychological, behavioral, or social in character. This broad applicability has many advantages, including the cross-fertilization across disciplines and professions that is thereby made possible. Because humans always function as coherently organized units in a context, successful analysis of one kind of dysfunction can be instructive in understanding others, and a variety of professionals can then devise collaborative modes of treatment. Such steps can bring a multidisciplinary and multiprofessional approach to helping people and to promoting human development closer to accomplishment.

The Basic Importance of Person-Social Context Dysfunctional Patterns

There are many purposes of significance to humans that they cannot achieve acting alone. Therefore, people form personal and social relationships to accomplish collectively what they are unable to do on their own. These unions are interpersonal—friendships, families, co-workers—and institutional—churches, corporations, communities. Individuals are not only living systems in their own right, but they also function as components of larger living systems.

For such groupings to be effective, they must serve their members' shared purposes and individual interests and ensure the occurrence of coordinated transactions among the group members. Groups that endure tend to develop consensus about the rules of conduct and types of behavior that are acceptable to the group in different types of behavior episodes. Such norms are considered to be binding on group members and usually constrain individuals' freedom to some degree in conducting their personal affairs. The rules of conduct vary from defining simple transactions, such as interactions between a sales clerk and customer, to more complex patterns, such as parents' treatment of their children, honoring of contractual agreements, acceptable sexual relationships. The behavior norms can be informal, defining conventional or expected patterns of action for people of different ages; they can be formalized in procedural or ethical codes; they can be codified into laws. Thus, parents can be held responsible for their children's welfare, rape and homicide can be forbidden, and divorce can be authorized.

When people depart from the social norms, their behavior impairs the collaboration and jeopardizes attainment of their own and others' goals. Behavior that is socially illegal, unacceptable, or inappropriate can be judged to be dysfunctional with respect to the goals of both the individual and the group. Disagreements can and do arise concerning the suitability of any given norm; comparable forms of behavior can be considered dysfunctional within one culture or historical period and appropriate at another time or place. However, people's happiness, health, and welfare are so embedded in their social relationships that social context dysfunctions are likely to be of pervasive importance in the concerns of psychotherapy clients.

Dysfunctional States

Dysfunctional processes do not occur singly or in isolation. Because of the structural and functional interconnections that systems display, a dysfunctional state in one aspect of a system is likely to affect other aspects as well.

Moreover, because living systems are self-organizing and self-corrective, disruption in one component will lead the system as a whole to attempt to compensate for that disruption with some modifications in its overall pattern of functioning. The extent to which other facets of the system will be modified in dysfunctional directions will be governed by the extent and severity of the disruptions and the network of interconnections that exist. Thus, clients' dysfunctional patterns are typically composed of some aspects that are a direct consequence of the type and degree of dysfunction—neurotic conflicts—and others that reflect compensatory processes and consequences—defensive patterns. These compensatory components can produce additional dysfunctional problems. Professionals seeking to assist troubled people should be alert to the manifestations in client functioning of such interrelationships.

NEXT STEPS

This chapter concludes the presentation of the propositional framework for representing the organization of humans' functional and dysfunctional development. It describes how the conceptual framework summarized in Chapter 3 typically operates in the daily episodes of life to construct recurrent functional and dysfunctional biopsychosocial patterns. One more set of propositions is necessary. As the purpose of psychotherapy is to facilitate desired changes in the day-to-day functioning of clients, therapists need propositions that represent the basic dynamics by which both stability and change can occur in humans. Propositions about processes that maintain stability and produce change underlie all proposals about procedures for producing change. These are discussed in Chapter 5.

Stability-Maintaining and Change-Producing Processes: A Comparative Propositional Framework

CHANGE OUTCOMES AND CHANGE PROCESSES

Two interrelated concepts in psychotherapy are psychotherapy outcomes and processes, a distinction analogous to the concepts of statics and dynamics in the physical sciences. These may be related to the concept of states. Chapter 4 defined a state as the values of all parts of a system at any moment in a given context. As system attributes vary from moment to moment, each state is temporary and transitory. A steady state is one that persists over time—a depressive episode—or recurs in similar circumstances—a phobia. Clients typically initiate therapy because they are unable to alter their dysfunctional steady states. Any steady state may be judged desirable or undesirable within some value framework; it can be considered well adjusted or neurotic.

CHANGE OUTCOMES

In physics, statics is the study of conditions under which entities display stability or constancy of state,—for example, an equilibrium or unvarying trajectory. Analogously, humans display stability or consistency in their functioning in different kinds of circumstances, illustrated by concepts such as habit and attitude. *Psychotherapy goals* are descriptions of desired patterns of steady state functioning, and *outcomes* are steady states whose emergence has been influenced by psychotherapeutic interventions.

CHANGE PROCESSES

In physics, dynamics is the study of the ways entities move or change when influenced by forces or energy. Similarly, studying humans' functional dynamics involves understanding how variations and changes occur when people are exposed to different influences, such as those that are material/energy based—drugs—and information/meaning-based—instruction. *Psychotherapy interventions* are procedures designed to stimulate variations from existing steady-state patterns, and to activate and guide clients' self-organizing and self-constructing processes so as to produce revised, elaborated, or new steady-state patterns.

Our 1963 analysis of psychotherapy approaches revealed that theorists' statements about therapy processes were usually descriptions of desired outcomes or goals of psychotherapy: reduce anxiety, increase self-confidence, alter troublesome thought patterns. These were in contrast to descriptions of processes by which such outcomes could be generated. When therapy strategies or methods were discussed, these were described by such words as interpretation or reflection of feelings. The discussions were usually limited to what therapists might do, with no specification of how those methods affected the processes whereby changes could be generated. Psychotherapy strategies and methods are environmental conditions, such as therapist behaviors, to which clients may be exposed and which are assumed to activate and guide change processes to generate desired results. To be complete, a psychotherapy theory must include propositions defining the ways its therapy strategies and methods are construed to influence change processes.

This chapter summarizes general propositions about stability-maintaining and change-producing processes that were synthesized from diverse human developmental sciences—that is, evolutionary and developmental biology, genetics, and developmental and learning psychology (see Ford, 1987, 1994; Ford & Ford, 1987; Ford, 1992; Ford & Lerner, 1992, for detailed discussion). The assumption was that if there are basic change processes underlying human development, different disciplines studying such changes would produce similar proposals about their nature. Our analyses revealed such convergence. Multidisciplinary approaches to understanding complex systems are producing similar ideas (e.g., Kelso, 1995; Thelen & Smith, 1994). Further, consensus was found across differing levels of analysis—physical, biological, psychological, behavioral, and social—which points to the utility of multidisciplinary approaches in explaining change processes within and between levels as well. If these phenomena are discovered to be basic and universal processes regulating stability and change in all aspects of human health and development, it follows that effective psychotherapy strategies and methods will represent some kind of application of these basic propositions.

ORGANIZATION-DISRUPTION-REORGANIZATION AND CHANGE-RELATED PROCESSES

Agreement on a key principle was found: It is a property of living systems, from cells to societies, to function so as to *create and maintain organization* within themselves, and between themselves and their contexts. Organization is adaptive; disorganization threatens life. This reality creates a dilemma. People are open systems, so the very processes of living and development in variable environments continually disrupt their organizational coherence. The processes involved in dealing with this continuous dilemma are actually the source of all change in living systems. *All stability and change in humans must result from processes that deal with discrepancies in, or disruptions of, existing states so as to create, maintain, and restore coherent organization within a person, in person-context relationships, and between intraperson and person-context patterns.*

Many ideas in the human sciences represent issues of organization, disorganization, and reorganization at different levels of analysis; these are seen in conflict, dissonance, illness, trauma, harmony, bonding, failure, dialectic, adaptation, marriage, and divorce. No pattern of functional organization can be disrupted unless it is occurring in the here and now. Therefore, a corollary of the organization-disruption-reorganization principle is that no pattern of functioning can be influenced to change unless and until it is currently operative in real time.

METHODS AND PROCESSES FOR ACTIVATING A FUNCTIONAL PATTERN

Chapters 3 and 4 explained that functional patterns or memories are not stored in a person's nervous system, like computer programs are stored in a computer. A pattern cannot be activated in precisely the same form every time, as is a computer program. Functional patterns are constructed within a framework of a current behavior episode. Therefore, unlike a computer program that is always the same, a reconstruction of a previously constructed functional pattern will not be identical from occasion to occasion because the conditions of a behavior episode are never identical; both contexts and individuals vary. A musical analogy can clarify this idea.

A piano has 88 keys—half-tones arranged in a combination of black and white keys. Those 88 keys may be struck in any combination simultaneously or in sequences; they may be struck at different rates and with different force;

pedals may be used to modulate or sustain the sounds produced. There are no musical compositions stored in a piano, yet musicians may play a nearly limitless number of songs on a piano, yet depending on how they activate its 88 keys. Small compositions can be combined to create a more complex composition, such as a sonata. Only one composition can be played at a time; it exists only while it is being played and is not stored in the piano when it is not being played. Moreover, each time the same composition is played, it will be different either because different pianists perform it or simply because no pianist can reproduce exactly a prior performance. With practice, pianists can learn to play a composition more fluently, efficiently, or expressively, to vary it intentionally, and to play it with less conscious attention to its elements. Then, they are no longer conscious of playing individual notes but instead work to produce dynamically shaped musical lines.

Consider the neurons in a person's nervous system as analogous to piano keys; each type can be tuned through learning to play different notes. There are many more neurons than keys, and the organization of neurons in relation to one another is far more complex, so the number of potential functional combinations or behavior compositions is far greater. Analogously, a specific functional pattern is created when the nervous system is selectively activated in a particular way. Any specific functional pattern does not exist—is not stored somewhere in the nervous system—when the nervous system is not activated in a particular way to create it. Learning functions to compose behavior patterns by organizing patterns of neural activation through selective attention, as with *neural networks.* Each neuron may be a functional component in different networks, just as each piano key may participate in many songs. The physical functioning of neurons provides the carrier on which information can be coded. It is the *pattern of coding* rather than the physical nature of neuronal operation per se that produces the functional pattern. At a neuronal level, the pattern of coding is manifest in the spatial-temporal patterns of neuronal firing. At a functional level, the pattern of coding is manifested in the content and organization of the thoughts, feelings, actions, and biological states represented by the concept, *behavior pattern.* Learning produces long-term potentiation of neural networks, making their activation as a network easier when behavior episodes occur that are similar to those in which the learning took place. When a new episode makes a particular functional composition relevant, it can be reconstructed as a unitary pattern. We have called such learned compositions behavior episode schemas (BESs).

Behavior Episodes as Activators of Learned Patterns
The concept of behavior episodes provides a tool for creating situations likely to activate a learned behavior episode schema composition. The living sys-

tems framework asserts that the way to activate reconstruction of a particular functional pattern and its organizing schema is to create a current behavior episode that is significantly similar to past episodes in which the pattern to be activated was probably learned. Much research supports this idea (e.g., Goldstein & Kanfer, 1979), and the concept of *retrieval cues* in memory research is illustrative. Creating behavior episodes to activate troublesome patterns and their guiding schemas is a delicate matter and requires great skill because activating troublesome patterns is typically upsetting to people, and powerful stability maintaining processes will operate to forestall such misery.

For example, an army veteran was walking with his wife when he heard a siren and an airplane (behavior episode). He threw his wife to the street and dragged her under a car because those two sounds, similar to wartime battle sounds, cued the activation of a severe fear-avoidance pattern (a behavior episode schema, called a phobia). Phobias are typically treated by creating a series of carefully designed therapy situations (behavior episodes) expected to activate the phobic pattern (behavior episode schemas) but in a form in which the fear component of the pattern is controlled to prevent the avoidance component. Similarly, remembering and talking about past behavior episodes called *episodic memories,* may activate some version of the behavior pattern that originally occurred in the remembered episode. If the cues in a behavior episode are changed, the behavior episode schema activated is likely to change. An illustrative application of that principle is called *reframing the problem,* which involves revising the way a problem is construed. This can activate alternate schemas, which may help the person form effective problem solutions and/or alternate plans of action. Some therapy interpretations probably serve a reframing function.

The proposition that functional patterns do not exist—and therefore can't be troublesome—unless they are activated suggests another strategy. Instead of trying to modify the troublesome schema itself, a lifestyle might be created that no longer provides the episode conditions that activate the person's troublesome patterns; these could include divorcing, getting a different job, moving to a place that does not activate the person's allergy. Stated differently, because habitual behavior patterns have been learned to deal with prototypical events of living, a habitual behavior pattern will not occur if the prototypical events to which it is functionally related no longer occur.

Two Strategies for Dealing with Behavioral Disruptions

There are two basic ways in which disruptions of organization, or disorganization, can be managed to maintain or regain organizational unity: (1) by forestalling or preventing disruption from occurring, or overcoming the disruption once it has taken place, or (2) by accommodating the disruption by creating some form of new organization. There are two ways in which a new organization can be created: (1) revise or elaborate some part of an existing behavior episode schema; or (2) create a new pattern by reorganizing previously learned components. Three types of change-related processes that emerged in humans through evolutionary processes are manifestations of these strategies: stability-maintaining processes, incremental change processes, and transformational change processes. Each is described in the next section, but remember that they are not mutually exclusive processes; they interact with one another to produce stability, variability, and change in human development and functioning.

STABILITY-MAINTAINING PROCESSES

The puzzling question that psychotherapists confront is why clients continue to behave in ways that produce distress, unhappiness, and ineffectiveness in important aspects of their lives. One would think that people would discontinue patterns that usually produce adverse outcomes. Moreover, when therapists try to help a person change such a pattern, they often encounter behaviors that divert or obstruct such change efforts. There appear to be powerful processes at work to maintain existing steady states and to prevent change. Indeed, there are!

MAINTAINING UNITARY FUNCTIONING

Chapters 3 and 4 described a model representing a person, with the person-in-context as the basic unit of reference. It asserts that people, as open systems, must maintain their structural and functional unity if they are to remain alive and adaptive (see Figure 3.2), and that requires the operation of each component, such as thoughts, feelings, actions, biological processes, and contexts, to be related to all the others so that they produce collective unity. This necessity poses a three-part problem: (1) Internal biological and psychological processes must be synchronized. (2) Actions in relation to contexts that vary, often unpredictably, must be synchronized. (3) The intraperson and person-context patterns must be synchronized. Because processes of living continually consume resources and continually face variable psychological, behavioral, and environmental conditions, disruptions of current organized states are inevitable. Maintaining unity must be a continual activity. Being results from a process of continuous becoming!

Suppose a person is walking in a city, crossing busy streets, climbing hills, and avoiding pedestrians, actions that require variations in the walking pattern to fit variations in the context. Variations in rate and intensity of walking require varying amounts of energy and place varying demands on different parts of the body. There must be variations in cell metabolism, oxygen intake, blood flow, breathing, and heart rate to support variations in effort. Perceptual/cognitive processes must be coordinated with actions and biological variability to guide the person toward his or her destination. Emotional processes may be activated to avoid anticipated dangers. Any disruption in the synchronized flow of activity will have a disorganizing effect: If the muscles do not get enough oxygen, people may get severe cramps and be unable to walk; if they misinterpret what they see, they may collide with a car; if they become inattentive, they can lose their way.

Human evolution has produced stability-maintaining processes that continuously operate to create and maintain personal unity in the face of varying, and often unpredictable, disrupting influences. Without them, life could not be maintained and effective living could not occur. No wonder they are so powerful. Thus, *processes that protect existing states are not pathological;* they are both natural and essential. However, they protect functional and dysfunctional patterns alike. For example, despite her unhappiness with her husband's treatment of her, Mrs. K constructed a steady-state pattern that maintains the status quo; she avoids confrontations with him, accedes to his demands, and sleeps in a separate room. Remember, *behavior patterns persist because they are performing some function,* no matter how dysfunctional they appear to others. To produce change requires overcoming or bypassing the stability-maintaining processes.

Stability Maintenance Through Negative Feedback Process

The role of negative feedback in maintaining unitary functioning, briefly discussed in Chapter 3 is examined more fully here. Recall that a person's functioning anywhere, at any time, is organized as a behavior episode in which all aspects of a person (see Figure 3.2) are functioning in coordinated, variable patterns flowing through time in relation to varying contexts. Each pattern of thoughts, feelings, and actions is organized to produce the desired outcomes specified in the active personal goals, within the possibilities and constraints of the person's current biological state and context conditions. These conditions will vary and may disrupt the content or flow of the pattern, so the person must be able to alter his or her thoughts, feelings, actions, and biological states while the episode is in progress if the person is to successfully accomplish his or her personal goals.

Negative feedback processes produce stability maintenance (steady states) by reducing discrepancies between current and desired or anticipated states.

The dynamics described are at the person level, but the same processes operate at other levels as well. For example, when a foreign substance invades a person's body, that biological-level disruption is responded to by the immune system to overcome or destroy the invaders and to restore the prior healthy biological state. At biological levels, these processes are regulated by material/energy based biochemical processes. At the person level, they are regulated by information/meaning-based processes, and diverse strategies may be used. For example, imagine a man who habitually assumes that other people consider him incompetent and unlikeable and are likely to exploit him. On a work project, co-workers treat him with respect and follow his lead. Their actions and statements contradict, and therefore may disrupt, his steady-state view of himself in relation to others. Several ways of dealing with that discrepant feedback, often called *defensive maneuvers*, can prevent it from disrupting his beliefs. He may avoid attending to their actions; if he does not notice them, they cannot be disruptive. He may interpret their actions to fit his beliefs, convincing himself that they have some hidden motive for acting that way. He may act to elicit rejecting behaviors from them, thereby confirming his beliefs. People are ingenious in creating ways to maintain their habitual behavior episode schemas.

Person-level dynamics operate as follows. Variables are continuously monitored that are indicators of desired outcomes—results to be produced or avoided, called a preferred state (PS). Those feedback signals represent the current state (CS) of the relevant aspects of the behavior episode: the person-in-context state. The current state and preferred state are continuously compared. That comparison process (the evaluative/regulatory function in Figure 3.2) influences either the continuation of or changes in the thoughts, emotions, and actions composing the current behavior episode pattern as follows:

1. If current state = preferred state (there is no discrepancy), then the current state continues unchanged to maintain the satisfactory state, or the behavior episode is terminated and a new one begun because the desired consequences have been produced.
2. If current state ≠ preferred state (there is a discrepancy), then the current state will be altered to try to better achieve the desired consequences, or the behavior episode will be terminated and a new episode initiated because the person concludes progress toward the preferred state is currently not possible.
3. If current state ➤ preferred state (the discrepancy is decreasing), then the current state continues unchanged or may be altered in minor ways to improve its efficiency.

4. If current state ◄- preferred state (the discrepancy is increasing), then the current state will be revised to try to reverse that trend, or it will be discontinued and a different behavior episode begun if no way of achieving the preferred state appears feasible at that time.

People are always functioning in some way, whether awake or asleep, as long as they are alive, so this stability-maintaining process is continuous. In habitual behavior episodes, these processes typically occur automatically and are not part of the current contents of consciousness, although they may be brought into awareness if a person directs attention to them.

Disruptions may occur at any level of person-in-context organization—cellular, person, or social interactions. Whether a disruption at one level becomes manifest at other levels as well will depend on the nature of the disruption and the stability-maintaining processes it activates. For example, the functioning of a single cell may become disrupted and initiate the kind of cell division called cancer. That biological-level disruption will not be manifested in disruptions at psychological or behavioral levels until the tumor elaborates to the point that it affects higher level physiological, psychological, or behavioral functioning. Similarly, an individual's interpersonal relationships may be disrupted without producing disruptions at biological levels. Whether a disruption is manifested at one level or at several levels has important diagnostic and treatment implications. Multiple-level disruptions activate stability-maintaining processes within each disrupted level as well as between levels and may require multilevel interventions to produce desired changes. The presenting symptoms of psychotherapy clients are typically combinations of disrupted states and ways of trying to maintain stability, often at biological, psychological, and interpersonal levels.

For example, a person in a therapy session may become nauseated. He or she will change behavior to try to reduce or eliminate the nausea, by drinking some water, changing the topic being discussed, breathing deeply, or leaving the session. If the disrupting influence is biological in nature—a "flu bug"—then information/meaning-based psychological/behavioral maneuvers are unlikely to reduce the nausea. However, if the nausea is the result of some psychodynamic process activated during the therapy episode, then psychotherapy methods may alter the psychological-level disruption and thereby reduce the nausea connected with it.

Stability-maintaining processes often operate on an *anticipatory* (feedforward in Figure 3.2) as well as a *reactive* (feedback) basis. Recall that people construct prototypic and habitual ways of dealing with different types of episodes, called behavior episode schemas (BESs). When they begin a new behavior episode, it activates some relevant, previously learned schema, and the person's functioning is then guided by the activated schema combined with current perceptions. That schema may lead the person to anticipate that certain conditions may produce unwanted consequences, as in increasing the deviation from preferred states, and cause him or her to behave in ways to prevent or avoid the occurrence of such potentially disrupting conditions. For example, a client may not show up for the next therapy session or may guide the session away from potentially disrupting or distressing topics as a way of preventing the kind of psychological disruption that triggered the nausea in the previous session.

Maintaining Stability in the Face of Motivational Conflict
One of the efficiencies in the ways humans function is that they typically pursue several outcomes simultaneously in any behavior episode, such as simultaneously trying to complete some task, obtain the approval of others, and avoid harm or physical discomfort (Ford, 1987, 1994; Pervin, 1991). Multiple motivational patterns create special adaptive problems. Because only one behavior pattern can occur at a time, that single pattern must produce multiple desired outcomes in the same behavior episode. Such *motivational alignment* produces higher levels of motivation by simultaneously serving multiple motivational patterns (Bergin, 1987; Ford, 1992; Winell, 1987). Humans construct such integrative behavior patterns day after day in many of their behavior episodes. Stability-maintaining processes operate to facilitate the construction of these successful behavior patterns, but serving multiple motivational patterns simultaneously can produce conflict. Each motivational pattern involves a combination of goals, values, and emotions (Ford, 1992). Therefore, motivational patterns can conflict in terms of their goals, as when you try to please rather than pleasing yourself; values, such as personal versus parental values; or emotions, such as affection versus fear. Successful motivational alignment within a behavior episode resolves or minimizes such conflicts.

Motivational balance across multiple behavior episodes is also important. All of a person's important motivational patterns cannot be pursued in each episode, so different ones must be constructed to serve different motivational patterns. A person typically has long-term goals that give continuity and meaning to the flow of life, intermediate goals that provide concrete objectives for organizing behavior, and short-term subgoals that provide for immediate achievement and recognizable progress toward intermediate and longer term goals. Motivational imbalances may occur (1) when people are successful in satisfying only some of their core motivational patterns, or (2) when their behavior is guided by short-term goals that are unrelated to their longer term purposes, thereby producing immediate satisfaction/pleasure but at the expense of longer term effectiveness and contentment. An example is enjoying temporary, drug-induced highs that lead to an addictive pattern, loss of job, and family breakup. Therefore, an effectively functioning person will display motivational balance across behavior episodes and across time (Winell, 1987).

Motivational patterns may focus on producing and maintaining cognitive or affective states such as pleasure or understanding; social relationships, such as belongingness or self-determination; or desired task outcomes such as mastery or material gain (Ford & Nichols, 1991, 1992). People typically have a relatively small set of core motivational patterns and a large proportion of their life satisfaction or dissatisfaction is a function of those central organizing concerns (Nichols, 1991). Individuals whose lives are dominated by too few or too many core motivational patterns are more vulnerable to dissatisfaction and distress than others (Ford, 1992).

When a person cannot accomplish motivational alignment and balance, conflict occurs. Stability-maintaining negative feedback processes then operate to resolve such conflicts. One possibility is to assign higher priority to some motivational patterns than others in a specific behavior episode so that a coherent behavior pattern can be constructed, and then to try to satisfy the other goals in a later episode. For example, a teenager may decide that it is more important to her to maintain her parents' respect and to protect herself than to obtain companionship and approval from her friends by taking drugs with them in a current behavior episode. She can seek their companionship and approval in a different kind of episode later on. Alternatively, one of her guiding goals or values may be abandoned; she may decide she no longer wants the friendship of certain agemates or that she no longer cares about her parents' approval. In a different scene, she may abandon the conflicted behavior episode and replace it with a different one to avoid having to resolve the conflict; she might pretend that she is ill and must go home. Last, the person may get stuck in the conflicted state, unable to find a satisfactory pattern, unable to withdraw, and struggling with approach/avoidance motivational conflicts. The concept of defensive behavior refers to different kinds of stability-maintaining strategies individuals use to defend their current states against disruptions. Pleasure, satisfaction, and other positive affective states are manifestations that a person is making progress toward the fulfillment of his or her currently operative motivational patterns. Anger, fear, depression, and other negative affective states are manifestations that a person's motivational patterns are not being satisfactorily fulfilled and/or that the person does not expect them to be satisfied.

People may seek the help of psychotherapists when distress and unsatisfactory outcomes are persistent and they consider themselves unable to construct more satisfactory patterns of living. However, current troublesome patterns persist because they are the best compromise among conflicting motivational patterns that people have been able to construct on their own to produce and maintain some preferred states or consequences, even though unwanted effects also occur. So, even though clients declare that they find their current patterns unsatisfactory in some ways, efforts to alter those patterns will activate stability-maintaining processes that will defend them against change precisely because the patterns came into existence in the first place to serve some of the clients' important motivational patterns.

If only negative feedback processes existed that protected and preserved existing patterns, people would be unable to change to cope adaptively with changing circumstances, and their adaptive viability would be severely limited. However, humans evolved with capabilities for changing as well as for maintaining existing patterns. One way to produce change is to harness the power of negative feedback processes to revise and elaborate existing patterns rather than to defend their current form. Such an arrangement is a key to incremental change processes.

INCREMENTAL CHANGE PROCESSES

Change occurs most frequently through successive differentiation and elaboration of existing structural and functional organization; examples are body growth or elaboration of a skill. This results in a step-by-step pattern of change or continuity in development. Recall that the essence of negative feedback processes is to identify and reduce discrepancies between existing and preferred states. Negative feedback processes produce stability maintenance when an existing behavior pattern is the preferred one and deviations from it are an undesirable discrepancy. Negative feedback dynamics then activate efforts to restore the status quo. Sometimes, though, existing habits are insufficient to overcome disrupting conditions, and variations on existing habits are tried to protect the current state. If one of these variants proves effective, it may be combined with the existing pattern, thereby producing incremental change in that pattern, or different means may be necessary to produce the same outcome in different circumstances. At a biological level, such incremental change is illustrated by the immune system. When the body is invaded by some infectious agent, the immune system operates to destroy it and to restore health. However, in the process, a new subset of immune system cells is produced especially sensitized to deal with future invaders of the same type. The incremental elaboration of immune system capabilities is the dynamic underlying the effectiveness of vaccinations against diseases.

GOAL SETTING, NEGATIVE FEEDBACK, AND SELF-GENERATED CHANGE

There is another way to create a discrepancy that can lead to incremental changes. A person may imagine and commit herself to trying to create a steady state different from one that presently exists. Imagined and desired future states are often called personal goals. Bernstein (1967) used the descriptive phrase "modeling of the future." Thus, goal setting can create a situation exactly opposite to the one in which the current state is defended. In defensive stability maintenance, the current state is the preferred state and is defended. In contrast, goal setting produces an evaluation of the current state as undesirable, thereby motivating efforts to change it to something different rather than to protect it. When a personal goal is activated, it specifies a preferred state. Then, negative feedback processes operate to evaluate the existing pattern as a deviation and facilitate activity to create the preferred state and eliminate the discrepancy.

Change-Producing Dynamics and Selection by Consequences

Change always starts with some existing state—behavior pattern. A person begins a behavior episode with an existing behavior episode schema and varies the approach if that doesn't work. Hilgard (1948) called such variations "provisional tries." However, why are only some of all "tries" learned? How is incremental change produced through goal-setting activity? It is through a process that Skinner (1981) called *selection by consequences;* response selection results from a reinforcing consequence. But, how is one to know which of the myriad of events always occurring within and around a person will function as a reinforcing consequence? Skinner defined it as a behavior-contingent event that altered the probability that the behavior would recur in future similar circumstances; an event can be identified as reinforcing only after the fact. Skinner defined a *consequence* as an event whose occurrence is contingent on—related to or influenced by—the activity of the particular behavior pattern being considered. Others have called this *generative causality.*

   The systems model being used here provides a basis for predicting in advance which kinds of events may produce selection by consequence: Only consequences the person evaluates as facilitating the reduction of discrepancies between desired and current states in an ongoing behavior episode will exert a selective influence. Those attempts that a person evaluates as producing progress toward achieving the personal goals guiding that particular episode will be learned; they will become more likely to recur in future, similar episodes. The consequences that will influence learning are a function of what the person is trying to do and of his or her perception and interpretation/evaluation of what is happening. In learning theory language, such a behavior episode is called a trial.

Construction of new behavior patterns is seldom accomplished in a single behavior episode; one trial learning is infrequent. Typically, a pattern is gradually learned in a series of similar episodes, through successive approximations. Extensive empirical evidence indicates that what is learned is a function of a sequence of episodes and the frequency with which these produce discrepancy-reducing consequences, called schedules of reinforcement in operant psychology. The special strength of this behavior modification technology lies in its careful design of a sequence of episodes aimed at producing specific kinds and sequences of incremental change. *Behavior shaping* is a procedure that arranges a series of subgoals to modify an existing pattern incrementally until a quite different pattern has been constructed.

Analogously, therapy sessions are a series of behavior episodes designed to facilitate client change. Moreover, each session may be thought of as guided by subgoals that cumulatively can lead to larger changes. However, if negative feedback dynamics are used with goal setting to initiate and regulate the process of incremental change, there must be client-therapist agreement about and commitment to the nature of preferred future patterns. The reason is that such goal setting creates the discrepancy that drives the negative feedback-based incremental change process.

Positive Feedback and Incremental Change

The possibility of change does not exist unless disruption of an existing steady state occurs; that is a necessary but not sufficient condition. Positive feedback functions to produce variations from an existing state; this disruption produces consequences that, through a selective iterative process, maintain and elaborate on those variations, like a snowball growing larger as it rolls downhill. In chemistry, this is called an *autocatalytic process.* Major changes can later result from the amplification of small initial deviations through such processes.

For example, suppose in some behavior episode in which her husband is criticizing and demeaning her for an error in their personal finances, Mrs. K becomes extremely angry. Instead of retreating to her room and feeling sorry for herself as she usually does, she fights back. Perhaps she tells him that he "screwed things up," that she won't straighten it out for him, throws the papers down before him, and then sits down in a chair to read a magazine. To her surprise, he stops attacking her, takes the papers, and straightens out the problem. In response to a verbal attack on her a few days later, she tells him that she won't let him treat her that way any more and leaves the house to calm down. When she returns, he initiates a pleasant conversation about something else. This reaction to her assertiveness emboldens her further, and in a confrontational episode a few days later she tells him that she is fed up with the way he treats her, and if he doesn't change she will do something about it. This escalation of assertiveness in the way she relates to her husband, fed by his reactions to these variations in her behavior, illustrates a positive feedback process in operation. However, such escalating deviations from the existing marital steady state create increasing instability in the two-person system. Deviation amplifying processes that are unrestrained can lead to destruction of the system, or necessitate some major reorganization to restore a greater degree of stability (to be discussed later as transformational change). For example, Mr. K could become so provoked with his wife's increasing assertiveness that he beats or divorces her.

Positive feedback processes can be a source of desirable incremental changes if linked to negative feedback processes that limit the extent or rate of change being produced. For example, physical growth spurts in children result from a kind of positive feedback process that then activates negative feedback processes to limit the rate and extent of physical growth. If Mrs. K were to pace her increasing assertiveness and do things to please her husband as he responds in ways she likes, then positive and negative feedback processes would be linked in a self-limiting, coupled way to produce incremental change in their previous steady-state relationship pattern.

TRANSFORMATIONAL CHANGE PROCESSES

Incremental changes occur through successive differentiation and elaboration of existing patterns, thereby maintaining coherent organization while change is occurring. Continuity and change typically coexist in human development, but sometimes such coexistence is impossible.

In physics, an equilibrium is a state of balance among opposing forces. Matter near equilibrium displays stability when exposed to some modest degree of perturbation. When the opposing forces become unbalanced, however, disequilibrium occurs. It may vary from a little to a lot, depending on the forces. When the opposing forces are far from equilibrium, the state is unstable; even a small perturbation may have a major effect, destroy the existing organization, and force the entire system to reorganize itself spontaneously into a new pattern or state. Many such critical transition states, called *bifurcation points* in chaos theory, have been demonstrated in the natural sciences. For example, the rate of flow of a fluid may progressively increase, but the pattern of the flow remains the same. However, at a critical rate of flow—a far from equilibrium state—a slight increase in flow rate will produce a dramatic change in the pattern of flow, called turbulence.

Analogous phenomena occur in people. Human behavior patterns may vary from being coherently organized and stable (a steady state) to being tenuously organized with precarious stability (a "far from equilibrium" state). At critical levels of instability, a small perturbation, or stressor may produce a major disorganization of biological, psychological, or behavioral states. Then, organizational coherence cannot be reestablished by incremental differentiation and elaboration of the existing state. At such critical bifurcation points, an alternate change process operates: Organization is restored through a reorganizational process called *transformational change,* or discontinuities in development. A psychotic break, and a sudden creative insight illustrate transformational change processes at work—in the disorganization-reorganization chain. Positive feedback processes, if not adequately limited by coupled negative feedback processes, can drive a system to such bifurcation points or transitional states.

An example is provided by the case of a woman who had some precarious personality patterns, constructed during her childhood relationship with an unpredictable, drunken, abusing father. In her mature years, daily stresses of her job escalated until they were nearly unbearable. Her mother developed a terminal illness and her marital relationship was difficult. Her sleep and eating patterns became disrupted. These persistent stressful circumstances, interacting with her precarious personality patterns, kept her in an ongoing and intense condition of stress. One day she fell and bumped her head. When she arose, she was in a new steady state; she could not remember who she was nor could she identify members of her family, her husband, her place of work, or her work skills. She had undergone a sudden transformational change, manifested as an amnesia, that markedly reduced her level of distress. This new steady state had functional utility because previously distressing thoughts and events no longer affected her.

Such rapid transformations need not be systemic in character. Cameron (1947) described a "crucial shift," which can take place in people with a paranoid orientation when they arrive at a sudden clarification by constructing a persecutory delusional system to account for their miseries and disappointments. Similarly, Fenichel (1945) has documented the crucial shift from world-destruction to world-reconstruction fantasies that signal the transformation of a schizophrenic condition from an acute to a chronic status.

Mrs. K's patterns of living are clearly in a precariously organized, far from equilibrium state. If incremental change processes do not begin to produce greater satisfaction and stability in her life and her distress grows, a transformational change might be triggered by some additional stressful event. At critical bifurcation points that lead to transformational change, multiple patterns of reorganization are possible and which will occur is unpredictable. For example, the positive feedback dynamic between her and her husband may continue to escalate: His criticism and rejection will increase her anger, depression, and withdrawal; this will further isolate him and expand his angry, rejecting behavior. The cycle will thus increase the instability and disorganization within each of them and in their marital relationship. At some point, a transformational change is apt to occur. Mrs. K could have a psychotic break, commit suicide, or shoot her husband in a fit of anger; or he might assault her during a drunken rage, divorce or abandon her, or run off with another woman.

Humans cannot tolerate or survive in highly distressed, disorganized states for extended periods of time; some transformational change is likely to occur, for good or for ill. People at such bifurcation points are said to be experiencing a crisis. Because the form of reorganization their life may take has not yet been determined, *crisis interventions* at such critical periods may be particularly powerful; in such states, a small perturbation such as a therapeutic intervention may have large effects. Once transformational change produces and consolidates a new state, producing change is much more difficult because the new state must be disrupted for the change to occur, and stability-maintaining processes will resist disruptions.

IMPLICATIONS FOR ANALYZING PSYCHOTHERAPY STRATEGIES AND METHODS

If these principles of stability and change are sound, then therapy strategies and methods must represent varied applications of them. Three kinds of implications of this view of change are discussed next: (1) the nature of the relationship between client and therapist, (2) the types of impact that interventions may be designed to produce, and (3) the different kinds of behavior on which different interventions may be focused.

THE PSYCHOTHERAPY RELATIONSHIP

The model of a person-in-context applies to therapists as well as clients. In therapy sessions, the behavior of each is motivated by their current personal goals; regulated by their values, self-evaluations, and emotions; and conducted with competencies and habits available in their respective behavioral repertoires. Each is a part of the other's context and that, along with their personal goals and biological states, activates a relevant behavior episode schema in each that organizes their functioning during the therapy session. Therefore, the behavior of each is affected by the other. The pattern of such mutual influences is typically called the *psychotherapy relationship*.

Shared Goals, Values, Expectations, and Commitments

Client-therapist relationships are a key tool for helping clients achieve desired changes because therapy sessions represent the behavior episodes designed to provide key change-producing experiences for clients; these will help them understand the change-producing episode they experience in their daily lives. If therapy is to be effective, client and therapist must function as a team, components of a two-person system. Therapy cannot be effective if they function as two separate systems with different goals and values and unsynchronized behaviors. A two-person system exists when the two function as collaborators who are committed to pursuing together the same general goals, who share values they use to regulate their collaboration, and who understand and value the special and complementary roles each is to perform and the skills they are to contribute to the effort.

They must agree that the primary purpose of the collaboration is to help the client achieve specified changes, an agreement that is likely to elaborate as therapy proceeds. They must agree to be open and honest in their communications and to treat their experiences together as confidential and privileged, because their communicative exchanges provide the feedback signals each must have to synchronize their functioning with the other effectively. If the feedback is not credible, it won't be used to regulate behavior. They must trust one another to carry out their roles conscientiously and effectively without malice or intentional exploitation or harm; otherwise, anticipatory, defensive, stability-maintaining processes will obstruct the change efforts. In particular, the therapist must refrain from using therapy sessions to pursue selfish goals and satisfactions; under such circumstances, the conditions for client change cannot be created because the therapist's goals rather than the client's goals become the focus of the relationship.

They must agree to work toward their shared goals on a regular basis and to give high priority to fulfilling that commitment to one another because change in complex and habitual behavior episode schemas can be produced only through a carefully orchestrated series of relevant behavior episodes— implied by concepts such as learning trials and schedules of reinforcement. When these general relationship conditions exist, therapist and client can function as two components in an integrated system and can synchronize their activities to serve the same objectives.

Specialized Roles and Competencies

The living system framework makes it clear that one person cannot produce changes in another. People change because of their own self-organizing and self-constructing operations. Both the therapist and client must understand that the therapist cannot do things to change the client—although that is what many clients initially suppose. The therapist can only facilitate the client's self-change processes. Therapists use their special knowledge and skills to create conditions that disrupt clients' troublesome steady states and to facilitate clients' motivated efforts to change themselves. A therapist may prescribe an antidepressant medication, but the client must take the medicine on a pre-scribed schedule; the client's body must biologically process and use the medication to produce the desired changes in biological state and to avoid unde-sired changes or side effects. Similarly, a therapist may guide communicative exchanges between them or arrange simulated (e.g., role playing) or real (e.g., "homework") behavior episodes to create experiences that clients may utilize to try to achieve psychological or behavioral changes in themselves. Therapists cannot change clients; they can only help clients change themselves.

Creation by therapists of change-facilitating conditions requires some un-derstanding of the nature and dynamics of the troublesome patterns to be changed. Only clients can provide the information from which that under-standing can be constructed; only they can demonstrate and/or describe the patterns considered troublesome and the conditions under which they usually occur. They do this through frank and honest self-report, self-descriptions on personality assessment measures, actions in therapy, role playing, and real-life actions. Therefore, clients bring three key kinds of expertise to the therapy rela-tionship: (1) relevant information and knowledge about themselves, (2) the abil-ity to perform the troublesome behavior patterns they wish to alter, and (3) their personal self-organizing and self-constructing capabilities. The creation of all these relationship conditions usually takes more than one therapy session and may require periodic reconsideration to ensure the most effective relationship.

Psychotherapy Sessions as Complex, Shared Behavior Episodes

Therapy sessions each represent a complex behavior episode of a special, highly personal nature, typically composed of both real and reconstructed episodes. The real behavior episodes are the actual interpersonal transactions between client and therapist. Each phase of a therapy session activates one or more relevant schemas in the client and therapist to guide their interactions in that episode. The activated schema serves to guide the aspects of the relationship within a two-person system as described above. Sometimes, however, the guiding behavior episode schemas lead the two people to behave toward one another not only as therapist and client but also as a surrogate for some other highly significant individual, such as a beloved parent or hated sibling. This is representative of the psychoanalytic concepts of *transference* by clients and *countertransference* by therapists.

The reconstructed episodes occur in several forms within the real therapy behavior episodes. The most common form is clients' description of episodes that have occurred, or may occur, in their real-life contexts. Such descriptions can activate within the therapy session a version of the schema that was constructed from and that guided the real-life episode; their description cues the reconstruction of an episodic memory. For example, a nurse described a wartime traumatic episode in a front-line hospital. During her description, her fear became intense, and the sights, sounds, odors, thoughts, feelings, and actions that occurred in that episode came flooding back into her consciousness. Some episodes created in therapy are designed to simulate real-life episodes; these include role playing and imagined or controlled exposure. Others are real-life episodes, such as in vivo exposure and homework.

Therapy Relationships May Involve Multiple People

Creating and maintaining a therapeutic relationship between a client and therapist is a complicated and delicate task. The same principles apply to therapy approaches that involve more than two people, such as group and family therapy or multiple therapist approaches. The task is even more complicated, however. Group or family therapy involves a multiperson system wherein each person functions as a component of a larger unit and where changes are sought in more than one person—the system component. This makes more complicated the task of meshing goals and values and of synchronizing multiple people's behavior to serve agreed-on therapy goals. Moreover, in many forms of multiperson therapies, the roles of client and therapist may alternately be performed by different members of the group; client members may perform some therapist functions from time to time.

TYPES OF INTERVENTION IMPACTS

Therapists are responsible for selecting and implementing intervention strategies and methods. Because a behavior pattern must be occurring to make modification possible, a therapy approach must have strategies and methods that will produce two interrelated impacts: (1) facilitating the activation of the behavior patterns to be changed, and (2) facilitating the disruption and change, or replacement, of the dysfunctional patterns.

Strategies and Methods for Selectively Activating Behavior Patterns
Every behavior episode activates in people one or more previously learned behavior episode schemas that organize and guide their behavior in that episode. To activate a particular schema, the new episode must be similar in salient ways to the kinds of episodes from which that schema was constructed. To selectively activate a client's dysfunctional pattern, the therapist must create an episode that provides salient cues for activating that pattern. These basic principles operate in all kinds of human relationships. When a parent gives a child instructions, a physician prescribes a medical regimen a patient is to follow, a teacher gives students test questions to assess their knowledge, or a highway sign provides direction, the presumption is that those context conditions will selectively activate a particular schema that will operate to produce a desired behavior pattern. If the cues are inadequate, the desired schema and behavior pattern are unlikely to be activated; this is sometimes called a miscommunication. For example, after an examination a student may say, "I knew the answer but the way the question was worded, I didn't know that was what you wanted."

Considerable knowledge about the nature of a client's repertoire of behavior episode schemas and skill in creating behavior episodes is required for the therapist to selectively activate relevant schemas. Therapists often rely on clients to identify appropriate episodes—clients' descriptions of phobic contexts. Knowledge about the culture in which a person's development was embedded and about his or her unique ontogeny are both useful, illustrated by the development of feminist and minority-oriented therapies. The utility of any attempt to influence people, as through advertising, can be increased by using knowledge about their cultural background—shared language, social institutions, beliefs and values.

Cultural knowledge alone may be insufficient for dealing with the kinds of dysfunctional patterns for which psychotherapy is sought. First, many individual differences exist in the nature and developmental timing of people's experiences from which they have constructed their repertoire of concepts, propositions, and schemas. Second, people don't respond the same way to similar experiences. Humans are self-constructing. People process their experiences uniquely. Two people may construct quite different schemas from a similar set of episodes. Therefore, a therapist must combine cultural and person-specific knowledge to understand each client's idiosyncratic schema repertoire and to skillfully design and conduct effective therapy sessions.

Clients' dysfunctional patterns are upsetting to them, so powerful stability-maintaining processes typically operate to defend the client from experiencing such distress. Unskillful efforts to activate troublesome behavior patterns can interfere with rather than facilitate therapy by activating defensive efforts to prevent the distressing patterns. Clients may shift to a safer topic, intellectualize about their problems, skip therapy sessions, or even terminate therapy.

Effective therapy approaches are likely to have strategies and methods for activating the behavior patterns to be changed, although therapists may not conceptualize their utility in those terms. Examples from approaches examined in the first edition of this book include Freud's free association technique designed to sneak past the censor, Rogers's nondirective interview strategy that enables a client to progress gradually toward distressing topics, and behaviorists' design of behavior episodes to activate patterns of behavior that could be reinforced and learned. Activating a behavior pattern is a necessary but not sufficient condition for producing change. Strategies and methods for influencing changes in patterns once they occur are also necessary.

Facilitating Change or Replacement of Dysfunctional Patterns
Client-therapist agreement about therapy goals creates the reference frame within which change dynamics can operate. It defines discrepancies between current unsatisfactory states and desired states, but not how to get there from here. Theoretically there are two ways of changing dysfunctional schemas to desired states. One is to change them in the direction of the desired state so they are no longer dysfunctional. The other is to discontinue their use and to replace them with more functional schemas already available in the client's repertoire or with newly constructed ones. Mrs. K can try to modify her dysfunctional marital relationship, or she can divorce her husband, create a separate life, and thereby terminate the need for her distressing marital schemas. Most psychotherapy literature focuses on changing rather than inactivating dysfunctional patterns.

Dysfunctional patterns for which clients seek help are habitual, steady state patterns that they have been unable to change on their own. The change principles summarized earlier assert that (1) the change process begins with some kind of disruption of the existing steady state, (2) which activates processes to overcome the disruption, and (3) which produces variability in the content of the troublesome state. Selection by consequence can then select alternate patterns from this variability and encourage the continued use of them. Not all variations a client might try will be of equal merit; some will have more functional utility than others. Therefore, some therapy techniques must selectively encourage the provisional try of alternatives likely to have greater functional utility for each client. Skill in such selective targeting of interventions rests upon knowledge linking idiographic information about a particular client to nomethetic knowledge about people in general. This means understanding the nature of their depressed states and the conditions that activate them such as linking this to the prototypical nature and dynamics of depressive patterns.

Mrs. K. consistently labels her distressful stomach tension and emotional experiences in her troublesome behavior episodes as anxiety or fear, and her behavior as functioning to forestall or alleviate her anxiety. Yet her descriptions of specific episodes raise the alternate possibility that they may be manifestations of anger rather than or in addition to fear, but that for some reason she does not construe them as anger. The therapist may slowly draw her attention to evidence in her own episode descriptions that she may be experiencing anger. That contradictory evidence introduces cognitive dissonance; it disrupts her troublesome schema and may trigger other possible interpretations. Once alternatives begin to occur, a different interpretation may be selected, thereby modifying the pattern.

Variability in functional patterns is a prerequisite to producing change in those patterns. We expect to find proposals about strategies and methods by which dysfunctional patterns may be disrupted and increased variability in the pattern may be facilitated. Carl Rogers's (1951) method of reflection of feeling focuses clients' attention on what Rogers considered to be salient aspects of their experiences. Reflecting contradictory feelings illustrates a method for facilitating disruption of psychological patterns. Sedation and shock therapy may be understood as biological interventions that function to disrupt an ongoing troublesome behavior pattern.

Change is not produced solely by variability, however. It is not enough for therapists to selectively facilitate potentially more adaptive variability in client functioning. Selection by consequences of alternative patterns must also be facilitated. Thus, we expect to find proposals about strategies and methods for helping clients discover that some alternative patterns produce desired consequences. For example, the authority and prestige of the therapist and the client's trust in and positive feelings for the therapist might be used as a selective consequence. Freud's method of interpretation may be such a strategy.

The most powerful form of selective consequences is the natural consequence of a pattern of behavior in real-life behavior episodes that are of personal importance to a person. We expect to find descriptions of strategies and methods designed to get clients to try out some alternate pattern in some personally meaningful episode and/or to capitalize on real-life tryouts that clients spontaneously perform. For example, a client may be asked to role play a different way of behaving in a simulated and therefore safe therapy episode. Clients may also be given homework to try out a different pattern in some real-life behavior episode. The therapist may actually accompany clients into a real-life episode to be supportive as they try out an alternative pattern.

Targets of Intervention Strategies and Methods

Strategies for facilitating change may activate a pattern to be modified, induce a client to try some alternate version, and selectively reinforce an alternative pattern. But on which aspects of the person's functioning should change efforts be focused: thoughts? emotions? biological functions? communicative or instrumental actions? That question is considered next.

System Change May Start with Any Component

Figure 3.2 emphasizes that a person always functions as a unified organization of structural and functional components in a context. A change in any part may lead to changes in other parts to restore unity of the whole, and it may alter the dynamics and the developmental pathway of the entire system.

If people's guiding goals or self-evaluations are changed, that may change what they try to do, how they try to do it, the contexts in which they behave, the consequences they experience, their evaluations of their effectiveness, and the feelings associated with their progress. If the way people act is changed, that may produce different consequences and feedback, which may alter how they think about themselves and the emotions they experience, producing further changes in the ways they act. If the biological substrate is altered, as with antidepressant medication, that may alter how clients feel, think, and act. If their contexts change, that may alter the consequences their actions produce, causing changes in the ways they think, feel, and act. Contextual changes may also create new possibilities for behavior that previous contexts prohibited or constrained, thereby activating and cultivating different schemas. If emotions change, evaluative thoughts may change, producing changes in the ways people think and act, and in the consequences they experience.

This rationale implies that similar psychotherapy outcomes may result from interventions that emphasize different cognitive, emotional, or behavioral interventions. *Equifinality* is a concept in biology meaning that different pathways may lead to the same developmental outcome. Folk culture recognizes this with phrases like "Many roads lead to Rome." This may be one reason that consistently different effects among psychotherapies have not been found.

The Potential Utility of Multiple Intervention Targets

It does not follow, however, that all approaches are equally efficient and effective in producing desired changes in every kind of dysfunctional pattern. The preferred starting point may differ depending on the condition or syndrome as well as the current state of the client and the context. Combining several interventions focused on different aspects of the person may be more effective than a single focus, at least for some dysfunctions; and multiple interventions might be combined simultaneously or sequentially. Thus, a therapist may try to help clients alter their depressive patterns by simultaneously combining antidepressant drugs with psychotherapy interviews focused on how they are thinking about and interpreting events in their lives. Medication might be combined with temporarily altering the context through hospitalization to reduce immediate life stresses. Psychotherapy sessions might be added later. It may be impossible to focus on only one component of a person at a time because all aspects of a person are always simultaneously operative in every behavior episode.

Psychotherapy Outcomes as Changes in Developmental Pathways

Clients typically enter psychotherapy wanting prompt relief from current, persistent distress, and the problematic conditions in their lives. They want to become happier and more effective people. Fulfilling such wishes is rarely possible. Producing changes in such patterns is not like pulling teeth; it can't be done quickly to get it over with. Clients' dysfunctional patterns were constructed through many episodes over an extended period of their lives; they are typically highly generalized across many contexts and current life episodes. Changing powerful habits takes time and practice of alternatives.

Therefore, desired changes cannot be fully accomplished within therapy sessions. Clients may come to think, feel, and act differently during psychotherapy sessions, but that does not necessarily mean that they will think, feel, and act differently in real-life situations. That can only come about through practice in the use of therapeutically altered schemas in significant real-life contexts. The processes whereby this takes place are referred to by learning theorists as *transfer of training* or *generalization*. Clients' lives go on continuously outside their therapy sessions, so therapy behavior episodes and real-life behavior episodes cannot be isolated from one another. Psychotherapy experiences are apt to stimulate variations in the ways clients try to lead their daily lives, and consideration of those efforts and their consequences becomes part of the therapy process. Desired changes in dysfunctional schemas result from an interaction of therapy-session episodes and real-life episodes; for enduring change to occur, the consequences of real-life episodes are the most important.

Psychotherapy outcomes should not be considered as final steady states but as ways of starting clients on somewhat different developmental pathways. Within-therapy changes can be consolidated and elaborated only through use by clients in their daily living. Moreover, because living is continuous and development is open ended, current changes can lead to other unexpected and unpredictable future changes. Outcomes that therapists and clients collaboratively seek may range all the way from constructing, consolidating, elaborating, and generalizing desired changes before they terminate therapy at one extreme to immediately alleviating current distress at the other. In between these extremes can be approaches aimed at producing some changes, and at starting change processes that clients can then elaborate through real-life experiences. These are long-term crisis intervention, and short-term approaches, respectively. Therapists differ in how they combine real-life and within-therapy change processes to help clients start down different developmental pathways.

Human development is a lifelong process for everyone. Patterns effective in one phase of life and set of contexts may be dysfunctional in other phases and contexts. Developmental flexibility to modify existing states as needed is highly adaptive. Psychotherapists may try to facilitate both specific changes and skill in using basic self-constructing capabilities.

EVALUATION OF PSYCHOTHERAPY PROCESSES AND OUTCOMES

The justification for expending the effort, time, money, and other resources required for psychotherapy ultimately hinges on the extent to which it works. Moreover, shaping therapy to fit clients' individual circumstances requires understanding of how it works. Other factors also need to be considered, such as differences in costs, efficiencies, and side effects.

TREATMENT EFFECTS

Sometimes the question of the effectiveness of a treatment is formulated in terms of effect versus no effect. This is inappropriate, however, because any intervention invariably produces some effects. The statement "The treatment had no effect," usually means that it did not generate the desired effects or that any other effects produced were not observed or detected.

A truism in technology evaluation is that any technology generates multiple effects that may be direct or indirect, primary or secondary, beneficial or detrimental, measurable or unmeasurable. Assessment specialists emphasize that (1) no information may be available on many of the effects of any intervention; (2) ways to monitor or assess many of the variables may not be available; (3) knowledge-based predictions either of potential effects or the ways in which they combine are often not possible; (4) potential intrusions from the contexts in which people live are difficult to foresee; and (5) often objectives have not been precisely stated and/or useful indices with which to assess progress toward objectives are often not available (Miller, 1970). If psychotherapy is assumed to generate multiple effects, then psychotherapy evaluations should be multivariate and should consider both intended and possible other effects; sometimes side effects may be as important as intended ones.

Types of Treatment Effects
Some types of psychotherapy effects people have identified are summarized in Table 5.1 to emphasize the wide range of effects that are possible. Not all of them can be considered desirable. Effective psychotherapies should generate specific effects in clients that (1) clearly result from the therapy, (2) constitute the primary effects intended, (3) are judged to be beneficial in character, (4) are accompanied by a minimum of undesirable effects, (5) are stable and can be sustained over a satisfactory period of time, and (6) are least costly to clients or to the agencies who sponsor them. The ideal is approaches that are high in beneficial effects and low in undesirable ones, and that have low cost characteristics.

TREATMENT EVALUATION

Both therapists and clients are continually evaluating the effectiveness of the therapy in which they are collaborating, even though such evaluations often remain informal, tacit, and unshared between the participants. For example, clients privately consider questions such as these: "How am I feeling? Am I making any kind of progress here? Should I continue?" Therapists are addressing parallel questions and formulating analogous judgments within sessions and from one session to the next. The purpose of evaluative processes is to guide decisions about what to do or not to do next—whether the treatment process should be continued, modified, revised, redesigned, or discontinued. Treatment evaluations are an essential ingredient of any therapy process. Without knowledge of results, therapists have no way of knowing whether their efforts remain on target or require some mid-course correction.

Table 5.1

An Illustrative List of Ways to Classify Different Kinds of Effects Produced by Psychotherapy Interventions

Effects Represented in Terms of Polarized Opposites

Intended versus Unintended Effects. The extent to which effects fit treatment objectives.

Positive versus Negative Effects. The extent to which effects are judged to be desirable (beneficial) or undesirable (detrimental) to the health, safety, or welfare of the client.

Direct versus Indirect Effects. The extent to which effects are judged to be the immediate result of the treatment, or are effects that are secondary; also referred to as primary versus secondary effects, or main versus side effects.

Short- versus Long-Term Effects. The extent to which effects persist over a period of time.

Immediate versus Delayed Effects. The extent to which effects can be identified relatively promptly or require a period of time to elapse before they become apparent; sometime referred to as lag or sleeper effects.

Stable versus Unstable Effects. The extent to which effects persist over a satisfactory period of time.

Effects Represented by Specific Designations

Order Effects. Effects that tend to occur in sequence; also called serial effects.

Incidental Effects. Outcomes that are regarded as trivial or inconsequential.

Residual Effects. Effects that persist beyond the termination of the treatment, typically used to refer to effects that are negative and secondary in character; also called aftereffects.

Summation Effects. Two or more outcomes whose combined effect is greater than either separately; also called combined or synergistic effects.

Contingent Effects. Effects that occur only under certain contingencies or conditions.

Partial Effects. Term used in instances when effects fall short of what was sought or intended.

Paradoxical Effects. Treatment results that are opposite to or discrepant from expectations.

Iatrogenic Effects. Effects attributable to characteristics of the therapist rather than the treatment.

Deterioration Effects. Results that are initially apparent at the completion of treatment but that tend to fade or disappear with the passage of time.

Rebound Effects. Instances in which the frequency or intensity of a behavioral process is initially reduced but subsequently recurs at even greater levels than initially observed.

Table 5.1 *(continued)*

Effects Represented by Specific Designations

Hawthorne Effect. Effects resulting from attention to clients rather than from the treatment procedures used; also called attention effects.

Transference Effect. Effects resulting from the personal attachment formed by the client to the person providing the treatment.

Placebo Effects. Effects following treatments incapable of generating the effects.

Habituation Effects. Initial results that are observable but that disappear with continued treatment.

Debilitative Effects. Negative effects that debilitate clients and render them no longer capable of effectively pursuing their ordinary affairs.

Hazardous Effects. Effects that place clients at risk with respect to health, safety, or welfare.

Morbid Effects. Effects that lead to clients' death.

For evaluation to make a positive contribution to treatment success and to confirming the effectiveness of the approach, it needs to be deliberately and intentionally pursued as a built-in, explicit, and regular part of the therapy process. Unfortunately, in most practitioner settings, treatment evaluations typically do not occur in any systematic or useful way. Appropriate treatment evaluation is perhaps the most frequently underemphasized aspect of day-to-day therapy practice. There are presumably many reasons for this. The complaint of excessive case loads is common: "We're much too busy; we're undermanned and underfunded." There is a tendency to justify the value of services with effort data—number of clients and interviews—rather than effects data—nature of client changes produced. The inadequacy of evaluation may reflect the field itself rather than the competence of individual practitioners. Proponents of each approach typically provide descriptions of their treatment techniques (procedural models) and how to apply them to particular types of clients or problems, but they typically give less attention to strategies and methods of evaluation. However, changes in service systems and the growing power of third-party payers is increasing accountability demands on therapy services. These can be adequately met only with more effective evaluation approaches.

Major Approaches to Treatment Evaluation
Treatment evaluation is far more than the exercise of a judgment; it involves a multifaceted process. To clarify this point, three major kinds of treatment

evaluation are considered. These differ with respect to (1) the purposes they are intended to serve, (2) the occasions on which they are performed, (3) the methods that are used, (4) the kinds of information that they generate, and (5) the results to which they lead.

First, there are the evaluations made as the treatment is progressing, sometimes called treatment monitoring. Technically they are called *process* or *formative evaluations* as the information they yield is used to evaluate what is happening during therapy and to inform, or reform, the intervention methods and processes being used. Such evaluations are made at intervals, preferably frequent, during treatment. Second, the purpose of *outcome* or *summative evaluations* is to provide information about the extent to which intended effects or therapy goals have been achieved, including both subgoals and larger goals and short- and long-term effects. Third, *follow-up evaluations* occur at varying time intervals after psychotherapy is terminated. Their purpose is to provide information about the extent to which client changes have been maintained without further treatment, and to determine whether different problems may have developed in the interim that require additional attention. Each type plays an important role in generating the knowledge of results needed if clients are to be adequately served and treatment approaches improved. Moreover, evaluations of effects, like any other treatment component, must be deliberately planned and pursued or they are unlikely to be done.

NEXT STEPS

The summary of the comparative framework that guides the comparative analyses has been completed. Next is presented an outline derived from it that will be used in analyzing approaches. Also described is the selection of approaches to be analyzed. Using the same outline for each chapter facilitates comparisons across approaches in the final chapters.

SELECTION OF APPROACHES AND ORGANIZATION OF ANALYSES

FAMILIES OF PSYCHOTHERAPY to be examined in this comparative study were defined in Chapter 1 in terms of their metaphysical and epistemological assumptions. These families are the following: traditional psychoanalysis; interpersonal, self-psychology, and object relations therapies; humanist approaches—existential, experiential, gestalt, and person-centered; behavior therapies; cognitive therapies; cognitive behavioral and skill-training therapies; behavioral medicine and behavioral health; eclectic and integrative approaches. It is impossible to analyze the more than 400 approaches others have identified; so exemplars of each family are examined. In addition, the outline for each chapter needs to be made explicit.

SELECTION CRITERIA

Just as members of a human family differ despite family resemblances, so too do approaches within a psychotherapy family differ from one another. The following criteria were used to select exemplars to represent and illustrate the general approach of each family.

1. They should have starting assumptions similar but not necessarily identical to those defining the family.
2. They should have a substantial number of current adherents among practicing psychotherapists.

3. They should be manifest in principal training programs, institutes, and workshops.
4. They should be widely disseminated in books and regularly published relevant journals.

Surveys of preferences for different approaches among practitioners and training programs during the past decade provide relevant information. In addition, the *Journal of Contemporary Psychology* and publishers' book lists were examined to identify relevant publications about different approaches. The sequence in which they are analyzed approximates the historical sequence of their emergence.

OUTLINE FOR THE COMPARATIVE ANALYSES

The outline, derived from the comparative framework, also reflects questions therapists might ask when considering an approach. Each chapter follows the same general outline to facilitate comparison of approaches in Section III. Each chapter begins by considering general questions. What are the underlying assumptions of the approach and its history of development? What basic types of client changes are typically targeted? An analysis follows of the conceptual content or human characteristics emphasized to answer questions such as these: What levels and units of analysis are used? To what aspects of people as defined in Figure 3.2 do its key concepts refer:

1. Biological, such as cellular or physiological systems
2. Psychological, such as consciousness, cognition, emotions
3. Transactional, such as instrumental or communicative actions
4. Environmental, such as natural, designed, interpersonal, and sociocultural
5. Complex patterns, such as lifestyles

Next, proposals about the ways different aspects of human life interrelate, influence one another, and change are analyzed by examining several questions.

1. To what extent do the theories emphasize proactive, anticipatory (feedforward), reactive (feedback), or other processes?
2. To what extent do they emphasize self-organizing dynamics (such as stability-maintaining processes), self-constructing dynamics (such as

incremental and transformational change processes), or other processes?

3. What models of normal and dysfunctional development are proposed?

Recommended strategies and methods whereby client changes may be facilitated and evaluated are analyzed next. A *strategy* is an arrangement of conditions, techniques, and activities, entailing considerable expenditure of effort, taking place over a sustained period of time, and directed toward accomplishing multiple and related changes in the state or behavior of the person with whom it is employed. *Methods* are means by which strategies are implemented; different methods may implement the same strategy. Illustrative questions are these:

1. How are therapy sessions designed as contexts for facilitating desired client change—Where? How often? How long? Expected duration of treatment? Roles of clients and therapists? Establishment of shared goals, values, and commitments?

2. What general strategies and specific methods are proposed for (a) selectively activating client patterns to be changed, (b) facilitating changes in or replacement of dysfunctional patterns, (c) facilitating the generalization of changes from therapy contexts to other relevant life contexts, (d) facilitating alterations in developmental pathways, and (e) evaluating client progress during therapy and final outcomes upon termination of therapy?

Finally, proposals for evaluating the adequacy of a theory are considered.

1. *Clarity* or internal coherence concerns the extent to which theoretical components fit together in systematic and logical ways: Is the procedural model clearly linked to the propositional model about functional and dysfunctional development?

2. *Comprehensiveness* or content value considers the extent to which the biological, psychological, transactional, and environmental aspects of life are encompassed.

3. *Accuracy* or truth value concerns the extent to which the theory is consistent with relevant empirical and clinical evidence.

4. *Utility* or heuristic value considers practical questions: To what extent does it help therapists understand clients' difficulties, design and implement therapy approaches, and produce desired outcomes? What are its resource and personnel requirements? Its costs? Its range of ap-

plicability? Its hazards, risks, contraindictions, and precautions that might be taken to reduce them?

Following is the outline used for each chapter to make comparison of models easier.

The Conceptual Model

Levels and Units of Analysis
Content of Key Concepts

The Propositional Model

Assumptions about Stability-Maintaining and Change Processes
Assumptions about Normal or Functional Development
Assumptions about Abnormal or Dysfunctional Development

The Procedural Model

Assessment or Diagnosis
Intervention Strategies and Methods
Evaluating Client Progress
Strategies for Evaluating the Approach

Other commentators have observed that therapists' descriptions of their procedural models may not fully correspond with what they actually do in therapy. Our analyses are based primarily on their descriptions rather than evidence of in-therapy actions, although published therapy protocols may sometimes be used as examples of their rationale in operation. Because of space limitations, issues and evidence concerning evaluation of effectiveness will be only briefly considered.

To help the reader distinguish between these theorists' terminology and our analyses of their proposals, we have typically placed quotation marks around their terms. Because they use their basic theoretical terms throughout their writings, we have not given specific citations or page numbers for most of those quotations. When longer quotations are used, specific citations and page numbers are given.

CHAPTER 6

Traditional Psychoanalysis

MORE THAN A century ago, Sigmund Freud began to create a new procedural model for treating neuroses. His conceptual and propositional models became a metapsychology to explain the nature, function, and dysfunction of complex mental processes. He called his new approach psychoanalysis. He attracted others who helped to elaborate and apply his approach to an increasing diversity of human problems. They were proud and strong-minded, men and women who saw themselves as revolutionaries in opposition to the medical establishment, working to create a new science of complex, mental, intrapsychic processes and new methods for treating psychological disorders—a view Freud encouraged (Sulloway, 1979). They established a clinically based tradition of science and therapy that could be used to understand human life at multiple levels—from individuals, to societies and cultures, and within a historical perspective. Creative, strong-minded, dedicated people often disagree and produce diverse ideas. Therefore, psychoanalysis has been modified and elaborated during its 100-year history, both by Freud and by the men and women who later joined in the effort (Mishne, 1993). Freud's disciples were often more rigid than he was in applying his ideas, so traditional psychoanalysis is both an elaboration of and a somewhat different version of his original proposals (Thompson, 1994).

HISTORICAL PERSPECTIVE

Freud was a prolific writer (see Strachey, 1953–1974). In addition to amount, two aspects of his writing make analysis of his model difficult: (1) He often used a rhetorical strategy of making strong, unqualified assertions of a seemingly firm principle in order to have an impact, and then introduced qualifications. Moreover, he used the same terms with different meanings and avoided formal definitions as a deliberate strategy of conceptual flexibility. This makes it impossible to take any of Freud's definitions literally (Holt, 1989). (2) He kept changing his views in the light of new evidence and ideas, but frequently did not make clear whether he had abandoned his previous views or had revised and/or absorbed them into his emerging conceptions (Holt, 1989; Sulloway, 1979). As a result, there is disagreement about what Freud really meant and the relative importance of his many proposals for both theory and treatment.

Legends or myths about the origins of psychoanalysis promoted its development and protected its belief system. Intentional institutionalization of psychoanalysis served to protect the authority and influence of Freud's proposals from erosion by others' ideas and to create a doctrine all psychoanalysts were expected to follow (Ellenberger, 1970; Sulloway, 1979). His followers saw him as a kind of messiah; "We knew all Freud's works by heart," his words took on "undreamed-of significance," and "there was an atmosphere of the foundation of a religion in that room" (Sulloway, 1979, p. 481). Two themes prototypic of hero myths were used to give the psychoanalytic movement a special institutionalized identity: (1) Freud was portrayed as a solitary hero struggling against a host of enemies who opposed him and his revolutionary views. (2) He was represented as an intellectual genius creating revolutionary ideas completely on his own, independent of contributions by other scholars of his time. Strong evidence contradicts both these myths (e.g., Ellenberger, 1970; Holt, 1989; Sulloway, 1979). Others assert that his theories are products both of his developmental history and personality and beliefs influential during that cultural period. Yet the myths persist: "Over four decades, Freud, independently and alone, conceptualized every one of his basic theories and techniques of psychoanalytic treatment" (Mishne, 1993, p. 4).

The heavily political nature of the psychoanalytic movement was a context conducive to conflict and theoretical fragmentation fueled by accusations and counteraccusations by "loyalists" and "dissidents" (Mitchell, 1988). Early in the psychoanalytic "revolution" Freud and his disciples became concerned that his vision of psychoanalysis might become contaminated or displaced over time by deviationist views (e.g., Adler; Jung). Therefore, a secret committee of loyal adherents was created to guard the movement's future by controlling training, publications, and psychoanalytic organizations, and by challenging and correcting those who attacked the accepted doctrine (Fine, 1979; Jones, 1953, 1955, 1957). Variations and elaborations by others of Freud's core ideas were acceptable, but basic alterations were not—except by Freud himself. The persistent ideological and political influence of the Freudian legend is revealed by a still frequently used tactic of psychoanalysts: Demonstration of direct conceptual lineage from Freud to new proposals increases their acceptability to traditionalists. Many psychoanalytic papers begin by citing Freud as having suggested a similar idea (Mitchell, 1988), and their authors can usually find something supportive in his extensive, diverse array of topics, ideas, and meanings, even though their proposals may contradict some other Freudian tenets (e.g., Modell, 1990).

This powerful institutionalization of traditional psychoanalysis has been both a strength and weakness (Fine, 1979). It has provided endurance and vitality for a century, but its defense of traditional doctrine has significantly limited its responsiveness to the extensive growth of knowledge about human development and psychotherapy since Freud's time. Much of the tension and conflict within psychoanalysis results from its traditional controlling legend, ideology, and political history. The 1970s saw an increasing rejection of the prevailing rigidity imposed by Freudian orthodoxy, even by mainstream psychoanalytic leaders:

> The crisis is a compound of escalating outer attack, of intense and literal therapeutic competition, of the disappointment of unfounded dreams of panacea, and of reactive, bristling orthodoxy . . . relinquishment of residues of a priestly omniscient taboo, insusceptible to criticism from within and without, will be in no sense a regression or a loss. It will indeed be a prodigious advance. . . . Cross-fertilization is not to be equated with contamination. (Stone, 1984 [1975], p. 434)

Psychoanalysis is not a single coherent model (Eagle & Wolitzky, 1992). Analysts have relinquished the idea of one "widely accepted theoretical paradigm and method of practice . . . espoused during Freud's lifetime" (Levine, 1995, p. 802). Pluralism and competition now exist. Contemporary psychoanalysis involves

> a proliferation of theoretical approaches, each with its own formulations, language, and perspective [and] of competing models, ideologies, and conceptualizations apparently bearing . . . an ambiguous relationship to each other. Adherents of each tradition focus on their own school, dismissing the value of alternate points of view. This threatens to dissolve psychoanalysis into cultish islands of devotional fealty. (Greenberg & Mitchell, 1983, p. 379)

"Disputes among adherents to different theories have come to resemble religious wars over contradictory dogmas rather than scientific disagreements over explanations of observational data" (Mishne, 1993, p. 377). This proliferation has led to calls for synthesis or integration within psychoanalysis (e.g., Mitchell, 1988; Pine, 1990; Skolnick & Warshaw, 1992; Wallerstein, 1990). However, the pluralism is primarily in conceptual and propositional models—*metapsychology*—rather than in the procedural model—clinical theory—used. This kind of pluralism began with Freud and Breuer (1957/1895) when they explicitly stated that they agreed about the observational data but disagreed about how to explain them.

Wolstein (1992) notes that empirically psychoanalysts

> observe, define, and make inferences about the conscious-unconscious dimensions of transference and countertransference, resistance and counterresistance, anxiety and counteranxiety, and the self: which makes their therapeutic inquiry psychoanalysis. Interpretively, they appeal to diverse myths and metaphors of contemporary pluralism about the conjectured and reconstructable meanings of those observations and inferences: which makes for their varieties of perspectives in psychoanalysis. (p. 327)

He illustrates multiple "interpretive and speculative metapsychologies of psychoanalysis" with Freud's instinct, Adler's power struggle, Jung's collective unconscious, Rank's absolute will, current ego, object, interpersonal and self models. He argues that different metapsychologies adopt for explanatory purposes different "cultural myths and metaphors" that reflect different aspects of human life such as "power, race, and will; adaptation, satisfaction, and security; self-fulfillment, self-realization, and mystical self-love" (Wolstein, 1992, p. 315). Freud's instinct/drive libidinal explanatory model used as its metaphor evolutionary biology. Ego, object, interpersonal, and self-perspectives use the metaphors of adaptation, consensus, individuation, and human uniqueness.

A shared procedural model unifies them.

> Psychoanalysis does not stand or fall . . . with the changing visions and revisions of such metapsychologies. Its structure of therapeutic inquiry is designed . . . to study the relation of conscious and unconscious processes and patterns arising directly within a unique and shareable field of experience that evolves in and through the self-supporting psychic connectedness of a particular psychoanalyst and patient. (Wolstein, 1992, p. 313)

One's beliefs influence one's actions, however, so analysts' conceptual/propositional model influences how they implement the procedural model, sometimes in severely limiting ways that produce gaps between analysts and patients or patients and their problems. When the meaning of everything is rigidly interpreted as representing one's guiding beliefs, the analytic process will be biased; analysts will see what they believe exists and will selectively direct patients' attention and self-interpretations toward what the analyst thinks is important; a highly intellectualized, distorted facsimile of a collaborative inquiry can result (Wolstein, 1992).

Two broad metapsychology approaches are dominant, with much variability within each, "reflecting the largest and longest split in the history of psychoanalysis, that between the 'culturalists' and the 'Freudians' " (Fine, 1979, p. 1). This is sometimes called the relational/structure and drive/structure models (Greenberg & Mitchell, 1983). This chapter focuses on *traditional psychoanalysis* or the drive/structure model; also called classical or orthodox, it is based primarily on Freud's ideas and methods with elaborations primarily from ego psychology. "Since 1923, all of psychoanalysis has been ego psychology" (Fine, 1979, p. 55). Chapter 7 analyzes self, object relations and interpersonal orientations that deemphasize or reject some Freudian concepts such as instincts and drives and emphasize human relationships and learning. Its current most influential forms are called *object relations* and *self-psychology*. Contemporary traditional psychoanalysis is a modified version of Freud's ideas. First his proposals are examined and are then related to current traditional psychoanalysis.

FREUD'S CONCEPTUAL AND PROPOSITIONAL MODELS

LEVELS AND UNITS OF ANALYSIS

Freud viewed the person as an entity distinct from the environment whose functioning results primarily from the individual's own inherent properties rather than being controlled by external stimuli or reality. Biological and psychological functioning are therefore the primary levels of analysis in his metapsychology—his conceptual and propositional models. Only his emphasis on transference in his procedural model implies a person-in-context level of analysis. His primary units of analysis represent patterns of biological functions—id processes—and psychological functions—ego and superego processes; unconscious processes. Instrumental and communicative actions are not included in any of his units, so he does not represent people as unitary, integrated entities.

HUMANS AS MECHANISTIC, REACTIVE BIOLOGICAL ENTITIES

Freud, trained as a physician/neurologist, adopted biologically based ideas dominant at the time (Holt, 1989; Sulloway, 1979). He created a metapsychology, a conceptual and propositional model, that was a physicalistic, reductionistic, deterministic, mechanistic representation of humans with emphasis on neurological functioning (Freud, 1887–1902 [1954b]). He sought to explain normal and dysfunctional behavior without assuming causal roles for any psychological attributes. His assumptions were these: (1) A person's nervous system is passive unless energized. (2) Behavior functions to reduce that energy. (3) Development results from stimulus ➤ excitation ➤ response patterns. Thus, his initial assumptions and those of the later behavioral revolt against psychoanalysis were similar. He never published his initial theorizing because it failed to account for clinically based observations and ideas to his satisfaction. However, it influenced many of his later proposals. Within his empiricist epistemology, humans were entities that could be understood through careful observation by an objective observer.

INSTINCTS AND THE BIOLOGICAL BASES OF BEHAVIOR

He increasingly relied on mentalistic concepts like the unconscious, primary and secondary process thought, ego, and superego. However, he did not abandon his initial mechanistic, reactive organism assumptions, and he persisted in his desire to account for human psychological and behavioral functioning in biological terms (id), but shifted his emphasis to evolutionary biology. He relied on Lamarckian assumptions of the inheritance of acquired characteristics. For example, he created an elaborate explanation that the oedipus complex was universal in humans because early in human evolution, parent-child love triangles took that functional form for adaptive reasons, and that experience became embedded in humans' biological inheritance (Sulloway, 1979). For him, biological development referred to phylogeny—the biological evolution of species and its influence on individual development (Holt, 1989).

It followed that all human thought and behavior was driven by such biologically based instincts or drives. He put the source of historical behavioral regularity inside the person (Freud, 1905 [1953b]). He initially assumed a dominant sexual instinct to be essential for preservation of life and the species. He frequently used the term *love* but never defined what he meant. Most frequently, it related to actual sexual desire and relationships. Throughout his career, he steadfastly proclaimed that sexuality is the one and only specific cause of neuroses. "Our observation shows us invariably . . . that the excitations that play this pathogenic part arise from the component instincts of sexual life. The symptoms of neuroses are . . . without exception either a substitutive satisfaction of some sexual urge or measures to prevent such a satisfaction" (Freud, 1940 [1964c], p. 186). Much of the rest of his theorizing was aimed at creating a model that explained how this came about.

He also posited *ego instincts* (Freud, 1940), self-preservation mechanisms that were autonomous from the sexual instinct. Later, followers built on this idea and created a greatly expanded conception of ego functions and development, termed *ego psychology*. Freud later added a *death instinct*, an organically based urge to restore earlier states, the ultimate such state being nonlife or death (Sulloway, 1979). He used this second instinct to account for regression to previously abandoned stages, for the persistence of some neurotic patterns through the repetition compulsion, and for the aggression pervasive in humans.

People innately function to satisfy their instincts, behavior called the *pleasure principle*. However, they had to tame these primitive urges analogous to "domesticating a wild beast", and make them compatible with their social contexts by channeling their expression into socially acceptable forms such as adult heterosexuality and socialized aggression; this is called the *reality principle*. Thus, people's personality was assumed to be shaped by forces acting on them from within and without to which they must react. Different forms of psychopathology resulted from unsuccessful ways of resolving conflicts among internal and external forces and their consequences.

Freud used Haeckel's biogenetic law—that is, ontogeny or individual development recapitulates phylogeny or species development—to justify his proposals about growth. He claimed that each infant traverses in a few years the same sequence of stages of sexuality he proposed to have occurred in the development of the human species over thousands of years (Holt, 1989; Sulloway, 1979). He stated that the seeds of adult psychopathology are sowed when transit through these early sexual developmental stages is unsatisfactory. It followed from these assumptions that humans' functioning and development are caused primarily by their inborn attributes rather than by their contexts.

UNCONSCIOUS PROCESSES AND THE TOPOGRAPHIC MODEL

The psychology of Freud's time equated thought with consciousness. In contrast, Freud assumed that dream symbolism, conscious thought, and behavior were surface forms, or manifest content, of underlying psychological functioning, or latent content. His objective was to discover the instinctually based, unconscious psychological processes lying behind conscious content. He assumed these to be the true causes of behavior, particularly dysfunctional behavior. To understand people's behavior, psychoanalysts must dig below the surface to psychological layers established early in life. This psychic determinism asserts that all observable behavior (e.g., symptoms) represents adaptations to or consequences of dynamic unconscious processes; all behavior is meaningful in some way. Symptoms manifest underlying compromise formations that use unconscious defenses to control unconscious, instinctually based sexual wishes. Depth psychology refers to unconscious causes that are fundamentally old and buried. Like good machines, people are unaware of the forces driving their behavior.

He proposed that *perceptual processes (PCPT)* reflected stimulation from inner or outer sources. Perceptual stimulation produces psychological products within processes bridging between unconscious and conscious functioning, called *preconscious (PCS)*. The contents of *unconscious (UCS)* functioning are available to *consciousness (CS)* only if they become part of the preconscious through inner-directed perception. At any given moment, the contents of consciousness are a selective sample of all that is available for potential use within the preconscious. (This sounds somewhat similar to the modern concept of working memory.)

The organization and dynamics of unconscious primary process and conscious secondary process thought were assumed to be different. Holt (1989) notes that this idea was "something known for centuries: The most logical and clearest thinking occurs in states of full awareness, with active attention to . . . the subject matter; and that thinking becomes most magical and bizarre in dreams, fantasies, and other nonvigilant states of consciousness" (p. 112). Freud said that *primary process thought* functioned to gratify instinctual drives without regard to reality. It is unreflective, irrational, and ungoverned by rules of logic; it follows no orderly time sequences, and tends to be imagistic with contradictory images and ideas coexisting. One image may manifest multiple meanings—called condensation—or may be a neutral substitute for another more distressing one—called displacement. Relationships among images and ideas are fluid and rapidly changeable. *Secondary process thought* functions to inhibit or control unconscious impulsivity through being rational and reflective, logically organized, anchored to reality, and making clear distinctions between past, present, and future. This unconscious, preconscious, and conscious classification of mental phenomena is called Freud's *topographic model* of mental functioning.

PSYCHIC ENERGY AND THE ECONOMIC MODEL

Trained in mid-nineteenth-century science, Freud considered explanations in terms of forces and energies to be the ultimate in scientific explanation (Holt, 1989; Sulloway, 1979). The nervous system was assumed to be passive unless stimulated, so he proposed that instincts exert their motivational influence by creating psychic energy in the nervous system, which functions as a drive. The psychic energy created by humans' sexual instinct he named *libido*. It has an instinctually based organic source, occurs in some quantity that exerts some degree of impetus for activity, and has an aim—appropriate satisfaction of the drive. The aim, however, can be realized only through linkage to some appropriate object—aspects of self or others.

Early in his theorizing, Freud adopted the widely accepted *principle of constancy:* "The nervous system endeavors to keep constant something in its functional relations that we may describe as the 'sum of excitation.' It puts this precondition of health into effect by disposing associatively of every sensible accretion of excitation or by discharging it by an appropriate motor reaction" (Freud, 1892 [1940], p. 154). He proposed that psychic energy motivated behavior: Increases in excitation are unpleasurable and decreases pleasurable (similar to the idea of drive reduction popular in psychological learning theory until the 1960s). His theorizing focused on how unconscious and conscious thought processes controlled this energy. He argued that all facets of personality, pathology, and activity—such as private thoughts; interpersonal interactions; and artistic, societal, and cultural creations—were direct or indirect expressions of instinctually based drives, primarily sexual, and their neutralization and transformation through reality-focused conscious secondary process thoughts, later called ego functions.

Quantities of psychic energy, called *cathexes,* can be discharged through actions, or controlled, inhibited, or neutralized by becoming cathected to psychic structures—organized patterns of thought—called *bound cathexes.* These are all intrapsychic phenomena, so libido does not become bound to people but to memories, thoughts, and fantasies about them. The larger the cathexis, the more powerful its potential influence on psychic structures and related behaviors, providing variations in intensity of unconscious motivation for thought and action. There is a limited amount of instinctually based psychic energy—libido. Unbound or uncontrolled libido (*free cathexes*) produces the conscious experience of anxiety, thus controlling psychic energy with thoughts and beliefs he considered essential for mental health. In primary process thought, this drive energy is manifested psychologically as an unconscious *wish,* a cognitive-affective concept representing a combination of meanings and pleasant or unpleasant outcomes of potential actions. Drive energy shifts automatically from idea to idea, pressing for immediate satisfaction—*the pleasure principle* (Freud, 1900 [1953a]).

One type of psychic energy can only be controlled by another, so to explain adaptive, purposive (secondary process) thought, Freud proposed another type of energy: Biologically based drive cathexes, manifested as unconscious wishes and experienced consciously as pleasurable or unpleasurable affect can be controlled by a mobile, manipulable energy of attention and consciousness, which he called *hypercathexis* (Freud, 1895a [1966], 1900 [1953a], 1923 [1961b]; Holt, 1989). Selective use of hypercathexis or selective attention enables people to do several things consciously: (1) They can inhibit their drive cathexes and make them focally conscious. Through attention cathexis, or logical, reality-oriented thinking (secondary process), they can produce a socially acceptable way of satisfying these drives—called *sublimation* or normal adaptation. (2) People can inhibit their discharge and access to consciousness, called *countercathexis* or *anticathexis*. Blocking the disturbing influence of uncontrolled cathexes from consciousness he called *repression*. This energy-based rationale is called Freud's *economic model* of psychic functioning.

Thus, Freud proposed that selective attention performs an organizing function to produce coherent, consciously self-controlled thought and action to satisfy motives in socially acceptable ways. Psychopathology results when this process is ineffective:

> We have found that one of the earliest and most important functions of the mental apparatus is to bind the instinctual impulses which impinge on it, to replace the primary process prevailing in them by the secondary process and convert their freely mobile cathetic energy into a mainly quiescent (tonic) cathexis. While this transformation is taking place no attention can be paid to the development of unpleasure; but . . . the transformation occurs on behalf of the pleasure principle; the binding is a preparatory act which . . . would be a preliminary function designed to prepare the excitation for its final elimination in the pleasure of discharge. (Freud, 1920 [1955a], p. 62)

What kind of mental apparatus could do this? His tripartite model answers that question.

Id, Ego, Superego, and the Structural Model

Freud's concept of structure is used with multiple meanings, like many of his concepts (Holt, 1989). Its defining feature is *organization*, but organizations can be composed of different kinds of parts. Any specific pattern of functioning is referred to by psychoanalysts as a *structure*—such as a specific pattern of thought, perception, or action. A second meaning is a consistent pattern or habit of psychological functioning that may include different kinds of content—for example, defense mechanisms. Such habits and specific instances of their occurrence may both be considered structures. A third meaning is a function by which different kinds of psychological and behavioral habits may be generated. Freud's concepts of id, superego, and ego are best thought of as groups of functions (Rubenstein, 1967) that operate on different kinds of content.

Freud's concept of id ("it") represents the biological basis of psychological functioning and includes humans' instinctually based psychic energies and processes by which they exert their influence on psychological and behavioral functioning. It is the source of all passions, the biologically innate in humans, and contains the core of the unconscious (Freud, 1923 [1961b]). It is "a chaos, a cauldron full of seething excitations, has no organization, produces . . . only a striving to bring about the satisfaction of the instinctual needs" (Freud, 1933 [1964b], p. 73). There is no concept of time; it operates by the rules of primary process thought. "The id . . . knows no judgments of value; no good and evil, no morality. . . . Instinctual cathexes seeking discharge—that, in our view, is all there is in the id" (p. 74). He assumed that ego and superego both developed out of the instinctually based, unconscious biological matrix of the id (Freud, 1923 [1961b]). He linked his topographic and structural models by proposing that their development from id functions meant that some ego and superego aspects could also function unconsciously. (Id functions appear somewhat analogous to some ideas in modern behavior genetics and sociobiology and to the biological components of our comparative framework.)

The concept of superego was created to represent self-regulating functioning, including self-observation, conscious maintaining of ideals, moral restraint, and standard setting (Freud, 1933 [1964b]). (This is similar to the regulatory function of the comparative framework used here.) It specifies both what one should not do and be, and what one should do and be. These functions have two developmental roots—one innate and the other learned. Based on his Lamarckian view of evolution and his adoption of the biogenetic principle, Freud (1923 [1961b]) proposed that conscience and other moral values were acquired phylogenetically out of the father-complex and had the same instinctual base as the oedipus complex. Building on this instinctual base, superego development is also influenced by the child's identification with parental authority, primarily the father who is the major source of prohibition of incestuous impulses. By learning and adopting parental values—identifying with their superego—the child successfully resolves the oedipus complex. As Freud put it, the superego is the heir to the oedipus complex (Freud, 1923 [1961b]). Its instinctual basis produces what he termed primal repressions, but its learned elaboration made possible learned or secondary repressions.

Freud (1923 [1961b]) described the ego as that part of the id "modified by the direct influence of the external world" by the influence of the "Pcpt-Cs (perception-consciousness)." It is "a coherent organization of mental processes" that regulate "the drives and adapt to reality" (p. 17). He preferred the German *Ich* to the term *ego* because it connoted self-observation. His elaboration of this concept came rather late in his career because it represents conscious control of behavior and he was trying to understand unconscious determinants (Holt, 1989).

Ego functions include monitoring and coordinating its constituent processes, controlling and organizing conscious thought (learning, thinking, memory), managing reality, controlling motility, and delaying motor discharge. Their operation manifests the rules of secondary process thought and the reality principle. The ego develops from "perceiving" and "obeying" instincts to "controlling" and "inhibiting" them; it stands for reason and "good sense" while the id stands for the "untamed passions" (Freud, 1933 [1964b]). (Note Freud's penchant for discussing groups of functions as if they were decision-making, action-performing entities. Such anthropomorphic reification carries seriously misleading implications.) Ego instincts provide an energy source that can oppose and control the drive energy of the id and the almost omnipotent pleasure principle (Freud, 1914 [1957c]) His concept of ego encompasses processes referred to in modern cognitive science as remembering, reasoning, problem solving, decision making, intelligence, and motor control (called control functions in the comparative framework used here).

His mechanistic assumptions led to his describing ego in passive, reactive terms "as a poor creature owing service to three masters and consequently menaced by three dangers: from the external world, from the libido of the id, and from the severity of the superego" (Freud, 1923 [1961b], p. 56). He implied some autonomy of ego from id functions by referring to individual differences in innate rudiments of the ego and the use of reality-based ideas and hypercathexes or selective attention as a means for controlling instinctual impulses and their affective manifestations, and behavior (Freud, 1957 [1964a]). Later, ego psychologists elaborated on these ideas, describing ego functions as a source of self-control and personal agency.

PROPOSITIONS ABOUT DEVELOPMENT

From the beginning, Freud (1895 [1954a]) sought to link normal and abnormal processes: "Actually, a satisfactory theory of neuropsychotic disturbances is impossible if it cannot be brought into association with clear assumptions about normal mental processes" (p. 120). Freud assumed that infant and early childhood development shapes adult personality—as the twig is bent, so the tree shall grow. He (1905 [1953b]) proposed that the sexual instinct has two aspects, the development of each of which could be traced. "Let us call the person from whom sexual attraction proceeds the *sexual object* and the act towards which the instinct tends the *sexual aim*" (p. 135). In infancy, the sexual instinct needs no object, but soon component instincts appear which "from the very first involve other people as objects" (p. 191). This is the origin of the concept of *object relations*. He asserted that people's sexual life emerges in two waves. The first wave reaches its peak when a person is five to six years of age. Then there is a period of latency followed by the second wave at the time of puberty (Freud, 1905 [1953b]). He assumed that this manifested an evolutionary pattern in which the human species descended from an animal that originally reached sexual maturity at the age of five. However, as humans evolved, alterations in patterns of social and sexual relations became adaptive. Family structures emerged, controlled by a tyrannical, all-powerful father who reserved heterosexual intercourse for himself. Children had to inhibit desires for sexual relations until they became older, producing a sexual latency period. Further evolution limited the father's tyrannical power, and adolescents could safely pursue sexual relations. He assumed that this species-constant developmental pattern of controlled or inhibited sexuality made possible the creation of human civilizations and was repeated in all present-day human psychosexual development (Freud, 1930 [1961a]). He considered this diphasic pattern of sexual development to be the source of all neuroses (Holt, 1979), and he based his developmental theory on it (Freud, 1905 [1953b], 1914, 1915 [1957a]).

The infant's own body is the initial sexual object, and stimulation of its erogenous zones is the instinctual aim, called *autoeroticism*. *Libido* or sexual energy can be released through functioning of these sensitive tissues, with psychosexual development sequentially emphasizing primarily the mouth, anus, and genitals. These continue throughout life as sources of sexual experience, but normally become integrated into mature adult sexuality. Initially, infants do not distinguish between stimulation arising from within and without their bodies, called primary narcissism, or self-love. The mouth is the infant's first source of pleasurable sensations, experienced in the oral phase. The desire to suck is partly the desire for the mother's breast, the first object of sexual desire, and obtaining gratification by eating is the first of a long sequence of mouth-based efforts to obtain sexual satisfaction, called the *oral receptive* phase. As teeth, chewing, and biting emerge during the first year, the child has a more aggressive capability, called the *oral sadistic* phase. Near the end of the first year, the anus becomes an important source of pleasurable sensations, called the *anal-sadistic* phase. Parental efforts at toilet training give this new phase increased emphasis. Around the third or fourth year, the genitals become a major source of pleasurable sensations, called the *phallic* phase. Children become aware of male-female genital differences, value their genitals, and are distressed by any real or imagined threat to them, called *castration fear*. Near the end of his career he dropped the idea of a rigid chronological sequence and noted that these phases may overlap or exist side by side (Freud, 1933 [1964b]).

Ego development and imagistic thought begins during the first year, providing another means of satisfaction (Freud, 1911 [1958b]). Whatever is thought of (wished for) is present in a "hallucinatory" way and wishes become means of gaining satisfaction. Initially, the infant functions as if its mental image were the real thing, and Freud considered this the prototype of all later forms of magical thinking. Infants soon learn, however, that wishing does not make it so and are forced to form conceptions of the real circumstance in the external world and to find ways of influencing them—the reality principle. Memory and remembering processes begin to develop.

Genital-based sexual pleasure combines with children's exploration of the world and their growing cognitive life in a search for other object relations (object = people in psychoanalysis) as sources of sexual gratification. Their first object is the child's own ego, called the narcissistic phase, which later shifts to the same-sex person—a homosexual object choice. Around the fifth year, this first phase of sexual development reaches its climax and activates the instinctually based heterosexual object choice, the parent of the opposite sex; this is called the *oedipus complex*. The child develops a wish for or fantasy of sexual relationships with that parent, which activates anxiety and guilt because of instinctual and learned taboos, and fantasied potential retaliation by the other parent. The child resolves this conflict during normal development by identifying with the same-sex parent, internalizing their values (thereby creating the child's own superego), and adopting masculine or feminine roles as their own, thus controlling or inhibiting the incestuous wish or fantasy. This resolution of the phylogenetically based triangular, mother-father-child oedipal conflict initiates the *latency phase* of psychosexual development in which the search for heterosexual gratification is subordinated to other forms of satisfaction.

The search for satisfying heterosexual relationships is reactivated by the increased intensity of the instinctual sex drive during puberty. If each psychosexual phase proceeds smoothly and the oedipus complex is adequately resolved, the adolescent has developed the rudiments of behavior patterns necessary for adult heterosexual relationships. These patterns are then more fully developed, leading to a mature, socially acceptable heterosexual *object choice* as an adult. It is important to recognize that Freud's model of development assigns a critical role to interpersonal relationships—relationships with parents during infancy and early childhood. However, he interprets their importance to be as objects of instinctual and drive gratification or frustration rather than as sources of healthy or pathological learning and socialization.

FIXATION AND REGRESSION

In each psychosexual stage there are prototypic patterns of behaving and of interpersonal (object) relations. Children usually integrate the preceding and new patterns as they move through these developmental stages and emerge with an adult synthesis of patterns learned at each stage. If children experience excessive anxiety during transitions from one psychosexual stage to the next, however, they may control the anxiety by continuing to rely on old habits rather than developing the patterns relevant to the next stage. This reliance on past patterns is called *fixation.* During a period of intense anxiety in later life, a person may revert to using patterns learned in an earlier stage, behavior called *regression.* For Freudians, the concepts of fixation and regression "are the explanatory key of psychopathology" (Etchegoyen, 1991, p. 541).

CHARACTER TYPES

People develop habitual ways of repressing, channeling, and sublimating sexual impulses; these various ways produce different personality types. Freud used his concept of fixation to identify several character types, reflecting his basic view that all forms of dysfunctional patterns can be traced back to unsatisfactory developmental transitions in infancy and early childhood.

Prototypic oral phase actions are eating and mouthing objects and having a dependent, trusting relationship with the mother. Fixation at this phase produces an adult *oral receptive character.* Such people are typified by a dependent, incorporating, or taking-in relationship to the world; they expect it to nurture and care for them. They have an attitude of friendliness and generosity, and beliefs that things will turn out all right without special effort by them. Their adult personality manifests a passive, helpless, but affectionate and friendly pattern. When children first get teeth, they can chew and bite; Freud interpreted this as the first manifestation of an aggressive and destructive way of relating to the world. Fixation at this phase was said to produce an adult *oral sadistic character,* manifesting aggressive, exploitive behavior, envy, ambition, rivalry, and anger. Fixation at the anal-sadistic phase, during which children must learn to control their eliminative processes, results in an adult *anal-*

retentive character. This character pattern is described as hostile, obstinate, possessive, stingy, untidy or meticulous, self-centered, destructive, fearful of throwing anything away, and often unproductive. This questionable strategy of generalizing by analogy from a physical act to a highly generalized personality style, such as biting-destruction-aggression, is typical of Freud. These character types significantly influenced formal psychiatric diagnosis. Prior to DSM-IV (APA, 1994), descriptions of various personality disorders in that manual were conceptual descendants of psychoanalytic character patterns.

Conceptual-Propositional Elaborations Typifying Contemporary Traditional Psychoanalysis

Freud initially used a reactive organism or mechanistic model: People are driven by instinctual drives and unconscious processes competing with contextual demands. Personality and psychopathology evolved as compromises among these competing influences. Introduction of the concepts of ego and superego in his structural model opened the door to an emphasis on proactive aspects of humans—their self-organizing, self-constructing, self-directing, and self-regulating capabilities—and of the influence of learning on development. Since 1923, theoretical elaborations of ego functions have been extensive, and traditional psychoanalysis now relies heavily on ego psychology (Fine, 1979; Mishne 1993). Learning was combined with instinct as the dominant influences on personality development. Freud's model of development emphasized movement from drive primacy to drive taming, and from self-love (narcissism) to interpersonal (object) love. Ego analysts emphasized movement from dependence to autonomy.

First, key ideas of pioneering ego psychologists (Anna Freud, 1936; Hartmann, 1958; Kris, 1951; Lowenstein, 1953; Rapaport, 1951; Erikson, 1950) are summarized. Then, more recent elaborations are considered, illustrated by Cramer (1991), Gabbard (1994), Greenspan (1989), and Weiss and Sampson (1986). Heinz Hartmann is considered the father of modern ego psychology (Mishne, 1993) because he introduced most of the key ideas. Thorough summaries, with extensive citations, may be found in Blanck and Blanck (1974, 1979), Etchegoyen (1991), Fine (1979), Ford and Urban (1963), Mishne (1993), and Yankelovich and Barrett (1970).

Hartmann, one of Freud's favorite pupils, had as his aim the fulfilling of Freud's hopes to establish a general psychoanalytic psychology (Lowenstein, 1966). He presented his ideas as extending rather than modifying Freud's views. That greatly facilitated their rapid acceptance in mainstream psychoanalysis. He assumed that humans begin life with an inborn biological base which, through maturational differentiation and elaboration, produces two groups of functions: (1) biologically based instinctual drives, their affective manifestations, and their dynamics (id); and (2) inborn capacities for learning from environmental interactions and subjective experience which he called primary autonomous functions of the ego or apparatuses of primary autonomy. These function to enable people to create and organize increasingly complex behaviors for effectively dealing with their contexts, called adaptation.

Inborn Autonomous Ego Functions
Inborn ego functions include sensory-perceptual, sensory-motor, consciousness, attention, cognitive and remembering processes, and capabilities for constructing representations and complex behaviors. This is similar to the directive, control, and information monitoring and processing functions of the comparative framework.

Inborn self-organizing and self-constructing functions are implied by phrases like "the synthetic, integrating, or organizing function," "the coordination and integration of experience and behavior," "centralization of functional control," "and "achieving solutions and directing actions." Anticipatory functioning is stressed as a basis for proactive, future-oriented behavior. There are several innate mechanisms for establishing and maintaining equilibrium among biological, psychological, behavioral, and environmental components, and that is the function of behavior (Hartmann, 1958). These ideas appear similar to the principle of unitary functioning and feedback and feedforward processes in our comparative framework. Effective operation of the "synthetic function of the ego" is a crucial characteristic of good adjustment: Play becomes freer, health better, sex more mature, and work more meaningful (Erikson, 1946).

Most behavior is intentionally directed toward consciously selected consequences that is, it is goal directed, and has gratifications unrelated to or far removed from instinctual drives. The mastery of difficulties, problem solving, and thinking all yield gratifications of their own (Hartmann, Kris, & Lowenstein, 1946). Hartmann brought Freud's concept of instinctual drives into the service of autonomous ego functioning by broadening the idea of sublimation into neutralization, or transforming instinctual sexual and aggressive energies to noninstinctual forms. The operation of autonomous ego functions yields learning of diverse behavior patterns, not as compromise formations to deal with intrapsychic conflicts as Freud emphasized, but as adaptations for obtaining gratifications through transactions with contexts, called the conflict-free sphere of ego functioning. Moreover, a person may even intentionally resort to using imagistic, childlike, less rational forms of thought or primary process as an adaptive tool; e.g., in creative activities, this behavior is called *regression in the service of the ego*.

Ego and Superego

Freud's concept of superego as special types of evaluative thoughts with the power to elicit emotional reactions is retained in ego psychology. Once initially established through resolution of the oedipus complex, this group of anticipatory evaluative thoughts is extensively elaborated through learning. Moreover, superego normal functioning "is constantly bound to certain activities of the ego and the further evolution of the superego does not diminish the developing ego's influence, but tends to increase it" (Hartmann & Lowenstein, 1962, p. 64). As in the comparative framework, the regulatory function or superego collaborates with adaptive directive and control function cognitive activity ego to produce effective, unitary functioning.

This elaboration of ego-superego functions and relationships rounds out the picture of human nature created by psychoanalysis to include both mechanistic, reactive organism assumptions of automatic behaviors produced by unconscious processes, and proactive organism assumptions of flexible instrumental behaviors initiated and learned through conscious, intentional, thoughtful planning and action. Reconciling the relation between these two seemingly contradictory views has been a persistent theoretical problem. Freud's emphasis on conflict-based functioning is supplemented by adaptive learning as an alternate pathway to development. The elaboration of ego functioning encompasses most of what the discipline of psychology studies and therefore provides a potential bridge between psychology and psychoanalysis. Freud's erroneous evolutionary biology view has been largely abandoned, resulting in a deemphasis of instinct theory. "Adherence to the idea of the centrality of infantile sexuality is no longer universal" (Abend, 1990b, p. 544). The concept of drive is still used but in more limited form. The idea of psychic energy is now largely ignored, and there is greater emphasis on the motivational influence of emotions, but psychoanalysts have not yet constructed a theory of emotions. The dynamics of conflict are still given prominence but more as products of learning than of instincts.

Examples of Contemporary Elaborations of Ego Psychology

Current psychoanalytic theory includes diverse elaborations of ego psychology ideas. Weiss and Sampson (1986) and colleagues describe a version they are subjecting to empirical evaluation. Freud's idea that most unconscious mental life results from psychic forces beyond people's control and without influence from their beliefs, thoughts, or appraisals of reality they call *the automatic functioning hypothesis.* This view has dominated traditional psychoanalysis. Weiss and Sampson contrast it with the idea that ego and superego functions play a key role in normal and pathological functioning, termed the *higher mental functioning hypothesis,* first discussed by Freud late in his career (Freud, 1940). It asserts that people may construct *pathogenic beliefs* that anticipate possible dangerous future events; activate distressing emotions such as fear, anxiety, shame, or guilt; and lead to learned ways of preventing the occurrence of pathogenic belief that produces distressing emotion patterns.

In Freudian terms, this is a pattern of ego ↔ superego functioning. Such patterns may become habitual, similar to a behavior episode schema in the comparative framework, and function unconsciously. It is a learned, habitual avoidance pattern. As a result, people may not do what they consciously would like to do, or may do things they consciously do not want to do. Pathogenic beliefs are not wishes or fantasies; they are grim and constricting and linked to reality. Because they are learned, many kinds of pathogenic beliefs in addition to sexual ones are possible. They are simple and compelling; once learned, they are difficult to change because people avoid experiencing disconfirming events. As ego and superego functions, however, they are potentially subject to a person's conscious control. By learning, a person can alter what he or she has learned.

Cramer (1991) interprets defense mechanisms and defensive behaviors as learned patterns or ego functions for dealing with distressing experiences (analogous to stability-maintaining processes in our comparative framework). Because distressing experiences are part of normal living, learning defensive strategies for dealing with them is part of normal development. Her proposals involve two types of development. First, from infancy through adulthood people's ego functioning and cognitive capabilities elaborate. The kinds of defensive behaviors of which people are capable will vary with their level of ego development. Different kinds of defense mechanisms are likely to be learned at different stages of development. Second, defenses do not emerge in full flower; they are learned strategies for coping with distressing experiences, and such learning results from multiple episodes. Defense mechanisms are adaptive strategies that display a developmental pattern. It is the nature of the way the defensive strategy is used to serve the larger pattern that determines whether it is considered pathological.

Vailliant (1993) links ego functions to mature, resilient functioning, analogous to the immune system. "Resilience conveys both the capacity to be bent without breaking and the capacity, once bent, to spring back . . . I like the definition . . . 'The self-righting tendencies within the human organism' "

(p. 184). This is similar to the concept of stability-maintaining processes in our comparative framework.

Examples of Elaborations of Developmental Propositions

The ego psychology theory of development differs in two key ways from Freud's. His developmental phases emphasize inborn maturational processes based on instinctual drives. Ego psychology acknowledges maturational influences but stresses learning as the primary source of development. Moreover, because learning can occur at any time, at least some kinds of development can occur throughout life. What happens in infancy and childhood is important, but it can be significantly modified through learning. The earliest developmental stages result from innate maturational sequences, but these quickly produce functional capabilities that infants immediately begin to use. Hartmann argued that infants are born into an *average expectable environment,* and each begins adapting to the other immediately, similar to the person-in-context unit of the comparative framework. For example, as infants' sensory-perceptual, sensory-motor, and cognitive capabilities emerge, they begin discriminating between themselves and their contexts, to anticipate future events such as being fed, and to direct attention and actions toward their contexts as well as themselves. They begin to construct habitual patterns of interaction with their contexts, producing the first object attachments. They form simple mental representations and then use them as memories and for organizing intentional behavior. As their ego function capabilities elaborate, they build increasingly complex cognitive, emotional, and behavioral patterns. Gradually an adult personality emerges, elaborates, and is modified across the life span.

Using the concept of ego identity and the ego's synthesizing function, Erikson (1946, 1950) created a stage model that emphasized people's lifelong efforts to create a coherent organization of their many and often contradictory representations of themselves, their relationships with others, and their ethnic, racial, religious, communal, and cultural identifications to produce a sense of continuity and persistent sameness of self (Erikson, 1956). Life involves a series of developmental challenges and transitions, so Erikson used embryology's epigenetic model as an analogy—that body organs develop in a fixed sequence. He extended this model into psychosocial development, proposing an orderly, maturationally emerging universal set of eight developmental tasks and related stages of development, adding adolescence, young adulthood, maturity, and old age to Freud's psychosexual and latency stages. The tasks and stages are universal, but each person's resolution of them may differ because of the influence of their social and cultural context. If a task and stage is inadequately resolved, it remains a point of arrest and may be partially worked through at a later point in development. His ideas have had more influence in social work and developmental psychology than in psychoanalysis.

Greenspan (1989) created a six-stage model of ego development in infancy and early childhood based on the idea of levels of ego organization. The capacity to organize experience is assumed to be present very early in life and increases with maturation. As a result, the complexity of ego organization of which the infant/child is capable emerges in phases. Greenspan proposes two basic types of experience: (1) sensory, involving contextual experience, and (2) affective-thematic, involving subjective experience of affects-meanings. Prototypic experiences must be organized in each phase. Infants initially directly organize both types of experience. Development proceeds from that base "to a higher plane, that of representation." Sensory and affective-thematic patterns are interpreted or labeled. Next, elaboration and differentiation of representations "create the basis for internal life to be symbolized and categorized along dimensions of self and nonself, affective meanings, time, and space." This provides the basis "for basic ego functions, new relationship patterns, relatively more differentiated and internalized conflicts, higher level defenses, and psycho-sexual advances" (p. 63).

Two early developments have special significance. Children begin experiencing themselves as a cause, creating a basis for the emergence of self-directed behavior and a sense of personal agency. They also begin to understand interpersonal communications and to use them to regulate interpersonal relationships. Affective experiences in social interactions are especially important in early development, and affective gestural communications play an important role. Greenspan (1989) assumes that increasingly complex patterns of functioning develop through three types of learning: (1) somatic learning—development of biological patterns such as sleep-wake cycles, arousal patterns, and body rhythms; (2) consequence-behavioral learning—development of person-context behavior patterns through processes like operant conditioning; and (3) representational/structural learning—the formation and organization of mental imagery and symbols into configurations that make possible thinking and cognitive problem solving. Individual differences in developmental patterns appear as a result of differences in ego capabilities and the contexts of learning.

DYSFUNCTIONAL PATTERNS OF DEVELOPMENT AND PSYCHOPATHOLOGY

Freud sought to answer two questions about psychopathology: (1) By what processes are neuroses (and later psychoses) produced? (2) Why do neuroses take different forms?

Processes Producing Psychopathology

Freud proposed that the process was the same regardless of the form of psychopathology. All persistent patterns of functioning result from conflict. Powerful unconscious forces seeking expression are continually monitored by opposing forces to prevent or control the form of their expression. Pathology results when (1) conscious thought—ego or secondary process—inadequately channels drive energy under constraints imposed by superego and ego/reality influences to satisfy wish fulfillment, and (2) drive-dominated processes operate unconsciously—id or primary process—to produce regression to infantile modes of functioning, psychic distress, and wish fulfillment in which fantasy rather than reality is the key source of satisfaction. "An invariable and indispensable precondition of every onset of a psychoneurosis is the process to which . . . the portion of the libido which is capable of becoming conscious and is directed towards reality is diminished, and the portion that is directed away from reality and is unconscious . . . is proportionately increased" (Freud, 1912b [1958c], p. 102).

Freud's basic formula was that *all neuroses and psychoses involve a defense against unbearable ideas* (Freud, 1924a, b [1961c]). This is called his conflict theory. He stated the conflict in different ways as his theory evolved: (1) an instinctually based wish and a defense against it; (2) an impulse opposed by awareness of reality contingencies; (3) conflicts among psychic agencies, such as the id, ego, and superego.

The way ego functions relate to reality determines whether a neurosis or psychosis results. Neurotic patterns result under these conditions: The defense involves ego functions or cognitive strategies for inhibiting or channeling id impulses and unconscious wishes to conform to the demands/constraints of superego influences, or evaluative thoughts, and ego influences, or reality-based ideas (Freud, 1924a [1961d]). In psychoses the withdrawal from reality is much greater; ego functions reject the nature of reality and create "a new external and internal world" that "is constructed in accordance with the id's wishful impulses" and "the motive for this dissociation from the external world is some very serious frustration by reality of a wish—a frustration which seems intolerable" (Freud, 1924a [1961d], p. 151). Psychotic symptoms reflect the nature of the artificial reality created.

Unbearable Ideas

At first, Freud assumed that the unbearable ideas were memories of real experiences, such as childhood sexual abuse by parents; he called this his trauma theory. However, he soon decided that the unbearable ideas represented imaginary rather than real events, i.e., were childhood fantasies or wishes. Later, as he tried to understand aggression and soldiers' persistent neuroses based in battle experiences, his trauma theory reemerged. However, he continued to assume that it was unbearable ideas, whether they were traumatic memories or fantasied events, that were the source of neuroses; the conflict is intrapsychic, not contextual.

Distressing Emotions

What distinguishes unbearable ideas from other ideas? They arouse distressing emotions. Emotions played an important role in psychoanalytic theory from the beginning, but Freud never proposed a theory of emotions. Affects he mentioned include love, pleasure, anxiety, fear, guilt, shame, hate, anger, and painful affect. Anxiety, however, is the only one he discussed extensively. Emotions, feelings, and affects link id and ego functioning because they are always conscious (Freud, 1915 [1958c]).

Freud proposed that unbearable ideas are unconscious wishes and meanings that represent forbidden modes of sexual expression and relationships; therefore, they are potential threats to the person's welfare if they become conscious and are implemented. As an example, castration threats and oedipal anxieties derive their terrifying force from phylogenetic residues of actual deeds. He postulated an inborn anticipatory reaction to danger that became manifest as a conscious state of anxiety and served as a signal that danger threatens, so he called it *signal anxiety* (Freud, 1926 [1959]). It indicates that a conflict exists between id impulses and ego controls. Later, he recognized the importance of guilt, depression, and hostility in some neuroses. He considered these manifestations of conflict between id impulses and the regulatory or punishing functioning of the superego—an id-superego conflict. They too signal dangerous conditions, but of a different type. Both represent approach-avoidance conflicts. The person wants to fulfill the unconscious wish—the pleasure principle—but also wants to avoid the anticipated undesirable consequences and distressing affects—the reality principle.

Defense Against Unbearable Ideas and Distressing Emotions

How can such dangers and distressing affects be avoided? Ego functions or thoughts directed with selective attention—hypercathexis—serve to inhibit conscious expression of forbidden ideas and to channel them into more acceptable forms. Defensive thought processes are unconscious, so people are unaware of the intrapsychic conflict, but are aware of observable manifestations or symptoms. Different strategies of thought, interpretation, and action, called defense mechanisms, serve to inhibit and control distressing manifestations (Freud, 1926 [1959]). The term *mechanism* represents an inferred habitual pattern; the actual behaviors that manifest a strategy are called *resistance* or defensive behaviors. In his structural model, they are unconscious aspects of ego functioning.

The basic defensive process is *repression*, or motivated forgetting. This results from an innate tendency to forget painful experiences, particularly in childhood. Freud (1914b [1957c]) considered it the cornerstone on which the whole structure of psychoanalysis rests. One way people avoid distressing affects such as anxiety or guilt is to avoid situations that produce them. Freud argued that when thoughts rather than events are the cause, the same process operates: Prevent the thoughts from occurring by response substitution—think other thoughts and perform other actions instead. *Primal repression* uses instinctually based responses; *secondary repression* uses learned responses (Freud, 1919 [1955b]). Most defense mechanisms function as different types of response substitution.

Anna Freud (1936) described different strategies. *Acting out* is a repetitive, compulsive action that functions to resolve a repressed psychological conflict by external means, often in the form of aggressive behavior toward self or others. *Compromise* is thoughts and actions that are substituted to make possible some indirect expression of the threatening ideas. *Displacement* is a form of compromise in which the forbidden impulse is expressed toward a substitute object: A woman expresses anger created by her husband at herself or children instead. In *sublimation*, forbidden impulses are expressed in some constructive and socially approved form such as artistic activity. *Denial* is a rejection of reality; thoughts/assertions that distressing ideas and events do not exist or did not occur are substituted for forbidden impulses such as "I don't hate my father." *Identification-introjection* occurs when a person's distressing thoughts and wishes about a parent are neutralized by the person's becoming like the parent, thereby rendering the parent harmless. Identifying with the threatening father and introjecting his values is the process proposed to establish the initial core of the superego. *Rationalization* involves using false explanations for the occurrence of forbidden ideas or behavior to prevent noxious emotions or consequences: "I was sleepwalking when I stole your money." In *Reaction formation*, responses are substituted for the forbidden ones that are their exact opposite; people prevent guilt by substituting loving thoughts and actions for hateful ones. *Projection* involves casting one's private devils out into the world, by attributing the forbidden ideas and impulses to someone else; instead of thinking "I am a bad person," the individual may think, "Other people are trying to persecute me." In *splitting or isolation*, distress is controlled by actively separating ideas from related, distressing affects, or by separating cognitions with opposite meanings—separating the beliefs that mother is pleasurable, good, and rewarding from beliefs that she is painful, bad, or punishing. With *undoing,* one symbolic act follows another with the opposite meaning as if to cancel the first one. It suggests, "that was not my intent."

The pattern of relationships among unacceptable impulses, ideas, and distressing affects and their controlling thoughts and interpretations Freud called a *compromise formation* because it was a compromise between what the id "wanted," what the superego "would approve," and what the ego and its interpretation of reality "would permit." *Neurotic and psychotic symptoms* represent compromise formations that persist because they make provision for both aspects of the conflict—the prohibited impulse and the defensive strategy used—even though they are only partly effective. This is similar to the interpretation of symptom syndromes of any disease; some symptoms manifest the disease itself, such as pain, and others the body's efforts to overcome the disease, such as increases in white blood cells. Symptoms persist because they produce two desirable consequences: (1) They ease the distressing affect, called *primary gain;* and (2) they produce nurturance from others or some escape from normal activities, called *secondary gain.*

Choice of the Form of Neurosis: Regression
The issue of how the same pathological process could result in different forms of psychoneurosis preoccupied Freud to the end of his career. He had adopted three basic assumptions by 1899: (1) The etiology of neurosis is always sexual and represents a repressed perversion: (2) The various forms of neurosis can be explained as a genetic (developmental) series: (3) Neurotic regressions to infantile libidinal stages mimic the archaic sexual patterns of humans' remote ancestors (Sulloway, 1979).

Two problems remained: Regression to what infantile sexual stage typifies each type of neurosis? What determines fixation at one stage rather than another, and a later regression to that stage? Freud (1916–17 [1963]) proposed three interacting causes: (1) Inborn psychosexual stages of development and individual differences in vulnerability to them are phylogenetically determined. (2) Infantile experiences of intense sexual conflict produce fixation at one of those stages. (3) Stressful experiences in adult life result in an inherent biological tendency toward regression to a fixated psychosexual stage. Adult experiences are stressful for neurotic people precisely because of their intense, repressed sexual conflict; that is why these individuals break down in the face of the same difficulties normal people successfully overcome (Freud, 1926 [1959]).

The form the neurosis assumes is determined by characteristics of the stage of fixation to which the person regresses and the related modes of secondary defense used, such as projection or repression. Freud linked four forms of neurosis to different stages:

dementia-praecox = autoerotic stage
paranoia = narcissistic-homosexual stage
obsessional neurosis = anal-sadistic stage
hysteria = phallic stage

His model of psychopathology was socially significant in two ways: (1) He asserted that neuroses were a potentially correctable psychological problem rather than a form of hereditary degeneracy or malingering. (2) Psychopathology and normalcy differ in degree, not kind, so neurotics and psychotics were restored to a place in society.

Neuroses Have a Developmental History
Not all approach-avoidance conflicts are pathological; only affectively intense ones lead to neuroses (Freud, 1900 [1953a], 1926 [1959]). He asserted that Neuroses (unlike infectious diseases) have no specific determinants; they result from many experiences, not from a single pathogenic factor (Freud, 1940 [1964c]). To understand a neurosis one must ask: What unconscious thoughts are in conflict? What affects are they generating? What cognitive and behavioral strategies are operating to prevent, or reduce the intensity of, the affects and to resolve or control the conflict? Why are they ineffective? Knowledge of the patterns prototypic of each psychosexual stage and of different kinds of defense mechanisms that people use will help the therapist understand the dynamics of each patient's neurosis. This view of psychopathology made formal diagnoses similar to those of medicine inappropriate and unnecessary.

CONTEMPORARY VIEWS OF PSYCHOPATHOLOGY

Two elaborations or modifications of Freud's assumptions about psychopathology have emerged. First, while the conflict model is still influential, the nature of the unbearable ideas that can distress people has been elaborated through ego psychology's emphasis on learned behavior. For Freud, the unbearable ideas were fantasies or wishes manifesting instinctual sexual or aggressive drives. Ego psychology legitimized the view that other kinds of pathogenic beliefs could be learned and provide a basis for psychopathology (Weiss & Sampson, 1986).

Second, ego psychology produced an alternate model; psychopathology may result from a weak ego (Fine, 1979), sometimes called a *deficit model* (Mishne, 1993). Ego psychology emphasizes development of people's capa-

bility for adaptation and for creating and maintaining coherent personality organization. Weaknesses in these capabilities make people vulnerable to development of pathological states. Ego weaknesses, deficits, or arrests may
occur in two ways. One way is through deficiencies in development. The
ideas, skills, and values people learn by which to manage their lives develop
slowly through experience and may be of limited adaptive value in some
later circumstances; in other cases, essential patterns may not have developed. For example, ego deficits may result in "impaired reality testing, poor
drive modulation, distorted object relations. . . . A paucity of adequate ego defenses explains affect intolerance, impulsivity, and panic states due to fears of
separation, disorganization, and the strength of wishes and impulses. Parallel superego distortions cause impairments in the capacity for internalization, render the individual dependent on external structure and objects as reinforcers" (Mishne, 1993, p. 191). The second way occurs when high levels of
prolonged stress, as in some prisoner of war camps, cannot be managed by
adaptive habits that have been effective in normal life circumstances; stress
may overwhelm adaptive ego functioning.

Greenspan (1989) suggests that maladaptive functioning, at least in early
childhood, results from inadequate mastery and integration of the sequential
levels of ego development. "In order to visualize this approach, picture these
four levels: engagement; purposeful, organized communication; representational elaboration; and representational differentiation. . . . The therapeutic
goal is to help a person function optimally at all levels at once in the context
of the full range of thematic-affective domains" (p. 136).

Gabbard (1994) suggests that different models of psychopathology may
be useful for understanding different kinds of dysfunctional patterns. He proposes that both descriptive and dynamic diagnoses be used with each person.
Descriptive diagnoses relate a patient's dysfunctional pattern to prototypical
patterns based on *DSM-IV* (APA, 1994) criteria. This is the classical medical
model, differential diagnosis approach. Dynamic diagnosis "is diagnosis in
the sense of understanding just how the patient is ill and how ill the patient
is, how he became ill and how his illness serves him" (Menninger, Mayman,
& Pruyser, 1963, p. 6).

FREUD'S PROCEDURAL MODEL:
THERAPY STRATEGIES AND TACTICS

Freud's voluminous writings gave limited attention to intervention; he was
not particularly interested in a theory of therapeutic action (Modell 1990). He
published 15 papers on this topic, mentioned it in only nine others, and de-

cided not to try to write a manual of therapy techniques (Thompson, 1994). His descriptions of specific cases gave additional clues as to methods. His therapy strategies evolved as his clinical experience and theories elaborated. From the beginning, the focus has been on the recovery of repressed memories or unbearable ideas beginning with hypnotic methods—making the unconscious conscious. The content of the memories to be recovered was specified by his instinct/drive theory. Memory recovery required overcoming defenses that kept them repressed, so that was the second key focus of his strategies. A widely accepted definition of traditional psychoanalysis is this: "Psychoanalysis is that technique which, employed by a neutral analyst, results in the development of a regressive transference neurosis and the ultimate resolution of this neurosis by techniques of interpretation alone" (Gill, 1954, p. 775). Grotstein (1996) states that psychoanalysis has suffered the fate of the Tower of Babel myth, but that Etchegoyen (1991) has produced a "monumental" analysis of the "disparate" psychoanalytic approaches, past and present, which should be the state of the art for psychoanalytic technique for years to come. Etchegoyen's volume has been a key source for our own analysis.

STABLE STRATEGIES AND FLEXIBLE METHODS

Freud usually described general strategies for intervention rather than specific tactics or methods. The same strategy can be implemented with different specific methods. The methods used may differ depending on each patient's problems and the phase of therapy, and analysts must implement the general strategies of psychoanalysis by flexibly selecting tactics appropriate for each patient. Freud emphasized the importance in effective psychoanalysis of "tact," "intelligence", and "sound judgment". He stated that the specific methods he described were suited to his personality: He couldn't stand having patients staring at him eight hours a day, so he sat behind them. Others should be flexible and use tactics appropriate to their own personality (Freud, 1912 [1958f]). His rules were "fatherly advice" about flexible, not rigid, tactics (Freud, 1913 [1958d]). Followers, however, turned them into dogma:

> "Recommendations on Technique" I wrote long ago were essentially of a negative nature. I considered the most important thing was to emphasize what one should not do, and to point out the temptations in directions contrary to analysis. Almost everything positive that one should do I have left to "tact." . . . The result was that the docile analysts did not perceive the elasticity of the rules I had laid down, and submitted to them as if they were taboos. (quoted in Jones, 1955, vol. 2, p. 141)

Classical psychoanalysis is thus more rigid in technique than Freud either recommended or practiced.

Four Strategies/Objectives
Freud's theories and four major therapy strategies evolved together in four broad time periods: (1) Make the unconscious conscious (1886–1905). (2) Work through transference and other resistances (1905–1914). (3) Where id was, ego should be (1915–1923). (4) Create optimal ego functioning (1923–1939) (Fine, 1979). This elaboration manifests a progressive expansion of therapy goals from symptom removal to personality reconstruction. It occurred because with his initial approach he found that symptoms disappeared during analysis but often returned after analysis terminated, suggesting that their real causes had not changed. Psychoanalysis is said to differ from other psychotherapies, such as expressive and supportive strategies, because of its objective of basic personality reconstruction through a focus on transference, resistance, and their interpretation to resolve unconscious, intrapsychic conflicts.

STRATEGIES AND METHODS FOR INITIATING PSYCHOANALYSIS

Selecting Clients
Psychoanalysis requires patients to commit lots of time and money. Therefore, Freud considered it unethical to accept a person for treatment if the analyst doubted the client's analyzability. He suggested that people of unreliable character, without sufficient capacity for honesty and candor, those too young or too old or in crisis, and friends might be poor patients. Good patients should have an inquiring mind, an openness to learning, a reasonable degree of education, an ego in touch with reality, and capacity to form a relationship with the analyst. They must be motivated, driven by their suffering and the wish to be cured that arises from it (Freud, 1911 [1958b]). He suggested that a brief "trial analysis" might help both client and analyst make the decision. He considered psychoanalysis appropriate for only certain kinds of neuroses and inappropriate for psychotics because it relies on transference; the artificial reality psychotics construct for themselves obstructs real-life interpersonal interactions.

Others have applied it to a greater diversity of psychopathology, but there is general agreement that psychoanalysis cannot resolve all psychological problems, so some selection criteria are necessary. The greater prominence of psychological over physiological factors, response to previous medical treatment, and type of illness should be considered. The desire of patients to know themselves and their motivation for analysis are decisive. Many consider important the ability to function in terms of the rules of the analytic setting, to form an alliance with the analyst, and to form transference relationships. Environmental factors may also be important, such as a social or family context that will sustain them in the analyst's absence. "A person who is completely alone is always difficult to analyze" (Etchegoyen, 1991, p. 25).

This selection process involves one or more *psychoanalytic interviews*. These differ from treatment sessions in both objectives and methods. They serve to facilitate the interviewee's free expression of his mental processes with the aim of determining whether analysis or some other treatment is appropriate. These interviews should end with recommendations concerning treatment and a brief summary of the reasons for the recommendations (Etchegoyen, 1991).

The Psychoanalytic Situation

Psychoanalytic treatment is accomplished through a carefully designed totality of transactions between analysand and analyst that include the setting and the relationship. These provide an interpersonal field within which the analytic process occurs. The setting is a framework of place, time, and rules of operation that remain constant throughout analysis. This includes a private place, regular frequency and duration of sessions, fees and payment arrangements, and general roles and responsibilities of each participant. The setting should be compatible with the larger cultural milieu—the therapist should observe traditional holidays and other relevant customs. The relationship has three components: transference; countertransference; and therapeutic alliance (Etchegoyen, 1991).

The Psychoanalytic Contract: Agreeing on the Setting, Roles and Responsibilities

The patient and analyst must begin by agreeing on an explicit understanding of the rationale of psychoanalysis and the rules by which their work together will be guided, often called the contract. Understanding what patients are expected to do and what they may and may not expect of the analyst provides the framework within which the psychoanalytic process evolves and can be understood. Patients' difficulties in abiding by the explicit rules such as missing appointments, challenging fees, unwillingness to free associate, can then be understood and interpreted as transference phenomena that reveal attributes of the patient's unconscious conflicts. Many of the rules are explicitly formulated at the beginning; others may not be mentioned until circumstances require them, such as rules about accepting gifts from patients (Etchegoyen, 1991).

Personality reconstruction requires time and intense effort, so Freud suggested meeting daily, except Sundays, for an hour. He said three times a week might be adequate for "slight" cases or during advanced treatment, and more than an hour might sometimes be fruitful. Contemporary analysts typically meet four to five times a week. Patients should pay promptly for every session, including missed ones, to facilitate their commitment to and a sense of responsibility for the activity, and to honor the analyst's need to earn a living.

How long should analysis last? Freud (1913 [1958d]) said that question is almost unanswerable. He noted that initially he tried to persuade patients to stay and later he couldn't get them to leave. He believed that analysis sets in motion forces that can't be predicted or controlled; thus, it may be "interminable" (Freud, 1937 [1964b]). Most of his analyses lasted less than a year; today, five to eight years is typical (Thompson, 1994). Freud emphasized that only patients could change themselves: "The doctor [analyst] has nothing else to do than to wait and let things take their course, a course that cannot be avoided nor always hastened" (Freud, 1914 [1958f], p. 155). One of his patients asked if understanding the dynamics of his childhood history would restore his psychic health. Freud replied it wasn't that simple and said that one can become well, but must want to become well. He used the analogy of buying a ticket that gives one the possibility to travel but one may choose not to travel. His general strategy was to let the patient decide when to terminate.

Selection of Goals

The general goals are implied by Freud's models of pathological and normal functioning, so they are the same for all clients. Pathology results from unconscious conflict among unbearable ideas, related affects, and defenses against them. Conscious, realistic organization and control of affect, thought, and action are the characteristics of well-adjusted people. Therefore, the general goals are to gain conscious control over distressing affects and unconscious conflict and to select or construct more satisfying ways of dealing with them and reality. However, patients must select the specific goals. Only they can identify the nature of their specific conflicts. The analyst may suggest possible new behaviors, but only patients can choose which to substitute for the old ones (Freud, 1916–17 [1963]).

STRATEGIES FOR ACTIVATING AND IDENTIFYING UNCONSCIOUS CONFLICTS AND THEIR CONSEQUENCES

Psychoanalysis requires making the unconscious conscious by bringing the motivating drive cathexes, unconscious wishes, distressing affects, and unconscious defenses under conscious control so they can become organized and controlled by more consciously controllable and adaptive forms of thought and action through the use of selective attention and reality oriented thought which he stated as "where id was, ego should be". The pathological patterns can be modified only when they are actually occurring; nothing can be slain "in absentia" or "in effigy" (Freud, 1912 [1958e]). However, unconscious conflicts and pathological patterns persist because patients have habitual patterns of thought and action that prevent their conscious expression and change. In the terms of the comparative framework, they are functional steady states protected by stability-maintaining processes. Therefore, direct approach to uncovering pathological patterns is not effective. Freud used strategies of free association and transference relationships to activate the troublesome unconscious conflicts.

The Fundamental Rule of Free Association
Freud decided that a key reason people could not solve their own problems was their habits of self-deception; "things are forgotten if one does not wish to remember them because they are painful, ugly or disagreeable, contrary to ethics and/or aesthetics" (Etchegoyen, 1991, p. 9). This motivated forgetting Freud called *repression* and *defense*. He described what is now called an approach-avoidance conflict. On the one hand, transference expresses the impulse and satisfies the pleasure principle, whereas the ego, governed by the reality principle, "tries to inhibit this process to avoid anguish, not to relapse into the traumatic situation" (Etchegoyen, 1991, p. 102). Freud developed the method of *free association* as a way for patients to sneak by their own defensive censorship and to activate in the here and now the pathological conflicts.

> Say whatever goes through your mind. Act as though, for instance, you were a traveler sitting next to the window of a railway carriage and describing to someone inside the carriage the changing views which you see outside. Finally, never forget that you have promised to be absolutely honest, and never leave anything out because, for some reason or other, it is unpleasant to tell it. (Freud, 1913, [1958d], p. 124)

Freud believed that both conscious and unconscious behaviors are highly organized and that by disclosing all thoughts and feelings, including those one usually conceals, unconscious conflicts will spontaneously become activated and work their way into consciousness. This is a difficult rule to follow, as people habitually edit what they say to others and themselves to avoid activating distressing affects and consequences. Adherence to the rule, however, serves two key purposes: (1) It cultivates a patient-analyst relationship based on principles of mutual trust and candor. (2) It is a way to gain access to the content of unconscious conflicts (Thompson, 1994). Dreams are another state in which unconscious conflicts may sneak by repression or defense. Patients are thus told to report dreams and then to free associate to their content (Freud, 1911 [1958b]) as another way of activating pathological patterns with the analyst. The unstructured activity of free association may also stimulate the occurrence of revealing dreams.

Free association produces these results only when used in the context of the traditional analytic situation and contract in which the analyst's activity is minimal so that patients' thoughts and statements are activated by their own dynamics rather than elicited by the analyst's behavior. Patients' free associations are the key source of information on which the analyst's understanding of the patient is based. A few supplementary information eliciting tactics are sometimes used (Etchegoyen, 1991). *Direct questions* may be used to elicit pertinent information or clarifications of patient meanings. *Indication* or *notation* draws patients' attention to something they have said or done and the meaning of which the analyst does not clearly understand. *Confrontation* shows patients two things in counterposition to encourage them to notice a contradiction and face a dilemma. Such tactics should be used cautiously and sparingly because they interrupt the flow of free associations and may change the dynamics of the desired, prototypical analytic context.

The Transference Relationship

The concepts of *transference* and *countertransference* were Freud's way of talking about what others often called the therapy relationship. What is transference? Freud (1912, 1915 [1958a,c,e]) argued that patients behave toward analysts with habitual interpersonal patterns built earlier in life, similar to the concept of the behavior episode schema in the comparative framework. "It must be understood that each individual, through the combined operation of his innate disposition and influences brought to bear on him during his early years, has acquired a specific method of his own in his conduct of his erotic life" (1912 [1958a], p. 99). Transference is a universal, spontaneous phenomenon

> which consists of joining the past with the present through a false connection which superimposes the original object on the present one. This . . . is linked to objects and desires from the past that are not conscious for the subject and that give his conduct an irrational seal, where the affect does not seem appropriate either in quality or quantity to the real, actual situation. (Etchegoyen, 1991, p. 82)

Not all transference is pathological. Seeking gratifying outlets for drives manifesting the sexual instinct is an inborn characteristic; instinctually libido seeks expression through an object; it becomes pathological only when it occurs in the service of the neurosis. Therefore, Freud subdivided habitual interpersonal patterns occurring in analysis into three types:

> Thus the solution of the puzzle is that transference to the doctor is suitable for resistance to the treatment only in so far as it is a negative transference or a positive transference of repressed erotic impulses. If we "remove" the transference by making it conscious, we are detaching only these two components. . . . The other component, which is admissible to consciousness and unobjectionable, persists and is the vehicle of success." (Freud, 1912 [1958a], p. 101)

Negative and positive are identified in terms of the affect involved, whether it is anger, anxiety, or sexual desire.

Negative and erotic positive transferences are manifestations of pathological patterns to be modified; that is, patients may feel and behave toward analysts with inappropriate habitual patterns of infantile desires, resentments, and guilt originally directed toward and learned in relationship to the father and mother as a result of the oedipus complex. Freud emphasized that although their origins lie in childhood experiences, they occur in the present in the form of real experiences in relation to the analyst. Real remembering isn't just a cognitive process; it involves the recurrence of habitual pattern. He called this *repetition.* It is a form of remembering in which "the patient does not *remember* anything of what he [she] has forgotten and repressed, but *acts* it out. He reproduces it not as a memory but as an action; he *repeats* it, without of course, knowing that he is repeating it" (Freud, 1914 [1958f], p. 150) So, "we must treat his illness not as an event in the past, but as a present day force" (p. 151). Repeating "as it is induced in analytic treatment . . . implies conjuring up a piece of real life, and for that reason it cannot always be harmless and unobjectionable" (p. 152). This is similar to our comparative framework's proposal that habitual behavior episode schemas are activated in relevant current behavior episodes, such as interpersonal interactions with an analyst. *Negative transference* involves ambivalence in which old feelings of anguish and resentment because of being deprived of a desired relationship in childhood recur in the present interactions with the analyst. *Erotic positive transference* is a recurrence in the therapy relationship of the intense infantile desire for a sexual, loving parental relationship.

The third component, *natural positive transference,* is called the working or therapeutic alliance by psychoanalysts. It manifests humans' innate desire for accepting, trusting, loving, and constructive relationships with other humans. It is "the relatively rational and non-neurotic *rapport* the patient has with his analyst" that facilitates analysis (Greenson, 1965, p. 157). It involves patients' wish to get well, feelings of confidence in and positive regard for the analyst, a willingness to collaborate in the analysis, the hope for a positive outcome, and a willingness to adhere to the rule of free association and an analytic attitude. "Thus the new sources of strength for which the patient is indebted to his [her] analyst are reducible to transference and instruction (through the communication made to him). [but] The patient . . . only makes use of the instruction in so far as he is induced to do so by the transference" (Freud, 1913 [1958], p. 31). Patients accept interpretations as credible and useful because of their positive regard for and confidence in analysts.

Freud considered patients' wish to escape their suffering a necessary but not sufficient motive for psychoanalysis. Strong positive feelings toward therapists, including confidence in their competence and commitment to their welfare, are essential ingredients to motivate patients to endure the intense experience and effort of psychoanalysis. Therefore, interpretations of resistance and pathological transference should be delayed until a proper rapport is established (Freud, 1913 [1958d]). Analysts cultivate this working alliance in several ways: They help clients understand and become committed to their role and responsibilities. (2) They cultivate patient trust by consistent honesty and nonmanipulativeness in the relationship. "Psycho-analytic treatment is founded on truthfulness. In this fact lies a great part of its educative effect and its ethical value" (p. 164). (3) Analysts maintain neutrality, by which Freud meant being objective and nonevaluative with regard to patients' thoughts and actions rather than completely avoiding self-disclosure as some followers have assumed (p. 164). (4) Analysts practice abstinence, by which Freud meant avoiding behavior that gratified patients' neurotic transference patterns or that gratified the analyst's own countertransference patterns, including sexual desires. He did not mean that analysts should abstain from all natural, positive interactions with clients, as some followers assume

Countertransference
Analysts, like all humans, react to interpersonal situations with their own history of habits, called countertransference when it occurs with a patient. Since it is what analysts say and do that influences patient change, it is important that analysts understand their own interpersonal habits so they can control their operation and influence on patients and can avoid unconsciously using patients to satisfy their own needs. To that end, a personal analysis is part of every analyst's training. Freud did not argue that countertransference should not occur, because that is humanly impossible. However, he believed analysts' understanding of their countertransferences can provide clues to understanding patients' conflicts and defensive maneuvers—What has the

patient done that has made me feel angry?—and that self-understanding can be used to help guide formulation of interpretations.

The objective is to activate patients' intrapsychic conflicts; therefore analytic sessions must be conducted so that the thoughts, feelings, and actions clients experience and display reflect their childhood-based pathological habits rather than being appropriate reactions to analysts' current behavior. For example, having patients free associate while lying on a couch, with analysts sitting out of patients' sight and listening but speaking infrequently, provides a kind of stimulus deprivation that reduces context influences on the content and flow of patients' thoughts and feelings. All analysts "think that the setting implies sensory deprivation, emotional frustration, limitation of the object world and infantile atmosphere" (Etchegoyen, 1991, p. 543).

These conditions annul the current object relation and facilitate a regressive process.

> The analyst's silence, and the patient's recumbent posture and free associative talk not only create the conditions for a certain kind of passivity in the patient— wherein experience will flow, unscreened, sometimes regressively—but equally can be seen as creating the conditions for a certain kind of activity—giving shape to experience in the absence of any external shaping demands. (Pine, 1990, p. 255)

Daily sessions quickly make the setting familiar and increase the likelihood that patients' own dynamics rather than the context will control their behavior.

Strategies for Helping Patients Learn to Control and Alter Their Pathological Patterns

The phrase, "where id was, ego should be," symbolizes desired changes. Unconscious conflicts and compromise formations influence patients' thoughts, feelings, and actions in ways they can't control and produce their symptoms. Change results from increased self-knowledge when: (1) Patients become aware of their unconscious conflicts and defenses, how these influence their current functioning, and how they are the result of faulty development in childhood, called insight. (2) Patients become able to consciously and intentionally overcome those habitual conflicts and defenses and to organize and control their thoughts, feelings, and actions to satisfy their basic drives in ways appropriate to the realities of their life. As patients remember and experience their unconscious conflicts and defenses through free association and transference experiences, the act of verbalizing them itself tends to create insight and self-understanding (Loewald, 1960).

If patients could cure themselves solely through self-talk, they would not have sought analysis. The key to patient change is analysts' ability to understand patients' troublesome unconscious psychodynamics, and to communicate that understanding to the patient in ways that help them overcome their defensive habits, elaborate their accurate self-knowledge, and use their increased understanding to alter their behavior. Traditional psychoanalysts slowly guide patients toward awareness and self-understanding of the nature of and relationships among their conflicts, defenses, and behavior. They do this through communicative strategies of providing factual information and clarifications, and conveying meanings lying behind patients' manifest thoughts, feelings, and actions through interpretations and constructions.

Because the goal is patient self-understanding and control, analysts use communicative strategies to help patients identify, evaluate, and choose from among possibilities they invent for themselves, rather than to propose better ways of functioning. The implicit assumption is that once patients decide on a course of action they have the skills necessary to execute it, so teaching interpersonal skills is not a component of psychoanalysis. All other aspects of psychoanalysis are intended to facilitate patients' understanding and constructive use of analysts' communications. Among these aspects are establishing a working alliance; frequency of sessions; the analytic attitude; the emphasis on honesty between patient and analyst; and the basic rule of free association.

The Strategy of Understanding

Analysts cannot help patients understand themselves until the analyst has an accurate understanding on which to base interpretations. Freud (1912 [1958e], p. 112) recommended that analysts avoid the biasing influence of selective attention by using evenly hovering attention to guide their observations. Analysts should be alert, take everything in, but not try to remember everything because

> as soon as anyone deliberately concentrates his [her] attention to a certain degree, he begins to select from the material before him; one point will be fixed in his mind with particular clearness and some other will be correspondingly disregarded and he [she] is in danger of never finding anything but what he already knows; and if he follows his inclinations he will certainly falsify what he may perceive. . . . It must not be forgotten that the things one hears are for the most part things whose meaning is only recognized later on. (p. 112)

No specific statement or act by itself is significant. It is an understanding of the underlying pattern or latent meanings of patients' manifest behavior that is the objective. Freud assumed that analysts' unconscious processes would discern the underlying meanings in the flow of patients' talk and actions, so the analyst "should simply listen, and not bother about whether he is keeping anything in mind" and "should withhold all conscious influences from his [her] capacity to attend, and give himself over completely to his 'unconscious memory' " (p. 112). He recommended against taking notes during a session for the same reasons.

Freud stressed the importance of focusing on patients' current, here-and-now conscious experience:

> It is of the gravest importance for the treatment that the analyst should always be aware of the surface of the patient's mind at any given moment, that he [the analyst] should know what complexes and resistances are active in him [the patient] at the time and what conscious reaction to them will govern his [the patient's] behavior. (Freud, 1911 [1958b], p. 92)

Dream interpretation should not be pursued "as an art for its own sake" but should only be used "subject to those technical rules that govern the conduct of the treatment as a whole" (p. 94).

Strategies of Providing Factual Information and Clarifications

Patients may have an ignorance of objective facts or extrinsic knowledge about the world, and that deficiency of information may be handicapping their efforts to resolve their concerns. Providing factual information to correct such errors may be appropriate and useful sometimes; a patient who reports blood in his feces may be told of its potential medical significance and a consultation with a physician recommended. There are risks—the patient may misunderstand the recommendation as support or a desire to influence or control him. Therefore, this tactic should be used infrequently and cautiously, and never with regard to psychological attributes of the patient (Etchegoyen, 1991). Sometimes patients may discuss something they know vaguely about themselves. Clarification may be used to help the patient apprehend that self-understanding more clearly.

The Strategies of Interpretation and Construction

Interpretation is the key strategy for psychoanalysts. Interpretation involves statements that convey to patients' the analyst's understanding of information and meanings that lie behind the manifest content of patients' statements and actions, and of which patients appear to be unaware. Analysts take diverse elements from the flow of patients' free associations, transferences, and communications and "produce a synthesis that lends a new meaning to his experience" (Etchegoyen, 1991, p. 325), often called insight. Analysts can only infer underlying, unconscious content, so interpretations should be considered hypotheses to be tested against patients' reactions to and uses of them.

Freud did not propose specific ways of making interpretations, in line with his belief that specific tactics had to be designed to fit the idiosyncratic nature of the dynamics of each patient, based on analysts' judgment about appropriate "tact," "dosage," and "timing." He implied that guiding patients toward relevant changes must be a slow, gradual incremental process, but he did specify the kind of content on which interpretations should focus. Because symptoms result from compromise formations to deal with the conflict between unbearable ideas and defenses against them, interpretations should help patients become aware of and understand the nature of that conflict and how it is influencing their current functioning. These are well established habits for patients, however, and their defenses operate to resist changing them. They function as stability-maintaining processes.

> The analytic treatment . . . seeks to track down the libido, to make it accessible to consciousness and, in the end, serviceable for reality. Where the investigations of analysis come upon the libido withdrawn into its hiding-place, a struggle is bound to break out; all the forces which have caused the libido to regress will rise up as resistances against the work of analysis, in order to conserve the new state of things. (Freud, 1912 [1958a], p. 102)

Interpretation must first help patients understand and overcome their patterns of resistance before they can face and cope with their unbearable ideas. The focus is on how, what, and why the patient is resisting. "The resistance accompanies the treatment step by step. Every single association, every act of the person under treatment must reckon with the resistance and represents a compromise between the forces that are striving toward recovery and the opposing ones" (Freud, 1972b [1958], p. 103). Resistance can occur in any part of the process, such as resistance to the rule of free association and other procedures, to recall, to interpretations, and to change as well as in the transference relationship (Freud 1914 [1958f]). Gaps, disturbances, distortions, and exaggerations of ongoing experiences are signs of resistance and of underlying conflicts. (See Greenson, 1967, and Wachtel, 1982, for a detailed discussion.) Luborsky (1996) reports studies of the occurrence during treatment of psychological and somatic symptoms that are indicative of brief impairments of usual functioning, and consequent to the occurrence of anxiety, helplessness, and/or hopelessness in clients.

Freud stressed that intellectual understanding was insufficient; the real experience of the resistance and conflict and understanding must be linked.

"One does not forget that it is in fact only through his own experience and mishaps that a person learns sense" (Freud, 1914 [1958f], p. 153). "We must treat his illness, not as an event of the past, but as a present-day force" (p. 151). This proposition is the basis for emphasizing transference interpretations. The essential, real experience of patients' intrapsychic conflicts occurs in the transference relationship. The feelings and behaviors of negative and positive erotic transference reenacted onto the analyst are not just fragments of a forgotten past; they are real-life, here-and-now efforts to satisfy clients' infantile wishes embedded in their neurotic conflict, and simultaneously to hide those wishes from themselves and their analyst. (This is analogous to our comparative framework's proposition that behavior episodes created during analytic sessions are guided by behavior episode schemas constructed from earlier experiences.) So, such transference episodes provide a testable reality for clients and analysts concerning the ways in which old habits operate in current life. Analysts use interpretations to direct patients' attention to those feelings, thoughts, and actions as they occur, to help patients understand the functions they are serving, and to link those real experiences to the patients' remembrances of childhood events and experiences that are the roots from which the current neurotic habits have grown. The timing of interpretations is thus important. The goal is to help patients learn to distinguish past from present relevance of those childhood patterns so they can control the patterns in the present and develop alternate patterns more appropriate to their current life.

Strachey's (1934) rationale for mutative interpretations describes conditions under which they are most likely to produce changes in existing "psychic structures." During transference, analysts do not behave like the original object or person with whom the pattern functioned during the patient's childhood, enabling the patient to become aware of discrepancies between the "archaic object" and the current one—the analyst. That awareness disrupts the existing "psychic structure" making change more likely. Mutative interpretations have two phases. First, the anxiety linked to the repressed conflict is mobilized and becomes conscious. That provides a key criterion for the timing of interpretations: Transference interpretations should be given at the point of "affective urgency" because that means the pattern to be modified is operating at that time. The second phase helps patients distinguish between the real object—the analyst—and the "archaic object"—transferred from childhood—which reduces the anxiety and leads to "structural" change.

The accuracy of interpretations, accuracy ("content"), their phrasing, ("tact"), the extent of ideas they encompass, their frequency ("dosage"), and the necessity of linking them to real, here-and-now experience ("timing") all influence their impact on the patient and require skilled judgment from the analyst. This is where the art of psychoanalysis is most evident. Differences among analysts in their guiding conceptual, propositional, and procedural models lead to differences in their decisions about these issues (see Etchegoyen, 1991, for many examples).

Construction is a special form of interpretation. It involves linking various elements to form a whole, usually involving something of historical significance in the person's life and its relationship to current patterns of functioning. This knitting together of diverse strands of a person's experience is sometimes called a complete interpretation. Such interpretations "should integrate all the levels the material offers: infantile conflict, present conflict and transference" (Etchegoyen, 1991, p. 424). The primary emphasis by some traditional analysts on historical reconstruction of the early life events and issues that produced patients' conflicts and defenses has led to what some consider an overintellectualization of the analytic process.

Separation Anxiety

Psychoanalysis involves patterns of reunion and separation. Every session has a beginning and an end. The sequence of sessions will be interrupted by holidays and changes in patient and analyst schedules, and then renewed. These shifts provide special conditions for transference reactions reflecting childhood patterns of separation and reunion. Patients often display anxiety when facing impending separations, and that provides another direct experience that can be interpreted to facilitate further understanding of their unconscious conflicts.

The Strategy of Working Through

Old habits are hard to change! This is particularly true of pathological patterns because they have a long developmental history, their dynamics are unconscious, they are heavily defended, and they produce some desired consequences, called secondary gain, which involves attention from others or protection from distressing affects. Changing these habits requires a lengthy series of relevant experiences; one interpretation is insufficient, no matter how accurate. Much of the skill of psychoanalysis involves facilitating such a series of learning experiences, analogous to relevant behavior episodes in the comparative framework. These experiences must be repeated to have a cumulative effect. "This working-through of the resistances may in practice turn out to be an arduous task for the subject of the analysis and a trial of patience for the analyst. Nevertheless, it is a part of the work which effects the greatest changes in the patient and which distinguishes analytic treatment from any kind of treatment by suggestion" (Freud, 1914 [1958f], pp. 155–156).

Progress is seldom smooth, and obstructions and setbacks frequently occur. Three types are common (see Etchegoyen, 1991, for details). *Acting out* by patients involves behaving in terms of some aspect of troublesome fantasies or memories rather than remembering them through the transference. Acting out is a way patients can avoid remembering and achieving insight about their behavior. *Negative therapeutic reaction* occurs when patients react to progress in treatment or to being told something positive about the course of treatment in ways contrary to what is expected. Instead of experiencing satisfaction and relief, they experience disappointment or anger. Paradoxically, instead of improving, they become worse. Freud (1923 [1961b]) described them as people who cannot tolerate any kind of praise, progress, or appreciation. *Reversible perspective* refers to thought processes patients use to try to avoid mental pain at any cost. They have fixed assumptions—analogous to schemas in the comparative framework—that control their interpretation of their experience. No matter the nature of the experience, e.g., what the analyst says, these patients will turn it around or reinterpret it to fit or confirm their guiding assumptions.

When such defensive strategies persist, they block any possibility of progress; this point is called an impasse. Progress is stalled; the road to cure is blocked. The analytic situation is preserved, but it does not create progress. The therapy involves incessant returning to the same problems without resolution. When a problem seems to be convincingly resolved through interpretation during a series of sessions, but then recurs intact, the analyst is probably confronting an impasse rather than a process of working through. An impasse may lead to termination or be resolved through further analysis so progress can be renewed.

Strategies for Facilitating Transfer to Real Life

Freudians generally assume that if changes become manifest during analytic sessions they will automatically generalize to real-life situations. Thus no strategies aimed at this objective are proposed. Working through during analytic sessions may involve patients' talking about real-life experiences, which may facilitate generalization.

ELABORATIONS OF THE PROCEDURAL MODEL IN CONTEMPORARY TRADITIONAL PSYCHOANALYSIS

Despite considerable theoretical elaboration, few major changes in the procedural model have occurred in contemporary traditional psychoanalysis (Abend, 1990a; Etchegoyen, 1991; Mishne, 1993; Simons, 1990; Weinshel, 1990). Stone (1984 [1951]) summarizes the "ensemble" of classical technique:

(1) practically exclusive reliance during the hour on the patient's free associations for communication; (2) regularity of the time, frequency, and duration of appointments . . . a clearly defined financial agreement; (3) three to five appointments a week . . . with daily appointments the dominant tendency; (4) the recumbent position . . . with some impediment to seeing the analyst directly; (5) confinement of the analyst's activity essentially to interpretation or other purely informative interventions such as reality testing or an occasional question; (6) analysts' emotional passivity and neutrality, specifically abstention from gratifying the analysand's transference wishes; (7) abstention from advice or any other direct intervention or participation in the patient's daily life; (8) no immediate emphasis on curing symptoms, the procedure being guided largely by the patient's free associations from day to day. (p. 7)

After Freud's death, a kind of rigid idealization of these techniques occurred supported by the authority of the training institutes. In particular, because of narrow interpretations of analysts' neutrality, abstention, and relative anonymity, some analysts displayed a "callous, aloof, arbitrary, withholding attitude," resulting in a "caricature" of Freud's theory of treatment (Eagle & Wolitsky, 1992, p. 141). They neglected Freud's original view that not all aspects of patient-analyst relationships represented problematic transference patterns learned in early childhood, and that the quality of the real patient-analyst relationship plays a key motivational role in effective treatment. Overemphasis by some on "objective" interpretation of all current behavior in terms of childhood roots and on verbalized insight produced an intellectualized process and a seeming disregard for the importance of current troubles. Sometimes differences in patient and analyst perspectives produced an adversarial rather than collaborative relationship because the analyst's view about what was going on was always right. Object relations and interpersonal approaches developed, in part, as a reaction to this highly impersonal, "mirror analyst" model of a nonrelating observer who simply interprets (Mishne, 1993).

Perhaps partially in reaction to such excesses, there has been growing rejection of the narrow interpretation of transference and countertransference as neurotic impediments to treatment, and renewed emphasis on the importance of the real relationship as well as neurotic transference between patient and analyst (Abend, 1990b; Gill, 1982; Modell, 1990; Stone, 1984; Weinshel, 1990). The concepts of transference and countertransference have been extensively discussed and Freud's distinctions between negative, erotic, and positive transference and countertransference have reemerged in contemporary thought and practice. In a workshop on the psychoanalytic process involving distinguished psychoanalysts "all the participants in the group were in agreement that the psychoanalytic process is interactional" (Boesky, 1990,

p. 564). Patients and analysts continually influence one another, resulting in "an extraordinarily intricate network of constantly shifting interactions" (Abend, 1990b, p. 547). Dorpat puts this emphasis in personal terms:

> Early in my psychoanalytic career I mistakenly believed that as long as I safe-guarded the analytic frame by adhering to the ground rules of analysis and by maintaining psychoanalytic neutrality, I could devote my complete attention to observing and interpreting what was occurring within the mind of the patient. Then I gradually and painfully began to realize that my steady preoccupation with what was going on within the patient often obscured what was occurring in my interactions with the patient. Now my aim is to shift flexibly between the intrapsychic and interactional perspectives" (Dorpat & Miller, 1992, p. xii)

There is also a renewal of Freud's emphasis on the "here and now" as the vehicle of change. Interpretation is emphasizing the current form and utility of transference patterns to the person (e.g., Cooper, 1987). Understanding patients' childhood roots, while still important, is given less emphasis; "the retrieval of old memories per se is no longer our principal goal" (Weinshel, 1990, p. 282). Dreams are no longer considered the royal road to the unconscious (Arlow & Brenner, 1988); dream interpretation receives less emphasis. Analysts' understanding of their countertransference reactions are believed to provide useful data about the meaning of patients' transference behaviors. Interpretation of resistance, conflict, and deficit is still the key strategy, and there are more discussions of methods—such as what, when, and how to interpret (e.g., Davison, Pray, & Bristol, 1990). There are also efforts to formulate models of the types and sequences of change that occur during psychoanalysis (e.g., Abrams, 1987; Boesky, 1990).

The inflated image of psychoanalytic results has been reduced in recent years. Analysts no longer speak of eliminating conflict, overcoming resistances, completely resolving transference, effecting cures, or of completing analysis (Weinshel, 1990). There is increased readiness to combine other treatments with analysis as appropriate (Simons, 1990). All these seem to be symptoms of greater flexibility and willingness to consider new proposals and developments. This may partly reflect concern over the relationship of current trends in the economics of psychotherapy in general to their traditional narrow client base (Cooper, 1991). Because traditional psychoanalysis lasts for years and is expensive, it is out of the reach of most people. As Stone (1984) noted, "In our private work we are, willy-nilly, . . . largely doctors for the prosperous and sophisticated. Through our clinics we reach an additional small number of those relatively adjacent to them. Blue-collar workers or their families are rarely seen" (p. 415).

Early in the development of psychoanalysis, Freud recognized the need to know that the changes observed in patients were stable; he abandoned hypnosis because he found the results capricious and unpredictable. His solution to evaluation of these changes relies on patient and analyst judgment. "First . . . the patient shall no longer be suffering from his [her] symptoms and shall have overcome his anxieties and his inhibitions; and . . . the analyst shall judge that so much repressed material has been made conscious, so much that was unintelligible has been explained, and so much internal resistance conquered, that there is no need to fear a repetition of the pathological processes concerned" (Freud, 1957 [1964a], p. 219). Freud acknowledged that the decision of when to terminate analysis was a difficult one. No other methods for making such judgments are proposed or used, such as evaluation by other observers; objective measurement.

Contemporary traditional psychoanalysis has introduced no new procedures. With the deemphasis on the concept of cure and an emphasis on personality reconstruction, establishing criteria for deciding when enough is enough is impossible. Only patients can decide when they are satisfied with their current personality dynamics, and they may never be satisfied because life confronts everyone with new and unpredictable challenges and stresses as it proceeds. Some analysts have adopted the procedure of scheduling follow-up interviews to try to assess the postanalytic status of their patients (Etchegoyen, 1991).

STRATEGIES FOR EVALUATING THE PSYCHOANALYTIC MODEL

Freudians say they have created a comprehensive psychology and the foundation for a unified science of man (Fine, 1979), so the epistemology, philosophy of science, and methods psychoanalysts use to verify their proposals are often criticized (e.g., Etchegoyen, 1991; Davar & Bhat, 1995). When analysts focus on psychological, ("intrapsychic") unconscious conflict, the turmoil is not available to objective observation, and unconscious phenomena are not even available to subjective observation. These conditions make application of typical empirical methods difficult.

Freud was well trained in inductive empirical science so he knew those methods. He argued that no science begins with clear and sharply defined basic concepts. Rather, scientific activity consists of "describing phenomena and then in proceeding to prove, classify and correlate them." Ideas are applied to help bring order from the data. These ideas must have "significant relations to the empirical material," relations which we "sense before we can clearly recognize and demonstrate them." Advancing knowledge "does not tolerate any rigidity even in definitions" (Freud, 1915 [1957a], p. 117). Freud applied this rationale throughout his career. He periodically modified his ideas to fit new observations and avoided formal definitions.

His database, however, was his clinical observations, which provided only anecdotal evidence. He did not take notes during analytic sessions. He conducted his therapy sessions, frequently numbering 10 to 12 a day, and then made notes about all of them at the end of the day. Even though Freud was a skilled observer, anyone who has conducted psychotherapy with a daily caseload cannot help wondering how accurate and complete such data recording can be, and therefore how sound are the conceptions derived from it. He used two other inferential strategies. He made observations of the same person in multiple analytic sessions (often called a single-subject design in current research), and then looked for consistencies across that large sample of occasions and observations. Thus, internal consistency appears to have been one inferential criterion he used. In addition, he considered his conceptualizations verified when patients said they fit their experience and helped them overcome their neuroses.

Contemporary Strategies for Evaluating Psychoanalytic Theory and Technique

This reliance on anecdotal data provided by unconfirmed clinical observation is still the primary way in which psychoanalysts try to verify their proposals. There appears to be growing recognition of the limitations of that traditional strategy. (Bellak, 1993; Macmillan, 1991). Analysts acknowledge that there is no sound, agreed-on method for reporting clinical material (Boesky, 1990), and that they have sorely neglected developing a real methodology of evidence (Comtom, 1990) Some psychoanalysts are trying to use more rigorous empirical methods (e.g., Luborsky, 1996; Weiss & Sampson, 1986). Some seek to interpret empirical evidence from other disciplines in support of psychoanalytic concepts (e.g., Cramer, 1991; Fine, 1979; Greenspan, 1989). Some suggest that psychoanalysis deals with reconstruction of personal narratives, so hermeneutic strategies might be used (Thompson, 1981). The evidence marshaled in support of theoretical proposals, however, is still primarily clinical reports by individual analysts about individual patients.

Formal research examining psychoanalysis is very limited, and there is almost no research on how analysts apply their different theories to treatment. In one study, there were differences in frequency and length of interpretations, the certainty with which they were made, and the content of interpretations (Fine & Fine, 1990). Given the evidence from psychological research of how interview content can influence the content of so-called memories reported by people, and that repressed memories recovered often turn out to be constructions rather than memories, one must wonder about the relationships between analysts' interpretations and how clients construe their difficulties and report their memories.

There are very few studies of long-term psychoanalytic treatment, and they all suffer from methodological deficiencies (Bachrach, Galatzer-Levy, Skolnikoff, & Waldron, 1991). They indicate that the majority of patients suitable for analysis benefited from treatment, but there are no control groups or comparisons with other psychotherapies. Therefore, evidence of the effectiveness of psychoanalysis rests primarily on ancedotal evidence provided by patients and analysts.

CHAPTER 7

Object Relations, Self-Psychology, and Interpersonal Approaches

C ONTEMPORARY PSYCHOANALYSIS DISPLAYS an increasing "tolerance for and assimilation of formulations that were once viewed as deviant and heretical" (Eagle & Wolitzky, 1992, p. 151). Increasingly influential alternative views represent a shift

> from drives and their transformations to relations with others [based] on the premise that the major motivational thrust [and] determinant of the patterning of personality and psychopathology is not the search for pleasure through drive gratification, but the establishment and maintenance of relations with others, real and imaginary, past and present. (Mitchell, 1994, p. 81)

Psychologists and psychiatrists have evolved similar views (Kiesler, 1996). Psychotherapy is the study of interpersonal transactions between patient and therapist and the intrapsychic consequences of those transactions (Strupp, 1982). This chapter analyzes three exemplars: psychoanalytic object relations, self-psychology, and interpersonal psychotherapy. Eisenthal (1992) notes a absence of psychoanalytic consideration of other interpersonal approaches despite their similarities.

PSYCHOANALYTIC OBJECT RELATIONS AND SELF-PSYCHOLOGY

HISTORICAL PERSPECTIVE

Traditional psychoanalysis links Freud's emphases on the developmental influence of children's instinct/drive-based fantasied sexual relationships with their parents with the ego psychology emphasis on reality relationships and the role of learning. That linkage facilitated the emergence in psychoanalysis of views that emphasize the role of interpersonal relationships in shaping development. These theorists agree with Freud that the seeds of pathological development are planted during the first few years of life, and that the nature of parent-child relationships is crucial. They differ from him, and among themselves, on four key aspects of traditional psychoanalysis: (1) What is the influence of instinctual and learning processes in development? (2) Which early years are developmentally most important? (3) What aspects of interpersonal experience are most important? (4) What epistemology is appropriate?

Freud acknowledged that in everyone's mental life, others are "invariably involved" as a "model," an "object," a "helper" or an "opponent" (Freud, 1921, [1961c]). However, he and traditional psychoanalysts propose that these "objects," or people, function to inhibit or facilitate the discharge of instinctual drives, or to serve as their target. Some analysts (e.g., Adler, 1924; Horney, 1939; Rank, 1945; Sullivan, 1953a; Suttie, 1935) openly rejected the instinct/drive model and adopted a socialization or learning model, leading traditional analysts to largely ignore their ideas. However, they were influential among psychiatrists, psychologists, and social workers—for example, Sullivan's ideas have had a major influence on the development of contemporary interpersonal psychotherapies.

Rather than rejecting the instinct/drive model, some analysts said they were elaborating it (Klein, 1932), or deemphasizing it and emphasizing social learning (e.g., Balint, 1965, 1968; Fairbairn, 1952; Kohut, 1977, 1984, 1991; Winnicott, 1958, 1965a,b). (These same references support the other learned generalizations described throughout the chapter, and will not be repeated each time.) Their controversial but less confrontational proposals were politically more acceptable, leading to wider consideration of their views within psychoanalysis. These object relations (OR) and self-psychology (SP) analysts argue that social experiences anchor the construction of mental life, and that learned patterns of relating to real or imagined others are the key force motivating behavior; they are the conceptual and interpretive hub of psychoanalysis. Ferenczi's emphasis on the damaging influence of maternal deprivation and parental deficiencies influenced most of these relational/structural theorists (Greenberg & Mitchell, 1983). The shift in emphasis from instinct to learning reflects a broader shift in science from nineteenth-century closed-system models to twentieth-century open-system models in which the influence of environments must always be considered.

Klein emphasized infancy; Balint, Fairbairn, Suttie, and Winnicott emphasized infancy and early childhood prior to the oedipal years that Freud stressed; Adler (1924), Horney (1939), Rank (1945), Sullivan (1953a), and Kohut considered child development to be crucial, but recognized development to be a lifelong process. All agree that the nature and history of relationships with others is the primary source of both healthy and pathological psychological development, but differ on which aspects of relationships are most important. For example, Freud (see chapter 6) assumed that all children feel helpless, are sexually attracted to their parents, and develop defensive wish-fulfilling, hallucinatory ideas and beliefs in the omnipotence of their thoughts and wishes to control their lust, anxiety, and hostility. Klein assumed that infants feel abandoned or mistreated by parents. Balint, Fairbairn, Winnicott, and Kohut believed that sound or pathological psychic development results when parenting is appropriately or poorly carried out during infancy and early childhood. Adler (1924), Horney (1939), and Sullivan (1953a) proposed that both parents and other family members, (e.g., siblings), plus the larger sociocultural context, influence psychological development.

Analysts also differ about the content and organization of the psychological "object" and "self" representations people construct and the relationships of those intrapsychic "structures" to real people and social transactions, ranging from a primary emphasis on the intrapersonal (e.g., Klein; Kohut) to a greater emphasis on the interpersonal (e.g., Horney, 1939; Sullivan, 1953a).

Epistemological disagreements also exist. Some (e.g., Horney, 1939; Sullivan, 1953b) adopt a form of empiricism that distinguishes among persons and contexts and emphasizes their interactions. Others (e.g., Adler, 1924; Kohut; Rank, 1945) adopt some form of idealism and phenomenology that emphasizes subjective rather than objective observation and experience. It is how people construe their interactions with others that is crucial rather than events themselves. They, like Freud, emphasize intrapsychic sources of psychopathology, such as representations of self and others, and criticize interpersonal relations models as giving too much emphasis to the influence of contexts and here and now events.

The guiding ideas of object relations and self-psychology analysts represent increasingly influential streams of theory and practice within psychoanalysis, reflecting "transformation of psychoanalysis from the constraints of nineteenth-century objectivist materialism to the greater freedom of a twentieth-century subjectivist contextualism" (Wolf, 1990, pp. x–xi). Consistent with Freud's focus on understanding complex mental processes, they emphasize intrapsychic phenomena, "but the intrapsychic is seen as constituted largely by the internalization of interpersonal experience mediated by the constraints imposed by biologically organized templates and delimiters," and assumes that "both outer world and inner world, both the interpersonal and the intrapsychic, play immensely important and interactive roles in human life" (Ghent, 1992, p. xiv).

This chapter does not summarize these theories using their own terminology. In addition to original sources, comparative summaries of object relations and self-psychology ideas are available (Bacal & Newman, 1990; Greenberg & Mitchell, 1983; Grotstein & Rinsley, 1994; Mishne, 1993; Mitchell, 1988; Skolnick & Warshaw, 1992). Rather, we identify the basic themes underlying their approaches by noting the shared meanings of their terms. Fairbairn, Klein, and Winnicott are the most influential object relations theorists. Guntrip (1961, 1969) is described as the foremost historian, synthesizer, and popularizer of their views (Greenberg & Mitchell, 1983). Kohut, who was originally an ego psychologist in the manner of Hartmann, created the self-psychology approach, which has an "uncanny resemblance" to Fairbairn's ideas (Robbins, 1994), and is considered "an extension" of Winnicott's key ideas (Modell, 1985).

CONCEPTUAL AND PROPOSITIONAL MODELS

Object relations and self-psychology theorists' ideas evolved over time and were presented primarily in papers on specific topics rather than as comprehensive theoretical models. These papers were later assembled in book form. Initially the theorists avoided direct rejection of basic Freudian ideas but later became less conciliatory and more critical of traditional psychoanalysis. Their models must be pieced together from multiple sources and decisions made concerning emphases on earlier or later formulations. Comparisons of their concepts and propositions is difficult because they use different labels for the same phenomena, the same labels for different phenomena, and sometimes terms that have metaphorical meanings, such as *mirroring.* They often retain key Freudian labels but with different meanings—for example, *libido; ego.* Therefore, we have tried to identify and compare the meanings to which their labels refer. Their jargon differences reflect metaphysical and epistemological differences. These range from combining realism and idealism with an empiricist orientation, to emphasizing idealism with a phenomenological orientation where concepts refer to contexts only indirectly through intrapsychic experience, such as "selfobjects".

ASSUMPTIONS CONCERNING INNATE COMPONENTS OF HUMAN NATURE

Object relations and self-psychology theorists all assume that infants enter the world with inborn biological and psychosocial characteristics and propensities. These provide starting points for, facilitate, and constrain the nature of human development, but they do not directly determine its content and form. This view could be considered a kind of instinct theory. Most of these theorists, however, reject Freud's assumptions about inborn sexual, aggressive, and death instincts and his faulty evolutionary theorizing (e.g., the phylogenetic origins of oedipal patterns). They justify their alternate assumptions with clinical observations and selected evidence from anthropology, ethology, and child development.

Infants Begin Life with an Elaborate Phylogenetic Inheritance
Psychologically, infants are not a blank slate on which experience writes a life story. Innate factors "prepare" them to be sensitive to and use certain kinds of experiences (e.g., visual and auditory preferences for human faces and voices; tactile preferences; intuitive empathic resonance to emotional states of others). These theorists emphasize different factors: libido as object seeking (Fairbairn, 1952); needs for satisfaction and security (Sullivan, 1953a); attachment (Bowlby, 1969). All agree that infants' innate abilities for using both inner and outer experiences to create psychological representations shape their developmental pathways, though few try to explain how such processes work. Most state or imply that emotions are inborn patterns that occur in reaction to different kinds of imagined or real human relationship conditions.

Humans Innately Seek Human Relationships
Western social and political philosophy has emphasized two views of human nature that represent starting points for the drive/structure and relationship/structure models. Traditional psychoanalysis assumes, as did Hobbes and Locke, that people are separate entities whose satisfactions and goals are personal and individual. Relationship approaches assume, with Rousseau, Hegel, and Marx, that humans are innately social and cannot meaningfully exist apart from others. Humans evolved to seek mutually supportive, protective, nurturing, affectionate relationships because such interpersonal patterns gave them a survival and reproductive advantage in evolutionary processes. Therefore, from birth onward, infants seek a positive relational matrix (Mitchell, 1988) or communal existence (Sullivan, 1953a); they experience anxiety, anger, loneliness or depression when deprived of it. This relational living is considered the fundamental source of human motivation; the sexual and aggressive patterns Freud emphasized are viewed as manifestations or derivatives of humans' social nature rather than being primary, instinctual drives.

Infants Are Innately Innocent
For Freud, babies' bestial impulses lead to difficulties unless tamed; *badness* is within them. Relational theorists (e.g., Fairbairn; Kohut; Winnicott) shift re-

sponsibility for "bad" development to the interpersonal context. Unempathic parents replace the bestial baby as the source of pathological development (Mitchell, 1988). An infant is "born innocent" and is "entitled" to be treated as a person (Grotstein & Rinsley, 1994); if cared for with good enough mothering in an average expectable environment (Winnicott, 1958, 1965a), or in a milieu of empathic selfobjects (Kohut, 1984), the child's development will be healthy. If the environmental niche of infants does not adequately match their inborn social predispositions, pathological development results.

Infants Are Innately Self-Constructing and Self-Organizing
Freudians incorrectly criticize these theorists as environmental determinists; they are constructivists, not mechanists. Humans do not merely react to experience; they proactively seek self-development through social relationships. Development does not result from unmediated experience—for example, conceptions of parents are not replicas of actual parents. People's ideas result from processing and refashioning experience with inborn perceptual-cognitive processes, illustrated by ideas such as fantasies and internal object relations (Klein), or endopsychic structures (Fairbairn). People use experiences to create psychological and behavioral patterns; people are a self-causing system (Pine, 1990). Mental functioning and the self develop through a process of transmuting internalization of interpersonal experiences:

> The foreign protein of the selfobject and of the self-object's functions [is] split up after being ingested; its constituents are then reassembled to form the self in accordance with those individual patterns that characterize the growing child's . . . specific psychic protein. These individual patterns derive from influences emanating from inherited patterns. (Kohut, 1984, p. 160)

Memories are "remodeled" or "retranscribed" with additional experience (Modell, 1990), recombining experiences, ideas, personal interpretations, and meanings into forms that may differ significantly from actual events and previous ideas.

The nature of these constructions, however, is constrained by innate organizational processes; an innate need and striving for organization (Bacal, 1990). Psychological dynamics operate to try to construct and organize psychological pieces so that they fit together producing cohesion, harmony and "preservation of the self" (Suttie), an "integrated" or "whole person" (Winnicott), rather than a collection of unrelated parts. Competing or fragmented organization is pathological. The ego seeks unified functioning from the beginning (Fairbairn); this unity requires harmonizing needs for development of the "true self," "nuclear self," or "guiding core" with needs for positive social relationships, both to become a person and to develop a "communal existence" or supportive "relational matrix." "Intrapsychic structures" are produced by inborn processes of differentiation, elaboration, and integration. When that fails, processes of *splitting, repression,* or *dissociation* create compromise organizations by separating satisfying, conflicting, or distressing ideas, such as the bad and good mother (Winnicott). This concept is similar to the self-organizing and unitary functioning propositions in the comparative framework used in this book.

LEVELS AND UNITS OF ANALYSIS

Object relations and self-psychology theorists reject Freud's one person psychology, which emphasizes individual autonomy, and adopt a multiperson psychology, which emphasizes the interaction of personal and social influences. The person-in-social context is their focal unit of analysis. Children are born "in a state of intense relatedness" to their contexts (Balint); the infant and maternal care "form a unit" (Winnicott); development proceeds from a state of "infantile dependence" to adults' "mature dependence" (Fairbairn); people exist and develop in an interpersonal field (Sullivan) or relational matrix (Mitchell, 1994); "observer and observed form an unbreakable unit (which is held together by empathy)" (Kohut, 1991, p. 464). Therefore, patterns of functioning or personality are context related both in origin and operation. However, their key concepts represent smaller units that represent different kinds of parts of their focal unit and which are a kind of cognitive representation, sometimes with associated emotions.

BASIC CONCEPTS

True to psychoanalysis as "a science of complex mental processes," most of the concepts of the object relations and self-psychology theorists represent intrapsychic, mental, or cognitive phenomena; they focus on perceptions, conceptions, interpretations, feelings, or experience rather than on what people do or say.

Structure

Psychoanalysts assume that people have and develop (habitual) psychological patterns, called structures, that organize their current psychic functioning, experience, and actions—similar to the behavior episode schemas in our comparative framework. Sullivan called them dynamisms to limit the danger of reification into real things. Object relations and self-psychology theorists assume that psychic structures result primarily from social learning that elaborates on some inborn starting points. Mind develops from "an interactive, interpersonal field" rather than as a set of predetermined structures emerging from "inside" a person, as Freud proposed (Mitchell, 1988; Sullivan, 1953a). Their concept of structures includes patterns of (1) stable, organized sets of psychological functions or "agencies of the mind," sometimes called *dynamic* or *ego structures;* (2) stable sets of ideas and psychological representations or mental content, often called *mental* or *intrapsychic structures;* or (3) both. For example, Freud's concept of ego includes both cognitive functions, such as learning, problem solving, and remembering, and guiding ideas and habits constructed through the operation of those functions, such as defenses. The primary structural concepts used by these theorists are self, ego, object, and various combinations thereof.

Self and Ego

Some object relations and self-psychology theorists use the terms *ego* and *self* as synonyms, so ego refers to a narrower set of phenomena than in Freud's usage. Others describe self as a subset of ego (e.g., Kernberg, 1982). The phenomena labeled *self* are not clearly defined. Sullivan's (1953a) personifications of self are patterns of images and ideas people have about themselves, such as good me; bad me; not me. For Fairbairn, representations of interpersonal experiences have three components: elements of self; others; and affective, purposive relationships between them. Kernberg's (1982) definition is similar: "I propose . . . to reserve the term 'self' for the sum total of self-representations in intimate connection with the sum total of object representations. In other words, I propose defining the self as an intrapsychic structure that originates from the ego and is clearly embedded in the ego" (p. 900).

The *original ego* is a unitary self-representation or psychic self that differentiates and elaborates through experience with others (Guntrip, 1961). Modifiers are used to specify the defining attributes of suborganizations of self-representations. For example, Winnicott (1965b) distinguishes between authentic, spontaneous, self-directed living, the *true self*, which includes "the inherited potential which is experiencing a continuity of being, and acquiring in its own way and at its own speed a personal psychic reality and . . . body-scheme" (p. 46), and overly compliant, conforming adaptation to demands and expectations of others, the *false self*. Kohut (1984) uses properties of organization—the "fragmented self"—or of developmental phases—"archaic" and "mature" mean initial and later phases—as defining attributes.

Kohut gives multiple definitions: The ego or self functions as "a unit, cohesive in space and enduring in time, which is a center of initiative and a recipient of impressions" (1977, p. 99). It consists of "three major constituents (the pole of ambitions, the pole of ideals, and the intermediate area of talents and skills)" (1984, p. 192). The self is not an "agency of the mind" but is "a content of the mental apparatus, . . . the core of our personality" (1991, p. 451). "The self is a structure which [strives] toward the realization of its own specific program of action [through] patterns of ambitions, skills, goals and . . . actions" (p. 454). Mitchell (1992) considers spatial metaphors misleading and defines self as the subjective organization of meanings one creates, including self-reflective ones. Integrated patterns of self-esteem; having personal ideals, values, and initiative, nuclear ambitions, being self-directed and self-sustaining, capacity for pleasure, with mature, satisfying relations with others, is the basis of mental health (Robbins, 1994).

Clinical examples accompanying such definitions suggest key defining features of the concept of *self* to be (1) a sense of personal agency manifested in personal goals and values; (2) habitual descriptive and self-evaluative thoughts about one's characteristics and competencies; (3) habitual beliefs and expectations about relationships with others; (4) the organization of all these elements. Integrated patterns are healthy and adaptive; fragmented ones are pathological and maladaptive. These features encompass the directive, regulatory and control functions, and idea of unitary functioning contained in the comparative framework used in the book. Different theorists emphasize different features.

Objects, Object Representations, Object Relations, and Selfobjects

As healthy and pathological personalities are considered to be products of human relationships, several key concepts refer to such relationships. They refer to people as *objects,* and cognitions of people as objects or *object representations.* Therefore, *object relations* can refer to actual interpersonal relationships between people, to cognitive representations of relationships with others, to relationships among one's object representations, or to a combination of these meanings.

Subcategories of object representations are created and modifiers are used to convey their meaning. For example, "true" or "external" object refers to a person, whereas "internalized" object refers to mental representations. Some theorists (e.g., Fairbairn; Winnicott) propose that "object representations" become organized into separate constellations distinguished by their evaluative qualities, both affective and cognitive, for example, "bad objects," "bad mother," or "good objects," "good mother," "ideal object." All emphasize "internal object representations and relations" but differ about how these are related to external objects or real people and self-representations.

Kohut's concepts reflect his phenomenological epistemology and the assumption that "all of us rightfully feel special and unique and that we cannot exist unless we feel that we are affirmed by others" (1984, p. 190). He focuses not on other people—object representations—but on how one interprets, evaluates, or experiences the personal significance of what others do and say. Thus, *selfobject* refers to "that dimension of our experience of another person that relates to this person's functions in shoring up our self" (1984, p. 49). Only those who evoke, maintain, or positively affect the sense of self through favorable, self-confirming feedback are selfobjects. "There are two kinds of selfobjects: those who respond to and confirm the child's innate sense of vigor and perfection [the *mirroring* selfobject]; and those to whom the child can look up and with whom he can merge as an image of calmness, infallibility, and omnipotence [the *idealized parent imago*]" (1991, p. 457). Parents, particularly mothers, are the first and most influential selfobjects; others may "later come to have a parental selfobject significance for us" (1984, p. 190).

No list of selfobject functions exists, but among the important ones mentioned are these: "attunement to affective states; validation of subjective experience—including temporary identification with the 'rightness' of the child's . . . perceptions; affect containment, tension regulation, and soothing; sustaining and organizing or restoring a weakened sense of self . . . and recognition of uniqueness and creative potential" (Bacal & Newman, 1990, p. 229). Feedback evaluated as negative—rejecting or critical—has deleterious effects, which Kohut calls *selfobject failures.* The implication is that only negative feedback given by people from whom one wants and expects self-confirming feedback has pathological impact. Nonselfobject relationships apparently have little influence on personality development regardless of their nature.

Through multiple occasions, people construct generalized representations of *object* and *selfobject* patterns of experience. These are then "experienced as parts of our self" and become functionally autonomous from their interpersonal source. Such representations can perform the object and selfobject functions, rather than needing outsiders to do so—that is, one can approve of oneself. It is confusing to have the same concept, object or selfobject, refer both to experiences of evaluative feedback by significant others and to mental representations of such experiences.

The many meanings of *object* and its variants are perplexing when one tries to understand and compare these theorists. Ogden (1994) tries to clarify and link their meanings, and to resolve a theoretical dilemma in object relations and self-psychology theories: How can mental representations (e.g., of "self" and "objects") carry out mental ("ego") functions such as thinking and evaluating? How can thoughts think? He summarizes their answer this way:

> The ego is split into parts each capable of generating experience and that some of these subdivisions . . . generate experience in a mode modeled after one's sense of an object in an early object relationship while others generate experience in a mode that remains fixed in a pattern congruent with one's experience of oneself in the same early object relationship. The two parts . . . remain linked and when repressed constitute an unconscious internal object relationship between self and others. (p. 89)

This is a version of Freud's (1940) idea that the ego differentiates into parts that combine function and content.

This kind of conceptual language is awkward because it retains Freud's tendency to reify cognitive functions, content, and organization into a thing-like existence, similar to an embryo that grows through differentiation and elaboration (e.g., "the ego [or self] acts to.."). The underlying meaning seems to be that people construct, from interpersonal experiences with significant others, generalized schemas that combine conceptual and propositional generalizations about properties of self and others and functional relations among them. A person might think, "I feel apprehensive, rejected, and angry with father in anticipation of his typical unaffectionate, critical behavior." Schemas with conflicting components may be constructed from inconsistent, unpredictable interactions: "I don't know whether father may be critical and unaffectionate or supportive and loving, so I feel hopeful, apprehensive, excited, angry, affectionate, and confused." Conflicting schema components are distressing, so people try to organize their schemas to remove contradictions: "I have a loving and supportive father, so when he is critical and unaffectionate it means I am a bad person." These are similar to the idea in this book's comparative framework that habitual behavior episode schemas are constructed to facilitate unitary functioning.

Because of their propositional elements, such mental representations or schemas function to enable people to anticipate, interpret, and shape real or imagined future social interactions. The term *internal object relations* refers to imagined rather that real relations. Greenberg and Mitchell's (1988) interpretation is similar: The broadest meaning of object relations identifies approaches "concerned with exploring the relationship between real, external people and internal images and residues of relations with them" and the influence of those constructed, habitual, subjective representations on a person's psychological and behavioral functioning (p. 12). This is similar to a behavior episode schema constructed from a set of similar interpersonal behavior episodes in the comparative framework used in this book.

Emotions or Affects

Like traditional analysts, object relations and self-psychology theorists provide no theory of emotions and only limited consideration of their intrapsychic or behavioral influence. *Emotion* is a term often absent from the subject index of their books; affect is sometimes used as a synonym for it. Freud considered *affects* to be manifestations of instinctual drives. Most object relations and self-psychology theorists reject that idea, and seem to consider them inborn response capabilities. One positive emotion, *love,* is emphasized. It is not sublimated sexuality, as Freud proposed, but is an affect of "affectionate tenderness" that manifests the need for human relationships by facilitating "affectional bonding." It naturally occurs in human relationships between people who display caring concern and positive regard for one another's selfhood, and motivates efforts to produce, retain, and restore such relationships.

Four kinds of negative emotions are emphasized: Anxiety, (fear); anger, (rage; hate); depression, and guilt. Each is described as occurring in relation to actual, anticipated, or imagined disruption, loss, or withholding of some desired aspect of object relations or affectional bonding. *Anxiety* is a reaction to interpretations of danger to self; *anger* to interpretations of anticipated frustration of interpersonal needs and insistence that others help remove the frustration; *depression* to interpretations of failure or loss of desired human relationships; and *guilt* to evaluations of oneself as bad in relation to others. This rationale is similar to the model of emotions in the comparative framework. The theorists discuss emotions as clues to the nature of underlying pathological "intrapsychic structures" or "object relations,"—how cognition influences emotions,—and as approach/avoidance facilitators,—how emotions influence thought and action. Because mental functioning activates these emotions, they can be controlled by constructing patterns of mental functioning to activate positive emotions, or to prevent, control, and alleviate distressing, negative emotions through processes termed *repression, splitting,* or *dissociation.*

Attention, Conscious, and Unconscious Processes

Object relations and self-psychology theorists use the concept of unconscious processes but do not define it. Most appear to implicitly accept Freud's view as summarized in Chapter 6. He considered consciousness a fact "without parallel," defying "all explanation or description," but said that unconscious functioning rather than consciousness is "the true essence of mental life." His mechanistic model assumes that unconscious, sophisticated mental operations and content, controlled by instinctual drives, occur in continuous streams and cause conscious behavior; we don't really know why we think, feel, and act as we do; a sense of personal agency is illusory. One becomes conscious of only a small portion of that stream and the contents of consciousness are constantly changing. Why? He described consciousness as a "sense organ" that "receives impressions" from both external and internal sources, through a process called attending; so we are only aware of what we attend to. But, pathological thoughts are not unconscious simply because they are unnoticed; some force or resistance keeps them from awareness, which he called repression. Freud changed his theory several times to try to provide a persuasive account of how unconscious processes are kept out of awareness.

Mitchell and Sullivan analyzed basic issues concerning these processes. Mitchell (1988) demonstrates that Freud's "structural model establishes an implicit infinite regress from which there is no escape," rather than solving the problem of repression and unconscious processes (p. 261). All psychoanalysts agree that much of psychological functioning occurs outside awareness; but, Mitchell points out, Freud's explanation of why, and of relationships between conscious and unconscious processes, is inadequate. Freud's mechanistic assumptions do not fit the object relations and self psychology model of humans as self-organizing and self-constructing; they do not adequately explain other clinical observations, and they contradict the key therapy objective of helping patients gain conscious control over their lives. The phenomena are real; the explanation is faulty. A different view is necessary and implied by other aspects of object relations and self psychology theories.

Sullivan (1953a) proposed an alternative view based on the concept of attention. He described attention and inattention, as "a universal bit of human equipment." It is manifested in the selective "focusing of awareness," "control over the contents of awareness," and "narrowing of attention," that produces a field of awareness composed of a "focus" and "margins." People function in varying contexts in complex, varying patterns. One can attend to and be aware of only a small portion of all those events at any moment, so selective attention simultaneously involves selective inattention. People are always unaware of most of the events occurring around and within them; unconscious processes are a normal part of living. It follows that people can become aware of many kinds of phenomena to which they can direct their attention. The contents of consciousness vary as the focus of selective attention varies.

People develop habits of attention and inattention that influence which aspects of their current functioning are conscious or unconscious. Sullivan assumed that the inborn reaction to anxiety is avoidance, and people learn avoidance habits. A key avoidance strategy is (1) to selectively fail to attend to anxiety-producing events, both internal (e.g., thoughts) and external (e.g., acts of others) events. (2) People also use substitutive processes; they selectively attend to or use other responses or events that activate neutral or positive affects. The more intense the anxiety, the stronger is the avoidance habit. Some habits can be easily overcome if desirable, but avoidance habits cannot. Strong avoidance habits result in *dissociation*—the barring from consciousness of some distressing psychological events; this is called a *dissociated system*. It is Sullivan's explanation of phenomena that Freud labeled *resistance* and *repression*, and which object relations or self-psychology theorists often call *splitting*. For Freud, *unconscious* refers only to such strong avoidance habits, which are also called *pathogenic beliefs* (Weiss & Sampson, 1986) and *habits of self-deception* (Shafer, 1981).

Others use similar ideas. Mitchell (1988) states that distinctions between conscious and unconscious events are closely related to typical distinctions between choice or free will and determinism: conscious = choice; unconscious = determinism. Both distinctions suffer from dichotomous thinking: Events are either conscious or unconscious; actions are either chosen free of constraint or are determined by prior causes. He thinks many object relations and self-psychology theorists preserve Freud's mechanistic, deterministic assumption that "the fate of the individual is generally a simple, direct, inevitable product of that person's experiences" (p. 256). He proposes a synthesis: "Our lives are composed of a sequence of choices, always within a particular context, always within a complex set of constraints" (p. 263). This idea is similar to the concept of open systems in the comparative framework. What distinguishes mental life is "its property of reflexivity, the capacity to represent itself to itself," which produces a "self-designing capacity" (p. 265). A "vast proportion" of the mental activity underlying choices "operates more or less outside awareness." So, "the problem is not so much accounting for how parts of mental life become unconscious, but how and under what circumstances portions of mental life become conscious" (p. 262).

Mitchell (1988) proposes that as choices are made they create "residues" that function to "screen out" past choices. "Repression is better understood not as a force but as a state, a condition generated by the obscuring of key past choices by subsequent and current choices" (p. 263). Anxiety plays a key role. "The content of the repressed lies concealed behind other mental content and processes which are granted greater focal attention and visibility. Repressed memories are not accessible because the analysand, although interested in them, is also not interested in them" because if they are attended to, anxiety and distress occur (pp. 263–264). He compares the idea that the contents of consciousness are only a part of much more elaborate underlying mental activity with ideas in cognitive science and artificial intelligence. These include the use of implicit knowledge in problem solving, simultaneous parallel processing activities, multiple intelligences, and creative thinking. No distinction is made between normal forgetting and repressed memories; in fact, the concept of forgetting is seldom mentioned by these theorists. The Mitchell and Sullivan proposals are similar to the model of attention and consciousness in the comparative framework of this book.

Communicative and Instrumental Actions
Surprisingly, most object relations and self-psychology theorists do not emphasize communicative and instrumental actions, even though the person-in-social context is their focal unit. A few, such as Sullivan, emphasize the role of communication in development and therapy. Some, such as Pine (1990), assert that the same actions may perform more than one function. They might produce self-esteem, elicit desired responses from others, and produce a practical result.

Biological Functions
The theorists assume genetically based biological starting points and acknowledge that individual differences in biological conditions may influence psychological functioning. But, these functions, do not play an important role in their theories.

Contexts
Interpersonal contexts, particularly early parenting, are heavily emphasized. The influence of other contexts is given little attention, except for the analytic setting itself.

PROPOSITIONS CONCERNING NORMAL DEVELOPMENT

Any theory of development must deal with three questions: What develops? When? How? The object relations and self psychology theorists define psychoanalysis as the science of complex mental processes, so their answer to "What develops?" is "psychic structures" and their organization. They stress psychological rather than behavioral, biological, interpersonal, or social development. There is nothing in these theories about how people learn to *do* things; they address only how people learn to *think* and *feel* about things. Their basic premise is that development flows from the interaction of a person's characteristics with his or her interpersonal or social contexts. As these characteristics and social contexts change, the content and organization of psychological development may also change—similar to the open system model in the comparative framework.

Most of the theorists assume that development may occur at any time, but the most important "when" is infancy and early childhood. Their answer to "how" is by socialization or learning (Mitchell, 1988). "Human experience, from the prenatal period onward, is what writes the software, . . . and in the earliest stages probably even modulates the very hard wiring that provides the capacities and limitations for the integration of experience" (Ghent, 1992, p. xviii).

Inborn Developmental Patterns

"All developmental models posit that human beings are prewired to follow general developmental patterns. The specificity, content, and emphasis of these patterns differ considerably" (Fosshage, 1992, p. 26). This variation is because of inborn differences such as temperament (Stern, 1985). Infants are constitutionally ready for reciprocal relationships—everyone needs to love and be loved, to be recognized and understood. Only through experiencing such relationships is the infant's "self" born (Scharff, 1992). Each person has an "intrinsic program of action" (Kohut, 1984), and this "guiding core" (Loewald, 1960), "true self" (Winnicott, 1965), or "nuclear self" (Kohut, 1984) activates "developmental strivings" (Fosshage, 1992) to elaborate that cohesively organized self in tune with relevant social contexts through "a continuous unfolding of an intrinsically determined social nature" (Stern, 1985, p. 234). As in embryological development, an inborn developmental direction is implied; this leads the person to develop satisfying, coherently organized goals, values, skills, and patterns of living that are accepted, valued, and socially confirmed by his or her "relational matrix."

Developmental Principles and Processes

The theorists are vague about the processes that produce change. Ghent (1992) proposes two basic opposing processes that "could be called expansive versus conservative [or] growth oriented versus status-quo oriented" (p. xxi). This concept is similar to the incremental/transformational change and stability maintaining processes in the book's comparative framework. All use a broad proposition about growth-oriented learning termed *incorporation, identification, introjection,* or *internalization,* but none clearly explains it. Freud compared this process to ingesting food. It appears similar to social modeling or imitation in psychological learning theory. Children take into themselves attributes of others—such as parental values—or self-other patterns—such as the way a parent helps the child control his or her distress—by constructing representations of these attributes. Children then use these representations to organize and regulate their own functioning. This implies that they create a copy of the real thing.

The idea of copying, however, conflicts with the theorists' assumption that "object" or "selfobject" representations are constructed from, rather than merely being copies of, perceptions of or experiences with others. Using the food analogy, they propose that representations of self and others result from "a constant symbolic digestion process that constitutes an important part of the cycle of exchange between the individual and the outside" (Benjamin, 1992, p. 52). The "foreign protein" of perception is "split up after being ingested" and then "reassembled" to create representations that are used to guide further development (Kohut, 1984). Identification and other processes appear to be selective, self-constructing procedures rather than simple imitation or social modeling.

A second proposition is that affective and cognitive evaluative aspects of interpersonal relationships influence learning. A key factor influencing the selection of attributes on which representations are based is the emotional nature of the interpersonal interactions (Winnicott). Experience has both a pleasant and a painful evaluative quality. Interactions may be gratifying or ungratifying, and representations of each type are constructed (Fairbairn). A child is particularly sensitive to the feeling states of its selfobjects (Kohut), but this sensitivity is bidirectional between mother and child so Sullivan called it an empathic linkage that produces a kind of "emotional contagion or communication." The child needs to experience the joy and approval of parents, called mirroring, and their attributes as desirable, called idealizing (Kohut). Similarly, parents experience their child in positive and negative ways; this influences how they behave toward the child. Interactions with a positive emotional or evaluative tone enhance growth and relationships; negative ones inhibit these processes. Positive consequences facilitate approach behaviors; negative ones facilitate avoidance.

A third proposition is that learning functions to create coherently organized patterns of intrapsychic and interpersonal functioning. Humans have "a pervasive tendency to preserve the continuity, connections, familiarity of one's personal [external and internal] interactional world" (Mitchell, 1988, p. 33). Their "mental structures" become organized in idiosyncratic "personal hierarchies" that differ in degree—from "tight" to "loose" or "fragmented"— or type of organization,—"cumulative," "transformative," "committed developmental directions." These compose one's personality (Pine, 1990). People are innately self-organizing. It follows that when organization is disrupted, a person will function to recreate coherent organization, thereby creating somewhat different functional patterns. When an existing pattern is a strong habit, functioning as a closed system, it prevents disruption and remains the same. Only when it functions as an open system so that it can be affected by outer reality is change possible (Fairbairn). Negative emotion-avoidance based habits tend to function as closed systems.

Kohut (1984) describes a process of "optimal failures," which lead to "transmuting internalizations" and results in "structure building." Although a relationship—such as parent-child or analyst-patient—may typically be understanding, caring, and supportive, there will be occasions when the adult figure behaves with irritation or lack of empathic understanding toward the other. Those instances are called optimal failures; although they disrupt the existing pattern of relationship, they occur in the context of a "good" relationship, and are "of a non-traumatic degree"; they are "understandable disappointments" rather than "traumatic frustrations." After an "optimal failure" disruption, the child or patient tries to change the pattern to accommodate the meaning of the disrupting event and restore coherent organization; this action is called transmuting internalization. The outcome is a modest change in the existing pattern, or structure building, similar to the process of incremental change in the book's comparative framework. However, if there is a "consistent mismatch" between current experience and the person's existing "perceptual-affective-cognitive schemas," the result may be "developmental derailment" and deficits in, or blocking of, normal developmental pathways (Fosshage, 1992).

A fourth proposition is that humans' functioning is largely anticipatory; people usually behave in terms of intrapsychic representations and expected consequences rather than as a reaction to actual interpersonal events. This behavior follows logically from their assumption that mental representations of "object/self relations" guide and organize current interpersonal functioning. People function in terms of memory and foresight. Foresight involves the anticipation that future interactions will conform to past experience. The basic link between "objects" and "self" is the anticipation and resulting experience of positive evaluations by others (Fairbairn). Anger is both a reaction to and an anticipatory effort to elicit desired responses from others (Suttie). A firm internalization of positive "self-selfobject representations" provides the basis for an expectation of positive responsiveness by significant others (Balint; Kohut).

Development Starts with What Exists
Infants begin life with a primitive but elaborate repertoire of capabilities. Initial development results from the interaction of these innate patterns with the flow of infants' experience, such as their capacity for constructing cogni-

tive representations and using them to guide future behavior. As cognitions of self and others are constructed, these facilitate and constrain creation of additional representations. Future development, including that occurring in analysis, always starts with existing structures; "analysis does not create, as in childhood, a self de novo but only a strengthening of preexisting structures" (Kohut, 1984, p. 217).

All the object relations and self psychology theorists assume that infants have a sophisticated and very active psychic life, but they differ over the nature of inborn characteristics and structures. For example, Klein assumed that infants have phylogenetically based, inborn, unconscious images and fantasies about object relations. While these can be modified through experience, she gives less emphasis to new experience than to unconscious fantasy in determining infants' basic outlook. Others assume that all self and object representations are constructed through experience in an interactive, interpersonal field.

Development Changes the Content and Organization of What Exists
Development results from differentiation, elaboration, organization, and reorganization of existing patterns. Infants' initial "objects" are "prepatterned" within "templates" provided by their developmental needs (Winnicott). Experience modifies infants' initial "object phantasies" (Klein). Infants' initial self is a product of their innate potentials and their selfobjects' expectations (Kohut).

Many assume that newborns do not distinguish between self and others; all experience is the same whether it comes from within or without the infants; everything is part of them, called an *autistic phase* or *infantile solipsism* (Suttie). Both their biological dependence on care by others and their innate social nature, however, immediately embed them in social interactions with their mother. The father is seldom mentioned. Mother is portrayed as both saint and villain in children's initial development. These are bidirectional or reciprocal relationships guided by an "empathic linkage" or "resonance" through which they sense one another's states (Sullivan; Kohut). Infants' innate need for affectional, nurturant attention elicits the mother's appropriate caring and approving responses; she performs a *mirroring function* (Winnicott; Kohut) that, in turn, gives her satisfaction. The psychologically important aspects of their relationship are not primarily physical; they consist of complex and mutual emotional needs (Winnicott).

Normally, the initial maternal environment performs self-sustaining, growth-enhancing functions for the infant. The "ordinary devoted mother" provides a "holding environment" composed of affectionate, caring, soothing, and self-confirming feedback. This helps the infant begin to become effectively self-directing and self-regulating. The mother doesn't need to be perfect, only a "good enough mother" (Winnicott). An occasional lapse from being a good "selfobject" provides "optimal failure" experiences—disappointments rather than traumas—that activate necessary "structure building" through "transmuting internalization" change processes (Kohut). These resemble what some learning theorists call a schedule of partial reinforcement which evidence indicates builds stronger habits than perfect consistency; the infant learns that "although mother is sometimes unaffectionate or irritable, she still loves me."

Infants construct self and object representations from these initial experiences centered around the *experience of merger with the mother* (Fairbairn), a fusion in subjective experience called *primary love* or *primary object relationship* (Balint), *archaic selfobject relationship* (Kohut), *subjective object* (Winnicott), or *primary identification* (Fairbairn). However, they soon begin to distinguish self from non-self. This distinction produces a developmental pathway of leading away from infantile dependence to adult independence. Others argue that autonomy is not the desired outcome: Separation is not a separation but a form of union (Winnicott, 1971). Humans' innate social nature requires positive, nurturing, sustaining interpersonal relationships from conception to death. Therefore, healthy development proceeds from infantile dependence to a mature interdependence that is mutual and without disparity (Fairbairn); the need for others continues, but the quality of the need changes (Kohut). The movement from infantile dependence toward mutual interdependence involves construction of self-other conceptions increasingly complicated in both content and organization. To learn about this progress, we examine the properties of these emerging structures.

Psychological Representations That Regulate Intra- and Inter-Personal Functioning

In the discussion, *psychological* is used instead of *cognitive* to show that the theorists' idea of a representation is a pattern of cognitive and affective responses involving self and others, and only partly present in the contents of consciousness. This concept is similar to the behavior episode schema in our comparative framework. Recall that the schemas are general perceptual-cognitive-affective-biological-action patterns that function in anticipatory, predictive fashion to organize and guide future functioning in similar situations. The emphasis of the object relations and self-psychology theorists on self or others differs, but that difference tends to disappear in clinical practice (Bacal & Newman, 1990). Representations of salient interpersonal situations or "selfobject" patterns are emphasized. The "basic relational configurations" involve "three dimensions—the self, the other, and the space between the two" (Mitchell, 1988, p. 33). But, "ego and object" are inseparable (Fairbairn); "the self is always defined in relation to objects [but] internal objects have no meaning except in relationship to the self" (Scharff, 1992, p. 24).

How are habitual intrapsychic structures constructed? Perceptual-affective-cognitive schemas are gradually built from interpersonal transactions. Once built they provide the frame within which subsequent life experience is organized and constructed, including transference (Fosshage, 1992). Children's interpersonal experiences, however, vary from occasion to occasion and person to person, resulting in different structures that can guide future functioning in different types of episodes, such as hostile versus approving ones, or with people with different styles, such as an affectionate mother and a cold father. A repertoire of self-other structures results, each of which will guide the child's functioning in new situations similar to those that led to their creation. "The patterns reflect learned modes of dealing with situations and are therefore always in some sense responsive to and shaped by the situations themselves" (Mitchell, 1988, p. 25).

Illustrative of the structures proposed are these: "good me," "bad me," and "not me" (Sullivan); "part objects," "whole objects," and "need-satisfying objects" (Klein); "libidinal ego—exciting (enticing) object," "anti-libidinal ego—rejecting (depriving) object," and "central ego—ideal (gratifying) object" (Fairbairn); "true self" and "false self" (Winnicott); and "mirroring and idealized selfobjects" (Kohut). Unified functioning, however, requires some form of intrapsychic organization of these component structures (Pine, 1990). "What ensues ultimately is an enormously complex perceptual, cognitive, affective and motivational system in which prior experience, by now patterned into templates that are unique for each individual, in turn molds and patterns experience" (Ghent, 1992, p. xix).

In the comparative framework used in this text, specific occasions of experience are called behavior episodes (BEs), termed *moments* by Pine (1990); his guiding "templates" or "patterns" constructed from them are behavior episode schemas (BESs). Kohut (1984) emphasizes the importance of distinguishing between people's experience in a specific episode, which he calls *experience-near acts,* and the general "template" assumed to be guiding such acts, which he calls *experience-distant principles.* He applied this distinction to analysts' theoretical model of what is normal or abnormal for an analysand and its relationship to their understanding of analysands' current experience. It can be equally applied, however, to understanding the relationship between analysands' experience in a specific behavior episode and the intrapsychic habits or behavior episode schema underlying that experience.

Properties of Healthy or Normal Development

A person's personality is composed of a repertoire of self-other representations. Both its content and its organization are important for healthy functioning. The general developmental pathway is from infantile, helpless dependence in which real or symbolic others regulate the person's functioning, to self-regulated, mutual interdependence. Children become able to regulate and organize their own emotional life, to monitor and soothe their tension and stress down to "tolerable" levels, to energize their own ambitions, goals and values, and to regulate their own self esteem (Jackson, 1994). The foundation structures are created in the pre-oedipal years of infancy and early childhood. Strong foundations lead to emotionally healthy adulthood; faulty ones make people vulnerable to later pathological development. Healthy adults are emotionally interdependent with others rather than maintaining the skewed dependence of infancy (Fairbairn). They live creatively and feel that life is worth living (Winnicott). They feel special and unique, confirmed by others and able to regulate their own functioning easily, effectively, and without conscious thought (Kohut, 1984).

Once formed, guiding representations become functionally autonomous from their developmental history; a person need not remember how they were learned. "Normal mental functioning . . . rests on smoothly interacting psychological structures" (Kohut, 1984, p. 160). Winnicott (as cited in Bacon-Greenberg, 1986, p. 384) assumes that "emotional and intellectual well-being rests on the ability to rework received experience according to one's inner inclinations" within "environmental provision of enough freedom to make one's mark and the resiliency of the environment to counter the individual's omnipotence." Pathological development results when psychic organization is faulty and the content is socially unsatisfying and maladaptive.

PROPOSITIONS CONCERNING PATHOLOGICAL DEVELOPMENT

Object relations and self-psychology theories grew from clinical work with patients thought to be more disturbed than the typical neurotic individuals from whom Freud's proposals were originally formulated—patients diagnosed as schizophrenic (Sullivan), schizoid (Fairbairn), borderline (Kernberg), or narcissistic (Kohut). At first, they considered traditional psychoanalysis satisfactory for neurotic patients, but like most therapy theorists, they progressively expanded proposals originally formulated to explain one type of disorder to try to explain many types. All forms of psychopathology reflect a deficit, defect, or distortion in development rather than primarily an intrapsychic conflict as assumed by Freud. A *deficit* refers to the absence of some interpersonal and psychic conditions essential for healthy development. A *defect* refers to a faulty way of functioning. A *distortion* is an indirect or compensatory way of trying to produce desired conditions when direct ways are not feasible.

Briefly, the theorists rationale is this:

1. The basis for psychopathology is established in infancy or early childhood as a result of faulty interpersonal experiences; if healthy self-other patterns are constructed, later life stresses are less likely to produce psychopathology.
2. Dysfunctional patterns result when parental behavior inadequately facilitates development of children's inborn social nature and their self and self-other guiding representations.
3. To control the distressing affects produced by faulty parenting and to try to create psychic organization that retains some sense of unity, children construct "mental structures" to segregate the distressing components of experience from positive or nondistressing ones.
4. Different forms of psychopathology result, depending on when efforts at segregation begin, the severity of distressing experiences, the kinds and organization of "mental structures" created, and the adaptive strategies used by the child.

Klein's (1932) approach is illustrative; the process starts at birth. The child feels every experience results from the acts of others or "objects" and has a positive or negative valence. Infants classify "objects" as good or bad based on their valence. This process leads to object relations in which "persecutory anxiety" and "ego splitting" predominate, with feelings of extreme omnipotence, denial, and idealization of the "good object" used to check the persecution. In this *paranoid* or *paranoid-schizoid position*, the anxiety results from fear of "ego destruction." As development proceeds, the infant begins to link good and bad representations and the feelings of love and hate toward each. In this *depressive position*, the anxiety results from fear that the good object will be destroyed and with it the infant's ego. Klein considered the depressive position basic to healthy development because it facilitates ego development, relations between subject and object, and relations with the world. Faulty parenting during the development of the paranoid position can make the child vulnerable for later serious psychoses. Faulty parenting during development of the depressive position can make the child vulnerable to later neurotic and other disorders.

Winnicott rejected the idea of inborn psychic structures, arguing that primitive emotional development encompasses the first six months of life, called *primary narcissism*. No distinction between self and object exists, and therefore there are no object relations. Successful primitive emotional development is the basis for constructing "self-object" patterns; faulty emotional development leads to creation of a "false self" to protect against "self-object" failures and distress. Theoretical differences have treatment implications. Because Klein assumed that ego functions and object relations exist from birth onward, she believed interpretation could be used in treating the infant/child. Winnicott argued that an interpersonal "holding environment" was needed within which the infant/child can regress to that earlier state where the developmental deficit can be remedied.

All these theorists agree that vulnerability to later psychoses results from dysfunctional development during the first years of life. Early faulty parenting prevents the infant/child from constructing functional patterns of self-other representations. They learn instead to protect themselves from distress with psychological barriers to self-other involvements (e.g., Winnicott's false self), creating roots for the isolation characteristic of schizoid states (Etchegoyen, 1991).

Faulty Parenting Properties That Facilitate Dysfunctional Development

Positive parenting is the sine qua non of emotional growth. When that is missing, development stops or is distorted, and the unsatisfied needs dominate subsequent living. Primitive emotional development is inconceivable without "good enough mothering;" children depend entirely on the mother to go through the difficult transition from primary narcissism to object relations (Winnicott). Children's innate needs for social relatedness and self-development are thwarted when parents are too often "emotionally absent, intrusive, or chaotic" (Fairbairn), display *selfobject failures* including unempathic, rejecting/critical/hostile, or unpredictable evaluative responding (Kohut), convey their anxiety and disapproval through moods and "tension states" (Sullivan), are troubled, inconsistent, compulsive or preoccupied (Winnicott), or unresponsive, erratic, vicious, threatening, rejecting, or absent (Bowlby, 1969). The content, evaluative nature, and organization of behavior are important aspects of faulty parenting. When parents are deficient, the content of their parenting is unempathic, vicious, or preoccupied; the evaluative nature is rejecting, disapproving, or hostile; and the organization is unpredictable, inconsistent, and chaotic.

Affective Reactions to Faulty Parenting

A child is thwarted when parental interactions are largely negative, unpredictably negative and positive, or absent. Persistent thwarting of children's needs for positive social relationships and self-development creates distressing, potentially traumatic affects. The object relations and self-psychology theorists emphasize one or more of four key types: (1) Faulty parenting thwarts the child's inborn social and self-development needs. As a result, the child feels unwanted, unloved and inadequate, and that his or her efforts to give love are not valued or accepted (Fairbairn; Suttie). (2) Vulnerability in self-esteem and the threat to the child's sense of self-cohesion produce feelings of anxiety (Guntrip; Kohut; Sullivan). (3) Thwarting may also produce hostility, manifested as hate, envy, or aggression (Fairbairn; Klein). "Earth hath no hate but love to hatred turned, and hell no fury but a baby scorned" (Suttie, 1935, p. 23). (4) Children evaluate their own hostility toward objects, or representations of them, whose love and approval the children want. They see their anger as being inappropriate, unfair, or self-threatening, and this realization activates guilt, shown as shame or humiliation (Fairbairn; Klein; Winnicott). The content and organization of children's self-other representations manifest their ways of trying to control distressing affects and still produce some degree of social acceptance and self cohesion.

Pathological Self/Object Representations
The theorists' proposal that psychopathology grows from psychological seeds planted during the first few years of life requires the assumption that infants and young children are capable of complex mental activity and construction. When others' behavior toward the infant/child and its experience of self-other interactions are both positive and negative as well as unpredictable, the infant/child is confronted with a confusing situation. He or she finds it difficult to construct representations of self, self-other, or self-selfobject patterns that combine contradictory satisfying and distressing experiences into a unified sense of self-in-social context. How can parents be both loving and rejecting, affectionate and hurtful, supportive and absent, good and bad? How is it possible to reconcile feelings of affection, satisfaction, anxiety, hostility, and guilt toward the same person?

These theorists propose that the children solve that dilemma by creating representations that separate or "split" the good from the bad portions of their experience. Although the theorists propose different types of representations, the underlying idea is essentially the same. For example, they construct "composite personifications" of nonanxious, tender experiences with others on the one hand—the "good mother"—and anxious, unaffectionate experiences on the other—the "bad mother." Self-personifications are also constructed based on the reflected appraisals of others—for example, "good me," "bad me," "not me" representations (Sullivan). Self or ego and object are "inseparable," so Fairbairn proposes three self-other structures: "libidinal ego—exciting (enticing) object; anti-libidinal ego—rejecting (depriving) object; and central ego—ideal (gratifying) object." The "true self" represents what one truly is or wants to be; the "false self" represents what others want one to be or the persona one presents to please others and protect oneself (Winnicott).

The organization of these self-other representations is also important because people struggle to create a unified sense of self-in-social context. Once this is created, people can regulate the impact of self-other relationships on their functioning by manipulating representations of them rather than the real relationships; self-other representations act as substitutes and solutions for unsatisfying relationships with real external objects (Greenberg & Mitchell, 1983). The greater the distress with natural objects, or real people, the greater the need to create psychic coherence by establishing relationships with internal objects (Fairbairn, 1952). People increasingly function in terms of the way they imagine things to be rather than in terms of how they are.

The psychic segregation of negative from positive representations, called *splitting,* is a mental maneuver that preserves the illusion of the goodness of the real parents and ignores or reinterprets the bad aspects as a means of gaining some measure of satisfaction of social and self-development needs and of avoiding distressing emotions. This appears to be a psychic avoidance pattern that disrupts *psychic unity* and creates the basic disunited *endopsychic situation* that makes one vulnerable to psychopathology (Fairbairn). These theorists propose different patterns of "splitting" related to their types of mental representations, such as *horizontal* and *vertical splits* (Kohut); forms of psychopathology reflect patterns of splitting. For example, Freud's oedipus complex is redefined as a product of segregating bad impressions onto one parent and good ones onto the other (Fairbairn; Sullivan).

A diversity of self-protective and adaptive mental maneuvers for dealing with segregated representations to prevent retraumatization (Fairbairn) have been proposed. *Projective and introjective identification* (Klein) have multiple and confusing meanings, a problem found with many analytic terms (see J. Scharff, 1992). For example the learning processes of identification and introjection are themselves not clearly defined. Frequent meanings are these: (1) *Projective identification* is a process by which some representations, usually negative ones, are fantasied or interpreted as representing aspects of some external object. They function to induce behavior in the other that the projector unconsciously identifies with. The projector can then seek to control those distressing self-other representations by controlling the objects to which they have been attributed. (2) *Introjective identification* involves people's taking in aspects of others as a way of adding to or controlling aspects of themselves, and then treating these aspects as if they were part of the self. To resolve contradictions in their representation of parents, children may blame themselves for negative parental behavior, thereby protecting their image of the good parent: "When, mother rejects me, it is because I am a bad person, not because she is bad" (Fairbairn, 1952; Winnicott, 1958). This is one of many possible forms of displacement. Ways of segregating good and bad representations and mental maneuvers for creating coherent organization among segregated representations are other ways of describing phenomena that classical analysts term *defenses*.

The object relations and self-psychology theorists agree that the nature of the organization of intrapsychic self-other representations is critical for mental health and illness; psychopathology is the study of the relationships of the "ego" to its "internalized objects" (Fairbairn). The theorists' versions of pathological intrapsychic patterns differ. The more intense the negative affect linked to a pattern, the more difficulty a person has in preventing it from disrupting the person's organized psychic functioning. Persistent, intense affect leads to segregation by an intense psychological avoidance pattern that blocks representations from consciousness; this avoidance is called *repression* or *dissociation*. The greater the proportion of representations linked to negative affect and the more intense the affect, the more difficulty the person will have in creating some sense of unified functioning. The individual's "self," "self-object relations," or "self-selfobject patterns" are said to be *fragmented* (Kohut) or *disunited* (Fairbairn). The more fragmented or disorganized the psychological patterns are, the more difficulty the person will have in creating and maintaining unified functioning, and the more vulnerable the person will be to psychopathology.

The most puzzling feature of psychopathology is its self-defeating quality. People persist in pathological patterns despite the distress and suffering these patterns produce. These theorists argue that humans' essential striving is not for pleasure but for social relationships. Therefore, pathological patterns persist because they serve a function; they are ways of trying to preserve some social connectedness through real or fantasied relationships, inadequate as they may be.

Etiology of Different Forms of Psychopathology
In general, these theorists propose that the same intrapsychic and interpersonal processes underlie the development of all forms of psychopathology. Different forms result from factors of (1) developmental timing, (2) the extent of intrapsychic fragmentation and distress, and (3) the intrapsychic strategies people use to deal with their distress. All psychopathological patterns are simply exaggerated versions of normal patterns of functioning and have a long history; they differ in degree but not in kind. A lengthy series of similar

distressing experiences is necessary to provide the "nutriment" that is "digested" and used to produce pathological mental structures and dynamics. The severity of pathology is a function of the extent of "splitting" of self-other representations and the portion of them that remain available to guide real-world instead of imagined relationships (Fairbairn).

The theorists propose somewhat different versions of the childhood conditions that make people vulnerable to different kinds of pathology. Different strategies may be used to control their negative affects toward parents and to preserve the sense of loving relationships, which is a matter of life or death for children. Each may lead to different forms of pathology: (1) Thinking that "Mother is good; if she hurts me it is because I am bad" makes people vulnerable to melancholia and feelings of inferiority and unworthiness. (2) When people reactivate the babyhood states of self and mother experienced as kind and good, they are escaping reality through fantasy and this may lead to psychosis. (3) In an extreme form, seeking a "good" substitute for a "bad" mother is a paranoid stance. (4) Anger and threat used to try to coerce the "object" into demonstrating love makes people vulnerable to delinquency, paranoia, or narcissistic personality disorders (Suttie). When children feel unloved and sense that the mother does not value or accept their love, they face a tragic situation of both being wary of offering love because it must be bad, and of accepting love because the love of others is not to be trusted. This is the basic schizoid conflict (Fairbairn).

Anxiety leads to pathological development in these circumstances: (1) It is excessively frequent and intense. (2) It is linked to circumstances the person both desires and fears, producing an approach/avoidance conflict. (3) The person has not learned an effective way of dealing with the conflict. Pathological patterns are composed of dysfunctional avoidant behaviors used in an effort to mitigate, control, or eliminate the disastrous effects of anxiety—the *self system*. However, they also prevent the occurrence of behaviors that might lead to satisfaction. A predisposition to serious disorder arises from massive avoidance of, and inattention to, interpersonal relationships. This avoidance results in significant dissociations from the relationships that are critical for the person's satisfaction and security.

The developmental period during which traumatizing parental or "self-object" failures occur also influences the type of disorder that may later develop; an example is a schizoid or depressive problem that predominates depending on whether the environmental failure occurs during the early or late "oral period" (Guntrip). If infants' *selfobject milieu* lacks *empathic responsiveness*, a *nuclear self* will not develop, providing a base from which psychoses may evolve. When it is partially adequate, an incomplete/faulty "nuclear self" may be created, making the person vulnerable to narcissistic behavior disturbances. Sound "selfobject milieus" in early childhood may produce a good "nuclear self" but faulty "selfobject relationships" in later childhood may produce conflicts that inhibit creative self-development, making the child vulnerable to structural-conflict neuroses (Kohut).

Because the theorists propose that different developmental conditions, occurring in different phases of development, produce different kinds of deficits, distortions, or defects, it follows that their interventions should be designed to fit the kind of developmental problems to be overcome.

THE PROCEDURAL MODEL:
THERAPY STRATEGIES AND TACTICS

Do the conceptual and propositional differences between traditional drive/structure and emerging relational/structure approaches lead to different procedural models? A clear answer is difficult

> because the privacy of the clinical setting and the ambiguity of technical concepts make it almost impossible for any analyst to know very much about how another analyst works. The drive model demands neutrality, but how neutral is neutral? The relational model demands participation, but how participatory is participation, and what form should it take? (Greenberg & Mitchell, 1983, p. 397)

Based on what the object relations and self-psychology theorists have written, we conclude that they have proposed no basic new strategies; they rely on strategies Freud initially proposed, but the tactics used to implement them differ from his, including their relative emphasis on the various strategies. For example, "self psychology does not advocate a change in the essence of analytic technique. The transferences are allowed to unfold and their understanding and explanation are central. It is the content and style of understanding and interpretation that is different" (Kohut, 1984, p. 208).

Key differences are these:

1. Greater emphasis on the patient-analyst relationship, particularly the dynamics of their real relationship, as a key therapeutic influence
2. Elaboration of tactics in addition to free association for obtaining an understanding of patients' difficulties and dynamics and for activating the patterns to be modified

3. A broadened view of the role and content of interpretations and the meanings they convey

THE PATIENT-ANALYST RELATIONSHIP

Analysts' neutrality, abstention, and anonymity stressed by traditional analysts is rejected "since it is the quality of early relationships that are . . . developmentally crucial [and] the quality of the analytic relationship that is . . . fundamentally therapeutic" (Greenberg & Mitchell, 1983, p. 391).

Relearning Through Relationship Experiences

In brief, the theorists' rationale is this: (1) All forms of psychopathology represent learned dysfunctional patterns, so effective therapy must provide relevant relearning experiences. (2) Because dysfunctional patterns were constructed to deal with faulty childhood interpersonal relationships, the relearning experiences provided by therapy must involve relevant kinds of "self-object" experiences from which patients can learn to modify their childhood-based intrapsychic dysfunctional self-other patterns. (3) Analysts must provide patients a relationship that is a model of good parental functioning that provides psychic "nutriment" that patients can "digest" and use to eliminate early developmental "deficits," repair developmental "defects," or revise "distortions" in development. Analysts must avoid repeating uncaring, hostile, and rejecting parental behaviors from which current dysfunctional "selfobject" or "object relations" patterns were initially constructed. Such analyst behavior would reinforce the dysfunctional patterns and prevent change.

Each theorist expresses this rationale somewhat differently. Analysts provide a specific type of interpersonal setting that "holds" the patient and that makes it possible for the "aborted self" of the patient to become "unstuck" and continue to grow (Winnicott, 1971). Analysts provide the crucial missing developmental experiences. Within the "actuating matrix" of the psychoanalytic situation the patient's "defective self" will function to complete its development (Kohut, 1984). This approach seems similar to facilitating self-constructing processes, explained in the book's comparative framework. The analytic situation enables patients to experience the analyst as a "primary object" for awhile so they can discover healthier patterns of "object relationships." Analysts must avoid the sense that they are powerful or knowledgeable, because that may revive patients' early experiences of oppressive inequality, and reactivate "the basic fault." Therapy helps "a frightened infant inside to grow up" (Balint, 1968, p. 171). It is the actual relationship between patient and analyst that constitutes the decisive factor. It includes not only the transference but also "a relationship with a reliable and beneficent parental figure" (Fairbairn, 1952, p. 377). Many analysts assume that "the central factor in therapy is not the achievement of intellectual insight but comprises an emotional experience of the difference between the therapist's attitudes and reactions and those of figures in his early life" (Bacal & Newman, 1990, p. 27).

The Primary Focus Is on Intrapsychic Change
Pathology is assumed to result from dysfunctional psychic structures representing "self-other" relations learned in infancy and childhood, though they may have been elaborated through later experiences. Like Freud, the object relations and self-psychology theorists focus on intrapsychic change rather than on cultivating interpersonal skills. There are two dysfunctional forms that require somewhat different change tactics; different theorists emphasize different forms (Mitchell, 1988). The *developmental arrest model* assumes a deficit exists. Faulty parenting produced a "developmental fixation" (Winnicott) or an interrupted "maturational push" (Kohut). Analysis seeks to make it possible for the stalled or interrupted development to begin anew. The *relational conflict model* assumes learned defects or distortions exist. Instead of "freezing" infantile needs in place, faulty parenting led to construction of dysfunctional "mental structures" or a poorly organized intrapsychic "world of object relations." Analysis seeks to alter those dysfunctional self-other "structures" (Fairbairn).

Functions of the Analytic Relationship
A good analytic relationship facilitates patient change in two ways. First, activating trust and positive affect toward the analyst inhibits activation of the negative affects such as anxiety, anger, or guilt that maintain repression or dissociation of faulty representations—the avoidance patterns. Then dysfunctional patterns can occur during analysis and patients can tolerate awareness of those patterns. The real relationship facilitates the transference relationship—that is, activation with the analyst of the patterns to be changed.

Theorists express in different ways this idea of reducing avoidance behaviors. It enables patients' "false," "compensatory," "defensive" adaptations "to collapse," thereby "freeing stalled development" and allowing their capacity for "self-cure" to pursue a healthier developmental pathway (Winnicott, 1958). It overcomes barriers to loving and feeling oneself loved (Suttie). Therapists should protect a patient's vulnerable self. They should not pursue areas patients are avoiding until trust in the relationship is established (Sullivan). The "split ego" evolved as an "internal closed system" to control effects of distressing early "object relations." Habitual defenses maintain such patterns as "closed systems." Effective therapy requires affecting them with "an open system of outer reality." Experiencing analysts as "good objects" is a necessary condition for patients to feel safe enough to "release" their "internal bad objects" from repression and to experience them with the analyst (Fairbairn). Analysts must provide therapeutic experiences that ease patients' need to defend themselves both by keeping their "bad objects" repressed and by blocking access to experiencing the analyst as a "selfobject" (Bacal & Newman, 1990). Defensive patterns are adaptive and psychologically valuable because they serve psychological survival. They function to save that sector of his "nuclear self," no matter how small or unstable it is, that he has created and maintained despite "serious insufficiencies" in childhood "selfobject experiences." "Transference resistances" must first be recognized and understood, and then dealt with by interpretation (Kohut, 1984). Therapy effectiveness is determined primarily by whether patients can tolerate becoming conscious of their sense of basic weakness and isolation, and can trust analysts to reach them "deeply" without hurting them as they were hurt as a child (Guntrip).

Even so, "all the evidence now available indicates that being nice, friendly, understanding, warmhearted, and in possession of the human touch cures neither the classical neuroses nor the analyzable disturbances of the self," at least as psychoanalysis defines therapeutic goals (Kohut, 1984, p. 95). Therefore, another function of the analytic relationship is to provide good, real-life interpersonal interactions from which patients can learn and which they can use to construct and reconstruct healthier psychological structures concerning self-other relationships.

Transference plays a key role in this process. All the theorists reviewed agree that clients' childhood-based pathological psychological habits must become active in relationship to their analyst if the habits are to be modified, but theorists' versions of the nature of those troublesome patterns differ. However, the activation in analysis of the old, dysfunctional patterns results not only from reducing negative affect but also from the analyst's behavior: The "events during an analysis are not determined by patients' associations and transference, or by analysts' interpretations, but by interactions between the two" (Balint, 1965, p. 285). For example, an analyst may do or say something that is similar in form to faulty childhood parental behavior linked to a patient's dysfunctional psychic patterns, thereby cueing activation of it. Activating transference patterns is a delicate matter, however, and can be deleterious rather than helpful, particularly with severely disturbed patients in very fragile condition, such as schizophrenics (Sullivan). It is important to distinguish an organized regression with the potential for unfreezing the failure situation from a pathological withdrawal accompanied by defensive splitting and dissociation (Winnicott).

Tactics for Understanding and Activating Patients' Dysfunctional Patterns

The basic therapeutic unit of psychoanalytic cure involves two interdependent steps: understanding and interpretation. Analysts must first understand their patients as a step toward helping patients better understand themselves. Object relations and self-psychology therapists reject the traditional assumption that analysts can function as objective observers gathering objective, verifiable information about a patient. They support an alternate view, with evidence from the natural sciences, that what is observed is a function of the act of observing. Patient and analyst function as a two-person, mutual causal system; each continually reacts to and influences the other through a flow of interpersonal transactions. The nature of their observations of one another is a function of those transactions. Therefore, they cannot be objective observers. They are *participant observers* (Sullivan), or make their observations through *relational participation* (Chrzanowski, 1982).

Empathic Understanding, Transference, Countertransference, and Intersubjectivity
The crucial information about patients lies not in their overt behavior but in their psychological functioning. Patients' immediate experiences with analysts result from interpersonal transactions that are influenced by their psychological functioning, called intersubjectivity. Intersubjectivity is "a field theory or systems theory in that it seeks to comprehend psychological phenomena not as products of isolated intrapsychic mechanisms but as forming at the interface of reciprocally interacting worlds of experience" (Stolorow, Atwood, Brandchafts, 1994). This is another way of talking about the reciprocal influence of phenomena that traditional analysts call transference and countertransference patterns.

Analysts become aware of their own "subjectivity" or countertransference through introspection. They try to understand the "subjectivity" of their patients through "vicarious introspection," by trying to understand patients' thoughts, feelings, and meanings by observing and interpreting their verbal and nonverbal communications using the patients' frame of reference. Kohut (1984) calls this *empathic understanding*. Empathy, an inborn human capability, is "the capacity to think and feel oneself into the inner life of another person" (p. 82), to experience that person's experience, though usually to an attenuated degree, and to understand the person's meanings, while "simultaneously retaining the stance of an objective observer" (p. 176).

Tactics for Eliciting and Communicating Understanding
To elicit the data on which their understanding of patients' private meanings and feelings can be based, these theorists use traditional free association methods supplemented with other methods, such as "targeted" free association. Here the analyst asks, "What comes to mind when . . ." or "Can you tell me more about that?" Another method is to ask direct questions. "Why do you suppose you are feeling angry toward me?" A third method involves dialogue with the patient. In general, these theorists are more flexible in the diversity of tactics they use, shape their tactics to fit patient dynamics, work in a more relaxed, less reserved fashion, and are more easygoing and willing to make themselves emotionally available if appropriate, than are traditional analysts (Kohut, 1984).

The resulting understanding of patients' current experience can be communicated to the patient to try to confirm that it accurately represents the person's actual experience in the current episode. Analysts describe their understanding of patients' current "inner state" as follows: (1) Convey the metamessage "you are understood," thereby cultivating a positive, trusting relationship. The patient's response would be, "This analyst really understands and cares about me." (2) Increase patients' accurate awareness of their own functioning. Most object relations/self-psychology analysts adopt a primary focus on patients' meanings, but some use the same procedure to examine patient-analyst concurrence. They probe the extent to which patient and analyst agree that those meanings correspond to the "actual character" of the events to which the meanings are attributed, a process called *consensual validation* (Sullivan). Some self-psychology proponents stress the experiential and tend to neglect explicit theoretical consideration of the "crucial role" of contexts, but they continue to recognize it in their clinical practice (Bacal & Newman, 1990).

Conveying empathic understandings to a patient, without evaluation of whether these are good or bad, right or wrong, significantly contributes to the first function of the relationship: to build trust and reduce defensiveness. This behavior implies a deep and empathic form of relatedness regardless of its content (Greenberg & Mitchell, 1983). Analysts must be able to feel and convey a sense of genuine personal relatedness (Guntrip, 1961). What is important is not so much what the analyst interprets but how he or she behaves (Winnicott). As patients grow in trust and feelings of security about the relationship, they feel freer to experience and express more distressing meanings. Transference of their bad habits to their interactions with the analyst become more likely. Accurately understanding current experience, however, is not enough. To endure change requires understanding and modifying causal intrapsychic patterns underlying current experience.

TACTICS FOR INDUCING ENDURING CHANGE

For analyst and patient to develop a shared understanding of experience in current episodes is helpful but insufficient. Kohut calls these *experience-near acts;* they are behavior episodes in our comparative framework. A single act or analytic episode cannot yield an accurate understanding of patients' dysfunctional patterns because no specific act of patient or analyst has more than momentary meaning; its meaning derives from the larger pattern of which it is a specific instance. Participant observation focuses on both the content and organization of the flow of patient-analyst activity. The analyst's objective is to identify and understand the consistent, generalized patterns—behavior episode schemas in our comparative framework—that guide the patient's functioning in specific analytic situations, or behavior episodes. Next, the analyst helps the patients to understand them. With a few exceptions, "It is not the understanding of the parts that explain the meaning and significance of the whole, but the whole that explains the meaning and significance of the parts" (Kohut, 1984, p. 127).

Self-Discovery
How can patients' understanding of their dysfunctional patterns (which Kohut calls *experience-distant principles*) be facilitated? One way is for them to discover such patterns themselves through shared understandings of their functioning in *experience-near acts* or specific analytic episodes, and then to use that explanation to revise their dysfunctional patterns. They can become "unstuck" and continue to "grow" through a "self-healing" process (Winnicott). The "maturational push" can begin to reassert itself "spontaneously" (Kohut).

Interpretation
Most patients require help in arriving at and using explanations of the causes of their specific acts in specific situations. Interpretation is the strategy serving that purpose. Conveying understanding focuses on patients' current states. *Interpretation* focuses on explaining the causes of those current states in "genetic" or developmental and more abstract or generalized terms. Analysts identify causal patterns and explain how patients' current thoughts and feelings are explained by "psychic structures" resulting from their experiences in early life.

The content of interpretations reflects theorists' conceptual and propositional models, so it varies because theorists use different explanatory configurations. For example, Kohut (1984) emphasizes "the essential importance" of patients "reexperiencing and working through the lethargies, depressions, and rages of early life via the reactivation and analysis of their archaic traumatic self-selfobject relationships in the transference" (p. 5). The focus of interpretations is the detailed examination of patients' "internal object relationships" that involve the analyst, and patients' associations in terms of experiences within the first few months of life (Klein). Patients must "regress in the transference" to a self-other state prior to that which produced the "basic fault." Starting with that early pattern, they can free themselves from their rigid, faulty "object relations" and construct better patterns through their relationship with their analyst; they step back to move forward on a different developmental pathway (Balint). Patients must experience a transference in which they enter a controlled "regression" back to their childhood "primary identification," so they can "regrow themselves" by relating to their therapist (Guntrip, 1969). Like the "good-enough mother," the "good-enough analyst" enables patients through transference to reach back and correct "the early disturbance," within the limits of the analytic setting (Winnicott).

The message or specific content of an interpretation is couched in the analyst's preferred theoretical terms, but the same meanings may be conveyed by different content. For example, to note that a patient appears to be angry toward the analyst for reasons similar to their childhood anger toward their parents, Klein might talk about "object fantasies," Fairbairn about "anti-libidinal ego," and Kohut about "archaic selfobject relationships." The timing of interpretations is also important. Their validity is tested against their power to explain immediate experience and to serve as tools for influencing future experience. Interpretations or explanations should occur only when patients' experience and current events in analytic sessions provide potentially convincing examples of the explanation in operation; a pattern cannot be influenced unless it is currently active. Change occurs primarily in incremental rather than transformational fashion, so it is usually best to focus on more superficial aspects of patients' patterns earlier in treatment and to move progressively and usually slowly toward "deeper" interpretations later.

Accurately understanding patients' immediate experience or causal intrapsychic habits is difficult, so interpretations will often be partially and sometimes totally wrong. Analysts may convey understanding of patients' current states but not act in accordance with patients' desires; analysts are not perfect. No single interpretation is critical, however, it is only necessary for patients to view their analyst as trying empathically to understand and to be right more often than wrong. In fact, occasional erroneous or contradictory interpretations or *optimal frustrations* may help by activating a transference pattern that can then become the focus of analysis, thereby facilitating understanding through *transmuting internalization,* and leading to *structure building* (Kohut). Both consistency in and occasional disruption of the relationship facilitate change.

Interpretations simultaneously have two meanings to patients that are components of an integrated experience: (1) Information and explanations are conveyed through messages' content. (2) Analysts' attitudes toward patients and their concerns are conveyed through tone of voice, facial and body gestures, and style of expression (Greenberg & Mitchell, 1983). Two kinds of impacts are possible. The content of explanations may influence patients' "intrapsychic structures," whereas analysts' thoughtful, objective, rational, caring manner provides a model for self-evaluation and understanding that patients can begin to incorporate and use on themselves. Analysts are *optimally responsive* when they provide a positive relationship, convey accurate understanding, and provide timely and useful interpretations (Bacal, 1985).

Conveying understanding and providing interpretations or explanations is a cyclical rather than linear process. Successful analyses require "countless repetitions of the basic therapeutic unit of understanding and explaining" (Kohut, 1984, p. 209). Patients' current dysfunctional patterns typically are the result of decades of learning and practice, and are heavily defended by strong stability-maintaining processes. Therefore, a lengthy learning process will probably be necessary to produce changes in such patterns.

STRATEGIES FOR FACILITATING TRANSFER TO REAL LIFE AND FOR
EVALUATING PATIENT CHANGE

Object relation and self-psychology theorists appear to assume automatic transfer of in-therapy changes to real life. They seem to believe that by using "the new psychic structures that have gradually been acquired over the years of treatment," patients can "learn the lessons of realism from life itself" (Kohut, 1984, p. 174). Although some analysts comment on the need for more effective evaluation, analyst and patient judgment is the primary method used to determine what enduring changes have occurred, as in traditional psychoanalysis.

STRATEGIES FOR EVALUATING OBJECT RELATION/ SELF-PSYCHOLOGY APPROACHES

The object relation/self-psychology theorists assert the importance of validating their theories but propose no ways of dealing with this issue different from those used by traditional analysts. There are unfortunate consequences to the lack of rigorous verification strategies. Once an approach has jelled, its major outlines become "dogmatic to adherents" who then defend it "vehemently," largely on ideological grounds. "Even though the claim of open-mindedness is always made," they display a "deep reluctance" to test their beliefs and consider alternatives (Kohut, 1984, p. 164). Because they focus on psychological phenomena "accessible only through introspection and empathy," the use of "experimental methods and statistical proofs" is precluded (p. 224).

CONTEMPORARY INTERPERSONAL PSYCHOTHERAPY

HISTORICAL PERSPECTIVE

Sullivan (1953a, 1953b, 1954, Ford & Urban, 1963) asserted that humans' functioning and development must be understood within its historical and current interpersonal contexts. Sullivan's views were largely ignored by analysts, but they significantly influenced psychiatrists and psychologists, leading to current interpersonal therapies. The initial impact in psychology was on theory and research about the social nature of personality development (e.g., Leary, 1957; Carson, 1969; Swenson, 1973). Psychotherapy applications followed (Anchin & Kiesler, 1982), and have recently grown into an influential stream (Andrews, 1991; Benjamin, 1993; Carson, 1991; Cashdan, 1988; Kiesler, 1988; Safran & Segal, 1990; Strupp & Binder, 1984). Kiesler (1996) provides a comprehensive summary and integration of contemporary interpersonal theory, research, and psychotherapy. His *Interpersonal Communication Psychotherapy*, which he also calls *Contemporary Interpersonal Psychotherapy*, is the exemplar we have analyzed.

CONCEPTUAL AND PROPOSITIONAL MODEL

Kiesler (1996) rejects the "Western world's myth of individuality" which ignores humans' "basic social embeddedness." His guiding assumption is that humans are innately social: "As social animals, we humans require transactions with others to satisfy our needs, attain our goals, and fulfill our potentialities" (p. ix). Unless otherwise stated, all Kiesler citations are to his 1996 book.

LEVELS AND UNITS OF ANALYSIS

Kiesler's (1996) basic level of analysis is an interpersonal transaction, which can be viewed in two ways: (1) In an "individualistic sense," it refers to people's actions in the presence of others; (2) in a "transactional sense," it refers to two people's "conjoint behaviors" which reciprocally influence one another. His approach is transactional; causality is "circular (rather than linear)." Behavior "is not . . . driven solely either by situational factors or by intrapsychic motivations"; relationships are "two-person groups in which members exert mutual influence (bidirectional causality)" (p. 3). Therefore, "the basic unit of interpersonal behavior is the interaction unit" (p. 6), which may vary in size, ranging from a single "cycle" to "phases" and "episodes," to lengthy sequences. However, "interaction units" can be "symbolic interactions" between "person and self schemas," such as fantasized interactions as well as real interactions (p. 8). Therefore, an intrapsychic level is also used, similar to simulated and instrumental behavior episodes in our comparative framework.

BASIC CONCEPTS

Kiesler's key constructs include the following: interpersonal behavior; the interpersonal circle, significant others, impact message, selective attention and perception, self and self-other schemas, interpersonal communication and the interpersonal transaction cycle. Each of these has subconcepts.

Interpersonal Behavior

Interpersonal behavior includes both overt, observable transactions between two people and interactions among psychological representations of "self and other." Kiesler's formal definition is, "Interpersonal behavior refers to recurrent patterns of reciprocal relationship present among two persons' *covert and overt actions and reactions* studied over some period (sequence) of their transactions with each other" (p. 67).

The Interpersonal Circle (IC)

The *interpersonal circle,* first proposed by Freedman, Leasy, Ossorio, & Coffey (1951) and Leary (1957), assumes

> that *human interpersonal behavior represents blends of two basic motivations: the need for control (power, dominance), and the need for affiliation (love, friendliness).* People continually negotiate two relationship issues in their interactions: How friendly or hostile they will be with each other, and how much in charge or control each will be in their encounters. (Kiesler, 1996, p. 8)

These appear to be evolutionary products, "a wired-in propensity for maintaining relatedness to others" that facilitates "survival of the species" (p. 69).

This idea is supported by Bakan's (1966) concepts of *agency* and *communion* and the "big five" factors of personality (Wiggins, 1996), as well as extensive empirical evidence. It is "an empirically based model" of the content and organization of interpersonal behavior "that specifies and organizes the full range of normal-to-abnormal interpersonal behavior" (Kiesler, 1996, p. 11).

The two dimensions of the circle are represented "as vectors in a two-dimensional circular space;" when "circumplex . . . and other trigonometric properties" are added, it "becomes a powerful structure for generation of theoretical propositions regarding interpersonal behavior" (Kiesler, 1996, p. 11). The control (dominance-submission) vector is the vertical axis; the affiliation (friendly-hostile) vector is the horizontal axis. Dividing the interpersonal circle into 16 segments, each representing a "trigonometric blend" of control and affiliation, creates a taxonomy of interpersonal behavior.

Interpersonal acts can also vary in their "intensity or extremeness," quantitatively as well as qualitatively. This feature is represented by the location of an act between the center and circumference of the circle. "The more extreme the act, the more maladjusted it is, and the more aversive its effects on interactants" (p. 16). Dividing each segment into four levels produces 64 patterns. For example, the mild to moderate version of one segment is termed *controlling-bold* whereas the extreme version is labeled *dictatorial-audacious;* the exactly opposite segment labels are *docile-timid* and *subservient-spineless.* Several questionnaires are used to describe people's actions or subjective reactions they produce in others. Correlated clusters of items describe the content and intensity of each pattern, which can be manifested overtly and/or covertly.

Significant Others

Kiesler (1996) says that people's *self-concepts* or *self-systems* emerge from and are maintained by "internalization" of what significant others—initially parents—communicate to them about themselves, particularly evaluative appraisals. *Significant others* "are those whose opinions about the [person] 'as a person' matter, with whom the [person] spends considerable time in either imaginary or real transactions, and who serve as potential sources of intimacy and regard in the [person's] life" (p. 73). Who functions as a significant other changes through life. The implication is that nonsignificant others have little influence on personality development.

Impact Message

In interpersonal transactions, one person's actions elicit psychological or "covert" responses in the other; this is called the *impact message.* There are four kinds: direct feelings or emotions; action tendencies; perceived evoking messages or relevant thoughts; and fantasies. Kiesler notes the "remarkable" similarity of these to the major components of contemporary theories of emotions, and concludes that "emotion is an essential component of the cyclical interpersonal transaction process" (p. 73).

Selective Attention and Perception

People's psychological responses to the behavior of another are a function of their perceptions and interpretations. (No model is provided of perception or its relationship to cognition.) What people perceive, think and feel results from *selective attention* and inattention. Kiesler (1996), like Sullivan (1953a; 1956), asserts that people prevent anxiety by not attending to anxiety-arousing events and by attending to other events. "The abnormal person operates from a selective inattention that ignores aspects of messages to and from others that are inconsistent with his or her constricted self-definition" (p. 127).

Self and Self-Other Schemas

Selective attention is guided by self-related schemas similar to the concept of the behavior episode schema in our comparative framework. Kiesler (1996) defines *self-schemas*—called self-systems or personifications of self by Sullivan (1953a)—as generalized patterns of psychological representations about the self constructed from self-related experiences, especially emotionally significant ones, with significant others: "Reflected appraisals" from significant others—what they "value, devalue and abhor in me"—define "what was 'good,' 'bad,' and 'not' me, my who-I-am template with which I now create my world" (p. x). Like a negative feedback loop (Andrews, 1991), they have self-confirming effects,: "They are readily activated with little information; they influence what we attend to, particularly self-consistent information; and they are used to actively solicit self-confirming evidence from others and to present ourselves in ways that will elicit such evidence" (p. 68). This is like stability-maintaining processes in the book's comparative framework. Thus, "our templates distort our experience of events in the world," so "experiences filtered by our templates cannot be directly perceived nor totally understood by anyone else." As a result, "In a real sense, we are isolated and autonomous beings insulated by our templates." But, our templates guide our interdependent interactions with others because "we conjointly create unexpected and reciprocally pleasurable shared outcomes" (p. x). People are simultaneously semi-autonomous units and parts of larger social systems—as described in the comparative framework.

People similarly construct "personifications of others" and of self-other relationships, or *interpersonal schemas*, that are learned ways of maintaining relatedness. "Humans are by nature attuned perceptually to detect any clues regarding the disintegration of interpersonal relationships and are programmed to respond with anxiety" and with "security operations" (Sullivan's alternative to defense mechanisms) to control such anxiety. One's self and self-other schemas may interact, producing psychological or fantasied interpersonal transactions—like behavior episodes in the comparative framework. Both kinds of schemas become habitual and operate unconsciously: It is "experimentally established that different forms of information processing routinely take place outside awareness" (p. 69).

Interpersonal Communication
Kiesler (1988, 1996) elaborates Sullivan's emphasis on communication: It is a "process of transmitting information (messages) from sender (encoder) to receiver (decoder), and the decoder's reciprocal response." Messages are conveyed both linguistically and nonverbally. Nonverbal communication is the basic way of "communicating emotional, relationship messages, including expressions of the encoder's attitudes about self and others—all of this being quite difficult for the encoder to distort or censor compared with his or her messages in the linguistic channel" (Kiesler, 1996, p. 209). This is like carrier–code distinctions in the comparative framework. Meaning is conveyed when messages evoke cognitive and/or affective responses from a "decoder"; linguistic and nonverbal messages can be inconsistent with or mesh with one another. Both participants simultaneously encode and decode messages from the other regardless of who is speaking at a given moment (p. 205). Thus, communication is a continuous mutual causal process that simultaneously conveys information and meanings, and defines the relationship—similar to the model of communication in the comparative framework.

Interpersonal Transaction Cycle
Carson (1969) proposed representing *interpersonal transactions* as an "unbroken causal loop" between the actions and reactions of two people relating with one another—analogous to coupling two open systems in the comparative framework. Kiesler (1996) states that each person's "who-I-am template" distorts his or her experience of the other. "What transpires between us is a moment-by-moment interactive process in which our . . . templates attempt to shape and alter each other's reactions in self-confirming directions" (p. x). The means is self-presentation: "the automatic, predominantly unaware, and recurrent manner in which we centrally view ourselves, which in turn leads to acted-out claims on others (evoking messages) regarding the kind of reactions and relationships we seek from them" (p. 4). Thus, the basis of the

process is interpersonal communication. Such encounters in "the here and now" function to both maintain and revise our "templates."

Other Aspects of People

Kiesler's theory is silent about humans' biological aspects, except for occasional reference to "genetic predispositions" and to examples of applications to health issues. Personal goals and personal agency beliefs are not discussed. We infer that they are part of the all-inclusive concept of self. Although transactional behaving is emphasized, there is little discussion of the nature or development of specific instrumental or communicative skills, or skills for monitoring relevant information. Interpersonal environments are emphasized, but the influence on people of sociocultural, designed, or natural environments is not examined.

PROPOSITIONS CONCERNING NORMAL DEVELOPMENT

Kiesler's (1996) interpersonal theory defines personality as "a complex set of interrelated intrapsychic and behavioral processes of persons that endure across time and situations (p. 38)"—specifically, patterns of interpersonal functioning. Therefore, personality patterns, such as self-other patterns, result from multiple experiences with significant others in interaction units called *interpersonal transaction cycles,* comparable to behavior episodes in the book's comparative framework. The dynamics of how development occurs is not explained. Kiesler's focus is on how personality operates once developed, and how it might be modified in therapy. The first developmentally important significant other transactions are with parents and siblings. Such relationships "grow and change, continue, develop, and even disintegrate" so "patterns of interpersonal behavior are influenced by different constraints and perform different functions depending on which phase of a relationship a particular dyad finds itself" (p. 50). This has implications for planning psychotherapy interventions.

Interpersonal Complementarity

Kiesler's (1996) basic assumption is that to create "comfortable (conjunctive, complementary) relationships" and avoid "uncomfortable (disjunctive, noncomplementary)" ones, people try "in automatic and minimally aware ways" to maneuver others to respond with control and affiliation actions "that are complimentary to, or reinforcing of" the pattern being preferred (p. 84). "Complementarity occurs on the basis of (a) 'reciprocity' [on] the control dimension . . . (dominance pulls submission, submission pulls dominance) and (b) 'correspondence' [on] the affiliation dimension (hostility pulls hostility, friendliness pulls friendliness)" (p. 91). Complementarity is an inference because it "springs from the psychological meaning attributed to others' overt behavior" rather than from the acts themselves (p. 110).

Both people in a transaction seek complementarity, so "whether a complementary outcome occurs for one interactant . . . depends crucially on what the other person concurrently wants, seeks, and is most comfortable with." *Complementarity* occurs if people's self-presentations "mesh and are mutually confirming"; *acomplementarity* results from partial meshing; when they clash, *anticomplementarity* results (p. 105). People learn different self and self-other schemas, so behaviors that produce complementarity for one dyad may not do so for another. Kiesler describes how his "interpersonal circle" model may be used to decide what would be complementary for a particular client's habitual interpersonal patterns. Types of complementarity have important implications for therapy relationships. Carson (1991) calls this an "interbehavioral contingency process."

This principle seems to represent Kiesler's view of change. Like Sullivan (1953a,b), Kiesler (1996) assumes that people function to create and maintain a coherently organized self-system and self esteem. When that is disrupted, they respond with anxiety and security operations to control it. "An individual bids for responses from others, and reacts to others, with responses that maximize feelings of security while minimizing feelings of anxiety. Interpersonal transactions that incorporate complementary behaviors reduce, eliminate or minimize interpersonal anxiety" (p. 90). (Producing complementarity is similar to negative feedback-based stability maintaining processes in the comparative framework.) "Transactions that include noncomplementary behaviors increase, exacerbate, or maximize anxiety" (p. 90), however, by disrupting the current interpersonal pattern. (Using noncomplementarity as a therapy strategy to facilitate change is similar to disruption-incremental change processes in the comparative framework).

Developmental Outcomes
Desirable developmental outcomes are not stated. Perhaps complementarity is desired, as it is "reinforcing and self-confirming to both participants," and can "minimize anxiety," "promote relatedness," and increase the likelihood of enduring relationships. Noncomplementary transactions, in contrast, "challenge existing behavior patterns," "are to varying extents aversive to both interactants," "increase anxiety," "interfere with relatedness," and "increase the probability of relationship disruption and termination" (p. 110).

Propositions Concerning Pathological Development

In contemporary interpersonal theory (Kiesler, 1996), "maladjusted behavior is defined as disordered, inappropriate, inadequate, and self-defeating interpersonal actions. It results originally and cumulatively from a person's not attending to (and not correcting) . . . self-defeating, interpersonally unsuccessful aspects of his or her interpersonal acts" (p. 128). Abnormal behavior manifests inappropriate or inadequate interpersonal communication" (p. 127). The dynamics by which pathological patterns develop are not explained. His reliance on Sullivan's "seminal" proposals implies dynamics of anxiety-based approach-avoidance learning in interpersonal behavior episodes.

Kiesler (1996, p. 133) describes seven attributes of maladjusted behavior:

1. *Extremeness:* the more intense the behavior, the more maladaptive and aversive
2. *Rigidity:* only a few interpersonal behaviors used, with little variability in behavior from one occasion to another
3. *Self-other perceptual discrepancy:* misperception by individuals of their own behavior and its impact on others, as well as misperception and misinterpretation of others' behavior
4. *Cross-channel incongruity or duplicitous communication:* conveying to, and eliciting from others, discrepant, mixed, and inconsistent messages and reactions
5. *Vicious self-defeating cycles or maladaptive transaction cycles:* maladaptive interpersonal behaviors that (a) evoke reactions from others that reinforce the maladaptive behavior, (b) are progressively experienced as more aversive by others, and (c) increasingly evoke messages of rejection and abandonment from others
6. *Tenuous stability under conditions of stress:* inability to use alternate interpersonal behaviors, and a tendency of individuals to escalate the extremeness and rigidity of their behavior under stress
7. *A higher level of interpersonal distress:* more interpersonal problems and more negative affect.

The Maladaptive Transaction Cycle (MTC)
Transaction cycles were described earlier. *Maladaptive transaction cycles* manifest attributes of the maladaptive behavior summarized above and produce a vicious cycle of self-defeating interpersonal transactions with significant others: "The covert and overt aspects of the maladjusted person's behavior . . . are chained circularly to the covert and overt aspects of the interactant's reactions" so as to produce escalating dissatisfaction for both, and "to recurrent

enactment of the cycle of maladaptive self-fulfilling prophecy and behavior" (p. 141). Why and how these cycles develop is not explained. The maladaptive transaction cycle and the interpersonal circle are key tools for diagnosing client difficulties and for guiding interventions.

THE PROCEDURAL MODEL: THERAPY STRATEGIES AND TACTICS

DIAGNOSIS

Kiesler (1996) stresses the role of diagnosis in planning treatment. "Basic understanding of both interpersonal diagnosis and intervention requires use of two conceptual models: the interpersonal circle, and the Maladaptive Transaction Cycle" (p. 201).

Diagnosis of the Type of Pathology
The *interpersonal circle* (IC) "specifies the range of individual differences in normal and abnormal interpersonal behavior" (p. 201). Assessments of the content, intensity, and important situational and temporal factors of a client's general interpersonal pattern (using measures constructed for that purpose) can be mapped onto the interpersonal circle to precisely link their prototypical maladaptive pattern of living to the generic patterns defined by the circle. This mapping facilitates a traditional psychiatric diagnosis by relating interpersonal circle patterns to *DSM-IV* (APA, 1994) diagnostic categories; it also aids identification of prototypical dynamics maintaining each pattern. Compare with a prototypic behavior episode schema for that type of pathology in the book's comparative framework.

Coyne's (1976, 1990) hypothesis about prototypic interpersonal depression is used by Kiesler as an example:

> "First, an interactant is pulled to express genuine reassurance . . . support . . . concern and helpful intent—in response to the depressed person's dysphoric behaviors" [complementarity on the interpersonal circle occurs]. "Second, . . . as frustration and irritation accumulate since the depressed person refuses to experience a healthy response to the increased attention (and the dysphoric behavior continues), the interactant's reassurance and support are now expressed less genuinely. [He] begins to feel angry and hostile, but [can't express] these feelings because of the vulnerability and suffering exhibited by the depressed person. The interactant is forced to respond with verbal assurances accompanied by nonverbal leakage of hostility, which the depressed person interprets as avoidance and rejection" [noncomplementarity occurs]. To try to avoid criticism or abandonment, the depressed person escalates dysphoric behaviors [to

try to restore complementarity]. "Finally, the interactant either avoids or eliminates contact . . . or the spiral continues . . . in a pattern of mutual manipulation.
(Kiesler, 1996, p. 145)

This example of the dynamics of depression is analogous to a positive feedback process as described in the comparative framework.

Diagnosing a Client's Specific Form of a Prototypical Pathology
The maladaptive transaction cycle (MTC) provides a way to depict specific
transactional patterns present in any patient's self-defeating relationships.
Kiesler (1996) assumes that "cyclically related patient-actions and therapist-
reactions [are] lawfully related and codetermined aspects of a central thematic interpersonal problem for the patient. This theme is exhibited not only
with the therapist but also with other significant persons in the patient's life"
(p. 239). Assessment, therefore, should include both the client's and significant
others' actions and reactions to one another, similar to a client's actual maladaptive behavior episode schema and others' reactions to it in the comparative framework. Kiesler (1996) states that "in the beginning stages of therapy,
the patient recurrently communicates his or her particular pattern of evoking
messages and enacts his or her pattern of rigid and extreme interpersonal behaviors" (p. 195). By observing specific examples of a client's maladaptive
transaction cycle and their own reactions—a set of relevant behavior episodes
in the comparative framework—and by obtaining similar reports from significant others of the client, therapists can identify psychological and behavioral components on which intervention should focus to disrupt the patient's
maladaptive transaction pattern.

   Once "the prototypic segments" on the interpersonal circle that define a
client's disordered pattern are identified, theoretically derivable interventions
can be specified. For example, "The goal of therapy is to facilitate an increased
frequency and intensity of interpersonal actions with significant others from
segments opposite on the circle to the segments that define the patient's pattern of maladaptive interpersonal behaviors" (p. 245).

INTERVENTION

Kiesler's (1996) basic assumption guiding intervention is that the content and
dynamics of the therapy relationship provide conditions within which clients
can learn revised or new self-other personifications, making them more encompassing, permeable, and flexible (similar to the psychoanalytic idea of a
corrective emotional experience) and can alter their maladaptive transaction

cycle into an interpersonal transaction cycle that is more flexible, adaptive, and satisfying. Three basic strategies are used: creating a positive therapy working alliance; activating and understanding the client's maladaptive transaction cycle in the context of that alliance; and providing an interpersonal transaction pattern that disrupts the client's maladaptive one and facilitates learning of an altered or different pattern.

Tactics for Creating a Positive Therapy Working Alliance
Kiesler's description of the relationship between client and therapist include the *working alliance*, the *transference-countertransference,* and the *real relationship.* A *positive therapy working alliance* has three components: "(a) mutual bonds of caring, liking, and trusting between patient and therapist; (b) their mutual agreement on the goals of treatment; and (c) their mutual understanding of the tasks necessary to accomplish the therapeutic goals" (p. 222). Relationship building is a "negotiation process" carried out through client-therapist communication patterns. Linguistic and nonverbal communication occur simultaneously. Information about the goals and tasks is conveyed primarily in the "linguistic channel" whereas information about mutual bonds is conveyed primarily in the "nonverbal channel."

Patients begin therapy by disclosing a "rehearsed story." Whereas the therapist's task is to help patients attend to, identify, and clarify missing elements of the story, that is not attempted in the beginning. In early therapy sessions,

> a "complementary transactional pattern" between patient and therapist mediates establishment of a positive therapeutic alliance, enabling clients to experience some level of acceptance and endorsement of their self-definition.

Activating and Understanding the Client's Maladaptive Transaction Cycle
Kiesler's (1996) "rock-bottom assumption . . . is that the client-therapist interaction . . . is similar in major ways to any other human transaction." So, within a working alliance, therapists function as "significant others" for clients. Then, clients' habitual maladaptive transaction cycle begins to function in relationship to the therapist, manifesting "the interpersonal dynamics that link self and other representations together in memory, which are displaced onto a new person" (p. 229). Sullivan called this *parataxic distortion* because it manifests interpersonal learning, while Freud's concept of transference connotes psychosexual drives.

The client's maladaptive transaction cycle includes an "evoking message" that elicits a "complementary impact message," or psychological responses, and overt behaviors in the therapist, like psychoanalysts' countertransference. The concept of the maladaptive transaction cycle includes both the client's and respondent's pattern. Therapists construct their understanding of clients' cycles by observing both the clients' behavior and the responses it elicits in them—the therapist—in multiple episodes of interaction. When possible, this observation may be coupled with reports of similar observations by significant others in the client's life. Therapists must distinguish between the two parts of their response pattern that psychoanalysts call objective and subjective transference. The "impact message" is analogous to "objective transference." Defensive and irrational reactions manifesting the therapist's own interpersonal history are analogous to "subjective transference."

Disrupting Clients' Maladaptive Transaction Cycles and Facilitating New Learning

When complementarity exists in therapists' responding, clients' maladaptive transaction cycles are being reinforced. Once an adequate working alliance is formed, therapists must begin to disengage from clients' maladaptive cycle. Kiesler (1996) states, "the cardinal therapeutic tactic is non-confirmation" of clients' maladaptive transaction cycle; "The essential therapeutic task . . . is to disrupt the patient's vicious circle of self-defeating actions" (p. 248) Such disruptions are produced by "noncomplementary metacommunications," or direct discussion of the patient's maladaptive cycle as it occurs with the therapist, including both the client's behavior and the reactions it elicits in the therapist.

Clients' thoughts and feelings can only be inferred by therapists, so statements about those parts of the client's maladaptive cycle should be phrased as "guesses" or "hypotheses." However, therapists can speak with authority about their own reactions, so descriptions of clients' "impact messages" can have more credibility with clients. Metacommunications are most effective when illustrated by specific events that have occurred in therapy episodes. "The success of metacommunication depends crucially on the commitment of the therapist to open, direct, unambiguous communication to the patient about the therapist's feelings, fantasies, and pulls as well as on the skill with which the therapist can provide feedback in a manner that is simultaneously confrontative and protective of the patient's self esteem" (p. 248).

Therapists may disengage from clients' maladaptive transaction cycle in several ways:

1. Privately observe and label the reactions clients are eliciting in them.
2. Discontinue complementary responding.

3. Verbally draw clients' attention toward missing elements in their rehearsed story that they have been inattending, including thoughts and feelings—the task elements—and habitual actions and messages—the transactional elements.
4. Metacommunicate information about both the positive and negative aspects and consequences of their maladaptive transaction cycle.

Noncomplementary responses threaten clients' "self" and "self-other" representations, so anxiety is activated and behaving to reduce it is intensified, called "resistance" or "countercontrol." This behavior may be realistic and conscious or automatic and unconscious. Such episodes are useful in helping clients understand their maladaptive transactions. Metacommunication should be descriptive rather than evaluative; empathic, problem-centered, spontaneous, and provisional, maximizing equality rather than superiority. This strategy is similar to stability-maintaining and incremental change processes in the comparative framework.

Kiesler's (1996) rationale implies that change occurs in two ways: disruption and self-reconstruction, and social modeling. "Through metacommunication, the patient begins to identify and understand his or her [maladaptive transaction cycle] as the first step toward healthier interpersonal alternatives. . . . By addressing their relationship directly, the therapist also models for the patient a powerful and unusual technique for communicating with those persons who are significant in the patient's life" (p. 286).

STRATEGIES FOR FACILITATING TRANSFER TO REAL LIFE AND FOR EVALUATING PATIENT CHANGE

Kiesler (1996) does not describe specific strategies for facilitating transfer. The implication is that these changes are expected to occur automatically as a function of in-therapy changes. A process view of change is described: "In . . . successful psychotherapy, the patient and therapist will move from rigid and extreme complementary transaction early in therapy, to noncomplementary positions in the change-oriented middle phases of therapy, to a later transactional pattern that exhibits mild and flexible complementarity. . . . in unsuccessful therapy, the patient-therapist relationship will remain bogged down in various degrees of complementarity throughout" (p. 261). "Adaptive client changes should be evident in more adaptive transactions with the therapist" (p. 242). They appear to rely primarily on client and therapist judgment as to whether change has occurred.

STRATEGIES FOR EVALUATING THE APPROACH

Kiesler (1996) does not explicitly discuss evaluation. However, his extensive citation and use of a very diverse empirical literature implies that he believes the strategies of empirical science should be used. He stresses that many of his proposals have yet to be empirically validated, and gives frequent examples of issues for which much more empirical research is needed.

CHAPTER 8

Humanist Approaches: Existential, Experiential, Gestalt, and Person Centered

A GROUP OF theorists, referred to as a "Third Force" in psychology and psychotherapy, stressed their sharp differences from psychoanalytic and behaviorist views of human nature. Three foundational schools are (1) The Client-centered (later called Person-centered) approach developed by Rogers (1942, 1947, 1951), (2) Gestalt therapy (initially called Concentration therapy) created by Perls and colleagues (Perls, Hefferline, & Goodman, 1951; Perls, 1969), and (3) Existential therapy created in Europe as Daseinanalyse (Binswanger, 1963; Boss, 1963) and elaborated in the United States by May (May, Angel, & Ellenberger, 1958) and Bugental (1967).

The distinctive emphases of this group remain influential. There are contemporary representations of the Rogerian approach (Bozarth, 1990), of existential strategies (Bugental, 1993; Bugental & Sterling, 1995), and of Gestalt theory (Korb, Gorrell, & Van De Riet, 1989; Simkin, Simkin, Brien, & Sheldon, 1993; Yontef, 1995). Experiential approaches build on these three traditions: Gendlin (1973, 1978, 1981, 1996) elaborates on the client-centered approach; Mahrer (1983, 1989) proposes an intensive experiential process mediated by exploration and discovery; Greenberg and associates (Greenberg & Safran, 1987; Greenberg, Rice, & Elliott, 1993; Rice & Greenberg, 1990) seek to integrate the three traditions within the framework of a theory of emotionality; and Assagioli (1965, 1973) extends the existential approach by proposing a higher consciousness and emphasizing transpersonal and spiritual aspects of human existence.

THE HUMANIST TRADITION

Analyses by Urban (1991), Rice and Greenberg (1992), and Shaffer (1978) reveal that these approaches manifest the centuries old humanist tradition. Socrates and Plato rejected the study of physical nature as a means of understanding humans, creating knowledge, or identifying intellectual and moral value. They viewed humans as having a material body and a nonmaterial, rational psyche or soul that inhabits the body as a pilot in a ship. Humans use their bodies to implement their innate tendency to seek the good, both for themselves and for others as they are by nature inherently social. The capacity for thought and rationality is humans' highest natural capability and the principal means for achieving the individual and collective good.

The influence of these ideas faded during the Middle Ages, reappearing during the Renaissance, when the term *humanism* was used to label a clear break from the dominant sterile authoritarian traditions that had accumulated within scholastic philosophy and theology. It emphasizes individuality, preservation and development of human life, the dignity and value of each person, the importance of subjective experience and rationality, human capacities for intentionality, the pursuit of valued purposes and goals, and the exercise of freedom and choice. Humanism affirms humans' unique nature and their perfectibility through collective exercise of rationality and accumulated knowledge (cf. Frank, 1977). Humanism has extensively influenced political, economic, social, and educational institutions of the Western world—such as its democratic institutions.

These theorists recognized that they shared this tradition. Rogers related person-centered therapy to humanism, Sartre (1947) linked existentialism to humanism, Bugental (1993) refers to existential-humanistic psychotherapy, and Rice and Greenberg (1992) consider the foregoing a coherent group. Mahoney (1991, 1995) identified humanist therapists as one of the principal metatheoretical clusters in his report of the combined results of 15 surveys of the theoretic orientations among U.S. clinical psychologists between 1953 and 1988. Recognition of their shared humanistic assumptions also reveals parallels with other approaches, such as Berne's transactional analysis (1961), Frankl's logotherapy (1962; 1967; 1969; 1975), Laing's radical therapy (1965; 1969; Ruitenbeck, 1962), and Whitaker and Malone's experiential approach (1953). It also links these theorists to an established tradition of inquiry in social and personality theory within the discipline of psychology—for example, Allport (1955, 1961), Buhler (1959, 1964), Erikson (1963, 1968, 1975), Fromm (1969), Maslow (1954, 1968), and Murray (1951, 1954, 1959; Murray & Kluckhohn, 1956).

The different names and theoretical terms used by these theorists imply basic differences in underlying models, but similarities among them are recognized (e.g., Pervin, 1960; Tageson, 1982). For example, Rogers noted similarities between his ideas and those of Adler and Rank, who broke from Freud to create subjectivist and goal-directed approaches. Perls (1973) acknowledged the existential nature of his Gestalt approach, but avoided the label because of the perjorative connotations it had acquired through the writings of Sartre and the association with nihilism. Urban's (1991) analysis of their shared humanist assumptions is summarized in Table 8.1.

Table 8.1
Shared Assumptions of Humanist Therapies (from Urban, 1991)

1. Humans must be viewed as distinct from all other forms of life and entities in nature.
2. A distinctive characteristic is the inherent capacity of humans for conscious experience and for awareness of that experience—that is, to be self-conscious and self-reflective.
3. Conscious experience includes a variety of processes, such as perception and categorization of experience, imagery, affect, conception thought, symbolization and language, recollection, anticipation and foresight, intentionality, choice and initiation of purposive action.
4. The contents of experience are continuously and rapidly changing, so that people are continually becoming something other than they presently are.
5. There are inherent human tendencies in each person to construct order and stability from the varied flow of experience, yielding organizations of experience of oneself and one's world, which constitute reality from that person's perspective.
6. The psychological organization each person develops enables the person to function as a unit; it is also necessarily individual, personalized, unique, and therefore of intrinsic value.
7. The psychological organization also exerts the principal influence upon what each person comes to be and do; each person, moreover, bears personal responsibility for both its properties and effects—the consequences produced.
8. In addition, each person is also inherently proactive, purposive, and self-directing in operation, defining both possible and desirable outcomes, and identifying goals that can provide value, significance, and meaning to one's existence.

Table 8.1 *(continued)*

9. Humans are also inherently self-regulating, constructing and using values to guide their choices among goals and choosing, initiating, directing, regulating, and sustaining courses of action intended to achieve those goals.

10. People function optimally when aware of the experiences produced from their transactions with themselves and their environments on a moment-to-moment basis, cognizant of their capabilities, open to all available possibilities and opportunities, and acceptant of the responsibilities inherent in living.

11. Problems in living arise when incongruities develop between the person's immediate and direct experience and their constructed psychological organization; recovery entails use of processes associated with optimal functioning.

12. Because each person's psychological organization is uniquely self-constructed and serves to guide behavior, a comprehension (understanding and explanation) of human action must be centered on the study of individual persons, taken one at a time.

13. This study requires a detailed inquiry into the organization of each person's subjective experience to which only that person has direct access; indirect access can be gained through reliance upon the person's subjective verbal report and the use of empathic or intuitive listening under specially arranged conditions.

METAPHYSICAL AND EPISTEMOLOGICAL ASSUMPTIONS

Recognition of their common roots in the humanist tradition helps one to identify the basic ontological, cosmological, and epistemological assumptions underlying the foregoing approaches.

ONTOLOGY

One can infer a commitment to an ontology of idealism that is manifested in a rationalist position of *phenomenalism:* The only reality humans can know directly is that which occurs in their personal experience. However, experience varies constantly, so humans try constantly to organize its diversity into some kind of meaning. By creating subjective networks of coherent meanings, people construct their models of reality and choose their modes of transaction with what they conceive reality to be. Physical science and technology are just such creations. Materialistic models are considered inappropriate for understanding humans: To treat them as objects of study, like any other object, is to dehumanize them, with inevitably deleterious effects. Extrapolation from studies of other species is considered biocentric and spuriously metaphoric in character.

Truth and Reality

Presuming a reality independent of humans is unnecessary. People's ideas about reality emerge from the meanings they construct from their experiences and intuitions, together with their impressions of others' experiences. Reality lies in the eyes of the beholder; it is particular and unique to the individual. Thus, there is no foundational theory of truth. Truth lies in the coherence among conclusions, courses of action, and people's experience, not in the correspondence between their ideas and an assumed objective reality.

COSMOLOGY

The humanists reject classical Newtonian assumptions about how reality is organized. Rather than seeing stability as the norm, with change construed to be a perturbation that requires corrective action, they see the universe as continually varying and changing. Only relative stability is possible; change is not caused by some force but is an innate tendency in all things. Traditional assumptions of linear cause-and-effect linked to a materialist view are rejected. Everything, including human experience, displays inherent organization; changes occur as successive transformations of organization. Through life, people remain coherently organized entities, even though changes of two types continuously occur. One type is change that follows intrinsic, never-ending sequences of progressive differentiation, producing an elaboration of parts and a more complex, organized whole—an organismic position. The second is change that occurs on a moment-to-moment basis as a person effects a creative adaptation to a varying personal and context-based experience, producing patterns different from those that existed before—a dynamic, or self-organizing view.

EPISTEMOLOGY

The humanists' emphasis on subjective experience does not mean that they reject science. They do reject any view of science that limits the study of humans to what can be precisely and objectively measured in multiple people under standard conditions—logical positivism—or that eschews any interest in subjective experience per se—traditional behaviorism. Nor do these approaches require one to assume that subjective processes occur within a bodiless mind. They assert the legitimacy and significance of subjective events as part of a total functioning person, regardless of whether biological correlates for those events are known. They acknowledge that most of people's psychological constructions and personalized meanings remain tacit and unverbalized. Only some of these can be consciously communicated to others, but someone may gain a reasonable understanding of another's subjective experience and private meanings by developing a special interpersonal relationship with that person and using participative listening and empathic or intuitive judgment.

Creators of these approaches (e.g., Rogers, Perls, Binswanger, Boss, May) continue to be cited, but the models they originated have been elaborated and developed by others. The present analysis focuses primarily on the more recent representations found in such sources as Bohart (1995), Bugental (1993), Bugental and Sterling (1995), Fischer (1991), Greenberg, Rice, and Elliot (1993), Korb, Gorrell, and Van De Riet (1989), Rice and Greenberg (1992), Yontef (1995), and Zimring and Raskin (1992). Analyses of original versions are available in Ford and Urban (1963). Summaries in the theorists' own terms are available elsewhere.

THE CONCEPTUAL MODEL

LEVELS AND UNITS OF ANALYSIS

The Person-in-Context

For the humanists, the person-in-context is the primary unit of concern. Humans can exist and function only within some kind of environment. "Being means being in the world"; trying to understand people separate from their world is an "ontological mistake" (Bugental & Sterling, 1995, p. 232). To talk about people as if they were completely free of their life contexts is meaningless (Bohart, 1995). Internal processes, such as the physiological and psychological processes, never operate in isolation but function in the context of the total environment (Korb et al., 1989). The person and the environment cannot be meaningfully separated but must be understood as parts of an organism-environment field, especially the interpersonal aspects of that field (Yontef, 1995).

The humanists consider relationships between people and their contexts in two ways. In the *interactional view,* what people come to be or do results from a dynamic interplay between themselves and their world (Bohart, 1995; Yontef, 1995). The *transactional view* conceives of a continual exchange, a condition of coconstitutionality, with the nature and meaning of each being shaped and modified by the ongoing dialectic or dialogue with the other. All events occur in dialectical relationships (Bugental & Sterling, 1995). These are dynamic units; no one is a fixed personality (Simkin et al., 1993); everything exists in process. Life is an ongoing and continually evolving process of moment-by-moment living (Bohart, 1995), a flow of events and changing interrelationships (Korb et al., 1989), continual dynamism (Bugental & Sterling, 1995). People behave in terms of what is currently important and salient to them.

People's interpretations and actions in a given situation are unified creations, in which individuals use their current experience and relevant learned psychological patterns. However, people never create precisely the same pattern twice, even in similar situations. Continuities exist, but all person-in-context patterns are continually evolving (Bohart, 1995). People continually explore and discover new ways of being and behaving (Bugental & Sterling, 1995), and changes are always occurring in the person-context field (Korb et al., 1989). In each situation, functioning occurs in organized units—for example, *gestalten*. These representations are similar to behavior episodes in the guiding comparative framework.

Person Components

The everyday concept of personality, reflecting the Aristotlean mode of an objective observer viewing the person as an object, is useless when one adopts the phenomenological view of the subjective observer (Bugental & Sterling, 1995). A phenomenological view focuses on psychological processes and plans that can be organized in diverse patterns. Examples of these processes are affects, sensations, perceptions, thoughts, evaluations, and intentions. However, the humanists assert that people should not be represented as composed of relatively fixed inner structures, such as basic values, beliefs, or traits, that are elicited under given conditions. To analyze people's dynamic complexity into simpler structures is to lapse into the fallacy of reductionism and spurious oversimplification; people always function as organized wholes (e.g., Korb et al., 1989). The assumed basis for unitary functioning varies; the most common is a proposed inherent movement or tendency toward organization (Rogers) or consistency (Adler). Compare the idea that people are self-organizing with the principle of unitary functioning in the guiding comparative framework. Initial knowledge of clients is fragmentary, but the meaning of the parts cannot be understood in isolation; they are all dynamically related.

Efforts to conceptualize such complex, unitary patterns usually yield relatively abstract analytic units and concepts, often termed *processes*. Therefore, the concepts of this group of theorists tend to be molar, organized in complex patterns, and qualitative in character, in contrast to the more molecular, discrete, and sometimes quantifiable units espoused by some other theorists.

Biological Characteristics: The Biological Person

Humanist therapists acknowledge but give little formal attention to the importance of humans' biological characteristics. Biological individual differences result from people's genetic inheritance, ecological niche, and life experiences; people differ in their biochemical tuning, height, neural and motoric capabilities, and physical handicaps. From an experiential view, it is not their biological or environmental circumstances per se that are critical. Rather, these are conceived to be conditions that constrain or facilitate the nature of people's experiences and thereby influence their plans and interpretations of possibilities and actions (Bugental & Sterling, 1995).

Biological and Psychosocial Needs

People have inborn needs for physical survival, safety, and functioning, such as the need for food and sex. Satisfying these needs or removing physiological deficits in them can be represented by homeostatic or drive models. Psychosocial needs, however, are just as basic and transcend people's animalistic needs of belonging, affection, competence, autonomy, and creativity. For example, infants are said to display a need for positive human relationships (Bowlby, 1969, 1982), which prompts them to seek from others contact/comfort and a basic sense of security (Greenberg, Rice, & Elliott, 1993). The humanists oppose models of psychosocial needs as derivatives of biological needs or secondary drives. Moreover, the relative influence of these two types of needs typically shifts from biological to psychological needs as people mature.

Psychological Characteristics: The Psychological Person

A phenomenological epistemology stresses psychological functions. Theorists of this persuasion rarely provide explicit definitions of their key concepts, but typically connotative meanings are implied. Prior experiences may be similar to and influence current experience, but the newness of each situation invariably produces novel elements. Each encounter is construed to be a dynamic constructive process and not simply an elicitation of routinized habits. Experience always occurs in a here-and-now form rather than as some learned permanent residues; therefore, concepts like memories, habits, or beliefs are not considered useful (Bohart, 1995). The focus of the humanists is on the "here and now" and "what and how" of behavior patterns rather than on their development. This emphasis is similar to the assumption in the book's comparative framework that only presently occurring events can be changed.

Consciousness, Awareness, and Attention
Being conscious or aware of one's experience is considered essential for effective functioning. Humanists seldom use the concept of unconscious processes. Some propose levels of consciousness, defined partly by content and partly by functions. Assagioli (1965, 1973) proposes a *lower unconscious* involving automatic processes at neurophysiological levels related to security and survival, and *higher unconscious* processes. This *superconscious* is responsible for feelings of love, joy, ecstasy, inner wisdom, and deep intuitive understanding. It exerts a natural pull within people toward personal growth, elaboration, intersubjective harmony with others, and planetary unity. Psychosynthesis is a therapy purporting to overcome barriers to people's access to these higher potentials. Rogers (1993) proposed a transcendental core or inner spirit that is indescribable. This spirit enables people to experience themselves simultaneously as a center of consciousness and with a sense of oneness with others. Thus, people's inner spirits can encounter each other, so that the barriers between one-ness and you-ness dissolve, and the relationship transcends itself and becomes part of something larger. Rogers does not explain how this occurs. Transpersonal psychotherapies use similar ideas. Space limitations here prevent further analyses of such proposals.

Humanists assume that attentional processes limit the content and range of people's awareness or experience, thereby facilitating or interfering with effective functioning. Clients' allocation of attention therefore becomes an important psychotherapy focus. The humanists seem to assume that selectivity of attention results from an inborn capability for self-direction. In their propositional models, they discuss the ways attention selectively influences experience and awareness.

Experience and Awareness
Humanists use experience and awareness as a way to conceptualize phenomena for which others others use concepts like perception and cognition. Awareness or self-awareness (Gestalt) and experience (person centered; experiential) refer to those aspects of a person's psychological functioning that constitute his or her current contents of consciousness. A phenomenological posture makes concepts stemming from objective modes of analysis inappropriate for understanding a person's existence. The analyst must take the

role of the "other" and understand clients from their own vantage point, called a phenomenological or subjective mode of analysis. As there is an infinite number of personal and unique constructions or existences that people can create, this epistemological strategy requires the therapist to accept as valid whatever clients present as their experience (Elliott & Greenberg, 1995; Yontef, 1995). Humanists avoid imposing a an *a priori* theoretical framework on clients' unique experience. Doing so would violate basic humanist assumptions (Shaffer, 1978). If the therapist emphasizes the essence of humanness rather than what people are like and do, the limits of human nature remain uncertain, and in this way, the therapist provides for the open-ended expansion and growth or self-actualization of which each client is capable.

All experience is a unified whole, so breaking it into components—perceptions versus images versus ideas—to understand it is to be misdirected by lapsing into the reductionistic error. Therefore, humanists do not make distinctions among kinds of experiences in their conceptual models. Treatment descriptions refer to what clients may have perceived, felt, thought, remembered, or decided, but these represent the concepts of clients rather than therapists.

Self-Experience and Self-Concept

Humanist theorists assume that people are self-constructing, but typically they do not describe how cognitive processes operate to construct patterns of personal meanings from the flow of experience and awareness. The content of experience varies from person to person, but some organizations of meaning appear to be universal, though the theorists do not explicitly state this. For example, person-centered therapists use the idea of self-concept, Gestaltists increasingly use it (e.g., Korb et al., 1989; Yontef, 1995), and existentialists periodically refer to an idealized or despised self-image (e.g., Bugental, 1978).

Rogers (1959) assumed that as soon as infants begin to have experiences, they become aware of themselves as separate entities. They begin to notice, attend to, perceive, and construct meanings from experiences based on "purely internal stimuli, memory traces, visceral changes and the like" (p. 199). He called this *self-experience*. Recurrent features are abstracted, first as images, then organized into concepts, and later encoded in verbal-symbolic terms, (such as "I am tall;" "I am strong;" "Other people like me"). These are not simply an aggregate of self-referent ideas, however. They become organized as a "consistent conceptual gestalt" (p. 201). Rogers (1959) considered the discovery that an alteration in one aspect of a person's self-concept could alter the entire pattern to be very significant for understanding psychological change processes.

Korb et al. (1989) argue that there is not one but a collection of self-concepts, ranging from relatively trivial and transient ones to more enduring and influential ones, and tending toward hierarchical organization. These are derived from multiple sources, including people's own evaluation of the feedback they receive about the adequacy of their efforts, comparative evaluations of themselves in relation to others, and evaluations from significant others. As people construct their own self-concepts, they are the ultimate source for self-concept change.

People also build representations that enable them to interact with their environment; these are representations of their world, a sense of the place within which they live, and of relationships between the self and world (Bugental & Sterling, 1995). These self and world models make up a person's existential reality. Watzlawick (1984) emphasizes that it is an invented reality—that is, not the truth in any metaphysical sense. These representations become interrelated into larger and more encompassing organizations, eventuating in the person's creation of a self-and-world construct system (Bugental & Sterling, 1995) or an interconnected set of internal models of self-in-the-world experience (Elliott & Greenberg, 1995)

Schemas

Some theorists use ideas from cognitive psychology. Wexler and Rice (1974) propose that people develop schemas to organize information about themselves and their world. They use new information to produce more differentiated and integrative schemas. Greenberg et al. (1993) use a schematic processing view of cognitive self-construction. People represent objects or events by configurations of their features. They organize these representations into schemas that are complex cognitive patterns (mental models) embodying their prototypical knowledge and ideas about themselves, and their contexts, and how those features relate to and influence one another. Abstracts of regularities—that which is generally true, what experiences have in common—is what becomes encoded in schemas.

Schemas operate outside of awareness as units; activation of any part activates the whole schema (cf. the comparative framework). An active schema guides perception, memory, and experience; automatically directs attention; it provides frameworks for organizing and preserving information and for cognitive constructions. New information is processed by means of a relevant schema to impose some structure on that information. Interaction of the schema with specific information about the current behavior episode enables a person to deal with current situations and to appropriately modify his or her schemas. Schemas are hierarchically organized; higher level ones serve as overarching organizations for more specific ones that function in a more context-specific manner, a rationale similar to one found in the comparative framework.

Finally, schemas are activated and used in remembering. Memory is construed to be a highly dynamic and reconstructive process and not simply a matter of the storage and retrieval of inputs. Reconstruction is better for material when it is related to the self and when it is imbued with emotion. Distinctions are drawn between *explicit* conscious, retrievable memory processes and *implicit* ones that influence current information processing, though they cannot be consciously remembered. People may attend to and clearly perceive events that are momentarily represented in their awareness, but these can become lost to conscious representation despite their assimilation into schemas. As a result, people possess a great deal of implicit procedural knowledge (know "how" as opposed to knowing "that"); they also have a tacit knowledge of patterns and rules such as the conventions governing the use of language. Some theorists distinguish between episodic, semantic, general, and autobiographical forms of memory. Reconstruction of episodic memories is facilitated when the event itself and its context is retrieved and linked with the representation of the self as agent or experiencer of the event.

Goals, Purpose, Choice, Freedom, and Responsibility
Humans have an inherent purposive nature—they are self-directing. This nature is implemented through cognitive functions that construct representations of desirable future states or personal goals. While the processes are generically human, the kinds of goals people construct vary greatly from person to person. They may be proximate or remote, few or many, and segmented or organized into patterns. The primary focus of these goals goes beyond biological survival. People seek to explore and confront challenges rather than to avoid pain and frustration, which they try to avoid only when they feel incompetent to deal with them (Bohart, 1995). This view is different from a teleologic framework that connotes the possibility of future events determining or influencing the present. All human activities occur in the present, so when clients talk about the past or future, the thoughts and emotions generated by the act of remembering, or anticipations of the future are happening in the present (Yontef, 1995). (Compare this with the idea in the comparative framework that only present events can influence one another.)

The humanists' discussions about goals are highly abstract. For example, James's (1995) list of "urges" includes freedom, autonomy and self-determination, comprehension and understanding, happiness and enjoyment, innovation and creation, authentic love relationships, and a sense of unity in some aspect of life larger than oneself. People have a "strong push" toward actualizing their potentials (Rice & Greenberg, 1992), implying that in everyone there exist states of being that are not now actual but that might become so. The processes through which such potential states become actual, called *actualization* or *self-actualization,* are not explained.

Some existentialists emphasize the importance for each person of developing a general guiding purpose that gives them an overall sense of value and significance; they consider this to be the critical life task. Some argue that there is no ultimate meaning or purpose inherent in life. People simply exist and must decide what to make of themselves, the purposes and conditions for which they shall live (Sartre, 1947). Frankl (1969) proposed a purpose or meaning to be inherent in each person's life. It is unique and specific for each person, can be discovered and fulfilled by them and none other, and can be discovered only through processes of living. In this respect, no person can be replaced; no life can be replicated by another. To define people's goals in advance is to circumscribe their unique potentialities. Each person's task is as unique as the specific opportunities he or she may have to implement it. Generic goal classifications are rejected, so therapists deal solely with goals that clients present during psychotherapy (Rice & Greenberg, 1992).

People are always in a situation of choice; both acting or not acting are choices. This condition exists even though the person cannot foresee all that will happen; to operate in terms of "maybe" is a "given of our choicefulness" (Bugental & Sterling, 1995, p. 233). Choices are guided by awareness of present and possible futures rather than by past events (Tageson, 1982); choices are also guided by the cognitive capabilities people use to solve problems, weigh alternatives, and form and execute plans—called control functions in the comparative framework. The ability to choose produces freedom, a state different from the deterministic laws of physical science (Bugental & Sterling, 1995). "Freedom is a basic principle, in fact, a sine qua non, of personality. It is by this characteristic that we separate human beings from animals" (May, 1989, p. 51). People are free to choose what they will attend to, how they interpret experience, what to value, what they do on specific occasions, and how to live (Warnock, 1970). Choice, however, always occurs within constraints and opportunities afforded by the immediate situation and the consequences that follow from one's choices.

Responsibility is "the child of freedom." Freedom to choose does not mean freedom from responsibility for the consequences of one's decisions and the resulting pattern of one's life, the good as well as the bad. People cannot be held responsible for events that befall them, but they are responsible for how they choose to respond to them. People may not be responsible for having undergone childhood abuse, but as adults they must understand that they can—and do—choose how to interpret and respond to that abuse. People are responsible to themselves and not to any group to support their standards: "one essential of the morally adult man is to create his own system of values, and to reject the stock morality of his group" (Warnock, 1970, p. 20). Thus, both biological and environmental determinism are rejected. That is why humanist theorists assert that freedom, choice, and responsibility lie at the center of human living (e.g., King & Citrenbaum, 1993; Tageson, 1982).

Choices do have to be implemented within the constraints and possibilities of people's current situations. Cognitive processes serve to construct and implement plans for doing so. For example, Yontef (1995) observes that Gestalt therapy is, among other things, directed toward facilitating clients' problem-solving capabilities by assisting them to acquire problem-solving tools. It accomplishes this by increasing the clients' ability to self-regulate and self-support. Contemporary humanist theorists typically discuss these issues at a general and abstract level, saying little about specific skills needed or therapist strategies and methods for cultivating them.

Some emphasize the existential uncertainty involved in living. Absolute clarity, predictive certainty, or unalterable truths are fictions. Typically, people face situations that are complex, obscure, and ambiguous. To be effective, people must avoid approaching situations with preconceived notions of what they will encounter, let go of the need to know, and be prepared to adapt to the unknown (King & Citrenbaum, 1993). The general frames, action strategies, or procedural rules people have come to rely on are never specific enough to determine what they can actually do in a specific situation. Thus, whatever they do must be a creative application of their current psychological patterns to the specific circumstances of the particular context they face, and this always results in something somewhat different from what existed before (Bohart, 1995).

Emotions

The concepts of emotion or feeling are frequently used in describing therapy sessions; methods related to emotions are often proposed. Person-centered therapists emphasize reflection of feelings. Gestaltists arrange for an intensification of experience to create a heightening of awareness or vivid experience to produce clear identification by clients of an emotion and its related need, which is said to automatically result in more complete meaning. Existentialists (e.g., Binswanger cited in Ruitenbeck, 1962; Boss, 1963; Yalom, 1981) propose that self-awareness automatically leads to intuitive perceptions of threats to one's existence, importance, or welfare, resulting in innate anxiety. This result produces restriction of behavior and a sense of guilt through intuitive recognition that one is not living up to one's inherent potential. It is therefore surprising how little theoretical attention these theorists give to emotions and affective experience. A reader looks in vain in the subject index of their books for reference to typical categories of emotion, such as anger, fear, or affection/love. The reluctance to classify experience may account for much of this lack of specification regarding differing kinds of emotion.

Rice and Greenberg (1992) argue that emotions are crucial to understanding people, and the central task of therapy is to facilitate emotional change, thereby enabling clients to construct new, more beneficial personal meanings. They note that humanist therapies stress awareness of feeling, but they propose no theory to explain its importance. They and their colleagues (e.g. Greenberg, Rice, & Elliot, 1993; Greenberg & Safran, 1987; Safran & Greenberg, 1991) seek to fill that gap with a theory of emotions similar to that described in our comparative framework. Based on recent theoretical and empirical work, they propose that humans have a limited set of inborn primary emotions mediated by genetically prewired *visceral brain circuits*. These emotions are biologically based action tendencies related to adaptation and survival, activated by automatic appraisals of the personal relevance of current situations. Different kinds of appraisals elicit different action tendencies: Emotions (1) can command attention, thereby influencing the salience of information, (2) are motivational in character, and therefore can influence the goals people pursue, and (3) convey information that can influence interactions with others.

Although emotions occur automatically, they cannot be consciously experienced until they are symbolized in awareness by images or words through people's cognitive capabilities. Complex patterns of emotions experienced by mature people evolve when their innate primary action tendencies become integrated with cognitions. Consciously experienced feelings are made up of a synthesis of information from multiple sources: (1) a physiologically based sensory/expressive motor system that operates without volitional control; (2) a semantically based emotional memory system, containing representations of prior emotional experiences; and (3) a verbally based language system, with a multifaceted conceptual and propositional organization, that uses conscious, volitional, and verbally mediated processes.

These are called emotional schemes (rather than schemas) to connote their embodied cognitive/affective/action organization (similar to behavior episode schemas in the comparative framework). Once developed, they can influence people by affecting their moods, thoughts, recollections, and what they encode from incoming information. The separation of cognitive and emotional processes is considered a false dichotomy because they are complexly linked so as to enhance human functioning; thought tends to be laden with feeling, and vice versa (Greenberg et al., 1993). Cognition is not inherently rational, nor is emotionality inherently irrational.

Some assume that attention to emotions is not essential in effecting client change. Bugental (1987) says "emotions are inevitable, valuable clues and to be respected [but] I do not see them as central, in themselves, to our work" (p. 8). He likens emotion in therapy to blood in surgery, both inevitable, both participating in cleansing and healing, both requiring respectful attention by professionals, but "neither is the point of the procedure" (p. 113). He argues that therapy seeks to increase people's consciousness of their own being, choices, powers, and limits, and that strong emotions—fear, guilt, hope, fulfillment—inevitably accompany such awareness. Emotions must be carefully managed as they arise in therapy, but they have no causal role. Their importance lies in their utility as clues indicating how well clients may be fitting into their lives, how they experience themselves, and how they relate to others.

Regulatory Processes

Humanists also assume that humans have inborn regulatory processes; people are innately capable of making direct evaluations, without conscious decision making, that serve both biological and psychosocial needs. Through an organismic (Rogers) or internal (Perls) valuing process, people differentiate subjective states characterized as comfort, pleasure, or satisfaction from those of discomfort, pain, or dissatisfaction. Choices are guided by values and valuing of consequences. Self-evaluations of people's acts and attributes lead to construction of self-efficacy beliefs (Bugental, 1987). Positive self-efficacy—a sense of agency—involves a positive view of oneself as well as one's potential and future, it leads people to believe they can meet and overcome a challenge (Bohart, 1995). Inappropriate self-evaluations are also possible, and these can contribute to personal difficulty. Thus, people can fashion alienated images of themselves; they can operate in terms of a despised self (being ashamed of themselves) or an idealized self (a grandiose positive sense of self) (Yontef, 1995). They can also function as a harsh internal critic, with an introjection-based rejection of self that prevents self-acceptance, healing, and growth (Bohart, 1995). This is similar to regulatory functions in our comparative framework.

ACTION CHARACTERISTICS: THE BEHAVIORAL PERSON AND ENVIRONMENTS

Humanist therapists provide no conceptual model concerning the ways people carry out transactions with their environments, whether observational, instrumental, or communicative. Consistent with their intrapsychic emphasis, they do not focus on changing how people act. They seem to assume that once clients construct more adaptive ways of thinking and feeling, more effective actions will naturally follow; skill training is unnecessary. The meaning of actions must be understood from the actor's perspective, however. Actions that appear to be pathological from an objective observer's perspective become reasonable and understandable when viewed from the perspective of the actor. They do not specify the ways experience may vary as a function of a person's actions—skilled or unskilled social behavior.

Despite their emphasis on the person-in-context as the focal unit and their assertions that environments provide different experiential possibilities, their epistemological assumptions lead them to avoid concepts about contexts and the actions by which people transact with them to generate experience. Clients' contexts are discussed in terms of clients' descriptions of them.

THE PROPOSITIONAL MODEL

Humanists assume that people create unique, personal lives, so they tend to avoid concepts about the *content* of human nature. However, the *processes* are considered uniquely human, so humanists do propose general propositions about them. Their discussions are typically quite general and abstract, consistent with their emphasis on human uniqueness (Shaffer, 1978).

HUMANS ARE INNATELY SELF-ORGANIZING

Experience occurs in a continual, varying flow and would produce a sense of uncertainty and instability were it not for an inherent human tendency to impose or create some coherent organization on the flow of experience. This self-organizing tendency exists at birth and persists throughout life. People need protection against "the disabling openness of possibility" and some organized way of dealing with "what is, at least latently, a perilous environment" (Bugental & McBeath, 1995, p. 112). The creation and maintenance of coherent patterns of psychological functioning results from the combined operation of the tendencies for self-construction and self-organization.

HUMANS ARE INNATELY SELF-CONSTRUCTING

Consensus exists that humans have an innate tendency, present at birth, to "grow, to expand, [and] to express potentialities" (Fromm, 1969). Infants are intrinsically curious, exploratory, and interested in developing their capacities for self-determination, autonomy, and choice (Bohart, 1995). Because self-constructing activity is an inherent inclination, neither sticks nor carrots are needed to prompt or elicit behavior (Rogers, 1961), and the tendency continues to function no matter how the environment may enhance or frustrate its operation (Maslow, 1970).

This is termed an *actualizing* or *self-actualization tendency* by Rogers (1961) and others. It is a master motive that both prompts behavior and gives it a directional trend, an inherent urge to maintain and enhance oneself by expanding and developing one's personal life organizations. Rogers later described this as one version of a formative tendency found throughout the universe: Everything, from crystals up, continually moves toward greater complexity and organization. Bugental's term is *searching:* A built-in, life-essential program, initiated when a person encounters unfamiliar situations for which they do not have practiced (learned) ways of coping, leading to acceptance of risk, exploration of possibilities, consideration of alternate pathways, and the experimental trial of efforts to resolve the situation (Bugental & Sterling, 1995). A basic motivation toward growth and development has also been a key idea in the Gestalt view. Bohart (1995) terms it a process of *self-righting.* The products of this self-constructing process are typically desirable (e.g., Rogers, 1961), but they can lead to good or bad constructions (e.g., Shlien & Levant, 1984); the potential to change is the key idea.

HUMANS ARE INNATELY SELF-DIRECTING

Humans are also assumed to be inherently purposive, intentional, or goal directed. They can identify goals and objectives worthy of pursuit, initiate and sustain action to attain them, and pursue their interests and purposes to enhance themselves and their development in desired ways (the directive function in the comparative framework). Humans are proactive; their activity is initiated from within and aimed at future states of being by a vision of the future; they do not reactively respond to situations (Bohart, 1995; Rice & Greenberg, 1992). Efforts to represent current behavior as caused by the past (e.g., early memories, habits, or fixations) are misdirected.

HUMANS ARE INNATELY SELF-REGULATING

Evaluations of one's goals, the available means for implementing them, the success of one's actions in producing the desired results, and one's overall capabilities and worth (called regulatory functions in the comparative framework) are all emphasized in humanist approaches. However, explicit theoretical formulations about evaluative processes are sparse. Everyone has an organismic (Rogers) or internal (Perls) valuing process. At each moment people make the best choices they can, doing what they feel to be possible and desirable (Bugental & Sterling, 1995); this implies that choices are based on evaluations of their value and feasibility. Bohart (1995) observes that adaptations occur on a moment-to-moment basis, through use of feedback to refine one's current interactions with people and tasks, and to elaborate one's generalized beliefs, concepts, schemas, and action strategies. People's choices are based on anticipations of the destination they want to reach, estimates of the possibilities for getting there, evaluations of their talents and skills for accomplishing the goal, and the obstacles they think they may encounter.

People construct such evaluative patterns in the course of living by incorporating elements from the expectations and evaluations of themselves by others, or by appraising their own efforts; Rogers called these *social* and *organismic valuing*. Some values become expressed as "shoulds," which can result in conflicts when opposed to one's "wants" (Rice & Greenberg, 1992). A number of theorists link the occurrence of anxiety to evaluative judgments. Anxiety represents a condition of uncertainty, resulting from people's evaluations that they are beyond their established modes of coping (Yontef, 1995), or when (1) they are called on by their environment to respond, (2) they feel unsure of their ability to do so, and (3) the outcome is evaluated to be of personal importance (Fischer, 1978). Anxiety is a signal of both danger and opportunity, so it is indicative of possibility and potentiality rather than pathology. Therapy should help people become aware of it rather than to eliminate it, thereby making it a constructive rather than destructive influence (May, 1981).

PRINCIPLES OF CHANGE

Humanist theorists view change as inherent in living—unavoidable and desirable. However, change implies stability: something exists that can be changed. They are vague about the specific processes that produce variability and change, and the relationships among them. They also differ in their emphasis on change and stability, and whether conflict between them is a source of dysfunction. Bugental and Sterling (1995) view self-organizing, self-maintaining processes as predominant. An individual's self-world construct system is laboriously created over many years, and resistance and defensive maneuvers to maintain it are to be expected. People strongly resist attempts by others to change their system because it provides satisfaction and prevents excessive stress. In contrast, Bohart (1995) argues that while stable patterns of organization do develop and provide for personal continuity over time, their continuing change and reorganization is what needs to be emphasized, despite apparent similarities from one occasion to the next. Yontef (1995) argues that people strive to strike a balance between stability-maintaining processes that foster personal autonomy and protect against harm, and growth or reorganizing processes that occur only through action-exchanges with environmental fields. Erickson and Rossi (1979) propose a natural tendency in humans to balance out opposites to achieve homeostasis.

Development or learning occurs on a moment-to-moment basis (Bohart, 1995). The person-centered tradition views it as a never-ending process of organization, differentiation, and reorganization—reintegration—resulting in progressively more complex patterns and greater functional capabilities. Psychological patterns undergo "schematic restructuring" (Elliott & Greenberg, 1995) or "shift and change" to deal with new information (Bugental & McBeath, 1995). These are complex, lived, whole-bodied changes occurring in an experiential manner (Bohart, 1995). Each new encounter leads to changes in intrapsychic patterns—sometimes slight, sometimes larger—unless additional processes prevent it.

How do changes occur? Despite emphasizing self-construction and self-organization, in discussions about change, the most frequently used terms are *assimilation, incorporation, introjection,* and *accommodation.* Their meanings must be inferred from their use, however, because formal definitions are not provided. *Assimilation* refers to using novel information or experience to elaborate existing psychological patterns. *Accommodation* refers to modifying existing patterns to take into account the effects of one's activity on others (Korb et al., 1989; Yontef, 1995). Both result in change or reorganization of psychological patterns toward more inclusive, complex, and better integrated frameworks for understanding one's self and world. *Incorporation* seems to be a synonym for assimilation, such as incorporating learnings into broader, more inclusive frameworks (Bohart, 1995). Assimilation and accommodation processes are selective—that is, rejection of information may also occur. This behavior implies that people use selection criteria for information to be used or rejected. Bugental and McBeath (1995) imply that evaluative judgments are made regarding the interplay between psychological patterns and contingencies in their contexts when they say that reorganization occurs when people try to become more effective in obtaining satisfaction and in preventing frustration. Bohart (1995) speaks of utilizing feedback to make adjustments in modes of interaction with people and tasks to become more effective in the future. Learning operates to continually refine and elaborate, or differentiate and integrate, generalized beliefs, concepts, and schemas, to define desired outcomes, and to enable people to predict the likelihood of their attaining given different action strategies. Despite the use of the term *reorganization*, it often appears to refer to an incremental change process.

Introjection refers to a wholesale adoption of the ideas, values, and practices of others, without analyzing or questioning them, and without integrating or assimilating them into existing psychological patterns (Yontef, 1995). Examples include the unassimilated moralisms and "shoulds" that youngsters acquire during their formative years. Although introjection may be necessary in childhood and useful in new situations, such as social modeling, some introjects that persist and remain outside of awareness may later influence dysfunctional development.

One other change principle is crucial. Although existing patterns can operate automatically, outside awareness, change requires awareness. Earlier it was assumed that becoming aware of inner and outer events is a passive and automatic process of perception, so clients needed to be helped to become open to experience. Some theorists continue to consider experiential awareness to be an effortless process; indeed, "good" experience (good Gestalt formation) is said to result from "spontaneous" awareness (Korb et al., 1989). Bugental's (1978) concept of *presence* is "being in a situation in which one intends to be as aware and as participative as one is able to be at that time and in those circumstances . . . by mobilization of one's inner (toward subjective experiencing) and outer (toward the situation and any other person/s in it) sensitivities" (p. 36).

More recently, selective control of conscious experience is often ascribed to attentional processes. Attention is considered an active process subject to volitional control, so it is a tool for pursuing personal goals. The selective influence of attention is considered inevitably biasing by some who argue that clients need to learn how to establish and maintain evenly deployed attention so as to remain open to all experience (Bugental & McBeath, 1995). Others advocate harnessing selective attention to bring certain elements of one's total experience into focal awareness by directing their perception toward particular targets—a process referred to as the focusing, or refocusing, of attention (Gendlin, 1996). Focal attention may be spontaneous, illustrated by automatic orientation toward an unexpected loud noise (labeled stimulus-driven attention capture in the comparative framework). It may also be purposely directed toward scanning information sources within and without the body (Korb et al., 1989). Bugental (1978), following May (1969), refers to this as *in-*

tentionality. Selectively directing attention results from choice, with or without simultaneous awareness that such choices are being made.

Greenberg et al., (1993) base on modern cognitive science their proposals that people can use information by both automatic—unconscious—and controlled—conscious—processing. Consciously attending to events can produce new experiences; however, attentional processes limit what can simultaneously be considered and necessitates serial processing of information. Humans' capability for parallel distributed processing enables them to use much larger amounts of information because limited attentional resources need not be allocated to automatic activities. (This view of selective attention is similar to the comparative framework.)

THE PROCESS OF NORMAL DEVELOPMENT

From birth, each person's existence is one of a continuing, varying flow of experience, with the person as the center. This experience is produced by sensory-perceptual information from sources both inside and outside the body. People use it to guide their activity (Rogers, 1951). Experience provides information both about particular objects and events—conceptual knowledge—and how they are related and operate spatially and temporally—propositional knowledge. All experiences occur in the present, although people often do not have a clear awareness of what they are doing or what is needed (Yontef, 1995). Memories of the past and anticipations of the future occur in the present, even though they represent past and potential future events.

Constructing Psychological Patterns from the Flow of Experience

There is an organic unity, an implicit wholeness (Bugental & Sterling, 1995), to each experience; it is a *gestalt* in which salient features stand out as figures embedded within a larger context, or ground (e.g., Korb et al., 1989; Simkin et al., 1993). These units include self-referents, awareness of oneself; other-referents, or awareness of one's context; and self-other referents, awareness of relationships between them. Some theorists (Bohart, 1995; Gendlin, 1981) emphasize that these gestalts are not merely cognitive but also have an affective tone, so people always experience a felt sense of each situation and how their lives are going. The term *feeling,* does not refer solely to emotions but to combinations of meanings plus the associated affective tone.

These units of experience have a general pattern. First, people become aware of some need or goal. They then scan the environment and themselves for possibilities, options, or choices available to meet the need. An option is selected, a course of action initiated, and the resulting experiences are either assimilated or rejected. The process leads to a sense of satisfaction and closure. Gestaltists call this pattern the Gestalt Experience Cycle (Korb et al., 1989). It is similar to the idea of a behavioral episode in our comparative framework.

All events and their spatial-temporal relationships are continually varying and changing, so none of them can ever recur in precisely the same form. Every experience episode is in this sense a new one, and if people had to live without memory or foresight, their adaptive capabilities would be rigid and ineffective. People's innate self-constructing and self-organizing processes produce a sense of stability and continuity; these processes facilitate unitary functioning by creating meaning and meaning patterns from the content and flow of experience episodes (Bohart, 1995). This is not a correspondence view that percepts yield concepts; meanings are constructed, not copied. Typically, the creative aspects are emphasized; meaning results from learning by discovery (Bugental & Sterling, 1995). These meaning patterns include goals, evaluations of the likelihood of attaining them, means for achieving them, evaluations of one's capabilities for achieving them, and anticipations of the obstacles that must be overcome in the process (Bohart, 1995). This is similar to the construction and content of behavior episode schemas in our comparative framework.

Once constructed, these psychological patterns operate primarily at implicit, nonverbal, and nonconscious levels. They are far more complex than conscious verbal/conceptual thought; hence, they are not easy to describe verbally (Bohart, 1995). People sense more complex patterns of meaning than they can ordinarily verbalize (Gendlin, 1964, 1969, 1996). The patterns encompass processes referred to as intuitive knowing, or the exercise of a nonconscious intellect, such that people know more than what their conscious minds are aware of (Rogers, 1993). Unconscious processes are normal, not pathological.

A person's sense of self in the world is not a stable, highly consistent structure. People's patterns of meaning continually change and elaborate through their flow of experience episodes (Bugental & McBeath, 1995), an activity termed the *self-in-process* (Rogers, 1959). The felt sense of oneself as a whole person at any moment is a creation resulting from interactions of meanings derived from experiences of a current episode with meanings constructed from relevant previous episodes—like the interaction of behavior episodes and behavior episode schemas in our comparative framework. Throughout life, such interactions produce modifications and elaborations in people's meaning structures and sense of self by "creative adjustment" (Yontef, 1995). This appears similar to the processes of incremental change in the comparative framework. People usually experience multiple selves within their varied life contexts, such as alarmed, amorous, or masterful selves.

Psychological Patterns Serve to Coordinate a Person's Behavior

Functioning outside awareness, these patterns, models, or schemas influence people's moment-to-moment activity, but they operate as tendencies or potentialities rather than as fixed habits (Bugental & McBeath, 1995). Their influence is probabilistic rather than mechanistic. They are never specific enough to determine what a person can or should do in a situation (Bohart, 1995). In each new episode, people experience a full range of sensations and perceptions, interacting with the meanings and memories prompted by those experiences (Rogers, 1959). The patterns function as a unit so that the activation of any part of one tends to activate the whole. Once activated, they automatically direct attention and provide a framework for organizing information and action. New information about specific instances is processed using relevant schematic prototypes that impose some structure on that information. Not all information is processed, however. A selection is made, based on the perceived degree of fit with the existing patterns. Actual behavior in any episode is a new creation resulting from the interaction of current information and previously constructed meanings (Greenberg et al., 1993).

Characteristics of Optimal Human Functioning

The secret to living a good life lies in the processes people use to participate in continually changing circumstances rather than in idealized outcomes. People construct their own unique outcomes, but some processes enable people to maximize their potentials better than others. This view defines the goals of therapy and provides criteria against which therapy progress can be evaluated. Optimal functioning (called the fully functioning person by Rogers, 1959) is not a state that one can achieve and maintain; one cannot always be fulfilled, content, or even happy (Bohart, 1995). Rather, it is a way of functioning that enables people to continuously test and modify their psychological patterns, thereby remaining open to seemingly infinite emergence and growth (Bugental & McBeath, 1995). The term being refers to what is actual or already exists, but not all existents are present at any one time. Those states that are not now actual, but might become so, are assumed to exist now as potentialities. Becoming is the process of potentialities continually coming into being—becoming actualized. Active participation in becoming is the key to optimal development.

Remaining open to experience (Zimring & Raskin, 1992) is typically among the first characteristics emphasized. The process of becoming requires one to be in continuing contact with oneself and one's surroundings because that is the source of relevant new experience (Yontef, 1995). People remain fully present (Bugental, 1986), continuously aware of their experiences, sensitive to inputs from each situation and the people in it, and living in the present. Openness to experience includes intuitive appraisals of what is "good" and should be assimilated, and what is "bad" and should be rejected (Simkin et al., 1993; Yontef, 1995).

People who embrace this openness are willing to be a *process,* a stream of becoming, rather than trying to be a finished product (Zimring & Raskin, 1992). They are flexible and capable of accepting change (Bohart, 1995), of experiencing the moment "in the here and now," and of moving on without "living in the past" or projecting into the future (Perls, Hefferline, & Goodman, 1951; Perls, 1969). In addition, to become the self one truly is, one must identify with and accept one's experiences (Rogers, 1961) by placing trust in their content and being able to consider data from all levels of oneself without fearing the possibility of mistakes (Zimring & Raskin, 1992). One must trust one's intuitive reactions and value them as effective guides, as these reflect one's inherent capability for effective self-regulation (Perls, 1973). Naturalness and acting spontaneously in accord with one's true nature is emphasized, but it is insufficient simply to know one's experience. One must identify with and accept one's self and characteristics as a growing and changing entity. Then, one can and will make choices that facilitate growth and development (Yontef, 1995). The implied assumption seems to be that people are innately good and adaptively effective unless distorted by faulty learning.

Openness to change leads to experiencing a flow of fresh perceptions (Bugental, 1986), and their ongoing assimilation leads to growth and development through continuing changes in self-organization (Yontef, 1995). This assimilation requires fluid and flexible information processing, people must hold ideas tentatively, and remain open to new opportunities, ideas, and possibilities (Bohart, 1995). For example, one should be able to forgo hard and fast conclusions about oneself, even those that appear positive, in view of the changing discoveries one continually makes about oneself and one's characteristics (King & Citrenbaum, 1993). People develop large and varied repertoires, which make them capable of richly differentiated reactions (Bohart, 1995).

Ideally, people are actively curious, interested in exploring possibilities and discovering more about their world and themselves, open to unknowns, willing to take risks and test their ideas and capabilities with new behavior in novel situations, persistent in the face of difficulty, able to appraise the result without making their sense of worth dependent on the outcome and to learn from the process (Bohart, 1995; Bugental & Sterling, 1995; Yontef, 1995). In so doing, they will experience themselves using their self-direction, self-regulation, and self-construction capabilities to make their own choices; they will recognize the freedom this behavior produces and will accept personal responsibility for the conduct of their lives (Bohack, 1995; Frankl, 1962, 1969; Elliott & Greenberg, 1995; King & Citrenbaum, 1993; Perls, 1973; Zimring & Raskin, 1992). Dysfunction results when this pattern of functioning becomes deficient.

The Process of Dysfunctional Development

Dysfunction is said to be present when people focus on protecting their *being* rather than on *becoming*. They cling to fixed forms of feeling, perceiving, thinking, and acting (Gendlin, 1969, 1996). The result is static, undifferentiated, unfeeling, and impersonal functioning; people are unable to learn or benefit from feedback and remain stuck in their misperceptions and inadequate behavior (Bohart, 1995). The humanists offer no theory as to why or how people become stuck or unstuck. Three aspects of this view should be noted: (1) The emphasis is on current functioning, and possible etiologies for the problems are deemphasized. (2) All forms of dysfunction are assumed to be ultimately reducible to one basic difficulty: an inability to function as an evolving process. (3) Intrapsychic aspects are stressed, with little attention given to the roles that biological, behavioral, or contextual factors might play. Fischer (1991) suspects that therapists create their own ways of understanding how such factors are taken up by people and how these factors play a part in people's psychopathology.

Only vague generalizations were found about kinds of dysfunctional patterns, such as a "failure to operate as an evolving process" (Bohart, 1995, p. 96). Some excluding criteria were identified. For example, dysfunction is not synonymous with having problems. Everyone has problems that arise from situations with which they do not have the resources to cope; these could be illness, loss of a job, or living among disputatious family members. People will be temporarily dysfunctional in such life circumstances (Bohart, 1995). Nor is dysfunction defined by particular kinds of responses, such as misperceptions, mistaken beliefs, or inappropriate or ineffective actions. These are features of everyone's activities.

Dysfunction occurs when people do not remain in contact with their experience, engage in inner listening, attend to their internal reactions, and symbolize them in awareness (Bohart, 1995; Gendlin, 1981; Greenberg et al., 1993;

Yontef, 1995). They are unable to be authentic and to function in terms of the actuality of their experience. This creates other difficulties. Inadequate experiential information makes people less adaptive in complex situations; it is like trying to solve mathematical equations with too many unknowns. Failure to remain open to experience and to use fluid, flexible modes of information processing precludes the possibility of change and the ability to adapt effectively to changing circumstances (Greenberg et al., 1993). Then, development of stress, feelings of helplessness, and perhaps depression are inevitable because the person's intrapsychic patterns will not generate sufficient satisfactions or will produce an excess of disappointment, hurt, or frustration (Bugental & Sterling, 1995).

To some extent, this condition can result from behavioral deficiencies such as inadequate attention by people to their experience; their focusing ability may be poor (Gendlin, 1981), or their verbal skills may be inadequate for representing their experience in awareness (Greenberg et al., 1993). Usually the condition results when people protect existing patterns by avoiding experiences: They may ignore aspects of experience, deny or prevent their occurrence, or distort them (Bohart, 1995). Bugental (1986) describes similar unsatisfactory ways of processing experience: People can distance themselves from important issues, deny emotional costs, and avoid confrontations with aspects of their experience. Gestaltists describe *projection*—attributing to others aspects of oneself; *deflection*—affective blunting of the impact of an interaction; and *retroflection*—accepting an impulse as one's own, but shifting its direction or the degree of its impact (Yontef, 1995). Such avoidance tactics interrupt or interfere with the flow of experience, so that one does not become aware of relevant perceptions, feelings, thoughts, or memories. (In the terms of the comparative framework, they function as stability-maintaining processes.) When awareness is blocked (Bugental & Sterling, 1995), it fails to unfold as needed, necessary learning does not occur, and more functional behavior is prevented (Yontef, 1995).

It is the organization, not the content, of dysfunctional patterns that creates difficulties. The concept of incongruence held by person-centered theorists refers to a form of dysfunctional organization. One type involves an incompatibility between people's current experience and their felt sense of self or their self-concept. People intent on maintaining their existing views of self and world cannot integrate disparate elements. For example, an anger experience may be considered incompatible with the kind of person one tries to be: Incongruence exists. The person turns away from unacceptable meanings, and self-deceptively struggles to reaffirm the threatened self-concept (Fischer, 1991). Gestalt theorists call disparate feelings a split; an example is simultaneous feelings of love and anger toward another that one is unable to reconcile (Simkin et al., 1993).

Incongruence is most apt to occur when people operate with rigid, undifferentiated psychological patterns that prevent assimilation and integration of discrepant experiences, and they screen out information (Wexler & Rice, 1974). They selectively attend, respond only to confirmatory experience, and inattend or distort discrepant experience to avoid disrupting their psychological patterns (Anderson, 1974; Greenberg et al., 1993). Their stability-maintaining avoidance tactics place severe limitations on their capacity to discover, shape, and make sense of their existence by keeping their patterns closed to reconsideration or modification. In this way, their psychological patterns are immune to change (Boss, 1963; Fischer, 1991; Gendlin, 1978). Entrenched modes of experiencing and responding are activated regardless of their suitability and are apt to be personally or socially detrimental (Gendlin, 1996; Yontef, 1995).

Another form of incongruence is generalized negative self-concepts that lead people to judge themselves harshly (Bohart, 1995). Some monitor their experience; subject it to analysis; criticize their thoughts, feelings, and reactions; and lecture themselves—that is, they try to self-engineer (Gendlin, 1969; Zimring & Raskin, 1992). Self-criticism generates a sense of shame, of being "not okay," or "not enough," and other incompatibilities that interfere with satisfactory decision making, autonomy, and growth (Yontef, 1995). Some theorists consider these reactions to result from earlier experiences in which parents, teachers, or others exposed the person to conditions of worth (Bohart, 1995). People feel worthwhile only when they conform to standards and values set by others, adopting a set of "shoulds" to guide their behavior. When disparities occur between what they think or feel versus what they think they should think or feel, they adhere to their rigid self-belief system, or *fixed gestalten,* which they maintain by interrupted contact and awareness (Yontef, 1995). This behavior results in a "closed system" of self-fulfilling "scripts" that fail to assimilate new experience. People can also create a false sense of self—a grandiose sense of their own self-importance—which can impede integration and inhibit growth (Yontef, 1995).

Other deficits arise from the automatic activation of patterns that persist despite being no longer appropriate. A person is "dominated by" (Fischer, 1991) or "holds onto" (Yontef, 1995) the past, continuing to function in terms of self-identities or patterns of interpersonal relationships that should have been surpassed, but whose operation prevents further development. Gestaltists refer to these as unfinished business; people have not completed an experience or formed a gestalt with some part of their past. In this view, co-herent self-organization requires closure. Once started, things need to be completed—fulfilling a need, settling a dispute, or resolving one's inner conflicts. Unresolved issues "bind energy" that could be better used to deal with new issues (Simkin et al., 1993). Yontef (1995) believes the more common of these is a failure to have fully expressed oneself, thereby remaining "stuck" with negative feelings that interfere with one's current life. Preoccupation with the past and excessive concerns with anticipated futures can be detrimental and can interfere with a person's remaining current with ongoing experience (Perls, 1969; Perls, Hefferline, & Goodman, 1951).

Greenberg et al. (1993) agree that most dysfunctions stem from incon-gruence in schematic processing; they propose a framework intended to encompass much of the foregoing. They identify six types of processing dif-ficulties, for which they have developed corresponding treatment proce-dures:

1. The automatic activation of psychological patterns that are discrepant from one's immediate conscious perception of a situation
2. Activation of two incompatible aspects of one's self, resulting in criti-cal self-evaluative judgments
3. Activation of two incompatible aspects of self that result in conflicts (splits) and the interruption of emotional expression
4. Automatic activation of patterns related to prior unresolved or trau-matic experience with others
5. Inability to symbolize the meanings one is experiencing, leaving one with an unclear felt sense
6. Activation of a private, previously unrevealed part of the self, which leaves the person feeling deeply vulnerable.

THE PROCEDURAL MODEL

Humanists assert that therapists cannot change clients; clients must change themselves (Bohart, 1995; Bugental & McBeath, 1995; Bugental & Sterling, 1995). Therapy is not something done to clients; rather, it facilitates operation of clients' self-change capabilities (Greenberg et al., 1993). Clients participate but remain free to use their own critical intelligence to decide what is valuable to preserve and what should be changed or relinquished, to capitalize on their discoveries in order to correct their own deficiencies, to grow and develop, to gain mastery and effective self-direction, and to cope effectively with their life circumstances.

Therapy Goals and General Approach to Strategy and Tactics

General Goals and Strategy

The goal for all clients is to free them to use their innate self-constructing, self-organizing, self-directing, and self-regulating capacities effectively so they can control and be fully responsible for their current being and continual becoming. These are process rather than content goals—the "how" rather than the "what" of optimal living. Clients identify and work toward their unique personal goals, but the goals are not to be limited to symptom alleviation, to dealing with some medical necessity (Yontef, 1995), or to facilitating other quasi-objective changes in clients' behavior. These theorists eschew the goals of behavior-oriented therapies, such as reconditioning of habits, and of psychoanalysis, such as gaining access to unconscious processes. They stress creation rather than repair (Bohart, 1995; Bugental & Sterling). Their strategies focus on creating relationship conditions and client-therapist dialogue that facilitates clients' use of their intrinsic processes of optimal functioning rather than on trying to change the content of clients' thoughts, feelings, and actions.

View of Tactics

All emphasize relationship-focused tactics. Some, especially the traditional nondirectivists, consider this sufficient, arguing that the therapist's role is to be a companion on the client's road to self-discovery in a relationship that facilitates clients' own thrust toward growth (Brodley, 1988, 1993). Others argue that one can remain faithful to the clinical philosophy of a humanist approach and at the same time utilize a large variety of tactics drawn from multiple sources to facilitate clients' processes of exploration. However, interventions are always offered in a nonimposing, nonauthoritative manner, as suggestions or possibilities, rather than as instructions or statements of truth (Elliott & Greenberg, 1995). Information giving is avoided: one does not bring news to the client (Bohart, 1995). Therapists do not treat client statements as something to be evaluated in terms of their truth, appropriateness, or dysfunctionality. Confrontations, challenges of assumptions or beliefs, or anything suggestive of argumentation are studiously avoided. Interpretation, attempts to offer clients insight into their motives and patterns of behavior or defense, is consistently avoided (Bohart, 1995; Bugental & McBeath, 1995; Elliott & Greenberg, 1995). Tactics should be considered experiments aimed at facilitating clients' self-discovery rather than methods intended to cause change (Yontef, 1995).

ABSTENTION FROM DIAGNOSTIC AND PRESCRIPTIVE JUDGMENTS

Humanists do not consider traditional diagnosis appropriate or useful because they do not agree that different processes produce different dysfunctions. Clients may describe similar experiences, such as anxiety, depression, or preoccupation with feelings of guilt. However, people are unique; there are no invariable rules about the etiology of different kinds of difficulties (Bohart, 1995). The humanists' phenomenological epistemology rejects inferences by therapists about causes of clients' dysfunctions, along with any theoretically based objective tools, such as a diagnostic system (Yontef, 1995). They typically do not attempt to gain detailed representations of client's symptomatic complaints, to collect psychosocial or case histories, to use psychodiagnostic tests, to arrive at a formal diagnosis, or to weigh the relative merits of alternate treatment methods.

Their objections to traditional diagnosis are several. Traditional diagnostic classifications are so broad and ambiguous that they obscure more than clarify the therapists' understanding of clients' unique constellation of personal characteristics. They also cultivate treating clients as objects to be appraised and evaluated. This violates a phenomenological stance in which only immediate experience is valid, precludes therapists from approaching each client with an openness to discovery of clients' unique situations, and interferes with the effective conduct of therapy (Bugental & Sterling, 1995; Yontef, 1995). Moreover, diagnosis is unnecessary because the general nature of clients' difficulties is already known: a failure to remain in satisfactory contact with, and creatively use, their flow of experience. There is one cause, but multiple developmental pathways are possible. Deliberations about the relative merits of alternate therapies are unnecessary because the appropriate remedy requires clients to use their processes of self-exploration and self-discovery to achieve self-initiated change.

Clients' entrance into psychotherapy is a self-selective process. The prerequisite client conditions for treatment are said to include the following:

1. Pain, stress, anxiety, or some other form of distress
2. Hope and yearning for a different life experience
3. Readiness to commit fully—time, emotion, effort, money—to therapy
4. Acceptance of the requirement to attend inwardly to bring about the desired changes (Bugental & Sterling, 1995)

Design of Psychotherapy Strategies and Tactics

Continued personal development are psychological processes, but humanists implicitly assume that external conditions, such as psychotherapy, can facilitate or impede their operation.

Establishing Client Understanding of and Agreement to Therapy Conditions
There is variation in the length of treatment judged to be necessary. Bugental and McBeath (1995) insist that intensive and long-term treatment is invariably required. They ask for such a commitment from clients at the outset, arguing that significant change means major and lasting life changes that cannot be attained if treatment affords only "add-on" effects to established and unchanged life patterns. Yontef (1995) says that treatment can legitimately range from brief psychotherapy of only a few sessions—short-term crisis interventions—to multiyear treatments, depending on the kinds of outcomes sought. The modal pattern of treatment is weekly sessions, although they range from several times a week to every other week or less. Gestalt therapists typically begin with individual sessions, often adding participation in various group procedures later. In general, the course of treatment is indeterminate because both the content and rate are left to clients' discretion and each client is unique. Only clients can decide when satisfactory progress has been made, so ultimately when to stop is a client decision (Bohart, 1995; Yontef, 1995).

Once getting-acquainted preliminaries are completed, therapists proceed directly into actions intended to establish a therapeutic relationship. The process begins "where the client is" (Yontef, 1995). Clients are encouraged to state their views of their needs and preferences, and their perceived strengths and difficulties. The therapy approach is explained and they are asked to agree to its conditions—to report their ongoing subjective experience; to explore their perceptions, thoughts and feelings; and to be honestly open and expressive on a moment-to-moment basis (Bugental & Sterling, 1995). A minority of clients is said to find this global task agreement unacceptable because they feel helpless and in need of direction from an expert, or believe they require specific interventions (Greenberg et al., 1993). Once agreement is reached, clients begin a process of searching and discovery, attending to and describing everything that enters their conscious experience. Some may have initial difficulty in doing this, although Gendlin (1996) reports that usually only a few sessions of practice are needed for them to learn the necessary attention-focusing skills. Centering exercises may be used to teach clients to become calm, to breathe easily, to orient themselves to the context, and to remain attentive to the subjective events in order to see what happens (Yontef, 1995).

Therapy Relationships: The Medium for Freeing Clients' Self-Changing Capacities
Humanist therapists agree that a special kind of client-therapist relationship
that is "intrinsically therapeutic," and from which "learning and growth usually result" (Yontef, 1995) is the "key curative element" (Bohart, 1995; Elliott
& Greenberg, 1995). A therapeutic relationship, alliance or bond is a real, authentic relationship. It is greater than the sum of the two participants and not
comparable to ordinary human relationships (Bugental & McBeath, 1995). It
is transactional; therapists are affected by the exchanges, both in their knowledge and understanding of the other and in expansion of self-knowledge.
Some note similarities between this kind of relationship and that called *inter-*
subjectivity by self-psychologists (Bugental & McBeath, 1995; Yontef, 1995).

Some adopt Martin Buber's terminology, defining it as an "I-Thou" relationship (Elliott & Greenberg, 1995; Yontef, 1995) in contrast to "I-It" relationships where people are treated as objects rather than as persons. It is said
that one cannot be in authentic dialogue with another if one aims at a result.
Thus, meeting with a client to achieve a goal, such as self-actualization, or a
cure, such as to eliminate depression, is an I-It relationship. In a genuine, authentic relationship, the meeting with another person constitutes an end in itself. To establish and maintain such a relationship, therapists engage in three
major types of actions.

1. *Empathy, empathic attunement,* or *inclusion* are intuitive capabilities that
enable therapists to do the following: (a) Abandon their previously formed
ideas about people in general, or about a client in particular. (b) Enter intuitively or imaginatively into clients' frames of reference and approximate as
fully as possible their subjective experience, such as perceptions, thoughts,
and feelings, while maintaining self-awareness as separate persons. (c) Remain abreast of clients' experience, grasping what is most crucial or poignant
for the client at each successive moment (Vanaerschot, 1990).

2. *Warmth, active caring, unconditional positive regard, unconditional accep-*
tance, prizing, liking, nonpossessive love, and respect are attitudes and actions
that convey affirmation of and appreciation for the client as a whole person.
They display a noncritical interest in and a nonevaluative tolerance for all
the client's characteristics. This attitude requires the therapist to maintain a
distinction between who the client is as a person and his or her behavior at
any given point in time.

3. *Presence* refers to actions representing therapists' sustained, direct, un-
reserved, and spontaneous communication with clients. It requires several
behaviors of therapists: (a) They must be consistently *genuine,* not trying to appear to be other than they are. (b) They must demonstrate *congruence*—main-

tain a correspondence among their perceptions, thoughts, feelings, and actions. (c) They must display *spontaneity,* allowing their dialogue to be neither controlled nor determined in advance. (d) They must show *transparence,* a willingness to be open and to share their own phenomenological experience (Bohart, 1995; Bugental, 1978; Bugental & McBeath, 1995; Elliott & Greenberg, 1995; Yontef, 1995).

Such relationships are assumed to have at least two beneficial effects. First, they reduce clients' avoidance patterns and facilitate openness to experience. Being liked and prized leads clients to feel safe to explore their experience, especially aspects they have been defending against, and to discover that their experiences make sense and are an intelligible consequent of the ways their experiences are organized. They begin to feel "less crazy" or "dysfunctional" as a result. Second, therapists' behavior provides clients with models for the way they should listen to their own experience. It helps them adopt distinctions therapists make, enabling them to differentiate between themselves as worthwhile persons distinct from their behavior, which may or may not be desirable; it helps them to adopt a more objective view of the relative merits of different actions available to them (Bohart, 1995). Put in terms of their change principles, clients assimilate or introject the therapist's modes of functioning; others call this social learning or modeling.

Dialogue: Facilitating Modification and Self-Control of Psychological Patterns
Humanists' rationalist ontology makes conscious control of thoughts, feelings, and actions the ideal. Client-therapist dialogues are intended to facilitate that ideal. Through dialogue, clients are enabled to focus consciously on aspects of their experience, such as perceptions, thoughts, affects, meanings, intentions. They do so as their experience unfolds moment-to-moment, identifying and symbolizing their inner experience more adequately, engaging in self-examination and self-discovery, integrating all their experience, and identifying with and accepting their experiences as trustworthy guides for living. The resulting increase in experiential awareness and self-acceptance permits each client to extract new and improved meanings, to forge new ways of synthesizing old experience, and to creatively reorganize ongoing experience in more productive and adaptive ways. Clients discover their freedom to make choices and to practice autonomy, and the necessity of accepting responsibility for their lives. They are empowered to try out new actions and refine their effectiveness through successive trials, thereby developing greater self-efficacy and competence for continual personal change, adaptation, and development in their lives.

The client controls the content of the dialogue—topics to be discussed, tasks to be undertaken—and the pace—whether to approach a painful subject or to try a particular method (Greenberg et al., 1993). Because there are no satisfactory predetermined pathways for clients to proceed from their present to their preferred states, psychotherapy is necessarily a process of search and discovery, of remaining open to the unknown, being willing to explore possibilities, experimenting with some that appear more likely. The client eventually finds a way to "resolve the situation" (Bugental & Sterling, 1995).

Therapists respond spontaneously to clients' statements, remaining current to whatever is happening in the moment between them and the client (Bohart, 1995). To what, however, should they attend? Bugental and McBeath (1995) advocate paying attention to the client's psychological process—the "how" rather than to the content—the "what". Yontef (1995) says that the therapist must attend to both. All agree that trying to elicit information about "why" is inappropriate. A view, the optimal pattern, of what conscious information processing ideally should be like guides their decisions about what to say during their dialogues with clients.

One method used to understand clients' psychological processing is monitoring body language. Therapists thus pay attention to clients' facial expressions, gestures, or breathing patterns in addition to what they say (Bugental & McBeath, 1995; Korb et al., 1989; Yontef, 1995). These movements are considered indicants of inner needs, feelings, or impulses apt to be less evident to the client and therefore not yet consciously experienced or verbalized. They are also useful to therapists in detecting calculated dissembling or manipulative maneuvers that clients sometimes employ.

Therapists use empathic reflections to facilitate exploration. These include *following responses;* these are simple acknowledgments that communicate to clients that they are being understood and encourage them to continue and to elaborate. Examples are "I see," "Mm-hmm," or head nods and smiles. *Empathic reflections* convey that therapists have grasped and accepted clients' emotional meaning and communicate that they are valued. These are intended to help clients accept their feelings, trust their own experience, and feel affirmed in their own existence. *Empathic explorations* focus on aspects of clients' communication that are most fresh, alive and central to their current experience to promote exploration of that which is unclear or most novel. These are intended to stimulate deeper experiencing and to facilitate symbolization of new aspects of experience not previously in focal awareness. *Empathic conjectures* express therapists' guesses as to what the client may be currently feeling but has not yet explicity stated (Greenberg et al., 1993). Such empathic reflections may focus on diverse affects, meanings, ideas, or complex experiences. Successful reflection is characteristized as an art, calling for the therapist to go beyond what clients have explicitly stated in an effort to express what they are experiencing but have not yet put into words. These must lie within clients' current range of experiential awareness (Bohart, 1995). In every instance, clients are the judge of their experience (Greenberg et al., 1993).

Some tactics assist clients to bring to focal attention what appears to be in the periphery of their awareness. Often this takes the form of a question. Yontef (1995) says that the classic inquiry is, "What are you feeling right now?" This focuses attention on the affective components of clients' experience and facilitates its verbal expression. *Attention suggestions* can be used to aid amplification or deepening of an affective experience, or to elicit associated cognitions (Greenberg et al., 1993). Such a suggestion would be "See if you can stay with the heavy feeling a bit longer." *Process observations* are also used to describe the manner of the client's verbal and nonverbal expression: "I'm aware that you're kicking your leg right now"; or "when you talk, your attention seems to be focused on other people rather than yourself" (Greenberg et al., 1993).

Some therapists advocate using self-disclosure—therapists' expression of their own subjective experience when it appears to resonate with the client's (Bozarth, 1984). This is called *transparency* by Lietaer (1991). An example is, "What I find myself experiencing as you describe your own feelings is . . . "; or, "As I listen to what you're telling me, I'm feeling moved to tears." Therapists are cautioned to ensure that what they say cannot be interpreted as critical or blaming. Yontef (1995) reports that Gestalt therapists are relatively self-disclosing as a way of exposing clients to different values, thoughts, feelings, behaviors, or skills; or as a way of providing feedback about how they are affected by the client. The content and timing of such disclosures are entirely discretionary. However, clients are never encouraged to imitate the therapist's way of being but rather to focus their efforts on developing their own.

Facilitating Activation and Client Exploration of Relevant Experiences

Clients' psychological patterns can be changed only when they are occurring (similar to the proposition in the comparative framework). A variety of methods help clients activate and experience patterns with which they are having difficulty; this is called *phenomenal experimentation* (Greenberg et al., 1993; Yontef, 1995). Such methods are often used by gestalt and experiential therapists; person-centered therapists are less likely to use them (Bohart, 1995). They address underlying process difficulties within clients and facilitate their recognition of some aspect of themselves. They are not aimed at creating specific client changes and are typically introduced with the general advisement, "Try it and learn" (Yontef, 1995). Gestaltists use methods thought to be unique to gestalt treatment, combined with techniques assimilated from every available source (Simkin et al., 1993). Many, if not most, interventions, however, are created by therapists on the spot. Indeed, therapist creativity and spontaneity is routinely encouraged (Yontef, 1995). Other therapists (e.g., Greenberg et al., 1993) try to specify the conditions, called *markers,* under which specific methods may be used, the preferred method to be used as each marker is identified, and the client end state likely to result.

Thus, when clients report distress over some episode in which they reacted in a problematic manner or in a way that did not make much sense to them, the therapist suggests that exploring it might be interesting or important. *Evocative* or *systematic evocative unfolding* helps clients reconstruct the situation, beginning just before the reaction was triggered. Then they engage in a detailed, slowed-down reexperiencing of the incident with as much vivid and experiential detail as possible. This includes the perceptions, thoughts, memories, and feelings associated with its occurrence (Bohart, 1995; Greenberg et al., 1993). (This process is similar to describing and reliving a past behavior episode in the comparative framework.) *Phenomenal focusing* is a comparable method used to induce clients to focus on the episode as if it were occurring now (Yontef, 1995). It helps clients to reconstruct the episode verbally in as much detail as possible, so as to reexperience the perceptions, thoughts, and feelings they had at the time.

When clients have a vague sense of an experience but are having difficulty articulating it, *experiential focusing* is used (Gendlin, 1981; Greenberg et al., 1993). This process involves six steps that the theorists describe in detail. Clients may report the simultaneous activation of two opposing psychological patterns involving mutually incompatible thoughts, feelings, or inclinations. These are called *splits* and either of them may lie outside of the client's awareness. When this situation occurs, the two-chair dialogue can be used. It is a form of role playing in which the client is helped to imagine one aspect in one chair and the incompatible aspect in another, and then to enact a dialogue between the two chairs (Bohart, 1995; Greenberg et al., 1993). This method is often used when clients experience societal expectations, or "shoulds", that are at variance with their own needs, goals, or personal concerns.

Clients sometimes reveal that a part of them is engaged in some kind of self-controlling action against another part "I just stop myself from feeling anything." At this point, a two-chair enactment may be useful. The client is helped verbally and nonverbally to role play the process of interruption, taking both the role of the "doer" and the "done to." This is a verbal and non-verbal rendition of wiping oneself out. This helps clients experience their responsibility for interfering with the experience and expressing their suppressed feelings (Greenberg et al., 1993).

Clients may report lingering, unresolved feelings toward significant others, such as a parent or spouse. They may be unable to express these feelings fully. Such feelings are considered indicative of "unfinished business." The clients are invited to use the empty chair method, in which they imagine the relevant person to be seated in an empty chair provided by the therapist. They engage in a dialogue with that person as if he or she were present. This enables clients to express their feelings fully rather than be interrupted. This expression facilitates their emotional relief and schematic reorganization based on the emergence of reciprocal views of self and other (Greenberg et al., 1993). It can also be used to assist clients to reenact an earlier episode, as with one's mother, but to experience more fully relevant affects and a "deeper level of experiencing" (Yontef, 1995). Expressive movement exercises are another way of helping clients amplify the intensity of affective expression through the use of physical as well as verbal expression. In this anger work, they might imagine a pillow to symbolize the boss at work, and express anger toward her by physically pummeling it (Yontef, 1995).

Sometimes clients have great difficulty in discussing some aspects of their experience, anticipating that strong negative emotions, such as anger or shame, will elicit therapists' criticism or rejection, or will overwhelm them with intensity. Then, therapists may use empathic affirmation, communicating that the hitherto unacceptable aspects of clients' experience are intelligible, acceptable feelings. They may even express genuine respect that clients have had the courage to share fully their difficult experience. Clients may also be encouraged to engage in outside-therapy poetry writing, artistic expression, or the maintenance of a daily journal as a way for them to safely identify, experience, and express feelings in verbal and nonverbal ways. Homework can be used to help clients try out new ways of thinking; for males, the assignment may be to speak to one woman per day without thinking of her as a prospective date.

The Implementation of Changes Under Real-Life Conditions

Humanist therapists assume that people's behavior is governed by their psychological patterns. When those change, clients' behavior in their daily life is expected to change automatically. Humanists explicitly avoid trying to guide or direct the way clients choose to use their new capabilities, though some may use homework to facilitate efforts.

EVALUATING CLIENT PROGRESS AND OUTCOMES

Humanists believe it is ultimately the client who decides when progress has occurred and when to discontinue therapy. This is because (1) humanists view the clients as the experts concerning their experience, and (2) they respect the freedom and integrity of each person. Termination is said not to be a problem because clients are motivated to move away from being dependent and to try to proceed on their own as soon as they feel ready (Bohart, 1995). Shared judgments by clients and therapists may be made on the basis of what both have observed of their "bodily and affective sense," and of the feedback from others who observe the client (Yontef, 1995).

Explicit and systematic criteria for evaluating client progress or the effectiveness of treatment are not provided, nor are formal evaluative procedures defined. In keeping with the emphasis on changes in processes of living rather than content, Bohart (1995) and Yontef (1995) list some prototypical client changes that may occur. These include increases in (1) access to their inner experiences, (2) self-acceptance, (3) self-trust, (4) clarity of self-definition, (5) self-disclosure, (6) self-initiative in making choices and acting on them, (7) tolerance and persistence in the face of difficulty, and (8) assuming responsibility for choices. These are similar to attributes of optimal functioning that apparently are not used as evaluative criteria.

Changes in the organization of psychological patterns are described; as examples, from new perceptions emerge new possibilities (Bugental & McBeath, 1995); clients become healed by bringing conflicting aspects of their life into harmonious wholes (Yontef, 1995) or by the creative synthesis of incongruities and experiences (Bohart, 1995); and clients create new psychological patterns through the synthesis of existing schemas with the new experiences generated during therapy (Greenberg et al., 1993). Some therapists use the term *insight* to refer to such creative integration, but there is limited agreement as to its meaning. It appears to result from intuitive rather than conscious cognitive processes and can only be partially represented in words. It includes intricate and whole-bodied changes that occur in an experiential manner (Bohart, 1995), is "the multi-level, polymeaningful, affective-cognitive-conative, pre- or trans-verbal recognition that comes to us at times of authentic inner awareness" (Bugental & Sterling, 1995, p. 247), or is the achievement of an integrated gestalt (Yontef, 1995).

EVALUATING THE THERAPY MODEL

Theoretical models about the nature of humans and psychotherapy can be created from philosophic, literary, and humanistic studies. Other methods are necessary for verifying one's models. Verification of their models by humanist therapists is typically limited to anecdotal evidence from therapists about their experience in using them on a case-by-case basis. Rogers and his associates (1954) proposed and used formal methods for evaluating his model, and some have continued that kind of effort into the present (e.g., Greenberg; Rice; Goldman). Generally, however, contemporary humanists do not appear to have followed his lead in systematically relating observational data to their theoretical models. In effect, outcome studies are restricted to idiographic accounts because initial presumptions regarding the unique properties of each client (and client-therapist pair), each therapeutic goal, and each treatment sequence preclude the use of normative studies of the effectiveness of humanist psychotherapies with various client-problem groups. The result, however, is that one's ability to generalize from the individual to the general case remains correspondingly limited.

CHAPTER 9

Behavior Therapies

EHAVIOR THERAPIES WERE the first approaches derived from the science of psychology, and proponents continue to emphasize the importance of maintaining a scientific orientation. Their continued vitality results, in part, from the continuing expansion of the theories upon which they are based. As a result, what began 50 years ago as a narrow set of principles about human nature and how it changes has become significantly more diverse and flexible (Franks & Barbrack, 1991). Critics often attack behavior therapies in terms of their narrower beginnings rather than acknowledge their current diversity (Eysenck, 1988). This chapter focuses primarily on current theoretical forms of behavior therapies (see O'Donohue & Krasner, 1995b, for a recent theoretical discussion), but a brief summary of their developmental history follows.

HISTORICAL PERSPECTIVE

As behavior therapies became mainstream, their developmental history and knowledge foundations were examined (see Fishman & Franks, 1992; Fishman, Rotgers, & Franks, 1988a; Franks & Barbrack, 1983; Glass & Arnkoff, 1992; Kazdin, 1978a; Krasner, 1971; Martin, 1991, for more detail). The initial guiding belief system was rooted primarily in two influential streams within scientific psychology: behaviorism and learning theory.

BEHAVIORISM AND LEARNING THEORY

Psychology has always held competing views about mind-body issues. Some like Titchener, emphasized mental phenomena, while Thorndike and others, using animal models to study learning, emphasized objectively observable behavioral and physiological phenomena. Behaviorism expanded the second emphasis, which dominated American psychology until 1960. Its initial metaphysical assumptions were materialistic, associationistic, mechanistic, and deterministic, and its *empiricist epistemology* reflected a philosophy of science called *logical positivism.* At the same time, the experimental study of learning was influential within psychology, and its guiding paradigm was similar to behaviorism. For example, consistent with a materialistic monism, it assumed that the principles of learning are the same for all organisms and behavior. Thus basic principles could be discovered by studying any organism from mice to humans, and any response from eyeblinks to actions. Two major streams of learning theory were influential in developing the behavior therapies.

One, illustrated by Pavlov's work and called *classical* or *respondent conditioning,* rested on the principle of contiguity, which Guthrie also emphasized. It proposed that if a naturally existing or *unconditioned* pattern of association between stimuli and responses occurred at the same time as some unrelated stimuli, those previously unrelated events could become associated with the original pattern—what Pavlov called a conditional relationship—and could then activate the responses in that pattern in the absence of the original unconditioned stimuli. The other, called instrumental or operant conditioning by Thorndike and Skinner, and solution learning by Mowrer, rested on additional principles of *contingency* and *reinforcement.* They proposed that, in addition to spatial and temporal contiguity, the environmental event had to be contingent on the occurrence of the response. There are two types of contingencies: Cues or discriminative stimuli signal impending events; consequences, or "rewarding" or "punishing" events, reinforce stimulus-response associations. Hull and others proposed that a consequence was reinforcing if it reduced a state of physiological imbalance, called drive reduction. Other ideas about learning were also proposed (e.g., see Hilgard, 1948) but were less influential in the development of behavior therapy. For 25 years following the advent of behaviorism, occasional efforts were made to apply learning theories to human problems, but public acceptance would require a cultural change to legitimize such applications.

THE LEGITIMIZATION OF APPLIED PSYCHOLOGY AND THE GROWTH OF BEHAVIOR THERAPIES

World War II presented the United States with a host of human behavior issues, ranging from selecting and training military personnel for specialized roles, through using propaganda to shape the beliefs of both friends and foes, to managing the consequences of wartime traumas. Using psychology to deal with these practical issues gained credibility as a result of psychologist's wartime work. By war's end in 1945 a more favorable cultural and socioeconomic climate was emerging for applied psychology (Glass & Arnkoff, 1992; Rimm & Cunningham, 1985).

Books and articles began to signal behavior therapies as alternatives to the dominant intrapsychically oriented psychotherapies (e.g., Dollard & Miller, 1950; Eysenck, 1957, 1959; Jones, 1956; Salter, 1949; Wolpe, 1952, 1953, 1958), and to challenge the effectiveness of psychoanalysis and other psychodynamic approaches (e.g., Eysenck, 1952). By the mid-1970s, behavior therapies had been applied to a diversity of human concerns and had gained respectability and acceptance as part of mainstream psychotherapy. The approach became institutionalized through a proliferation of practitioners, journals, and professional societies. The initial missionary zeal for behavior therapies declined as acceptance and success grew. Subsequent years brought about elaboration, change, and disagreements among behavior therapists.

INFLUENCES PRODUCING CHANGES IN AND ELABORATIONS OF BEHAVIOR THERAPIES

Three kinds of development produced changes in and elaborations of the methods and guiding assumptions of behavior therapies: therapy experience; development of a negative social image; changes in learning theory and broadening of the knowledge base and methods.

Therapy Experience

Deficiencies in their initial formulations became apparent to behavior therapists as they applied those principles to real-life problems and people. The assumptions that behavior was under automatic stimulus control of environmental contingencies and reinforcers and could be changed without considering psychological events became increasingly difficult to maintain. Although therapists recognized the influences of emotions on behavior, they were defined as physiological or autonomic rather than psychological responses. Cognitions were initially considered epiphenomena, and not causally related to behavior or biological events such as neural processes.

Therapy experience and analyses of behavior therapy practices, however, revealed that therapists actively dealt with cognitive events as means of influencing behavior. They accomplished this by using client self-reports for assessing the nature and dynamics of problems, by reviewing client self-monitoring to assess behavior change progress, by motivating and encouraging them to faithfully follow behavior change procedures, by having clients use mental imagery, and by prompting introspective reports of subjective states such as fear (e.g., Fishman & Lubetkin, 1983; Klein, Dittmann, Parloff, & Gill, 1969; Wilson, 1980; Wolpe, 1958). Cognition was conceptualized in two ways to fit conditioning models: (1) Thoughts were considered "covert behavior"; the learning of thoughts and overt actions or physiological responses were presumed governed by the same principles, so they could be altered through covert conditioning techniques (e.g., Cautela, 1967; Cautela & Kearney, 1990). (2) What people said and what they thought were the same, or at least tightly linked, so verbal behavior made thoughts objectively observable and conditioning of verbal behavior corresponded to changes in related thoughts (Goldiamond & Dyrud, 1968; Kanfer, 1968). Razran's (1939) earlier demonstration of semantic conditioning—conditioning related to the meanings of words rather than to the words themselves—was ignored.

Development of a Negative Social Image
The early assumption that behavior was stimulus controlled and could be shaped with environmental manipulations influenced the development of a negative social image. The initial deemphasis upon consciousness and thought, and the promotion of a materialistic, mechanistic metaphysics contributed to public misconceptions about and resistance to behavior therapy (Glass & Arnkoff, 1992). It was sometimes represented as an inhumane approach that encouraged totalitarian behavior control. Movies depicted it as cruel, enforced behavioral control; the popular press confused it with unrelated methods like psychosurgery, brainwashing, and torture (Turkat & Feuerstein, 1978). Proponents argued that behavior therapy was humane because it emphasized teaching clients how to reach their goals (Mahoney, Kazdin, & Lesswing, 1974; Wolpe, 1981), and that it reflected a kind of utopianism because it emphasized planning social environments to encourage the best of human behavior (Krasner, 1988). Such arguments probably did less to counteract negative beliefs than did changes in learning theory and the broadening of the knowledge and methods used by behavior therapists.

Changes in Learning Theory and Broadening the Knowledge Base and Methods
A growing body of evidence led some to doubt the adequacy of principles such as reinforcement in accounting for empirical observations (Premack, 1965; Viken & McFall, 1994). Disagreements about the conditions necessary for learning to occur (Koch, 1959), and doubts that any laws of learning had been empirically confirmed (Erwin, 1978), led some to reject the idea that conditioning automatically strengthens stimulus-response connections. They

proposed that the *information value of conditioning contingencies* underlies learning. In other words, people acquire information about relationships from events although this knowledge may not be immediately manifested in behavior (Kamin, 1969; MacIntosh, 1984; Rescorla & Wagner, 1972). One review concluded:

> At one time conditioning appeared to be defined as an unconscious, non-cognitive, and automatic process . . . the contemporary approach recognizes a role for representations and beliefs about predictive and causal relationships even in the case of animal conditioning . . . [It] allows for the idea that inappropriate and maladaptive beliefs may well have arisen through a conditioning experience and that such beliefs may be changed through conditioning procedures. (Dickinson, 1987, p. 77)

Accompanying the challenges to traditional learning theory was the growing realization that therapy was a setting of social influence; thus, findings from social psychology were also potentially relevant (e.g., Goldstein, Heller, & Sechrest, 1966; Krasner, 1971).

A new theory, compatible with these trends, emerged called *social learning theory* (Bandura, 1969, 1977). Its key idea, "social modeling," resembled the concept of *imitation* (e.g., Miller & Dollard, 1941); that is, it proposed that a person could learn new behaviors by observing others perform them. It was compatible with the behavior therapies' original emphasis on learning, but was less mechanistic and legitimized both psychological and behavioral events as well as non-conditioning-based methods as part of the therapy process. It, and cognitive approaches, now represent the mainstream of current behavior therapies (Fishman & Franks, 1992).

CONTEMPORARY BEHAVIOR THERAPIES

The evolution of behavior therapy has produced a variety of approaches (called "paradigm drift" by Kendall & Bacon, 1988) and controversy about their applicability to the movement. For example, some behavior therapy pioneers worry that cognitive approaches have strayed beyond the boundaries of behavior therapy into the realm of "mentalism" against which the movement initially rebelled. They also argue that behavior therapy's original paradigm included variables now called cognitive (Krasner, 1988; O'Donohue & Krasner, 1995b). These tensions led Franks and Rosenbaum (1983) to ask, "Will the coming years see behavior therapy fragmented into numerous self-contained fields? Or will some common underlying behavioral theme be found to encompass them all?" (p. 9).

There are some similarities among behavior therapies. Hallmarks are "accountability, openness to alternatives, and appeal to data rather than authority." (Franks & Barbrack, 1983, p. 509) Nine assumptions typify current approaches (Fishman & Franks, 1992; O'Leary & Wilson, 1987):

1. The same principles guide acquisition and maintenance of normal and abnormal behavior.
2. Most abnormal behavior can be modified by applying social learning principles.
3. Assessment is continuous and focuses on current behavior determinants.
4. People are best described by what they think, feel, and do in specific life situations.
5. Treatment methods are precisely specified, replicable, and objectively evaluated.
6. Treatment outcome is evaluated in terms of (a) initial behavior changes produced, (b) its generalization to the real-life setting, and (c) its maintenance over time.
7. Treatment strategies are individually tailored to different problems in different individuals.
8. Behavior therapy is applicable to a broad range of clinical and educational problems.
9. It is humanistic as therapy goals and methods are agreed on, not arbitrarily imposed.

The official definition of behavior therapy developed by the Association for the Advancement of Behavior Therapy fits those assumptions:

> Behavior therapy involves primarily the application of principles derived from research in experimental and social psychology for the alleviation of human suffering and the enhancement of human functioning. Behavior therapy emphasizes a systematic evaluation of the effectiveness of these applications. Behavior therapy involves environmental changes and social interactions rather than the direct alteration of bodily processes by biological procedures. The aim is primarily educational. The techniques facilitate improved self-control. In the conduct of behavior therapy, contractual agreement is negotiated, in which mutually agreeable goals and procedures are specified. Responsible practitioners using behavior approaches are guided by generally accepted principles. (Franks & Wilson, 1975, pp. 1–2)

Note that no human aspects such as consciousness or cognition nor any methods such as introspection are excluded, and no metaphysical model is specified. Their empirical and largely realist epistemology may be the key characteristic linking them as a family of approaches. Most contemporary behavior therapists are methodological or neobehaviorists who acknowledge the importance of both behavioral and mental events (e.g., see Franks & Barbrack, 1983; Mahoney & Kazdin, 1979; Martin, 1991). They differ about the role and influence of cognition in neuroses and therapy. Onken and Blaines' (1991) illustrate the behavior therapies' diversity by saying, "The term behavioral therapy is used here in the broadest sense, and refers to psychosocial therapeutic interventions, including operant and classical behavior therapy, cognitive therapy, and other forms of psychotherapy" (p. 143). This chapter examines the approaches initially derived from conditioning theories of learning. Later chapters examine cognitive, cognitive-behavioral and skill training, and behavioral medicine/health approaches.

Some behavior therapists espouse a technological or eclectic orientation that views technology and science as related but separable. They seek to identify empirically the effectiveness, feasibility, and efficiency of specific strategies and methods for specific problems, clients, and settings without necessarily trying to explain why they work: "The measure of a technique is not its scientific lineage, but its efficacy" (Kendall & Bacon, 1988, p. 150). Thus, therapists can use any method derived from any model without having to adopt its theoretical and empirically unsubstantiated rationale" (Lazarus, 1969). This produces a functional autonomy of methods from the theories that spawned them. In other words, the same strategies and methods can be used in different approaches. Eclectic approaches are analyzed in a later chapter.

The first behavior therapies were derived from applications of a classical conditioning model, or Skinner's classic operant conditioning model, usually called behavior modification or applied behavior analysis. Social learning theory and social psychology produced elaborations and legitimized the consideration of psychological events in behavior therapy. Among the initial leaders of this movement were Albert Bandura, Alan Bellack, Hans Eysenck, Cyril Franks, Michel Hersen, Frederick Kanfer, Alan Kazdin, Leonard Krasner, Howard Rachlin, and Joseph Wolpe.

Krasner (1971) described the result as a set of "specific techniques derived from the experimental laboratory, usually based on learning theory" that become effective "only within the context of maximum social influence," and where therapists function as "a compound social reinforcing and discriminative stimulus" (p. 486). Contemporary behavior therapists (1) focus on current rather than historical determinants of behavior, (2) emphasize overt behavior change, (3) objectively specify treatment to make replication possible, (4) rely on basic research in psychology to generate treatment strategies and methods, and (5) are specific in definition and accountability, treatment, and measurement. (Kazdin, 1978b; Mueser & Liberman, 1995). The two most distinguishing features of contemporary behavior therapy are (1) its emphasis on the direct modification of behavior rather than intrapsychic patterns, as emphasized in psychoanalysis, and (2) the recognition that stability and behavior change are under stimulus control, which is primarily environmental.

THE CONCEPTUAL MODEL

Behavior therapists consider diverse kinds of responses and stimuli in their emphasis on specifying each client's idiosyncratic patterns, but there is no general conceptual model of the content and organization of human behavior to guide these analyses. This reflects two guiding assumptions that seem to make a conceptual model unnecessary. First, the same learning principles govern all behavior regardless of kind, so specifying different kinds of responses is unnecessary (note that no response-defined concepts are included in Kazdin's 1989 glossary). Second, the possible ways of associating specific stimuli and responses through contiguity and reinforcing consequences are almost limitless.

LEVELS AND UNITS OF ANALYSIS

Behavior therapists argue that assessment of the content and dynamic organization of each client's idiosyncratic behavior patterns provides the basis for planning treatment. This requires specifying the *particular kinds of responses and environmental events* involved in the pattern, and their *functional antecedent and consequent relationships*—what elicits, reinforces, and maintains the pattern. Diagnostic classifications have limited utility because similar dysfunctional patterns such as depressive states, may have different antecedents and consequences. Because environment and behavior are assumed to be interdependent, the focal level of analysis is the person-in-context. They consider complex behavior patterns to be constructions of behavioral and environmental elements; therefore, they use *multiple levels of analysis*. That is, they measure specific stimuli and responses and their combination into units of varying complexity without proposing standard units of analysis. Their analyses of specific cases implicitly use the taxonomy for different kinds of responses traditionally used in the science of psychology (O'Connor, 1987), and one similar to our comparative framework. Similarly, no taxonomy of environmental events is proposed. Each therapist uses the kinds and complexity of environmental units considered appropriate for each client, so the taxonomy used may vary from client to client and therapist to therapist.

Behavior therapists emphasize A(ntecedent)-B(ehavior)-C(onsequent) analyses of behavior patterns, so their units of analysis include a temporal element. Rachlin (1988) argues the importance of this and believes it creates serious problems for molecular analyses. These analyses postulate chains of conditioned stimuli and responses to account for the influence of phenomena not specifically present in the current situation. Rachlin asserts a need for units of analysis representing "temporally extended patterns of behavior," termed *molar behaviorism*. Similarly, Hallam (1987) argues for "a macroscopic level of analysis in which behavior is chunked into units that extend far beyond the usual time-limited definitions of a response" (p. 325). Emphasizing meaningful behavior "acts or actions in situations" would preserve the unity of complex behavior and "the integrity of the actor" (p. 324) and "can be construed as an unfolding reflection of a dramatic plot" (p. 325). Thus, they believe people are best described by what they think, feel, and do in specific situations (O'Leary & Wilson, 1987). (This is similar to the behavior episode and behavior episode schema units in our comparative framework.)

Problems are created when levels and units of analysis are idiosyncratically specified and differ from client to client. When is something a response or stimulus, and when a complex pattern: Is fear a response or a pattern of responses? Inadequate behavior analysis results in ineffective treatment when important eliciting and behavior-maintaining conditions are inadequately specified (e.g., Rachlin, 1988; Wolpe, 1990). Therefore, a direct link exists between the units and levels of analysis used and the selection and effectiveness of interventions. Without agreement on appropriate levels and units of analysis, the ability to generalize from one client to another about the relevance and effectiveness of treatment approaches is compromised.

CONTENT OF KEY CONCEPTS

Behavior therapy stresses three concepts: *Behavior/response; environment;* and *stimulus.*

Behavior/Response
These terms are used as synonyms by behavior therapists to lump together units of different size and content. For example, a rapid heartbeat and a phobia are both responses. Behavior and response are usually defined in terms of observational methods rather than content or pattern, in keeping with an empiricist epistemology. Thus, responses are functions that can be objectively ob-

served by someone other than the actor; they are overt rather than covert. Contemporary behavior therapists broaden this definition to include both overt actions and observable manifestations of covert processes, such as affects and thoughts. (Fishman, Rotgers, & Franks, 1988b). For example, Kazdin (1989) defines behavior as "any observable or measurable response or act . . . [it] is occasionally defined to include cognitions, psychophysiological reactions, and feelings, which may not be directly observable but are defined in terms that can be measured" (p. 337).

The respondent conditioning model defines unconditioned and conditioned responses as activities that are functionally related to *antecedent* stimuli. In contrast, Skinner introduced the concept of an operant response, defined as "spontaneously emitted" behavior that "operates on" or influences the environment, and that is controlled primarily by its *consequences* (Kazdin, 1989). None of these definitions identifies qualitatively different kinds of responses, or distinguishes between molecular—a smile—and molar—a clinical depression—units.

Shapiro (1964) combines content with the vantage point of observation and proposes categories typical of a monistic behaviorism. All responses are of two types: *Excitatory responses* are glandular and muscular activations; these are material-based processes that can be directly observed or inferred. *Inhibitory responses* are experimentally demonstrated suppressions of excitatory responses. Wolpe (1990) defines a response in biological terms as the activation of a specific "set of neurons" and the consequences of such activations as "muscle contractions" or "perceived images." Knowledge is learned in the form of "engrams" that are "complex, integrated neural-response systems" (p. 22), and "pleasure" is a "subjective correlate of additional neural excitation." (p. 16) This terminology implies a form of biological determinism, because it reduces all psychological events to byproducts of biological processes. For example, learning alters neural patterns directly and psychological events indirectly.

Translated into our comparative framework, the behaviorists concept of behavior or response refers to the behavioral person, including ingestive, eliminative, motoric, communicative, information collection, and behavioral monitoring behaviors. It also includes some aspects of the biological person, such as neuronal (central nervous system and autonomic nervous system,) and glandular functions. Aspects of the psychological person, such as emotions and thoughts, are manifested in objectively observable behavioral—verbalizations—or biological—blood pressure—responses. "Although emphasis is placed on behavior, or what people do, this does not mean that problems are viewed solely in terms of overt actions. How people feel (affect) and think (cognition) are often central to the specific problems brought to treatment" (Kazdin, 1989, p. 2). The tradition of behavior therapy emphasizes causal roles for behavioral and environmental rather than psychological events, reflecting its origins as a revolt against the psychoanalytic's view of causality: "Behavior modification often focuses on behavior both as an end in itself and as a means of changing affect and cognition" (1989, p. 3).

Anxiety/fear is a specific kind of behavior that behavior therapists have emphasized from the beginning. Many consider it a key to understanding neuroses, particularly in treatments for phobias. Behavior therapists typically consider fear and anxiety to be synonyms for one kind of emotion. Although a diversity of interventions have been devised focussed on this emotion, the concept is seldom defined and often not included in subject indexes.

It is considered an unconditioned or unlearned response that can come to be elicited by any stimulus through learning. It is aversive, linked to avoidance responses, and often defined in biological rather than psychological terms. For example, Wolpe (1990) defines anxiety as a person's "characteristic pattern of autonomic responses to noxious stimulation" (p. 23). He views the psychological experience of anxiety as a correlate or manifestation of the autonomic pattern. Because people's autonomic patterns may differ, the experience they call anxiety may also differ. Eysenck (1987a) summarizes proposals that fear/anxiety "could best be regarded as consisting of at least three loosely coupled (response) systems—subjective, behavioral, and physiological" but notes that the subjective component would be rejected by some because of "the well known objection to introspective evidence of most behaviorists" (p. 13). (Eysenck's summary is similar to the comparative framework's model of emotions.) Other emotions, such as anger and depression, have attracted increased attention as behavior therapists have addressed a growing diversity of problems, but they, too, have remained generally undefined. "Positive" emotions such as affection/love and happiness/joy are seldom mentioned.

Verbal or *language behavior* is another kind of response increasingly emphasized in conditioning models. This is the way many behavior therapists convert cognitive processes into overt and objectively observable behavior. Their discussions of the conditioning of verbal or language behavior seem to assume implicitly that thought occurs in linguistic codes, so changing what a person says results in changing what they think (e.g., Eifert, 1987).

Perception is a kind of response that Wolpe (1990) argues is the basis of cognition. "A person's knowledge of the world consists entirely of private events. An individual's first response to an object is the perception of it. Images evoked in the absence of objects . . . are conditioned perceptions. Together, immediate perceptions and conditioned perceptions make up cognitions" (p. 19). In this formulation, he maintains his monistic, antimentalist assumptions in two ways: (1) The possibility that humans can construct and manipulate representations that are not direct perceptions is rejected; cognition is limited to environmentally-linked perceptual processes. (2) Perceptions have no causal role; they are manifestations of nervous system activities, and it is patterns of nervous system functioning—which he calls *engrams*—"arousable by systematically variable combinations of sensory inputs" (p. 22) that influence actions.

Other psychological processes such as attention, problem solving, self-evaluation, or moral reasoning are not considered in conditioning-based approaches, consistent with theorists' avoidance of mentalism and introspection. For example, concepts like memory are deemed unnecessary because learning is assumed to occur automatically without involving mental representations. However, therapists using a social learning rationale do focus on some psychological phenomena, such as self-efficacy. The cognitive function of goal setting is implied in their emphasis on client-therapist collaboration in deciding on the goals or behavior change toward which therapy should be directed. Some have begun to refer to some biological characteristics—genetic factors (Eysenck, 1987b) and neurohormones (Kelley, 1987). As behavior therapists have applied their procedural model to a greater variety of human problems, they seem to be progressively elaborating their conceptual model to encompass more of the psychological and biological components included within this book's comparative framework.

Environment

Behavior therapists initially assumed that behavior was controlled or caused by social/environmental conditions rather than by intrapsychic phenomena. Krasner (1988) referred to these as "the clashing conceptual models of human nature . . . as 'inner' and 'outer' explanations of locus of causation of behavior (the perennial nature vs. nurture controversy)" (p. 27). Despite this environmental emphasis, definitions and taxonomies of environmental determinants have not been proposed. Behaviorists stress specific, proximal, immediate, environmental conditions, but may also use a hierarchical model and include "ecological and broad-scale environmental assessment . . . factors such as economic or occupational opportunities, architectural design, public transportation systems, nutrition, environmental pollutants, and recreation facilities" (Wilson & O'Leary, 1980, p. 37).

Contemporary behavior therapists are less doctrinaire. Just as theories of development have shifted from nature versus nurture to nature and nurture, so too have most behavior therapists shifted to the view that both environmental and person variables play influential roles as antecedents and consequents in eliciting and maintaining behavior patterns (Martin & Levey, 1987; O'Connor, 1987). This shift is reflected in discussions of the concept of stimulus.

Stimulus

Phenomena represented by the concept of stimulus are defined not in terms of kinds of events but rather in terms of their relationships: "A stimulus is the antecedent of a response" (Wolpe, 1990, p. 13). More generally, a stimulus is "a measurable event that may have an effect on a behavior" (Kazdin, 1989, p. 347). This view is consistent with a cosmology of mechanism in which responses are reactions to events or stimuli. However, this kind of definition creates the difficulty that an event cannot be identified as a stimulus until it has been observed to have elicited or influenced a response. Moreover, such a functional definition does not exclude any kind of event from operating as a stimulus. So therefore, in behavior therapy theory both environmental events and responses may function as stimuli for other responses. Interestingly, except for Bandura's social learning model, this formulation has not been extended to include the idea that responses may also function as stimuli for environmental events. Stimuli may differ from one another and across occasions in terms of qualities or differences of kind, intensity, duration, and frequency. Each of these properties may have a differential influence on behavior.

SUMMARY COMMENTS

In general, the conceptual model of behavior therapies focuses on the organizational properties of behavior patterns rather than the content: Behavior or responses are defined as reactions to stimuli, and stimuli are any events that elicit or affect responses. True to an associationistic model, learning creates organizations of elements—stimuli and responses—thereby producing different kinds and levels of complexity of behavior patterns. Their propositional model, thus, should explain how such organizations can be created and modified.

THE PROPOSITIONAL MODEL

The propositional models of traditional behavior therapies use three principles proposed in their guiding learning theories: *Contiguity, contingency and consequence,* and *observational or vicarious learning.* Each refers to different aspects of behavior and environment interactions, but they share some basic assumptions about change processes.

ASSUMPTIONS ABOUT STABILITY-MAINTAINING AND CHANGE PROCESSES

They share a general mechanistic, associationistic model of people as reactive entities, so they emphasize feedback or reactive processes. The roles of feedforward—anticipatory, proactive—processes have historically not been equally emphasized, perhaps because they contradict the reactive organism model. Feedforward is indirectly represented in concepts like cue and discriminative stimulus and receives significant emphasis in more recent social learning formulations (e.g., Bandura, 1986). The propositional models also emphasize incremental change and stability-maintaining processes but ignore the possibility of transformational change. They all assume that (1) only presently occurring events can affect and be affected by learning processes, (2) change results from modifications and elaborations of presently occurring patterns, and (3) behavior episodes provide contexts within which change occurs. They create specific situations (behavior episodes in our comparative framework) that facilitate occurrence of some responses and constrain others, and then arrange for contingencies and consequences to occur that increase or decrease the probability that the target stimulus-response pattern will occur.

Types of Contingent Relationships

When the occurrence of one event is related to or influenced by another event, a contingency exists. These learning theories stress three kinds of contingent relationships, which is their way of representing the dynamics of human behavior.

Contiguity is a contingency of simultaneous covariation: Events occur at the same time and place; when one occurs, so will the other. Such a contingency implies the possibility but does not require that the two events are functionally related. Some other event may be influencing the occurrence of both, or their covariation may be accidental. The respondent conditioning concept of conditioned stimulus (CS)–unconditioned stimulus (UCS) relationships illustrates contiguous association. In a *predictive contingency,* the occurrence of one event signals the probable future occurrence of another. It represents sequential rather than simultaneous covariate contingencies between events—the flow of events through time—and does not require that they be functionally related. This is illustrated by the concepts of discriminitive stimuli and cue. In a *causal contingency,* some events influence the occurrence of others.

Our comparative framework proposes two kinds: In a *facilitating contingency,* one event fosters the occurrence of another. In a *constraining contingency,* one event limits or prevents the occurrence of another. The assumption that stimuli elicit responses represents facilitating contingencies. The concepts of inhibition and avoidance represent constraining contingencies (e.g., Wolpe's idea of reciprocal inhibition).

Conditioning models stress different contingencies. Respondent conditioning focuses on contingencies between antecedent stimuli and responses: stimuli elicit responses (an S ➤ R contingency). Instrumental/operant conditioning uses both S ➤ R predictive—or discriminative—and causal R ➤ S contingencies in the relationships of responses to their antecedents and consequences. A brief summary shows how these emphases appear in each learning model.

CONTIGUITY: CLASSICAL OR RESPONDENT CONDITIONING

Classical or respondent conditioning starts with the assumption that organisms, such as humans, have unlearned, built-in behavior patterns, called unconditioned responses (UCR), that are innately activated or elicited by specific stimuli, called unconditioned stimuli (UCS). Thus, a UCS-UCR pattern is considered a basic, unlearned person-in-context pattern that functions as a unit. This serves as the theorists' basic unit of analysis. All other learned patterns are considered to be based on or derived from these innate, unlearned behavior patterns. A fear pattern is illustrative: It is innately activated in infants by stimuli such as sudden loud noises or loss of support. Through learning, fear patterns can come to be activated by almost any other kind of event.

Learning New Elicitors for Existing Behavior Patterns

When activated, unlearned UCS-UCR units occur in a larger context that includes other environmental and response elements that are not a part of the inborn pattern. Because these elements occur in *spatial-temporal contiguity,* they may become associated with that behavior pattern. The new association is assumed to occur automatically—without conscious effort or cognitive involvement. Learned elicitors are called conditioned stimuli (CS) and the behavior patterns they elicit are called conditioned responses (CR). Beginning with Pavlov's stress on the importance of language, as a "second signaling system", this conditioning model acknowledges the existence of language and thought and the possibility that they might come to function as conditioned stimuli through learning. However, the potential role of cognition in classical conditioning arrangements was not emphasized in American behaviorism in which behavior therapy was initially rooted.

There are two somewhat different classical conditioning arrangements, called Pavlovian A and B (Eysenck, 1985). In the A arrangement, a particular motivational state is activated in animals or people—for example, they are deprived of food to make them hungry. Then, when food (an unconditioned stimulus) is presented, eating behavior (an unconditioned response) follows. Some other event—a conditioned stimulus—that occurs at the same time as the unconditioned stimulus becomes capable of activating preparatory behavior, such as salivation—a conditioned response—which is linked to but not the same as the unconditioned response, such as eating behavior. The conditioned stimulus, however, cannot substitute for the unconditioned one because it does not directly elicit the unconditioned response. The newly learned association will not occur if the relevant motivational or drive state does not exist. In this arrangement, a conditioned stimulus-conditioned response association represents a predictive contingency for the unconditioned response, analogous to a discriminative stimulus in operant conditions. It is predictive of but does not elicit the unconditioned response. In terms of our comparative framework, such conditioned stimuli perform a feedforward function.

In the B arrangement, no prior motivational state is activated, the unconditioned stimulus activates an unconditioned response that functions as a motivational state—fear. Some other event (conditioned stimulus) occurring simultaneously with the unconditioned stimulus also becomes capable of eliciting the unconditioned response: the conditioned stimulus can substitute for the unconditioned one, so a causal contingency between the conditioned stimulus and the unconditioned response has been created. For example, an infant who experiences fear—an unconditioned response—when accidentally dropped—an unconditioned stimulus—by a visitor—a conditioned stimulus—may later react with fear in that visitor's presence. The B arrangement is considered the format for learning fear-based neuroses. Additional elicitors may be learned in both A and B arrangements if they occur contiguously with the original unconditioned stimulus-unconditioned response pattern, or with a previously learned conditioned stimulus-conditioned response pattern (called higher order conditioning). This process incrementally elaborates the stimulus elements of a person-in-context unconditional stimulus-unconditioned response unit. Notice that reactive contiguity-based learning models do not address the question of how the *content* of a person's behavior may become diversified and altered, but deal only with ways to alter or elaborate its *predictive* or *eliciting stimulus conditions*. Accordingly, this is sometimes called *respondent conditioning*.

Unlearning Learned Elicitors

Inborn patterns—unconditioned stimulus/response relationships—evolved and persist because they have important adaptive utility. Learned patterns (conditioned stimulus-conditioned response and conditioned stimulus-unconditioned response) persist as long as they retain a link to the original unconditioned stimulus or unconditioned response. They may be unlearned by eliminating their contiguity relationships. In the A pattern, this unlearning involves arranging for the conditioned stimulus to occur in the absence of the unconditioned stimulus to which it is linked. This eliminates the predictive contingency value of the conditioned stimulus. In the B arrangement, it is necessary to arrange for the conditioned stimulus to occur in the absence of the unconditioned response to which it is linked so as to eliminate its causal relationship to the unconditioned response—such as fear. This assumed automatic process of progressive weakening of stimulus-response associations is called *extinction*. For example, if the feared visitor is with the baby in situations that do not elicit fear in the child, the likelihood decreases that the visitor's future presence will elicit fear.

Some responses are assumed to be inherently incompatible, so they cannot occur simultaneously; if one takes place, the other cannot. One way to extinguish the B pattern is to activate in the person some other response that prevents the occurrence of the unwanted unconditioned response, such as fear, in the presence of its eliciting conditioned stimulus. This is often called *response prevention* or *reciprocal inhibition*. For example, the baby may be playing a game that elicits pleasure, thereby preventing the fear response in the visitor's presence. This is a key idea in Wolpe's systematic desensitization therapy. No criteria are proposed for identifying incompatible responses.

Why Are Associations Learned and Unlearned?

Consistent with their cosmology of mechanism, traditional classical conditioning models assume that new stimulus-response patterns result solely and automatically from the contiguity of events. Why, then, do only some of all the environmental and response events that occur contiguously with the original pattern become associated with it and function as conditioned stimuli? Some kind of selection processes must be operating. Although they seldom mention it, behavior therapists implicitly assume that clients are alert and notice events that function or come to function as unconditioned or conditioned stimuli. In therapy practice, instructions to clients and other procedures facilitate *selective attention*. The resulting *selective perceptions* provide the feedback signals for reactive learning processes and are probably important in the selectivity of classical conditioning procedures. Concepts like discriminative stimulus and discrimination are the behaviorists' indirect ways of talking about selective attention and perception. In classical conditioning arrangements, however, the person's behavior has no influence over the events that occur.

Contingency and Consequence: Instrumental or Operant Conditioning.

The instrumental/operant model of learning stresses that people's actions do influence what happens, and that adaptive acts function to control their consequences. Contingent relationships do exist among stimuli, behavior, and its consequences. These are represented in four basic propositions: *reinforcement*, *punishment, discriminative stimuli,* and *extinction.*

Reinforcement

Learning is a selection process. A diversity of responses may occur in any situation, or behavior episode. The resulting consequences make some responses more likely to occur in future, similar episodes and others less likely. Why are some responses selected in and others selected out? The operant model proposes that it depends on the consequences produced by each response pattern—on *response-consequence causal contingencies.* The only responses that are learned are those that display instrumental or adaptive value. They produce positive consequences, called positive reinforcement, or they terminate or avoid negative ones, called negative reinforcement. The term *reinforcement* carries only propositional meaning; it identifies a causal relationship between events, but not event content. The word *reinforcer* implies a specific event but is meaningless as to what kind because the model proposes that any kind of environmental or response event can acquire reinforcement value. Reinforcement is assumed to be an automatic process that involves neither conscious effort nor the use of cognitive processes.

　To increase the likelihood that a person will behave in a particular way in a particular behavior episode, one must (1) predict what kind of event will serve as a reinforcing consequence (RC) for the person in that episode, and (2) devise behavior episodes in which the desired behavior occurs and is immediately followed by the reinforcing consequence. The consequence must follow immediately if the person is to react to the causal contingency; contiguity is a prerequisite for contingency; behavior change always occurs in the here and now.

　How can one determine which kinds of events will function as reinforcers for a particular person in a particular situation? Empirical evidence makes it clear that no event will function as a reinforcer in all kinds of behavior episodes, nor will it always have the same reinforcement value in similar episodes. The operant answer is that an event's reinforcement value can only be determined empirically—by observing whether it increases relevant response frequencies in particular behavior episodes. The problem with this answer is that it makes the selection of reinforcers a trial-and-error process because it provides no criteria for predicting in advance what events might be reinforcing in a particular situation.

Two operant model-based strategies for dealing with this dilemma are proposed. First, certain consequences are assumed to be *innate reinforcers* for everyone in certain kinds of episodes: Food is a positive reinforcer when a person is hungry, and pain termination will always have negative reinforcing value, since it terminates an outcome the person dislikes. Such primary or unconditioned reinforcers can be used with everyone in relevant behavior episodes. However, no taxonomy of innate reinforcers is provided, nor any criteria for identifying them. Second, *acquired reinforcing value* can result for any environmental or response event if it occurs in a behavior episode in contiguity with an event that already functions as a reinforcer. They become *secondary or conditioned reinforcers.* Thus, secondary reinforcers are learned by the same process as conditioned stimuli in respondent conditioning. One special arrangement of primary and secondary reinforcers is called a *token economy.* In it, something that has no intrinsic value for the person (a token) can be used to obtain something that does have intrinsic value, the token functions as a *primary reinforcer.* Through its causal contingency with a primary reinforcer, a token can come to function as a *secondary reinforcer.* In a sense, tokens function as immediate subgoals that help obtain a distal, primary goal.

Everyone has a history of specific behavior episodes in which some events have served as reinforcing consequences; these represent a person's reinforcement history. Selection of a reinforcer for a new episode can be based on knowledge of a person's reinforcement history, but how can therapists know what that is? In practice, they rely on client report, although they sometimes also try to observe directly what is reinforcing in relevant natural or simulated behavior episodes. Their practice-based terms and procedures, however, imply a predictive criterion—that an event's potential reinforcement value is a function of a person's evaluative responses. For example, a positive reinforcer is often described as a favorable, and a negative reinforcer as an aversive or noxious event or stimulus. Favorable or noxious for whom? The client, of course. Therefore, in commonsense language, an event is likely to function as a positive reinforcer if it is something a client wants or likes, and a negative reinforcer if it is something the client does not like or wants to avoid.

Procedures for selecting reinforcers confirm this implication; therapists' assessment procedures identify clients' positive and negative preferences for different kinds of events (e.g., Cautela & Kastenbaum, 1967; Wilson &

O'Leary, 1980). Thus, in practice, behavior therapists appear to rely on what our comparative model calls the directive and regulatory or evaluative functions for identifying consequences likely to have reinforcing value for a client. Wants, likes, and preferences are attributes of the psychological person. Therefore, such terms have been avoided in traditional behaviorist models. Later, we will summarize more recent formulations of conditioning theory and human learning that reinterpret the dynamics of conditioning contingencies so as to include information/meaning-based learning.

Punishment

The behaviorists' concept of punishment does not refer to attributes of events, as does everyday usage, but to a functional relationship between events. A consequence is punishing if it decreases response probability. There are two types: (1) presentation of an aversive event, such as being burned by touching a hot object, and (2) removal of a positive event, such as suspending driving privileges. These are contingent on the occurrence of a target response. Note that the terms *positive* and *aversive* imply people's evaluations of the impact of an event on them. In commonsense terms, people stop behaving in ways that produce consequences they don't like or want, or deny them consequences they do like or want. Ethical concerns have limited the use of punishment procedures by behavior therapists.

Discriminative Stimuli

Type A respondent conditioning describes how stimuli come to signal the probable occurrence of responses. Operant models use the concept of *discriminative stimuli* to deal with the same issue. If stimulus X consistently precedes behavior that is followed by a reinforcing or punishing consequence, and stimulus Y does not, a *predictive contingency* exists. People can learn that X signals that the same behavior-consequence pattern is likely to follow and Y does not. Then, their behavior is under stimulus control. To get a person to perform or inhibit the target behavior, present a learned discriminative stimulus. You can't influence behavior that isn't occurring, so prompts and cues—instructions, gestures, demonstrations—function as discriminative stimuli to elicit target responses so they can be reinforced or punished. Thus, discriminative stimuli perform a feedforward function enabling people to anticipate rather than just react to reinforcing or punishing consequences.

The concept of generalization represents a related form of predictive contingency. If the stimulus conditions of a new behavior episode are similar to previous ones in which a particular response has been effective, the probability that the previously effective response will occur may be increased.

This is called *stimulus generalization* and is a very important issue in psychotherapy: how to get desired behavior patterns that occur in psychotherapy sessions to occur in relevant real-life episodes. Similarly, if a response has consistently been effective in a particular type of episode, the probability of a similar but not identical response occurring in that type of episode may be increased; this is called *response generalization*. This similarity is important because creating alternate ways of accomplishing similar outcomes has considerable adaptive utility, as no two episodes are ever identical. In commonsense language, a person will try effective habits in new situations for which they seem relevant, or will, in a familiar situation, try some version of a kind of behavior that has been effective in that kind of situation in the past.

Two other ideas are related to the concept of discriminative stimuli: response shaping and chaining. People cannot use a behavior pattern to achieve reinforcing consequences if that behavior pattern isn't in their repertoire. Procedures are necessary for helping people learn new, more complex behaviors. In *response shaping*, a behavior episode is designed to elicit and reinforce a particular pattern of behavior. However, rather than waiting for the complete pattern to occur, reinforcement is provided for any behavior that is in some way similar to the desired pattern. The same episode is repeated over and over, with successive approximations toward the desired behavior pattern being reinforced until the complete pattern has finally been constructed through learned association of its elements. Some consequences require a sequence of behaviors to produce them. In chaining, responses that lead up to the behavior that will be reinforced are conditioned to be discriminative stimuli or secondary reinforcers, beginning with the response closest to the reinforcing consequence. Thus, a sequence is constructed and maintained by the predictive contingency that each response brings one closer to the reinforcing consequence.

Extinction
Unlearning existing patterns requires breaking learned associations, the predictive and causal contingencies between stimuli and responses. This *extinction* can be accomplished by creating behavior episodes in which a once-effective behavior is no longer followed by a reinforcing consequence, or the predictive contingency no longer exists. With repeatedly nonreinforced episodes, the probability that a learned pattern will occur declines, as a predictive or causal contingency no longer exists. In commonsense language, people usually cease to behave in ways that no longer work, even if those behaviors used to be effective.

OBSERVATIONAL OR VICARIOUS LEARNING: SOCIAL LEARNING THEORY

Social learning theory emerged from several sources, but Bandura's (1969, 1977) version is considered to have had the greatest influence on the practice of behavior therapy.

Constructing Cognitive Representations of Behavior-Context Possibilities
The core assumption is that people do not have to actually perform responses for learning to occur; they can also learn by watching others behave in relevant behavior episodes, called *modeling* (like observational behavior episodes in the comparative framework). Bandura (1977) says three kinds of cognitive representations are constructed through vicarious learning: (1) behavior possibilities; (2) predictive contingencies about behavior-consequence relationships, called *outcome expectancies;* and (3) predictive contingencies about the likelihood that people can behave effectively in that way, called *self-efficacy expectancies.* The modeling process may be made more elaborate by adding verbal explanations, which clarify for the client the general rules that guide effective behavior in that kind of episode. Rule-guided behavior provides more generative flexibility than simply modeling a specific behavior pattern. Bandura proposes that if people know what to do, believe they are capable of doing it, and believe that the behavior will produce desirable consequences, they are more likely to behave that way in the future.

Bandura (1977) says this solves a practical problem in operant procedures: A response has to occur to be reinforced; but suppose the desired response is not in the person's repertoire? Then, no matter how long the therapist waits, it will not occur. The operant strategy of response shaping is a slow and often impractical process. Through observational learning, people can quickly learn a new response possibility and response-consequence contingency. This can then be elicited by asking them to try to behave that way in a similar behavior episode, a process called *participant modeling.* The episode may be created under real-life conditions or it may be simulated, as in role playing. Once the response is performed, discriminative and reinforcing contingencies can be applied. The most powerful reinforcers are real-life consequences; but approval of therapists and others—as in group therapy—are important social reinforcers in the social learning model.

Thus, cognition is proposed to play a causal role in the learning and performance of actions. Bandura (1972) asserts that environment, behavior, and cognition influence one another and that learning results from this triadic reciprocal determinism rather than from a single cause. By combining social learning with conditioning theories, behavior therapy retained its roots in learning theory and gave cognition a role in influencing behavior, but conditioning principles retained their influence in guiding treatment methods.

As originally formulated, certain learning was considered to involve automatic, nonconscious processes in which mental events such as thoughts played no role. These types were respondent conditioning and operant conditioning. Conditioning terminology reflects the mechanistic assumptions of a reactive organism and excludes mentalistic connotations. Beginning 30 years ago, researchers reported that verbal stimuli, instructions, and general background features of laboratory settings significantly influenced the acquisition of responses (e.g., Prokasy, 1965).

They concluded that accumulating evidence challenged the operation of automatic reinforcement, indicating that more complex processes must be involved in conditioning (e.g., MacIntosh, 1984). "We have found that even the simplest forms of conditioning appear to involve cognitive processes, that learning can occur without reinforcement within the conditioning paradigm, and that even where reinforcement operates, strict contiguity between the response or stimulus and the reinforcer is neither necessary nor sufficient for conditioning" (Dickinson, 1987, pp. 57–58). Some behavior therapists raise similar criticisms:

> The special status accorded reinforcement procedures is difficult to understand . . . in light of the available empirical evidence. Outside of the unique circumstances found in institutional settings, reinforcement procedures have surprisingly weak support in the behavior therapy literature. Ironically, the view of reinforcement held uncritically by many behavioral practitioners today was found incomplete and in need of revision by experimental learning theorists decades ago. (Viken & McFall, 1994, p. 121)

New Explanations for Conditioning Processes

Some behavior therapists concluded that traditional conditioning theories are unproven and do not provide a sound base for therapy (e.g., Erwin, 1978; Franks & Barbrack, 1991). This does not mean that respondent and operant procedures do not influence learning; it only means that empirical evidence does not support nonmentalistic, reactive organism explanations about *why* they work—that is, how contiguity, contingency, and consequence influence learning. For example, Timberlake (1995) proposes a causal system reconceptualization of reinforcement processes.

The emerging view assumes that humans evolved capabilities for detecting, representing, and using information about environments and their relationships to them, making it possible to predict and control adaptively important events. This suggests that

> development of the conditional response reflects the acquisition of knowledge about the relationship between the events in a conditioning experience rather than ... direct strengthening of a response or behavioral disposition posited by reinforcement theory. Knowledge about event or stimulus relationships must involve some form of internal or mental representation of these stimuli. (Dickinson, 1987, p. 58)

Changes produced by conditioning methods are mediated by people's use of perceptual and cognitive representations of the predictive and causal contingencies among environmental and response events to guide their behavior. Representations result from participation in specific situations, so there is still merit in behavior therapies' focus on behaviors in specific episodes as a source of learning (and of cognitions—e.g., Eysenck, 1988); and this observation shows that conditioning and social learning are similar.

Elaborations of Social Learning Theory
Bandura's (1986) elaborated view continues to emphasize that learning and performance of behavior patterns is a product of mutual causal processes among environmental, behavioral, and cognitive factors, called *reciprocal determinism,* and that learning results from both direct and vicarious experience, within individuals' biological limits. The role of cognition is enlarged, so he now calls his view a *social cognitive theory of thought and action.* He proposes that humans have five innate cognitive capabilities (similar to the information processing, governing, and feedforward functions in our comparative framework):

1. *Symbolizing Capability*—"Through symbols people process and transform transient experiences into internal models that serve as guides for future action" (Bandura, 1986, p. 18).
2. *Forethought Capability*—"Future events cannot serve as determinants of behavior, but their cognitive representation can have a strong causal impact on present action. Images of desirable future events tend to foster the behavior most likely to bring about their realization. Forethought is the product of generative and reflective ideation" (p. 19).
3. *Vicarious Capability*—"The abbreviation of the acquisition process through observational learning is vital for both development and sur-

vival . . . virtually all learning . . . resulting from direct experience can occur vicariously by observing other people's behavior and its consequences for them" (p. 19).

4. *Self-Regulatory Capability*—"People do not behave just to suit the preferences of others. Much of their behavior is motivated and regulated by internal standards and self-evaluative reactions" (p. 20).

5. *Self-Reflectivity*—"Reflective self-consciousness . . . enables people to analyze their experiences and to think about their own thought processes" (p. 21).

Bandura uses a unit similar to the behavior episodes in our comparative framework. "Goals and standards [are] cognitive representations of desired futures. By making self-satisfaction conditional on fulfilling selected goals, people give direction to their actions and create self-incentives to persist in their efforts until their performances match their goals" (Bandura, 1986, p. 233). Episodes occur in specific contexts and are organized and guided by personal goals. "It is because behavior is selected, organized, and sustained by cognized future outcomes that it retains coherence and direction, despite dissuading momentary effects" (p. 239). Variable activity transacts with environments' facilitating and constraining conditions for the desired outcomes. The resulting contingencies and consequences provide information for construction of cognitive representations of the content and organization of behavior-environment events. "By observing the differential outcome of their actions, people eventually construct conceptions of new behavioral patterns and the circumstances in which it is appropriate to perform them" (Bandura, 1986, p. 111). "Successful courses of action tend to be selected and ineffective ones discarded" (p. 106).

Our comparative framework specifies three types of behavior episodes: transactional, observational, and thought or simulated episodes. Bandura (1986) uses the first two. *Enactive learning* results from carrying out transactional activities. This is the kind of episode used in both respondent and operant conditioning. *Observational learning* results from episodes in which people observe others performing actions. It is the same learning process; people construct cognitions of relationships among environmental and response events, but the data sources differ. Self-performance produces some self-referent feedback that observation does not, so people do not learn specific responses as implied by the concepts of imitation or reinforcement: They construct propositional models that function as rules that can be used to guide construction of useful behavior patterns in future episodes. "A generative conception serves two functions: It provides the rules for producing appropriate response patterns, and it provides the standard for improving performance on the basis of perceived discrepancies between conception and execution" (Bandura, 1986, p. 111).

The regulatory function of internal standards and self-evaluative reactions is stressed. *Perceived self-efficacy* is a pattern of evaluative thoughts about whether one can act effectively to produce desired outcomes in particular situations. Even if people have the skill, they won't try or will give up quickly if they believe they can't perform appropriately. Therefore, erroneous evaluative beliefs persist because people avoid behavior episodes that might produce disconfirming outcomes. *Outcome expectations* are predictive beliefs that the environment will yield desired consequences if one performs competently. Even if people believe they are competent, they will not try if they believe the environment will not be responsive. As an example, "They won't hire me because I'm female".

Thus, Bandura emphasizes two of the three components of the comparative framework's model of motivation: personal goals and personal agency beliefs. What about the motivational and regulatory function of *emotions?* He discusses how emotions may be activated, but he proposes no theory of how they work. And what about *skilled actions?* His observational learning involves four processes: *attention, retention, production,* and *motivation. Production processes* "govern the organization of constituent subskills into new response patterns" (Bandura, 1986, p. 51). Bandura assumes, as in the operant model, that the person is already capable of skilled action; it is only necessary to activate existing skills in the right combinations. He implies that practice plays a role in his descriptions of cybernetic-like processes: "Transforming symbols into actions involves learning how to organize action sequences, to monitor and compare enactments against a symbolic model, and to correct evident mismatches" (Bandura, 1986, p. 90). The nature of the correction process in motor skill learning remains unspecified, however.

REINTERPRETATION OF TRADITIONAL CONDITIONING MODELS IN MODERN LEARNING THEORY TERMS

The updated propositional framework appears to be as follows. Type A respondent conditioning (stimulus—stimulus relationships) appears to occur through the person's constructing a representation of a predictive contingency—a conditioned stimulus—which then serves a feedforward function to produce relevant anticipatory responses—conditioned response—in future similar situations. Type B appears to occur through the person's constructing a representation of a causal contingency—conditioned stimulus—which then functions to activate the unconditioned response to which it has become linked. Learned elicitors of fear are a prime example. Operant conditioning—stimulus-response and response-stimulus—relationships appears to occur when people construct representations of both predictive (discriminative stimuli) and causal (response-reinforcement) contingencies, and use them to guide instrumental actions. Patterns of sequential covariation that appear to be created by a person's actions are the basis for causal attributions called *generative causality*, that is, "I can cause it." Once learned, propositional models serve a feedforward function in organizing behavior in anticipation of consequences. Of course, the representations formed may not reflect real contingencies. Accidental covariation may lead a person to construct faulty anticipatory or causal attributions, and then to behave in ways dictated by those faulty beliefs.

This formulation may help explain the differential impact of schedules of reinforcement. Responses that are always reinforced are more easily learned and extinguished than periodically reinforced ones, called partial reinforcement. For 100% reinforcement, only a few nonreinforced episodes can convince a person that the contingency no longer exists. Partial reinforcement produces an expectation that the reinforcement will not always occur. Therefore, more unreinforced episodes must occur before a person recognizes that the contingency has changed. People often try to produce multiple outcomes with the same behavior. As a result, the beliefs guiding any behavior episode are likely to include multiple predictive and causal contingencies related to the multiple outcomes sought. Learned patterns persist because they produce some outcomes the person values, even though unwanted outcomes may also occur that make the behavior seem dysfunctional to others.

In instrumental conditioning, behavior is modified through successive approximation until the desired consequence or reinforcement occurs. A reinforcer, then, is any event representing a consequence a person values or is trying to produce—one that reduces the discrepancy between symbolized (desired) and actual consequences. Learning combines propositional or cognitive and procedural or behavioral components into functional units that can occur automatically without conscious cognitive guidance. Complex combinations of patterns may be learned. For example, through Pavlovian B arrangements some event, a conditioned stimulus, may become a learned elicitor of fear; through instrumental conditioning, responses may be learned that prevent or terminate the fear. Then, the entire pattern may become automatic and function as a unit, such as a phobia.

The approach is still behavioral because it stresses person-in-context patterns of action, or instrumental behavior episodes. Observational episodes may be used to facilitate construction of propositional models, but those models will not be effectively linked to patterns of action until people actually perform the actions in instrumental episodes and verify for themselves the utility of the predictive and causal contingencies they observed by watching others. Moreover, behavior therapy's emphasis on the importance of careful behavioral analysis is still important because (1) careful analysis of the conditions that selectively activate and terminate a behavior pattern provides a basis for inferring the predictive and causal beliefs guiding the person's behavior in that context, and (2) the propositional model itself can change if the predictive and causal contingencies it contains are contradicted by those that actually occur.

Conditioning and social learning theories have evolved, therefore, so that mental events are considered key components of the learning process. Those who express concern over the intrusion of mental events into the original behavioral paradigm (e.g., Eysenck, 1988; Krasner, 1988; Rachlin, 1988) apparently do not fully accept the empirically based theoretical elaborations that have been made in the very models of learning that initially spawned behavior therapy. Rampant mentalism, however, has not returned because changes in, and the influence of, mental events is linked to actions in behavior episodes.

ASSUMPTIONS ABOUT NORMAL OR FUNCTIONAL DEVELOPMENT

Behavior therapies rest on a process model stressing how behavior develops rather than what develops, so no theory of normal or functional development is proposed. Except for inborn behavior patterns (such as unconditioned stimulus–unconditioned response, and operants), all behaviors are assumed to be learned according to the same set of principles, and all learning occurs in incremental fashion. Therefore, all behavior is functional in the sense that it is learned because it has some kind of adaptive value: It is linked to some desired consequence. Why, then, would anyone need therapy?

ASSUMPTIONS ABOUT ABNORMAL OR DYSFUNCTIONAL DEVELOPMENT

A behavior pattern is considered abnormal or dysfunctional if it produces undesirable consequences, but that is an evaluative judgment requiring some criteria specifying why and by whom a pattern is judged dysfunctional. The same behavior may be evaluated as functional in one type of episode and dysfunctional in another. For example, striking a person is considered dysfunctional in a marital relationship, but functional in a boxing match; fear is dysfunctional when it occurs in benign situations, but functional if one is endangered. Behavior therapists provide no theory or criteria defining dysfunctional development. The implicit criterion seems to be that the person, or those around him or her, believe that the behavior makes the person or others miserable or interferes with effective instrumental behaviors. Consistent with their emphasis on the analysis of specific patterns, behavior therapists seek to describe specific dysfunctional patterns. Included in these are eating disorders, substance abuse, conduct disorders, depression, sexual dysfunction, or chronic pain. They do this rather than propose general models for psychopathology (e.g., Bellack, Hersen, & Kazdin, 1990; Mueser & Liberman, 1995; Turner, Calhoun, & Adams, 1992). This is their form of differential diagnosis and treatment. Theories about neurotic patterns are exceptions.

Development of Neurotic Patterns
Behavior therapies gained their initial credibility by helping people unlearn dysfunctional fear patterns (e.g., Eysenck, 1957; Wolpe, 1958). Any pattern that includes inappropriate fear or anxiety elicitors, fear itself, and behaviors learned to prevent or terminate the fear, is defined as neurotic. Biologically based disorders or psychoses are not classified as neuroses. Neurotic patterns such as phobias, panic disorders, posttraumatic stress disorders, and obsessive-compulsive disorders differ in the nature of the eliciting conditions, attributes of the fear pattern, and/or the kinds of behaviors used to prevent or terminate the fear. The following summary relies on formulations by Bandura (1986), Eysenck (1985), Levis (1985), Reiss and McNally (1985), and Wolpe (1990).

All these behaviorists propose an anxiety model of neurosis, but differ somewhat on the specifics. All start with the assumption that fear/anxiety patterns are innate, become activated under prototypic conditions, and serve an adaptive function by leading to behavior that protects or extracts the person from potentially harmful circumstances. Fear is normal and adaptive in relevant situations in everyday life. However, fear is an aversive state; people don't like it. Therefore, they try to terminate it by escape behavior, or to prevent its occurrence by avoidance behavior. Behaviors that effectively produce either of those consequences are learned and become activated when similar fear-eliciting conditions occur. A person may interpret the experience of fear so that it elicits further fear; for example, a frightened person may notice a rapid heartbeat and think, "I'm having a heart attack." This observation may prolong and intensify the fear through a positive feedback process.

The behaviorists agree that anything can become a learned elicitor of fear, a conditioned stimulus; these include both environmental events and one's own responses or anticipatory thoughts. One form of learning is through actual experience in behavior episodes in which strong fear occurs, such as an automobile accident. This is called the *trauma model*. Through a Pavlovian B process, hearing screeching brakes or getting into a car can come to elicit fear. Another form of learning is through social modeling. A child may become afraid of snakes through watching her mother react with strong fear in the presence of a snake. Through explanation or instruction, parents may teach a child to be afraid of some circumstance. An event may be interpreted as a signal—a discriminative stimulus—that some dangerous consequence may occur, thereby eliciting fear. For example, novice flyers sometimes become frightened when they interpret some noises as signs that something is wrong with the plane.

Extinction or unlearning does not occur under typical conditions because the elicitor, the conditioned stimulus, does not occur without the fear response, the unconditioned response, thus reconfirming the causal contingency each time. Such reconfirmation may increase the frequency or strength of the fear and elaborate the eliciting conditions through stimulus generalization or further conditioning. Moreover, the learned escape/avoidance behaviors prevent exposure of the pattern to new learning conditions that might alter the representations of causal contingencies. Because neurotic patterns may be learned in different ways, it seems plausible that different intervention approaches might be necessary to fit the original learning conditions and the current dynamics.

THE PROCEDURAL MODEL

A procedural model specifies the "how to" aspects of therapy: (1) how to identify the nature and dynamics of the dysfunctional behaviors, called assessment or diagnosis; (2) how to change them, called intervention strategies and methods; and (3) how to verify what changes have occurred and what caused them, called therapy evaluation strategies and methods.

ASSESSMENT OR DIAGNOSIS

Behavior therapy stresses careful, accurate behavioral assessment or functional analysis before beginning therapy because the design and evaluation of interventions depend upon clearly specifying the content and dynamics of the patterns to be changed (e.g., Mash & Hunsley, 1990; Mueser & Liberman, 1995). The objectives of a sound behavioral assessment are these:

1. To determine whether the client's problems may have an organic basis for which a medical treatment might be necessary.
2. To identify precisely (a) the specific behavior patterns, or target behaviors, to be changed, (b) the specific stimuli (the behavior episode conditions) that activate those patterns, and (c) the specific conditions or reinforcers that maintain the dysfunctional patterns and prevent their extinction.

Client and therapist collaboration is essential in selecting therapy goals so that clients understand and are fully committed to the effort.

Diagnosis in the traditional sense—identifying a phobia or depressive pattern—is considered insufficient because it only identifies similarity to a prototypic pattern of signs and symptoms. That may provide useful clues, but it cannot replace careful behavioral assessment. Designing effective behavior therapy requires specifying the stimuli, responses, and reinforcers that provide the current idiosyncratic dynamics of clients' difficulties. Identifying conditions under which a dysfunctional pattern initially developed—its etiology—is useful only if it provides clues about elicitors and reinforcers currently maintaining the pattern. When behavior therapy seems ineffective, it is said to result from inaccurate or superficial assessment, so that the methods used did not influence the associations between stimuli, responses, and reinforcers that needed to be altered (e.g., Wolpe, 1990). Therapy should begin with a careful assessment, and if the desired changes do not occur, therapists should consider the possibility that the original assessment was incomplete and may need to be revised or elaborated. Moreover, additional goals and interventions may need to be added as clients reveal important new problems during therapy (Sorenson, Gorsuch, & Mintz, 1985).

Under the surface of this seemingly simple and straightforward idea lie several problems. "Behavioral assessment means different things to different people, and although such pluralism may indicate the vitality and flexibility of the field, it makes the description of behavioral assessment a difficult task" (Mash & Hunsley, 1990, p. 89). Some problems involve behavior content and organization, and other epistemological assumptions and assessment methods.

Behavior Content and Organization
Behavior therapies rely on a process model and do not provide a conceptual model for behavioral content and organization, so they provide no conceptual tools for guiding behavioral assessment. Therefore, therapists must individually select or invent a taxonomy of behavior and stimuli to use in their assessments. This condition naturally leads to assessment disagreements. For

example, their strategy requires first identifying the behaviors to be changed, so that the eliciting and reinforcing conditions can be analyzed. However, assessors often disagree in their definition of which behaviors should be targeted (Wilson & Evans, 1983).

A related issue is the selection of the levels and units of analysis to be used in behavioral assessments to represent relevant behavioral organization. Because the theoretical model provides no guidance, behavior therapists must invent their own solutions, with disagreements likely. For example, they initially emphasized small units composed of discrete, observable responses and stimuli—movements, anxiety symptoms, verbalizations, presentation of food, or exposure to phobic stimuli. As limitations of this method appeared, assessment moved toward larger units that represented patterns of covariation among multiple stimuli and responses (e.g., Kanfer & Phillips, 1970; Lazarus, 1973), thereby creating the possibility of linkages to the tradition of syndrome analysis (e.g., Mash & Terdal, 1988). This growing emphasis on organized patterns of variables and their causal relationships has led to an emerging interest in systems models of behavioral organization as having potential utility (Mash & Hunsley, 1990).

Epistemological Assumptions and Assessment Methods

The behaviorists' assessment methods began with direct observation, unstructured and structured interviews, ratings by others, and psychophysiological methods. Later, behavioral checklists and questionnaires, self-monitoring procedures, analogue methods including role playing, and some more traditional psychometric procedures have been added (Mueser & Liberman, 1995). Epistemological biases influence the methods each therapist uses—for example, those with antimentalistic epistemologies give less attention to internal mediators of overt behaviors than others more willing to accept the potential causal role of cognitions and affects. Multidimensional or systems assessment is growing; multiple methods yield information about most of the kinds of responses in our comparative framework, including biobehavioral interactions. Computer-based assessment procedures are being used to produce more effective analyses and to create multidimensional databases for planning and evaluating therapy, as well as for training therapists in assessment skills (Mash & Hunsley, 1990).

Despite the emphasis on careful analysis as a basis for designing interventions, "there is astonishingly little information on the process, reliability, or utility of functional analysis" (Mash & Hunsley, 1990, p. 100). Without agreement on specific taxonomies for stimuli and responses, however, or on the levels and units of analysis that should be used, generating information representing more than the individualized approaches of specific therapists will be difficult.

INTERVENTION STRATEGIES AND METHODS

A *strategy* is a general plan for accomplishing specified objectives; *methods* are specific techniques for implementing a strategy. The same strategy can be implemented with different techniques. Behavior therapists have created a great many methods (see Bellack & Hersen, 1985, for descriptions of over 150 techniques), but these are actually varied ways of implementing a limited number of strategies that reflect behavior therapy's learning theory base. Many, but not all, of their strategies and methods are examined next.

A STRATEGY OF DESIGNING SPECIFIC LEARNING EPISODES

The assumption that maladaptive behaviors are learned requires the creation of relevant learning experiences to change them. Regardless of the problem content, all behavior therapy uses a model similar to behavior episodes in our comparative framework, both as a means of activating dysfunctional patterns and of facilitating learned changes. A sequence of therapy sessions is a series of such episodes, carefully designed and sequenced to produce learning outcomes that incrementally change the targeted behavior patterns in desired ways and/or that result in learning more adaptive patterns. Two kinds of behavior episodes are involved, with the second embedded in the first, like a plot within a plot. The first kind seeks to create a therapeutic relationship and alliance that facilitates client participation in the learning episodes. Within that context, the second kind creates learning conditions tailored to produce specific changes in the troublesome behavior.

A STRATEGY OF SOCIAL INFLUENCE: THE RELATIONSHIP AND THERAPEUTIC ALLIANCE

Behavior therapists cultivate all three components of the model of motivation in our comparative framework: positive emotions, clear goals, and positive personal agency beliefs.

The Relationship
Behavior therapists' emphasis on the intentional design of learning episodes and their mechanistic model led others to conclude that they ignored the in-

fluence of the therapy relationship. That impression is incorrect. From the beginning Wolpe (1958) argued that all therapies, including his, must create a special type of human relationship in which positive and potentially therapeutic emotions and attitudes toward the therapist are evoked in clients to provide a context favorable for learning. He stated that this relationship, by itself, may produce some changes, so evaluation of the effectiveness of different approaches must demonstrate that their methods yield changes beyond those resulting from such nonspecific factors. Frank, in *Persuasion and Healing* (1961), argued that psychotherapy is a context within which social influence facilitates change. Goldstein, Heller, and Sechrest (1966) abstracted from social psychology's scientific literature empirically supported principles that could guide the use of social influence in therapy. Krasner's (1971) review of behavior therapies asserted that its specific techniques became effective "only within a context of maximum social influence," and described therapists as "a compound social reinforcing and discriminative stimulus" (p. 486).

Schaap, Bennun, Schindler, and Hoogduin (1993) link principles of social influence to the nature and influence of the therapy relationship in behavior therapies and describe empirical evidence that behavior therapists are rated higher on relationship variables than are psychodynamic and Gestalt therapists. By listening attentively; taking client concerns seriously; treating clients with respect; accepting them unconditionally with warmth, concern and empathy; and encouraging and enabling them, behavior therapists activate in clients positive emotions, trust that the therapist won't hurt them, and hope that their distress may be alleviated. Positive emotions facilitate a willingness in clients to try new experiences.

The Therapeutic Alliance

The two other essential motivational components—clear goals and positive personal agency beliefs about the learning tasks and their role in them—are facilitated through a therapeutic alliance. The initial phase of behavior therapies, organized around the functional analysis of clients' dysfunctional patterns, is designed to produce these motivational conditions and a shared action plan. Therapists' reputation, skill, and competence, revealed when the therapists function as expert guides and teachers, elicit in clients the respect, confidence, and trust essential to facilitate their influence with clients.

Client and therapist should agree on the goals of therapy toward which their joint efforts will be directed. Clear goals enable people to effectively organize relevant behavior patterns and provide criteria against which to evaluate their progress. Wolpe's (1990) description is illustrative.

The patient is given a general outline of what behavior therapy attempts to do. He or she is told that since neuroses are a matter of emotional learning, it makes the best sense to treat them by using scientific knowledge of how habits are made and broken. The procedures that come from this knowledge are called behavior therapy. But to be as effective as possible, the therapist must know exactly what things, or thoughts, or feelings are the triggers to the neurotic fear responses. The triggers differ from person to person, and the therapist applies his or her expertise to determine their make-up (p. 90)

Through collaboration in the functional analysis of the client's problems, therapist and client construct a shared view of the content and dynamics of the problem behaviors and of the goals of therapy.

Clients must also understand and agree to a plan of action that specifies the means to be used—the relearning episodes necessary to reach their shared therapy goals. Even though a client has clear goals, and likes and trusts the therapist, effective participation in therapy will not follow unless supportive personal agency beliefs also exist; clients must believe they can do it (Bandura's self-efficacy beliefs) and that therapy will be effective (positive context beliefs). This view is cultivated by the therapist in several ways:

1. Clearly explaining what clients will have to do.
2. Expressing confidence in clients' capabilities.
3. Promising to be by clients' side throughout the process.
4. Using their status as an expert to convince clients that the approach works.
5. Training clients in the skills required, if necessary.

The therapy relationship and alliance is a dynamic and potentially changeable state, so therapists must continually cultivate and maintain it.

A good relationship/alliance is not sufficient for effective therapy. Specific relearning experiences must also be created. Several strategies for creating this second type of behavior episode are used.

CONTROLLED EXPOSURE: A STRATEGY FOR ALTERING NEUROTIC FEAR PATTERNS

Fear/anxiety is a noxious experience, one that people dislike and want to terminate or avoid. Fear elicitors may be learned by (1) direct experience, (2) social modeling, or (3) direct teaching. Once an elicitor-fear pattern has been learned, additional elicitors for it may be learned, technically called second-order conditioning. Sometimes an aspect of the fear response itself is interpreted as dangerous; as an example, a client may interpret dizziness as going crazy. Such a response can become an additional elicitor that increases fear through a positive feedback loop, which can escalate fear into a panic attack.

Fear is aroused by a predictive contingency, a signal that some harmful consequence may occur. Normally fear is adaptive because it enables people to withdraw from, or avoid, circumstances that might hurt them. Once a person acquires an elicitor-fear pattern, they learn behaviors that will terminate it or prevent its future occurrence, a causal contingency called an avoidance pattern. Notice that it is fear reduction that is the immediate reinforcer, not escape from some actual event. Thus, the fear-avoidance pattern may actually become stronger each time the eliciting conditions activate fear, which is then reduced by the escape/avoidance behaviors, even though nothing bad actually happens. Avoidance patterns prevent people from acting to discover the inaccuracy of their fear-eliciting, anticipatory or predictive propositions.

To unlearn a neurotic pattern, clients must have experiences that extinguish their faulty predictive and causal beliefs; they must break the links between the learned elicitor (the conditioned stimulus), the fear response (the unconditioned response), and the behaviors used to prevent or reduce the fear (the conditioned response). To accomplish this, people must expose themselves to the fear-eliciting situation and inhibit their avoidance pattern long enough to recognize that their predictive and causal beliefs about that situation are unsound. The generic label for this basic strategy is *exposure therapy*. It involves creating specific behavior episodes that (1) contain the fear-eliciting stimuli, (2) control the occurrence/intensity of the fear so that the escape/avoidance parts of the pattern do not occur, and (3) enable clients to stay in the episode long enough to learn that they can control their fear and that nothing bad happens, thereby weakening the influence of their faulty beliefs.

Several methods have been created to implement this strategy. Some rely on real-life behavior episodes called in vivo exposure; others create imagined, simulated, or observational episodes. Contact desensitization, systematic desensitization, flooding, paradoxical intention, and abreaction are labels for different methods (Bellack & Hersen, 1985; Wolpe, 1990, 1995). They differ in the design of the episode used to elicit the fear-avoidance pattern, in the ways they try to control the anxiety that occurs so that the client can endure the episode, and in the duration of each episode.

Contact desensitization and *flooding* typically involve instrumental episodes in which the real, fear-eliciting conditions actually occur. Through client report and sometimes direct observation and exploratory trials, situations that elicit the fear pattern are identified and usually ranked in terms of the intensity of fear elicited. For example, going out on their porch, standing on the sidewalk in front of their house, walking a block away, or taking a bus downtown will each elicit fear, but of different intensities, for agoraphobic people afraid to leave their homes. Clients are first asked to participate in the episode that elicits the lowest intensity of fear: going out on the porch. One method of controlling the fear is to use the positive impact of the therapist's presence to inhibit fear intensity and to enable clients to endure the experience. The exposure in an episode must be maintained until the client reports that the fear has significantly diminished or disappeared, often requiring 30 to 60 minutes. It is this lengthy, continuous exposure to relatively high levels of anxiety that resulted in the label *flooding*. The total sequence of behavior episodes is experienced over a period of days or weeks until clients' fear responses are eliminated or significantly reduced, even in the most severe episode. In effect, clients learn that nothing bad happens and that they can deal with the previously distressing situations; their propositions of predictive and causal contingencies in that kind of episode have been extinguished.

Several variations are used. Clients may be taught behavioral methods to use as ways to help control their anxiety while enduring the fear episode. An example is breathing retraining to promote relaxation and to prevent hyperventilation. In *participant modeling*, the episode is first modeled by someone else; clients watch the model, observe that nothing bad happens and that the person is unafraid. They then perform the same behavior. Participant modeling may be carried out in real-life or simulated episodes, such as role playing in the therapist's office. Another variation is to have clients practice facing fear-inducing episodes without the therapist—with a friend or by themselves, often called homework. This may be counterproductive unless the therapist can be sure that the client's fear will be successfully controlled in the episode.

Clients are sometimes also trained to practice a form of *reciprocal inhibition*, wherein they are taught to think about things that activate positive feelings while enduring a fearful episode; they might concentrate on how much fun they can have once they are no longer afraid to leave their homes. This behavior both inhibits the occurrence of fear and encourages learning of new, positive responses to the old fear-eliciting circumstances. Of course, clients are also given explanations about what to expect and why the treatment works. They can rehearse these to themselves as another way of controlling their anxiety. Another variation, often used to deal with ritualistic behavior that is part of obsessive-compulsive patterns, is to combine exposure with *response prevention* by prohibiting the client from performing the rituals while enduring the fear-eliciting episode.

The client's situation may be more complicated. As Wolpe (1990) points out, neurotic fears may have a combination of elicitors, some of which may be erroneous beliefs that resulted from misleading teachings, misinterpretations, or observational learning. For such cases, the therapist will need to supplement the exposure treatment with cognitively focused methods designed to help clients alter their faulty thinking and interpretations. For example, their interpretation of their racing heart as signaling a potential heart attack can be changed by helping them to understand the physiological changes that accompany a fear pattern.

Wolpe's (1958, 1990, 1995) *systematic desensitization* was probably the first behavioral version of exposure therapy. It differs from exposure therapy in three ways. First, Wolpe found in vivo exposure was often difficult if not impossible to arrange, so he substituted *imaginary exposure*. He asked clients to describe a set of episodes that differ in the degree of fear activated, called an *anxiety hierarchy*. These do not have to be episodes clients have actually experienced; they only need to contain the fear-inducing stimuli. Clients then expose themselves by imagining a behavior episode, beginning with the least intense fear-inducing episode, extinguishing its fear response, and then proceeding to the next one, until they can imagine the most intense episode without significant fear.

Second, to try prevent or limit the fear that occurs, Wolpe applied the learning principle of *reciprocal inhibition* or *counterconditioning*. Certain kinds of responses cannot occur at the same time. So, he reasoned, if clients were in a state that involved a response incompatible with fear when they began to imagine an episode, fear could not occur. He chose deep muscle relaxation as the competing response, and trained clients in relaxation procedures. Then, before beginning an imagined episode he asked clients to create a relaxed state in themselves on the assumption that this would inhibit fear when they imagined a frightening episode. He states that other competing responses can be used: positive emotions activated by the therapist's presence, autogenic training, transcendental meditation, yoga, or electromyographic biofeedback. If clients already have a well-practiced competing response they can activate, then using that is efficient.

Third, systematic desensitization differs from flooding in that the duration of each exposure is very brief. When imagining a scene, clients are asked to raise their finger when the scene is clear. After 5 to 7 seconds, they are told to stop the scene. They are then asked to report the amount of fear they experienced, using a subjective scale Wolpe created. If they experience any fear, that imagined episode is repeated until no fear is experienced; then they imagine the next episode in the hierarchy.

Note that the contingencies in imagined episodes are between cognitive representations of events, rather than real events, and the fear response itself;

they are imagistically coded rather than abstractly coded thoughts, as defined in our comparative framework. Therefore, they are more like actual perceptions of real events. This could be considered a limited form of cognitive-
behavior therapy, where the cognitive representations are analogous to
imagistically coded episodic memories. Does the extinction of associations between thoughts and the fear response generalize to real events? Wolpe says
that it does, but "real life exposure is routinely encouraged in coordination
with standard desensitization" (1990, p. 210) using homework assignments.
In the assignments, the client practices in real life the imagined episodes for
which fear has been extinguished. Thus, Wolpe explicitly trains for generalization to real-life episodes. Systematic desensitization may not succeed if
(1) the client is unable to activate deep muscle relaxation or some other effective competing response, (2) the anxiety hierarchy being used is not accurate,
or (3) the client is unsuccessful in using imagery to activate the fear pattern.

POSITIVE AND NEGATIVE REINFORCEMENT: A STRATEGY FOR
CULTIVATING DESIRED ACTIONS

The exposure strategy helps extinguish faulty fear-based habits, but many
problems of living result from deficiencies or inadequacies in people's habitual actions. Therefore, strategies and methods are necessary for helping people to learn adaptive instrumental habits. People learn new habits if the habits
produce outcomes that they like and want (positive reinforcement), or if they
terminate or prevent outcomes that they dislike and do not want (negative reinforcement). This strategy, often called *contingency management,* involves
(1) clear specification of the desired actions, (2) selection of consequences considered desirable or undesirable by the client that can be made contingent on
the desired actions, and (3) creation of behavior episodes with appropriate
discriminative stimuli; these enable the client to behave so as to experience the
episode's causal contingency with the positive or negative consequence. It is
most efficient for clients to be aware of the response-consequence contingency
so they know what they need to produce that consequence.

Several methods for implementing this strategy have been created. They
differ in terms of the kinds of instrumental actions they are designed to cultivate, the nature of the reinforcing events, who is in control of the reinforcers
—the client, therapist, or others—and the kinds of episodes used to activate
the behavior to be learned. *Contingency contracting* involves developing a written statement, collaboratively produced by the parties involved, defining the
responses to be performed and the consequences or reinforcers that will follow, contingent on those actions. The contract is signed by the person who is

supposed to perform the actions—such as the client or a child—and by those who control the consequences—therapists, parents, a spouse, teachers, hospital staff. The contract is then a public commitment and makes possible a public record of success. Putting clients or children in control of their own reinforcers, which requires their commitment to play by the rules, has the desirable feature of cultivating self-control.

A token economy differs in the design of reinforcing contingencies. Clients do not receive the desired consequence after each successful performance; they receive a substitute—a token or secondary reinforcer. After receiving a certain number of tokens, they can trade them in for an instance of the desired consequence, such as watching their favorite TV show. *Skill training*, such as assertiveness training, is a method, described in Chapter 9, used when clients do not have the desired responses in their behavioral repertoire. *Covert conditioning* (Cautela, 1967; Cautela & Kearney, 1990) uses imagined rather than real episodes as the learning context, similar to Wolpe's use of them. Clients are asked to imagine a particular situation, acting in a particular way in that situation and experiencing certain consequences contingent on their actions. Any learning arrangements possible with overt behaviors can be simulated in this covert version. The approach assumes continuity between covert and overt behaviors such that what is learned through this imagined practice will be used in real, appropriate situations. This strategy is popular in sports psychology now, in a form called mental imagery or rehearsal. Because of their antimentalist assumptions, behaviorists prefer the term *covert* to *mental*, but the method clearly assumes that thoughts can exert a causal influence on actions.

AVERSIVE CONDITIONING: A STRATEGY FOR INHIBITING UNDESIRED BEHAVIORS

People develop many habits that they wish to get rid of; substance abuse, eating disorders, and self-injurious behaviors, and others. Aversive conditioning is a strategy designed to help people learn to inhibit unwanted behaviors. It is called *aversive conditioning* rather than punishment, because the latter term carries controversial or undesirable social meanings, including child abuse and the death penalty. There are ethical concerns linked to the use of this strategy, yet avoidance of aversive conditions has great adaptive value as a part of our evolutionary heritage. We need to avoid eating food that smells or tastes bad because it may make us sick or kill us. Moreover, aversive conditions are a basic tool of our culture: If you perform poorly you may lose your job or fail in school. Some argue that it is an appropriate treatment strategy as long as it is used humanely and with clients' informed consent. Aversive conditioning seems to train a person in what not to do but provides no facilitation of alternate preferred behavior. Therefore, it is considered less useful when used by itself than when combined with methods for cultivating desired alternate behavior patterns.

This strategy requires collaborating with clients to specify the behavior to be inhibited, the conditions that activate it, and events that they consider aversive or undesirable. This information is used to design behavior episodes so that an aversive event occurs when the unwanted behavior is performed. In this way, a causal contingency is created between the undesired behavior and the aversive experience. To avoid the latter, the person must learn to inhibit the former. What is aversive for one person may not be so for another, so selection of aversive events must be individualized. There are two broad types, however: (1) Presentation of an event the person doesn't like—such as a putrid taste or odor; and (2) removal of an event a person does like, called response cost—such as taking away his or her driver's license (Kazdin, 1989). Humans' evolutionary history may make it easier for some kinds of associations to occur, called preparedness (Marshall, 1985). For example, events that occur within functionally related body systems appear to be more readily associated, such as linking aversive odors, tastes, or nausea-producing substances to eating or drinking. It is important to avoid using as an aversive consequence an event linked to other desirable behaviors; giving a child extra homework as an aversive consequence may make all homework an aversive task.

Making the aversive event more intense does not seem to improve learning; the event is sufficiently aversive if it is intense enough for the person to recognize an unwanted causal contingency. Varying the kind of aversive event—using reprimands for one episode, removing a privilege for another—seems to facilitate learning the causal contingency. A method called *time out* involves removing the person, often a child, from all sources of positive reinforcement for a brief period whenever the unwanted behavior is performed. The causal contingency seems to be learned more quickly if the child is kept in the situation where the desired consequences can be obtained while prohibiting actions through which they could be obtained. Aversive conditioning can also use imagined episodes rather than real ones; this is called *covert aversive conditioning*.

STRATEGIES FOR MODIFYING COMPLEX PATTERNS AND
FACILITATING TRANSFER TO REAL-LIFE CONTEXTS

Clients often bring multiple problems to therapy. That is probably the rule rather than the exception, because they usually do not seek therapy until their problems have become relatively severe and have persisted over an extended period of time. Through careful functional analysis, behavior therapists specify the group of faulty habits for which change is desired, the conditions under which each change may be produced, and the strategies and methods likely to be most successful for each type of change. With any client, a behavior therapist is likely to use multiple strategies and methods (e.g., Hersen & Last, 1985; Turner, Calhoun, & Adams, 1992). This raises another question: In what sequence should the various changes be attempted?

The key strategy for facilitating transfer to real-life contexts is to use training episodes as nearly like clients' real-life behavior episodes as possible. In vivo training episodes—that is, homework—are likely to be most effective in this regard. In addition, behavior therapists argue that their type of therapeutic alliance represents a model clients can use to deal with future problems without a therapist; this gives them control of their future behavior by cultivating self-direction and self-regulation.

STRATEGIES FOR EVALUATING CLIENT PROGRESS AND THERAPY OUTCOMES

A fundamental feature of the procedural model in behavior therapy is a clear and explicit specification of the behavior changes client and therapist agree are to be sought. This specification provides concrete criteria for monitoring client progress. Behavior therapists evaluate client progress by collecting information about declines in frequency of the unwanted behavior and increases in frequency of the desired behaviors both in the therapy episodes and in relevant real-life episodes, during the course of therapy, and at several junctures—such as at the termination of therapy and on follow-up over various periods of time. Formal assessments are sometime used, but client and therapist observations appear to be the most frequent source of evaluative evidence.

STRATEGIES FOR EVALUATING THE BEHAVIOR THERAPY MODEL

Behavior therapists have, from the beginning, been committed to two basic ideas: application of known psychological principles to intervention development and experimental evaluation of the effectiveness of those applications. Basing the development of therapy approaches squarely on psychological science has had a profound impact on clinical psychology. Behavior therapists propose a multistage evaluation strategy. First, they suggest that propositions should be tested and verified by basic, experimental research, with both animal and human subjects, before being applied to therapy clients. Second, they advocate careful assessments of, and comparisons between, both process and outcome measures of different strategies and methods used with clients, similar to medicine's method of field trials. Third, they believe that each therapist should collect evidence about outcomes with each client to verify the effectiveness or ineffectiveness of the strategies and methods used, to identify needs for alternate methods, and to show where further research would be helpful.

Although these empirically based strategies are stressed, leaders of this approach express concern that too many practitioners do not practice what they preach. Too few are sufficiently conscientious in collecting relevant evidence concerning their own practice and in keeping up with the empirical literature that may be relevant to their work.

CHAPTER 10

Cognitive Therapies

HISTORICAL PERSPECTIVE

Cognitive processes have been a focus of psychotherapy theory and practice since Freud created psychoanalysis. Behavior therapies deemphasized cognition, but within the last 25 years the causal influence of cognitive processes has been reemphasized. For example, in a survey of 800 clinical and counseling psychologists, "cognitive-behavioral" was ranked second behind "eclecticism" as the preferred approach (Smith, 1982). Cognitive approaches assume that (1) cognitive processes play a mediational role; (2) cognitive appraisals of events can affect people's responses to those events; (3) cognitive activity can be monitored and changed; and (4) changes in people's assumptions, interpretations, and thoughts can lead to changes in their actions (Dobson & Block, 1988; Kazdin, 1978). Theorists differ, however, as to the kinds of cognition they emphasize.

The diversity of concepts is truly overwhelming; these include thoughts, ideas, prototypes, meanings, beliefs, schemas, mental models, assumptions, expectancies, rules for living, attitudes, self-statements, self-efficacy beliefs, cognitive distortions, and illusions (Dobson & Block, 1988). Moreover, the concept of cognition is often used "in different ways to refer to different phenomena" (McFall, Treat & Viken, 1997, p. 176), such as a "thing"—for example, a belief or schema; an "event" or "experience"—for example, to expect or perceive; or a "process" in the dynamic operation of a complex system—remembering, or automatic versus controlled processing. The similarity among cognitive approaches is evidently unclear (Kendall, Vitousek, & Kane, 1991).

TYPES OF APPROACHES EMPHASIZING COGNITION

The label *cognitive-behavioral* has been proposed for all approaches that reject the idea that behavior is determined primarily internally, as with Freud, or primarily externally, as with Skinner, and that seek to integrate both views (Meichenbaum, 1977), making it desirable to combine cognitive and enactive methods (Kendall & Hollon, 1979; Kendall, Vitousek, & Kane, 1991; Mahoney, 1977a; Mahoney & Arnkoff, 1978). The relative emphasis on cognition and behavior varies greatly among these approaches, however. Others—for example, Kazdin (1978a)—distinguish between therapies that primarily stress modifying cognitions with the expectation that overt behavioral changes will readily follow, called *cognitive* or *cognitive-semantic therapies,* versus those therapies that emphasize both cognitive and behavioral methods, seeking overt behavioral change as the primary result, called *cognitive-behavioral therapies* (Lehman & Salovey, 1990).

Mahoney (1988) listed 17 subtypes, including earlier approaches, such as Kelly's personal construct therapy and Frankl's logotherapy, and more recent ones, such as Lazarus's multimodal therapy, problem-solving therapies, Guidano's constructivist cognitive therapy, and Mahoney's own cognitive development therapy. Dobson (1988b) added others, such as, cognitive-interpersonal therapy (Safran & Segal, 1990) to his list of 22. They agreed that most of these therapies could be viewed as one of three major variants: covert conditioning, information-processing, and cognitive-learning approaches. A fourth, cognitive-structural approaches, was added by Dobson.

Covert Conditioning Approaches
The covert conditioning approaches are conditioning models applied to problems such as unwanted ruminations, smoking, overeating and obesity, alcohol abuse or phobias. They are called *covert counterconditioning, covert modeling, covert sensitization,* and *covert reinforcement.* They approach covert behavior within a traditional behaviorist perspective but move beyond metaphysical behaviorism to address mediational processes. We examined these approaches in the analysis of behavior therapies in Chapter 9.

Information Processing Approaches.
Some approaches view people as information processing systems, actively collecting, interpreting, and appraising information about themselves and their environments, and making decisions and initiating actions based on their estimate of the best way of dealing with each life episode. These theorists assume that cognitive processes can be disaggregated and subjected to self-monitoring, self-correction, and improvement by supervised training and practice. Examples are the stress appraisal model (Lazarus, 1966; Lazarus & Launier, 1978; Lazarus & Folkman, 1984), anxiety-management training (Suinn & Richardson, 1971), Meichenbaum's self-instruction training (1973)

and stress inoculation training (1977, 1985), and the problem-solving therapies of DiZurilla and Goldfried (1971) and Spivack and Shure (1974). Dobson (1988b) and Mahoney and Arnkoff (1978) group these into two types: *Problem-solving* therapies focus on the reasoning aspects of cognition, such as problem analysis and evaluation. *Coping skills* approaches emphasize the learning of new and more adaptive ways of dealing with specific types of problems. The latter are examined in Chapter 11.

Cognitive-Structural Approaches

Key exemplars of the relatively recent cognitive-structural theories are constructivist cognitive therapy (Guidano, 1984, 1987; Guidano & Liotti, 1983, 1985) and cognitive developmental therapy (Mahoney, 1980, 1985, 1991). Proponents of these approaches assume that people develop underlying cognitive structures that, although tacit and unverbalized, serve as models that guide both the content and process of their thinking; they provide coherence and stability to people's personal knowledge, emotional experience, and behavior. However, the metaphysical and epistemological assumptions of the cognitive-structuralists differ significantly from the other three subtypes (Dobson & Shaw, 1995) as they adopt post-rational or post-modern assumptions (Neimeyer, 1993a, 1993b). They are examined as exemplars of integrative approaches in Chapter 13.

Cognitive Approaches

The cognitive approaches are called *cognitive semantic therapies* (Kazdin, 1978; Lehman & Salovey, 1990), *cognitive learning or restructuring therapies* (Mahoney, 1974; Mahoney & Arnkoff, 1978), or simply *cognitive therapies*. Aaron Beck's cognitive therapy (CT) and Albert Ellis's rational-emotive therapy (RET) are exemplars that are examined in this chapter. Their developmental pathways were more distant from the behavior therapy movement than most of the others. Their proponents assume that people's behavior is governed primarily by internal cognitive processes rather than environmental contingencies and they subscribe to the following:

1. Each person acquires a variety of cognitive components—such as assumptions, beliefs, schemas, rules for living.
2. These components are influential cross-situational reaction tendencies.
3. They can be inappropriately or poorly formed, producing cognitive errors and distortions within the person.
4. Such faulty processes lead to cognitive conflict, emotional distress, and/or distorted or otherwise ineffective behavior.

The proponents assert that they are also behavioral—note that Ellis renamed his approach rational-emotive *behavior* therapy—but their theoretical models remain primarily cognitive.

GUIDING ASSUMPTIONS

Rational-emotive therapy and cognitive therapy start with similar metaphysical and epistemological assumptions. Both proceed from a dualist ontology—both body and mind exist; from a realist epistemology, in which the environment is viewed as reliably given to the senses, thereby producing valid mental representations; and from a rationalist view of knowledge, in which knowledge is authorized to be valid by means of reason and where the higher cognitive or rational processes can and should exercise supremacy over other events, such as feelings or actions.

We have inferred Ellis's metamodel assumptions as he has not made them explicit (Mahoney, 1988; Neimeyer, 1995b). However, Beck (1976) explicitly describes his metaphysical and epistemological position. He has no quarrel with commonsense assumptions concerning the nature of reality, and expresses impatience with psychoanalytic and behaviorist skepticisms concerning the validity of conscious ideation and subjective report. Acknowledging that his view is mentalistic and materialistic, Beck argues for the validity of accepting clients' reports of their ideas, feelings, wishes, and other psychological events at face value, and their interpretations of events as basic, rock-bottom data. He argues for a representationist epistemology, somewhat different from Ellis's presentationist stance. He asserts that perceptions can serve only as rough approximations of reality because inherent limitations of people's sensory apparatus permit only a small sampling of events. Also, events are interpreted with the inherently fallible modes of cognitive processing that are influenced by physiological and psychological processes. These can include drugs, fatigue, diminished consciousness, or states of high arousal and can significantly alter people's perceptions and interpretations. Thus, conceptions of self and contexts are constructions, so they will correspond in varying degrees with conceptions created by others. They can be usefully tested against alternative hypotheses about reality before they are accepted as reliable knowledge. Assuming that one's ideas are identical to the events they purport to represent can lead to errors of interpretation and action by both clients and therapists.

The similar approaches of Ellis and Beck emerged from their similar backgrounds. Both had extensive training and experience in psychoanalysis but later became spokesmen for practitioners who had become impatient with traditional psychoanalysis, particularly its procedural model. Ellis joined others (e.g., Eysenck, 1969; Luborsky, Singer, & Luborsky, 1975; Rachman & Wilson, 1971) in questioning whether psychoanalytic procedures resulted in durable changes in client behavior. Gradually Ellis (1957, 1962) formulated a theory of emotional disturbance in which he proposed that people habitually filter their perceptions through the distorted ideas or beliefs they hold about themselves and the world, rather than reacting in an objective manner to external events. When these beliefs become cast in absolute or imperative terms, dysfunctional behavior results. He created techniques intended to attack and alter such beliefs actively and directly.

Beck's early work with depressed clients (Beck, 1961, 1963; Beck & Hurvich, 1959; Beck & Ward, 1961) led him to conclude that the data did not correspond with the traditional Freudian model of "anger-turned-inward," and that an adequate model must provide for the *contents* of the depressed person's negative thinking. He created a cognitive model (Beck, 1967) that assumes distinctive, distorted forms of thought characterize depressed people; they have consistently negative views of themselves, their worlds, and their future. These negative thoughts produce the affective, motivational, and behavioral deficits of the depressive syndrome. Beck created methods to alter the kinds of cognitive distortions that such clients had constructed.

Over the past thirty years, cognitive therapy and rational-emotive therapy have been applied to diverse problems, have generated many publications for both professional and lay audiences, and have become the major treatment in centers for research and practice through which many practitioners have been trained. Each has attracted a large following of practitioners. Some surveys rank them among the 10 most influential psychotherapists of the century (Smith, 1982).

THE CONCEPTUAL MODEL

Levels and Units of Analysis

In the approaches of Beck and Ellis, two levels and units of analysis are emphasized: the person and component functions.

The Person as the Primary Level and Unit of Concern
Consistent with trait models of personality, the theories of both Beck and Ellis identify the person as the primary focus, without specific linkage to people's contexts. Ellis describes people as a "complex, bio-social organism [sic] with a strong tendency to establish and pursue a wide variety of goals and purposes," who construct and seek to attain goals they value in order to bring a

sense of meaning or significance to their lives (Dryden & Ellis, 1988, p. 217). Beck emphasizes *personality*, which he defines as a "relatively stable organization composed of systems and modes" where systems are considered "interlocking structures (cognitive schemas) organized according to the functions they perform (e.g. affective schemas; action schemas) and according to their content (mode)" (Beck, Freeman, & associates, 1990, p. 32). Both models recognize that adaptive behavior, successful pursuit of personal goals, and the construction of guiding beliefs and schemas require a variety of exchanges with the material and social environments, so the person and the context must interact.

The principle of *unitary functioning* in this book's comparative framework is explicit in some—and implicit in many—discussions of the models. For example, Ellis and Dryden (1987) state that for convenience of analysis, one may refer to separate categories of events, such as emotion, thought or behavior; however, these are rarely experienced in isolation, and they often overlap to a significant degree. They are more properly understood to be interwoven patterns, each including important elements of the others, continually interacting with and affecting one another.

Component Functions

Despite the theorists' emphasis on the person, it is units of analysis below that level on which their interventions are primarily focused. The person is conceived of as a complex organization of biological, psychological, and behavioral components, but habitual patterns of cognitive-affective functioning play the key role in creating person-level patterns. Therefore, their conceptual models explicitly emphasize some components in our comparative framework, whereas the role of others is more implied than made explicit.

BIOLOGICAL CHARACTERISTICS: THE BIOLOGICAL PERSON

Biological processes are considered important and influence psychological functioning; the models assume an interactive dualism. However, proposals are vague about the nature of such influences.

Rational-Emotive Therapy Assumptions

Ellis (1970) "believes in the biological underpinnings of behavior," (p. 52), and assumes there are inborn functional tendencies. Humans are innately purposive, "equipped with goals, purposes, and desires," particularly personal survival goals and "living in a happy and unfrustrated manner" (Ellis, 1986, p. 278). People are innately hedonistic, governed by two basic goals, "to stay alive and be happy" (Dryden, 1987, p. 7). Ellis posits inborn "biological tendencies" for cognition that enable people to formulate rational and irrational ideas, cognitions, and beliefs. He stresses that people can think and be-have effectively, but also that humans "are born to think crookedly," or "with a tendency to be disturbed," influenced by the tendency toward "short-range hedonism"; "unless we fight our biology, this short-range hedonism, and our tendency to go to extremes and to think crookedly . . . we don't get very far" (Ellis, 1970, p. 59). Note the similarity to Freud's assumption that people's neuroses result from phylogenetically based instincts and drives that will produce dysfunctional behaviors unless properly channeled by the ego and superego. The form is similar; Ellis assumes different content for the inborn influences.

Ellis assumes that significant individual differences in biological functioning exist, and that many people malfunction because of strong innate vulnerabilities or biological tendencies to over- or underreact to environmental influences, thereby exaggerating or minimizing the importance of events, especially traumatic ones (Ellis, 1986). Biological factors can thus limit psychological and behavioral functioning, as in rational-emotive therapy clients "compromised by organic brain pathology." He considers it possible to assist a person with schizophrenia, for example, but not be able to correct the "underlying biological thinking disorder" (Ellis, 1970, p. 63).

Cognitive Therapy Assumptions

Beck views human functioning similarly. He refers to "hallowed notions of human nature and biology," positing both instincts and basic biological drives (1986, p. 14). Among the former, he cites an instinct for self-preservation, a maternal instinct, and the social instincts, such as "attraction to other people, love, and affection." Basic drives are illustrated by hunger, sleep, and sexual urges. He also suggests that human biological functions are inherently directed toward attaining goals, which include maximizing pleasure and minimizing pain. He summarizes this in terms of a *pleasure principle* and a *reality principle*, and the avoidance of danger—defined to include both physical and psychosocial harm—or the attainment of safety.

Beck et al. (1990) assume that complex functional patterns result from differentiation and elaboration of humans' genetically determined inborn strategies resulting from their phylogenetic heritage. Using the language of ethology, Beck defines strategies to be highly patterned, stereotyped forms of programmed behavior, involving both underlying processes and overt actions, designed to promote the biological goals of survival and reproduction, such as the perception of danger, the arousal of the autonomic nervous system, the fight/flight pattern. Like the idea of unconditioned responses in conditioning models, inborn patterns provide the base upon which more varied and complex patterns are constructed.

Beck (following Scarr, 1987) assumes that individual differences exist in inborn patterns, that maturational development evolves from them as genes are selectively turned on and off, and that these in turn influence the nature of people's experiences in relation to their contexts. For example, research reveals that relatively stable patterns of temperament and behavior such as shyness or rebelliousness are identifiable at birth and persist through developmental periods (Kagan, 1989). Beck does not specify what is genetically programmed and what is learned. Knowing which is which might be of practical importance in conducting psychotherapy. Interacting factors produce a person's psychological state, "including innate, biological, developmental and environmental factors" (Beck & Weishaar, 1989, p. 23). In depression, for example, there may be both predisposing factors—such as hereditary susceptibility, or physical disease leading to neurochemical abnormalities—and precipitating factors—such as physical disease, and chronic or acute stress.

Use in Therapy

Case examples of rational-emotive therapy and cognitive therapy reveal that biological aspects of client functioning are both recognized and addressed in the conduct of psychotherapy. For example, Ellis, McInerney, DiGiuseppe, and Yeager (1988) describe the use of intoxication by abusers of alcohol and other substances to alleviate a range of discomforts (such as fatigue, pain, depression, and anxiety), they also cite physiological effects induced by persistent intoxication, such as high blood pressure. Physiological components are included in the diagnosis, assessment, and treatment processes of cognitive therapy. For example, descriptions of depressive states include inappetence, insomnia, or anergia; panic states include palpitations, dyspnea, vertigo, or hot/cold flashes. Treatments for anorexia and obesity entail a concern with the client's physiological status. In practice, though, biological components appear to be considered on an ad hoc, as-needed basis rather than constituting a systematic component of the more general models guiding practice. This neglect may stem from a presumption that biological symptoms manifest effects rather than causes. For example, Beck (1976) describes vegetative signs of depression, such as inappetence, anaphrodisia, and insomnia, as physiological concomitants of an essentially psychological disturbance, analogous to the autonomic nervous system manifestations that accompany anxiety.

PSYCHOLOGICAL CHARACTERISTICS: THE PSYCHOLOGICAL PERSON

Cognitive therapists emphasize psychological functioning. The extent to which they consider the kinds of psychological phenomena in our comparative framework is examined next.

Consciousness and Attention

Neither consciousness nor attention is explicitly used in the rational-emotive therapy or cognitive therapy conceptual models, but they are mentioned occasionally by Ellis and Beck as awareness or attentional selectivity. Consciousness seems to be a given. The contents of consciousness—beliefs, or thoughts—are the focus of interest. Ellis and Beck were trained in psychoanalysis, but neither uses the concept of unconscious processes. Ellis does not refer to it. Beck is explicitly critical of Freud's view and uses the term (as did Adler) to refer to content that is implicit, tacit, and unverbalized but potentially accessible to the person's awareness. The processes that direct and regulate attention are not discussed. Beck (1976) once used the control systems idea of feedforward processes, but he does not link this to the anticipatory functioning of selective attention as described in the comparative framework used here.

Emotions and Affective Experience

The concepts of emotions and affective experience are often used, but differences in their meanings are unclear. Beck, for example, refers to crying spells, sadness, loss of gratification, lethargy and apathy as affective states. Emotions involve both feelings and "visceral or bodily events," but no theory about the nature of emotions is stated by either theorist. Ellis and Beck both appear to adopt psychology's traditional classification of kinds of emotions. Their discussions and examples imply that emotions perform regulatory functions, as in our comparative framework, but their discussions obscure important functional differences among kinds and levels of emotions.

Ellis groups emotions into two types: positive and negative, he treats them as corollaries to his assumption that hedonistic processes—maximizing pleasure, and minimizing pain and discomfort—govern human functioning. Positive emotions are manifested in subjective states such as pleasure, relief, or satisfaction; negative states of displeasure or dissatisfaction manifest emotions such as sadness or depression, anger or annoyance, guilt or regret, frustration or disappointment, and shame or embarassment (Ellis, et al., 1988). Emotions are rarely pure and unalloyed, but represent biological, cognitive, and behavioral patterns (Ellis, 1986). Dryden (1987) proposes blends of emotions.

Beck's (1976) view is similar. He considers emotions to be distinctive and identifiable events, even though he does not clearly specify their nature. He sometimes refers to them as an emotional response and at others times as a process. He, too, divides them into positive and negative subtypes, with positive emotions including such states as joy, pleasure, or happiness, and negative ones including emotions like sadness, anxiety, and anger. He says they have both physiological and behavioral concomitants—for example, a panic state is described as an abrupt episode of miserable feelings, sweating palms, pounding heart, trembling, and nausea. Beck is not clear as to whether emotions invariably occur in relation to activity or whether different kinds of emotions occur only under some circumstances.

Hedonism always operates, so some level of positive, negative, or blended emotions is always present. Both men state that variations occur in the amount of arousal—its frequency, amplitude, or duration—but they do not explain the role of such variations. Appropriate versus inappropriate or realistic versus unrealistic emotions differ in both kind and amount—their intensity and duration. For example, concern is different from anxiety; it is typically more realistic—in a person's best interests—to experience concern over an anticipated outcome rather than to become overly concerned, be anxious, or experience panic. Regret is preferable to guilt, and annoyance is more realistic and appropriate than anger. Appropriate levels of positive and negative emotions are less painful to experience, are less likely to alienate other people, and facilitate pursuit of individuals' objectives and ability to perform (Ellis, 1985, 1986). Therefore, an important objective of rational-emotive therapy is to enable clients to experience less disruptive emotions and thereby to perform better.

Cognitive Characteristics

For Ellis and Beck, cognition is the key concept because they conceive of human functioning as organized and regulated primarily by cognitive processes (Dobson & Block, 1988; Lehman & Salovey, 1990). Consistent with their metaphysical assumptions, they view healthy, well-adjusted, and effective people as functioning cognitively like good scientists. They gather empirical data, formulate rationally ordered models and hypotheses free of illogicalities, and objectively test these ideas against publicly observable outcomes. However, people frequently deviate from the principles of careful empirical observation and rationality, and they form conclusions about themselves, other people, and the future that are irrational, illogical, distorted, overgeneralized, or absolutistic. They can also display inadequate reality testing of their ideas in their real-life contexts. Both Ellis and Beck propose that deficiencies in conceptual models and hypothesis-building and testing processes are the primary source of clients' dysfunctional behavior.

Ellis (1977a) uses a variety of concepts about cognition; these include imaging, expectancy, will, attribution, insight, fantasy, self-rating, and self-evaluation. Three, however, receive primary emphasis: personal goals, choice, and beliefs (Ellis & Dryden, 1987). Ellis considers these to be inborn cognitive tendencies whose content is influenced by sociocultural experiences and people's innate propensity toward short-range hedonism, particularly early in life (Ellis & Greiger, 1977).

The emphasis on personal goals or purposes, stems from his proposal that humans tend to be goal directed; they are happiest when they have succeeded in establishing important life goals and purposes, and actively strive to attain them. (This view is similar to the directive function in our comparative framework.) Ellis does not explain how personal goals develop, why different kinds develop, the relationships among them, how they might be manifested in awareness, or how a person might be able to reconcile differences or discrepancies among them.

The importance of choice derives from the assumption in rational-emotive therapy that humans control their own lives, not only by the way they interpret events but also by how they pursue their purposes and deal with their life circumstances (Ellis & Greiger, 1977). Choice, therefore, represents cognitive processes of reasoning, solving problems, selecting options, forming conclusions, making decisions, and selecting courses of action (similar to control functions in the comparative framework).

Belief is the concept given most emphasis; it is basic to the rational-emotive treatment model, but no formal definition is given. Beliefs (Bs) are considered the primary determinants of emotions and actions. Ellis says beliefs are a kind of cognition "adopted or created" by a person over his or her life course; whether they arise with or without conscious intent, they can be "strongly held." They are not empirically based facts; they are hypotheses or models that can be challenged and are potentially testable. Ellis's belief lists reveal that they are descriptive, anticipatory self-evaluative concepts and propositions; examples are "I am incompetent"; "If I fail at any important task, I'm a total failure, and completely unlovable." Beliefs may exist in nonlinguistic forms, as attitudes or images (Ellis et al., 1988). Beliefs can be general—"I must succeed at all important tasks"—or specific—"I must succeed at this particular task" (Dryden, 1987). Specific beliefs may be special cases of general beliefs—that is, they may be hierarchically organized (Wessler & Wessler, 1980). Beliefs appear to be organized, as Ellis refers to "belief systems." Their key role in people's functioning is attributed to their governance of an immediate outcome, in the form of beneficial (self-helping) or detrimental (self-defeating) emotional and/or behavioral consequences. Therefore, in rational-emotive therapy, anticipatory, evaluative beliefs seem to perform cognitive regulatory functions—as in our comparative framework.

Rational-emotive therapy relies heavily on two subconcepts: rational (rBs) and irrational (iBs) beliefs. At first, Ellis thought the distinction was self-evident, and he simply provided lists of types often found in clients. Others, however, criticized his examples as neither self-evidently rational nor consistently adaptive, so he tried to clarify the concepts (Ellis & Dryden, 1987). Beliefs are rBs under these conditions: (1) The person understands them to be hypotheses. (2) They lead to "appropriate feelings." (3) They can be verified with empirical evidence, and (4) They contribute to attaining the person's goals. They express a person's preferences, hopes, and desires; they are conditional rather than absolute, are in accord with available empirical evidence, and demonstrate functional or self-helping utility.

Beliefs are iBs under these conditions: (1) They are absolutistic assertions and commands, such as the idea that one must have love or approval from all that one finds significant, and that one must be adequately competent and achieving at all times (termed a kind of "mustabatory ideology") (Ellis & Harper, 1975). (2) They lack empirical evidence to support them or are contradicted by existing evidence. (3) They result in inappropriate emotions, such as severe anxiety or depression. (4) They lead to self-defeating actions (Ellis, 1986; Ellis et al., 1988). These beliefs are dysfunctional; they interfere with or detract from a person's attaining personal or collective goals (Ellis et al., 1989).

Each person is unique, so many individual differences exist in people's habits of thought, but Ellis notes a remarkable sameness in the iBs people construct. He identifies 10 to 13 basic types of iBs manifesting diverse illogicalities, such as all-or-none thinking, non sequiturs, and overgeneralizations. However, all can be reduced to absolutistic evaluations of perceived events, formulated as dogmatic "musts, shoulds, have to's, got to's, and oughts" (Ellis, 1977a, p. 14). These habits of thought have five commonalities:

1. *Demandingness*—placing rigid, absolutistic requirements on oneself and others
2. *Awfulizing*—exaggerating the seriousness of events
3. *Low frustration tolerance*—assuming one is unable to tolerate discomfort or distress
4. *Rating self and others*—assuming people's worth to be contingent on their deeds and accomplishments
5. *Overgeneralizing about the future*—adopting pessimistic expectations about future attainments

Such irrational anticipatory evaluations lead to intense, extreme inappropriate feelings and actions (Ellis et al., 1988). Therefore, habitual irrational evaluative thoughts and the emotions they activate—the regulatory function in our comparative framework—are considered the basis for all psychopathology.

Dysfunctional iBs do not represent all of any person's beliefs; even persons susceptible to emotional disturbance have acquired rBs as well. Nor do iBs invariably occur, as they are activated only in certain kinds of situations, analogous to activation of schemas in relevant behavior episodes in our comparative framework. However, iBs are widespread in American society because of the so-called nonsense characterizing contemporary culture (Ellis, 1970). People with emotional problems differ in degree, but not in kind, from their fellows. Attempting to address what critics term Ellis's conceptual imprecision, Dryden (1987) defines beliefs as evaluative conclusions of personal significance that result when "people get what they believe they want" or "don't get what they believe they must have" (p. 14). That evaluative meaning directly impacts emotions and behavior. However, his use of "believe" in defining "belief" reveals that definitional problems remain.

Despite emphasizing concepts of goals, choices, and beliefs, the corpus of Ellis's writing reveals the use of many other cognitive concepts on an as-needed basis. For example, people are said to be capable of both experiencing and observing part of themselves and can detach their "observing self" from their "experiencing self" with the former instructing the latter—giving "self-instructions" (Ellis, 1986, p. 279). Also mentioned is the necessity for teaching clients the importance of distinguishing between observations and inferences, of errors in causal attributions, of the faulty predictions they so often make, and of problem-defining, consequential thinking, means-end thinking, and perspective-taking operations involved in successful problem solving. This is similar to the control functions in the book's comparative framework. Although these cognitive activities are discussed as independent processes, Dryden (1987) argues that they overlap and interact with one another. No model is provided, however, to explain how all these aspects of cognition are interrelated. Rational-emotive therapy continues to place beliefs at the center of these interacting cognitions, and Ellis contends that teaching clients specific cognitive skills, such as decision-making and communication skills, is fruitless unless their disturbed patterns of thought and emotion are corrected first (Ellis et al., 1988).

Beck also assumes that cognitions organize and regulate all other functions (Beck et al., 1990). His key concept is *schema*, which he considers similar to Kelley's "personal constructs." Schemas are cognitive structures, made up of "deep" tacit assumptions at subconscious levels, so they are outside the ordinary range of awareness. He assumes (1) that people construct these internal models of the self and the world from multiple experiences in specific behavior episodes, and (2) that their basic form is typically established early in life. Schemas function to shape people's perceptions and interpretations of the meaning of events, to organize experience, and to guide behavior—similar to behavior episode schemas in the comparative framework. They are adaptive insofar as they facilitate more efficient information processing, linking new information to that previously acquired, and recognition and recall of information (Goldfried & Robins, 1983). Schemas become organized into larger cognitive patterns—that is, a belief system (Beck, 1976). This concept appears similar to the principle of unitary functioning in the comparative framework.

Beck assumes that the flow of sensory input is admitted into awareness by the process of perception. For him, perception involves identifying, recognizing, focusing and reflecting on, and evaluating events, whether they are external, subjective sensations or psychological ones. He combines in one concept perceptions of discrete events with cognitive interpretations of their meaning, and he often calls this complex unit an *interpretation* or *perceptual interpretation.* He says it is important to distinguish between public and personal/private meanings of an event. The public meaning is the formal, objective definition of an event; private meanings are informal, subjective, and laden with a network of a person's experiences, ideas, and associations. Private meanings can be judged to be inaccurate, unrealistic, and lacking in authenticity." *Deviant interpretations* are those that consistently depart from reality.

Schemas include organizing processes or a *program of rules* as well as the content and organization of events and interpretations (Mahoney, 1995). Such rules enable people to code and evaluate their experiences. Schemas selectively screen, sort, and integrate the flow of experience, enabling people to construct, guide, and regulate their behavior patterns. Schemas represent categories of experiences, and are hierarchically organized. Beck does not formally classify kinds of schemas but describes them as organizations of psychological and behavioral functions in relation to contexts—like the behavior episode schemas in the comparative framework. Schemas may include constructs and rules about one's personal, familial, occupational, religious, or cultural activities. Moreover, because people function with relatively stable patterns of different kinds of responses, Beck suggests that they have corresponding subschemas—that is, cognitive, affective, motivational, and action schemas. Within each of these there may be subsubschemas, such as self-evaluation or memory schemas (Beck et al., 1990). Ellis's concept of *belief* might be thought of as such a subschema operating within a larger integrative schema. The organizational properties of schemas include breadth, flexibility or rigidity, or density—their prominence in the cognitive organization—and valence—the extent to which they may become active in any situation. They can be rated from active—degree of valence—to inactive—dormant or latent—, and from impermeable to changeable (Beck et al., 1990).

The content and rules of schemas largely function outside people's awareness—that is, they represent tacit knowledge. However, their products—specific thoughts and images—are more readily accessible. The thoughts Ellis (1962) referred to as "internalized statements" or "self-statements" and Maultsby (1984) labeled "self-talk", Beck calls *automatic thoughts* because he thinks that term more adequately reflects the way they are experienced, which is by reflex and of necessity. They are spontaneous and fleeting; they carry a sense of inherent validity. They are so habitual as to be functionally automatic in specific contexts; in these contexts they represent immediate, unpremediated interpretations that occur spontaneously and without apparent volition and shape both the person's emotional reactions and actions. Though they occur within the realm of consciousness, automatic thoughts are generally inattended and therefore unrecognized. Beck proposes that people can be taught to shift their attention to monitor such habitual thoughts consciously through self-observation. Teaching clients to attend, monitor, and evaluate their automatic, unexamined thoughts and to learn to distinguish between appropriate and maladaptive ones is a key strategy in cognitive therapy. Close inspection of a person's automatic thinking when dealing with different kinds of life episodes provides clues as to the nature of the person's underlying schemas.

Beck has tried to adhere to these definitions and to distinguish between schemas and their consequences; he sees both spontaneous and fleeting automatic thoughts as schema products (Beck, Rush, Shaw, & Emery, 1979). However, he notes that in many representations of cognitive therapy, such distinctions have become eroded. Freeman, Pretzer, Fleming, and Simon (1990) observe that in the literature on cognitive therapy, "the terms dysfunctional beliefs, underlying assumptions and schemas, have been used interchangeably to refer to the person's unspoken and often unrecognized assumptions . . . no consistent distinctions are drawn between these closely related terms" (p. 4). They concluded that it was appropriate for those terms to be treated as synonyms.

Although cognitive therapy is considered an important theory (Arnkoff & Glass, 1992), its conceptual model has suffered considerable criticism. Dobson (1988b) criticized Beck's use of schema, originally developed within cognitive psychology (cf. Neisser, 1967), used in social cognition (Markus, 1977), and subsequently applied to clinical problems where a variety of idiosyncratic attachments have adhered to the concept. Others have criticized Beck's use of schema as vague and imprecise, asserting that the scope and conditions of activation of a schema remain unclear. Likewise many different elements have been proposed as components of such schemas. Thus, Freeman et al., 1990, consider "many aspects of cognition" relevant including self-statements, irrational beliefs, expectations, basic assumptions, attributions, mental images, and current concerns. How such cognitions are similar or different, or how they are organized into schemas, remains unclear. Finally, the assumption that the nature of people's schemas can be accurately inferred from observation of their behavior and history or from interview data has been questioned. The risk of inferential error and the assumption of direct correspondence between what people overtly say and do and what they think—covert schemas—remain inadequately addressed.

Safran (1984a, 1984b, 1988; Safran & Segal, 1990) criticizes that view of schemas as too reliant on an information-processing model. He argues that people should be studied from an ecological perspective: The psychological patterns people develop are constructed in relation to their real-world contexts, which are largely interpersonal in nature. During their development, people create interpersonal schemas that are generic cognitive representations of interpersonal events based on "interactions with attachment figures [enabling] the individual to predict interactions in a way that increases the probability of maintaining relatedness with these figures" (Safran, 1988, p. 13). They are created and maintained on the basis of their functional utility and are composed of cognitive, affective, and action components that are intrinsically related—like the behavior episode schemas in our comparative framework. Rather than a distinctive approach, this is characterized as a refinement in the theory and practice of cognitive therapy (Safran, 1988; Vallis, 1991).

BEHAVIORAL CHARACTERISTICS: THE BEHAVIORAL PERSON

Both cognitive therapy and rational-emotive therapy often use the term *behavior,* but neither clearly defines its meaning. Sometimes, the concepts of *performance* and *skills* are used instead, but they too are only illustrated—as relaxation or assertive skills—rather than defined. *Action* and *behavior* seem to be considered synonyms (see *Thought and Action in Psychotherapy: Cognitive-Behavioral Approaches* by Kendall, Bemis, & Kane, 1991). Dryden's (1987) summary of rational-emotive therapy substitutes *actions* for *behavior;* Dryden describes actions as purposive, intended to bring about a change in the person's state, or in his or her physical and interpersonal contexts. *Action tendencies* are generalized types of actions, such as a tendency to withdraw, and *response options* are specific action possibilities. Later, we describe the use of behavioral assignments in the two therapies.

We infer that Ellis and Beck implicitly accept the traditional materialist, behaviorist view that defines behavior as objectively observable physical movements and communicative acts, and biological functions observable through the aid of instrumentation. In this definition, behavior is *body* and they emphasize *mind,* but they provide no propositions about how mind influences body or vice versa. They argue that intrapsychic processes govern behavior. By assuming that when beliefs or schemas change, clients will construct or use different behavior patterns, they sidestep the necessity of specifying a conceptual model of behavior. However, distinctions among different kinds of behavior are of practical significance. Ellis (1986) argues that hard and fast distinctions between such categories as emotion, thought, and behavior cannot be legitimately drawn because each invariably includes elements of the other. Nevertheless, he does refer to behavior as if it were a distinct and independently identifiable class of events.

Environmental Characteristics
Both Ellis and Beck cite Epictetus's saying that people are moved not by things, but rather by the views they take of them. Thus, the prospect of death may alarm one who construes it to be the end of existence, and elicit hope in another who views it as a transitional phase to an even better existence. Neither Ellis nor Beck denies the importance of environmental events; they propose that the impact of contexts is mediated by cognition, and so the mediating processes, rather than the events themselves, are of primary importance (Dobson & Block, 1988). Both acknowledge that adverse and challenging life events occur—such as social rejection, pressures at work, loss of one's job, unemployment, divorce, or death of a loved one. Clients may react to these with intense, negative emotional reactions, but it is their thoughts and beliefs about the events, not the events themselves, that govern how they respond.

Ellis asserts that all individuals retain innate capacities to change their thinking so they can lead happy and productive lives, even in the face of what many others might consider adverse contexts (Ellis, 1962, 1971, 1985; Ellis & Bernard, 1983, 1985; Ellis et al., 1988). He notes that environmental obstacles to client progress can arise during therapy in the form of a difficult and uncompromising mate, or a pressure-laden job. It may be necessary to encourage clients to distance themselves from those persons or situations if the situations cannot be modified. Even so, contexts only limit clients' opportunities to attain happiness; they do not directly cause psychological problems: Clients' beliefs are the primary culprit (Ellis, 1985; Ellis & Dryden, 1987; Dryden, 1987). Sometimes Ellis refers to the people and things around each person as a system (Ellis, 1970). He sees the relationship between persons and contexts as reciprocal in nature: People are affected by the system in which they develop and live, but they also intentionally affect the people and the things—the system—around them (Ellis, 1986).

The nature of different types of contexts—physical, interpersonal, or sociocultural—their reciprocal interactions, and their implications for client functioning are not explained. For example, in couple therapy, rational-emotive therapy focuses on the individuals in the relationship rather than on their interactions or the larger system in which they function. Ellis asserts that mates are disturbed not by one another's actions or by life's rough breaks, but by the views each takes of such events. Therefore, the thinking of each person must be changed to alter the couple's disturbed feelings and actions (Ellis et al., 1989).

Explicit references to environments and/or their properties are also rare in the writings of Beck and his associates, although contexts are mentioned in case examples. The importance of contexts, however, is clearly implied in cognitive therapy as in rational-emotive therapy. For example, to judge beliefs as irrational and expectations and interpretations as incorrect (Ellis) or as consistently departing from reality and therefore unrealistic and lacking in authenticity (Beck), it must be assumed that the validity of clients' beliefs, expectations, or schemas can be checked by comparing them with clients' actual contexts. Two methods are used for making such judgments: (1) a comparison of clients' view of their real-life circumstances against the criterion of someone considered more capable of assigning an objective and public or consensual meaning to such events—such as the therapist; and (2) the implementation of some action in the real world to test the validity of clients' cognitions. Neither theorist defines environments, proposes a classification of them, or specifies the nature of reciprocal relationships between people and their environments. In discussions and case examples, both Ellis and Beck emphasize interpersonal contexts as playing a key role in the development and operation of dysfunctional patterns, but they give little theoretical consideration to how different kinds of contexts may have different effects on people.

This completes our analysis of the conceptual components of rational-emotive therapy and cognitive therapy. We turn next to consider the "hows"—their propositional models.

THE PROPOSITIONAL MODEL

ASSUMPTIONS REGARDING CAUSALITY

As in most therapy theories, cognitive therapy and rational-emotive therapy do not explain the implications of their metaphysical assumptions for understanding how the parts of humans are linked to and influence one another. Mahoney (1988) and Niemeyer (1995a) describe how cognitive therapies use a view about the organization of phenomena, termed *associationism*, that has been dominant in psychological and behavioral sciences for nearly a century. In this view, complex patterns are created by linking elements together. This leads to a view of causality in which events are understood to be temporally and spatially related in linear chains of cause-and-effect. The occurrence of any particular event—a consequence—is presumed to be caused by other events that occur before it—antecedents. Change is explained by identifying the antecedent events (A) that impinge on the relevant responses (B) to produce the change or consequence (C), often termed ABC analysis. The cognitive models of Beck and Ellis were developed within the decades 1950 to 1970 when such a view was dominant. Our 1963 analysis of psychotherapies also used that associationistic view of linear causality.

Others criticize that causal model as oversimplified and inaccurate. Karl Lashley noted as early as 1951 that psychological processes usually occur far too rapidly for one element to function as an antecedent or stimulus for subsequent events in a sequence. He believed that other explanations have greater merit. He suggested that actions could be viewed as ensembles of simultaneous events, no element of which is intelligible when removed from the ensemble of which it is a part; this idea is illustrated by concepts like states, state transitions, behavior episodes, and behavior episode schemas in the book's comparative framework.

PROPOSITIONS CONCERNING THE ORGANIZATIONAL DYNAMICS OF HUMAN FUNCTIONING

Ellis and Beck provided propositions about the organization of human characteristics that reflect an associationistic model. The most important ones are described below.

A person is a complex organization of parts, and innately functions to create and maintain unitary patterns of functioning. The assumption that humans inherently tend to create coherent intraperson and person-context patterns of functioning, and that poorly organized patterns are dysfunctional and cause people distress, is clearly implied in both cognitive therapy and rational-emotive therapy, but it is not explicitly stated. The assumption undergirds Ellis's and Beck's basic rationale that *beliefs* and *schemas* function to integrate perceptions, emotions, and actions into coherent patterns. This is similar to the principle of unitary functioning in the comparative framework. Although their concepts are somewhat different, both consider these parts to be interrelated so that people function in a unitary and purposeful fashion in pursuit of goals and objectives—survival and happiness (Ellis, 1970), or avoidance of danger, self-preservation, maximizing pleasure, and minimizing pain (Beck, 1976). Ellis argues that although it is conceptually useful to think in terms of the different parts of humans, in practice they cannot be separated from one another.

People function both to create and to protect coherent patterns. For example, both theorists describe examples of self-fulfilling prophecies, wherein people's beliefs, schemas, or assumptions are said to lead to actions that produce outcomes they then interpret in terms of their expectations—like stability-maintaining processes in the comparative framework. Goldfried and Robins (1983) suggest that a bias exists in people toward the encoding and retrieving of schema-consistent information, so that assimilation of new information to existing schemas occurs more readily than accommodation of schemas to new information. Although Ellis and Beck both sometimes refer to organizations of responses as systems, such as belief systems, they do not use that concept in any technical way.

Cognitive processes create and coordinate humans' behavior patterns. Ellis and Beck assume that cognitions not only occur antecedent to but also determine people's emotional responses and their actions, summarized in the aphorism, "As ye think, so shall ye feel and act."

Human perceptions—a form of cognition in their view—are considered relatively valid mental copies of aspects of the real world (cf with the realists' epistemological assumption). Collectively, perceptions provide the basis for the construction of people's thoughts and ideas concerning themselves and their world. Once created, these ideas influence how people construe each new situation, the emotions that will occur, and how they choose to act. These are the assumptions of rationalism as summarized by Shanon (1987). Accurate ("realistic") perceptions, and logical, orderly ("rational") thinking are the key to effective behavior and appropriate feelings. Therefore, alleviating a person's difficulties involves both altering faulty cognitions, such as inaccurate perceptions or irrational beliefs, and activating rational cognitive processes, such as logical problem solving or empirical hypothesis testing, to replace illogical ones, such as habits of overgeneralization and faulty causal attributions.

Information flows from the environment to the person and is assimilated, integrated, and reconstructed into patterns of cognitions on the basis of similar characteristics and regularized contingencies—for example, schemas and rules (Lyddon, 1995). As development proceeds, these cognitive organizations—assumptions, beliefs, schemas, modes of thinking—become habitual, and then operate to determine the person's interpretations of succeeding events, to shape the emotional responses that occur, and to instruct and guide the focus and direction of the person's behavior (Freeman et al., 1990). Much of the content of such cognitions is tacit and unconscious, but their operation can be identified through their manifestations, called automatic thoughts (Beck, 1976) or self-statements (Ellis, 1977a). These immediate, unpremeditated interpretations of events occur spontaneously and without apparent volition. Cognitive therapies tend to espouse a soft determinism, describing cognitions as tending to shape or influence people's perceptions, emotions and actions rather than completely dictating their occurrence.

Ellis's version of the ABC form of analysis represents his view of how events are functionally related. He proposed that people go into situations in their system or environment equipped with goals, purposes and desires, "especially the goals of personal survival and living in a happy and unfrustrated manner" (Ellis, 1970, p. 50). What takes place—that is, what the person judges to take place—constitutes an Activating Event (A). It leads to evaluative judgments that are governed by the person's rational (rB) or irrational (iB) Beliefs and related "self-talk," and are often both in the ordinary person (Ellis, 1970). When adverse or less-than-desirable Activating Events (As) occur, the rBs that occur take the form of evaluative or wish statements: "I don't like this failure, and I wish it had not occurred." If rBs predominate, they lead to appropriate and self-helpful consequences (Cs), such as appropriate feelings of frustration or disappointment rather than anger or depression, and effective actions. If iBs occur, they prompt inappropriate affect and self-defeating behavior, with emotional disturbance and ineffective adaptation the result. Maultsby's (1984) ABC model is similar; repeated pairings of a perception (A) with evaluative thoughts (B) leads to rational, or irrational emotive and behavioral reactions (C).

Many of Ellis's colleagues found it necessary to elaborate his ABC model, so, even though he liked its simplicity, he finally responded to criticisms that it glossed over important distinctions between different types of cognition (Wessler & Wessler, 1980) by creating an expanded schema (Ellis & Dryden, 1987). Surprisingly, he stated that "there is . . . no absolutely correct way of conceptualizing clients' problems according to such an expanded schema" (p. 8).

The schema explicitly provides for the operation of personal Goals (G's) in organizing behavior episodes. Equipped with innumerable Beliefs (B's), including "cognitions, thoughts, or ideas," people seek out an environment in which to try to fulfill their goals (G's). Activators (A's) result which can include people's "perceptions of present or current events," "their own thoughts, feelings or behaviors about those events"; "they may be embedded in memories or thoughts (conscious or unconscious) about past experiences" (Ellis & Dryden, 1987, p. 8). These A's can be categorized into those that contribute to versus those that interfere with successful achievement of the person's goals, but they do not directly cause cognitive, emotional, or behavioral consequences. It is the person's Beliefs that mediate between A's and C's, and directly cause or create C's. Ellis also tried to be more specific about the kinds of cognitions considered to be Beliefs, with special attention given to those that result in self-helping or self-defeating kinds of behavior. This expanded schema appears similar to the interaction of behavior episodes and behavior episode schemas in our comparative framework. With his primary emphasis on Beliefs, Ellis gives cognitive regulatory functions the key role in influencing how people behave.

The ontological dualism of rational-emotive therapy and cognitive therapy assumes that mind can influence body, but the theorists are unclear about how this causal influence is exercised. They typically describe sequential cause-effect patterns thus: goals → cognitions or activators → evaluations or beliefs → emotions → actions. Neither theorist, however, seems wedded to a linear associationistic model. For example, Ellis asserts that although he uses sequential depictions, the three elements (A, B, and C) are mutually influential, even though rational-emotive therapy usually "attacks" the B in this ABC triangle. Others (e.g., Freeman et al., 1990) argue that Beck also posits mutual causality among psychological, emotional, and behavioral functions. They note that emotions can influence cognition—for example, perception and recall may be biased in a mood-congruent way; also, actions can affect evaluations of a situation, either by changing it or by eliciting different consequences from it. However, the proposition of reciprocal causality remains undeveloped in both therapy theories.

Sometimes Ellis's and Beck's descriptions are suggestive of an information processing feedback loop. Others have suggested that the components of their models correspond to the basic information processing framework of input (perception), throughput (cognition) and output (behavior). Beck has increasingly used feedback and feedforward terminology in his writings, as in depicting the self-fulfilling characteristics of depressive states. The negative view depressed people have of the world, themselves, and their future leads to negative emotions and physiological states, such as sadness and anergia. Their negative evaluation of these symptoms feed back into the psychological system, resulting in a continuing vicious circle with a positive feedback effect—the condition becomes progressively worse. Extensive use of feedback cycles in representations of a range of clinical disorders appears in recent analyses (Beck et al., 1990; Freeman, et al., 1990). Processes akin to feedback are implied in Ellis's discussions of current actions and evaluations as influencing appropriate emotions and self-helping actions on the next occasion (Ellis, 1970).

Feedforward processes are implied in rational-emotive therapy discussions of how anticipatory beliefs selectively influence functioning. Assertions that people "prejudicially view or experience . . . (events) in the light of their biased Beliefs (expectations, evaluations)" (Ellis & Dryden, 1987, p. 8), or that people's beliefs color their perceptions of and inferences about reality (Ellis et al., 1989) are illustrative. Feedforward processes are also implicit in many of Beck's clinical analyses, such as his proposal that people with anxiety disorders are excessively preoccupied with the maintenance of their physical well-being, which leads them to selectively attend to bodily cues (Beck & Emery, 1985). Beck has commented on the utility of the relatively new concept of feedforward in cognitive psychology as a way of representing the anticipatory features of cognitive schemata (Beck et al., 1990).

Emotions are aroused by descriptive and anticipatory evaluative thoughts. Emotions are considered important in both theories. Beck and Ellis agree that emotions are aroused by evaluative thoughts appraising the potential good-bad, beneficial-detrimental personal impact of currently perceived events or imagined possibilities. For Beck, evaluative thoughts are components of schemas. Like Lazarus (1991), he proposes that *primary appraisal* evaluates the potential personal impact of events, and *secondary appraisal* evaluates one's potential capability for coping with that possible impact. For Ellis, *Beliefs* perform this evaluative function. In his recent elaborations, emotional arousal is elicited by evaluations about the extent to which current personal goals are being attained: Positive emotions result from people's evaluations that they are getting what they want or are avoiding what they don't want; negative emotions result from their evaluations that they aren't getting what they want or aren't avoiding what they don't want. This implies that some kind of emotion will occur in every purposive action.

Ellis and Beck assume that different kinds of evaluative thoughts arouse different emotional states. For example, the evaluation that progress toward desired consequences is occurring stimulates positive feelings such as pleasure. Positive feedback loops can escalate such feelings up to levels of euphoria. Sadness results from evaluations that something of value has been, or will be, lost. Anger results from evaluations of direct, indirect, or potential assaults on one's personal domain, including obstructions of goals. Fear—whose affective correlate is said to be anxiety—arises from evaluations of real or anticipated damage, either physical or psychosocial in nature (Beck, 1976).

Although their propositions about emotional functioning are sketchy, the descriptions appear generally compatible with our comparative framework.

Once constructed, cognitive patterns tend to become habitual and automatized, and hence not ordinarily part of the contents of consciousness. People are usually not aware of the ways their underlying assumptions, beliefs, expectations, or schemas determine how they perceive events, choose their actions, and evaluate the consequences of their actions. People are usually aware of what they are doing and how they are feeling, but typically they do not pay attention to, think about, or try to verbalize the ideas that are organizing their behavior; they do not articulate to themselves the rules and concepts guiding their interpretations and reactions (Beck, 1976; Ellis, 1970). People can thus unwittingly behave in ways that are detrimental to themselves and their goals. When asked about their guiding ideas, people often find it difficult to identify and describe them without considerable help and effort.

Beck (1976) suggests that some parts of people's schemas are initially adopted in tacit form and never made consciously explicit. Thoughts, feelings, or wishes may flash briefly into consciousness, but the underlying schemas are not conscious despite their habitual nature (Beck, et al., 1990). However, both cognitive therapy and rational-emotive therapy propose that habitual beliefs and schemas can become consciously verbalized through introspective analysis, thereby becoming susceptible to change. This view implies that people were once aware of these beliefs before the beliefs became automatic. As long as habitual, guiding cognitions remain tacit and unstated, they function independent of the person's conscious control and are resistant to change (Ellis, 1970).

Unconscious cognitions are manifested in consciousness in affective experiences and certain kinds of thoughts. Ellis describes a person as a "self-talking animal"; human "intrachange"—people communicating with themselves—is comparable to interpersonal interchanges, occurring in simple sentences (Dryden & Ellis, 1988, p. 223). Conscious thinking consists primarily of short, verbal phrases, or simple exclamatory sentences (Ellis, 1970). Ellis seems to assume that thinking and talking use the same symbolic code or verbal language. That direct correspondence implies that one can infer what people are thinking from what they say, and one might modify the way people think by changing the way they talk about their thoughts.

Beck (1976) says that immediate, unpremeditated interpretations of both external and inner events occur spontaneously and without conscious volition throughout behavior episodes. These *automatic thoughts* manifest the underlying schemas from which they stem and may occur in linguistic or imagistic forms (Beck, 1976). Beck differs from Ellis in proposing that people think with constellations of meanings, and that words are tools for manipulating, modifying, and communicating meanings (similar to the comparative framework used in this book). Meanings are encased in thoughts or images and derive from networks of ideas and associations. Underlying schemas can be inferred from people's verbal reports about their automatic thoughts.

Two conditions must be present for cognitive patterns to be modified: (1) The person must become aware of the cognitive pattern that needs changing and must focus attention on the aspects of it that need correction: (2) The cognitive pattern must be perturbed by an encounter with discrepant information or experience. Cognitive therapists call processes of cognitive change *cognitive restructuring;* it is assumed to be a normal part of adaptive living. People are continually honing and shaping their ideas, clarifying and changing assumptions and beliefs, and shedding portions that are no longer useful. Rational-emotive therapy and cognitive therapy assume that conscious, rational control of behavior produces adaptive functioning. Habitual cognitive patterns, such as beliefs or schemas, that exert their influence outside of awareness and produce unwanted consequences are considered the basic source of maladaptive functioning. The first condition for modifying a cognitive pattern is that the person must become aware of it and how it influences his or her emotions and actions. Both Beck (1976) and Ellis and Dryden (1987) assume that people can become aware of their underlying thoughts by focusing attention on them while they are occurring: Cognitive patterns can be changed only when they are occurring and the person is aware of them (as in the comparative framework used here). By stating habitual thoughts in explicit, conscious terms, one can gain conscious control over them and thereby gain control over the emotional and behavioral consequences to which they lead.

Even with awareness, however, change will not occur unless some experience, information, or interpretation occurs that contradicts some part of the habitual pattern. That cognitive dissonance disrupts the coherence of the cognitive pattern—as with overgeneralized beliefs—and the relationships among cognitive components, such as faulty rules of reasoning. The innate tendency to create and maintain coherent organization then operates to overcome the disruption: The discrepant influence may be ignored or reinterpreted to fit and maintain the habitual pattern; some components may be altered; new components may be added or old ones eliminated; or the entire pattern may undergo reorganization. (A similar process appears in our comparative framework.)

Neither theory makes clear how cognitive restructuring occurs. Change processes are discussed either in terms of intervention methods used—what the therapist does—or of effects on clients—how clients change. Explanations of the processes by which interventions produce effects are not provided. Discussions of change in case examples use phrases such as "she revamped her thinking," "he became aware of the logical inconsistencies in his belief system," "she was able to see the fallacy of her beliefs and consequently realized she had other options," and "the patient learns to challenge the validity of these negative thoughts" (Beck, 1976).

Also implied, though not explicitly stated, is that once cognitive restructuring occurs, changes in the person's larger cognitive-behavioral organization will automatically take place, producing changes in relevant emotional, communicative, and action patterns. Only occasionally must a person be coached in using preferable patterns of behavior. Once a change appears, however, what determines whether it will become established as a permanent functioning alternative to the dysfunctional pattern?

Cognitive changes must be validated in the person's real-life experience in order to become firmly established and subsequently used. Ellis (1970) quotes John Dewey as saying that one does not really believe something until one acts upon it. He asserts that "there is no other way to get better than to work and practice," which justifies the use of "homework assignments" since "to really depropagandize himself, the person has to act" (p. 62). Action by itself is insufficient, however, because learning results from selection processes in relation to consequences. Both Ellis and Beck propose that behavior is goal directed; this view implies that the achievement of goals through the use of the changed cognitive patterns produces preferred consequences and positive emotions rather than the misery of their previous patterns. Experiencing the functional utility of a cognitive restructuring facilitates enduring change in clients' cognitive-behavior patterns, as implied by their case descriptions. For example, therapists' rely on clients' reports of success in real-life behavior episodes as one basis for terminating therapy.

Beck (1976) suggests that multiple beneficial effects stem from cognitive restructuring. He notes that sound assessment of improvement in a depression requires establishing that desired changes have occurred in affect, motivation, cognition, physiological functions (sleep and appetite), and overt behavior. He implies that these are outcomes in keeping with the client's goals. More recently, he refers to *cognitive-affective-behavioral organizations* to stress his view that emotional consequences play a key role in clients' acquiring and maintaining changed patterns. He proposes a direct relationship between basic biological goals and pleasure-pain centers, and he suggests that activities that contribute to survival and reproduction goals, such as eating or bonding, generate gratifying affects such as pleasure. This is an automatic mechanism that serves to reinforce those activities and to produce expectations of pleasurable consequences in the future (Beck et al., 1990). It is not clear whether Beck means that all personal goals are linked to those biological goals, or that these emotional mechanisms operate with other types of personal goals. Clearly, in this more recent formulation he attributes to emotions a regulatory function similar to the one in our comparative framework.

PROPOSITIONS ABOUT NORMAL OR FUNCTIONAL DEVELOPMENT

Neither Ellis nor Beck provides propositions about normal development. They say little about influences before birth or in infancy, childhood, adolescence, or aging phases, or about the impact of varied environments on people's developmental pathways. A key source of this relative neglect of developmental issues is probably the theorists' emphasis on analyzing adults' current cognitive functioning, which is the typical focus of psychotherapy. The psychoanalytic emphasis on historical sources of people's difficulties is typically eschewed, replaced by careful specification and analysis of here-and-now functioning. One can create speculative answers to the question of how current patterns may have been acquired, but that may be irrelevant to the question of what is needed to effect a change under present conditions.

There does appear to be general agreement about preferred outcomes of individual development, defined in terms of effective adult functioning. Humans behave by virtue of their knowledge. Preferably that knowledge consists of well-defined symbolic mental representations, organized into well-formed meaning-structures. The use of that knowledge determines people's capabilities for dealing effectively with themselves and their world. The acquisition of preferred forms of knowledge and its effective use is typified by the problem-solving strategies of natural scientists: The well-adjusted person gathers empirical data free of observational distortions, formulates rationally ordered hypotheses free of illogic, and conducts unbiased, objective testing of those hypotheses against publicly observable outcomes. The accuracy of one's perceptions is determined by how well these perceptions correspond with the real world, with what is actually there. The suitability of one's ideas and beliefs, understood to be hypotheses, is determined by their adherence to accepted forms of reasoning as well. People must always be ready to test their beliefs and to abandon them in the face of persuasive evidence that they are invalid (Neimeyer, 1995b; Shanon, 1987).

Well-adjusted people engage in continuing, active disputation and reality testing of their assumptions, beliefs, expectations, and schemas so they can process information accurately and adapt effectively (Niemeyer, 1995b). Adherence to such principles enables people to continuously generate cognitive-affective-behavioral patterns that have maximal functional utility. The phrase, "the human as a personal scientist" (Mahoney, 1977c) characterizes this view and serves as an overarching framework for formulating the goals of treatment for any particular client.

In cognitive therapy, an allegiance to the logico-empirical methods of positivist science appears to be considered sufficient for people to live effectively with a minimum of emotional distress. Ellis, however, considers such a representation to be limited, failing to address critical issues, such as these: What constitutes ethical conduct? What are the preferred characteristics of human relationships? His background in social and moral philosophy led him to place the "personal scientist" role in a larger framework that he calls rational philosophy. This is a set of assumptions, beliefs, and operating principles that he asserts have greater functional utility than alternate ways of thinking. People who adopt this philosophy are more likely to reach their goals within their network of interpersonal relationships and to undergo the least emotional disturbance in the process.

Reflecting what he calls ethical humanism, responsible hedonism, and rationality (which he considers the distinctive feature of humans), Ellis defines rational philosophy as going beyond scientific thinking to include enlightened self-interest; social interest; high frustration tolerance; long-range hedonism; self-direction; self-responsibility; self-acceptance; acceptance of responsibility for one's thoughts, feelings, and actions; commitment to creative pursuits; risk-taking; acceptance of uncertainty; and nonutopianism (Ellis, 1979; Ellis & Dryden, 1987). This philosophy seems to reflect the emphasis on individualism typical of the culture of the United States. Therapists may have to content themselves with more limited changes in clients who are interested in immediate benefits; more basic and long-lasting improvements require a comprehensive philosophic restructuring of their belief system so they can adopt rational philosophy.

Propositions About Dysfunctional/Abnormal Development

Origins of Dysfunctional Cognitions

Both Ellis and Beck provide little theorizing about how dysfunctional beliefs or schemas develop—whether taught by adults; learned through social modeling of patterns used by one's family, peers, or cultural group; or discovered by trial and error learning. Rational-emotive therapy provides no elaborate view about development of psychological disturbance (Ellis & Dryden, 1987) but proposes that it is ultimately a matter of individual decision and choice (Ellis, 1986). Ellis considers the construction and elaboration of adverse cognitive habits to be inevitable. He assumes that humans are innately fallible because they have a strong biological tendency to think irrationally, especially for thinking in absolutistic terms. Humans naturally make errors and behave in self-defeating ways. He cites 10 ways in which irrational thinking is historically universal across all social and cultural groups to justify this view. He counterbalances this gloomy view of people by positing a second biological tendency; the ability to think about one's thoughts and to work toward changing one's irrational thinking.

Beck speculates that there may be an interactive effect between nature and nurture. People with a strong inborn sensitivity to rejection may develop intense fears and beliefs about the catastrophic meaning of such an event, particularly if the rejection is especially potent, occurs at a vulnerable time, or is repeated (Beck et al., 1990). He mentions that an unfortunate life history may be a factor in the development of personality disorders. He does consider processes thought to be responsible for some developmental transitions—for example, from steady-state conditions of maladaptive cognitions to more severe states, such as depression or anxiety. He proposes that a *cognitive shift* occurs, in which transient and situation-specific beliefs become accentuated or intensified and generalized to include a wider range of situations; as a result, they become more absolute and extreme (Beck et al., 1990). The conditions under which such transitions occur are not specified.

The Content and Dynamics of Dysfunctional Cognition

Cognitive therapists agree that clients create their own misery and distress (Dobson, 1988b). The psychological wounds from which they suffer are primarily self-inflicted, the emotional sufferings they undergo their own doing, and their behavioral inefficiency and ineffectiveness their own creation. All are traceable to the ways they think. It is primarily the beliefs and schemas they have constructed and continue to use that produce their dysfunctional patterns of living: It is the person's crooked thinking (Ellis, 1970), or inaccurate and distorted information processing (Beck, 1993) that is the source of emotional and behavioral difficulties.

Reality exists, but people select and interpret what they consider real with varying degrees of accuracy; they often deviate from principles of valid empirical observation and form conclusions about themselves, others, and the future that are absolutistic, overgeneralized, or illogical (Beck et al., 1979). The greater the cognitive misrepresentation or distortion, the greater the problems they are likely to develop since their guiding schemas include those errors. Misinterpretations can result in a web of incorrect meanings, which are labeled deviant when they depart from so-called reality (Beck, 1976; Beck et al., 1979). Thus, the validity of a person's beliefs or schemas can be judged by their accuracy in representing real-world events.

Once distorted schemas exist and function, incoming information must be distorted, misrepresented, or otherwise biased to fit them (Robins & Hayes, 1995). When memories are processed, they may undergo misrepresentation as well. To maintain the established cognitive organization, the person may also resort to making logical errors, thereby deviating from principles of rationality as well (Beck et al., 1979). Ellis lists a variety of cognitive distortions that he believes to be derived from the basic "musts": all-or-none thinking; jumping to conclusions and negative nonsequiturs; fortune telling; focusing on the negative; disqualifying the positive; allness and neverness; minimization; emotional reasoning; labeling and overgeneralization; personalizing; phonyism; and perfectionism (Dryden & Ellis, 1988). Beck's (1967, 1976) list includes these: dichotomous (polarized) thinking; overgeneralization; selective abstraction (selective sensitivity); personalization; catastrophizing (exaggeration or magnification); overinclusive labeling; global undifferentiated judgments; arbitrary inference (mind reading); and minimization. Typically, maladaptive ideation is linguistic in form, but Beck believes it can also be imagistic—for example, visual fantasies. Disqualifying the positive and "should" statements are errors others have proposed (Freeman et al., 1990).

Types of cognitive distortions are defined both by their content (what one thinks), and by the logical errors of thinking used (how one thinks). Self-statements (Ellis) or automatic thoughts (Beck) manifest people's guiding beliefs or schemas, making it possible to evaluate them as dysfunctional when they disrupt internal harmony by generating inappropriate, excessive emotionality, discomfort and suffering, and/or ineffective behavior that is self-defeating because it interferes with the person's attainment of important objectives (Beck, 1976).

Persistence of Dysfunctional Patterns
Both theorists try to explain why dysfunctional patterns tend to persist; this persistence is called stability-maintaining processes in our comparative framework. Ellis (1986) states that irrational beliefs tend to be strongly held without defining what that means. Sometimes, he implies feedforward processes—observing that demandingness and other absolutistic beliefs are retained in the face of starkly contradictory reality because they color people's perceptions of reality and their inferences about it (Ellis et al., 1989). Anticipations of failure, hidden agendas, and difficulties in thinking about thinking are additional proposals used to account for the persistence of dysfunctional patterns.

Consistent with the rational-emotive assumption that irrational beliefs (iBs) cause dysfunction, Ellis proposes that specific irrational beliefs function to maintain dysfunctional patterns: They perform a function similar to that of defense mechanisms in psychoanalysis. He provides these illustrations:

1. People mistakenly assume that their dysfunctional patterns are attributable to situations (A causes C) rather than to their absolutistic beliefs (B causes C):

2. They attribute their problems to events in the past rather than to their constant reindoctrination of themselves in the present with their absolutistic beliefs:

3. They believe that simple acknowledgment of an irrational belief should be sufficient to produce change, whereas interrelated changes in cognitions, emotions, and actions are all required to break an established pattern:

4. People adhere to a philosophy of low frustration tolerance, are committed to short-term hedonism, and avoid the short-term discomfort necessary to achieve long-range goals:

5. They have created secondary and sometime tertiary concerns about their disturbances—such as becoming depressed about their depression, or anxious about their anxiety:

6. They rely on classic defense mechanisms, such as rationalization or projection, to redefine their problems or to minimize the problem severity rather than honestly taking responsibility for their problems:

7. They believe there are certain benefits linked to maintenance of their ideas and actions: Always expecting the worst avoids the misery of unexpected disappointments:

8. People act according to their beliefs and expectations, eliciting responses from themselves and others that they can use as evidence to confirm their views—the self-fulfilling prophecy.

Through such beliefs people are assumed to perpetuate their problems; cling to self-defeating, habitual patterns; and remain resistant to change (Ellis & Dryden, 1987, pp. 22–24).

These beliefs might be summarized as (a) misidentification of the nature of the problem (1, 2 and 3), (b) escalation of the problem through positive feedback processes (4 and 5), (c) examples of the functional utility of the dysfunctional patterns (6 and 7), and (d) self-generated negative feedback processes. Ellis argues that because people forcefully preserve their irrational patterns, forceful methods of intervention are required if significant and durable changes are to occur.

Beck and his associates have also catalogued a variety of processes that function to maintain dysfunctional patterns. First, there is the coherence characterizing established schemas; they are held firmly in place by networks of cognitive, behavioral, and affective elements, making them difficult to alter (Beck et al., 1990). This condition is especially true when schemas function as a "closed system," as in a depression. There, contradictory information is screened out, only selected memories are processed, thinking is repetitive and recurrent, and the effects of one's actions are interpreted as confirmation of one's biased expectations.

Second, people often do not have conscious access to the cognitive organizations that govern what they do. For example, people who typically avoid situations that upset them—phobics, for example—will not be aware of their maladaptive ideation as long as they maintain a comfortable distance from the phobic situation (Beck, 1976).

Third, it is always hard for people, including scientists and therapists to make a paradigm shift from a model or schema that is sometimes accurate to another that is strange, unfamiliar, and productive of either discomfort or even anxiety (DiGiuseppe, 1986). Finally, established schemas display some functional utility, yielding short-term benefits, despite their distorting biases and longer term limitations (Freeman, 1987; Freeman & Leaf, 1989).

Ellis proposes that the same basic irrational beliefs underlie diverse disorders, earning criticism for inattention to diagnostic issues and for failing to design differential treatments for different syndromes (Kendall & Bemis, 1983). Discussions of applications of rational-emotive therapy to specific conditions—alcohol and substance abuse, marital discord—apply the same basic theoretical model.

Beck argues that a person's cognitive organizations, including the rules for processing information, predispose them toward certain modes of adjustment and adaptation. Therefore, each type of disorder manifests prototypical schemas, cognitive distortions, and recurrent cognitive biases (Robins & Hayes, 1995). Prototypical cognitive-emotional-behavioral patterns for major clinical disorders are described in terms of their maladaptive or dysfunctional content and their typical distortions (Freeman et al., 1990). A convenient listing of 14 typical beliefs associated with each kind of personality disorder is provided (Beck et al., 1990). These descriptions are used in differential diagnosis and in targeting key beliefs for therapeutic change. For example, depressed patients are said to display a negative view of their world, a negative concept of themselves, and a negative appraisal of their future—a set of symptoms termed the cognitive triad. Their ideation is saturated with the notion of loss—past, present, and future—prompting cynicism, self-criticism, pessimism, and feelings of sadness and behavioral apathy, marked by the inclination to avoid, escape, and give up (Beck, 1976; Beck et al., 1979). People with paranoid conditions covertly maintain hostile and critical views of others, believing others to conceal malevolent intentions behind an agreeable facade. Those struggling with paranoid ideation often adopt a posture of wary suspicion and distrust to avoid being misled. This distortion in turn can prompt a variety of others, such as rejecting apparent signs of approval, interpreting ambigious interpersonal cues as provocations, or seeing other people's actions as deliberate, direct impingements upon their personal domain (Beck, 1976).

THE PROCEDURAL MODEL

The general objective of cognitive psychotherapy is to identify dysfunctional habits of thought and modify or restructure them to help the patient develop and use desired patterns of thought, emotion, and action. Clients are trained to replace maladaptive beliefs with rational beliefs and habits of thought (Ellis & Dryden, 1987); they are also helped to revise dysfunctional schemas and faulty information processing to formulate more effective patterns of functioning (Beck, 1995; Freeman & Simon, 1989).

Overview

Beck and Ellis have independently devised general therapy strategies that are similar in substance though differing somewhat in terminology. These strategies are described variously as structured, active and directive, semantic or insight-oriented, educative or reeducative, and time-limited methods for alleviating psychological and behavioral problems (Beck et al., 1979; Ellis, 1970; Ellis & Dryden, 1987). The term *structured* connotes a planned and deliberate approach rather than implying a defined sequence of procedures that must be followed in lock-step fashion. The theorists describe a general strategy but are less explicit about specific tactics.

General Strategy

Their broad strategy has several aspects. After deciding that their approach is suitable for the client's problems, agreeing on general treatment goals, and briefing the client on the nature of the approach, the strategy addresses the following specific subgoals:

1. Describing the dysfunctional patterns and the kinds of behavior episodes in which they occur
2. Identifying the cognitive elements evaluated as dysfunctional, whether distorted, irrational or illogical
3. Making the client aware of the dysfunctional cognitions as they occur during specific behavior episodes
4. Rendering explicit the links between the dysfunctional cognitions and their unwanted affective and behavioral consequences
5. Disrupting the operation of those cognitive components by providing additional, or contradictory, rationally and empirically based information
6. Modifying or reorganizing dysfunctional patterns to accommodate the new information, thereby increasing the patterns' functional utility and the likelihood that clients can achieve their goals
7. Ensuring that changes are regularly implemented in real-life situations.

This logically ordered summary does not mean that therapy is actually conducted in that specific sequence. Rather, therapy is an iterative process, particularly when more than one pattern is to be altered.

Because the process requires clients to modify their dysfunctional beliefs, schemas, and habitual ways of processing information, the targeted changes are in clients' personal conceptual and propositional models. Ellis considers the modifications to be partly intuitive, a condition he calls insight, but he also recognizes changes to be semantic as well; changes occur in meanings clients construct concerning people and events. Beck also interprets the crucial changes to be semantic in nature, relying on modification of clients' networks of meanings. A leadership role and active participation by therapists is essential; their knowledge and experience are needed to determine the direction in which therapy should proceed. Both theorists refer to the educative aspects of the therapist's role, described as "teaching" or "training" clients in more effective ways of thinking about themselves and their problems. Clients must collaborate, following the rules described by the therapist, and make committed efforts to specify and change their troublesome patterns. A basic optimism underlies both therapies: Few clients are considered immune to the possibilities of an educative approach; everyone can learn to control the content and organization of their thoughts, emotions, and actions.

Describing the strategy as time limited may be a way of characterizing it as a targeted, contrasted to open-ended, approach. Termination of treatment occurs when patterns targeted for change no longer occur within relevant behavior episodes and preferred patterns occur instead. In rational-emotive therapy terminology, treatment can be terminated when clients successfully identify, challenge, and counteract their irrational beliefs and no longer experience inappropriate negative emotions or act dysfunctionally when they do (Ellis & Dryden, 1987). Although cognitions are the direct targets of cognitive therapy, success is measured by corresponding and desired changes in emotions and behavior (Freeman et al., 1990). Ellis's strategy is said to accomplish results relatively quickly, often requiring no more than 15 to 20 sessions. However, depending on the nature of clients' problems, their motivation for change, and the intricacies of their life situation, therapy may last for several years (Freeman et al., 1990).

Specific Tactics

Both theorists argue that specifying a standardized treatment is a mistake. What cognitive therapists actually do in the privacy of therapy is unknown (Golden & Dryden, 1986), but all agree that much variation in practice exists and there is not a slavish uniformity among practitioners (Arnkoff & Glass, 1992). Initially, Ellis proposed few specific methods, based in part on his view that "there is no one-to-one relationship between theory and practice" (Ellis & Dryden, 1987, p. 47), and perhaps also because he opposes "the formulation of absolute, dogmatic therapeutic rules" (Ellis, 1985, p. 316). Dryden (1987); Ellis & Dryden (1987); and Walen, DiGiuseppe, & Wessler (1980) report more specific methods which have subsequently been developed. Techniques have been freely borrowed from other approaches and used as needed to carry out rational-emotive therapy's strategic tasks. Ellis describes this as an eclectic and multimodal approach, which he considers an advantage (Ellis & Dryden, 1987).

Beck and his colleagues also reject an emphasis on technique and insist on procedural flexibility adapted to clients' life circumstances. Therapists must understand the conceptual and propositional model of cognitive therapy and be familiar with the wide range of techniques available. The emphasis is on the assessment of clients' status and the design of treatment plans specific to their situation, considering both their problems and their unique ways of integrating and using information, because clients learn in different ways. Techniques can then be selected from all those available, many of which are not exclusive to cognitive therapy. Therapists may have to improvise, as some trial and error is often necessary, and a degree of artistry is involved (Beck et al., 1990; Freeman et al., 1990).

Flexibility of technique may be desirable, but when theorists provide no basis for deciding which methods are most useful for what purposes, under what conditions, there is no link between the conceptual and procedural components of the model.

Although therapists may seek to achieve similar results, they may go about it very differently. Beck's colleagues acknowledge that cognitive therapy and rational-emotive therapy show similarities in theory and strategy, but they consider differences in therapy relationships and therapy methods to be of major significance.

Establishing a Therapeutic Relationship
Both theorists believe establishing and maintaining a therapeutic relationship to be a necessary but not sufficient condition for therapy success and that building the relationship begins with the first contact. Ellis advocates an *authoritative teacher-respectful student* model, whereas Beck proposes a *friend and adviser collaborative* model. The relationship is both a precondition for and a part of the process of psychotherapy as it involves cultivating client attitudes and behaviors essential for successfully pursuing other therapy goals. Four client relationship roles are discernible in both procedural models:

1. A willingness to be candid in disclosing details of their personal lives
2. A confident trust that the therapist will work in their best interests
3. Openness to the information, advice, and suggestions provided by the therapist, and a readiness to implement prescribed tasks
4. The development of a calm and deliberate method of problem solving in imitation of the model the therapist consistently provides

Ellis's description of therapist relationship roles is similar to those proposed by others (Ellis & Dryden, 1987). Therapists must provide a good role model for the client (Ellis, 1970), remaining calm and composed, informal, easygoing and relaxed, capable of being humorous when appropriate, and unruffled by whatever irrationalities, criticisms, or hostilities might arise. They should behave in a consistently open, warm, genuine, and caring fashion. Undue warmth is to be avoided, however, lest some clients' excessive needs for love or approval be unwittingly reinforced. Genuineness can be conveyed by a willingness to disclose personal information when appropriate, such as giving personal examples of similar problems and how the therapists resolved them. Unconditional acceptance should be extended to clients in simple recognition of their existence as fallible human beings, but this should not prevent therapists from being evaluative or critical of some aspects of clients' thought and behavior. Acceptance should be reflected in patience with clients' efforts to progress and an encouraging optimism regarding their capabilities for doing so. Therapists should also offer not only affective empathy but also philosophic empathy, demonstrating that they understand the philosophic rationale lying behind clients' feelings. As teachers, therapists should speak from a position of knowledge and confidence and be capable of conveying empirical facts and logical thinking in clear and incisive ways. Therapists speak authoritatively but never as authoritarians.

Ellis recommends a forceful, directive style, including forthright, vigorous confrontation, argumentation, and disputation of clients' habitual modes of thought. He recognizes that some rational-emotive therapists disagree—for example, Garcia (1977) and Young (1977) advocate a more gradual, gentle, and considerate style. Ellis, however, argues that forceful methods are needed to counter clients' powerful adherence to their habitual irrational beliefs. (Compare our comparative framework, in which stability-maintaining processes are difficult to overcome.) Ellis does accept the possibility that different styles may be useful with different kinds of clients as an empirical question that should be addressed with research (Ellis & Dryden, 1987). A minilecture orients clients to the nature and process of rational-emotive therapy. Brief descriptions of therapist and client roles are included, and clients' active participation is stressed. The ability of clients to choose to work at "undisturbing" themselves is emphasized.

Beck's view of therapist relationship roles recognizes that therapists inevitably serve as role models for clients, but he suggests that therapists function as friend and adviser rather than as confident, authoritative teacher. This role should be conveyed by a patient, sensitive, sympathetic, understanding, considerate, and tactful manner. Empathic respect for but not necessarily agreement with clients' thoughts and ideas is conveyed to signal acceptance of all client thoughts, even farfetched, superstitious ones (Haaga & Davison, 1991). This openness will instill trust and a willingness in clients to collaborate.

The preferred relationship is described as a collaborative inquiry in which therapists and clients jointly proceed through a process of guided discovery as opposed to direct confrontation or instruction. In this process, they both work to unravel clients' assumptions and beliefs, explore the meaning of distressing events, and facilitate awareness and verbal articulation of clients thoughts and images. In doing so, therapists maximize clients' participation, minimize the impression that the therapist seeks to impose ideas or values, and reduce chances of client resistance and noncompliance. This process, termed *collaborative empiricism*, enables clients to develop a general problem-solving approach for use in addressing future problems (Beck, Freeman, & associates, 1990; Freeman, Pretzer, Fleming, & Simon, 1990). In the terms of our comparative framework, clients are helped to construct a behavior episode schema through social modeling in successive therapy sessions; this schema then serves as an umbrella for guiding effective problem solving in other life episodes that are causing clients difficulty.

A collaborative relationship is more than mere cooperation; in such a dyad, the respective participants make different but equally important contributions to the achievement of a common purpose. Rational-emotive therapy proponents might argue that their model is a type of collaborative relationship—teacher and learner—but they have not done so.

Diagnosing Problems and Prescribing Treatment

Traditional clinical practice calls for an initial specification of clients' presenting condition, called a diagnosis (*dia* = thorough, *gnosis* = knowledge) and conceptualized as the client's current dysfunctional states. Next, therapy goals are established that specify alternative, preferred states to be sought. Selecting optimal and feasible forms of intervention to help the client move from dysfunctional to preferred states completes the prescriptive phase of the process.

Ellis spends little time gathering diagnostic information about clients' dysfunctional patterns. Clients may be asked to complete (1) a biographical information form, giving information on their personal, occupational, and family background; presenting and past complaints; estimates of personal strengths and assets; and prior treatment history, and (2) a personality data form to elicit prototypical irrational beliefs they use, and to reveal which of these may underlie their problems (Ellis & Dryden, 1987). This information only supplements within-session analyses. Ellis does consider it important to explore clients' preferences for and expectations of the service they would like to receive so that unrealistic anticipations and/or preferences can be corrected by the therapist. This seems to be Ellis's way of describing how therapy goals are established. He does not provide descriptions of the kinds of goal statements needed. It is apparent that the diagnostic and prescriptive process used in other therapies is omitted; in rational-emotive therapy, treatment begins in the first session.

Ellis is often criticized for failing to follow diagnostic and prescriptive processes, but if, as he proposes, the general nature of clients' problems is known in advance—that is, their reliance on one or more kinds of irrational beliefs—no formal diagnosis is necessary. He assumes that correcting those irrational thoughts will alter related dysfunctional emotional and behavioral states; therefore, consideration of the advantages and disadvantages of alternative therapies is not required. Without a clear statement of intended outcomes, however, there are no explicit criteria against which treatment effectiveness can be assessed by therapists, clients, and others.

Beck and his associates advocate a comprehensive diagnostic and prescriptive process without expending excessive time or sacrificing development of a good working relationship. These therapists do suggest an outline for such an evaluation (Freeman et al., 1990). It includes gathering information about presenting problems; current life situations; and developmental, medical, and psychiatric background. A correspondence is sought between the client's presenting condition and standard psychiatric syndromes, such as those presented in the *DSM-IV* (APA, 1994), because each disorder is presumed to involve a characteristic set of dysfunctional beliefs and faulty information processing modes (Beck, 1995). This comparison defines the general form of the problem domain. Analysis of clients' specific dynamics occurs during treatment. Therapy goals should be made explicit, including both the problems to be overcome—the dysfunctional states—and the positive outcomes desired—the preferred states. Multiple goals should be prioritized, with more readily achieved goals given higher initial priority. Provision is made for dealing with clients' questions and concerns before beginning therapy (Freeman et al., 1990).

Both cognitive therapy and rational-emotive therapy assume that some kind of dysfunctional habits of thought underlie dysfunctional emotional and behavior patterns. However, not all of a client's habits of thought are faulty, so the task is to discover the ones that are. The basic strategy for doing so uses various methods to encourage clients to describe specific episodes in which their problems have occurred. This process activates in the therapy setting the dysfunctional thought habits, like behavior episode schemas, that govern and direct their dysfunctional patterns. Once faulty schemas are activated, clients can be helped to identify and describe them explicitly.

Teaching the Client an Analytical Model

Both Ellis and Beck believe it is useful to teach clients a model with which to understand the troubling events. Ellis teaches his ABC model using minilectures and relevant books, accompanied by in-session practice to cultivate skill in its use. Beck thinks it is better for clients to learn to use his model through exploring events specific to their own experience. Didactic explanations can be used, preferably with clear examples, when clients encounter difficulty in providing the kinds of information the therapist needs. Providing clients with a conceptual model not only guides the process but simultaneously reassures the client that his or her problems can be analyzed and understood, and replaces the client's negative evaluations of helplessness and hopelessness with positive hopes and expectations (Meichenbaum, 1985). There are also books about the cognitive therapy approach that can be used with clients to facilitate their participation.

Activating the Dysfunctional Patterns
In keeping with the principle that behavior always occurs in the here and now and can be changed only when it is occurring, the strategy of Beck and Ellis is to seek to elicit clients' descriptions of specific day-to-day behavior episodes when adverse emotions and unsatisfactory behavioral outcomes occur. They use four kinds of behavior episodes:

1. Past episodes
2. Episodes currently occurring in clients' daily lives, including therapy sessions
3. Imagined episodes that clients anticipate may occur in the future
4. Behavior episodes linked to the unfolding therapy process that occur under real-life conditions

In rational-emotive therapy, clients' temptation to dwell on childhood events is discouraged because the focus is on how current patterns function rather than on their origins. Clients are also dissuaded from an endless outpouring of their feelings, as affective catharsis is not considered helpful. Clients must focus on the habits of thought that generate those feelings. Ellis asks clients to describe current behavior episodes in which the dysfunctional patterns occur, then he moves promptly to analyze them into their ABC components. He seeks a brief working description of A (the most pressing event associated with the distress), not as it was but as the client viewed it. Then, a description is sought of the emotional and behavioral consequences (Cs) that the client supposes to be caused by A. These are not disputed but are accepted as natural consequents of the client's irrational beliefs; emotions are trusted as indisputable facts about a client's experience. However, differences are noted between appropriate versus inappropriate feelings, and self-helping versus self-defeating actions. Next, the therapist poses questions to elicit the client's ongoing self-talk assumed to intervene between A and C, which manifests the underlying beliefs (Bs), both rational and irrational.

The therapist's skill and persistence are required over several sessions, as clients often confuse affective with cognitive descriptions: They describe how they feel rather than how they think, and they tend to report rational beliefs first. For the client to identify irrational beliefs, the therapist must usually continue questioning until the client's absolutist musts and grandiose demands on himself or herself, on others, and on the world are recognized. The process is simplified by the finite number of prototypical dysfunctional beliefs all clients use. Once the dysfunctional beliefs are identified, change procedures begin (Ellis & Dryden, 1987; Haaga & Davison, 1991).

This part of Beck's strategy—defining the problem areas—should be completed early in treatment. The methods used in a process of guided discovery are called the *cognitive probe* because they function to identify dysfunctional cognitive components. As client and therapist collaborate in generating detailed accounts of affective, behavioral, and cognitive events occurring in each problematic episode, the therapist uses three tactics: (1) facilitating the client's retrospective recall and reconstruction, (2) prompting the client to use imagistic representations, and (3) training the client to engage in self-monitoring to track the contents of his or her experience during relevant behavior episodes.

Retrospective discussion relies on clients' episodic memories of salient past behavior episodes and is the primary tactic used. Such memories, however, are often fragmentary and incomplete, so therapists must engage in a process of filling in the gaps. They use questions to prompt a complete report of all aspects of the episode—for example, the emotions that occurred. Cognitive components are of special interest, so the therapist uses probes to activate dysfunctional ideation or automatic thoughts he or she expects to have taken place during the behavior episode and to have caused the troublesome emotions and actions (Beck, 1976). If this tactic is unsuccessful, the imagery technique can be used. With imagery, clients are encouraged to imagine the episode as if it were happening right now. Often they will then experience the automatic thoughts just as they would in the real episode. Alternatively, they can be asked to imagine a similar future episode to try to activate their maladaptive beliefs and emotions. The therapist looks for the possibility of idiosyncratic, stereotypic, and dysfunctional interpretations of these experiences, as these can indicate the ultimate meaning of the event to the client and point to the core dysfunctional schemas underlying the client's overall reaction.

Clients differ in their effectiveness in using these methods, so they usually need training to become proficient in observing their functioning in behavior episodes and in reporting their observations. When they make their thoughts verbally explicit, these thoughts become part of clients' awareness and are thereby susceptible to change. Training focuses on self-monitoring of ongoing experience, particularly subvocal verbalizations—the self-talk or automatic thoughts that cognitive therapists assume always to occur in association with behavior. Clients are instructed to use these monitoring skills on a daily basis and to bring what they learn to subsequent therapy sessions. To overcome the fallibility of memory, cognitive therapy practitioners ask clients to keep records—such as a journal—make audiotapes, or use a Dysfunctional Thoughts Record (DTR) form to record a brief description of an episode, their emotional response, and the automatic thoughts they had. They are also requested to rate on a scale of 0 to 100 the intensity of the emotion and their degree of certitude or belief in each automatic thought. These ratings are intended to overcome clients' tendencies to think about events in categorical, all-or-none rather than dimensional terms. The records advance the collaborative inquiry in therapy sessions into the details of the client's problems.

To identify underlying core schemas that produce the client's automatic thoughts and behavior, Beck recommends that the therapist scan for recurrent themes or patterns among the thoughts, infer the underlying commonalities, and offer these as a hypothesis, seeking the client's feedback concerning its merits. A downward arrow technique (Freeman et al., 1990) can also be used, with the therapist choosing an apparently important automatic thought as a starting point and pursuing its implied guiding schema with the client.

Some assume that cognitive therapy limits itself to "intellectual" change. Beck (1987) argues that cognitive change depends on a certain level of affect and that clients must not only articulate dysfunctional beliefs but must also experience the related affect if their faulty thought habits are to be changed. Similarly, Ellis asserts that clients hold onto "mustabatory" beliefs "strongly, forcefully, and vehemently," therefore requiring a reindoctrination that is also done "forcefully and vividly with dramatic impact" (Ellis & Dryden, 1987, p. 30). In other words, all parts of a dysfunctional pattern must be activated to ensure that the total pattern can be influenced by the intervention. (This is comparable to the principle of unitary functioning and is analogous to activating a behavior episode schema as defined in our comparative framework.) What constitutes a "sufficient level" of emotion and how the therapist can determine that it occurs is unclear.

Restating the Problem

Once dysfunctional patterns become explicit and intelligible, client and therapist can seek agreement about the client's cognitions that need to be altered. In cognitive therapy terms, clients recognize the effects of their automatic thoughts and dysfunctional schemas on their emotions and actions (Freeman et al., 1990). In rational-emotive terms, they recognize the recurrent link between their irrational beliefs and dysfunctional affective and behavioral consequences, and realize that other ways of thinking would be better (Ellis, 1970; Ellis & Dryden, 1987). Ellis terms this the attainment of *intellectual insight* by the client, a necessary step although in and of itself insufficient to achieve emotional and behavioral change.

Disrupting the Operation of Dysfunctional Patterns
The basic strategy for altering dysfunctional beliefs or schemas involves disrupting them with contradictory information the client has ignored or misinterpreted, and/or presenting incompatible new information. If the client accepts the validity of the contradictory information, the dysfunctional thought habits are disrupted. He or she develops doubt about the habitual meanings or beliefs. Self-organizing tendencies then begin to function to restore coherent psychological organization. In Beck's (1976) terms, when clients recognize maladaptive cognitions and their discrepancy from reality, they have a tendency to correct them automatically by finding a way to reorganize or restructure them to create an integrated pattern that appears more likely to be useful in achieving personal goals.

Therapists play an active role in selecting the disrupting information and guiding clients toward desirable cognitive restructuring. In addition to changing specific dysfunctional patterns, a broader objective is to teach clients to be more effective personal scientists, as described earlier. For Ellis, the strategy relies on the "logico-empirical method of scientific questioning, challenging and debating," to induce clients to surrender their irrational beliefs (Ellis, 1979, p. 73). Beck refers to it as the implementation of a rational, empirical outlook, best pursued in a collaborative manner with the client—that is, *collaborative empiricism* (Beck, 1976).

Many errors or dysfunctions exist in clients' habits of attending to, interpreting and evaluating, thinking and reasoning about, and anticipating events. Therefore, a diversity of methods is necessary to fit the kinds of errors to be corrected; each has been named; for example, reattribution, decentering, distancing, reverse role play, time-projection techniques. They are too numerous to be described completely; for convenient summaries, see Beck et al. (1990), Dryden (1987), Ellis and Dryden (1987), and Freeman et al. (1990). We have summarized them here in groups that aim at influencing each type of cognitive functioning represented in our comparative framework:

1. *Methods Focused on Information Collection Functions:* Clients are taught the importance of maintaining distinctions between observations ("I see") and inferences ("I think"); their perceptual distortions are questioned and challenged and more accurate perceptions identified.

2. *Methods Focused on Cognitive Directive Functions:* Faulty goal setting is addressed by helping clients consciously formulate their guiding purposes and

intentions when they have not made their goals clear to themselves, or by challenging unwarranted expectations and demands—such as Ellis's "must" and "has to."

3. *Methods Focused on Control Functions:* Dysfunctional problem-solving habits are changed (a) by teaching clients to distinguish between observable "facts" and their interpretation, and between hypotheses ("I assume") and tests for verification ("I have confirmed"); (b) by showing clients the fallacy of thinking in dichotomous rather than dimensional terms, of thinking stereo-typically of themselves and others, of overgeneralizing from a limited obser-vations, or of assuming that they are the central focus of events; (c) by re-hearsing clients in the skills of alternative thinking, such as by examining varied hypotheses to account for the behavior of other people; (d) by chal-lenging clients' means-end and consequential thinking by taking their as-sumptions to ludicrous extremes; (e) by marshaling contradictory evidence to refute clients' erroneous conclusions; and (f) by questioning the benefits or secondary gain that clients derive from maintaining dysfunctional beliefs.

4. *Methods Focused on Cognitive and Emotional Regulatory Functions:* Clients learn to use rules of evidence to question their expectations or assumptions of helplessness and futility, to challenge their assumptions of personal respon-sibility for all the outcomes that occur, to identify and critique inappropriate evaluations of their characteristics, capabilities, or performance—such as un-warranted or excessive self-criticism—and to test such evaluations against consensual reality. Alternative, more realistic evaluative habits of thought may be suggested and practiced. Emotions also regulate peoples' behavior, so emotions whose habitual occurrence is inappropriate are identified and cri-tiqued, and the cognitions that activate those emotions identified, challenged, and restructured.

Reorganizing or Restructuring Dysfunctional Patterns
As habitual dysfunctional patterns of thought are disrupted, raising clients' doubts as to their utility, alternative ways of perceiving and thinking are si-multaneously considered. However, additional methods are necessary to en-sure that alternative, more effective patterns are adopted and become coher-ently interrelated.

Beck asserts that clients cannot entirely relinquish their dysfunctional habits until they have incorporated new adaptive beliefs and strategies to take their place (Beck et al., 1990). Rational-emotive therapy calls for clients to reorganize their cognitive habits by substituting or replacing dysfunctional components with others that have greater functional utility—such as substi-tuting realistic desires, preferences, or wishes for unrealistic, overgeneralized demands. When this shift occurs, changes in emotions and behavior are assumed to follow.

Two broad types of restructuring methods are used: (1) helping clients discover what is needed through discussion and evaluation; and (2) pointing it out to them if they are unable to discover it on their own. Ellis often uses (2), ranging from providing general information and advice to prescribing specific ways for clients to think, and using various persuasive tactics to induce them to adopt his suggestions. Homework assignments may help clients cultivate the use of his suggestions, such as rehearsing rational self-statements between sessions. Clients may also be induced to devise their own self-statements and then to record and verbally recite them, on the presumption that these eventually become internalized by repeated usage (Ellis, 1970). Beck prefers (1), seeking shared decisions in finding desirable alternative patterns. Both procedural models seem to assume that desirable patterns of thinking are already available, as from clients' prior experience with others, or can be discovered by clients through therapy discussions. Changes in emotions and actions are expected to follow automatically from cognitive restructuring.

Additional methods are often used to ensure that revised patterns include coherent cognitive, affective, and action components. Clients are led to practice new ways of thinking through *cognitive rehearsal techniques,* this strategy enables them to experience the different feelings that result and to consider the different actions that are implied. *Imagery techniques* (imagining relevant behavior episodes) or role playing (simulating relevant episodes) are other forms of rehearsal. When clients have difficulty constructing effective action-patterns, therapists may demonstrate how they might act, by standing, gesturing, and speaking, and have clients emulate the pattern; this is called modeling. Such methods enable clients to try a behavior in the safety of the therapy context before using the new patterns in the real world. Finally, skill training may be used in those instances where extensive coaching seems needed, as in assertiveness training, social encountering, or communication skills. Ellis (1980) is skeptical of the utility of skill training and warns against its use before clients' dysfunctional cognitions are altered.

Facilitating the Implementation of Changes Under Real-Life Conditions
Some clients are eager to try out new patterns in the real world, but others are ambivalent, hesitant, and fearfully resistant to risking such exposure. The most frequently used method to foster such generalization is *homework assignments.* These are designed to expose clients to specific contexts, with the expectation that using their restructured patterns will produce desired consequences, serving to validate the new patterns' functional utility and to encourage more frequent use of them.

Ellis actively encourages clients to take chances and to try things, even though they are difficult—such as seeking opportunities for social interactions. To cultivate persistence in the face of uncertainty, he prescribes "stay in there" exercises that enable clients to discover they can tolerate discomfort. Antiprocrastination exercises demonstrate that benefits accrue from doing things promptly. Shame-attacking exercises—such as publicly doing silly and outlandish things—enable clients to discover that catastrophic results do not invariably follow. Where external rewards are not immediately present, he teaches clients to reward—and penalize—themselves.

Beck also advocates scheduling goal-oriented activities with clients; an example is trying an "empirical experiment" such as reciting positive self-statements for a week and evaluating the result. He asserts that collaborative planning and breaking assignments into doable chunks work best. He begins with easier assignments so clients can experience and be credited with success. Small successes cultivate their belief in their capability to proceed independently in the future, and encourage them to engage in joint planning of additional steps. Arranging such activities is considered particularly important early in the treatment of depressions to generate some degree of pleasure and an elevation of mood as a means of counteracting clients' assumptions that they can derive neither enjoyment nor a sense of competence from their actions.

Facilitating Alterations in Developmental Pathways

Neither rational emotion nor cognitive therapy specifically proposes that therapy may start clients on an altered developmental pathway that could lead to further changes through normal processes of living and learning. Ellis sees his ABC analysis strategy to be a generic skill that can be a powerful tool for further healthy development after therapy ends. He arranges opportunities for clients to practice it to develop skill in its use as a preferred problem-solving strategy. He induces clients to teach the model to others, undertaking to "talk them out of" some of their ill-founded beliefs. He also uses role-reversal, during which clients guide the therapist through a problem using the ABC strategy. Recognizing that most clients tend to slip back into familiar but dysfunctional patterns, Beck and others propose relapse prevention methods (Beck et al., 1990). These include reviewing gains made and successful strategies used, remembering cautions against unrealistic expectations of future problem-free living, encouraging anticipation of problems, and teaching trouble-shooting methods.

Evaluating Client Progress and Outcomes

Hundreds of judgments are made during therapy: How is the process going? Is a mid-course correction needed? Have our goals been attained, or achieved to the client's and therapist's satisfaction? However, the bases for such judgments and the processes by which they are made are not clearly specified in either therapy.

Ellis says little about process evaluation; Beck gives it some attention. His recommended format identifies the points at which evaluations should occur, the kinds and sources of data that should be collected, including clients' reports, but not the criteria therapists should use for evaluating progress. He says each therapy session should begin with solicitation of client reports of their current status and events of the previous week, followed by their evaluation of the prior session and a review of the results of their homework assignments (Feeman et al., 1990). After the main agenda items are completed and new homework assignments planned, the therapist should seek the evaluative reactions of the client regarding the current session before it ends. Client feedback is thus solicited at two points in each therapy session. This involvement helps maximize the collaborative participation of clients; it also helps therapists evaluate progress and decide whether changes in strategy or methods are needed.

There is some attempt to specify outcome criteria for deciding when to terminate therapy. To paraphrase Ellis, this state has been reached when clients can (1) identify their dysfunctional cognitions—irrational beliefs; (2) replace them with more functional or rational ones; (3) perform effective, self-helping actions; and (4) experience appropriate emotions in the process (Ellis & Dryden, 1987, pp. 60–61). Therapists have direct observational evidence about these outcomes from clients' functioning during therapy sessions and indirect evidence from clients' reports. Therapists appear to have the responsibility for deciding whether a satisfactory outcome has been attained. Only two evaluative conclusions are implied: Plan either to terminate or to continue treatment. Ellis recommends follow-up sessions and evaluations after termination to determine the client's condition and to remove any remaining obstacles to sustained improvement (Ellis & Dryden, 1987). If long-lasting changes are sought in clients' philosophical orientation, the task of evaluation becomes more intricate and difficult.

Beck's cognitive therapy approach is similar. Conditions appropriate for terminating therapy are described as "corresponding and desired changes in emotion and behavior" (Beck et al., 1990, p. 284) or "better adaptive ability" (Freeman & Simon, 1989, p. 360). Consistent with their collaborative approach, cognitive therapists advocate consensus judgments for process evaluations; they look for substantial agreement between clients' self-report and therapists' observations, and the reports of significant others when appropriate. If clients, their associates, and the therapist say things are better, then they are better. It is suggested that termination of treatment be accomplished slowly (a tapering process) so as to allow for ongoing modifications and corrections. The frequency of treatment sessions should change from weekly to biweekly, and then monthly, with follow-up sessions scheduled at three- and six-month intervals, and booster sessions scheduled on an as-needed basis.

EVALUATION OF THE APPROACH

Cognitive therapies advocate use of empirical scientific investigations to evaluate theories and methods. Therefore, one might expect their conceptual and propositional models to have been tested against and modified by the evolving knowledge base in the human sciences. That has not been the case. Cognitive therapies emerged either before or coincident with developments in the cognitive sciences and were driven by the practical experiences of professional applications, ahead of many developments in relevant scientific fields (Mahoney, 1995). Proceeding independently of scientifically established knowledge is the norm in the history of psychotherapy (Dawes, 1994; Freedheim, 1992; Lazarus & Davison, 1971). Beck and his colleagues have not attempted a detailed comparison of their model with the relevant scientific knowledge base. Ellis (1977b) attempted to demonstrate that rational-emotive therapy was confirmed by existing empirical evidence, but Mahoney (1977b) demonstrated that Ellis's review was highly selective. He showed that it included many references of only remote relevance to rational-emotive theory and was relevant to the merits of cognitive approaches in general, rather than to rational-emotive therapy in particular. He noted that science can only disconfirm theories, not prove them true.

The importance of cognitive processes in human functioning is now widely accepted, but how best to conceptualize these processes and their relationships to other aspects of humans and their contexts remains a problem (Meichenbaum, 1995). The rational-emotive and cognitive models have been commended for having broken important ground, but these plaudits have been accompanied by criticisms of their multiple shortcomings. For example, Ellis's ABC strategy has been faulted as unidirectional in form, despite his disclaimers, and far too simplistic, even though clinically useful. Beck's view of schemas has been criticized for being vague and imprecise, and hence incapable of being adequately tested and subjected to verification (Kendall & Bemis, 1983). Detailed critiques of the conceptual and propositional aspects of the two approaches are available (e.g., Arnkoff & Glass, 1982; Guidano, 1988; Mahoney, 1988; Neimeyer, 1995a).

Beyond the theoretical soundness of these models lies the question of the utility of their procedural approach. Evidence that clients benefit from a treatment does not prove that the theoretical model that spawned it is valid. Therefore, empirical process and outcome evaluations of the procedural models are important, regardless of the soundness of the conceptual and propositional models. Despite enthusiastic claims for its clinical efficacy, rational-emotive therapy has been described as the least adequately tested of all the major psychotherapy approaches (Hollon & Beck, 1994). Some outcome evaluations have begun to appear (e.g., DiGiuseppe, McGowan, Simon, & Gardner, 1990; Finn, DiGiuseppe, & Culver, 1991). Cognitive therapy has been more extensively studied, apparently demonstrating it to be equally effective or superior to alternate treatments. A widely cited meta-analysis of 28 outcome studies of unipolar depression (Dobson, 1989) showed cognitive therapy to have outperformed pharmacotherapy, behavior therapy, "other" psychotherapies, and a wait-list condition. However, the methodological merits of meta-analyses remain controversial. Many additional studies that appear to document its utility in the treatment of depression have been considered promising (Segal & Shaw, 1986), but others have considered them so conceptually and methodologically flawed as to preclude any legitimate conclusions (Abramson, Alloy, & Metalsky, 1988). Determining which ingredients may be responsible for clinical improvements remains a problem, and comparisons with other therapies are confounded by the eclectic use by cognitive and rational-emotive therapists of methods from many approaches. For example, researchers studying their use with other conditions, such as panic disorder and bulimia, have been unable to determine whether patients symptomatic improvement can be attributed to changes in their models of cognitive processing or to behavioral modifications sought simultaneously (Haaga & Davison, 1991).

CHAPTER 11

Cognitive-Behavioral and Skill Training Therapies

HISTORICAL PERSPECTIVE

Humanistic/nondirective and psychodynamic/psychoanalytic approaches, though different, share some implicit assumptions: (1) People behave incompetently because their "sickness", or intrapsychic conflict, obstructs the use of other effective and satisfying behavior patterns. (2) Patients' behavioral repertoire include those more effective responses, but they are not used or are used in dysfunctional ways. (3) Those other behaviors would occur if the obstructing "illness" or "habits" were removed or altered (Goldstein, 1995). Even behavior therapies focus primarily on altering dysfunctional behaviors, although their behavior shaping methods are aimed at teaching new behaviors. Some theorists questioned these assumptions and proposed instead that people were sick or dysfunctional because they behaved incompetently, rather than behaving incompetently because they were sick (Phillips, 1985). Often, people did not know how to behave competently; they did not have the necessary responses in their repertoire.

This shift in assumptions led to related views about psychopathology or abnormal behavior and intervention strategies. The signs and symptoms manifest in a pathological pattern were interpreted as adaptive attempts gone awry—as errors in the ways a person had learned to try to deal with different kinds of life situations or tasks. What lay behind these ways was not a disease process but rather "healthy urges" to produce desired consequences (Waters & Lawrence, 1993). These responses are the best the person has been able to do within his or her personal learning history. The person is considered deficient, or at least weak, in skills necessary for effective, satisfying daily living (Goldstein, 1995). The behaviors are signs of incompetence rather than of illness or abnormality.

In this view, the appropriate intervention strategy would be to help people learn more adaptive ways of producing the consequences they desire in their lives. This approach requires a proactive focus on cultivating competence by learning new skills rather than a primarily remedial focus on eliminating or modifying maladaptive patterns. The traditional sequence of *abnormality (or illness)* ➤ *diagnosis* ➤ *prescription* ➤ *therapy* ➤ *cure* was contrasted to the skills approach of *client dissatisfaction or ambition* ➤ *goal setting* ➤ *skill teaching* ➤ *satisfaction or goal achievement* (Authier, Gustafson, Guerney, & Kasdorf, 1975). Therefore, a model in which trainers or educators help people or trainees learn new skills was more appropriate than a medical model of therapists curing patients. Prompting, shaping, and related operant procedures were methods created in behavior therapies to cultivate new behaviors, but growing evidence of their limitations made the need for other proactive methods increasingly apparent.

Approaches using this rationale are called cognitive-behavioral, skill training, or educative therapies. Several edited volumes summarize them and their applications to different populations and problems (e.g., Cartledge & Milburn, 1985; Curran & Monti, 1982; Dobson, 1988b; Hollin & Trower, 1986; Kendall, Vitousek & Kane, 1991; L'Abate & Milan, 1985; Larson, 1984; Meichenbaum, 1974, 1977, 1995; O'Donohue & Krasner, 1995a; Spence & Shepherd, 1983). Proponents of cognitive therapies also call their approaches cognitive-behavioral because the approaches also consider behavior (see Chapter 10). For example, rational-emotive therapy is now called rational-emotive behavior therapy and its primary journal is now called the *Journal of Rational-Emotive and Cognitive-Behavior Therapy.* However, the theoretical and procedural models of these therapists are different from skill development approaches, and the term *cognitive-behavioral* is used here in that sense. This analysis focuses primarily on five versions that have been extensively tested both empirically and clinically. They exemplify the diversity of pathways that led many professionals to create skill training/psychoeducational approaches. They are represented in our discussion by the work of Goldstein, Meichenbaum, Guerney, Trower, and Gambrill.

Arnold Goldstein, an early leader of this family of approaches, was impressed with growing evidence of the ineffectiveness of the dominant therapy approaches for people of lower socioeconomic status (SES) and less education. He viewed insight-oriented therapies as singularly middle to upper class in their philosophies, rationales, and therapy methods. They fit the typical middle-class YAVIS clients—those who were young, attractive, intelligent, verbal, and successful (Schofield, 1964)—whose childhood socialization emphasizing intentions, motivation, inner states, and self-regulation provides them with skills, resources, and motivation that fit such therapies. In contrast, the socialization experiences of lower SES patients emphasize action, consequences rather than intentions, reliance on external example and authority, and a restricted verbal code. These qualities suggest that effective therapies for them should recognize their different attitudes and behaviors. Thus, Goldstein sought alternatives (Goldstein, 1973). His *Structured Learning Therapy* or *Psychological Skill Training* is less verbal, conceptual, and introspective, and more action and interpersonally oriented. It was first applied to chronic hospitalized adult psychiatric patients (Goldstein, Sprafkin, & Gershaw, 1976; Sprafkin, Gershaw, & Goldstein, 1993). Bellack et al. (1997) have recently presented an elaborate sophisticated self training approach for treating schizophrenia. Later, Goldstein's interest shifted to problems of aggression (Goldstein, Monti, Sardino, & Green, 1979), child-abusing parents (Goldstein, Keller, & Erne, 1985), and aggressive adolescents. It was elaborated and applied to treatment of children and adolescents, and the training of various types of professionals (Goldstein, 1981, 1988; McGinnis & Goldstein, 1990). Recently, Goldstein has focused on the prosocial training of aggressive, delinquent, and drug-using adolescents in communities, institutions, schools, and gangs (Goldstein, 1990, 1991; Goldstein & Glick, 1987; Goldstein & Huff, 1993; Goldstein, Reagles, & Amann, 1990). Extensive empirical and clinical evidence supports the utility of his approach.

Meichenbaum (1974, 1977) set out to "bridge the gap" between cognitive-semantic and behavior therapies. Using theory and research about relationships of overt and inner speech and thought by Russian developmentalists (e.g., Sokolov, Vygotsky) as well as the work of Americans on the self-guiding function of private speech, he created ways of teaching people how to control their behavior through overt and covert self-talk. These efforts evolved into *Stress Inoculation Training* (SIT), a comprehensive, multifaceted, multilevel, flexible approach with applications to children and adults in diverse settings with varied problems (Meichenbaum, 1985, 1986). It is an exemplar of this family of approaches for these reasons: (1) Meichenbaum's "transactional perspective" assumes that cognition, affect, behavior, and context occur in dynamic, changing patterns that can be modified through skill training. (2) Stress inoculation training views remediation as a preliminary step toward elaboration of adaptive skills that "make clients better problem solvers to deal with future stressful events as they might arise" (Meichenbaum 1985, p. 30). Extensive empirical and clinical evidence supports the efficacy of this therapy.

Guerney (1977, 1984; Guerney & Guerney, 1985), a pioneer of family-focused skill training, began with a Rogerian approach and evolved an educative strategy through clinical experiences resulting from involving parents in the resolution of their young childrens' adjustment problems, a strategy called *Filial Therapy*. From this evolved approaches for marital or *Conjugal Therapy,* and parent-adolescent *(PARD)* relationships. General strategies and methods emerged for resolving or preventing interpersonal problems and for enriching existing relationships, called *Relationship Enhancement Therapy.* Extensive research and clinical experience supports its effectiveness (e.g., Guerney, 1984; Guerney, Vogelsong, & Coufal, 1983; Ross, Baker, & Guerney, 1985), and a meta-analytic comparative review (Giblin, Sprenkle, & Sheehan, 1985) concluded that it demonstrated by far the largest effect sizes of any of 23 marital and family interventions studied.

A fourth pathway emerged in England with roots in work on human-machine interactions (Welford, 1966, 1980) and social psychology (Argyle, 1967; Argyle, Furnham, & Graham, 1981). Through a research program at Littlemore Hospital, Oxford, Trower and colleagues developed and tested a rationale, strategies, and methods for helping patients with various kinds of social inadequacies (Trower, 1982, 1984; Trower, Bryant, & Argyle, 1978). It was based on Argyle's (1967) analogy that the prototypical organization of both motor and social behavior is as a goal-directed act regulated by feedback. Trower (1995) evolved that into a *social skills training* model and provides evidence of its effectiveness with three diagnostic groups for whom social skills training has been best developed: shyness/social phobia, depression, and schizophrenia.

The context of social work traditions provided a fifth pathway. Gambrill (1977) started with behavioral approaches, but she discovered the work of Trower and others while she was a visiting scholar in London (Gambrill, 1984). She designed skill training approaches for problems of shy, socially anxious adults and the elderly, and for teaching assertion skills to adults (Gambrill, 1985, 1986, 1995a, 1995b). Her approach is supported by an integration of empirical and clinical evidence from multiple sources, along with evidence from her own research program.

CONCEPTUAL MODEL

The skill training/psychoeducational theorists discuss their procedural models in detail, but their conceptual models about the nature of humans are mostly implied. Therefore, we have pieced together their conceptual models based largely on descriptions and justifications found in their procedural models. They use multilevel concepts that encompass all the kinds of behavior in our comparative framework, but with minimal attention to biological aspects, and the interpersonal/sociocultural aspects of environments.

LEVELS AND UNITS OF ANALYSIS

The Person-in-Context and Behavior Episodes
The primary unit of analysis of the skill training/psychoeducational theorists is comparable to the person-in-context unit of our comparative framework, but different names are employed. Meichenbaum's (1985) *transactional perspective* says: "Stress is a particular dynamic relationship between the person and the environment as they act on each other" (p. 3). Using interpersonal models, Gambrill (1984), Guerney (1984), and Trower (1995) call this unit an *interpersonal transaction* or *interaction* or *situation* or *context,* and emphasize "the mutual influence between persons and environmental factors" (Gambrill, 1984, p. 106). "Situations provide the context—the rules, the roles, and goals—in which episodes and their elements are identified, defined, and understood" (Trower, 1982, p. 406). In each goal-directed episode "the individual consciously monitors the immediate situation and his or her behavior and modifies his or her performance in the light of continuous external feedback and internal criteria such as a desired outcome" (p. 418).

Goldstein, Gershaw, and Sprafkin, (1985) speak of *personal and interpersonal life tasks* with which people must cope in school, at work, in the community, with peers, family, and authorities. McFall's (1982; Schlundt & McFall, 1985) concept is *task,* defined as an episode of behavior within a context that is an organization of component processes, such as behaviors or social skills. *Social competence* is a task-oriented pattern of behavior that effectively accomplishes the goals of the task. Different tasks require different patterns of component *social skills* because tasks differ in their guiding goals and functional contexts. Task goals, while different, are often related (Graham, Argyle, & Furnham, 1980), so tasks are related in various ways. One task may be prerequisite for or facilitate success or failure in another; several may be subtasks of a superordinate task in a hierarchical organization; or tasks may be conflicting or independent of one another. Different kinds of tasks make up a person's *life space* and the relationships among them produce a *complex, interrelated life system* (Schlundt & McFall, 1985).

The theorists' prototypical procedural model operationalizes this unit in a form similar to behavior episodes as defined in our comparative framework as well as McFall's concept of task. They do this by defining, assessing, modeling, and having clients practice specific exemplars of relevant interpersonal transactions, tasks, or situations—by experiencing problematic behavior episodes.

Component Functions
The skill training/psychoeducational therapists also use units of analysis below the level of the person. People have component behaviors, functions,

or specific skills whose synchronized interactions produce different patterns of interpersonal transactions. No classification system for component functions is stated, although the concept labels employed appear to reflect the taxonomy in common use in society and/or in the discipline of psychology—for example, perception, cognition, emotion, and action.

Social Groups

Units at a level above the person are also used, primarily interpersonal units or relationships, as with parents, spouses, children, and co-workers. Most skill training focuses on teaching people to deal effectively with such relationships. The therapists refer to other contexts, such as work settings, and recognize that interpersonal relationships are embedded in different sociocultural contexts that prescribe or foster prototypical ways of dealing with interpersonal issues such as conflict.

CONTENT OF KEY CONCEPTS

Skill training models use three broad concepts to represent relevant aspects of humans and their environmental contexts: *competence, skill,* and *interpersonal contexts.* Different patterns of psychological and behavioral functioning are conceptually represented as different kinds of skills.

Competence

Skill training models focus on cultivating "effective and satisfying" behavior in "critical life situations" (Goldstein, 1981; Goldsmith & McFall, 1975), symbolized by concept labels such as *competence, performance competence* or *socially competent behavior.* A shared definition of competence, however, has been difficult to attain, partly because what is considered competent behavior is linked to socioculture norms (Conger & Conger, 1982) involving evaluative judgments about outcomes and means of producing them (Schlundt & McFall, 1985).

The concept of competence is used in five different ways in the psychological literature (Ford, 1985):

1. As a motivational construct (such as competence motivation) referring to the formulation of and persistent, effective pursuit of goals
2. As a behavioral construct referring to a repertoire of skills that a person can flexibly organize/perform

3. As a self-concept construct referring to personal agency beliefs, such as self-efficacy; these are anticipatory self-evaluative thoughts about probable behavioral effectiveness
4. As a cognitive-behavioral construct of effectiveness in obtaining valued goals
5. As a goodness-of-fit construct about patterns of functioning in which diverse person-components function smoothly together, as in internal equilibration, and in synchrony with the opportunities and demands of their contexts, as in external equilibration

The broadest meaning is any effective behavior pattern—for example, personal grooming or musical performance. In skill training models, however, competence refers primarily to social competence (Curran, 1985). M. Ford's definition captures the meanings used by most social skills approaches. Based on the idea of behavior episodes, he specifies five domains of variables that a definition of social competence must encompass:

1. The desired consequences or goals of the person
2. The social system and context within which the goals are to be accomplished
3. Variable skills or means for accomplishing the goals
4. The boundary conditions and values limiting the means that may be used
5. Both the immediate results and their personal and social consequences for future functioning

The resulting definition is this: "Social competence is the attainment of relevant social goals in specified social environments, using appropriate means and resulting in positive developmental outcomes" (M. Ford, 1987, p. 202).

This definition combines Trower's (1982) concepts of *social competence*—possession of the capability to generate relevant skilled behavior—and *social performance*—the production of skilled behavior compatible with social realities of specific situations. Trower used Carver's (1979) cybernetics model (similar to our comparative framework) to describe competent functioning. Meichenbaum's three-part social competence model—*overt behaviors, cognitive processes,* and *cognitive structures*—combined with his transactional view stressing social environments (Meichenbaum, 1985; Meichenbaum, Butler, & Gruson, 1981) includes most of Ford's criteria. Marlowe's (1985) model of social intelligence includes *social interest* and *social self-efficacy* (motivational components) and *social skills* (implementation components).

Social Skills

Trower (1995) identifies two subtypes of social skills. *Social skills* are overt communicative and instrumental actions people can perform in relevant situations (called transactional functions in our framework). *Social skill* refers to psychological functions used to construct skilled action patterns guided by rules, goals, and social feedback. Trower and others (e.g., McFall, 1982; Wallace, 1982) view information processing models as focusing on social skill—for example, decoding or receiving, decision making or processing, and response selection or sending. These are analogous to cognitive control functions in our comparative framework. Some theorists (e.g., Pierce, 1995) use Lazarus's (1991) strategy of grouping skills by the goals at which they are aimed—by function rather than content. Skills aimed at altering psychological responses are called emotion-focused, cognitive coping, or palliative strategies, and those aimed at altering person-context relationships, are called problem-focused coping. Both may involve combinations of psychological and behavioral skills.

Such broad categories are insufficient, however. All skill approaches combine content and function to identify precisely the specific skills to serve specific goals in specific contexts. The approaches differ in the specific skills they emphasize because they focus on different populations and goal-context combinations. Examples of the types of problems addressed are these: control of stress, anger, and aggressive behavior; family relationships; and addictions and chronic pain problems. Types of populations include divorced people; physically and psychologically impaired people; hospitalized psychiatric patients; children, adolescents, adults, and elderly people with social problems; and people being trained to conduct social skills training (L'Abate & Milan, 1985; Curran & Monti, 1982; O'Donohue & Krasner, 1995a).

Because skills are means for producing desired outcomes, the skills effective for producing the same outcome may differ with context, population, and developmental attributes. For example, conflict resolution skills effective in adolescent ghetto gangs may differ from those effective among five-year-old preschoolers or among upper socioeconomic families having marital conflicts. Approaches also differ in the simplicity or complexity of the skills defined. Some, referred to as *Micro* skills, are quite specific, such as using facial gestures or maintaining eye contact; alternatively, *macro* skills are complex patterns, such as selectively attending to, accurately interpreting, and emphatically responding to the emotional states displayed by others. Macro skills may be taught as units or as sets of micro skills. All the specific skills addressed by different approaches cannot be described here, but there is considerable agreement about the general importance of several kinds of skills in social tasks or behavior episodes. Because the skill training therapists focus on person-level functioning, the generic skills for which they have developed training procedures usually involve patterns of multiple kinds of responses. The basic skill concepts of our five exemplars are briefly described next. We relate these concepts to our comparative framework by listing the relevant components of Figure 4.2 (see Chapter 4) in parentheses after each skill. Here we focus on the basic macro skills. The references cited earlier provide more detailed descriptions of the micro skills that make up each macro skill.

The first two exemplars of the cognitive-behavior/skill training therapies to be considered are Trower and Gambrill. Their approaches are examined together because they are conceptually related. Both theorists consider behavior to be competent when it accomplishes goals, so behavior is not effective if a person cannot formulate appropriate, clear goals (cognitive directive function). Goals vary in scope, from starting a conversation to going out on a date, but one must also be able to use problem-solving behaviors to flexibly and creatively construct sound plans for achieving goals (remembering, information processing, and cognitive control function). People must then be able to implement their plans through skillful interpersonal self-presentations and verbal and nonverbal behaviors (communicative and action functions). Effective social behavior is situation specific and situations differ in the rules, roles, and statuses typical of the larger social contexts within which they occur (interpersonal and sociocultural environment). People regulate their behavior by monitoring relevant feedback about their and others' behavior (selective attention; information collection; perception). They must then translate accurately the meaning of that feedback (evaluating, remembering, anticipating, and information processing). Organizing and modifying the flow of their interpersonal transactions is facilitated by expectations and imaginatively taking the role of others (feedforward from anticipatory regulatory and control cognitions). The behaviors of others in interpersonal transactions can be influenced by selective use of reward and reinforcement (evaluative communicative acts of approval/disapproval or pleasure/displeasure).

Skill deficiencies in any component processes reduce people's interpersonal effectiveness, so training may be needed in any or all of them. Each skill is only one part of a person-in-context unit, so skills must be learned as parts of patterns of effective behavior in meaningful social situations or tasks (behavior episodes). People differ in the kinds of episodes in which they behave incompetently and the nature of their skill deficiencies. Therefore, the skills to be taught must be defined to fit each case and situation. Still, generic integrated programs of skills can be constructed for people with similar deficiencies. For example, skills for overcoming shyness include listening-receiving skills and sending-asserting skills. Among the listening-receiving skills are these: selective attending, providing encouragements; asking questions, paraphrasing content, and reflecting feelings. The sending-asserting skills include self-disclosure, asking favors, disagreeing, expressing negative feelings such as anger, expressing positive feelings such as affection, refusing requests, and responding to disagreement and to negative or positive feelings (Trower, 1995). Assertion skills training helps people learn to deal with prototypical interpersonal tasks (e.g., refusing unwanted or tempting requests, responding to criticism, requesting changes in annoying behaviors or negative events, apologizing, disagreeing with others, initiating and maintaining conversations, making small talk, giving and receiving compliments, expressing positive emotions, complimenting others, asking favors, and ending interactions). The specific effective skill content for each task will vary depending on differences in interpersonal contexts, such as different subcultures (Gambrill, 1995a).

The third exemplar of the cognitive-behavioral/skill training group is Guerney (1977). He stresses interpersonal relationships as the key unit of analysis and individuals as subunits in that larger "system." The skills emphasized are those that enable people to function effectively as a part of a social unit rather than skills focused primarily on their self-interest. Guerney assumes that the resolution of interpersonal problems and conflicts, and the cultivation and maintenance of satisfying interpersonal relationships, rests primarily on people's capacity to generate honest and compassionate communications to and from others—interpersonal feedback and feedforward processes—and to participate in collaborative problem solving. Both require an accurate, conscious understanding of self and others.

For Guerney, understanding is a nonjudgmental "appreciation of relationship-relevant needs, desires, preferences, aspirations, values, motivations, and emotions of one's own self and one's partners" (1977, p. 12). Notice that the emphasis is on explicit awareness (consciousness, selective attention) of personal goals (cognitive directive function), self-evaluative thoughts (cognitive regulatory function), and emotions (arousal function). Moreover, appreciation of relationships among all those factors requires thought processes that identify and interpret their implications and interrelationships (cognitive problem solving, remembering, information processing).

Guerney uses concepts representing all the functions identified as psychological functions in our comparative framework. Emotions (arousal functions) are stressed but are not defined. He seems to use the prevalent commonsense taxonomy (e.g., anger, fear, guilt, affection, or love). Consciousness of and selective attention to one's own states and those of others are considered prerequisites for effective behavior because they give people intentional control over what oftentimes are unconscious, reflexive, interpersonal behaviors. Guerney assumes that people function as goal seekers (cognitive directive function). People have a strong need "to know where they are headed," and satisfaction results from fulfilling goals guiding an interpersonal relationship. Positive self-concepts and self-esteem (cognitive regulatory function) are favorable anticipatory evaluative thoughts about one's capabilities and characteristics and about how one is viewed by others. Motivation refers to patterns of clear goals and evaluative expectations that one can behave in ways that will produce satisfying outcomes. Conservation of energy refers to another kind of anticipatory evaluation like the expectancy-value models of motivation—that is, how hard people will work is a function of the value they place on the result.

Compassion is a psychological pattern of sympathetic, supportive attitudes and emotions about people's concerns, positive evaluations about their hopes, and a willingness to try to protect them from distress. Combining compassion and understanding yields empathic understanding whose accuracy and utility rests on several kinds of behaviors. First, careful and accurate observation (selective information collection and perception) of communications, feelings, and actions of self and others is essential for obtaining the data from which empathic understanding can be constructed. Second, for empathic understanding to influence interpersonal relationships, it must be conveyed to others through empathic communication (communicative acts) that accurately or "honestly" convey one's empathic understanding, phrased in compassionate terms. Mutual empathic communication produces interpersonal relationships characterized by mutual trust, openness, affective and attitudinal warmth, and collaborative problem solving.

Interpersonal conflict is another concept whose meaning is not made explicit. Conflict resolution results from collaborative problem solving (cognitive control functions, remembering, information processing, communicative acts). Personality is one's "relatively enduring preferred ways of dealing with emotions, people, and self-concept-related thoughts" (Guerney, 1984, p. 175). (This is similar to one's repertoire of interpersonal behavior episode schemes in the guiding comparative framework.)

Guerney defines five macro skills for constructing empathic understandings, for communicating them honestly and compassionately (empathically), and for collaborative problem solving. Each uses psychological and behavioral components. *Expressive skill* combines empathic understanding and communication to increase people's conscious understanding of their own self-concept, emotions, conflicts, problems, desires, and goals, and to increase their ability to communicate those things to others in ways that elicit in others conscious, compassionate, collaborative understanding and responding. Subskills include these:

1. Phrasing statements as personal views rather than objective truths to reduce defensiveness on the part of others.
2. Stating past, present, or anticipated feelings, such as emotions and evaluative thoughts, if they are important to the issue.
3. Phrasing statements in terms of specific events (for example, "When you did that it . . .") rather than in terms of generalizations and conclusions (such as "You always . . .") to reduce defensiveness.
4. Stating positive assumptions, attitudes, expectations, and feelings about the other related to the specific issue being considered to encourage positive rather than defensive responding.
5. Stating precisely your requests for the other to change so he or she clearly understands, and describing the positive feelings such changes would produce. Expressive skills are used to convey ideas and feelings to which others are expected to respond.

People use *empathic skill* to respond to others' communications so as to increase their own personal attractiveness to others by making the others feel respected, understood, and appreciated. People also use empathic skill to elicit self-revealing statements from others to facilitate their own understanding of their self-regarding attitudes, emotions, conflicts, problems, desires, and goals; another use is to help others understand themselves better and therefore be able to better select realistic and effective courses of action. Subskills of the empathic skill include these:

1. Listen intently.
2. Convey interest and understanding while others are talking.
3. Try to absorb other people's mood; concentrate on their subjective world.
4. Try to understand the meaning of things from the other person's point of view.
5. Consider possible differences between their reactions and yours.
6. Imagine a tentative statement that will convey your understanding honestly and compassionately.
7. Evaluate this imagined statement from the other's perspective and screen out potentially threatening words or phrases.
8. Communicate the statement declaratively without using first-person pronouns.

9. Monitor the other person's reactions as you make the statement and modify it accordingly.
10. Accept corrections readily.

Mode switching involves the *discussion and negotiation skills* of recognizing when to shift back and forth between using expressive skills and functioning as an empathic responder to facilitate mutual understanding and respect and effective collaborative problem solving. Guidelines for when to switch from expressive to responder skills are specified and taught.

Interpersonal problem/conflict resolution skills assume that the most realistic and enduring problem/conflict resolutions are those that best serve the goals and attitudes of all concerned and that consider all relevant factors, including emotional ones. There are several subskills:

1. Ensuring that all are satisfied that they have clearly expressed all relevant personal concerns and have been empathically understood.
2. Determining whether current conditions are favorable for initiating problem solving or whether different ones need to be created.
3. Trying to imagine possible solutions that would adequately serve the interests of all parties rather than mere compromise or splitting-the-difference.
4. Sharing and evaluating solution proposals using all expressive, empathic, and mode-switching skills.
5. Clearly specifying the details of what, where, when, and so on of any solution agreed on.
6. Imagining possible difficulties and exceptions and agreeing in advance about how to handle them to avoid negative feelings and misunderstandings.
7. Agreeing on a follow-up process to facilitate implementation and modification if necessary.

Facilitation or teaching skill uses expressive, empathic, and mode-switching skills to elicit, encourage, teach, and reward the use of relationship enhancement skills by others. Explicit description, modeling, and favorable evaluative communications are key subskills taught. *Self-change skill* helps people to implement changes in their own psychological and behavioral patterns in relevant interpersonal contexts to implement interpersonal agreements and objectives. *Helping-others-change skill* is used to help others implement agreements to change their psychological and behavioral patterns in relevant contexts. *Generalization and maintenance skills* function to cultivate long-term use of changed patterns of functioning, and of the entire package of relationship enhancement skills, in real-life relationships and behavior episodes after relationship enhancement training is completed. Learning and using these skills involve prospective thought and both simulated and real-life practice.

The fourth exemplar is Meichenbaum. His rationale for Stress Inoculation Training (SIT) reflects a *transactional perspective*. For example, stress is neither stimuli nor responses, but a pattern of mutually influential person and context factors. Intervening in "the cognition-affect-behavior-consequences chain" is necessary to alter stress patterns (Meichenbaum, 1986, p. 347). Meichenbaum's key concepts encompass cognition, affect, consciousness and attention, behavior, environment, stress, and coping.

Cognition includes all psychological processes called governing functions in our comparative framework. Several subconcepts refer to different aspects of cognition. *Cognitive events* are the flow of current contents of perception and thought that are conscious or can be readily made conscious as they occur during behavior episodes (also behavior episodes in our comparative framework). These events include perceptions of subjective states and environmental interactions, current intentions/goals, attributions, expectancies, and task-relevant and irrelevant thoughts. They include not only thoughts but also "images, symbolic 'words,' and gestures and their accompanying affect" (1986, p. 348). The content and organization of such events within a behavior episode, which he labels *self* or *internal dialogue*, "can influence how one feels and behaves" (Meichenbaum, 1985, p. 7). A key method by which people manipulate and control the content and organization of cognitive events (thought processes) is by the use of language in private speech or self-talk, called a mediational process.

Cognitive structures are a person's repertoire of previously learned "tacit assumptions and beliefs that give rise to habitual ways of construing the self and the world. The individual's personal schemata, current concerns, hidden agenda, and personal goals influence the way information is processed and the way behavior is organized" (1986, p. 348). Each structure or schema includes both ideational and affective components (like behavior episode schemes in our comparative framework). From among a person's total repertoire of structures or schemas, specific ones are activated within and organize each behavior episode. They operate like a "paradigm" that selectively influences the content and organization of perception, thought, and action, and like "selective filters" that influence a person's interpretation and appraisal of events.

Cognitive event flows and creation, change, or elaboration of cognitive structures, is influenced by *cognitive processes* (Meichenbaum's label for remembering and information processing); these are the ways people "process information including search and storage mechanisms, inferential and retrieval processes" (1985, p. 7). People use multiple information processing strategies (Meichenbaum & Gilmore, 1984) that typically operate automatically and unconsciously, but they can become knowledgeable about their repertoire of information processing strategies and can consciously use and control them for different kinds of tasks, which Meichenbaum calls *metacognition*.

Problem-solving strategies (cognitive control functions) select and selectively organize ideas, perceptions, and memories to imagine potential courses of action to solve problems or produce desired outcomes. *Confirmatory bias* (his term for the stability-maintaining processes in our comparative framework) is a self-fulfilling prophecy process, in which people selectively perceive, remember, and interpret experience to filter out information that might disconfirm existing beliefs or schemas; it usually occurs automatically and unconsciously. Because this bias is not employed consciously and intentionally, it plays a key role in maintaining maladaptive behavior patterns.

Appraisal processes (cognitive regulatory functions) play a critical role in stress. Following Lazarus (1991; Lazarus & Folkman, 1984), stress inoculation training uses two subconcepts. *Primary appraisal* is anticipatory evaluative thoughts about the potential impact on or threat to the person of some current, imagined, or anticipated events. *Secondary appraisal* is an anticipatory evaluation of the person's capabilities for dealing with those events—of his or her *coping resources and options*. These are similar to the concepts of personal agency or self-efficacy beliefs. *Affect* is stressed but is never clearly defined. It refers to emotional states, such as fear, anxiety, and anger, and may include physiological manifestations of arousal, such as pain, tenseness, or gastric distress. Affects are considered stress responses resulting from appraisal processes, so positive affects are seldom mentioned, and the role of affects in behavior patterns other than stress is not discussed.

Consciousness and attention are also key concepts. People are assumed to behave usually in "mindless and scripted" or habitual ways, using unconscious processes. Therefore, they are often unaware of the cognitive structures, processes, personal goals, evaluative thoughts, problem-solving habits, or aspects of their communicative and instrumental behavior—gestures or vocal expressions are examples—that guide, organize, and direct much of the moment-to-moment flow of their daily behavior. However, people can usually become aware of events within and around them by using selective attention to produce selective observations (information collection). This is a key to the development of adaptive, and the modification of maladaptive, behavior. Enactive experience enables people to discover that "old cognitive structures are questioned and unwarranted" and to reconstrue "one's self, the world, and the commerce between the two," because it produces feedback information that influences changes in previously learned "structures." Thus, change requires consciously directed selective attention to relevant cognitive, affective, and behavioral habits, environmental events, and information to "interrupt the automaticity of their acts" or "the scripted nature of their behavior" (Meichenbaum, 1986, p. 349). (This is like the proposition in the comparative framework that learning requires awareness of relevant events.)

Behavior refers to all communicative, instrumental, and information collection acts through which transactions with the environment are carried out. Speech is of special importance because others use it to regulate a child's behavior, and practitioners of stress innoculation training adopt the assumption of developmental theorists like Vygotsky that such experiences provide the basis for the child's learning to regulate his or her own behavior with self-talk and later with private speech. *Coping* refers to a "constellation" of many specific acts organized to deal with stressful situations.

Stress refers to a complex pattern of person-context transactions. Its components include (1) A challenging or threatening environment, or *stressor*; (2) *appraisal,* or anticipatory evaluative thoughts, of the potential impact on the person of that stressor, and his or her ability to cope with it; and (3) emotional, physiological, and cognitive *stress reactions* activated by the appraisal. People deal with stress through two types of coping responses. *Intrapersonal or emotion-focused coping responses* are attempts to alter their stress reactions and cognitive appraisal processes. *Interpersonal or problem-focused coping responses* function to deal with or modify the stressor. Note that these concepts refer to the targets of the coping responses rather than the kinds of responses used. Stress inoculation training does not propose a single preformed kind of coping response; which should be used depends on the nature of the stressor, the characteristics of the persons involved, and the sociocultural context. The skills taught are aimed at helping the person anticipate stressful situations and prevent stress reactions, which Meichenbaum terms *stress inoculation.*

The last exemplar of cognitive-behavioral/skill training therapy to be reviewed is Goldstein. His definition of skills training specifies his key concepts: "Psychological skills training is the planned, systematic teaching of the specific behaviors needed and consciously desired by the individual in order to function in an effective and satisfying manner, over an extended period of time, in a broad array of positive, negative, and neutral interpersonal contexts" (1981, p. 3). Goldstein's focus is not on cultivating rigid habits that will operate in different kinds of social situations but on teaching specific skills and how to combine them flexibly in different ways for different situations. This knowledge empowers people to organize and regulate their actions consciously and adaptively to serve their purposes.

Goldstein stresses the teaching of specific overt behaviors or interpersonal skills (communicative, instrumental, and information collection actions) by which people can influence different kinds of interpersonal contexts, such as communication, relationship, leadership, and conflict management skills. Psychological factors such as self-understanding, values, attitudes, or insight, which are the focus of traditional psychotherapies, may also change if new skills produce different results, but they are not primary targets of skill training. However, Goldstein assumes that actions are selectively directed, organized, and regulated by subjective responses, so his basic skills include psychological components. *Personal skills* are emotional, observational, and cognitive skills such as self-control, decision making, goal setting, moral reasoning, and setting problem priorities. *Emotions,* both a person's own and those of others, are very important in interpersonal relationships; examples of these are anger, fear, and embarrassment. Learning how to observe them accurately and control them are important skills. Like others, Goldstein does not define or provide a taxonomy of emotions, nor does he explain how the emotions relate to other psychological or behavioral components.

Skill training will be ineffective unless trainees are motivated to learn; sufficient competency motivation must be present to drive them. Implicit in Goldstein's formulation is a hierarchical model of motivation. First, there must be some interpersonal states or outcomes that a trainee wants to attain (personal goals). Trainee effectiveness and satisfaction in achieving these goals is the objective. *Effectiveness* refers to producing desired impacts on others (environmental consequences) whereas *satisfaction* refers to the "inner consequences" of "pleasure, gratification, or personal satisfaction" resulting from effectiveness (positive evaluative thoughts and emotions). However, skill training focuses not on teaching personal goals but on teaching the means or skills by which goals can be specified and achieved in different kinds of interpersonal situations. Trainees must believe that their current skills are inadequate and that the skills to be taught will succeed. They must "need" and "want" to learn those skills and must believe they can learn them (personal agency beliefs). Clients must adopt learning the new skills as a subgoal necessary for achieving their primary goals.

Trainee motivation must be a conscious commitment to goals and subgoals. Training will not be effective unless trainees can selectively attend to relevant variables within and around them to produce accurate observations (information collection, perception) about the training task. They must also be able to observe their own and others' thoughts, feelings, and actions in that situation; this helps to guide their learning and performance and to maintain their motivation. Although the social situations (interpersonal and sociocultural contexts) with which people must cope are diverse, some recur in many kinds of behavior episodes. Goldstein constructed 10 detailed groups of skills for prototypical interpersonal situations; he called these *The Prepare Curriculum for Teaching Prosocial Competencies* (Goldstein, 1988). Ten macro skills are defined, each involving a set of subskills, which in turn are composed of micro skills. Each set of skills and training procedures resulted from an extensive review of relevant empirical evidence and professional experience and were subjected to careful empirical evaluation in applied situations by Goldstein and his colleagues.

The 10 macro skills and their major subskills are summarized in four groups. Macro skills are organizations of psychological and behavioral components specified in his basic concepts.

Group I: Some skills are useful in most if not all interpersonal situations.

1. *Problem-solving skills* undergird the use of other skills because they are "tools" for making "judicious decisions" about how to behave in any situation. Problem-solving steps include these: *Stop and think* carefully about the nature of the situation and your reactions; *identify the problem; gather information from your own and others' perspectives; identify possible alternatives* for dealing with it; *evaluate potential consequences and outcomes* and use that evaluation to choose an alternative. These skills may be used as a private cognitive problem-solving process (cognitive control function), or collaboratively through communication with others.

2. *Interpersonal skills* are patterns of cognitive, observational, and communicative skills generic to effective human interactions, and are similar in many ways to what others call assertiveness skills. There are 50 subskills organized into six groups: *Beginning social skills* (communicative skills); *advanced social skills* (carrying out collaborative activities); *dealing with feelings; alternatives to aggression; skills for dealing with stressful situations;* and *planning skills.*

3. *Situational perception training* teaches selective attention, observation, and perception skills for obtaining accurate information about what is going on in, and one's reactions to, interpersonal behavior episodes so that accurate understanding can guide behavior and misperceptions can be avoided.

Group II: Some skills are useful for dealing with episodes in which anger and aggression may occur.

4. *Anger control training* teaches skills for controlling one's own emotional state of anger because it often functions as a precursor to aggression.

5. *Moral reasoning training* involves skills for dealing with "values-relevant" but ambiguous situations that raise questions about what values are worthwhile, how to apply one's personal values in that situation, and what to do when two values conflict.

Group III: Some skills are useful for people in recognizing and dealing with their own and others' emotions.

6. *Stress management training* teaches physical and mental activities to control and reduce the hormonal, chemical, cardiovascular, digestive, muscular, and related physical/physiological manifestations of the stress response (biological functions), thereby enhancing the person's ability to cope adaptively with stressful situations.

7. *Empathy Training* provides skills for accurately perceiving and non judgmentally understanding what others are feeling or thinking and for sympathetically conveying that understanding to them.

Group IV: Social groups have rules and processes by which they operate, so effective social group participation requires skills for understanding and using group processes.

8. *Recruiting supportive models* teach skills for identifying, seeking out, establishing, and maintaining relationships with others who encourage prosocial functioning and who, in their own lives, effectively use or model prosocial skills, because a responsive environment is essential both for maintenance and transfer of newly learned skills.

9. *Cooperation training* teaches skills for performing effectively in cooperative task structures that involve working with others for mutual benefit.

10. *Understanding and using groups* provides skills for understanding how groups operate and the "group forces" that influence their behavior, and how to use that understanding to try to gain a measure of control over the content and outcomes of group interactions.

Interpersonal Contexts

All the skill training theorists assume that maladaptive or psychopathological patterns for which no organic cause exists are faulty learned ways of dealing with social behavior episodes and personal psychological responses to them; in other words, these patterns are faulty cognitive, emotional, and coping patterns that are a function of the environments in which they were learned and presently occur. While the theorists recognize that all interpersonal interactions occur in larger sociocultural contexts, their rationales and intervention strategies emphasize qualitatively different behavior episodes that involve direct interpersonal transactions with significant others; they believe that maladaptive patterns can be modified by altering the behavior pattern and/or the environment. Of the four categories of environments in our comparative frameworks, Meichenbaum emphasizes interpersonal and sociocultural ones. The content and strategies occurring in interpersonal transactions reflect the current sociocultural context within which they are embedded, and the sociocultural backgrounds of the participants.

For Goldstein, *interpersonal contexts* refers to the broad array of positive, negative, and neutral interpersonal behavior episodes a trainee may confront and which differ in terms of demands and opportunities they present the trainee. Included are episodes with peers, teachers, parents, co-workers, authorities, or community groups aimed at different kinds of goals and regulated by different kinds of rules. For example, there may be group pressure and forceful persuasion to conform to group goals or values and to behave in ways contradictory to the person's own goals and values. Because the effectiveness of skills is determined by the response from the context to their use, the most powerful training approaches involve both teaching the skill and influencing the context to be appropriately responsive to the performance of the skill. Skill training occurs in specific contexts or behavior episodes. A trainee may become skillful in a training episode, but if the skills are to be used over extended periods of time, called *maintenance,* and across a broad array of behavior episodes, called *transfer,* the training must occur over time in samples of simulated and real-life interpersonal situations. The people trainees choose to associate with in turn provide contexts that will support or reject the use of the prosocial skills they have learned. Trower (Hollin & Trower, 1986) emphasizes that "behavior is inseparable from the moral context and moral rules of conduct of the community—the structuring rules that give the behaviour inter-subjective and negotiable meaning . . . all such rule systems operate in an essentially public domain" (p. 252).

Different approaches focus on different kinds of interpersonal contexts. For example, Gambrill, Trower, and Meichenbaum have focused primarily on kinds of problematic social situations faced by adult and elderly people; Guerney emphasizes family and family-like social relationships; and in his recent work, Goldstein has focused on problematic interpersonal contexts faced by adolescents. Meichenbaum and Goldstein also emphasize differences in cultural contexts and how they may influence interpersonal transactions embedded within them.

PROPOSITIONAL MODEL

All these approaches adopt a propositional model similar to that of our comparative framework. Trower and Gambrill use control system models proposed by Argyle (1967; Trower, Bryant, & Argyle, 1978) and Carver (1979; Carver & Scheier, 1984). Goldstein and Guerney rely on Bandura's social learning model and Rogerian, Sullivanian, reinforcement, or modern educative approaches. Meichenbaum combines social learning, developmental models of relationships between language and thought, and behavior therapy principles of learning. Bandura's (1986) latest description of the propositional foundation of his social learning model is very similar to our comparative framework. His presentation is relied on in this analysis because these theorists primarily discuss applications rather than the propositional assumptions of his model. Sometimes they discuss their propositional models, but much is often implied in their description of their procedural models, so we rely on those implications as well.

All aspects of a person are dynamically related so a person can function as a unit. The principle of unitary functioning means that both intra- and interpersonal aspects must be coherently interrelated. For example, for Meichenbaum (1985), cognitive interventions are only one of several possible "points of entry into what are essentially interrelated processes (emotions, physiological reactions, behavior, social consequences)" (p. 58). Gambrill (1985), following Trower, argues that it is essential to focus not only on what people do and say in interpersonal contexts but also on the processes that organize the use of those skills, including "attention to goals and plans, perception and translation of social signals, feedback, self-presentation, ability to take the roles of others, knowledge about the rules for appropriate behavior in specific situations as well as verbal and nonverbal skills" (p. 327). Goldstein (1981) and Guerney (1984) similarly emphasize the unity of the person, as proposed by Bandura (1986): "Social cognitive theory embraces an interactional model of causation in which environmental events, personal factors, and behavior all operate as interacting determinants of each other" (p. xi).

Humans are capable of self-direction and self-regulation. The assumption of personal agency is basic to understanding and changing people's behavior patterns, often referred to with the term *motivation.* Humans are proactive in seeking preferred states and consequences through effective relationships with their contexts rather than simply reacting to environmental demands and constraints. Most human behavior is purposive—it is oriented toward producing future states and consequences; it is "motivated and regulated by internal standards and self-evaluative reactions. . . . Self-directedness is exercised by wielding influence over the external environment as well as enlisting self-regulatory functions" (Bandura, 1986, p. 20). People change their behavior patterns through an intentional mediational process that involves the self-directed and regulated interaction of private speech and thought. A key way to change affect, thought, and behavior is to change a person's selective attentional and appraisal habits (Meichenbaum, 1977). People are "goal seekers"; "The trick is to find out what the clients want and what they do not want for themselves, and then to show them that the things you wish to teach them will help them to get what they want and avoid what they do not want" (Guerney, Brock, & Coufal, 1986, p. 170). Psychological helping methods are designed to help people "fully develop their potentials and capitalize on the opportunities available in their social environment, or change their attitudes to accept what is beyond their power to change" (Kanfer & Goldstein, 1991, pp. 1–2). Each individual is a self-regulating, goal-directed system that continually monitors its performance and makes decisions about how to behave based on that feedback (Hollin & Trower, 1986, vol. 2). How is this accomplished?

Cognitive and emotional functions exert a causal, organizing influence on behavior. The content and strategies of thought influence emotions and the content, organization, and execution of actions; emotions affect thought processes and variations in biological functioning in both anticipatory and reactive ways. That is the basis for psychological-behavioral unitary functioning and personal agency. In Trower's and Gambrill's control system model, *motivation, goal,* and *translation* refer to cognitive processes continuously specifying consequences toward which a current behavior pattern is directed and interpreting motivational inputs and perceptual feedback to produce effective behaviors. For Meichenbaum, *internal dialogue* refers to cognitive processes that interpret current *cognitive events* (specific perceptions, emotions, and thoughts) in the framework of currently operative cognitive structures (goals, self-evaluations, schemas). To do this, a person uses *cognitive processes or strategies* (problem-solving heuristics) that produce relevant *coping responses.* Goldstein (1973) encompasses these cognitive functions within Bandura's concepts of *incentive-motivational components, retentional components,* and *motor reproduction components.* Cognitive personal skills include *emotional* and *self-control, decision making,* and *goal setting* (Goldstein, 1981). Guerney's concepts of *empathic understanding and communication,* and *collaborative problem solving* reflect this assumption of cognitive causality.

Conscious regulation of thought processes makes intentional change possible. Repeated practice of psychological-behavioral patterns makes them automatic so they can be performed as a unit without forethought, conscious control, and regulation. Such habits are useful because they efficiently produce effective patterns of functioning in frequently experienced life situations. Some habits, however, can be maladaptive and self-defeating. The initial learning of a habit, or changing an existing habit, requires directing attention to its content and organization, and to the conscious formulation and practice of preferred patterns in relevant contexts.

People usually behave in a mindless and scripted way (Meichenbaum, 1985). Habit "is a much more common determinant of social behavior than cognition" and most social transactions are guided by habits or learned rituals; "to change a behavior then we must think before we act . . . [because that] 'deautomatizes' the maladaptive behavioral act" and makes possible the learning of more adaptive behaviors (Meichenbaum, 1977, p. 210). Interpersonal responses trigger reactions in others. "Usually, this triggering action takes place automatically and unconsciously—that is, outside our awareness, [but] by learning to be acutely aware of what has hitherto been unconscious . . . and by learning to understand and to alter responses accordingly, people can gain control over what previously has been mysterious and has worked mainly at an unconscious, 'reflexive' level"). People's capacity "to consciously control those interpersonal behaviors that they initiate and those that they make in response to the interpersonal behaviors of others" increases their effectiveness (Guerney, 1984, p. 176). Goldstein, Gambrill, and Trower stress conscious understanding and acceptance of the training rationale, conscious commitment to goals and processes of training, and carefully directed attention to conscious monitoring and interpretation of feedback signals about relevant aspects of themselves and their contexts.

Language is a learned tool for the conscious regulation of thought, emotion, and behavior. Language is a pervasive auditory (speech) and visual (writing) perceptual experience, but by itself it is meaningless. It becomes a tool for manipulating and conveying meanings when perceptible patterns of linguistic symbols are systematically linked to imagistically and abstractly coded experiences and ideas through personally, socially, and culturally shared coding rules—such as word definitions, grammatical rules, and syntax. Individuals learn the code through socialization; hearing speech is linked to the flow of a person's experiences and actions from birth onward. They also learn through formal instruction, as in schools. Language is thus used to consciously organize and regulate interpersonal relationships and patterns of psychological functioning across the life span. Cognitive-behavioral and skill training theorists all rely on this proposition in both the formulation of self-regulation and communication skills, and in their skill training methods. Not understanding other people's language code is an important source of interpersonal misunderstandings. Because of language differences between client and therapist "their very thinking about or conceptualization of" symptoms, feeling states, and behaviors may differ (Goldstein, 1973, p. 48).

Some theorists explicitly make this a core proposition. Guerney (1984) asserts: "The resolution of interpersonal problems and conflicts rests mainly on a person's capacity to generate honest and compassionate communications to and from others" (p. 177). Interpersonal conflict or problem resolution results from collaborative problem solving that is accomplished through "a complex dialogue" conducted through using mutual patterns of expressive and empathic responding skills. Meichenbaum (1977) rejects the idea that thought is "nothing but talking to oneself." He avoids "equating inner speech with thought" but describes "inner speech" as one important aspect of thinking (p. 13). He asserts:

> In short, I am proposing that behavior change occurs through a sequence of mediating process involving the interaction of inner speech, cognitive structures, and behavior and their resultant outcomes. Mediational processes involve recognition of maladaptive behavior (either external or internal) and this recognition must come to elicit inner speech that is different in content from that engaged in prior to therapy. The altered private speech must then trigger coping behaviors. Some clients require explicit teaching of such coping responses and this is where the technology of behavior therapy is of particular value (p. 218)

People construct representations of possible behaviors and consequences by observing the behavior of others. How do people become aware of potential new behavior patterns that are not already in their repertoire and the potential efficacy of these? How do they learn to use existing behaviors in new ways? One way is through self-initiated trial and error experience. The skill-training approaches, however, all propose that the most efficient way is through watching others effectively perform in relevant social situations, called *modeling*. Bandura's (1986) rationale is illustrative: "By observing others, one forms rules of behavior, and on future occasions this coded information serves as a guide for action" (p. 47). However, he asserts, such representations are not rigid scripts or specific responses. Rather, they are generalized representations or models containing both conceptual and propositional knowledge about predictive and casual contingencies among specific kinds of behavioral and environmental events; they are the rules and strategies that can guide the generation of a version of that pattern shaped to fit the specific situation in which it is performed. (This is similar to the functioning of behavior episode schemas in our comparative framework.)

Modeling may function as an instructor, inhibitor, disinhibitor, facilitator, stimulus enhancer, or emotion arouser, and these effects occur in combinations (Bandura, 1986). *Observational learning,* considered the source of most new behavior patterns, is manifest "when models exhibit novel patterns of thought or behavior which observers did not already possess but which, following observation, they can produce in similar form" (p. 49). *Inhibitory or disinhibitory effects* strengthen or weaken inhibitions over performance of behavior that has been previously learned. *Response facilitation effects* occur when others' actions increase the likelihood that an observer will perform previously learned behaviors they have not used "because of insufficient inducements, rather than because of inhibition" (p. 49). *Environmental enhancement effects* result from attention-directing rather than behavior-cueing functions of modeling. Observers' attention may be directed to objects, environmental events, or settings that they may subsequently use to serve their purposes. *Emotional arousal effects* occur if emotions are vicariously aroused in an observer when a model displays emotional reactions.

Performance skills result from successful practice of modeled behaviors. It is one thing to have an idea about how to behave and quite another actually to skillfully do it. Learning to behave skillfully in interpersonal situations requires practicing the use of one's conceptual model of how to behave to organize and guide one's actions in relevant situations in ways that produce desired consequences. The actions must be rewarded or reinforced; this is called *enactive learning* by Bandura (1986). (This is like the proposition in our framework that behavior can be learned only when it is occurring.) Practicing in relevant imagined or simulated behavior episodes is called *rehearsal* or *participant modeling*. Successful practice produces several results: (1) It links guiding conceptions and performance skills into integrated packages that can function as a unit when activated. (2) It increases the skill with which the behaviors can be performed with variations as necessary to fit different social situations because situations are similar but they are never identical. Therefore "skilled activities are seldom performed in exactly the same way; they must be varied to fit different circumstances" (Bandura, 1986, p. 111). (3) Practice may reveal inadequacies and produce changes in guiding beliefs: "Change in one's cognitive structures is most likely to occur by discovering through enactive experience that old cognitive structures are questioned and unwarranted and that the adoption of new, more adaptive structures is rewarding" (Meichenbaum, 1985, p. 9).

The learning and performance of social skills is regulated by their social consequences. All five theorists agree that people learn skills when feedback following their use indicates that the skills work, are reinforced, or are rewarded—that is, they produce consequences that serve people's guiding goals and values. This is true for all kinds of skills (Trower, Bryant, & Argyle, 1978). For example, chronically aggressive youth have discovered that aggressive behavior" is very often richly, reliably, and immediately rewarded. It works; it pays off; it is reinforced—thus making it behavior that is quite difficult to change" (Goldstein, 1988, p. 2). Note, however, that the goals, skills, and consequences implied in this statement would typically be labeled antisocial: dominating others, stealing or damaging others' property, or hurting or exploiting others for personal gain. Thus, value judgments are involved by both client/trainee and therapist/trainer concerning which kinds of goals, skills, and consequences are judged desirable (Guerney, 1977).

The focus of the approaches, discussed here is on prosocial skills for cultivating positive interpersonal relationships and intrapersonal comfort and satisfaction; therefore, the desired consequences represent the "attainment of valued social goals" (Gambrill, 1995b, p. 268). "A primary goal . . . is to provide the client with high expectations that when the client emits the behavior being taught, it will result in gratification of very significant needs—that is, social needs (Guerney, 1984, p. 177). All five theorists implicitly assume that basic social needs or goals for everyone are approval, acceptance, affection, encouragement, and support by significant others. Providing such consequences contingent upon specific kinds of behavior will be rewarding and will lead to the learning of a causal contingency between that behavior and those consequences. It follows that relationships with significant others who are supportive of and who model the desired social relationships will facilitate maintenance and generalization of the use of those behaviors (Goldstein, 1988).

Practice of skills in diverse contexts increases their maintenance and use in new contexts. Following World War II, psychotherapists typically assumed that once clients problems' were straightened out in therapy, those gains would automatically transfer to their everyday lives. Unfortunately, the overwhelming result of many studies of psychotherapy outcomes was that "much more often than not, transfer and maintenance of intervention gains did not occur . . . gains did not persist automatically; transfer and maintenance did not necessarily follow" (Goldstein, 1995, p. 384). This discovery led to the conclusion that specific strategies and methods were necessary to facilitate generalization to new settings, called *transfer,* and over time, called *maintenance.* A set of principles and guidelines for facilitating maintenance and transfer were abstracted from relevant theoretical and empirical literature (Goldstein, 1990, 1995; Goldstein, Heller, & Sechrest, 1966; Goldstein & Kanfer, 1979). All five approaches examined here include strategies and methods in their procedural models that use those principles and guidelines.

In significant relationships, the behavior of one person tends to be reciprocated by others. Guerney (1984) is most explicit about this proposition:

> Interpersonal interactions are very largely reciprocal in nature . . . "like elicits like" on certain critical dimensions of attitude and behavior. Affection, openness, love, cooperativeness, and, in general, positive interpersonal responses generally elicit positive responses from others. Hostility, competitive / uncooperative, deceptive, and, in general, negative interpersonal responses likewise elicit negative responses from others. (p. 176)

Similarly, Gambrill (1995b) says, "The enjoyment experienced in social exchanges is related to the enjoyment offered to others" (p. 219). A review of hundreds of studies about interpersonal consequences of empathic responding empirically confirms that it is consistently a potent promoter of positive relationship attributes such as interpersonal attraction, dyadic openness, conflict resolution, and individual growth (Goldstein & Michaels, 1985). This proposition is implicit in the theorists' descriptions of the attributes of the trainer-trainee relationship that are prerequisite to an effective collaboration. Through displays of empathic understanding, expressions of confidence in the worth and capabilities of the trainee, and clear explanations of the rationale for and potential payoff of learning new skills, trainers try to elicit trainee trust. They work to build trainees' confidence in them—the therapists—and the approach, and to strengthen the trainees' commitment to and cooperation in the training. They encourage trainees to be less defensive and more open and honest in their interpersonal transactions.

ASSUMPTIONS ABOUT NORMAL OR FUNCTIONAL DEVELOPMENT

All five skill training theorists assume that skills are learned because they are useful for some purpose. However, they propose no models of what is considered prototypically normal. In fact, they stress that what is considered desirable is a function of value judgments that vary with cultural contexts, implying that there is no prototypically normal pattern of development. What develops will be whatever functions to produce a satisfactory, dynamic fit between person and contexts.

There appear to be some implicit assumptions about what is desirable reflected in the theorists' descriptions and justifications of the skills they emphasize, although these may reflect the values of the Western cultures within which the approaches were created. For example, Trower, Bryant, and Argyle (1978) suggest that people can be considered socially adequate if they typically affect others in ways they intend and society accepts. In Guerney's (1977) belief, while value judgments are involved, there is widespread support for the values represented in the forms of behavior that generate empathic human relationships. Goldstein (1988) implies a model of preferred development in his Prepare Curriculum skills: "It seeks to teach empathy to the insensitive, cooperativeness to the uncooperative, problem solving to the inadequate, negotiating skill to the acting-out, anger control to the impulsive, allocentrism to the egocentric, group processes to the isolated, stress management to the anxious, social perceptiveness to the socially confused, and more" (p. 1). Meichenbaum (1985) suggests that what may differentiate so-called normal people from client populations is not the absence of stress or of irrational thoughts but the availability of a repertoire of flexible coping skills for producing intraperson comfort and satisfaction and desired interpersonal relationships in ways that are socially acceptable.

ASSUMPTIONS ABOUT ABNORMAL OR DYSFUNCTIONAL DEVELOPMENT

The skill training therapists reject the use of medical models, so they propose no theories of pathology. Patterns are judged dysfunctional when they produce intra- and interpersonal effects the person or the social context considers unacceptable, and the person is unable to control the patterns consciously. Guerney (1977) distinguishes dysfunctional patterns that have a genetic and biochemical basis from others; he asserts that psychotherapy is not appropriate for the former, but it may be useful to people in helping them cope with the emotional and interpersonal consequences of "biochemically based" disorders. Gambrill (1995a) recognizes possible genetic influences but takes a modern behavior genetics stance: "Genetic predispositions toward shyness may interact with nonoptimal social environments in ways that encourage the development and maintenance of social anxiety and reticence in social situations" (p. 257).

Trower, Bryant, and Argyle (1978) propose that at least some forms of "mental disorder" may be "caused or exacerbated" by social incompetence in two ways:

> "Failure of social competence is primary, leading to rejection and social isolation, which in turn produces disturbed mental states; . . . Other kinds of mental disturbance affect all areas of behaviour, including social performance; social inadequacy results in rejection and isolation, thus adding to the original sources of stress and leading to deterioration." (p. 1)

In discussing theories of social anxiety, each of which he suggests has some merit, Trower (1986) lists a skills deficit model, a cognitive self-evaluation model, a classical conditioning model, a personality trait approach, and a self-presentation approach. This listing suggests that social anxiety may have its origins in a deficiency in any part of the person represented in our comparative framework. (see Figure 4.2).

All five skill training theorists seem implicitly to assume the following: (1) Humans evolved as social creatures; being embedded in positive relationships that are accepting, supportive, affectionate, and compassionate is essential to their well-being and happiness. (2) Absence of positive relationships or presence of pervasive negative relationships produces subjective distress and related coping responses; these elicit further social rejection and lead to dysfunctional patterns or psychological/behavioral disorders. For example, "Social relating is fundamental to individual and species survival" (Trower, 1995, p. 58), and lack of intimately relating to others is a "serious difficulty" (Gilbert & Trower, 1990). The form and severity of the disorder is a function of the extent and intensity of the social rejection by and isolation from significant others. Therefore, psychopathology is defined interpersonally.

PROCEDURAL MODEL

All skill training approaches use highly similar procedural models (e.g., Gambrill, 1995a, 1995b; Goldstein, 1981; Guerney, 1984; Meichenbaum, 1985; Trower, 1986). As Trower (1986) put it, "The technology of skill acquisition has now become a standard package of procedures" (p. 53).

Their procedural models reflect the skill training theorists' person-in-context unit of concern. Taking a single component skill—such as goal setting, problem solving, selective observation, moral reasoning, empathic responding, emotional control, accurate and effective communication, or specific social skills—and teaching it alone is not considered likely to be effective by itself. Rather, they emphasize combining component cognitive, motivational, communicative, and social skills into complex, flexible patterns. They report also that some skill combinations are more difficult to teach than others. For example, problem solving and communicative skills are easier to teach than are skills of moral reasoning linked to moral behavior (Gibbs, Potter, & Goldstein, 1995; Goldstein, personal communication).

The therapy strategies and methods of the skill training theorists are often grouped into three sequential, iterative phases. First is the "introductory" (Guerney), "reformity prescription" (Goldstein), "conceptualization" (Gambrill; Meichenbaum), or assessment" and "instruction" (Trower) phase. Next is a "skills training" (Gambrill; Goldstein; Guerney; Trower) or "skills acquisition and rehearsal" phase (Meichenbaum). Finally, there is an "application and follow through" (Meichenbaum) or "generalization and maintenance" (Gambrill; Goldstein; Guerney; Trower) phase. Each phase serves certain goals and uses an array of intervention strategies and methods, but they overlap and interact. For example, while client motivation is a key objective of phase I, it requires continued attention, and skills may be added during training. The fine procedural models are summarized next around the phase formulation, but it is only a useful heuristic for understanding what is a carefully integrated approach to facilitating behavior change. The same procedural model is used for skill training with both individuals and groups, but conducting training in groups adds the interpersonal value of practicing with and gaining feedback from others in a similar situation.

INTRODUCTORY AND CONCEPTUALIZATION PHASE

The objectives of the introductory phase are to establish a positive, collaborative relationship, to encourage trainee motivation, to identify skills needed, to teach the training rationale, to reconceptualize trainees' concerns within the rationale, and to help trainees understand what will be expected of them.

Establishing a Positive, Collaborative Relationship

A positive relationship is considered a necessary but not sufficient condition for effective skill training; it provides a framework within which coping skills can be "nurtured" (Meichenbaum, 1985). Trainees' confidence in their instructor is especially important early in training before natural, real-life consequences of using their new skills demonstrate their value (Guerney, 1984). A positive relationship helps trainees accept training, understand their problems, and increase trainers' potency as a model and "reinforcer" (Trower, Bryant, & Argyle, 1978). A positive relationship helps trainees construct a view of the trainer as competent, enthusiastic, warm, genuine, empathic, and trustworthy (Guerney, 1984)—a person by whom trainees feel accepted, understood, and liked (Meichenbaum, 1985).

How do positive interpersonal attitudes and emotions influence training? Their powerful *prosocial potency* (Goldstein, 1988) facilitates approach and minimizes avoidant or aggressive behaviors. Positive attitudes facilitate honest revelation of private hopes, self-evaluative thoughts and feelings, and commitment to collaborate in the training. When trainees like and trust trainers and believe in what they say and do, this connection gives greater credibility to trainers' explanations and evaluative feedback about trainees' capabilities and performance. A strong, good connection has powerful social reinforcing value that significantly facilitates learning. Extensive empirical evidence (e.g., Waterhouse & Strupp, 1984) supports the beneficial therapeutic impact of this kind of relationship. On the other hand, self-protective processes are activated when people feel threatened, criticized, misunderstood, or rejected. The usual result is some form of uncooperative, non-self-revealing, antagonistic, and resistant behavior; this attitude makes learning new skills virtually impossible (Goldstein, 1988; Guerney, 1977; Meichenbaum, 1985; Trower, Bryant, & Argyle, 1978).

How can trainers cultivate this positive relationship schema? First, they should consistently use empathic understanding and communication (see Guerney's conceptual model). Goldstein (1988; Goldstein & Michael, 1985) and Guerney (1977, 1984) extensively describe and summarize evidence about empathy and its functions. It is a four-component process. The first part involves use of trainee statements and behavioral cues to infer trainees' feelings and thoughts accurately. The trainer then tries to imagine experiencing the other's cognitive and affective subjective states unfettered by value judgments, stereotyping, or explanatory speculations. Next, trainers consciously try to distinguish which of the parts of that simulated experiencing are their own feelings and which are like those of trainees. Finally, trainers clearly and sensitively convey to the trainees the resulting understanding (Goldstein, 1988). Assessment and teaching roles must be skillfully performed to elicit trainee confidence in the trainer's professional expertise.

Trainee Motivation
The view of motivation within the cognitive behavioral/skill training approach is similar to our comparative framework model. Trainees must formulate and commit themselves to *clear goals,* including (a) primary goals representing interpersonal consequences they desire and (b) subgoals defining specific skills for producing them. There must be *personal agency beliefs* (PABs) that if trainees use those skills, others will respond as desired (positive context beliefs) and that trainees can develop and use those skills (positive capability or self-efficacy beliefs). Such personal agency beliefs result from confidence in the trainers' expertise, persuasive examples that have meaning in the trainee's life, and discussion of research evidence. Goals and personal agency beliefs must be supported by positive affect elicited by the therapy relationship and anticipations of desired outcomes. Inducing and maintaining motivation is the most fundamental part of a skills training process (Guerney, 1984).

Assessment of Skills Needed
Assessment of clients' current contexts and specification of skills needed is considered a collaborative task. Skill trainers use a differential diagnosis and differential treatment model; interventions should be tailored to the needs of clients rather than representing a standard approach to all clients—what Goldstein calls a "reformity" rather than a "conformity" prescription. There are large individual differences at different phases of life in the skills people need. Trainees have different purposes, subcultural contexts, and skills, and these must be accommodated. Extensive attention has been given to identi-

fying effective assessment methods (Gambrill, 1995a; Meichenbaum, 1985; Schlundt & McFall, 1985; Trower, 1995) Assessment is considered a multi-method, collaborative task that may involve interviews, imagery-based recall, self-report and other formal measures, self-monitoring, role play and behavioral observation, peer and expert ratings, and physiological monitoring. The way it is conducted significantly influences relationship formation and trainee motivation. True to their basic person-context unit, skill trainers not only assess trainee skills but also the contexts within which those skills are to be used.

Goldstein has constructed many skill training components. His approach is to identify trainees' specific skill deficiencies and then to design appropriate training by selecting relevant components from his total skill curriculum. Guerney has constructed generic relationship process skills that he considers generically useful for dealing with any kind of interpersonal problem, so assessment simply involves a yes or no decision as to whether potential trainees consider his approach appropriate. In our comparative framework, synchronization of interactions among system components results from selective communication of relevant feedforward and feedback signals. Guerney implicitly uses this idea, as his training involves teaching people how to understand and communicate with one another skillfully so they can effectively synchronize their functioning as parts of a larger unit—an interpersonal relationship.

Teaching Training Rationales and Reconceptualizing Trainee Concerns
The skill training theorists stress peoples' conscious, thoughtful direction, regulation, and control of their own behavior. Trainees come with private beliefs—some are conscious; others are tacit; they have previously constructed or were taught these beliefs to help them deal with their concerns and interpersonal relationships. Their existing beliefs usually mislead them in important ways, so they must become aware of the inadequacies of their beliefs to understand the need to alter or replace them. Trainers explicitly provide trainees a rationale for what they are doing and why. First, by using educational procedures of explaining and discussing, and sometimes visual aids and reading assignments, trainers teach trainees a general conceptual and propositional model representing the nature and dynamics of interpersonal transactions and how people's thoughts and feelings affect and are affected by those transactions. The rationale for the design of the training procedures and their effectiveness is explained within this framework. The objective is to construct a general schema that trainees can use to guide their efforts and to help trainees cultivate the confidence that it will work. This framework is then used to help them realize how their existing beliefs are inaccurate and

self-defeating. Their concerns are reconceptualized using the new rationale, and that revised view is then used to explain how the proposed training can help them with their concerns. The way this is done influences relationship dynamics and motivation. Meichenbaum (1985) explains that a "hard sell" is likely to make a trainee defensive and resistant; instead, trainees should be involved as collaborators in the reconceptualization process. The new view must appear credible, plausible, and useful to trainees if they are to use it to guide their efforts.

Teaching Trainees Their Roles and Responsibilities

Trainees' apprehension about what they may have to do, whether they can do it, whether they may be embarrassed, and how much time they have to invest may reduce their motivation and cooperation. Frank discussion, clear explanations, and use of examples can help alleviate such concerns, further strengthen their motivation, and enhance their feelings of being in control of themselves and their actions.

SKILLS TRAINING PHASE

The same basic training strategy is used for all skills. It involves creating a series of relevant simulated and real behavior episodes within which the skill can be observed, practiced, and polished. Trainees must follow these steps:

1. Have a clear, conscious understanding of what a skilled performance should look like, the results it should produce, the kinds of situations in which it could be used, and be motivated to learn it.
2. Observe skilled performances in prototypical situations.
3. Consciously and intentionally practice it in specific training behavior episodes.
4. Monitor their performance and its consequences, along with the trainer and perhaps other trainees and use that feedback to revise and improve their guiding schema and their performance.
5. Practice in relevant real-life behavior episodes.
6. Monitor their performance and its consequences, and discuss that information with the trainer to improve their guiding schema and their performance.

Explanation and Motivation

The purpose of the explanation and motivation component is to help trainees construct a preliminary cognitive schema representing the skill that they can later use to guide their practice efforts. They accomplish this through educative strategies and methods. Spoken and written descriptions of the skill, its desired consequences, and contexts in which it might be used help trainees develop an abstract understanding of it, including principles and rules for generating the skill when appropriate and additional motivation for believing it will be effective.

Demonstration, Modeling, and Discussion

Having an abstract understanding of a skill is one thing; performing it skillfully is quite another. Social learning strategies of *observational learning* and *modeling* are used to help trainees learn "how to do it." Skills are complex behavior patterns designed to produce desired consequences in specific contexts. Sometimes it is useful to demonstrate how to do parts of it without concern for context before modeling the entire pattern. As an example, showing trainees the phrasing of communications or expressive gestures may help produce the desired impact.

The theorists' person-in-context focus stresses learning to perform the skill as a unit, so *modeling* gives trainees specific examples of how to do it by having them observe others behaving skillfully in relevant interpersonal situations. In terms of our comparative framework, the trainer creates simulated behavior episodes that are similar to real-life behavior episodes in which the trainees hope to use the skills. Simulated episodes are used initially because they can be controlled as to length, content, and consequences and provided in a supportive, nonthreatening context. The modeled behavior episode should include a context similar to relevant real-life ones, the antecedent behavior of the other person that creates the problem situation, the performance of the skill to deal with it, and the other person's response to show the impact of the skill. The last is important because observing the occurrence of the desired consequence adds credibility to and motivation for learning the skill. A diversity of modeling methods can be used; live performances may be used, with the trainer or others role playing the skill. Recorded versions can also be done, using audiotape or videotape. Goldstein and Guerney have constructed training materials that others can use for the acquisition of these skills.

Demonstration and modeling are linked to discussions of trainee observations and interpretations. This focuses attention on relevant events and helps trainees cultivate the cognitive interpretive aspects of the skills. Demonstration, modeling, and discussion—observational learning—result in elaboration of the preliminary abstract idea into a functional schema that trainees can use to guide skilled behavior. This training may be repeated as necessary to allow trainees to cultivate a sound functional schema before asking them to perform the skill.

Practice, Monitoring, and Feedback in Simulated Behavior Episodes
Observational learning can produce a schema, but only *enactive learning* can link that schema to performance skill. Trainees must practice the skill in a relevant simulated behavior episode while they and the trainer—and perhaps others—monitor their performance. Practice is followed by discussion of the performance based on trainees own observations and those of others aimed at maintaining motivation and improving performance and its guiding schema.

Evaluative interpersonal feedback has significant motivational effects on trainees' emotional and personal agency beliefs and how these influence their motivational patterns. Trainers should provide encouraging comments to help maintain trainees' motivation. Even if their performance is poor, trainees can be complimented on their effort, reminded that they should not expect perfect performances immediately, and encouraged to believe that practice will bring improvement. Performances may be videotaped so trainees can see themselves as others see them. Substantive feedback provides information about skill aspects that are functioning well, and those needing improvement. The trainers' assumption is that discussion of feedback by the trainee and others will lead to a refinement of guiding schemas and to more effective self-monitoring. It also helps convert interpersonal talk into private self-talk as a means of self-guidance and improvement of future performances both before and while they occur. This training increases trainees' self-regulation and self-control capabilities and their positive personal agency beliefs, all of which are essential for effective functioning in real-life situations without the guidance and support of a trainer. Simulated behavior episodes are usually repeated several times to polish performance skill before trainees try the skill in real-life situations where no two interpersonal episodes are ever identical. The nature of simulated behavior episodes in which trainees practice is varied to cultivate more flexible use of the skill. They are designed to involve different people, different contexts, and different interpersonal problems in preparation for use of the skill in real-life situations.

Practice, Monitoring, and Feedback in Selected Real-Life Behavior Episodes
After-session practice is termed *homework* or *in vivo practice*. Trainees and trainer collaborate in identifying daily life behavior episodes in which trainees might practice the skills they have learned in simulated episodes. Trainees try out new skills when relevant real-life episodes occur, monitor their performance and its consequences, and discuss the results in their next training session. The objectives of these discussions are the same as the objectives for simulated behavior episodes. It is important for trainees to experience success when they first use new skills in real life. Therefore, care is used initially to se-

lect episodes where there is a high likelihood that the skills will produce desired reinforcing consequences so as to maintain and strengthen trainee motivation. As in vivo practice yields success, progressively more challenging homework episodes may be selected, both to cultivate greater trainee skill and to strengthen trainees' personal agency beliefs. In real life, desired consequences do not always result from using the skills. To further cultivate their self-regulation, trainees are taught to expect occasional failures and how to think about and deal with them if they occur.

GENERALIZATION AND MAINTENANCE PHASE

The skill training theorists assume that skills are learned through practice in specific behavior episodes to produce desired consequences in specific contexts. What is learned are generalized schemas (or behavior episode schemas) for creating and guiding skilled performance in future similar behavior episodes—that is, the schemas are intitially context specific. These theorists reject the underlying assumption of other therapies that changes manifest in the therapy context will automatically transfer to and be maintained in future real-life behavior episodes. Therapy follow-up studies support rejection of this automaticity assumption. Analysis of 192 therapy outcome studies revealed that only 14% reported maintenance or transfer of therapy outcomes after therapy terminated (Goldstein & Kanfer, 1979).

The skill training approaches argue that unless there is systematic use of techniques that are *transfer-enhancing*—that encourage use of the skill in different situations—and *maintenance-enhancing*—that encourage continued use after therapy ends—maintenance and transfer are unlikely to occur. This step is discussed here as a final phase, but its strategies and methods need to be used throughout the process. Goldstein (1990, 1995; Goldstein, Heller, & Sechrest, 1966; Goldstein & Kanfer, 1979) has given more detailed consideration to this issue than others; his work encompasses the proposals of the other theorists, so his comprehensive approach is summarized here. To construct it, he conducted an extensive search of both basic science and therapy literatures, looking for empirical evidence that supported the both the guiding principles and the practical methods of transfer and maintenance. He identified procedures for enhancing transfer and maintenance, but he asserts that they are coupled processes, so any of the procedures may contribute to both.

Transfer-Enhancing Strategies and Methods
Six principles and related training methods are described. They all help trainees learn guiding schemas (behavior episode schemas) that are flexible

and likely to be activated and used in diverse real-life behavior episodes. *Sequential modification* involves training people to perform a skill in one context, such as at home, and then in another, perhaps at work. In this way the trainees progressively learn to use the skill in diverse settings. *Provision of general principles* involves teaching trainees the rules, general strategies, or organizing principles used to generate skilled performances. This step is similar to some of the self-regulatory mediational methods cultivated by cognitive therapies. Empirical evidence indicates that the more often an effective behavior is practiced, the more likely it is to occur in other, future behavior episodes. Therefore, *overlearning* by repeated practice beyond that which produces initial learning will increase *response availability*. The greater the diversity of behavior episodes practiced—with different people, varied contexts, and different interpersonal issues, called *stimulus variability*—the more likely is transfer to new situations. A fifth principle is called *identical elements*. The more similar to significant real-life episodes are the behavior episodes in which the skill is practiced and learned, the more likely it is to transfer to those real-life episodes. One strategy designs simulated behavior episodes to be as similar as possible to those relevant in real-life so they feel like the real thing to the trainee. The similarity can be 100% if real-life behavior episodes are used for skill practice, as in a phobic context. *Mediated generalization* strategies teach trainees to use several context-bridging, self-regulation skills, such as Meichenbaum's self-regulation through self-talk. Methods include self-recording of what happens in relevant behavior episodes, self-instruction about how to behave at those times, and self-reinforcement or punishment for adequate or inadequate performances.

Maintenance-Enhancing Strategies and Methods
Persistence, durability, and maintenance in real-life of the skills learned during therapy is said to be primarily a function of the patterns of reinforcement during training and later in their natural environment. Stated differently, one aspect of the guiding behavior episode schema that trainees construct is the expectations or propositions about the probability that the desired consequences will occur when the skill is used. If they assume that it should always be used successfully, a few failures can lead them to stop using the skill. If, on the other hand, they expect it to work only some of the time, they are more likely to persist in its use when occasional failures do occur. Seven intervention strategies and their associated methods are used to teach the second kind of expectation through what conditioning models call a schedule of partial or intermittent reinforcement. The key is to have enough successes for the trainee to believe the skill continues to be valuable, but enough failures to learn how

to endure occasional setbacks. The propositions may need to be different for different trainees.

Thinning of reinforcement involves designing a series of training behavior episodes so that the frequency of success is progressively reduced to an intermittent pattern the trainer believes to be typical of the trainee's natural environment. In the early stages of skill training, it is desirable for reinforcement to occur contingent on and immediately following the skill performance. As training proceeds, it is useful to introduce *delay of reinforcement* so the trainees modify their expectation from immediate gratification to the probability of delayed gratification if they persist. This step is necessary, because in real life desired consequences often do not immediately follow actions.

Trainers often facilitate learning through coaching or prompts—by using reminders or suggestions. *Fading of prompts* serves to progressively increase trainees' self-control in skill performance. *Booster sessions* on planned or as-needed schedules periodically reintroduce trainer-guided training behavior episodes to support and encourage continued refinement and use of the skills. *Preparation for failure in the natural environment* involves helping clients realize that skills will not always prove effective or satisfying and prepares them for coping with that eventuality. For example, clients can learn to use self-reinforcement when their skills are well performed but are unrewarded by the context: "I did it right even if they didn't respond the way I wanted." When failure results because their behavior was inadequate, they can learn evaluative thoughts that help keep them from getting too discouraged. Designing homework assignments so that trainees initially experience a high degree of success and then practice progressively more difficult behavior episodes may also help inoculate them from too much discouragement when they experience occasional failure.

The strategies and methods described so far rely on helping the trainee to think and act in specific ways. However, the person-in-context unit implies the possibility of changing the context so that it responds differently to the trainee's efforts. *Programming for reinforcement in the natural environment* trains significant people in the trainees' natural environment to recognize, understand, and appropriately reinforce the behavior patterns being taught. For example, Guerney systematically trains couples or parent-child dyads to respond to one another in ways that mutually reinforce desired relationship functioning. Goldstein suggests that at macro levels, changes in institutional policies and practices—at school or in the workplace—may be necessary.

Another approach is to *use natural reinforcers.* It is often said that the best teacher is the natural consequence of the act. If therapists understand the social context and subculture in which trainees lead their daily lives, they can anticipate how that context may react to different patterns of behavior. That knowledge can be used to design behavior episode schemas for training so they fit the reinforcing contingencies that are a part of the trainees' natural environment. Even within trainees' daily life space there can be considerable diversity in the ways different people react. Therefore, one way people can maximize the likelihood of reward for particular ways of behaving is to spend their time in supportive rather than unsupportive contexts. They can choose to focus on some interpersonal relationships and limit participation in others. Goldstein's version of this, called *recruiting supportive models,* is based on empirical evidence that youth who are more resilient in difficult environments are those who have continuing relationships with adults who support and model prosocial behavior.

EVALUATING CLIENT PROGRESS AND OUTCOMES

One feature of these approaches is that desired outcomes are clearly specified in terms that can be directly observed—a skilled performance—so a clear criterion is available against which progress can be evaluated. The evaluations of progress and outcomes rely on client, therapist, and sometimes others' observations of the extent to which specified skills are performed in ways that produce desired outcomes in simulated and real-life episodes.

EVALUATION OF THE APPROACH

Cognitive-behavioral skill training theorists subscribe to an empiricist epistemology. Therefore, they rely primarily on traditional scientific methods to evaluate their approaches, and rely less on anecdotal clinical evidence than do practitioners of many other approaches. More than many other theorists, they have tried to identify and apply relevant empirically supported knowledge and techniques from the human sciences. Goldstein has been particularly effective in this regard. The cognitive-behavioral group have generated an extensive empirical literature about the effectiveness of their approaches based on careful research designs applied to real trainees (clients) and teaching skills applied to real-life concerns. The evidence, reported in publications cited in this chapter, is more extensive and persuasive regarding the effectiveness of their approaches for their objectives than is the case with most other approaches. The specificity with which they define the outcomes they seek to generate—specific kinds of skills—facilitates evaluation and accountability for their work.

CHAPTER 12

Behavioral Medicine and Behavioral Health

HISTORICAL PERSPECTIVE

Behavioral medicine and behavioral health emphasize two types of objectives for health-focused interventions. *Behavioral medicine* is the application of psychological and behavioral interventions, in contrast to surgical or pharmacological ones, to the remediation of or rehabilitation from consequences and sequelae of physical injury or illness. *Behavioral health* interventions seek to cultivate healthy development and to prevent health problems. The sources from which they developed are somewhat different, but they are merging into one broad stream of effort. Strictly speaking, they are not a different family of approaches. Rather, they apply strategies and methods developed primarily by the behavioral, cognitive, and cognitive-behavioral or skill training approaches to the remediation, rehabilitation, or prevention of biological dysfunctions, or to cultivating optimal biological functioning. These goals stand in contrast to the typical psychotherapy focus on psychological and behavioral outcomes.

The growing popularity of these approaches to illness and health represents a renewed credibility of a centuries-old idea (Pattishall, 1989). Ancient Chinese wrote of the relationship of lifestyle to health. The ancient Greek god, Aesculapius, was the god of the healing arts. His daughter, Panacea, was concerned with healing the sick, while her sister, Hygiea, represented wise living and healthy behavior. Hippocrates argued that health results from states of harmony with one's environment and in oneself, and that mind and body influence one another. Galen's formulations extended that view. The influence of this early, integrative, person-environment view of health and illness declined as Descarte's philosophical doctrine of mind and body as separate entities gained dominance. It provided the conceptual foundation for the development of medical interventions that implicitly assumed health problems were problems of the body—solely biological—and so medicine could focus on methods for altering the body—material-energy-based interventions—without concern for the mind. As a result, modern medicine became defined as biomedical science, and physicians' training was tied to understanding the physical and biological sciences and the human body (Flexner, 1910). Advancing knowledge about correlations between brain structures and different kinds of behavior led to the proposition that at least some psychological and behavioral dysfunctions had organic origins. "Diseases of the mind" were allocated, therefore, to a specialty within medicine called psychiatry.

However, the idea that mind might influence health did not die (Pattishall, 1989). Within medicine, some continued to explore the possibility that certain health problems had psychological antecedents. For example, a merger of Freudian psychoanalysis and psychiatry produced a dynamic, as contrasted to organic, psychiatry culminating in the concept of psychosomatic medicine. The credibility of that view eroded, however, for lack of solid empirical evidence that psychological functioning produced physical illnesses—for example, that ulcers result from anxiety—and that physical illnesses could be cured through psychological changes. What did result was consultation-liaison psychiatry aimed at helping other medical specialists with the psychiatric, psychological, and social problems of medical patients.

To assist in this process, psychiatric departments began to employ behavioral scientists to capitalize on their expertise in measurement and research, expertise and to assist in teaching behavioral science to medical students. In contrast to psychiatry, behavioral scientists stem from disciplines with strong research traditions and growing, empirically-grounded knowledge bases and technologies about human development and functioning. Their special competencies earned them increasing recognition and acceptance from a diversity of hospital medical departments. This eventually led to the establishment of behavioral science departments separate from psychiatry in many medical schools. The National Board of Medical Examiners established a behavioral science section of the basic science examination for medical students in 1973, following the recognition that knowledge of the biological person was insufficient for dealing with health and illness; the psychological and behavioral aspects of people must also be understood. From this fertile environment of clinical medicine, behavioral medicine emerged.

As the scientific biomedical model for diagnosing and curing illnesses evolved, a focus on health promotion and disease prevention emerged (Matarazzo, Weiss, Herd, Miller, & Weiss, 1984). Some people argued that it was less expensive, more humane, and of benefit to more people to focus on preventing illness and on cultivating healthy development than it was to wait until people became ill and then try to cure them. This public health movement credo produced effective interventions aimed at preventing rather than curing illnesses, such as purification of water, environmental sanitation, and immunization for infectious diseases.

As infectious diseases, malnutrition, and environmental hazards declined as causes of morbidity and mortality, heart disease, cancer, stroke, arteriosclerosis, suicide, substance abuse, and accidents became key health problems. However, growing evidence from clinical, disciplinary, and epidemiological research reveals that such health problems are powerfully influenced by people's own behavior and psychological reactions. Hippocrates' view has reemerged in a more sophisticated form. It follows, therefore, that promotion of healthy lifestyles should lie at the heart of efforts to gain control over the current major disablers and killers of humans.

The blossoming of this perspective has spurred the development of behavioral medicine/health. Helping people learn to control their social behavior, what they ingest and inhale, patterns of exercise and rest, emotions and reactions to stress, and the ways they think about themselves, their tasks, and their social relationships are key strategies for dealing with or preventing cancer, hypertension, cardiovascular disease, and other health problems. Evidence also indicates that healthy people are less vulnerable to infectious illnesses, and if they become ill they show better response to lower doses of medication and recover more quickly. The quantity and diversity of relevant literature is growing rapidly (e.g., Adler & Matthews, 1994; Araki, 1992; Carlson & Seifert, 1991; Carr & Dengerink, 1983; Kaptein, van der Ploeg, Garssen, Schreurs, & Beunderman, 1990; Matarazzo et al., 1984; Miller, 1983; Pattishall, 1989; Rodin & Salovey, 1989; Sarafino, 1994; Snyder & Forsyth, 1991).

The rationale, strategies, and methods of the behavioral medicine/health movement have a multidisciplinary base, but *health psychology* is a key source of knowledge and intervention methods for it (Carmody & Matarazzo, 1991). Behavioral medicine/health provides no distinct conceptual model because it relies on existing therapy models to influence *indirectly* the biological states of health and illness by *directly* modifying psychological and behavioral processes. However, additional concepts emphasizing biological interactions with psychological, behavioral, and environmental factors are introduced, and their propositional and procedural models emphasize mind-body interactions more than the psychotherapy approaches from which they borrow. The conceptual models of the approaches applied by behavioral medicine/health were summarized in Chapters 9–11, so only key supplemental concepts are analyzed here.

CONCEPTUAL MODEL

LEVELS AND UNITS OF ANALYSIS

Consistent with the approaches they utilize, practitioners of behavioral medicine and health therapy use multiple levels and units of analysis. The emphasis on integrated patterns of psychological, behavioral, social, environmental, and biological influences on states of health and illness means the *person-in-context* is the focal unit. Many specific interventions, however, emphasize *component function* relationships. The latter include relaxation training to control stress reactions, facilitating immune system functions, or promoting participation in social groups, such as social support networks. The various interventions have multidisciplinary roots in anthropology, sociology, psychology, and biology, which reflect this multilevel conceptual orientation.

CONTENT OF KEY CONCEPTS

Behavior therapy was a key impetus in the development of behavioral medicine (e.g., Miller, 1983; Carr, Funabiki, & Dengerink, 1983). *Skill* training and cognitive-behavioral models have also been influential, particularly in the self-management of chronic conditions, control of stress reactions and emotions, self-regulation and compliance with treatment regimens, and emphases on prevention and optimal health (e.g., Hollin & Trower, 1986; Karoly, 1991; Pierce, 1995; Turk & Rudy, 1995). However, behavioral medicine/health approaches emphasize some aspects of humans more than the approaches from which their applications are drawn.

Brain-Behavior Relations
This movement changes traditional medicine's most basic assumption—that is, it rejects Cartesian dualism and assumes unitary functioning (like the comparative framework used in this book. It stresses causal interactions among psychological, biological, and behavioral functions with its cornerstone concept of *brain-behavior relations*. The nervous system is the component that makes possible these mutually influential relationships (Womack, Vitaliano, & Maiuro, 1983). Like our comparative framework, it identifies humans' autonomic nervous system (ANS) and central nervous system (CNS) as providing the biological base that makes possible information/meaning-based integration of human functioning within humans themselves and with their contexts. The autonomic system organizes internal functioning through interrelated neuronal and biochemical processes. The central nervous system

creates organized person-context transactions through interrelated processes of anticipating and collecting information, constructing meaning, remembering, linked with skeletal-muscular processes regulated through feedback and feedforward dynamics. Unitary person-in-context functioning is made possible by multilevel structural-functional linkages among these two branches of the nervous system and the hypothalamus-pituitary-adrenal (HPA) axis. That HPA linkage, tied to the brain's limbic system role in emotional arousal, makes it possible for psychological and behavioral processes to affect biological functioning through regulation of the release of biochemical compounds, such as hormones, into the circulatory system as well as through direct neural linkages (Gellhorn & Loofbourrow, 1963).

The most complex and flexible linkages of the autonomic and central nervous systems are in the brain, so neuroscientists see the brain as the organ of the mind. It provides material carriers for information/meaning-based functioning and for producing integrated biosychosocial patterns of functioning. Damage or dysfunctions in brain structures may disrupt some aspects of brain functioning, and psychological/behavioral dysfunctions may disrupt some aspects of brain functioning; examples are neurochemical dynamics or biologically based addictions to ingested or inhaled substances. This basic shift in assumptions leads to an emphasis on several other concepts.

Somatization

A condition in which physical complaints exist but are not produced by organic pathology is called *somatization* (Katon & Dengerink, 1983). Empirical evidence indicates that up to 50% of primary care patients have psychological rather than biomedical precipitants for the symptoms that lead to their visit. The discomfort reported is usually real, rather than fictitious so some kind of intervention is warranted. The causes of such physical symptoms, however, are likely to be faulty psychosocial patterns rather than physical disease; the symptoms typically result from natural physiological processes that are part of stress reactions.

Stress and Coping

The human meaning of the concept of *stress* results from an analogy to its traditional physical meaning of a force that impacts on and disrupts the existing state of an entity, and/or the deformation or disruption of the entity's state caused by the force. In human terms, the *force* is some physical, social, or task demand to which a person must respond, called the *stressor*. Infectious diseases, ingested or inhaled substances, wounds, physical exercise, temperature changes, and prolonged activity without sleep illustrate *physical demands*.

Work, interpersonal interactions, thinking and problem solving, supervising and training others, dating, marriage and child rearing illustrate *social task demands*. The deformation or disruption to physical demands is the resulting shift in biological processes; for social and task demands, it is the way people interpret, evaluate, or appraise the demand and mobilize their biological, psychological, and behavioral resources to respond, typically called the *stress reaction*.

Stressful demands are part of the nature of open, living systems, so stressors and stress reactions are natural and necessary parts of effective, adaptive living and a source of change and development; stress is useful and life without stress is impossible (Selye, 1976; Lazarus, 1991; Pierce, 1995). Why, then, does the concept of stress have a negative connotation—distress? People usually do not refer to situations as stressful when they are having fun or when they are succeeding at a task, even though such circumstances do involve significant demands and efforts.

People usually limit the concept of stress to behavior episodes with two negative features: (1) The stress reaction includes uncomfortable or noxious subjective experiences, such as pain, gastric discomfort, fear, fatigue, or anger. (2) People appraise their efforts to deal with the demand adaptively as unsuccessful or yielding undesirable consequences, or they anticipate that such unwanted consequences will occur. Therefore, whether negative stress occurs is a function of how a person interprets, evaluates, and deals with the demand, typically called *coping responses* (Lazarus & Folkman, 1984; Pierce, 1995). Each behavior episode involves demands, stressors, and stress reaction mobilization to support coping behavior. Adaptive completion of demanding behavior episodes removes those stressors and demobilizes the stress reactions. Thus, in healthy, day-to-day living, stressors and stress reactions are ubiquitous but temporary.

Lifestyle

People develop consistencies in their patterns of anticipations, evaluations, interpretations, and coping behaviors when they are faced with tasks and demands; such habitual patterns are called their lifestyle. People's lifestyles influence their health status and vulnerability to future illness and injury (Matarazzo, 1984a). For example, people with good health habits usually live over a decade longer and have better general health than those who do not have those good habits. Such healthy people generally (1) sleep seven to eight hours daily, (2) eat breakfast almost every day, (3) never or rarely eat between meals, (4) are at or near prescribed height-adjusted weight, (5) never smoke cigarettes, (6) use alcohol moderately or not at all, and (7) have regular physical exercise (Belloc & Breslow, 1972; Breslow & Engstrom, 1980). Negative habits of thought and emotional reactions increase people's vulnerability to accidents and illness (Carmody & Matarazzo, 1991). Moreover, if one shifts the focus from identifying pathogens and how they cause illness—called pathogenesis—to identifying causes of good health—called salutogenesis by Antonovsky (1984)—lifestyle factors that facilitate healthy development in general can be identified. For example, personality factors such as a sense of coherence, hardiness, and resilience are generalized habits of anticipatory and evaluative thought and skills that serve as generalized resistance resources to protect people from developing health problems (Antonovsky, 1979; Kobasa, 1982). Diverse bad habits, functioning as parts of one's lifestyle, increase morbidity and mortality risk.

Risk Factors and Behavioral Pathogens

A *pathogen* is a specific causative agent for a disease. In traditional medicine, it refers to microbiological, chemical, or physical entities typically associated with acute and chronic infectious diseases caused by microorganisms; physical health problems are assumed to result from material causes (Antonovsky, 1984). Recognition that people function as integrated biopsychosocial units in a context, and that lifestyle characteristics can influence development of physical health problems has expanded the concept of pathogen to encompass psychological and behavioral causes as well; these are known as *behavioral pathogens* (Matarazzo, 1984b). Moreover, evidence has become persuasive that illness typically results from combinations of causes. For example, if 1,000 people smoke cigarettes extensively, only some will develop lung cancer. Why don't the others?

A *multivariate causation model* replaces traditional medicine's *one cause-one cure model* (Weiss, 1992). For an illness to develop, multiple pathogens or influences must be operating. This is the concept of *risk factors*. A risk factor is any material, psychological, or behavioral agent or process that contributes to the development of a particular illness, but by itself will not cause that illness. For example, if a person smokes, has a genetic vulnerability, is overweight, in bad physical shape because of poor dietary, exercise, and sleep habits, and suffers from persistent psychological stress, that person is more likely to develop a cardiovascular disease than a person with a healthy lifestyle, excellent physical and mental health, and without a genetic vulnerability. This concept implies that treatments should also be multivariate, aimed at altering multiple risk factors. Kozlowski (1989) illustrates this with interventions for tobacco health hazards.

Psychoneuroimmunology

Psychoneuroimmunology illustrates the kinds of concepts being developed to transcend the limitations of traditional medical organ and physiological system categorizations. Behavioral medicine/health approaches use basic bio-medical classifications but combine them with classes of psychological/be-havioral functioning to try to produce more integrative units of analysis to represent systemic patterns of mind-body functioning. Psychoneuroim-munology studies interactions among psychological, behavioral, neural, en-docrine, and immune processes, and how stress reactions, including dis-tressing emotions, may influence alterations in immune system functioning (Ader, 1981; Borysenko, 1984). The immune system is a key defense against material pathogens, so weakening those defenses through erosion of im-munological response capabilities makes people more vulnerable to illness (Ader & Cohen, 1993).

Self-Management and Compliance
People typically administer their own biomedical or health care, except for those infrequent periods when an illness is in an acute or crisis stage, or surgery is required, leading to hospitalization and direct care by others. Even hospital treatment requires some patient self-management in forms such as in-formed consent and cooperation in the procedures. In most instances, physi-cians diagnose and tell patients what to do; then the patient is expected to go home and do it. Sometimes they do not, and this lack of *compliance* with health care regimens is a significant problem (Brigham & Dengerink, 1983). Self-care is even more pervasive when the objective is developmental or preventive. Karoly (1991, 1995) defines *self-management* as a process by which people de-liberately employ cognitive and behavioral skills to accomplish something that they would not otherwise accomplish, because social forces or their own habits and lifestyle impede or prevent their achieving that goal. Self-management is a cornerstone concept for behavioral medicine/health inter-vention strategies and methods.

Types of Health and Illness Objectives
Behavioral medicine practitioners use the existing biomedical classifications or diagnostic categories for different types of illnesses when specifying their illness intervention targets, such as hypertension, headache, addiction, stroke, atherosclerosis, and asthma. They use existing biomedical physiological sys-tem classifications when specifying their health intervention targets, such as respiratory, cardiovascular, nervous, and immune systems.

Kinds of Psychological, Behavioral, and Environmental Characteristics
Behavioral medicine practitioners use concepts to represent psychological, behavioral, and environmental factors that have been created by other disci-plines, particularly psychology,—for example, cognition, emotion, and social support.

PROPOSITIONAL MODEL

Behavioral medicine/health approaches rely primarily on the propositional models of the approaches they apply. Rather than repeating all of those, we discuss a few that are particularly emphasized in these health-focused applications.

Psychological, behavioral, and biological responses occur in mutual causal patterns. This is like the principle of unitary functioning in our comparative framework. It reflects the rejection of Cartesian mind-body dualism and the adoption of a transactional model of human nature that recognizes the reciprocal nature of interactions among biological, psychological, behavioral, and social factors in health and illness (Carmody & Matarazzo, 1991).

Habits of functioning and lifestyles are learned and can be altered through learning. Basic patterns of biological functioning—such as respiration, circulation, and digestion—emerge through genetically regulated maturational processes within a healthy environment during fetal and infant development. Critical deviations in fetal biochemical environments resulting from toxic material/energy influences on the mother's biological state can produce fetal and infant health problems (LaBarba, 1984). When basic biological processes become operative, the infant begins to learn and elaborate information/meaning-based psychological-behavioral patterns to organize and regulate his or her environmental transactions and internal states. Because complex information/meaning-based patterns include biological components, and because mutual causal processes operate in those patterns, it follows that the kinds of biological responses that occur within each such pattern can be influenced by learning (Miller, 1983; Schwartz, 1984). Patterns of biological responses that occur as components of emotional arousal patterns may be influenced by learning because of their involvement in stress responses (Turk & Rudy, 1995).

Lifestyles serve both immediate and delayed consequences and these may conflict. Habits are learned and maintained because they produce outcomes people want and/or terminate or help avoid others they don't want. People usually seek multiple consequences with the same behavior pattern: For example, they eat to satisfy their hunger, because they enjoy the taste of food, because they enjoy the companionship that generally accompanies eating, and to help maintain their health. Multiple causes usually influence every behavior pattern (Schwartz, 1984). Some consequences or goals are immediate—the taste of a delicious dessert; others are delayed—gaining weight. Short-term and long-term goals may conflict, and producing one may prevent the other; an example is the immediate pleasure of smoking and the long-term maintenance of health. Immediate consequences are more influential in a person's learning and maintaining habits than are delayed ones, sometimes called a *gradient of reinforcement.* When they conflict, short-term goals and consequences will be more likely to guide behavior and learning (Miller, 1983). For delayed consequences or long-term goals to influence current behavior they must be linked to some immediate consequences or short-term goals; subgoals function as steps toward more distant goals (Karoly, 1991; Pierce, 1995; Schwartz, 1984).

Health problems can be produced by faulty habits of thought and action. People produce stress reactions and health problems in themselves through their actions and anticipatory and evaluative thoughts; through learning, these patterns can become habitual (Katon & Dengerink, 1983; Rodin & Salovey, 1989). For example, habits of eating or inhaling substances may cause health problems by placing excessive stress/demands on healthy, steady-state biological functioning. Such habits are risk factors in certain conditions:

1. The substance is infectious or toxic, such as poisons or viruses.
2. The substance cannot be removed through metabolic and excretory functions and progressively accumulates until it becomes disruptive; as an example, excessive breathing of coal dust produces "black lung" disease.
3. Biological processing of excessively ingested materials produces persistent changes manifested as unhealthy biological steady states, as with addictions, obesity, deposits in arteries, cirrhosis of the liver.

Evolutionary processes have produced bodies organized to support frequent, persistent, and high levels of physical activity. For example, arterial blood movement results from a "pump"—the heart—but blood return to the heart through the veins results from physical activity. If appropriate levels of physical activity are not maintained, biological processes will shift into a lower gear, muscular atrophy will occur, and the efficiency of biological processes such as respiratory and circulatory processes—may deteriorate. If high levels of physical activity persist without sufficient periods of rest so the body can recover from the resource depletion that results from excessive demand, changes may occur that result in unhealthy biological states. Habits of thought may cause health problems when they persistently activate autonomic nervous system and hormonal patterns that normally function as temporary states, such as components of emotional states, causing these to become habitual. This situation produces chronic conditions manifested in somatization; an example is type A personalities (Novaco, 1995; Turk & Rudy, 1995).

People can consciously use thoughts and actions to influence their biological responses. Complex patterns of biological, psychological, and behavioral responses are learned, so learned changes in those patterns can alter their biological components. People can learn to intentionally focus their attention on organizing different states of thinking and acting to produce and maintain a desired biological state (Carlson & Bernstein, 1995; Novaco, 1995; Turk & Rudy, 1995). They can regulate their progress toward that goal with selective observation of changes in indicators of the desired biological state, called *biofeedback* (Schwartz, 1984; Schwartz and associates, 1995). Selectively focused attention and awareness of relationships among relevant factors are essential for such biobehavioral self-management (Novaco, 1995; Turk & Rudy, 1995). Such goal setting and biofeedback-regulated change processes are similar to the concept of behavior episodes and negative feedback dynamics described in our comparative framework.

ASSUMPTIONS ABOUT NORMAL OR FUNCTIONAL DEVELOPMENT

The behavioral medicine/health literature gives little attention to specifying the nature of normal, functional, healthy development, yet health promotion approaches require specifying what should be promoted. They appear to rely on ideas about normal development primarily from the fields of developmental biology and psychology and related applications, such as pediatrics and pediatric psychology (Roberts, Maddux, & Wright, 1984; Jessor, 1984; Woods & Birren, 1984). There are efforts to specify healthy psychological and behavioral outcome states—such as healthful patterns of exercise, eating, sleeping—and psychological or personality patterns—such as a sense of coherence (Antonovsky, 1979) and self-efficacy (Schunk & Carbonari, 1984). Often this topic is discussed in terms of health as an absence of illness, or in terms of eliminating risk factors.

ASSUMPTIONS ABOUT UNHEALTHY OR DYSFUNCTIONAL DEVELOPMENT

Three rationales are used for causes of health problems: learned faulty lifestyles; learned faulty stress and coping patterns; disease and injury. Learning is assumed to occur through conditioning, social learning or modeling, and cognitive restructuring.

Learned Faulty Habits and Lifestyles

During their life course, people may learn habits of living that produce some immediate satisfying consequences but that also produce some health problems over time. For example, habits of eating and drinking, nonexercise, and substance abuse may give individuals immediate pleasure, but in the long term produce health problems such as obesity, cardiovascular disease, cancer, emphysema, and debilitating addictions (see Belloc & Breslow, 1972; Breslow & Engstrom, 1980). Moreover, one health problem may help cause another—hypertension as a consequence of obesity, or malnutrition resulting from alcoholism. A child's family and sociocultural milieu may provide customs and models that cultivate illness-producing behavior patterns; examples are family eating patterns and teen peer pressure to drink alcohol, smoke, or use drugs. There is nothing abnormal about the ways such habits are learned and function. They are learned the way all adaptive habits are learned; they are effective in producing desired immediate consequences. They are called dysfunctional only because they produce other unhealthy long-term consequences, often called side effects.

Faulty Stress and Coping Patterns
Behavioral health theorists consider stress to be a natural and necessary part of adaptive living; but if coping with day-to-day stressful episodes is ineffective, normal stress reactions may persist over more extended periods of time and produce steady-state changes that are unhealthy. This happens when daily living produces a series of behavior episodes that a person evaluates as unsuccessful, threatening, or thwarting, resulting in a continuing mobilization of stress reactions, called *cumulative stress*. Without periodic demobilization of stress reactions to permit restoration of normal steady states, a person's adaptive capability may erode.

Humans' bodies limit the effects of cumulative stress by shifting to a different steady-state pattern (Selye, 1976), and some normal temporary reactions may become persistent symptoms. For example, somatization may occur (Katon & Dengerink, 1983). Emotional states, such as anger, fear, or depression, are usually components of stress reactions (Lazarus, 1991; Novaco, 1995). Through brain-behavior interactions, emotional arousal activates biological processes to support coping behavior; among these processes are increased heart rate, blood pressure, and respiration; vasoconstriction; metabolic and immune system changes. If such biological mobilization persists because of unsuccessful coping, those temporary states may come to function as new, habitual steady-state parameters—for example, hypertension—and result in somatization, manifested as headaches or tachycardia (Adler & Matthews, 1994; Carmody & Matarazzo, 1991; Katon & Dengerink, 1983; Miller, 1983; Pierce, 1995; Snyder & Forsyth, 1991). Cognitive evaluations of symptoms may produce further stress that exacerbates the problem, as in a positive feedback process. For example, tachycardia may be interpreted as a heart attack, producing a panic reaction or illness behaviors to avoid the anticipated disaster.

Disease and Injury

Disease and injury place direct physical demands and stress on the body, and these automatically activate biological stress reactions to cope with the disruption. Such reactions appear as immune system, body temperature, and circulatory changes. The resulting disruptions may be exacerbated or attenuated by psychological/behavioral responses to both temporary and chronic conditions. For example, smoking produces circulatory changes that slow down the healing process following surgery; anticipatory evaluations of the potential consequences of a disease or injury may activate a fear-based stress response or behaviors that interfere with recovery; conversely, positive emotional states or attributions of being able to deal effectively with circumstances important to one's self may facilitate recovery from or prevention of illness (Antonovsky, 1984; Karoly, 1991; Strickland, 1984). Patients typically play a key role in implementing treatment regimens, and if they fail to do so responsibly, a behavior called *noncompliance*, their recovery or rehabilitation may be negatively affected. Chronic conditions, such as diabetes or pain, can be exacerbated by faulty lifestyle habits (Turk & Rudy, 1995). Thus, psychological/behavioral interventions can significantly influence treatment of and rehabilitation from traditional health problems that are initially caused by disease/injury rather than psychological/behavioral disruptions when patients are helped to learn and use different lifestyle and coping habits (see Johnston, Weinman, & Marteau, 1991).

PROCEDURAL MODEL

Behavioral medicine/health applies procedural models that have been developed by other approaches to influence biological functions and health and illness states. These strategies have been applied to every basic human physiological system and to diverse health problems involving them. Although a large and growing body of evidence supports the efficacy of these methods for influencing some biological processes, this is an emerging field and there is much yet to learn (Araki, 1992; Caddy & Byrne, 1992; Carlson & Seifert, 1991; Carr & Dengerink, 1983; Kaptein, van der Ploeg, Garssen, Schreurs, & Beunderman, 1990; Matarazzo et al., 1984). These procedures emphasize careful specification of the changes to be produced, and creation of a therapeutic relationship with and motivation of clients to facilitate their effective participation in therapy.

Collectively practitioners of behavioral medicine/health approaches use combinations of direct feedback, corrective thought and action, and social modeling that assume a reciprocity of influence among biological, psychological, behavioral, and environmental factors similar to those represented in this book's comparative framework (Thoresen, 1984). The treatment strategies appear to share a fundamental assumption: Desired changes will result not from what someone else does to the patient, but from the patient's own efforts; the role of others is to help patients learn to regulate their own functioning. Therefore, an important side effect of effective treatment can be clients' increased belief in their own efficacy. Most behavioral medicine/health applications can be grouped into three strategies: biofeedback; controlling emotions and stress reactions; and modifying coping skill components of lifestyles. In practice, they are combined with varying emphases on each. For example, biofeedback strategies also use the other techniques. Patients are taught to believe that biological processes can be influenced or controlled by thoughts and actions, and that they can learn to control their biological symptoms by using biofeedback strategies; this is cognitive restructuring. They are taught to selectively attend to and monitor relevant biofeedback signals—coping skills—and are motivated to use relaxation methods and variations in their thinking activity as means of influencing the target biological state, which is controlling stress reactions and emotions.

BIOFEEDBACK

Biofeedback is a generic term for strategies in which a person consciously and intentionally monitors an observable indicator of some biological state and uses that information to regulate the psychological-behavioral activity so as to influence that biological state (Steger, 1983). Because different kinds of phenomena and levels of organization ranging from micro to macro are involved, biofeedback must be understood from "a comprehensive, multitheoretical, multidisciplinary, and multilevel framework" (Schwartz, 1984, p. 308).

Biofeedback uses a model of negative feedback-based regulation like that of our framework. It requires the following steps:

1. Identifying the relevant aspects of a specific biological system to be influenced, and the state to be produced or maintained.
2. Specifying observable indicators of the relevant biological responses the person wants to control and how he or she can monitor them.
3. Defining behavior episodes in which the client's goal is to think and act so as to produce a desired value of the monitored feedback signal on the assumption that the signal will reflect the desired biological state.
4. Practicing in relevant behavior episodes until the desired biological state can be intentionally produced in appropriate real-life episodes.

Each aspect of this basic strategy can be varied (Schwartz and associates, 1995).

Identifying the Biological Function to Be Controlled
Biofeedback training has been focused on every major biological system: circulatory, gastrointestinal, immune, muscular, and neural. Different aspects of each system may be targeted for control. For example, biofeedback has been used to control blood pressure, heart rate, and peripheral vasoconstriction or dilation, and to control the entire skeletal muscle system through relaxation training, or tension in specific muscle groups, as in relieving muscle tension in the head and neck to alleviate headaches.

Specifying Relevant Feedback Signals and How to Monitor Them
There are two defining attributes for a relevant feedback signal. First, it must reflect the biological state to be controlled in such a way that it will change when the targeted state changes. Thus, selection of a relevant feedback signal requires one to have a model of the organizational dynamics of that biological system from which such relationships can be predicted. For example, because the heart's pumping action moves blood through the arterial system, the temporal patterning of blood flow in an artery—the pulse rate—reflects the temporal patterning of heart action. Second, the signal must be perceptible by the person if he or she is to focus attention on it selectively. Of course, there are individual differences in perceptual acuity in different modalities.

Sometimes monitoring can occur through natural observation. For example, patients can kinesthetically observe variations in specific muscle tension by concentrating attention on those muscles, or they can observe their heart rate by holding their fingers against an artery. Many biological functions, however, are difficult to monitor through direct observation, so instruments may be used for real-time measurement of them and to provide perceptible signals a person can monitor. Several monitoring technologies have been created and used: (1) cardiovascular for cardiac function and blood pressure monitoring, (2) electromyographic (EMG) for muscle activity monitoring, (3) peripheral vasomotor for monitoring vascular dialation or constriction, (4) electroencephalographic (EEG) for monitoring brain functioning, and (5) electrodermal (GSR) for skin conductance or resistance monitoring (Schwartz and associates, 1995; Steger, 1983).

The timing of feedback signals may vary in relation to activity to influence them. For example, feedback signaling changes in blood pressure may be observed while the activity is in progress, whereas feedback signaling weight loss or gain may involve significant time lapses between the activity and observation of relevant feedback signals. Prompt feedback is the most influential. Sometimes an extended period of time must elapse before feedback signals indicate that the desired state—such as significant weight reduction—is occurring. In these cases, it is desirable to have more frequent feedback signals or subgoals for substates to signal progress toward the ultimate desired state. These small signs are needed to maintain the person's motivated effort; examples are indicators of increased exercise, decreased caloric intake, and small but progressive amounts of weight loss.

Theoretically, any biological function that provides feedback signals people can consciously monitor might be influenced by psychological or behavioral activity. For example, physical connections exist between the nervous system and components of the immune system that provide structural bases for each to influence the other. Also, evidence is growing that psychological/behavioral functioning can produce some kinds of immune system changes and that the immune system may affect brain functions (Hall & Kvarnes, 1991; Cohen & Herbert, 1996). However, a person cannot monitor such changes in real time because of limitations in current monitoring methods.

Defining Training Episodes
Learning intentional, conscious control of biological functions occurs through practice in specific situations in which a pattern of contingencies and consequences can be arranged to facilitate the occurrence and effectiveness of desired patterns. Careful design of the behavior episodes used for training, and preparation of patients to participate in them actively are essential. Clients must have clear goals and evaluative criteria for regulating their efforts, must understand the feedback signal and how to monitor it, and must be able to do what is required. If instruments are used to monitor feedback signals, the training episodes may be constrained to laboratorylike settings, although portable monitoring technologies are becoming available for some biological functions (Carlson & Bernstein, 1995; Turk & Rudy, 1995).

Practicing Relevant Behavior Episodes
A series of behavior episodes or learning trials is typically required for the desired learning to occur. However, learning to control a biological function in an artificial situation designed by a therapist does not mean the client will automatically be able to control that response in real-life situations. Once clients can control the function in the behavior episodes during training, additional training in more natural episodes is desirable to facilitate transfer to and maintenance in real-life situations of their new, self-management capability (Turk & Rudy, 1995).

Controlling Emotions and Stress Reactions

Many health problems and somatic symptoms are products of cumulative stress in which emotions are important components. Therefore, alleviation or prevention of such problems can often be accomplished through control of emotions and stress reactions. Two ways are used and typically combined in practice: (1) biological regulation, and (2) cognitive regulation.

Biological Regulation

Stress and emotional states linked to social and task demands usually involve heightened arousal states; these are manifested in increases in sympathetic nervous system activity and muscle tension in preparation for increased action (Carlson & Bernstein, 1995). Frequent, persistent activation of the sympathetic nervous system without adequate reduction through effective behavior can produce health problems and somatization. Some kinds of behaviors cannot occur simultaneously: people cannot stand and sit at the same time. If people can activate responses that are contradictory to unwanted ones, such as stress and emotions, they can prevent or interrupt these responses. A strategy frequently used for this purpose is the induction of self-controlled states of relaxation.

What is relaxation? Diverse evidence suggests that an integrated pattern of neurological and biological functioning exists that is contradictory to sympathetic nervous system and motoric activation, which produces decreases in respiratory rate, muscle tension oxygen consumption, and heart rate, and increases in skin resistance and alpha wave activity (Benson, 1975, 1984; Carlson & Bernstein, 1995; Davidson & Schwartz, 1976). For example, electrical stimulation of portions of a cat's hypothalamus results in pupil constriction, decreased muscle tension, blood pressure and respiratory rate—and a relaxed cat (Hess, 1957). Hess interpreted this "trophotropic response" as a "protective mechanism against overstress," which promotes a "restorative process" in opposition to "ergotropic reactions" involving increased "oxidative metabolism and utilization of energy" (p. 40). If people can activate a relaxation state, then stress reactions and emotional states that typically prepare them for action will be inhibited or demobilized, including their biological components.

Multiple relaxation methods exist that are a form of biofeedback regulatory control (Benson, 1984; Hillenberg & Collins, 1982). In *progressive relaxation*, the assumption is made that relaxing skeletal muscles will produce feedback signals through the ascending reticular activating system (ARAS); these signals will result in changes in neural—such as hypothalamic—activation and reduce sympathetic nervous system activation. People can learn to relax any group of skeletal muscles intentionally by attending to the feel of the muscles' tension, and using that subjective experience as the feedback signal for consciously controlling the muscle state. Other biological processes may be intentionally controlled to make them function as they would in a relaxed state; these include rate and depth of breathing, cardiac regulation, and feeling of skin warmth. *Autogenic training* (Luthe, 1969) illustrates such a multivariate approach.

The roots of *meditation methods* are in Eastern religions, such as yoga, zen, and transcendental meditation. If muscle tension, stress, and emotional states are regulated by perceptual and thought processes and if one eliminates all or most perceptual and thinking activity—particularly anticipatory evaluative thinking—a relaxed state should occur. Muscle relaxation and controlled breathing may also help produce such a meditative state. Meditation methods differ somewhat, but they usually have some version of four basic elements (Benson, 1984):

1. Eliminating perceptual input by locking attention onto some monotonous stimulus, such as a sound, word, or phrase repeatedly thought or spoken, or fixed gazing at some object
2. Disregarding thoughts that may intrude into the meditative state
3. Assuming a relaxed posture to decrease muscle tonus
4. Meditating in a quiet context, usually with eyes closed, to reduce external stimulation. This is analogous to a state of stimulus deprivation.

Relaxation is assumed to follow naturally the elimination of perceptual and cognitive activity, as in sleep. *Hypnosis* is another method for inducing relaxation states through severely limiting and controlling perceptual and cognitive activity.

Cognitive Regulation

Meditation methods seek to reduce stress and emotional reactions by eliminating perceptual/cognitive influences. *Cognitive regulation* has the same objective but seeks to accomplish it not by eliminating such influences but by changing their content. Cognitive regulation is involved in all human behavior, so the key issue is what kind of regulation is operative (Karoly, 1991). Cognitive therapies assume that troublesome stress and emotional reactions result from faulty beliefs, appraisals, and attributions, particularly anticipatory ones. If more adaptive cognitions replace faulty ones, a procedure frequently called *cognitive restructuring,* reduction in troublesome stress and emotional reactions should follow. Evaluative and anticipatory cognitions about the nature and causes of health and illness significantly influence how people deal with their health issues (Rodin & Salovey, 1989).

Cognitive regulation has been used with diverse health issues (see Kendall & Turk, 1984). For example, when people are faced with stressful medical treatment or diagnostic procedures, such as surgery, chemotherapy, or cardiac catheterization, their anticipatory thoughts about the impending experience and potential consequences can activate stress reactions. Helping patients adopt less stressful thought patterns enables them to control their fear and cope more effectively with the experience. Cognitive regulation methods have also been used to help people cope with chronic conditions, such as pain, insomnia, or asthma, through tactics such as attentional diversion, thought substitution, thought stopping, and problem solving; these tactics help them construct coping strategies (Kaptein et al., 1990). Symptom alleviation may result from cognitive restructuring if the symptoms are somatic manifestations of stress reactions.

MODIFYING COPING SKILLS

Effective self-management in coping with health and illness involves "patients' control over their awareness and expression of symptoms, their reaction to illness triggers (e.g., stress, fear), their display of high-risk (usually addictive) behavior patterns, and/or their day-to-day performance of complex and effortful, therapeutic regimes or preventive health-care activities" (Karoly, 1991, p. 581) Skill training strategies and methods are useful for teaching coping skills. Karoly (1991) illustrates the application to health issues of seven categories of intervention: (1) early-stage motivation enhancement, (2) behavioral enactment training, (3) cognitive regulator development and/or modification, (4) pre- and post-performance monitoring and evaluation training, (5) environmental manipulation, (6) affect management, and (7) persistence training. A skill training strategy is particularly relevant to efforts to modify addictive and lifestyle patterns that contribute to health problems and to rehabilitation activities.

EVALUATING CLIENT PROGRESS AND OUTCOMES

The outcomes to be produced are always defined in terms of some biological state and/or behavior patterns linked to that state. These outcomes are specified as therapy goals and subgoals during treatment planning. A key facet of behavioral medicine/health interventions is explicit monitoring of the variables to be changed, through both direct observation and technological monitoring. The therapy itself continuously produces data showing how much the target states have changed. As psychological/behavioral functioning is the means by which biological/health states are influenced, process evaluations of the extent to which the patient is behaving appropriately are essential—for example, is the patient complying with the diet plan? Monitoring treatment compliance is a key process evaluation, as considerable time may have to elapse after relevant psychological/behavioral changes have occurred for the desired biological change to occur—such as weight loss.

EVALUATION OF THE APPROACH

Like the therapies that undergird their approach behavioral medicine/health practitioners adopt an empirical epistemology and emphasize empirical verification of the models, strategies, and methods, employed. Perhaps this is even more critical for these practitioners because of the need to demonstrate the credibility of their interventions to traditional medical professionals. Experimental designs with nonpatient subjects, such as testing methods for consciously influencing blood pressure, can sometimes be used to collect empirical evidence that their interventions do produce the desired effects. Practitioners of behavioral medicine/health also draw freely from any discipline with knowledge and know-how of potential applicability to some health issue; they avoid becoming doctrinaire in either conceptualization or method. In that sense, they might be thought of as part of the more general movement toward integration in psychotherapy. Because the dependent variables upon which they focus are biological in nature, they can capitalize upon an accepted theoretical model of human biological structures and functions, and extensive methods for measuring those functions, to guide their work. A theoretical model for psychological and behavioral functioning capable of achieving consensual endorsement has yet to be developed.

CHAPTER 13

Eclectic and Integrative Approaches

HISTORICAL PERSPECTIVE

The fields of psychology, psychiatry and social work took a quantum leap forward once the idea gained credibility that some human difficulties can be ameliorated by psychological as well as medical methods and procedures. After this point, psychotherapy approaches began to proliferate. Over 400 different approaches have been created during the 100-year history of psychotherapy (Karasu, 1986), each purportedly unique and superior to others. Each approach "developed its own jargon that confounds dialogue across orientations and widens the theoretical rift. Isolated language systems and rival definitions encourage clinicians to wrap themselves in semantic cocoons from which they cannot escape and which others cannot penetrate" (Norcross, 1990, p. 218). "Most school adherents display a staunch unwillingness to consider the possible merits of opposing positions" (Lazarus, 1996, p. 59). Therapy approaches, "like battling siblings, competed for attention and affection in a 'dogma eat dogma' environment" (Norcross & Newman, 1992, p. 3).

The continuing proliferation of approaches has prompted a growing call for some kind of synthesis. The rationale: All approaches deal with human functioning; basic change processes must be the same for all humans; a finite number of general principles should underlie the surface diversity, even as each approach may also have something unique to offer. Efforts to produce some form of synthesis are currently called *eclectic* or *integrative approaches.* Historical detail about this movement and its characteristics may be found in Arkowitz (1992), Beutler and Clarkin (1990), Gold (1996), Goldfried (1995), Kazdin (1996), Lazarus (1996), Norcross and Goldfried (1992), and Stricker and Gold (1993, 1996).

478

There is resistance to such efforts. Some theorists argue that metaphysical and epistemological differences underlying diverse approaches are so basic as to prevent sensible integration of them (e.g., Fischer, 1995; Lazarus, 1995a), and that "there appear to be no data to support the notion that a combination of different theories can result in a more robust therapeutic technique" (Lazarus, 1996, p. 59). However, practitioners apparently ignore these objections, as typically about half report using an eclectic or integrative approach (Jensen, Bergin, & Greaves, 1990). There is both clinical and experimental evidence "that the activities of experienced therapists of differing orientations are becoming similar, even though their conceptualizations of cases may be articulated quite differently" (Norcross & Newman, 1992, p. 30). Practitioners appear to use methods that work regardless of the "school" that developed them (Garfield & Bergin, 1994). Safran and Messer (1997) have criticized integrationist strategies, arguing for "a more contextually based, pluralistic approach toward psychotherapy integration," and "an atmosphere of confronting and discussing difference rather than shunning it." They warn that "a theoretical system is always in danger of becoming a fossilized remnant of what was once a vital insight," resulting in a withering of creativity (p. 149).

FACTORS INFLUENCING INTEGRATIVE EFFORTS

Eight factors are said to be pressing psychotherapists toward integrative efforts (Norcross & Newman, 1992):

1. Creation of many purportedly different approaches
2. Evidence that each approach is useful with some but not all types of problems
3. Evidence that psychotherapy is superior to no treatment, but lack of evidence that any approach is consistently superior to others, except for a few specific types of problems (Lambert & Bergin, 1994)
4. Increased communication among therapists from different "schools" facilitating acceptance of, and opportunities to experiment with, different approaches
5. Growing belief that factors common to many approaches influence desired outcomes
6. New socioeconomic influences such as the prevalence of third-party sources of fees accompanied by increased demand for accountability and documentation of the effectiveness of an approach
7. Increasing interest in and development of short-term treatments aimed at specific types of problems, influenced by managed care efforts to reduce health care costs

8. Institutionalization of integration efforts through organizations, publications, and professional meetings

Like other professions promoting a professional service, psychotherapists must be responsive to the needs and expectations of a more knowledgeable public about the service they are being offered (see *Consumer Reports*, 1995). Therapists whose approaches typically involve several years of continuous treatment, as in psychoanalysis, are increasingly concerned that economic pressures will erode their potential client base.

TYPES OF INTEGRATIVE EFFORTS

The comparative framework in this book reveals that integration might occur at different levels.

1. Guiding assumptions—ontology, cosmology, and epistemology
2. Conceptual models—the aspects of people emphasized
3. Propositional models—how things are related, function, and change
4. Procedural models—how things may be influenced

There is immense heterogeneity in the psychotherapy integration movement and multiple paths toward integration are being explored (Norcross & Newman, 1992). This upheaval results in concern that the integration movement will simply add to the proliferation of psychotherapy approaches rather than reduce the current heterogeneity. The multiple pathways toward integration currently followed can be grouped into three categories (Arkowitz, 1992): *common factors* (focused primarily on 4 in the list above); *technical eclecticism* (emphasizing number 4 of this list), and *theoretical integration* (concentrating on 1, 2, and 3). Exemplars have been chosen to illustrate each category.

METAPHYSICAL AND EPISTEMOLOGICAL ASSUMPTIONS

The theorists to be discussed often fail to be explicit about their metaphysical assumptions. They do consider important the interactive influences among clients' biological, psychological, behavioral, and social/environmental factors, so their implicit ontology combines the materialist and idealist positions and imply a psychophysical interactionism. They assume that all aspects of people and their contexts are mutually influential, calling this transaction *cir-*

cular or *cyclical dynamics,* and argue that a change in any aspect of a person such as cognitions or actions, or the person's context may lead to changes in other aspects. This view is similar to the open systems model of the comparative framework used in this book.

The eclectic theorists adopt a *representationist* or *constructivist epistemology* of realism; they believe that empirical criteria are primary in clinical decision making. Lazarus (1992) contrasts this view with a pure epistemology of idealism:

> Given the fact that observations do not occur in a vacuum but are influenced by our viewpoints . . . is it, in fact, possible to separate observations from theories? According to extreme views of social constructionism [Gergen, 1982], we create what we observe to the extent that we cannot discover what is inherent in nature; rather, we invent our theories and categories, and view the world through them. (p. 234)

Even though observation and theory cannot be totally separated, the distinction is useful. " 'Observations' refer to notions that call for minimal speculation"—he hit his boss and left—whereas "theories" involve a "range of assumptions"—his castration anxiety linked to his father is expressed toward his boss as displaced conflictual impulses—that make them "quantitatively and qualitatively different." "The point at issue is that observations do not have to constitute pure facts in order to be separable from theories. If it were deemed impossible to ever separate the two, how would we ever test our theories?" (Lazarus, 1992, p. 234) This view is similar to the distinction in this book's comparative framework between perceptions as imagistically coded representations resulting primarily from selective sensory-perceptual processes, and conceptions as abstractly coded representations resulting from cognitive self-organizing and self-constructing processes.

COMMON FACTORS

Schools of psychotherapy stress their differences to convey what they consider to be their unique value. For six decades, beginning with Rosenzweig (1936), others have focused on similarities among approaches (Arkowitz, 1992; Goldfried & Newman, 1986). Our *Systems of Psychotherapy* book (Ford & Urban, 1963) sought to identify similarities and differences among 10 approaches. Empirical evidence that different approaches yield comparable effects implies that similar outcomes may be produced by similar interventions. The *common factors* approach seeks to discover "the profile of factors that are *most strongly associated with positive therapeutic outcome*" as a basis for improving psychotherapy (Arkowitz, 1992, p. 275).

Whereas common factors might be sought at all four levels identified by our comparative framework, similarities in procedural models have been stressed; these are strategies and methods for influencing change. For example, Goldfried (1995) recommends focusing on the level of *clinical strategy* lying between theory and technique. In his view common strategies must represent robust phenomena as they have survived the "biases" of different metaphysical and theoretical models. Arkowitz (1995) argues that the objective of common factors should be the development of propositions regarding the processes of change that serve to specify the nature and interactions of both common and specific factors. Strupp (1995) considers the most challenging questions to be, What are the essential ingredients of therapeutic influence? How does change come about?

A number of issues are concerned with common factors: What are they? How many are there? Are their influences additive or interactive? Are different combinations of common factors manifested in successful treatment of different kinds of patients and problems? (See *Clinical Psychology: Science and Practice*, 1995, 2, (1), for discussions.) Weinberger (1995) describes five empirically supported factors: (1) the therapeutic relationship; (2) expectations of therapeutic success; (3) confronting or facing the problem; (4) providing an experience of mastery or cognitive control over problems; and (5) attribution of therapeutic success or failure. Goldfried (1995) includes (1) culturally induced expectations that therapy can be helpful; (2) participation in a therapeutic relationship; (3) the possibility of obtaining an external perspective on oneself and the world; (4) encouragement of corrective experiences; and (5) opportunities to repeatedly test reality. Lambert (1992) grouped diverse lists into *support, learning,* and *action factors* that he believes to represent a developmental sequence presumed to operate in many treatment approaches.

EXEMPLARS OF COMMON FACTORS

Approaches often cited as including a common factors view (Arkowitz, 1992; Norcross & Goldfried, 1992; Gold, 1996) are those of Beitman (1987, 1992), Frank (1982), Garfield (1980, 1992), and Prochaska and DiClemente (1984, 1992). Frank defined *demoralization* and *restoring morale* as the common client problem and goal. Therapeutic components include a confiding, emotionally charged relationship with a helpful person, a healing setting, a rationale or myth used to help clients understand themselves and their problems, and a ritual for helping them resolve their problems. Garfield's guiding assumptions (1992) include these: (1) Most apparently successful approaches rely on common factors for many of their positive outcomes. (2) Therapy must be guided by an understanding of each client's unique patterns of functioning. (3) Theory and methods chosen should fit each client's particular problems and patterns. We have selected Beitman's and Prochaska and DiClemente's approaches as exemplars.

CONCEPTUAL MODEL

Beitman, and Prochaska and DiClemente, stress the commonalities among therapy strategies and tactics rather than propose specific conceptual models. In that sense, they resemble the thought of learning theorists who assumed that learning principles and processes are the same for all kinds of behavior in all kinds of species, so a conceptual model was not required. For Beitman and Prochaska and DiClemente, the stages and levels of treatment, as well as the assumed reciprocal relationships between pharmacotherapy and psychotherapy (Beitman, Hall, & Woodward, 1992) imply a model including all kinds of behavior—a biopsychosocial model. This view enables them to deal with varied conceptual models of other approaches. Beitman seeks flexible models that can "assimilate new ideas generated from patients, other psychotherapies, other psychotherapists, colleagues, personal life experiences, and research," and accommodate each therapist's "psychotherapy schemas" and the "schemas" of each patient (1992, p. 202). Beitman, however, does emphasize two specific concepts: *core interpersonal schema* and *unresolved trauma*.

Core Interpersonal Schema (CIS)
Schemas are considered "conceptual maps" used by people to interpret and construct reality; the core interpersonal schema is one type. It "is based upon early experiences with caregivers and modified by subsequent intimate relationships. It represents the self in relationship to others and carries with it both self-identity and the manner in which interpersonal relationships are to be formed" (Beitman, 1992, p. 207). Therefore, intra- and interpersonal functioning are guided by the same schema. Its basic elements are two figures in a dynamic equilibriated relationship with one another; they create "a dialectic tension seeking resolution, and the degree of psychopathology appears to be dependent upon the degree of this power differential" (p. 208). Superego-id or grandiose-depreciated self (psychoanalysis), topdog-underdog (Gestalt), rescuer-supplicant (existential) all refer to this duality. It includes "buttons" that when "pushed" activate certain emotions, thoughts, and/or actions, and "scripts" that represent potential patterns of actions and consequences. The concept of the core interpersonal schema is similar to the behavior episode schema in our comparative framework, but a core interpersonal schema is a

highly generalized schema that is activated in all imagined or actual interpersonal episodes. The person does not possess different schemas for different relationships.

Unresolved Trauma

Trauma refers to very distressing events such as sexual, physical, and emotional abuse, rape, and early caregiver loss through death or separation. *Unresolved* means that the effects of those events continue to influence the person.

> The painful emotions are walled off from consciousness but enter consciousness indirectly when some environmental event bears sufficient similarity to the old hurtful situations to trigger its associated feelings. Patients usually have no idea about the origin of these feelings, which usually present as symptoms. (Beitman, 1992, p. 206)

It is not clear whether this is a separate trauma schema, or whether the trauma manifests itself through the person's core interpersonal schema.

Propositional Model

The primary attention of these three theorists is on intervention—the development of a procedural model. An explanation or theory of why or how those interventions influence change—a propositional model—is not provided.

Beitman does propose a proposition called *interpersonal loops*. A person's core interpersonal schema "is played onto the environment through expectations and behavior" which induce others "to fit their role expectations through a variety of subtle clues" called *metacommunication* (Beitman, 1992, p. 208). One person's metacommunications interact with those from another person, producing interpersonal loops that some call vicious cycles, or virtuous cycles, or cyclical psychodynamics. Interventions can be made at different points in such loops, to provide different consequences, encourage alternate actions, or cultivate different thoughts. This proposition is similar to the control systems model in our comparative framework and to habitual behavior episode schemas influencing the content and dynamics of specific behavior episodes. The implication is that disrupting habitual interpersonal patterns activates change, but the nature of that change process is not explained.

Prochaska and DiClemente assert that effective change can result only from intentional activity by the client. "Clients have potential resources as self-changers, which must be used in order to effect a change. In fact, clients need to shoulder much of the burden of change and look to the therapist for consultation on how to conceptualize the problem and ways to free themselves to move from one stage to another" (Prochaska & DiClemente, 1992, p. 315). This assertion appears similar to the proposition in our comparative framework that people are self-organizing and self-constructing.

PROCEDURAL MODEL

Beitman's Model

Enduring psychotherapeutic change results from helping patients correct faulty self-representations, behavior patterns, and interpersonal cycles resulting from unresolved *traumatic experiences* and maladaptive *core interpersonal schemas* (Beitman, 1992). It occurs through a four-stage process: (1) engagement or relationship building; (2) searching for patterns in client functioning, similar to problem definition and acceptance in other approaches; (3) instigating personal/interpersonal change that occurs in three substages of (a) giving up the old pattern, (b) beginning a new pattern, and (c) maintaining the new pattern; and (4) preparing for termination. Two basic strategies are emphasized: *self-observation*—awareness of the pattern as it occurs—and *exposure*—occurrance of the pattern under altered conditions. These strategies are similar to our comparative framework assumptions that new learning requires client awareness of and disruption of a pattern while it is occurring; change can occur only in the here and now.

Self-observation "while new information is available in the environment" in relation to current core interpersonal schema functioning is a key to changing that schema. It involves becoming aware of and describing "very personal experiences" as targets for pattern analysis and change. "A kind of dual vision is required with one eye on new information and the other eye on the core schema, so that the new light exposes the darkness of old thinking" (Beitman, 1992, p. 209). Facilitated by the working alliance, the therapist's "other-observer aligns with the self-observer of the patient" producing a coupling of "insight" with "outsight" (Beitman, 1992, p. 209). Altering faulty script components of the core interpersonal schema is a "crucial aspect" of change. This is accomplished by "playing out" the script in therapy sessions, such as transference patterns, so the patient can discover that the script does not end as the faulty core interpersonal schema predicts. Thereby, the patient is able to change that script.

Exposure is "controlled exposure to reality" so that unresolved traumas and "distorted schemas" can be altered or "corrected." "New information to dysfunctional schemas is like oxygen to a wound. Once the oxygen reaches the malfunctioning area, healing can begin. Acceptance of the devastation of traumatic events lead to their resolution" (Beitman, 1992, p. 209). Multiple exposures are necessary for change to occur. Somehow awareness and acceptance of new information alters the old and change takes place, but no proposition is suggested to explain how this occurs.

These two strategies can be implemented with a diversity of tactics. One significant way in which psychotherapy approaches differ lies in the tactics they use. Which tactics should be used with a specific patient in different phases of therapy is a function of patients' idiosyncratic patterns. Therefore, Beitman considers assessment or diagnosis an important part of the process. He states that he has not yet tried to evaluate the soundness of his model empirically.

Prochaska and DiClemente's Transtheoretical Model
The transtheoretical model has evolved from a detailed analysis of 24 popular psychotherapy theories and from empirical and clinical evidence about different approaches (Prochaska, 1984). This procedural model rests on a three-dimensional strategy: (1) identification of *levels of change;* (2) specification of *stages of change,* and (3) selection and use of *processes of change* (Prochaska & DiClemente, 1984, 1992).

Levels of change refers to *types of problems.* Symptoms or syndromes can be identified, but they occur within "complex, interrelated levels of human functioning" (1992, p. 306). Prochaska and DiClemente identify five hierarchically organized and interrelated levels of psychological problems: (1) symptom/situational problems, (2) maladaptive cognitions, (3) current interpersonal conflicts, (4) family systems conflicts, and (5) intrapersonal conflicts. Starting with (1) is useful because change tends to occur more quickly with these problems, which are often the primary reason a person seeks therapy. Prochaska and DiClemente prefer "to begin at the highest most contemporary level that clinical assessment and judgment can justify" (1992, p. 397). The further down the hierarchy, the deeper the level, and the further removed from awareness are the causes of the problems; thus, the longer and more complex therapy is likely to be. Levels are interrelated, so any change may produce changes at other levels. Interventions should fit the levels or kinds of problems targeted.

Prochaska and DiClemente provide no theory or empirical evidence to justify these levels, either as different problem levels or as hierarchically organized. On the surface, these levels appear to represent a classification of different problem content—that is, kinds of phenomena. Some phenomena others consider important are not on their list—for example, inappropriate and maladaptive kinds or degrees of emotion, skill deficits, or biological patterns. Why are "intrapersonal conflicts" considered "deeper" than, say, "maladaptive cognitions?" Moreover, if these different kinds of functions are interrelated, a model of organization is implied, but left unstated.

Stages of change is similar to what others call *phases of therapy*. The two theorists identify five: (1) precontemplation, (2) contemplation, (3) preparation, (4) action, and (5) maintenance. Each stage is defined by an invariant set of tasks and a period of time needed to move to the next stage. For example, to move from precontemplation to contemplation, a client must (1) become aware of the problem; (2) take ownership of it; (3) confront its habitual aspects, including defensive maneuvers, that make it difficult to control; and (4) recognize some of its negative aspects. These "tasks" might also be thought of as specific therapy subgoals. Clients differ in their current stage at the time they enter therapy. Some may have traversed the first three stages on their own or through other programs and are ready for action interventions (stage 4). Others may still be at stage 1 or may have struggled on their own to stage 2. Different interventions are effective at different stages because the tasks differ. Therapists need to identify each client's current stage of change so they can select appropriate interventions. Prochaska and DiClemente note that psychotherapists too often assume that all clients are at the same stage when they enter therapy, with undesirable consequences, such as early termination.

Processes of change, is a term which actually refers to *intervention strategies*. The two theorists specify 10 separate and distinct processes of change used by different approaches and supported by empirical evidence: (1) consciousness raising, (2) self-liberation, (3) social liberation, (4) counterconditioning, (5) stimulus control, (6) self-reevaluation, (7) environmental reevaluation, (8) contingency management, (9) dramatic relief, (10) helping relationships. "These are best understood as a middle level of abstraction" between theoretical assumptions and techniques. They represent "types of activity initiated or experienced by an individual in modifying thinking, behavior or affect related to a particular problem" (Prochaska & DiClemente, 1992, p. 302). Diverse client coping activities and therapist techniques can be understood to be a use of one or more of this "finite set" of "basic change processes"; the same strategy can be implemented with different tactics or methods. For example, confrontation provides new information, challenges current thinking, and offers feedback, facilitating more accurate client information processing. All, however, represent the consciousness raising change process. The two theorists provide no propositional model or theory to explain how and why these strategies work—why does "consciousness raising" influence change?

Different strategies and their tactics of implementation are more effective with different levels of problems and stages of change. Different therapies stress different strategies, so Prochaska and DiClemente propose and illustrate how each is most useful with particular combinations of type of problem and stage of therapy. It is often necessary to intervene at multiple levels—types of problems—and they propose three approaches. A *shifting levels strategy* focuses initially on one type of problem such as symptom/situational, and then on another such as maladaptive cognitions. A *key-level strategy* is useful when "available evidence points to one key level of causality of a problem, and the client can be effectively engaged at that level" (Prochaska & DiClemente, 1992, p. 308). A *maximum-impact strategy* is useful in complex cases where "it is evident that multiple levels are involved as a cause, an effect, or a maintainer" of problems (p. 308). Interventions with different types or levels of problems may have synergistic rather than sequential effects.

"In summary, the transtheoretical approach sees therapeutic integration as the differential application of the processes of change at specific stages of change, according to identified problem level" (Prochaska & DiClemente, 1992, p. 307) Accurate assessments of a client's stage and level are essential for selecting intervention strategies. The therapy relationship is considered important but is not included in the theorists' list of processes of change. They apparently view it as a prerequisite for all intervention strategies and propose that the kind of relationship conditions needed will differ for different combinations of stage of change and type or level of problem.

Empirical evaluation of Prochaska and DiClemente's procedural model is extensive and ongoing. Because of the nature of their research funding, most of their evaluations have been focused on behavioral health problems such as smoking, alcoholism and other addictions, obesity and weight control.

> "Research has been highly supportive of the core constructs. . . . Longitudinal studies have supported . . . predicting premature termination and short-term and long-term outcomes. Comparative outcome studies support the potential of stage-matched interventions to outperform the best alternative treatments available. Population-based studies support the importance of developing interventions that match the needs of individuals at all stages of change [and] the relevance of this approach for generating participation rates that are dramatically higher than traditionally reported." (Prochaska & DiClemente, 1992, p. 328)

TECHNICAL ECLECTICISM AND ASSIMILATIVE APPROACHES

Eclecticism is often considered an atheoretical stance and defined as selecting what seems best from different alternatives. It is a fundamental error, however, to assume that technical eclecticism is anti- or atheoretical (Beutler, 1995). "There are vast differences between a haphazard, subjective, smorgasbord conception of eclecticism (known as *syncretism*)" and one based on psychological science (Lazarus, 1992, p. 232). Therapists need "a superordinate theory of human functioning" to guide the selection of interventions, but the theories used are "directed by one's personal preferences" (Beutler & Consoli, 1992, p. 282) and are theories of personality and pathology without adequate theories of change. Technical eclectics guide their work with different personality theories, but "seek a common theory about how to facilitate change." These are "if-then" theories that "rely on empirical evidence in identifying what variables should be included and in determining when and what strategy or procedure is applied" (Beutler, 1995, p. 80). The eclectic theorists believe that integration should occur at the procedural rather than theoretical level, and that interventions are not dependent for their effectiveness on the theories that generated them.

Maintaining one theoretical model but incorporating strategies and techniques from other approaches, called *assimilative integration* (Messer, 1992), is a way many therapies are being elaborated. For example, Stricker and Gold (1996) describe an assimilative psychodynamic approach in which diverse strategies and methods are freely used based on therapists' ongoing assessment of the patient's psychodynamic status. Two widely known exemplars of technical eclecticism are multimodal therapy (Lazarus, 1989, 1992, 1995b) and systematic eclectic psychotherapy (Beutler, 1983; Beutler & Clarkin, 1990; Beutler & Consoli, 1992).

CONCEPTUAL MODEL

Lazarus
Lazarus' has labelled his approach *multimodal,* because his conceptual model represents people in terms of seven interactive "modalities of functioning," or kinds of responses. These are his key concepts, symbolized by the acronym BASIC I.D. (1989, 1992):

1. **B**ehavior (skills, instrumental and communicative actions)
2. **A**ffect (emotional states, moods)
3. **S**ensation (perceptions of distressing biological states, such as headaches, nausea)
4. **I**magery (dreams, vivid imagistic memories, and hallucinations)
5. **C**ognition (attitudes, values, opinions, and ideas that interfere with happiness)
6. **I**nterpersonal relationships (bothersome interactions with other people)
7. **D**rugs/biology (drugs being used, illnesses, and health problems)

Lazarus notes that psychologists traditionally use these response classes. His definitions and examples, however, do not include a number of traditional categories (Lazarus, 1985). Deficits in attention, consciousness, and memory processes are not specified, although *nonconscious processes* and *defensive reactions* are "addressed as necessary" during therapy. Perceptions of psychological (affects) and biological (sensations) states are stressed, but perceptions of contexts are not. Interpersonal contexts are emphasized, but the influence of political, sociocultural, and other "macroenvironmental events" must be considered (Lazarus, 1985) He stresses the anticipatory and evaluative aspects of cognition—like feedforward and regulatory processes in our comparative framework; goal setting, information processing, reasoning, and problem solving—directive and control functions in our comparative framework—are not emphasized, although *analytical, planner,* and *thinker* are terms used in his structural profile inventory. Lazarus assumes that these different kinds of responses are in continual "reciprocal transaction," but concepts representing organized patterns of them, such as personality patterns, are not used, perhaps because he stresses individual differences and the idea that everyone constructs his or her own unique patterns.

Beutler

Beutler does not propose a conceptual model but seeks integration among "eclectic models of treatment selection" others have created (Beutler & Clarkin, 1990). He "combines the clinical wisdom and empirical underpinnings of four theories" (p. 15): common factors; prescriptive psychotherapy; differential therapeutics; and systematic eclectic psychotherapy, which includes multimodal therapy. Beutler believes a therapist's "formal theory provides both the foundation for communicating with other professionals and constitutes the philosophy of life that is taught to the patient," and "one theory is considered as 'true' as another, the value resting more on its usefulness and believability than upon its truth" (Beutler & Consoli, 1992, p. 267).

In discussions of therapy, Lazarus uses concepts representing diverse human attributes and their contexts; these include feelings, actions, emotions, intellectual capacity, thoughts, levels of ego integrity, beliefs, unconscious wishes, medical problems, family, and social support systems. The concepts imply a biopsychosocial, person-in-context conceptual model encompassing all the kinds of human functioning studied in psychology. Beutler uses three superordinate concepts with subtypes, designed to facilitate treatment selection, and to encompass predisposing patient personal characteristics, patient problems, environments, and life circumstances.

Three types of *predisposing patient personal characteristics* are identified. *Expectations* reflect "observed or experienced cause and effect relationships";

they are constructed from each person's "unique personal history" and reflect the person's "sociodemographic environment." The characteristics may be situation specific (states) or general (traits). They are "the building blocks both of coping ability and the enduring response patterns we define as 'personality' " (Beutler & Clarkin, 1990, p. 59). This usage is similar to the principle that propositional knowledge functions as a feedforward (anticipatory) process in our comparative framework. Beutler identifies two types: (1) social role expectations—sexual, authority, and family—that influence both daily life and within-therapy functioning; (2) treatment specific expectations about the nature of therapy, the therapist, and potential outcomes that influence the therapy process. *Coping ability* is reflected in problem severity: the effectiveness of one's coping methods to keep anxiety and stress from impairing social and interpersonal functioning, and a person's position or location in the problem-solving process (defined by Prochaska's "phases of change").

Personality characteristics are "recurrent but dynamic patterns that are enacted in . . . new and often threatening experience" (Beutler & Clarkin, 1990, p. 66), similar to our comparative framework's concept of behavior episode schemas. The characteristics vary in "historical significance and generality," degree of "personal sensitivity or receptivity . . . to interpersonal sources of influence or support," and "methods" used in problem resolution (Beutler & Consoli, 1992, p. 272). Four response-specific personality styles that influence motivation and compliance in therapy activity are particularly relevant to treatment planning:

1. Problem severity involves impairments in a person's ability to deal with social, occupational, or interpersonal demands of everyday life and to keep anxiety and distress within manageable limits, as manifested in acute, intense, situation-specific aspects of people's difficulties requiring immediate attention.

2. Problem complexity is the extent to which presenting problems are generalized habits that are repeated as themes of underlying dynamics across situations and are represented symbolically in patients' complaints.

3. Reactance level is the tendency to respond oppositionally to demands, varying from being easily threatened by a perceived loss of autonomy to a high tolerance for such threats.

4. Coping style is one's preferred pattern of interrelated defense mechanisms. Internalizers use self-devaluation and self-blame, compartmentalization of affect, and idealization of others. Externalizers attribute responsibility for their difficulties to external objects or others.

Repressive styles avoid recognizing harmful circumstances. Cyclic styles vary among these styles or from passive to active defenses.

Systematic treatment selection must be based on reliable and valid description of *patient problems* that are the targets of change. *Diagnosis* represents patients' symptoms in terms of accepted syndromes, as in the *DSM-IV* (APA, 1994). Beutler considers this of limited value, particularly with biologically based problems and treatments. However, planning treatment for a specific patient's problems—that is, symptom complex and/or potential underlying conflict syndromes not included in *DSM-IV*—requires describing the content and organization of clients' specific thoughts, feelings and behaviors, and their antecedents and consequents—for example, Lazarus's BASIC I.D. approach.

Therapy theorists differentially emphasize the influence of past or present *environments and life circumstances* on patients' problems. Two sets of context factors are considered relevant to treatment planning. Past and current *environmental stressors* are significant in the development and current functioning of patient problems. The nature of *environmental resources*—sociocultural, family, and social support networks—can significantly influence persistence and change in patient problems and the efficacy of different kinds of intervention.

PROPOSITIONAL MODEL

Multimodal Therapy
Lazarus (1992) relies upon social and cognitive learning theory (Bandura, 1986) because

> its tenets are open to verification or disproof. The efficacy of [many techniques is] readily explained by social and cognitive learning principles. . . . Remaining theoretically consistent but technically eclectic enables therapists to spell out precisely what procedures they use with various clients, and the means by which they select those particular methods. (p. 232)

See Chapter 9 for a discussion of social learning theory.

Like Bandura, Lazarus assumes that the component modalities of functioning operate in patterns of reciprocal influence to produce coordinated patterns, analogous to the principle of unitary functioning in our comparative framework. It follows that faulty functioning in any component modality can produce psychological and behavioral disturbance, and the more faulty the component functions, the more complex will be the disturbance. No propositions about how such reciprocal influence is exercised are offered. The proposition of *firing order* states that a reliable pattern lies behind the ways each person generates negative affect, resulting in habitual vicious cycles—certain thoughts may trigger negative emotions that activate certain actions that produce consequences that confirm the instigating thoughts (see Lazarus, 1985, for examples). This view appears similar to the ideas of the behavior episode schema and behavior episode in our comparative framework.

Systematic Eclectic Psychotherapy

Beutler (Beutler & Consoli, 1992) construes psychotherapy as "a social-influence or persuasion process"; therapists' theories specify "the content of *what* is persuaded" and their "technology functions as the *means* of influence." The quality of the relationship "defines the limiting influence of the procedures used" (p. 266). They are "more a collection of empirical observations than of explanatory constructs," so "models of social influence are sufficiently flexible to encompass a broad array of explanatory theories" (p. 268).

Persuasion or social influence theory, largely from social psychology (e.g., Goldstein et al., 1966), provides propositions about change (Beutler & Clarkin, 1990; Beutler & Consoli, 1992):

1. People differ in their receptivity to direct persuasive efforts.
2. The effectiveness of methods for producing desired persuasion is partially dependent on how they fit recipients' characteristics, such as methods effective with one style of coping may be less effective with others.
3. The effectiveness of methods is a function of the degree to which they manage arousal levels and focus efforts.
4. The degree to which a persuader is viewed as "a safe, knowledgeable, trustworthy, and credible" person affects the degree to which "receivers" will be influenced; for example, empathic, credible, supportive, and caring aspects of a therapy relationship represent underlying but created experiences in effective treatment.
5. Other things being equal, discrepancies between a valued persuader's views and those of willing recipients will predict the amount of attitude change produced. The amount of discrepancy motivates change; the content provides a direction for change.

This is similar to the idea in our comparative framework that disruption of existing steady-state patterns is a prerequisite for change. Beutler does not address the nature of psychological disturbance (psychopathology) but the nature of the interpersonal forces and mechanisms that instigate or inhibit change" (Beutler & Consoli, 1992, p. 267). Each therapist's theory of symptom development provides the patient with an explanation of change and a focus for intervention.

PROCEDURAL MODEL

Interventions are not selected based on their propositional models. Instead, eclectic theorists tend to use two selection criteria: (1) Interventions must be appropriate to target problems, client and therapist characteristics, and the phase of therapy; these decisions require careful individual assessment of clients' unique patterns for which traditional diagnoses, such as those in the *DSM IV,* are not useful. (2) The value of interventions for specific purposes should be supported by empirical evidence and by clinical experience.

Multimodal Therapy

Lazarus's (1990) assumption that everyone is unique and that therapy must be tailored to each individual is the cornerstone of his approach. It follows that one must first identify a client's unique patterns of difficulty through multimodal assessment. Then, the therapist must select and implement interventions specific to that pattern rather than "molding patients to preconceived treatments," as Lazarus believes many other approaches do. A warm, caring, and flexible patient-therapist relationship is the "soil" that enables techniques to "take root," rather than a cause of change, as some assume (Lazarus, 1992). Varying relationship properties in different phases of therapy and with different patients may be desirable. Initially a "neutral, accepting and open atmosphere" is created to cultivate accurate reporting of difficulties in each modality, but as the interviews proceed it is necessary "to gauge how best to augment the level of rapport" with each patient (p. 222). This requires clinical judgment based on careful observation of what patients say and how they say it, and on observing the impact of each intervention.

A multimodal assessment is accomplished during the initial interviews to answer 12 questions (Lazarus, 1992):

1. Are there signs of psychosis?
2. Are there signs of organicity?
3. Is there evidence of depression or suicidal or homicidal tendencies?
4. What are the presenting complaints and what precipitates them?
5. Why are patients seeking therapy now?
6. What are important antecedents?

7. What seems to be maintaining patients' troublesome patterns?
8. What do patients want from therapy?
9. Is a particular therapeutic style indicated or contraindicated?
10. Is individual, group, or/and family therapy most appropriate?
11. Can this therapist create a facilitative therapeutic relationship with this patient, or should the patient be referred elsewhere?
12. What positive attributes/strengths do the patients have?

Interview data plus a *Multimodal Life History Inventory* provide information on which an analysis and profile of current problems in each modality—that is BASIC I.D.—can be based. Sometimes a *Structural Profile Inventory* is also used to provide quantitative ratings of the relevance of each modality. Modality profiles "are far superior to traditional psychiatric diagnoses for guiding treatment selection" (Lazarus, 1992 p. 241). In the assessment process "there is no slavish attention to order," and sometimes "the complete assessment and treatment of the BASIC I.D." is not necessary. It is also useful to identify the consistent patterns with which people generate negative affect in themselves, called the *firing order*. Sometimes an impasse is reached during therapy, and a second order BASIC I.D. assessment may be necessary to identify the source of the difficulty (see Lazarus, 1990, for examples).

Once problems are identified, a comprehensive treatment approach can be planned. The emphasis is on (1) *treatments of choice* for each problem in each modality, based on research about differential effectiveness for specific problems, (2) *tailored interventions* selected to fit patients' beliefs, goals, coping styles, life contexts, affective reactions, and resistances, and (3) *therapists' styles* that match treatment styles to specific client characteristics. Lazarus notes that sometimes adequate research evidence is not available, and the therapist must rely on clinical judgment and straddle the fence between art and science

Different techniques are appropriate for different modalities, but "one cannot elicit or change affects or emotions directly"; they can only be reached through other modalities. Lazarus provides a list of "main hypothesized mechanisms of change" for each modality (Lazarus, 1992, p. 238):

1. Behavior = positive and negative reinforcement; punishment; counterconditioning; extinction
2. Affect = acknowledging, recognizing, and clarifying feelings; abreaction
3. Sensation = tension release; sensory pleasuring
4. Imagery = coping images; change in self-image
5. Cognition = heightening awareness; cognitive restructuring
6. Interpersonal relations = modeling assertive and other social skills; dispersing unhealthy collusions

7.   Drugs/biology = treating medical illness; substance abuse cessation; better nutrition and exercise; psychotropic medication

To call these mechanisms of change is misleading. They include ways therapists might facilitate change, as by reinforcement, clarifying feelings, modeling, medications. They show desired outcomes, such as tension release change in self-image, substance abuse cessation. They do not, however, specify ways of producing them; for example, is relaxation training the preferred method for facilitating tension release? Elsewhere (Lazarus, 1990) illustrates techniques he considers to have received empirical support: modeling and observational learning procedures; social skills training; flooding and exposure; response prevention; cognitive restructuring; desensitization; self-regulatory methods; relaxation training. Most techniques are drawn from cognitive-behavior therapy as research findings indicate that they are the most effective for many kinds of problems in his judgment.

A basic rule is to start with the specific problems of the patient that are most amenable to change or that require immediate attention, so as to augment the therapist's credibility. Problems to be addressed and methods to be used are usually selected through therapist-patient discussions. It would be naive, however, to assume that patients always know what is best and that therapists must always comply. It is initially desirable to follow the patient's "script" fairly closely to help establish good rapport. Later it will be "more acceptable and less threatening" for the therapist to influence choices, but suggesting goals that patients are unlikely to attain should be avoided.

In *bridging*, the therapist deliberately "tunes in" to the patient's preferred problem modality; he or she starts where the patient is. This approach avoids making the patient feel misunderstood and alienated. Once good rapport is established, the therapist can shift the focus to other modalities. It is usually more productive to intervene in the same sequence as the patient's "firing order." Patients decide when to terminate therapy, and most do so before all the issues in their modality "problem profile" are resolved; they often feel capable of dealing with the remaining issues on their own. The task-oriented nature of this therapy seems to avert the development of undue dependency that may create difficulties in termination in other approaches.

Systematic Eclectic Psychotherapy

Beutler and Clarkin (1990) specify decisional criteria for planning discrete treatments targeted at specific problems and considering patient characteristics and environmental conditions. The procedural model is summarized in three domains of decisions: *context of treatment, therapy relationship,* and *strategies and techniques.*

Selecting a *context of treatment* involves three types of decisions. What should be the *treatment setting?* Therapy may be provided in diverse places: inpatient and outpatient, clinics, private offices, patients' homes, and feared situations. Inpatient settings are often necessary for severe acute and chronic problems where psychotherapy may be combined with medical treatments. Less restrictive settings are preferred when feasible.

Should the *treatment mode and format* be psychosocial, medical, or some combination? Individual, family, and group psychosocial formats may be used individually or in simultaneous or sequential formats. Medical formats typically use drugs for psychotic confusion, anxiety, depression, and mania. Medications have side effects and only influence some aspects of patients' problems, making it desirable to combine them with psychosocial formats.

What should be the *treatment intensity,* the frequency and duration of therapy? The first option considered should be no treatment unless proof of the need for treatment is persuasive, and criteria for that decision are provided. As a general rule, symptom-focused treatments require a lesser frequency and duration than do those focused on underlying conflicts. Therapists tend to be biased toward longer term treatment, but treatment plans should recognize that most patients seek only short-term treatments.

The *therapy relationship* has two facets. The first is *patient-therapist compatibility.* Evidence relevant to the guiding theory of social persuasion is interpreted to mean that a complex pattern of initial and background similarities and differences is desirable. Similarities in demographic background and in attributions concerning therapist credibility, competence, and trustworthiness, and some differences in beliefs, values, and interpersonal patterns appear to facilitate establishing a therapeutic relationship. Pairing patients and therapists in terms of such compatibilities can be useful. However, therapists may be able to overcome "problematic initial relationships" with two types of skills for enhancing and maintaining the therapeutic alliance. Moreover, enhancing the fit between patient attributes and treatment conditions is required throughout therapy, and involves continuous "process diagnosis" in order to make the moment-to-moment decisions that are necessary. The goal is to cultivate a positive affective, attitudinal, and behavioral relationship, this may require different methods with different patients at different phases of therapy.

Role induction skills help patients learn how to function effectively as patients. These skills are desirable both when treatment begins and when new treatment methods are introduced. Typical procedures include written and verbal explanations, instructions and examples, observation and participatory learning methods such as role playing and therapeutic contracting. *Relation-*

ship management skills are used to alter the therapy environment to accommodate patient expectations. Situational stimuli, such as the arrangement and decor of the therapy space, availability and behavior of supporting staff, and administrative procedures can fit or contradict patient expectations and personal styles. Different nonverbal styles, such as eye contact, body posture, facial expression, and physical touch, may facilitate or constrain the therapeutic relationship. Verbal behavior style—what is said, the prosodic aspects of speech, and the amount of talk—can influence the quality of the relationship in different ways at different times; sometimes quiet patience is needed; at others active discussion is helpful.

Therapy strategies and techniques are selected using a four-level hierarchical decision-making model, which include "(1) the breadth of the focal objectives, (2) the depth of experience level targeted for change, (3) the mediating phases and goals required by the intervention, and (4) the intratherapy structure required for initiating and maintaining productive work" (Beutler & Clarkin, 1990, p. 222). *Focal objectives* are of two broad types. If the problems seem to be primarily faulty habits maintained by environmental factors, then symptom-focused goals are appropriate. If the patients manifest underlying unresolved conflictual experiences, then conflict resolution goals are primary.

Therapists' technical expertise makes psychotherapy more than the comforting support of a good friendship or caring relationship. Once the focal objective is selected, decisions must be made about the *level(s) of intervention* to be emphasized. The level or depth is defined in terms of the extent to which patients are aware of and capable of controlling their behavior, ranging from conscious experience, contemporary determinants, and voluntary behavior to unconscious experience, historical determinants, and involuntary behavior. Four levels are proposed: overt behavior, cognitive habits, feelings, and unconscious motives. Different interventions appear effective with each, and with patients with different coping styles. This classification confounds kinds of phenomena with awareness of and ability to control them. Presumably people can be unaware of any aspect of their functioning.

The focal objective is not accomplished all at once; it is achieved through *mediating goals and phases of psychotherapy.* Beutler uses Beitman's four therapy phases, each of which involves specific tasks or mediating goals: (1) facilitating patient-therapist engagement, (2) searching patterns to identify the objectives of change, (3) instigating change, and (4) preparing for termination. Beutler added (5) maintaining progress and preventing relapse. Methods are categorized according to the combinations of types or levels of experience and mediating goals with which they are most effective. *Conducting therapeutic work* refers to moment-to-moment decision making that is necessary in the flow of patient-therapist interactions during therapy sessions. There are two broad aspects to "therapeutic work"—"managing arousal level" and "therapeutic focus." "If the therapist is successful in keeping the patient within the range of therapeutic arousal and is able to maintain focus upon the intrasession or extratherapy experiences that are significant to the symptomatic or conflictual dynamic of the problem, success is likely" (Beutler & Clarkin, 1990 p. 284) Procedures should be used that match patient distress or problem severity, reactance level, and problem-solving phase.

THEORETICAL INTEGRATION

The principal objective of theorists who seek to integrate psychotherapeutic models is to develop overarching conceptual and propositional representations of human functioning that can (1) provide for the integrated operation of all biological, psychological, behavioral, social, and environmental aspects of human living, development, and change; and (2) provide a framework for synthesizing diverse models of psychopathology and psychotherapy that others have created (Dobson, 1988).

Three exemplars are analyzed. Each manifests different aspects of dynamic systems models in different ways. Wachtel's (1977) attempt to integrate psychoanalytic and behavioral approaches gave early credibility to the possibility of theoretical integration. This led to an integrative approach he calls *cyclical psychodynamics* (1987, 1993; Wachtel & McKinney, 1992; Wachtel & Wachtel, 1986). Frederick Kanfer and associates (Kanfer, 1971, 1977; Kanfer & Gaelick-Buys, 1991; Kanfer & Karoly, 1972; Kanfer & Schefft, 1988) created a systems-based *self-management approach. Constructivist approaches* are described in recent compendia (Dobson, 1988a; Mahoney, 1995; Neimeyer & Mahoney, 1995).

CYCLICAL PSYCHODYNAMICS

Wachtel's training in psychoanalysis led to his dissatisfaction with what he considered to be an overemphasis on early experience and insight; an insufficient attention to current patterns of functioning, social skills and current environments; and a vagueness about change processes. Psychodynamic therapists emphasized the "inside-out" direction of causality and tended to ignore "outside-in" influences that behaviorists emphasized (Wachtel, 1977). Wachtel found bases for integration by examining the meanings or phenomena to which the terminology of each refers. The result, called *cyclical dynamics,* "seeks to synthesize key facets of psychodynamic, behavioral, and family systems theories" (p. 335) that can embrace all the significant phenomena encompassed by their diverse concepts, and as many types of clinical interventions as can be coherently employed. (Note: Strupp and Binder, 1984, also call their approach *cyclical psychodynamics*.)

Primary Unit of Analysis

In his synthesis, Wachtel (1993) recognizes the importance of all the psychological, behavioral, and environmental component processes featured by different approaches, but places emphasis upon their interrelationships. Therapists must attend "to the precise details of how the person is presently living his life and to how unconscious psychological structures and the patterns of daily life reciprocally interact with and maintain each other" (p. 19). "People live in contexts, and our behavior, both adaptive and maladaptive, is always *in relation to* someone or something" (p. 24). Thus, the person-in-context is his primary unit of analysis.

Conceptual Model

Wachtel utilizes the conceptual models of the three approaches upon which he builds rather than creating one of his own. The concept of anxiety and related distressing affects plays a key role in his propositional model of psychopathology: "In large measure, people seek psychotherapy because they have become afraid of aspects of the world or aspects of their own experience" (Wachtel, 1993, p. 37). He does not describe a theory of the nature of anxiety or the conditions that produce it; he seems to rely on Freud's revised theory of anxiety.

Propositional Model

The distinguishing feature of Wachtel's approach is the "central role it gives to repetitive cycles of interactions between people and to cycles of reciprocal causation between intrapsychic processes and the events of daily living" (1993, p. 17) The circular nature of causality means that people's behavior produces consequences that help shape their behavior; it is a kind of self-fulfilling prophecy; people are proactive and self-constructing, not just reactive.

Such *interaction cycles* are the basic form of normal development, called the "continuous construction model," in which "patterns of internal subjective experience and patterns of relating to others are derived from past relationship experiences but are continuously operating in the present" (Zeanah,

Anders, Seifer, & Stern, 1989, p. 657). The idea that development is a continual, interactive, and mutually influential process between people and their contexts serves to reconcile theories that emphasize the importance of early life experiences, such as psychoanalysis, with the evidence that negative experiences occurring during the first few years of life do not inevitably and irrevocably shape later development. Change occurs throughout the course of life (e.g., Brim & Kagan, 1980). Early experiences are important because they initiate a development pathway that leads a person to act in ways that facilitate an elaboration and perpetuation of that pathway, but developmental pathways can be altered by future experiences. Unless this were so, psychotherapy would be ineffective.

Typically, people's intentions guide their functioning so as to produce consequences they intend to achieve. Feedback from repeated episodes of similar intention-action-consequence cycles leads to the construction of habitual ways of dealing with that type of episode. People are often unaware or unconscious of their habitual patterns, particularly the psychological aspects of them. (Interaction cycles and the patterns they produce are similar to the feedback and feedforward system dynamics, and the behavior episode and behavior episode schemas in the comparative framework used in this book.)

Learned cyclical patterns normally develop further through experience. Wachtel uses Piaget's ideas of schemas, assimilation, and accommodation to explain change processes. Interaction cycles are linked to *schemas*. "No act or experience is ever completely new, uninfluenced by previous schemas. And none is ever completely the same" (Wachtel, 1993, p. 57). When people face a new behavior episode, they use their existing schemas to *assimilate* and *interpret* current events and to guide their actions toward them. This behavior produces stability and continuity in patterns of functioning, but no episode is exactly like any previous one. Therefore, people must adjust their existing schemas to the different aspects of the current episode. This process of *accommodation* is a source of variation and change in existing schemas. Both occur in every behavior episode, but their balance varies. For example, "transference reactions [are] the product of schemas in which assimilation predominates over accommodation" (Wachtel, 1993, p. 58). (Assimilation and accommodation are similar to stability-maintaining and incremental change processes in our comparative framework.)

Wachtel uses a fear-avoidance model of psychopathology. People are said to have an inherent tendency to avoid anxiety. If they can help it, they "do *not* walk around anxious all day." Life is "bounded by invisible markers" to which one responds "with exquisite sensitivity and with scarcely any awareness of being anxious or even of avoiding" (Wachtel, 1993, p. 31). Every child develops fear-avoidance patterns, so "neurosis" is a matter of degree but "loving support, dependability, and encouragement of gradually increasing growth and independence" from family, peers, and friends typically lead to reasonably satisfactory "adaptiveness and attunement to reality" (p. 34).

Psychopathology results from faulty interpersonal fear-avoidance patterns, called *vicious circles* or *cycles*. Wachtel rejects the psychoanalytic concepts of *developmental arrest* and *fixation*—that faulty childhood intrapsychic patterns persist, unchanged by later life events, and automatically operate in adult life. Patients' faulty patterns are not expressions of "a childhood mental state or process" but are elements in vicious circles "in which both the defense and the defended against, both the unconscious psychological forces and the way of life with which they are associated, determine each other in a continuing cycle of confirmation and reconfirmation." The causes "lie not in the distant past but in the interactive present" (Wachtel, 1993, p. 23).

Neurotic avoidance patterns distort further development by producing other outcomes: "Crucial skills of living . . . are impaired because the person is driven by anxiety to avoid the relevant experiences" and behaviors; "clear thinking is disrupted because anxiety-provoking *thoughts* are avoided [leading to] a compelled reaching of false conclusions" that control anxiety in the short term, but produce further problems in the long term; and "clear appreciation of one's own desires, aspirations, concerns, and subjective experience is disrupted, leaving the individual without a rudder" and likely to think, say, and do things "antithetical to [his or her] nature" (Wachtel, 1993, p. 32).

Behaviors used to avoid anxiety are called *defenses*. Ironically, they often produce the very interpersonal and psychological consequences they seek to avoid, thereby perpetuating and elaborating the problem. For example, a patient who fears expression of his anger may control it by behaving submissively toward others, leading them to ignore his needs or desires, increasing the anger he experiences. (This set of circumstances is similar to positive feedback processes in our comparative framework.) Thus, neurotics influence others to act as unwitting accomplices in maintaining their faulty patterns; interpersonal patterns persist because of the behaviors of both participants.

The Freudian idea of *repetition compulsion* assumes that neurotics unconsciously but intentionally cause the trauma to recur persistently so they can try to master it. Wachtel assumes the opposite; the neurotic "does not *aim* for the consequences he encounters; he produces them despite—yet because of—his vigorous efforts to prevent them" (Wachtel, 1993, p. 23). That is why he calls it a vicious cycle. No matter the origin of the pattern, "it will perpetuate itself so long as he keeps living the way he does. And . . . he keeps living that way because he is *afraid* not to" (p. 22).

Procedural Model

Because neurotic patterns are persistent, faulty *vicious cycles,* therapy must be designed to alter them. The process of *diagnosis* focuses on identifying the psychological, behavioral, and contextual content and dynamics of patients' vicious cycles. No specific diagnostic strategies and tactics are proposed. Because vicious cycles are functional units, change in only one part is insufficient. "Internal change and change in overt patterns are not really alternatives. They are two facets of one process, and neither alone will yield reliable and satisfying results" (Wachtel, 1993, p. 256). This is a "synergistic process" in which new behaviors produce consequences and different feedback; this in turn facilitates the formation of new insights, which can then lead to trying more new behavior (like the open systems model in our comparative framework).

Wachtel's three interrelated *intervention strategies* are consistent with his propositional model, and each may be implemented with diverse tactics or methods. First, the vicious cycle to be changed must be identified and activated. Then, it must occur under current circumstances that disrupt its typical operation and effectiveness: "Almost all of the interventions described in this book can be seen as part of an effort to interrupt the vicious circles in which the patient is caught" (Wachtel, 1993, p. 267). Finally, as patients try to accommodate the disruption, therapists must facilitate desirable changes. The key questions are these: Why is the patient so afraid? How can he or she be helped to become less afraid? Evidence indicates that the most powerful corrective is "the direct experience of safety in the presence of what he fears," called *exposure* (Wachtel & McKinney, 1993, p. 41). Exposure combines the strategies of activating and disrupting vicious circles. It involves activating the vicious circle under conditions in which the anticipated consequence and associated fear do not occur, thereby disrupting the vicious circle. Because the current experience and guiding schema do not match, accommodation change processes are activated. The therapist can facilitate these with relevant suggestions, explanations, and guided practice.

Wachtel emphasizes a principle of *gradualism.* Clients have learned and maintained faulty patterns through many specific experiences, and many repeated experiences are required to change them. Change in old habits occurs slowly; it is necessary "to undergo repeated extinction trials for the anxiety to these cues" or "to participate in working through" (Wachtel & McKinney, 1992, p. 340). Moreover, people "impose an order" on their experience, and "vigorously" seek to create and defend a coherent view of self and self-esteem (similar to our framework's proposition that people are self-organizing and self-maintaining). Gradual, incremental change makes it easier for patients to maintain a sufficiently coherent self-organization while simultaneously undergoing change.

Some contexts and aspects of the cycle itself can activate vicious cycles, such as phobias. Therefore, the cycle can be activated by placing the person in that context, called *in vivo exposure;* an example is flooding. As the fear occurs in anticipation of rather than in reaction to a frightening event, the context must be designed to prevent the anticipatory fear from occurring. This constraint limits the defensive or avoidant behaviors that prevent the patient from learning that unwanted consequences do not follow. Positive and negative affective states cannot occur simultaneously. Thus, a therapist using behavioral approaches activates positive states by creating a positive relationship with the client and by teaching clients skills for the self-activation of positive states; these include relaxation techniques and imagery. *Graded exposure* is also used to inhibit fear by initially using exposure contexts that are only a little bit like the feared context, such as systematic desensitization. Desired changes are facilitated by repeated exposure to a relevant range of contexts and by therapists' encouragement, explanations, and skill training.

When fearfully anticipated events are represented in subjective experiences—patients' thoughts, wishes, and feelings, as assumed in psychodynamic approaches—an exposure strategy requires different methods. Vicious cycles must be activated within safe and positive patient-therapist relationships where patients can discuss their private experiences, past and present, and therapists can respond in facilitative ways. The relationship itself does not produce change, but it serves as a catalyst for other change processes. Activation of such vicious cycles may occur in two forms. One is a remembering process; the discussion of relevant experiences activates the vicious cycle in experiential, not just cognitive, form similar to a simulated behavior episode in our comparative framework. The other is a real-life interpersonal behavior episode, in which vicious cycles are activated as patients interact with therapists—that is, in transference reactions. "Transference provides an opportunity for therapeutic learning to occur in the context of a vivid *in vivo* experience" (Wachtel, 1993, p. 96), but it is not solely a result of patients' neuroses as traditional psychoanalysis assumes. It is "the individual's idiosyncratic way of construing and reacting to experiences, rooted in past experiences, but always influenced as well by what is really going on . . . all transference reactions are reactions *to* something" (Wachtel & McKinney, 1992, p. 345). Therefore, therapists must understand both the events patients are currently reacting to and why, based on past history, they react to such events in that way. This conception is similar to our proposition that any behavior episode schema is activated only in current behavior episodes that are somehow like the ones from which the schema was constructed.

Wachtel stresses "two important realities" regarding verbal interventions. First, words themselves are meaningless, so the impact of therapists' comments ultimately results from meanings that the words activate in patients: "It is essential to be clear that the meaning *to the patient* of the therapist's comment is not objectively given in the comment itself. The patient will inevitably experience the comment 'in his fashion,' filtering it through his past experiences, expectations, needs, fears, and working models of human relationships" (1993, p. 4). People in similar cultures acquire certain shared meanings that can be activated by words, so that what clients experience "is significantly determined by the actual shape and tone of the therapist's remarks" (1993, p. 5). This idea is similar to propositions about communication in our comparative framework. Wachtel, like many theorists, fails to define the term, *meaning*. He extensively describes and illustrates how therapists' phrasing of their comments or interpretations serve a variety of functions. Some can "evoke and intensify the incipient feeling so that it becomes a more complete experience" (p. 43). Others, such as reframing and relabeling, disrupt the cycle so that accommodation processes are activated. Still others, such as attribution and suggestion, facilitate client construction of new ways of interpreting events, experience, and action.

Insight is essential in helping clients achieve a "central aim" of cultivating a "true sense" of personal agency so that one can "experience himself as the vital center giving direction to his daily actions and choices" (Wachtel, 1993, p. 49). This is similar to the idea of self-direction in our comparative framework. There are many "true" interpretations of what is going on in a patient's life, however. This approach "seeks to go beyond the naive view of a single truth that is simply 'discovered,' " to achieve "a version of the truth that will help the patient to see new possibilities for his life" (Wachtel, 1993, p. 69). Insight alone is not sufficient. There is a "synergistic interaction" between achieving insight, experiencing and controlling emotions, and learning to act differently. Change in one aspect facilitates changes in the others because of "the complex feedback loops that link and maintain them" (p. 270). This is similar to the open system model in our comparative framework.

Since vicious cycles are maintained by patients' repetitive patterns of interaction in their daily lives, much of the significant process of change must occur outside therapy. Therapists must help patients develop "the *crucial skills in living* that have been impaired by the patient's anxieties and attendant avoidances" (p. 65). This requires therapists to understand "the 'cast of characters' in the patient's life" and "the systems (family and other) in which the patient participates" (p. 63). (See Wachtel, 1977, 1982, and Wachtel & Wachtel, 1986 for examples.)

"The research evidence supporting cyclical psychodynamic theory is still only indirect" (Wachtel & McKinney, 1992, p. 354), but Wachtel asserts that a significant body of research in social and developmental psychology supports his theoretical model.

SELF-MANAGEMENT THERAPY

Primary Unit of Analysis

Kanfer argues that biological, psychodynamic, humanistic, cognitive, behavioral, and developmental approaches each provide *microtheories* about some, but not all, important aspects of human development and functioning. A *metatheory* is needed that can link these microtheories about different aspects of people so as to represent humans as coherently organized entities. Kanfer and colleagues argue that systems models are currently the best available approach for that purpose, and also for integrating research and practice, because they convey "that it is the concerted interactions of variables in the environmental, psychological, and biological domains that result in a particular psychological state or behavior of a client at a given time" (Kanfer & Schefft, 1988, p. 30). The *person-in-context* is their key unit, operationalized as descriptions of *states* (similar to behavior episodes in our comparative framework). Clinicians have to make decisions concerning selective interventions targeted on different aspects of people. Systems models facilitate such decisions because they are *multilevel* and can represent states as organizations of component processes. Therefore, Kanfer's approach also uses *component process units of analysis,* such as cognition and action, while recognizing their interrelationships in states.

CONCEPTUAL MODEL

Kanfer uses psychology's traditional classification system, but with his own terminology. *Behavior* includes instrumental and communicative actions that result from three interacting sets of influences. *Alpha variables* "include all influences that originate outside the person [including] the entire social, cultural and physical environments and infrastructures" (Kanfer & Schefft, 1988, p. 36). *Beta variables* are the mediating processes initiated and maintained by the person at the psychological level. *Gamma variables* are "the genetic and biological factors that contribute to human behavior" (p. 36). Kanfer borrows concepts from the relevant disciplines to represent subclasses within these four large groupings—such as verbal statements-alpha; memories-beta; en-docrine glands-gamma. He provides no explicit models about these different phenomena—for example, cognition—but there seems to be an implicit reliance upon existing models in relevant scientific disciplines.

Propositional Model

Kanfer uses a control system model with feedback and feedforward processes to represent a person as a dynamic unit; he refers to it as a *self-regulatory system* (similar to our comparative framework). Such a system is goal directed, guided by a preferential hierarchy of values. As people act in a context to produce some consequences, their functioning is represented as a three-stage sequential model of person-mediated control: (1) *self-monitoring* involves attending to their behavior and its consequences; (2) *self-evaluation* involves comparing the feedback information generated by their self-monitoring processes with the *performance criteria* and *personal standards* guiding that particular behavior episode; (3) *self-reinforcement* involves their cognitive and emotional reactions to their self-evaluations. Self-reinforcement has both *feedback effects* influencing the learning of that behavior pattern, and *feedforward effects* influencing clients' expectations and behavior on future occasions (Kanfer & Gaelick-Buys, 1991). Karoly (1993, 1995) has elaborated these components to include cognitive functions of direction, control and regulation, arousal functions, information collection and processing functions, action functions, and biological functions. Emotional arousal, including biological aspects, results from the feedback-evaluation, self-regulatory phase of the process and functions as a motivational state. Positive emotions correlate with progress in reaching goals, enhance goal striving, and strengthen beliefs in one's competence. Negative emotions indicate lack of progress in attaining goals and activate efforts to terminate them, either by overcoming obstructions or avoiding the conditions that produce them (similar to the model of emotions in our comparative framework).

The operation of this self-regulatory model in daily life is represented by a *problem-solving model* in which a preferred state is identified and the problem to be solved is how to produce it. Cognitive, behavioral, emotional, and biological processes are organized into specific patterns of functioning in specific contexts that continue until preferred states are produced, or the person stops trying to solve that problem (similar to a behavior episode in our comparative framework). Solving unfamiliar problems requires intentional, conscious effort; continuing attention to relevant personal and context variables; and choosing among alternative approaches, called *controlled processing*. It is the "creative" aspect of information processing (similar to the idea of information/meaning-based self-construction in our comparative framework). Repeated solution of similar problem situations by means of controlled processing results in well-learned, quickly executed, habitual behavior patterns, linked by previous experience, performed with minimal attention or concentration, and occurring simultaneously with other activities.

When familiar problem situations arise for which habitual patterns exist, the problem-solving process is guided by those patterns, called *automatic processing*. If the situation changes so that a habitual pattern is disrupted and ineffective, self-regulatory processes are activated using *controlled processing*, similar to conscious control processes in our comparative framework, to create an effective approach (Kanfer & Schefft, 1988). This behavior results in new learning, typically in the form of revision, differentiation or elaboration of the relevant habitual pattern. (This is similar to the concepts of behavior episodes and behavior episode schemas and their interactions in our comparative framework.) *Self-regulatory cycles* (similar to behavior episodes in our comparative framework) may be either *corrective* or *anticipatory.* Corrective cycles are actual behavior episodes in which current feedback is used to modify the behavioral pattern; anticipatory cycles are imagined behavior episodes in which imagined consequences and feedback are used (similar to instrumental and simulated behavior episodes in our comparative framework).

Behavior disorders or psychopathology result from dysfunctional self-regulatory habits. Automatic processing is a dominant feature of symptoms presented by clients with behavior disorders, consisting of patterns that may have been useful to the person at one time but are inadequate or maladaptive in his or her current life. Automatic processing patterns are difficult to modify because they operate outside the person's awareness, and *awareness is required for change.* That is why dysfunctional patterns impede change to preferred states, and why clients have been unable to alter their troublesome patterns on their own. Dysfunctions in any part of the self-regulatory pattern can lead to behavior disorders or psychopathology. Deficiencies in self-monitoring, such as neglect of biological cues of fatigue or affective cues of anger, inappropriate evaluative thoughts, such as excessively high standards and expectations, deficits in self-evaluation, such as selective attention to only self-congratulatory or self-demeaning information), or impaired self-corrective feedback, such as inattention to the effects of one's behavior on other people, can all lead to ineffective self-regulation and interfere with effective problem solving. Identification of component dysfunctions can guide targeted interventions.

Procedural Model

"The client's capacity to evaluate and guide her own behavior, and thereby to influence both herself and her environment, is the core component of psychological treatment" (Kanfer & Schefft, 1988, p. 35). (This view is similar to our comparative framework's ideas about self-direction and self-construction.) Effective therapy "has as its core the development of self-regulatory skills" to help clients reach realistic, attainable goals that meet their needs and are acceptable to their society. It assumes "the goal of changing regulatory *processes* rather than just behavioral outcomes" in specific situations (p. 59). This process can include changes in setting goals and evaluation standards, self-monitoring ability, relationships between intentions and self-regulatory actions, planning and problem-solving style, self-reward and self-criticism habits, and appreciation of relationships between choices and success in achieving them. Automatic processing maintains dysfunctional patterns, so a shift to controlled processing is a goal.

A process model for assisting clients to shift from automatic to controlled processing has matured into a *seven-stage sequence:*

1. Role structuring and creating a therapeutic alliance
2. Developing a commitment for change
3. Conducting the behavioral analysis
4. Negotiating treatment objectives and methods
5. Implementing treatment and maintaining motivation
6. Monitoring and evaluating progress
7. Effecting maintenance, generalization, and termination of treatment.

Each stage has three to five steps (Kanfer & Grimm, 1980; Kanfer & Schefft, 1988). Three basic *strategies* use behavioral, cognitive, and skill training *tactics:* (1) guiding clients through a process that leads to the disruption of ineffective or self-defeating automatic processing patterns; (2) using self-regulatory behaviors, problem solving, decision making, and similar complex activities to facilitate changes in the faulty patterns and/or creation of new, more satisfactory patterns; and (3) rehearsing and practicing until those patterns are overlearned and stabilized (Kanfer & Schefft, 1988). The therapeutic alliance does not itself produce change, but it establishes conditions of positive affect and interpersonal support that facilitate change efforts and activities.

Treatment involves applying general problem-solving model developed by Kanfer and his associates, beginning with a functional analysis to carefully define the faulty self-regulatory patterns to be changed. Traditional psychiatric diagnoses are not very useful for this purpose. These analyses are guided by an antecedent–behavior–consequence (ABC) model of causal relations. A diversity of diagnostic strategies and methods useful for this purpose are described (Kanfer & Schefft, 1988, pp. 169–214). Specific tactics for the various treatment stages are detailed in Kanfer and Goldstein (1986), Kanfer and Schefft (1988), and Kanfer and Gaelick-Buys (1991). These stages include establishing therapeutic relationships, learning goal and value clarification methods for specifying treatment goals, using specific tasks and assignments, formulating behavioral contracts, or changing self-generated behavioral consequences (reinforcement). Kanfer and associates believe that any method can be considered that has demonstrated utility for any of their therapy subgoals in any phase of treatment, regardless of its origins.

Evaluation of patient progress is accomplished through collaborative decision making between patient and therapist. This process appears to rely on interview data and personal judgment. No specific procedures are proposed. Research validating the approach is considered important. Some has been directly aimed at aspects of this approach, but principal reliance is placed on empirical evidence generated within several basic disciplines and on research on cognitive, behavioral, and skill training approaches whose strategies and methods the therapists use.

Constructivist Approaches

A group of psychotherapies are emerging whose proponents have evolved from different theoretic antecedents—behavior, cognitive, and personal construct therapies. Despite their diversity, they have begun to recognize that they share some basic ideas that Mahoney and Neimeyer are trying to define (see for example, Neimeyer and Mahoney, 1995). The view is emerging that current similarities lie primarily in their metaphysical and epistemological assumptions, and their theoretical implications. A suitable name is under debate. From among dynamic systems, autopoietic, complex systems, process-oriented, post-rationalist, developmental, self-organizational, cognitive constructivist, and constructivist, Mahoney (1996) thinks *constructivist* is becoming the preferred name.

Neimeyer (1995b) believes that constructivist approaches have been influenced by a post-modern era *zeitgeist,* a period of paradigm shifts and epistemological soul-searching. Affinities are noted between constructivist views and emphases on (1) the inevitability of multiple meanings within postmodernist philosophy, (2) the social construction of knowledge within social constructivism, and (3) the need for interpretive and reflective methods of inquiry advocated by hermeneutics. Similarities are noted with trends in feminist theory, cultural diversity movements, and nonpathologizing ways of accounting for human differences.

Metaphysical Assumptions

Ontologically, the constructivists assume, as did Kant, that reality is ultimately *noumenal;* it exists but is not directly knowable by the human mind. People construct ideas about reality that they use to guide their functioning in relation to it. Constructivists adhere to a dualist ontology similar to psychophysical interactionism. They reject a mechanistic cosmology with its assumptions of reductionism, associationism, and linear determinism, and the organismic assumption that people's development is determined by their own qualities and moves toward an ultimate outcome. The view of the constructivists is similar to a *self-organizing open systems cosmology* emphasizing reciprocal interdependence and codevelopmental processes. They stress change processes that produce system transformations in the direction of progressively more complex, higher order patterns of organization, but the process is open ended. There is no predetermined final outcome as proposed in organismic models. Relations between entities, or people, and their environments are inherently transactional. Rather than a billiard ball view of linear cause and effect, environments are understood to affect systems and their behavior, and also to be affected and modified by what the systems do; influence is reciprocal; change processes are codetermined. Thus, relations between people and their world involves complex, dynamic exchanges of influence, a natural *catallaxy* or open-exchange dynamics (Mahoney, 1988).

Epistemological Assumptions

Neimeyer (1993b, 1995b) argues that constructivists share an epistemological view. They reject the positions of realism or presentationism. They consider as misguided the logical positivist empiricism upon which much of contemporary science has relied. They assume that humans cannot directly know reality. People use phenomenal representations that they construct to try to discern meaning, order, and predictability in the events that give rise to their subjective experience. This is called *critical constructivism* (Efran & Fauber, 1995; Mahoney, 1988) because it assumes a reality exists that people increasingly approximate through their cognitive constructions, even though they are unable to access it completely. Theirs is a *representationist* or *constructivist* form of empirical epistemology. Others espouse a *radical constructivism,* implying an idealist ontology and a phenomenalist version of a rationalist epistemology that stresses experience as reality.

Both emphasize the organization of the world as manifested in human experience. Each person is the primary agent in creating his or her own knowledge. Therefore, constructivists adhere to a *constructive alternativism,* the view that reality can be construed in multiple ways; there are *multiple realities,* each a product of the *personal meanings* that people create. Reality is neither singular, nor stable and neatly external; it is multiple and relative, a set of complex, dynamic patterns subjectively constructed. People, and clients in particular, must recognize that their knowledges about reality are human creations, that none can make a legitimate claim to absolute truth, that all are subject to continual revision or replacement. It is important for clients to understand how their realities are created and the consequences that follow from their personal constructions (Feixas, 1995; Mahoney, 1988; Meichenbaum, 1995; Neimeyer, 1990).

It is virtually impossible for people to know whether their ideas correspond to an independently existing reality because people can never escape "embeddedness" in their own representations to compare them to an external standard of truth or reality (Rosen, 1993). In the extreme, this could lead to the dead end of *solipsism:* the belief that the only reality people can know are their subjective experiences and mental creations. Solipsism is avoided by assuming that all forms of knowledge and belief are ultimately *social constructions,* whether they deal with personal, religious, political, or scientific matters. Knowledge is culturally mediated, intertwined with social action, constructed through activities linked to achieving socially important goals, and continuously sustained by social processes. People can come to share a social reality that they construct together and which they collectively experience as their real world.

How is this possible if experience and knowledge construction is a within-person, subjective phenomenon? How can one person know what another is experiencing or thinking? The constructivists' answer is that humans share a symbolic world. Languages and other symbol systems enable people to share and influence one another's private meanings—like the relationship between language and thought in our comparative framework. What is basically subjective—one's experience and patterns of representations or meanings—can become a culturally mediated, socially shared phenomenon through symbolic communication; consensus is a form of confirmation. Therefore, although they reject a correspondence theory of truth and its corollary—that any beliefs that do not correspond to objective reality are by definition dysfunctional—the constructivists adopt what might be called a *social correspondence theory of truth.* Two criteria are proposed for evaluating the merits of individual and socially shared ideas. The first is *viability,* or their demonstrated adaptive value in organizing people's functioning to produce desired, and to avoid undesired, consequences. Multiple views may be viable; different ones may be more or less viable for different individuals and social groups, in different settings, and at different phases of life. The second is *coherence,* or their internal consistency with the larger set of personally and socially held beliefs into which they are incorporated (Mahoney, 1988; 1995; Rosen, 1993).

People's representations—their knowledge and beliefs—evolve; they develop toward a progressive modeling of more and more of the human situation, toward enhancing the likelihood of survival through the anticipation of unwanted perturbations and learning to minimize their effects. This view assumes that human knowledge and ways of knowing undergo evolutionary development analogous to biological evolution; hence, it is called *evolutionary epistemology* (Guidano, 1988).

The Principle of Unitary Functioning
Constructivists acknowledge humans' biological aspects, but view body and mind as interdependent and inseparable. People are construed to be *somatopsychic entities*—unified systems. People are also described as *embodied theories of life* (Mahoney, 1990), psychological organizations incorporated in a physical form or body. Humans do not have constructs, so much as they function as interpretations of their worlds, external and internal. As an embodied theory, each person's actions are the ongoing construction processes that others—cognitivists—have tried to localize in the head.

The Person-in-Context as the Focal Unit
Unitary functioning means that the key level of analysis is the person-in-context. Not only are all aspects of people and their contexts related, but also the organization of both individual and group functioning is co-constituted so that the personal meanings of individuals cannot be understood separate from the sociocultural contexts in which they developed and currently function. It follows that conversations between client and therapist can never occur in isolation, as they resonate with themes of the larger community and reflect the community's progress in defining how people are to live with one another (Efran & Fauber, 1995). At a practical level, conceptual units are needed that represent unified patterns of functioning rather than kinds of responses and how they might be associated.

Conceptual Models
Constructivist theorists are generally critical of the scientific and psychotherapeutic traditions of classifying human attributes into different kinds of responses—sensations, perceptions, thoughts, feelings, or actions. For example, some echo Kelly's objection to the Aristotelean trichotomous division of thoughts, feelings and actions, as an "arbitrary cleavage that confuses everything, and clarifies nothing" (1969, p. 91). This traditional set of concepts is

considered a legacy of dubious value. If used at all, these categories should be understood to be different aspects of what are essentially unified attempts by the person to adapt, to develop, and to survive. They are better understood as interdependent expressions of holistic, systemic processes (Efran & Fauber, 1995; Mahoney, 1988, 1995).

The traditional distinction between cognition and emotion is also challenged. If it is retained, constructivists argue that emotions are more powerful because of the importance of affective aspects of all experience. Emotions are considered dynamic expressions of the processes involved in the development of all constructs and are not the culprits or the causes of psychological dysfunction. The nonpathologizing approach to emotions embraced by these theorists stresses the naturally adaptive significance of all affective experience, including affects that others characterize as pathological. For example, anxiety has functional utility, occurring when the events one faces lie outside the current boundaries of one's construct system; depression and anger are useful and instructive because they indicate important impending transitions in the person's construct systems (Neimeyer, 1990). This is somewhat similar to the model of emotions in our comparative framework.

Despite such objections, the constructivists do not propose a clear alternative and often use the traditional concepts in their case descriptions. There is a genuine effort to create concepts that reflect their emphasis on the person-in-context as the focal unit. The term *construct* is often used to represent the complex, holistic patterns of person-in-context functioning. The theorists agree that constructs are not the same as concepts, which refer solely to cognitive phenomena, and that all constructs are system organizations of some kind that function as integral wholes (Mahoney, 1990). They differ, however, in the phenomena to which the term *construct* refers.

For example, for Feixas (1995), constructs are assumptive beliefs linked in hierarchical self-organizing systems. Others consider constructs to be hypothetical models. Humans function like scientists. Constructs are hypotheses that people construct to make their lives understandable, predictable, and controllable. They are organized in complex construct systems or theories (Neimeyer, 1987) that people test through their actions, within the limits imposed by their understandings (Neimeyer, 1990). The metaphor of "man, the scientist" describes the *cycle of experience* that can be summarized in terms of a feedback loop (Feixas, 1995). Efran and Fauber (1995) define constructs as *embodied programs of action*—patterns of biological, cognitive, affective, and behavioral processes that are context dependent. Constructs are not automated programs because each occurrence is a socially situated creation. They operate as *process loops* that do not necessarily have identifiable beginnings or ends, and specific cause-effect sequences cannot be specified. This idea seems similar to the behavior episodes and behavior episode schemas in our comparative framework.

Guidano (1987, 1988, 1991, Guidano & Liotti, 1985) proposes that people continually organize and revise the flow of their experience into a single, elaborate, coherently organized *self-construct* that coordinates and integrates their overall cognitive growth, development, and emotional differentiation. This concept is suggestive of the self-organizing and unitary functioning propositions in our comparative framework. Because all experience has self-reference, it all contributes to this complex construct. Because it is dynamic and continually changeable as a result of new experience, Guidano calls it a process. It is more elaborate than the traditional idea of self-concept. It represents integrations of self-reflective experiences (the "Me") with those of agency (the "I") into interrelated organizations of sensory, perceptual, cognitive, emotional, and motoric patterns.

The self-construct begins with *self-recognition,* or self-differentiation, in infancy and early childhood, and continues to evolve across the life span. It yields *self-identity,* composed of inherent feelings of uniqueness and historical continuity, which enable people to maintain continuous and coherent self-perceptions and self-evaluations in the face of "temporal becoming" and "mutable reality." Maintaining internal coherence in one's identity is the fundamental self-organizing invariant because without it people would be rendered incapable of proper functioning and would lose the very sense of reality. For example, resistance to psychotherapy occurs because any disruption of self-construct organization activates processes to maintain it—like the stability-maintaining processes in our comparative framework. The nature and continuity of relationships with significant others play a key role in self-construct development, illustrated by Bowlby's attachment theory. If the self-construct is distorted or rigid, the person is unable to assimilate experiences effectively, leading to cognitive dysfunction, emotional distress, and maladjustment.

Narrative is another concept used by some. For example, Meichenbaum (1995) and Goncalves (1995) follow Bruner (1990) in proposing that people construct privately developed story lines, or *self-narratives,* to explain themselves and situations, and to provide the options and consequences for dealing with problematic situations. These theorists suggest that humans are inherently storytellers, that narratives are natural forms for thinking and remembering, and that humans represent their most basic information about themselves and their realities in the form of stories. Recollections are considered to be narrative inventions, and the stream of consciousness is described as a stream of stories. People have idiosyncratic ways of organizing knowledge, typified in certain types of narratives that assume a role for them of best examples, or prototypes, or root metaphors to account for their experiences. Each person's narrative also constitutes that person's life as he or she conceives it, and the person's sense of self-identity is dependent on the content and cohesiveness of his or her life story. The psychological understanding of a person requires the identification and analysis of his or her prototypic narratives.

Whereas the *contents* of these diverse constructs differ—that is, the construct systems, embodied programs of action, self-construct, narrative—the *functions* they are said to perform are quite similar. All are changeable with new experience, operate to create coherent organization and generalized meaning out of the flow of transient experience, and help to organize people's behavior.

Meaning and *experience* are key concepts. People are meaning-making agents and use meanings to guide their actions, but the meaning of *meaning* is not provided. Guidano (1991) defines it as

> an *ontological understanding* in which the perceived recursiveness of one's ongoing affective-physiological modulation is consistently recognized and appraised as unitary and continuous in time, through the structuring of basic categories (self-identity, truth-falsity, competency-control, etc.) of exchanges between self and world able to produce and assimilate coherent experiences. (p. 31)

This quotation illustrates the high level of abstraction, complexity, and vagueness often found in constructivists' writing. *Experience* is the raw material for construct building, but it remains undefined. We infer that *experience* refers to the moment-to-moment contents of consciousness resulting from transient perceptions of current internal and external events, and *meaning* refers to the relating of those perceptions to people's organization of constructs so as to interpret their personal significance.

Some propose that there are at least two levels of the knowing process: *explicit* and *tacit*; these are said to be hierarchically related (Mahoney, 1995; Guidano, 1988; Guidano & Liotti, 1985). This is the constructivists' version of what others call conscious and unconscious processes. The *explicit level* includes all those conscious processes—expectations, beliefs, selective attention, and actions—that mediate one's transactions with one's environment. Their functioning is said to be governed by "deep structures" that are tacit and unstated or unconscious. They include basic assumptions, implicit causal theories, and tacit rules of inference that provide the apperceptive scaffolding for the person's constructions, and abstraction rules that enable the person to construe a pattern of organization among events. They serve as ingrained beliefs and judgments, which are in actuality hypotheses and theories. As such, they allow for the transformation of deep ordering rules into explicit processes and thereby constrain the content and form of what takes place on the surface that makes up the person's conscious experience and behavior. Thus, unconscious processes are not pathological; they are an essential part of normal functioning.

Propositional Models

Constructivist theorists share several assumptions that provide the foundation for their explanations about how people function and change. We have paraphrased and reordered those enumerated by Guidano (1988), Guidano and Liotti (1983), Mahoney (1991, 1996), Mahoney, Miller, and Arciero (1995), and Neimeyer (1993, 1993b, 1995a, 1995b).

People function as self-organizing and self-constructing living systems. Humans are an instance of complex living systems in general, constantly active and in process, temporally becoming, governed by principles of dynamic equilibrium, and operating as autonomous units. They maintain their unified identity through self-organizing or autopoetic processes, and elaborate and change themselves through self-constructing processes. Humans are not primarily reactive entities whose behavior is determined by events within and around them but are anticipatory and literally *constructive*—that is, form-giving—in operation.

Subcomponents of the person also demonstrate self-organizing and self-constructing capabilities. In particular, the human knowing system—the mind, which includes cognitive, emotional, and motoric aspects—is said to be a subsystem with autopoetic properties, functioning by means of generative processes to construct and then protect the internal coherence and integrity of its own psychological organization—self-maintenance. The system also functions through processes of self-renewal to elaborate and develop those organizations to assimilate new information and to cope with perturbations arising from its exchanges with its contexts.

The patterns of psychological organization that people construct are the principal components governing human activity. Humans engage their environments in terms of what the environments mean to them. There are no meanings in nature, so the meanings must be human creations. The human knowing system's function is to construct meanings that can guide the person's actions; people are meaning-making agents. The mind is not a passive receptor that incorporates, processes, and uses incoming information. Rather, it is an active, constructive system, capable of producing its inputs, including the sensations that lie at the base of its own constructions, and outputs that it generates. This view is similar to motor theories of the mind (Hayek, 1952; Piaget, 1970; Weimer, 1982) that (1) advocate abandoning conventional sensory models that depict mental processes as collectors of sensory information and presume that the information collected resides in the external world, and (2) conceives mind to be "intrinsically a motor system, and the secondary order by which we are acquainted with external objects as well as ourselves . . . a product of what are, correctly interpreted, constructive motor skills" (Weimer, 1977, p. 272).

This proactive, anticipatory mode of operation is considered basic to the processes of human knowing. People are *intentional, goal-directed, and purposive* in orientation. The regulation and control of the mind's inputs entails the use of both feedback and feedforward mechanisms that function actively to constrain and influence the moment-to-moment experiences people generate. These processes of self-direction, self-organization, and self-construction are basic characteristics of humans that continue throughout life, producing life-span development that results in progressively more complex constructions. This view projects the mind of the knower onto the forms of the known, and within the dynamics of knowing itself.

Change processes are stressed because humans are dynamic systems. Exploration is a key activity for functional adaptation and development because it results in novel variations and creatively different styles of "being in the world" (Mahoney, 1990). Mahoney (1988) asserts that processes are continually activated within people that operate to maintain their integrity and viability. These processes are "dialectical," with new patterns emerging out of interactions among contrasting patterns. Most of these psychological organizations, and the processes that generate them, operate at unconscious levels. All significant psychological change involves a change in the meanings that make up the person's private reality.

There are first-order and second-order processes that produce incremental change. First-order processes involve the assimilation of current experience into existing patterns that constrain the nature and range of phenomenological content. Accommodation is a second-order process occurring when new experience can not be made to correspond with expectations and memory structures, requiring their proactive modification. Finally, knowing processes are open, self-organizing, and developing systems that transform their own basic organization when the system's dynamic equilibrium is sufficiently challenged by perturbations. Disorder and disequilibrium are natural phenomena that play an integral role in the system's transformation toward higher order and more viable forms of organization. These change propositions are similar to the stability-maintaining, incremental, and transformational change processes in our comparative framework and to their activation by disruption of current steady states.

Dysfunctional development can be a product of these change processes. Progressive development typically represents a transformation to higher order constructs and metacognitions. *Regressive development* follows from an entrenchment into prior "knowing structures." In open systems, there is an indeterminate directionality to developmental pathways. Dysfunctional or regressive development stems primarily from a failure to modify one's constructions to accommodate feedback contradicting the viability and coherence of these constructions. People become "stuck" in the process of elaborating their personal constructs. Preoccupied with maintaining what they have, they attempt to function with construct systems that are no longer viable. Dysfunctions usually appear as conflicts between a person's mode of construing with the modes of other people rather than with physical facts. Constructs may be problematic for the individual and group, not because they are invalid, but rather because they are (1) internally contradictory—they don't fit with other knowledge structures, (2) inconsistent—they don't agree with social consensus, (3) nonintegrative—they fail to interrelate effectively with components of the person, or (4) nonadaptive or nonviable—they fail to promote the person's maintenance and survival (Neimeyer, 1990).

Theorists who use the personal narrative as the principal organizational unit emphasize the nonviable yet powerful stories that some people construct and maintain. Their stories include bleak self-portrayals, inexorable plots, narrow themes, and demoralizing meanings that are well rehearsed, backed by selective negative evidence, and so persuasive that the person does not judge them to be stories at all but real slices of life (Omer & Alon, 1996). Such people need alternate narratives that are also compelling but more viable or adaptive.

Procedural Models
Constructivists' procedural models are generally undefined, stemming from a commitment to abstract levels of theorizing and a reluctance to describe interventions in denotative, specific terms. As a result, much of their discussion of intervention is couched in terms of change outcomes to be produced rather than how those changes can be facilitated. Guidano (1987) protests the "tyranny of technique." Neimeyer (1993b) describes constructivist psychotherapy as more of a philosophical context within which treatment is done, rather than a body of procedures and techniques that can be described and implemented. Efran and Fauber (1995) describe therapy as a context for in-

quiry, not a technology for retraining particular behavior patterns. Mahoney (1995) says the emphasis should be almost entirely on general guiding principles rather than on routine prescriptions. Discussions of intervention are at the strategic rather than tactical level. The constructionist's adopt *technical eclecticism*, as their general model, making possible the use of any technique regardless of its origins (Neimeyer, 1990).

The power and importance of the *therapeutic relationship* is emphasized. It is a special relationship with a helping professional unlike other relationships clients experience (Neimeyer, 1990). It is collaborative because each participant brings different but equally important contributions to the accomplishment of the therapeutic tasks. Meichenbaum (1995), Rosen (1993), and Spence (1984) refer to therapists as *co-constructionists* who collaborate with clients in the construction of new meanings or more meaningful personal narratives. Harter (1995) believes the creation of a safe, collaborative relationship is crucial, as it provides a context within which clients can feel safe enough to ask the kinds of questions needed to challenge and recreate their habitual roles. Constructivists emphasize active participation by clients, paying attention to clients' ways of construing and their phenomenological experience, and showing respect toward clients' current modes of representing themselves and their world (Mahoney, 1990). The style of engagement with the client is collaborative rather than directive or disputational; exploratory rather than structured; reflective, elaborative, and personal rather than persuasive, analytical, and technically instructive (Neimeyer, 1995b). Despite an unwillingness to specify techniques, constructivists appear to be describing the relationship as a facilitative context for other kinds of interactions aimed at helping clients reconstruct dysfunctional patterns or construct new patterns.

Specific therapy goals are typically not identified. In general, these theorists emphasize strengthening clients' awareness of all aspects of their experience and their self-organizing, self-constructing, and self-directing capabilities. The objectives are said to be more creative than corrective, aimed at facilitating clients' unique development rather than at eliminating dysfunction (Neimeyer, 1995b). Dynamically complex changes in broad construct systems or personal narratives are sought rather than more specific changes in thought units or behavior patterns. In that way, they resemble psychoanalysts more than practitioners of most other approaches.

Constructivists attempt to help people become truly responsible for answering their own questions (Efran & Fauber, 1995). The therapist helps clients to recognize themselves as the source of their own constructions, which is fundamental to exposing their specific constructs to invalidation, revision, and re-creation (Harter, 1995). Clients are also encouraged to experience, explore, and express a broad range and complex mixture of affect, and exercises and techniques traditionally associated with experiential therapies are used for this purpose. Significant changes are said to involve reorganizations in clients' personal meanings concerning themselves, their personal reality, their values, and their capabilities (Mahoney, 1990).

Guidano (1987, 1988, 1991) stresses modification and transformation of "deep tacit structures," so his therapy requires several years. Early phases are devoted to clients' exploration of their developmental history in order to identify the origins of their most basic assumptions. The objective is modification and reorganization of the "core structures" relevant to clients' sense of self, identity, and the world. The tacit, unconscious level of personal knowledge structures must become conscious and linked to clients' personal identity in order to become part of their explicit beliefs and thought procedures. This makes possible clients' reorganization of the self and their experience of the world. The nature and extent of change largely depends on the nature and extent of self-awareness clients develop. Guidano assumes that "while thinking usually changes thoughts, only feeling can change emotions" (1991, p. 96), so the differentiation, recombination, and integration of basic affective themes to facilitate new emotional experiences is emphasized. This activating of the emotions is said to facilitate self-regulation, modification of patterns of self-perception, and a reordering of personal meaning processes. Some have noted the underlying similarity of Guidano's approach to psychoanalytic strategies.

Personal narrative approaches (Goncalves, 1995; Meichenbaum, 1995; Shafer, 1981) view therapists and clients as co-constructionists for the identification, deconstruction, and reconstruction of clients' narratives. Clients are helped to reframe stressful experiences and to normalize their reactions. Through reconceptualization, clients formulate a healing theory of what happened to them and why. They are helped to relate stories in which they effectively used strengths, resources, and coping abilities to fill out the rest of the story. They are helped to reconstruct new assumptive worlds and new ways of viewing themselves and the world and thus enabled to construct narratives that fit their present circumstances, that are coherent, and that are adequate in capturing and explaining their difficulties. Thus, they "retell their tale in a way that allows them to understand the original meanings and significance of present difficulties, and moreover to do so in a way that makes change conceivable and attainable" (Shafer, 1981, p. 38). Constructivist approaches suggest that changes come slowly and with difficulty because the self-maintaining processes of living systems by nature resist changes. The therapist follows up on changes by helping clients experiment with new behavior outside the therapy situation, making sure that the changes remain consistent with clients' core identity constructs (Neimeyer, 1990). *In vivo* activity—implementation of new actions—is described as an important element in effective therapy. Changes in psychological patterns lead to changes in actions in real-life settings.

EVALUATION OF CLIENT PROGRESS AND OUTCOMES

All eclectic and integrative theorists—with the exception of the constructivists—propose that a careful specification or diagnosis of each client's specific dysfunctional patterns be made at the beginning of therapy and that preferred states be identified. This diagnosis provides criteria for evaluating progress and outcomes. Constructivists seem to avoid this kind of precision and to encourage emergence of preferred outcomes as part of clients' self-constructing activities during therapy. All theorists reviewed in this chapter, however, rely primarily on client and therapist judgments during therapy to evaluate progress and outcome, with the view that evaluations should be a collaborative activity. Some advocate follow-up sessions as a means of evaluating the extent to which changes are enduring after therapy ceases.

EVALUATION OF THE APPROACH

Advocates of common factors, eclectic, and integrative approaches typically support the scientist-professional model proposed for clinical psychology and stress the importance of relying upon evidence rather than authority for selecting alternate approaches. Evidence produced through formal research is considered most reliable, and clinical criteria in addition to client self-evaluation are viewed as important in evaluating therapy effectiveness. Most of these therapists rely on traditional empirical scientific approaches. However, eclectic approaches have not yet produced a body of research that supports its claims of superior efficacy (Lambert, 1992), and there is a "conspicuous absence" of good empirical data supporting the value of psychotherapy integration (Lazarus, 1995).

Constructivists argue that the traditional, objectivist view using logical and empirical methods to identify verifiable facts is too constricting. Critical constructivists accept the objectivist's pursuit of reality but assert that it can never be absolutely known. Radical constructivists deny the objectivists' external reality and assert that all experience is personally constructed. Both assume that each person's reality is a language-defined construction whose inherent method is qualitative and depends heavily on narrative (Snyder, 1996).

They argue that scientific methods more compatible with emerging meta-physical and epistemological assumptions should be sought. Snyder (1996) believes that their theory of reality is so similar to humanist approaches that it is "old wine in a new bottle," so perhaps some of the research strategies and methods created by humanists like Carl Rogers might be useful. Mahoney (1991, pp. 451–452) suggests four general research themes for the future:

1. Expansion of traditional research methodologies "to include qualitative, process-sensitive measures of human change" with more stress on development of "phenomenological research" and "measures of personal experience that are sensitive to both changes and continuities"
2. Extension of our understanding of individual differences and their influence on different life-long developmental pathways through "a creative synthesis of idiographic (individual-focused) and nomothetic (group-focused) concepts and methodologies" because "subject variances . . . are too often disregarded as 'error variances' "
3. More intensive longitudinal studies and greater creativity "about the measures and meanings we use to study human lives in process"
4. Expansion by therapy researchers of "their collaborative relationship with practitioners and their clients"

More than most, eclectic and integrative theorists advocate using theory and evidence from the human sciences to help construct, evaluate, and improve therapy theory and practice. However, their conceptual, propositional, and procedural models reflect infrequent use of large bodies of relevant theoretical and empirical knowledge about emotions, perception, cognition, developmental processes, and the brain.

COMPARISONS OF PSYCHOTHERAPY APPROACHES

W E EMERGE FROM our analyses of contemporary models of psychotherapy with admiration and respect for the accomplishments of these theorists and therapists. We are impressed with their collective inventiveness, creativity, and range and quality of thought. They have demonstrated remarkable ingenuity in the variety of explanations, strategies, and methods they have developed. Our own experiences as psychotherapists make us aware of the difficulties one encounters in developing an effective conceptualization and treatment for each client and in constructing general models of psychotherapy as well. Clinical practice is demanding and leaves little time for careful scholarship.

We admire the way most current theorists present their models as attempts to forge improvements in theory and methods rather than presenting their approaches as the only "right way." In general, they recognize that all theories are, in principle, provisional, imperfect, and subject to revision and improvement. Thus, all models we examined have undergone elaboration and change in their theoretical and procedural models; only a few purists continue to adhere to the initial models. This flexibility is particularly evident in the various procedural models, where all borrow methods from one another; each is integrative in that sense. Usually, however, the theorists have not altered their metaphysical, epistemological, and theoretical models to fit the implications of their elaborated procedural models. A few therapy theorists have displayed excessive hubris, and still fewer have lapsed into the fallacy of presumptive truth. As a rule, criticisms are directed toward the ideas of others, not on their competence or intent. The absence of *ad hominem* arguments illustrates the scholarly maturation of the field.

Section III identifies similarities and differences among approaches and considers their implications for future efforts. The objective is to lay groundwork to help others find ways of consolidating the ideas held in over 400 approaches into fewer theoretical and procedural models that can advance the effectiveness and credibility of therapy theory and practice. We assume that because they are all dealing with the same basic phenomena—the nature of humans and how they function and change—it is unreasonable to suppose that the hundreds of different approaches that have been proposed are completely different from one another. If psychotherapy's Tower of Babel continues to grow without a clarification of the relationships among approaches or adequate documentation of their utility, its role and influence in the emerging context of managed care, and its financing may erode. Two related sets of ideas are presented. First, we use our comparative framework as a tool to compare the ideas in the exemplars analyzed. Second, we express our own views about implications of those findings for future work. We try to be explicit about which is which. We state generalizations we have abstracted from our comparative analyses, then, we document the validity of these generalizations by identifying the ideas of theorists whose views illustrate each generalization. Because of the extensive number of sources cited in Section II, we have not tried to be exhaustive in specifying every therapist's position on every issue discussed. Rather, we have used examples from each family of therapies to document the generalizations we propose and indicate in parentheses which theorists and/or families provide examples of that generalization. We have tried to use enough examples to make our generalizations plausible. Full references for these citations are not repeated here, so as to make the material easier to read; they may be found in the relevant chapters in Section II. Hopefully, readers will be prompted to construct additional generalizations suggested by our analyses.

Section III contains four chapters that mirror the major sections of our general outline: (1) metaphysical and epistemological assumptions, and (2) conceptual, (3) propositional and (4) procedural models. An epilogue contains some broader comments. Each chapter contains brief summaries of parts of our comparative framework most relevant to that chapter to facilitate presentation of and understanding of our comparative analyses. Some readers may find it helpful to reexamine Section I for a more detailed review. To avoid repetition of the cumbersome family names, we use the acronyms created in Chapter 1 to link our comparisons and generalizations to ideas in the various families that support the generalizations. The acronyms are: PT (traditional psychoanalysis); ISCT (interpersonal and sociocultural therapies, including neoanalytic self-psychology and object relations); HT (humanist therapies, including existential, experiential, gestalt, and person centered); BT (behavior therapies); CT (cognitive therapies); CBST (cognitive-behavioral and skill training therapies); BMHT (behavioral medicine/health therapies); and EIT (eclectic and integrative therapies).

CHAPTER 14

Metaphysical and Epistemological Issues

C HAPTER 1 SUMMARIZED the metaphysical and epistemological assumptions created by philosophers, discussed their scientific and professional implications, and examined their selective influence on the kind of psychotherapy model one chooses to pursue. Before discussing the guiding assumptions used by the theorists reviewed in this book, we comment on some limitations imposed by the typical interpretation of those assumptions.

METAPHYSICAL AND EPISTEMOLOGICAL
ASSUMPTIONS AS HUMANLY CREATED BELIEFS

Most psychotherapists and scholars follow the tradition of philosophy and consider these assumptions as axiomatic; they are propositions regarded as self-evident truths and accepted on the basis of their intrinsic merit. As such, they are treated as unquestioned givens. It is often asserted that many of these axioms are incompatible; not all can be simultaneously correct. Historically, the positions became pitted against one another, and people chose sides. One must be either a materialist or idealist, realist or representationist (constructivist); mechanist or wholist; one cannot be both. The belief that different metaphysical and epistemological assumptions are basic, irreconcilable axioms has led many to conclude that integration of theories based on them is impossible because that would violate the axioms on which they stand. In our view, such "either-or" thinking about metaphysical and epistemological assumptions is unsound and self-defeating, and should be abandoned for several reasons.

First, these metaphysical and epistemological categories should be recognized for what they are and are not. They are neither god-given or immutable. Like all classification systems, they were created by people and should be subjected to the same kinds of evaluations as any other humanly created way of construing things. They are "as-if" constructions, as are all other kinds of models designed to represent one of many possible ways of construing human experience or reality. That they tend to fall at the most abstract and inclusive levels with which humans think and communicate with one another does not alter the fact that they are still models or tools. They can be subjected to the same epistemic criteria as models in general; they can be evaluated in terms of their correspondence with observations of objects, events, and subjective experience as well as their internal consistency, coherence with the cascade of more particular models with which they are related, fertility in generating discoveries, predictive accuracy, viability, and the like.

Second, most of these assumptions are centuries old, created by philosophic reasoning prior to our immense progress in the scientific understanding of our universe, our world, and ourselves; they emerged before much scientific knowledge existed about humans' biological, sensory, perceptual, cognitive, emotional, behavioral, and contextual patterns of functioning. These old assumptions should no longer be considered immune from redesign in the light of advancing knowledge, or be allowed to continue to constrain contemporary thinking. For example, recent knowledge about the nature of, and relationships between, perceptual and cognitive processes makes inappropriate continued complete separation of realist and idealist epistemologies—as still proposed by radical constructivists.

Third, as noted in Chapter 1, emerging ideas in the natural and social sciences (and incidentally in the procedural models of these psychotherapists) suggest alternate views that can reinterpret the traditional assumptions. That is what led Pepper (1972) to propose near the end of his career that the new "root metaphor" of a dynamic, self-regulating system may be "the most fruitful or even the correct one for a detailed synthetic comprehension of the structure of the universe" (p. 548). It is time for psychotherapists to formulate metamodels that encompass all aspects of humans manifested in both science and psychotherapy and the processes of daily living.

METAPHYSICAL AND EPISTEMOLOGICAL ASSUMPTIONS OF
OUR COMPARATIVE FRAMEWORK

The comparative framework described in Chapters 3, 4, and 5 incorporates multiple metaphysical views. It encompasses material phenomena (biological attributes; physical actions; contexts) and immaterial phenomena (properties of organization; information; psychological functions; human communication). Both types are accepted as ontological realities. There is utility in both materialist and idealist views; body and mind are different but coupled phenomena. Humans are construed to be multilevel, integrated organizations of different kinds of structures and functions, operating as unified entities—a psychophysical, interactive dualism—continually embedded in, and in transaction with, similarly organized contexts—an open system. Within such an open, dynamic systems model, cosmological assumptions of mechanism, such as reflexive responding, and organism such as embryological development, are considered subtypes of organization within a self-organizing, self-constructing systemic organization. A pluralistic epistemology is espoused in which multiple observational vantage points are considered useful, with perception providing the kind of information realists emphasize, cognition-producing thoughts as stressed by idealists, and clear, scientifically grounded proposals specifying mutually influential relationships between perception and cognition.

PSYCHOTHERAPY MODELS' METAPHYSICAL ASSUMPTIONS

Our analyses of these psychotherapy theories reveal that many theorists have not made their metaphysical assumptions explicit nor addressed the degree of influence of such assumptions on their theoretical models. Presumably, many take their implicit assumptions for granted. A few, such as the constructivists, Beck, the behaviorists, have discussed their guiding assumptions extensively and have compared them with alternate views. For many of the theories, however, it was necessary to infer their metaphysical positions from the conceptual, propositional, and procedural models they espouse. We found that often their procedural models imply a broader metaphysical view than do their theories.

ONTOLOGICAL ISSUES

In the first half-century of psychotherapy development, ontological differences were tightly drawn (see Ford & Urban, 1963). A key way each set of theorists sought to establish a distinctive identity was to stress their ontological differences from others. Initially, Freudian psychoanalysis and behaviorist approaches stressed different aspects of a materialist ontology: Biologically

based instincts and drives impelled people from within (Freud), or physiological functions, actions, and contexts drove them from within and without
(behaviorists). Behaviorists deemphasized cognition whereas Freud initially
described cognition as manifesting the functioning of instincts and drives.
Both acknowledged the occurrence of thoughts but did not assign thoughts a
major causal role in people's functioning. In contrast, humanists and existentialists stressed an idealist ontology; human thought processes, in the form of
personal goals and cognitive evaluations, were the primary causes of people's
functional patterns. External and biological stimuli did not directly influence
behavior; only people's interpretations of such events functioned as causal antecedents. Interpersonal and sociocultural approaches (see Horney or Sullivan) emphasized a form of dualism, with thoughts, affects, and contextual
events all influencing behavior in interactive ways.

As therapists have tried to help and have learned from increasingly diverse populations of clients and problems, they have become more willing to
learn from therapists of different persuasions, and earlier constraints on their
thinking have steadily eroded. Experiences with diverse clients continually remind therapists that people are complicated, and that biological, psychological, behavioral, and contextual factors are always simultaneously occurring
and in transaction with one another. As a result, therapists have moved toward using metaphysical frameworks that can encompass all these factors.
Thus, we find that contemporary psychoanalysts emphasize cognitions as
significant causes—for example, ego functions—and give greater attention
to the roles of behavior and contexts, such as reality testing; behaviorists now
also consider cognition and emotions important; cognitivists and humanists
add a consideration of behavior and contexts, although some humanists still
emphasize an idealist ontology. All acknowledge the operation of biological
factors but vary in dealing with them in their procedural models. A few theorists, such as the radical constructivists, still try to maintain the narrower
metaphysical positions.

We found that the procedural models of virtually all contemporary psychotherapies adhere to the common sense ontology or its formal version: a
psychophysical interactionism. Few espouse monist or other views. All presume materialist—biological, environmental—and idealist—psychological—
functions to be interrelated in important ways. There are differences in the nature of the relationships proposed, but virtually all acknowledge the need for
some kind of connection between the two. There are differences in the extent
to which their procedural models reflect this more encompassing ontological
view, but continuing to argue over whether a realist *or* an idealist view is
true—whether phenomenal experience is the only "reality" *or* whether an ob-

jective reality exists—is of little value. These different terms point to different phenomena. Both are useful; what matters is the nature of their linkage. Our analyses reveal that most contemporary psychotherapy models are moving toward an ontological position similar to that described in our comparative framework.

COSMOLOGICAL ISSUES

The metaphor of the machine as the basic model for representing the "structure of the universe" dominated most of science until near the middle of the twentieth century. As no surprise, it was also the most influential metaphor in the initial development of the psychoanalytic and behavior therapies. The early humanist, interpersonal, and sociocultural therapies (see Rogers; the Gestalists; Sullivan; Horney) rejected this reactive organism, robot-like model of humans and espoused a more proactive, pilot model that emphasized dynamic patterns rather than discrete elements linked in linear causal chains. Thus, the debate within theoretical physics between Einstein and Bohr regarding the nature of reality appears to have had its parallel within the field of psychotherapy theory. Einstein argued that reality consists of substances whose properties are unaffected by their relationships to other objects. Bohr proposed that no such autonomous entities exist; reality consists of relations among substances, and thus every occurrence and every event varies as a consequence of its relationships with other simultaneously occurring events (Pauli, 1994). Psychotherapy theorists have had a similar debate and have moved toward a cosmology more like the one Bohr espoused.

Rather than assuming that objects and events are organizations of discrete elements that can be disaggregated into their elements to be understood—a process called reductionism—more recent psychotherapists seem to have collectively concluded that they need to think in terms of complex, dynamic, unitary organizations or configurations, in which the constituents are influenced by their interdependence; the whole cannot be fully understood by removing elements from the assemblage and examining them separately. Theorists now appear to think in terms of causal fields rather than causal chains. There is a general movement toward Pepper's (1972) final root metaphor of a dynamic, self-regulating system that can encompass contextual models and that also fits within the emerging cosmological view of the natural sciences. A broad, implicit consensus about cosmological assumptions is emerging among psychotherapy theorists that is similar to those of our comparative framework.

This consensus can be illustrated by citing the many conceptual/propositional proposals used by these theorists that all seem to convey similar meanings:

- Through the ego's synthesizing function, patterns and levels of ego organization are produced (psychoanalysis).
- The notion of complex, dynamic organization is discernible in the concepts of organism-environment fields (Yontef), gestalten, and gestalt experience cycles (Korb), interpersonal circles (Kiesler), interpersonal loops (Beitman), transaction cycles (Carson, Guerney) or life tasks (Goldstein) that function as causal loops.
- People are a process that displays a tendency toward organization and a purposive nature (humanists; constructivists).
- People function like a control system (Trower) in self-regulatory cycles (Kanfer) that are manifested as goal-directed acts regulated by feedback (Gambrill, Trower).
- People must be understood as being basically socially embedded (object relations).
- People are embodied programs of action (Efran & Fauber), or embodied theories of life (Mahoney).
- Human behavior is organized in multimodal patterns of reciprocal influence with a firing order (Lazarus), in terms of cyclical psychodynamics (Wachtel), or cycles of experience (Feixas).
- Behavior patterns result from mutual causal processes among environmental, biological, behavioral, and psychological factors, called reciprocal determinism (Bandura), behavioral therapy, cognitive-behavioral and skill training therapy, and behavioral medicine/health therapies).

This restructuring does not mean that mechanist and organismic models of organization no longer have utility. They can still serve as useful tools in understanding certain kinds of behavior patterns. For example, some aspects of human functioning can be usefully represented in terms of linear processes or antecedent-consequent sequences: for example, if one shines a light in a person's eye, the pupil will contract. Even some aspects of the operation of complex systems, such as a control system, can be usefully disaggregated into linear and parallel sequences. We argue, therefore, that different cosmological models may be useful for representing different kinds of human functioning at different levels of organization. The most useful view of the way things are organized may be to assume a general model of complex, dynamic, self-organizing, self-constructing, open, contextually embedded systems, within which certain components may be appropriately represented by means of mechanistic or organismic models. This can be considered a *pluralistic cosmological position.*

EPISTEMOLOGICAL ISSUES

An either-or mentality has also pervaded discussions of the merits of different epistemological views appropriate for psychotherapy. The metaphysical model we see becoming the consensus view in contemporary models of psychotherapy makes a continuation of either-or arguments about epistemology inappropriate and fruitless. A persistent allegiance to one as opposed to others is misplaced when therapists' theoretical and procedural models both actually rest on a *pluralistic metaphysical view.*

Albert Einstein articulated the principle that all observations are relative to the vantage point of the observer. Different and equally valid observations of the same phenomenon are possible. However, what is observed will always vary as a function of the position of the observer relative to the target of observation. It follows that one can significantly expand one's knowledge of phenomena by examining them from a variety of observational vantage points, using a variety of observational methods. This diversity requires that one recognize the limitations of the kinds of knowledge each vantage point can yield, however, and that one also finds ways to combine the knowledge gained from each. Physicians use this principle when they rely on a combination of information generated by different means from different vantage points of observation; examples are patients' symptomatic complaints, physicians' observations of clinical signs, and data obtained by means of instrumental and laboratory studies. Similarly, the growth of empirical science stemmed from the realization that no single method—no sense experience, intuition, or reason alone—is infallible, and that the formation of usable knowledge results from the skillful art of combining all these methods. Multimethod measurement of variables is an example of the application of this principle in formal research designs.

A directly analogous situation exists within psychotherapy. A person's functioning can be viewed from the objective vantage point of an outsider watching it occur—the therapist—from the subjective vantage point of the person in whom it is taking place—the client—or from the vantage point of a significant other—a spouse or friend—or of measuring instruments. Client reports—the subjective observer—can provide information about events such as values, wishes, affects, or goals, to which no one else can have direct access; viewing the same person from an external vantage point—the therapist as an objective observer—can identify events of which the client may be unaware. For example, her eyes may redden without her knowing it, her postural changes may go unnoticed because her attention is focused elsewhere, or she may not recognize the common pattern in the varied thoughts she is expressing.

Using two or more observers has other benefits. With two observers, the possibility of convergent validity exists, the consensual validation of observations supplemented with formal measures. With only one observer there is no way of determining observer bias. The content of observations from different vantage points will also differ; that is their value. One need not argue that one is right and the other wrong. One's understanding of what is taking place can be significantly enhanced when information from multiple points of vantage is taken into account. As most clinicians know, in general the greater the range of observations from varied persons—client, therapist, spouse, employer, teacher, co-workers—about the behaviors of concern, the greater is the safeguard against the likelihood of error. These comments illustrate a *realist view.*

Observations, regardless of the vantage point, are only *perceptions* of some events at a moment in time; each is a snapshot of reality that cannot, by itself, reveal the plot line, narrative, pattern, or meaning of which it is a part. To understand the rest of the story, one must organize and interpret the content and flow of the perceptual data provided by one's observations; this is a *conceptual act,* often called *meaning making.* Such cognitive acts have served as the basis for an *idealist epistemology.* The interpretation of specific observations requires linking observations to some general model, theory, or interpretive frame that one already has. It follows that different people may interpret the meaning of the same observations differently because they have constructed and use different conceptual interpretive frames. Just as observations from different vantage points can be compared to seek consensual validation, so too can interpretations using different models be compared to seek shared understanding of the meanings most usefully attributed to those observations. The procedural models of these therapy theorists make it clear that they have consistently moved toward an *epistemological pluralism* comparable to that of our comparative framework.

The procedural models often stress the utility to clients of "new information" provided by perceptions; their theories of change rely on the disrupting influence of new information on clients' habitual patterns. They use both clients' and therapists' observational vantage points, and sometimes formal measurement and other observers as well. Virtually all stress the need to understand the interpretive frame each client uses to attribute meaning to specific observations, variously referred to as a schema, construct, self-concept, belief, object representation, psychological structure, template, narrative, or self-regulatory habit. Changing clients' interpretive frames is part of their cure. The models also assert that obtaining relevant observations should be a shared, collaborative activity, and that the process of interpreting the significance of those observations are best shared as well; they recommend that therapists function as co-constructionists of meanings.

The use of pluralist metaphysical and epistemological assumptions should be reflected in the conceptual, propositional, and procedural models one develops. We proceed next to examine the extent to which this has proved to be the case within and among the psychotherapy families we have analyzed.

CHAPTER 15

Conceptual Models: Aspects of Humans Emphasized

ESIGN CRITERIA FOR our comparative framework were summarized in Chapter 2. Two general issues with regard to conceptual models were discussed: What is the nature of the units used? What kinds of phenomena do the units emphasize and what is the content of their concepts?

THE NATURE OF UNITS USED

Our world and the people in it are organized in a complex manner; they are continually varying, changing entities composed of many kinds of phenomena. It is impossible to consider all phenomena at once, so people conceptually break them into chunks that they find useful for different kinds of purposes. Every theory selects certain phenomena as its primary focus, remaining selectively inattentive to the rest. Phenomena are hierarchically organized, so one must decide what levels of that hierarchical organization will be the focus: for example, to study humans one might focus on cells, organ systems, or recurring patterns of thought or action. The units used may differ in size and content; they may represent phenomena within one level, or sets of phenomena across levels.

Levels and Units of Analysis in Our Comparative Framework

Our comparative framework asserts that psychotherapists must deal with at least three levels of analysis: (1) the person-in-context as a unified entity; (2) different kinds of structures and functions that compose a person, such as thoughts, actions; and (3) the larger contexts of which people are a part, such as families. Some may focus on other levels as well. As an example, non-medical psychotherapists seeking prescription privileges imply a focus on neurochemical processes at cellular levels. We emphasized that a multilevel approach requires models that can represent both intra- and interlevel relationships—for example, how do physiological events influence emotions and how do emotions influence a person's interpersonal transactions?

We noted that historically much psychological theorizing reflects a mode of analysis in which properties of an object determine its behavior—a ball rolls because it is round—represented as *B=f(P)*. The tradition of trait psychology is illustrative. Our open, living systems model stresses that it is impossible for a person to exist separate from a context; human behavior results from mutually influential person and context relations, represented as *B=f(P ↔ E)*. For example, a client's behavior in a therapy session is a function both of attributes of the client and of the therapy session, which includes attributes of the therapist.

Therefore, our comparative framework's focal level of analysis and unit of reference, representing an open system model, is a *person-in-context*. Both persons and contexts are organizations of component structures and functions, so *biological, psychological, and behavioral components* of persons and *natural, interpersonal, designed, and sociocultural components* of contexts represent other levels of analysis. People also function as components of social units, so a higher level of analysis is also potentially useful in psychotherapy theories, such as the dynamics of family patterns. These basic conceptual units are highly generalized abstractions. To be useful to either professionals or scientists, they must be operationalized as units of analysis that can be used to understand and represent the flow of a specific person's functioning in a specific context.

Person-in-Context Operational Units: Behavior Episodes and Behavior Episode Schemas.

In Chapter 4, we described two operational units derived from our living systems model to represent the person-in-context level. Behavior always occurs in the here and now to serve specific purposes; it cannot occur yesterday or tomorrow. A *behavior episode (BE)* represents a system's states in real time in a specific situation and is the natural unit in which human functioning is organized. *Behavior* means a pattern of biological, psychological, and behavioral functioning; *episode* refers to the flow of that pattern through time in a specific context, organized by a central theme that is defined by the intentions guiding the episode. The specific content of perceptions, emotions, and actions will vary, but remains organized around the guiding theme. A behavior episode begins when some specific intentions or personal goals begin functioning to organize one's behavior. It ends when (1) the actor concludes that the intended results have occurred, or that no further progress can be made at that time, (2) some current events interrupt that episode and activate a shift to different controlling intentions, or (3) the desired outcomes are judged to be unattainable.

Behavior episodes are transitory. Each one begins and ends, never to recur; no two are identical. Some are similar in the goals or intentions that guide them and the contexts in which they occur. This similarity enables people to construct generalized versions of their experiences in sets of similar episodes, including anticipations about probable futures, that they can then use to guide their functioning in a new but similar behavior episode. Those generalized representations we call *behavior episode schemas (BES)*. The term *schema* denotes a generalized, prototypical pattern of functioning; the term *behavior episode* means that a schema includes all the components of behavior episodes; it is not just a conceptual representation. A person's actual functioning in any episode results from the interaction of behavior episode events with the behavior episode schema active during that episode. Thus, the "past" and "future" as represented in the behavior episode schema and the present as represented in current behavior episode experiences and conditions are combined to guide a person's immediate functioning. Behavior episodes and behavior episode schemas vary in scope and duration; more complex ones can be understood as organizations of smaller ones guided by subgoals.

Component Units

The major component units in our comparative framework were defined by relating each major component of a living system model to one basic attribute of humans as defined in the basic human sciences:

Physical structures and processes = biological structures and functions
Governing functions = cognitive and information processing functions
Energizing functions = attention/consciousness, emotions, and activity arousal
Information collection functions = sensory/perceptual processes
Transactional functions = instrumental and communicative actions
Environment = natural, designed, interpersonal, and sociocultural contexts.

Each of these has subcomponents. For example, cognition is subdivided into three kinds of thinking: directive—example: goal specification; regulatory—

example: self-evaluative; and control—example: problem solving. Several different kinds of emotion are specified. A model for each component was constructed from relevant basic scientific and clinical literature. These are conceptualized as qualitatively different phenomena, but they cannot occur separately because a person always functions as a unit in a context. Each can be observed only in the context of some behavior episode.

Social Units
Our comparative framework suggests that social units, such as families, may also be understood as systems, and that intimate relationships may be understood as two-person systems, as in a therapy relationship. No specific units are proposed, however.

LEVELS AND UNITS OF ANALYSIS IN PSYCHOTHERAPY MODELS: THE PERSON-IN-CONTEXT

All three levels described in comparative framework are used by all these theorists, but the relative emphasis given to each level and related units differs somewhat among theorists and in their conceptual and procedural models. We have tried to identify how they are similar and different.

The Aristotelean notion that people's behavior is caused primarily by their own characteristics is deeply woven into the thinking of Western culture, so it is not surprising that it also appears in these theories. We noted a tendency in the theorists' discussions of cases and therapy procedures for them to describe clients' behavior as resulting from some personal attribute, such as intrapsychic conflict, belief, self-concept, schema, or construct, independent of their behavioral contexts—that is as a *person unit*. Our analyses reveal, however, that in both their theoretical models and key aspects of their procedural models, most of them use a *person-in-context unit*.

CONCEPTS REPRESENTING PERSON OR PERSON-IN-CONTEXT LEVEL UNITS

The contemporary use in traditional psychoanalysis of Freud's theory can be interpreted as analogous to a control system model, like our comparative framework, created before control systems theory existed. The concepts of *id and ego instincts* include phenomena similar to some biological functions of our framework. The concept of ego, as elaborated by ego psychologists, includes phenomena similar to those called cognitive directive and control functions, attention/consciousness, information processing and remembering, and perceptual monitoring functions in our framework. The emphasis in ego psychology on the *conflict-free ego sphere* adds a purposive or directive function to PT. The concept of *superego,* and its relationship to ego functions and emotions, is analogous to the *cognitive regulatory function* in our comparative framework. The view of *emotion* linking id (biological functions), ego (cognitive directive and control functions), and superego (cognitive regulatory functions), and their operation as anticipatory responses that regulate approach-avoidance behaviors, is somewhat similar to the tripartite model of emotions in our framework. Whereas Freud's theory ignored the role of environments, ego psychology and PT's procedural model of traditional psychoanalysis recognize its importance with ideas like reality testing, and the careful design and conduct of analytic sessions to facilitate change. Transactional functions are theoretically ignored, but communicative acts are very important in their procedural model—for example, free association, the analytic relationship, and therapist interpretations.

The key role PT gives defense mechanisms and resistance as processes that protect the psychological status quo when it is threatened with disruption is like control systems' negative feedback stability-maintaining processes. The inclusion of anticipatory functioning, such as signal anxiety, recognizes the role of feedforward processes. Positive feedback is the only process in our comparative framework that is not included in PT. The key idea of transference in the psychoanalysts' procedural model can be viewed as an operational version of a person-in-context unit, analogous to a behavior episode schema.

Interpersonal and sociocultural (ISCT) therapists stress inborn needs for intimate, nuturing, caring social relationships as the dominant "instinctual" human motive rather than the sexual and aggressive drives emphasized in traditional psychoanalysis. The interpersonal and sociocultural analysts and psychotherapists stress interpersonal contexts as essential for newborns to become human—and ignore other types of contexts—so theirs is a *person-in-social context* unit: Babies exist in "a state of intense relatedness" to contexts (Balint,); infant and maternal care "form a unit" (Winnicott); observer and observed form an "unbreakable unit" (Kohut); people develop from "infantile" to "mature" interpersonal "dependence" (Fairbairn), in interpersonal "fields" (Sullivan), or "circles" (Kiesler), or a "relational matrix" (Mitchell). From the start, the ego seeks unified functioning (Fairbairn); there is an "innate need and striving for organization" (Bacal), to produce "cohesion," "harmony" and "preservation of the self" (Suttie), and an "integrated" or "whole person" (Winnicott).

These theorists do not describe in detail their unit's prototypical content and dynamics. They stress interpersonal contexts; for some it is a social level unit, a two-person system. It is clear that people's behavior is aimed at eliciting desired behaviors from others and is influenced by others' behavior. Interpersonal transactions function as "unbroken causal loops" (Carson). Kohut's definition of ego is illustrative: a unit "cohesive in space and enduring in time" that is "a center of initiative" (feedforward functions) and "a recipient of impressions" (feedback functions) (1977, p. 99). It has a "pole of ambitions" (directive function), a "pole of ideals" (regulatory function) and an "intermediate area of talents and skills" (control and transactional functions) (1984, p. 192). We conclude that their broad though vague descriptions are similar to our comparative framework's open systems unit.

Whereas proponents of the humanist therapies (HT) espouse an idealist, phenomenological ontology and epistemology, they stress a person-in-context unit. "Being" means "being-in-the-world" so trying to understand people separate from their context is an "ontological mistake" (Bugental & Stirling) and is meaningless (Bohart). People are part of an "organism-environment field" (Yontef), so component processes never operate in isolation but function as "organized wholes" in the context of the "total environment." To analyze people into "simpler structures" is to lapse into spurious oversimplification (Korb, et al.). In terms of dynamics, all these theorists emphasize change rather than stability; they see people as a "process" (becoming) rather than a "stable existence" (being), so they emphasize here-and-now functioning rather than past experiences. They recognize that both stability and change exist (Bohart); people try to strike a balance between them (Yontef); there is a natural tendency to balance out opposites to achieve homeostasis (Eriksen & Rossi). Stability-maintaining self-organizing and self-maintaining processes—resistance or defensive maneuvers—predominate (Bugental & Stirling); people are innately "self-righting" (Bohack). However, innate *self-constructing processes* drive human development forward.

The theorists all agree that people's behavior is organized by their innate purposiveness and inborn valuing processes—the directive and regulatory function in our comparative framework. These processes guide people's continual searching (Bugental & Stirling) and their innate "self actualizing" or "formative" tendency (Rogers). Their theoretical descriptions of this unit are highly abstract and vague, but they do operationalize them in their procedural models. For example, the Gestalt experience cycle is a general pattern (Korb et al.): People become aware of a need or goal. They scan their environment and themselves for options for meeting the need. They select an option, initiate an action, and either assimilate or reject the resulting experiences. The entire pattern leads to a sense of satisfaction and closure. We conclude that their basic idea is similar to the living system unit in the book's comparative framework.

Contemporary behavior therapy (BT) theorists focus on current rather than historical determinants of behavior and emphasize overt behavior change. They stress the interdependence of behavior and contexts, analyzing clients' dysfunctional patterns into the particular kinds of responses and environmental events involved, and specifying their functional antecedent and consequent relationships. Response components of patterns may be "overt," demonstrated by actions or statements, or "covert," such as perceptions, thoughts, or emotions. Their model now combines biological and psychological functions with their original emphasis on behavior and environmental functions, leading some to propose larger, more integrative units than the traditional stimulus and response elements organized into "chains:" Units are needed that represent "temporally extended patterns" called *molar behaviorism* (Rachlin); emphasizing actions in situations would preserve the unity of complex behavior as an unfolding "dramatic plot" (Hallam); people are best understood in terms of what they think, feel, and do in specific situations (O'Leary & Wilson).

The behavior theorists' propositional model about change or learning stresses feedback processes, such as reinforcement, punishment, and extinction; it implies the operation of anticipatory feedforward processes in concepts like cue and discriminative stimuli. BT increasingly relies on Bandura's social learning model. His latest version provides an integrative person-in-context view similar to our comparative framework. BTs procedural models explicitly operationalize that unit: They (1) design "learning" or "training" episodes that explicitly activate "habitual" dysfunctional patterns under environmental conditions conducive to their change, or that enable practice and learning of new patterns. (2) They repeatedly expose clients to those conditions in a series of "learning trials" or "episodes." Thus, BT relies on a person-in-context unit that is similar in many ways to our comparative framework's living system unit.

Cognitive therapy (CT) theorists recognize that effective functioning requires exchanges with environments, so the person and the context must interact. Their theoretical discussions, however, focus on the *person* as the key unit, without specific linkage to contexts: People are "complex bio-social organisms" that construct a "variety of goals and purposes" which they pursue to "bring a sense of meaning" to their lives (Dryden & Ellis); personality is a "relatively stable organization" that is composed of "systems" or "interlocking structures" that perform functions, such as thinking, and "modes," the content of "structures" (Beck). *Actions* are purposive, aimed at changing the person's state or context (Dryden). *Beliefs* integrate perceptions, emotions, and actions into coherent patterns, or "cognitive-affective-behavioral" patterns in the pursuit of "survival" and "happiness" (Ellis), or "avoidance of danger," "self-preservation," "maximizing pleasure" and "minimizing pain" (Beck). *Schemas* are organizations of psychological and behavioral functions in relation to contexts (Beck).

Stability-maintaining negative feedback dynamics are described as "self-fulfilling prophecies" and feedforward dynamics operate through "expectations" or "anticipatory beliefs" (Beck; Ellis). In recent analyses, Beck makes extensive use of the idea of "feedback cycles" in representing diverse disorders, and the ideas of "vicious circles" and positive feedback dynamics to explain why a condition becomes progressively worse. Both Beck and Ellis operationalize this theoretical unit in their procedural models in essentially the same way; clients are asked to describe in detail specific, recent episodes in which the dysfunctional pattern occurred, including the context; what they thought, felt, and did; and what happened. Both theorists use "homework assignments" that are specific behavior episodes designed to facilitate practice of preferred patterns of functioning. We conclude that their theories and practices reflect a unit similar to that of our comparative framework.

Cognitive-behavioral and skill training theorists (CBST) merge behavior therapy, cognitive therapy, and educational theory and methods into explicit person-in-context units. Meichenbaum's "transactional perspective" assumes that cognition, affect, behavior, and context occur in dynamic patterns changeable through skill training. Trower and Gambrill use a control system model similar to that of our comparative framework; they stress the "mutual influence between person and context factors" (Gambrill), and "goal directed episodes" in which people consciously monitor the immediate situation and his or her behavior and modify their performance based on "continuous external feedback" and "internal criteria" (Trower). Goldstein defines "personal and interpersonal life tasks" as patterns of component processes that are episodes of behavior within contexts. Guerney's key unit is an "interpersonal communicative transaction" in which two or more people function as a social unit and communicative interactions serve to synchronize their thoughts, feelings, and actions. In their procedural models, all these theorists operationalize this unit as specific training episodes. We conclude that their unit is very similar to that used in our comparative framework.

Behavioral medicine/health therapy theorists (BMHT) draw on behavior therapy, cognitive therapy, and cognitive-behavioral and skill training and borrow units from these approaches. They stress the ways psychological and behavioral functions can influence biological functions.

Eclectic and integrative therapy (EIT) theorists display "immense heterogeneity," but their objective of psychotherapy integration appears to have led to the use of integrative units. "Core interpersonal schemas" guide the content and functioning of "interpersonal loops" that "play into the environment" to induce others "to fit their role expectations" (Beitman). Patterns of human behavior involve complex, interrelated levels of functioning that include psychological, behavioral, situational, and interpersonal/social components (Prochaska & DiClemente). Behavior patterns are "multimodal"; they involve behavior, affect, sensation and perception, imagery, cognition, interpersonal relations, and biology. These patterns occur in "continual, reciprocal transaction" to produce "coordinated patterns" according to learning principles, particularly social learning (Lazarus). Beutler combines other integrative and eclectic approaches, a combination that implies a biopsychosocial unit. People live in contexts so behavior is always in relation to someone or something, and organized in "cyclical dynamics" manifest in episodes of "intention-action-consequences" that involve "circular causality;" stability maintaining processes are manifest in "vicious cycles" (Wachtel). Kanfer uses a systems model to guide his approach (which uses all the components of our comparative framework) because it specifies how the "interaction" of environmental, psychological, and biological variables produce "a particular psychological state or behavior" at a given time.

Constructivist theorists conceive of humans as unified, "somatopsychic" entities, or "embodied theories of life" (Mahoney). Patterns of individual and group functioning are "co-constituted" so that people's "personal meanings" cannot be understood separate from their sociocultural contexts (Efran & Fauber). People's sensory-perceptual, motoric, and cognitive activities as they interact with their environments are the source of all knowing; to "know" a context means "to act upon it" (Guidano). Different kinds of responses should be understood as "interdependent expressions" of "holistic, systemic processes" (Efran & Fauber; Mahoney). "Constructs" are "system organizations" that function as "integral wholes" (Mahoney), and are organized in "construct systems" or "theories" (Neimeyer); they are "embodied programs of action" that are context dependent patterns of biological, cognitive, affective, and behavioral processes that operate as "process loops" (Fauber). The "cycle of experience" can be summarized as a feedback loop (Feixas). People continually organize their experience into a single, elaborate, coherently organized "self-construct" that coordinates their psychological growth, development, and differentiation. Maintaining "internal coherence" in that identity is the "fundamental self-organizing invariant" (Guidano), like stability-maintaining negative feedback dynamics in our comparative framework. People are also constructive (form-giving), able to elaborate their functional patterns (Guidano; Mahoney; Neimeyer). The descriptions by EIT theorists vary from explicit control system models to being quite abstract and vague, but their collective view seems to represent or imply a unit similar to the living systems model in the comparative framework used here.

Operational Units: Behavior Episode Schemas (BES)

How have all these theorists operationalized their person-in-context level concepts? Are their operational units similar to the behavior episodes and behavior episode schemas in our comparative framework? The theorists usually describe their operational units in their procedural models. Units similar to the behavior episode schemas are considered first.

The general concept of "structures" is used by many of these theorists to refer to persistent or habitual patterns of functioning that organize and guide people's current patterns of behavior, so the *function* of structures is similar to the function of the schema in our framework. Theorists differ in the way they describe the nature of the "structures" they propose, but most limit their *content* to psychological components. Typically, "faulty structures" are considered the source of psychopathology.

In PT, Freud's key "structure" is "intrapsychic conflict," with specific content designated by concepts like "oedipus complex." Ego psychology added "ego structures" (habitual directive and control function patterns) created from reality-based experiences rather than instinct-based influences. An ego psychology based structure that is an alternative to "intrapsychic conflict" is "pathogenic beliefs" (Weiss & Sampson). The guiding structures of object relations and self-psychology (ISCT) analysts are learned habitual psychological patterns (like ego structures) that are generalized representations about oneself and interpersonal relations, including "self," "object" or "object relations," and "selfobjects" (Balint; Kohut; Fairbairn; Winnicott). They are also referred to as "guiding templates" (Pine) and "experience distant principles" (Kohut). ISCT models call guiding structures "dynamisms" or "personifications" (Sullivan) and "interpersonal circles" or "self" and "self-other" "schemas" (Kiesler).

HT theorists stress continual development, so they tend to talk about "processes" rather than "structures." However, two structural concepts are frequently used: (1) "self-concept" (Rogers; Bozarth; Gendlin; Korb et al), which some elaborate into a person-in-context concept, "internal models of self-in-world experience" (Greenberg & Rice) or "self-and-world construct system" (Bugental & Sterling); and (2) "schema" (Greenberg, Wexler, & Rice), which embody prototypical knowledge and ideas about one's self and one's context, and how those features relate to and influence one another. "Personal goals" are another structure whose organizing function is sometimes stressed (Bohart, Yontef).

BT theorists represent the organization of behavior in terms of patterns of different kinds of component responses and stimuli linked by predictive and causal contingencies. In their view, many different kinds of patterns may be learned, so rather than proposing key structures, they try to identify the specific kind of habitual pattern that is creating problems for each client as well as patterns typical of different kinds of disorder (examples are agoraphobia and depression). In contrast to several therapy families, their structures are similar to behavior episode schemas. In that sense, the behavior therapy theorists do not restrict their descriptions of structures to psychological components.

CT theorists' key structural concepts emphasize types of cognitive functions: "belief" and "belief system" (Ellis), and "schema" (Beck). Beliefs are "strongly held hypotheses" composed largely of habitual self-evaluative expectations or demands, so in that sense they are similar to PT theorists' super ego structures. Schemas are "internal models" of self and world that include both content and "a program of rules" or propositions that function to shape perceptions and interpretations of events, organize experience, and guide behavior. Like BT theorists, they emphasize the view that many kinds of "beliefs" and "schemas" can be learned, and different kinds of disorders may have "beliefs" and "schemas" with different kinds of content and propositions as their antecedents. The function of their key concepts is similar to the function of a behavior episode schema but the content of their concepts is more limited.

CBST approaches stress teaching "effective and satisfying" behavior in "critical life situations" (Goldstein; Goldsmith & McFall), termed *competence, performance competence, interpersonal competence,* or *socially competent behavior.* Competence involves capabilities for both generating and performing relevant skilled behavior compatible with specific situations (Goldstein; Trower; Meichenbaum). Skills may be psychological (such as problem solving), behavioral (such as actions) or interpersonal (such as communication), so a competent pattern is an organization of relevant skills. There may be many different kinds of competence patterns that organize and guide people's functioning in different kinds of situations. BMHT theorists use a multivariate causation model. Their concepts of "stress and coping patterns" and "lifestyles" refer to enduring prototypical patterns of anticipations, evaluations, emotions, interpretations, and actions that people use when they are faced with tasks and demands. Thus, the central concepts of CBST and BMHT theorists seem similar to the behavior episode schema of the comparative framework.

EIT theorists tend to use some form of "circular," "cyclical," or "interpersonal transaction" dynamics similar to the behavior episode schema unit. "Core interpersonal schemas" include "buttons" which when "pushed" activate specific emotions, thoughts and/or actions, and "scripts" representing potential patterns of actions and consequences; "unresolved traumas" are analogous to PTs "intrapsychic conflicts" (Beitman). Symptoms or syndromes occur within "complex, interrelated levels of human functioning" (Prochaska

& DiClemente). Lazarus's "BASIC I.D." refers to enduring patterns of seven, mutually influential "modalities of functioning." Beutler sees such enduring patterns as resulting from interactions among "predisposing patient personal characteristics," "patient problems" and "environments and life circumstances." Wachtel's "cyclical dynamics" psychological, behavioral, and contextual (such as family systems) variables and synthesizes them into complex, enduring patterns of mutually influential component functions that he sometimes calls schemas (following Piaget). Kanfer's "self-regulatory system" and "problem-solving" models combine to produce learned "enduring states." Constructivist theorists tend to use highly abstract and inclusive concepts. One used by many of them is *construct*. "Constructs" differ from concepts (which have only cognitive content) because they are "system organizations" that function as "integral wholes" (Mahoney). "Constructs" may differ in content, but all function as "embodied programs of action" (Efran & Fauber) patterns of biological, cognitive, affective, and behavioral processes that are context dependent.

Operational Units: Behavior Episodes

All the theorists discussed agree that any pattern of functioning can be learned or changed only while it is occurring in the here and now, and that arranging for special conditions to operate while the pattern is occurring is the key to learning or change. Therefore, all their procedural models operationalize their guiding structures—similar to behavior episode schemas—in specific remembered, observable, simulated, or real-life episodes, much like the concept of behavior episodes in the comparative framework.

Freud's concept of "repetition" refers to the recurrence of habitual pattern in a current specific situation. He called it a form of "remembering" in which the "memory" is "acted out" rather than cognitively recalled. A very important form of "repetition" occurs when a patient's "unconscious intrapsychic conflict", as in the "oedipus complex," is "acted out" in specific analytic episodes, called "transference" (and "countertransference" when therapists "act out" their "intrapsychic conflicts" toward patients). A related form is habitual "unconscious defenses," which a patient acts out to "resist" becoming aware of their conflict. In Freud's view, dysfunctional patterns can only be influenced to change while they are occurring; they cannot be slain in absentia or in effigy. Therefore new learning requires a series of specific behavior episodes in which "transference" and "resistance" occur and are analyzed, a process called "working through."

ISCT theorists assert that dysfunctional patterns result from faulty social learning; therefore, relearning requires new, relevant social relationship experiences, which therapists must provide in psychotherapy sessions, called "experience near acts" (Kohut), "moments" (Pine), or "causal loops" of "interpersonal transaction cycles" (Carson; Kiesler). Self-psychology and object relations analysts rely on "transference" as a key kind of experience near acts. Interpersonal therapists use a similar idea, but Sullivan calls it "parataxic distortion" to connote that it reveals interpersonal learning rather than "psychosexual drives" as Freud proposed. Kiesler calls it a "maladaptive transaction cycle" to indicate that both client and therapist behaviors are involved; his process is analogous to the analytic combination of "transference" and "countertransference".

HT theorists stress "processes" and "current functioning"—that is "moment-to-moment" living (Bohart); change can occur only in such "moments." In each behavior episode, functioning occurs in complex patterns, as "gestalten," or a "Gestalt experience cycle" (Korb et al.). The humanists assume that only clients can change themselves, so these therapists create a therapy relationship that consistently and repeatedly provides learning experiences that free clients' self-changing processes. HT theorists, especially experiential and gestalt therapists, may create special "experiential" therapy episodes to help clients become aware of and deal with specific kinds of problems. During therapy sessions, clients are asked to describe and to relive past significant behavior episodes, called "evocative" or "systematic evocative unfolding" (Bohart; Greenberg et al.), or "phenomenal focusing" (Yontef). To facilitate elaborating vaguely experienced episodes into more vivid experiences, "experiential focusing" is used (Gendlin; Greenberg et al.). Simulated episodes may also be created through "role playing," "two-chair dialogues," "empty chair" or "two-chair enactments," and "expressive movement exercises" (Bohart; Greenberg et al.; Yontef).

BT theorists' propositions about change processes are the most explicit and extensive of all the approaches analyzed. These theorists assume that dysfunctional patterns are learned, so clients must experience new, relevant learning "episodes" or "trials" to unlearn or relearn. BT creates and conducts such specific learning episodes. The content of episodes will vary, depending on the learning objectives. There are two broad types: (1) "Relationship experiences" in therapy sessions are used to motivate clients to try to change; and (2) "Controlled exposure" to relevant learning conditions is used to facilitate desired behavior change. Exposure may take two forms: (1) Observational learning results from watching someone else demonstrate illustrative behavior. This technique is often called social modeling. (2) Enactive learning requires a client actually to behave in relevant behavior episodes, either within therapy sessions or in real-life situations.

CT theorists advocate the careful identification and analysis of each dysfunctional pattern. Then, therapy sessions directly target those patterns, in contrast to the free association employed in PT. Clients are asked to describe in detail—thereby reexperiencing to some extent—specific episodes of daily living in which the dysfunctional pattern operated. These include (1) past episodes, (2) current episodes in their daily life or in therapy sessions, (3) imagined episodes that might occur, and (4) real-life episodes linked to the therapy process. It is during those periods of describing and reexperiencing such behavior episodes that change becomes possible through "cognitive restructuring." In addition, therapists create learning episodes to help clients cultivate specific skills. These episodes may be simulated—for example, "cognitive rehearsal," "imagery," "role playing," or "modeling"—or real—as in homework assignments.

Theorists in the CBST and BMHT approaches use specific training episodes designed to help clients learn specific skills, skill combinations, and to flexibly create useful skill combinations. These therapists use both observational and enactive behavior episodes in careful combination, moving from social modeling, to practice in simulated episodes, to practice in real-life episodes.

EIT theorists differ in the explicitness of their change proposals, with constructivists being the most vague. Activation of "core interpersonal schemas" under therapeutic conditions, analogous to PT's transference, enables clients to learn how their core interpersonal schema is invalid (Beitman). A patient's "BASIC I.D." is manifested as a "vicious cycle" that perpetuates itself. Therapy focuses on activating and altering those "cycles," relying primarily on modeling and enactive learning episodes (Lazarus). Faulty vicious cycles must be identified and activated in therapy sessions under conditions that disrupt them; "exposure," particularly "in vivo exposure," is the most effective change method. "Transference" is a kind of "vivid" in vivo exposure experience. Then, therapists must facilitate clients' efforts to change their vicious cycles (Wachtel). Kanfer uses behavioral, cognitive, and skill training methods, with a focus on (1) identifying, activating, and disrupting ineffective, self-defeating, "automatic processing" "self-regulatory" patterns, and (2) using "problem-solving strategies" with "controlled processing" to create and implement needed changes. For constructivists, faulty "embodied programs of action" (Efran & Fauber), patterns of "being-in-the-world" or "embodied theories" (Mahoney), or "deep tacit structures" (Guidano), are clients' sources of difficulty. They operate in therapy sessions through clients' discussions of dysfunctional ways they currently organize their "personal meanings" in "personal narratives" or "construct systems." Exposure during therapy episodes to new experiences and meanings that disrupt existing "structures" enables clients to change their "narratives" or "construct systems" by "first order" (assimilation) and "second order" (accommodation) processes (Mahoney).

COMMENTARY

This analysis illustrates how different therapy theorists may express the same general idea with different terminology, and the problem that creates for clinicians who are trying to understand, compare, and use different approaches.

Generalized Patterns as Guiding Units

There is widespread agreement among theorists that some generalized, habitual functional units organize and guide clients' patterns of functioning in their current contexts (analogous to the concept of behavior episode schema in the comparative framework). When these units are faulty, dysfunctional behavior results. There is also general agreement that these units involve multiple kinds of responses—for example, personal goals, evaluative thoughts, emotions, and plans for action. The theorists differ in what they name their units and in the descriptions of the content of those units. Thus, one important focus of future theoretical and empirical study should be to identify and reach agreement about the most useful ways to represent and name these "guiding structures." For example, is there only one general form, as some suggest—an all-inclusive self-concept, narrative, or interpersonal transactional cycle? Are there multiple forms as others suggest—multiple schemas, constructs, or selves for different interpersonal or other kinds of behavior episodes? If there are multiple forms, how are they related? Are they completely independent or are they interrelated, and if so how—such as hierarchically or some other way? What is their content? Is their content solely cognitive? (and if so what kinds). Do these structures also include habitual emotions, actions, selective attention, or biological states? Do they become active only in certain kinds of situations, or are they so general they operate in all kinds of contexts? What are the relationships among the parts of these general units? We suggest that our comparative framework and its person-in-context behavior episode schema unit might be useful tools in the search for answers to such questions.

Theorists also agree that the guiding units operate in specific situations, and that learning, or relearning requires creating and using such episodes—analogous to the behavior episode unit on the comparative framework. They differ, however, in how they describe and name them: "transference," "interpersonal" or "experience" cycles, "learning trials." Because all theorists rely on specific behavior episodes as their tool for change, progress in theory and practice could result from careful analysis and comparison of the types actually used by therapists of all persuasions, and the purposes for which they are used. The objective would be to try to identify generic types with specification of the ways each type can be used to facilitate different kinds of change—for example, episodes that are "recalled," "observed," "imagined," "simulated," "enacted with therapists," or "enacted in real-life contexts." First, however, the theoretical nature of the guiding structures must be clarified as a prerequisite for clarifying the potential therapeutic utility of different kinds of specific behavior episodes. This means that discussions of how to produce change must be related to what is to be changed. Our comparative framework provides one way to conceptualize the content of and relationships between units similar to behavior episodes and behavior episode schemas.

LEVELS AND UNITS OF ANALYSIS IN PSYCHOTHERAPY MODELS:
COMPONENT LEVEL UNITS

The comparative framework used in this book also encompasses all the basic kinds of biological, psychological, behavioral, and environmental factors given prominence in the human sciences; it proposes a minitheory for each one, constructed from relevant disciplinary and professional literatures, and provides a model for how these components are related and interact. The concepts embodied in the basic therapy theories stress psychological—especially cognitive—components, communicative actions, and interpersonal contexts. Biological and action components and other kinds of environments tend to be neglected by many, but not all.

BIOLOGICAL COMPONENTS

Comparative Framework Units and Therapy Theory Units
Our comparative framework adopts the model of human physiology widely accepted in biology and medicine and used to integrate knowledge about different parts of biological functioning. The biological person is represented as an organization of material/energy-based structural/functional subsystems: circulatory, respiratory, central nervous, autonomic nervous systems, and others. All therapy models analyzed mention the importance of biological factors, but few translate that belief into their conceptual models, nor do they explicitly use the biomedical model of human physiology. Conceptualizations of biological components typically remain fragmented, vague, poorly

substantiated if substantiated at all, and seldom explicitly related to therapy procedures. In a few approaches, some attention is given to biological factors in their developmental theories and procedural models.

Developmental Theories and Inborn Starting Points

All theorists who propose a developmental theory start by assuming or implying that humans have inborn repertoires of functional capabilities—"genetic factors" or "predispositions"—that provide a starting point for future development. They assume that these include both inborn *patterns,* such as "instincts," "drives," "social needs," and "strategies," like fight or flight; "emotional schemes;" "gamma" factors and *processes,* "ego functions;" "primary and secondary process thought," "conscious experiencing;" "self-righting," "self-maintaining" or "self-organizing;" "meaning-making," "learning" or "self constructing;" "purposive," "a sense of agency" or "self-directing;" "hedonistic" or "valuing;" "choice" or "problem solving"). Therapy theorists differ in the kinds of inborn characteristics they stress.

In growing bodies of evidence in disciplines like behavior genetics, developmental psychology and biology, sociobiology and ethology, extensive support exists for the idea that people's inborn biological nature influences their development and functioning. Wide individual differences in inborn characteristics are also being documented by the basic disciplines. However, therapy theorists seldom use such knowledge to evaluate or justify their assumptions. For example, there is little scientific support for the evolutionary theories of Lamarck and Haeckel, which Freud used to support his proposal that the oedipal complex is universal, but considerable evidence supports the idea that humans evolved as social organisms.

The choice of different theories of development has practical significance; it implies the use of different kinds of interventions to facilitate individuals' development. For example, if the oedipus complex is learned rather than genetically determined, only some people are likely to learn that faulty belief and it can be changed by further learning. Therefore, different diagnoses would be necessary for different people, and knowledge of etiology may be relevant to treatment design. Moreover, modern behavioral genetics stresses individual differences in two ways: It provides evidence that people may differ significantly in their genetic inheritance; it points out that even where a genetic predisposition exists, it will not necessarily flower into functional patterns unless it interacts with key environmental conditions, (such as contexts in which alcohol is available and used by a person genetically vulnerable to alcoholism.

Knowledge continues to grow about inborn attributes and how they can facilitate and constrain different kinds of developmental pathways. Therapy theorists could profit from relating their assumptions to the more detailed and sophisticated bodies of theory and evidence in behavioral genetics, developmental biology, and developmental psychology, where different metamodels of development have been created and evaluated (e.g., see Ford & Lerner, 1992, for an overview). Models of development in therapy theories are analyzed in Chapter 16.

Procedural Models and Biological Components.
Therapists' evolving procedural models give more attention to biological factors than do their guiding theoretical models. Once therapists acknowledged that not all symptoms have biological causes, a psychophysical parallelism view initially dominated therapy practice. Fifty years ago, psychotherapists assumed that they should not begin therapy with a patient until a physician had determined that the symptoms were not problems of the body. *Body* and *mind* were considered independent; physicians took care of the body and psychotherapists took care of the mind. That metaphysical view still seems implicit in much therapy theorizing, as in the view that biological and psychological functioning can be treated separately, so all biological problems should be referred to a physician, and vice versa.

In therapy practice, however, the frequent use of drugs to alter dysfunctional cognitive or emotional patterns, such as psychotic or anxiety states, illustrates recognition that biological functioning directly influences psychological and behavioral functioning. Now, the preferred treatment for serious depressions combines biological and psychotherapy interventions. The use of "photo therapy" to alleviate seasonal affective disorders, relaxation training to control emotions or alleviate headaches, and psychological interventions to facilitate dealing with and recovery from illnesses and surgery are all now widespread and imply a metaphysics of mind-body interaction. There is also an expanded emphasis on using psychological/behavioral (information/ meaning-based) interventions for health promotion and disease prevention. Many medical schools as well as psychiatry departments now include behavioral science. Thus far, only BMHT theorists make theoretically explicit the proposition that states of "body," "mind," and "context" are mutually influential and that biological states such as symptoms may be altered by psychological and behavioral interventions, as well as the reverse.

All the theories that were analyzed emphasize cognitive and emotional processes. However, those processes are made possible by the brain's biological functions, and these in turn can be altered by psychological and behavioral functioning. Therefore, psychotherapists may profit from energetically exploring the interface between brain sciences, neurochemistry, and psychological functioning. At a practical level, that interface undergirds clinical psychologists' desire for prescription privileges. Psychotherapists who assume they can ignore biological factors when dealing with cognitive and emotional functioning, and physicians who assume the reverse, are using a discredited and outdated metaphysics of psychophysical parallelism.

PSYCHOLOGICAL COMPONENTS

Our comparative framework specifies three groups of interrelated psychological functions that are analogous to three basic functions of self-organizing systems. *Arousal functions* selectively energize all other functions: Activity arousal fuels all activity patterns; consciousness and attention arousal selectively organize the nervous system to carry out information processing functions; emotional arousal temporarily augments the first two and provides subjective experiences that are evaluative and regulatory in nature. *Information monitoring, collection, and processing functions* selectively generate perceptual experiences and construct, revise, elaborate, or combine cognitive and behavior patterns. Directive, regulatory, and control *governing functions* select, use, and organize cognitive information/meaning-based representations to create and guide behavior episodes.

PSYCHOLOGICAL COMPONENTS: AROUSAL FUNCTIONS

Activity Arousal: The Comparative Framework and Therapy Theory Proposals
Our comparative framework assumes that activity is continuous in humans at all levels of functioning—from cellular operations to complex transactions with their environments. The theoretical problem is how to account for qualitative and quantitative variations in activity, rather than why it occurs or what may start or stop it.

Few contemporary therapy theorists adhere to the initial emphasis of Freud (PT) and Watson (BT) that people are passive unless energized by some stimulus. For Freud, it was an inner stimulus (instinctually based drives); for early behaviorists it was an outer (environmental) event. Most contemporary approaches including BT consider both inner and outer influences to be important and stress the proactive nature of human activity. Some, such as the HT and EIT view the person as part of a never-ending spatial-temporal flow of varying events ("becoming;" "being-in-the-world"). Activity is considered a basic property of life, but the potential significance of variations in level or intensity (relaxed, lethargic, hyperactive, fatigued, and alert), and their conscious manifestation in affective experience, are rarely addressed.

Therapy theorists give little attention to variations in activity arousal, despite its significant influence on humans' development and functioning. For example, individual differences in energy-generating metabolic patterns—for example hypo- or hyperthyroidism, and circulatory functioning as in high or low blood pressure, can produce differences in activity level and temperament ranging from largo and legato to staccato and prestissimo, that can have major impacts on how people feel and behave, how others behave toward them and, as a result, the kinds of habitual patterns they develop.

Consciousness/Attention (CA) Arousal and Perception:
Comparative Framework Proposals
Our framework describes consciousness attention arousal as a state of activation of the nervous system that allows people to intentionally monitor and use information/meaning-based representations to construct, guide, and revise different kinds of functional patterns. This arousal is accompanied by a subjective experience typically called being awake or aware. A person in a coma or deep (NREM) sleep cannot perform information processing functions—coordinated perception, thought, and action are impossible. Consciousness is analogous to the state of a record player that one has turned on before a specific record has been selected to play. It is a state of arousal that is content free.

Creation of coherently organized patterns of activity requires a selection process that uses some kinds of information/meaning-based forms and ignores others, and orchestrates a specific pattern of central nervous system activation and inhibits others. Attention is a function of consciousness states that performs these selection operations. Attention is analogous to the act of selecting a specific record to be played on the record player, and the volume and tone settings to be used. Where does the content of the music come from that one hears when playing a record? It comes from the record, not the record player. Similarly, what is the origin of the contents of consciousness—what you are aware of? These thoughts come from the sensory or cognitive sources on which selective attention is focused. Selective attention produces feedback signals, the conscious contents of which are called perceptions or thoughts (see Figure 3.2).

Perceptions are conscious representations of what occurs at each moment as revealed by the sources to which sensory perceptual structures and functions are directed by selective attention. What exists changes from moment to moment, and so will perceptions. As momentary, transient pieces of information, perceptions have limited adaptive utility unless their potential meaning is interpreted using previously constructed ideas. Therefore, perceiving and thinking are coupled but different information/meaning-based processes. Perceptions tell us what is happening now; interpretations are thoughts that tell us how that phenomenon might affect us, what might follow, and how we might influence future events. Dysfunctional behavior may result either from faulty interpretations or inadequate perceptual data, and it is important for treatment to distinguish between the two.

Selective attention also performs feedforward functions by selectively activating different patterns of functioning—complex patterns of actions, communications, or thoughts. Thus, attention selectively organizes input, throughout, and output to create unitary patterns. When a new pattern of functioning is being constructed, a person must be aware of its components, learning without awareness is not possible. After a pattern is well learned, however—has become an automated habit—it can be activated as a functional unit without a person's being aware of its content. Therefore, unconscious functioning is a normal and useful mode, but the cues that activate the unconscious functioning of a habit are perceptions that can result only from selective attention. Although the habit may function unconsciously, a person can be aware of the current conditions that activated it and some of its manifestations. In fact, people can intentionally activate unconscious content by consciously manipulating some part of that habit of which they are aware, the way a person steers a car by turning the steering wheel. Because learning requires that people be aware of what they are trying to learn, to change an automated habit requires the person first to focus selective attention on it so it can be consciously examined and modified.

Consciousness/Attention Arousal and Perception: Therapy Theory Proposals
All the theorists under discussion share the idea that *conscious control* over one's current functioning and development is the key to psychologically healthy, happy, and effective living. For many theorists, however, this idea is only implied. HT make it most explicit with concepts such as "freedom," "purposiveness" or "sense of agency," "choice" or "problem solving." The procedural models of all the approaches we analyzed use methods that resemble our comparative framework model of relationships among consciousness, selective attention, perception, and learning. However, the theorists' conceptual and propositional models about these processes and the relationships of the processes to thought and language are generally vague or only implied. As a result, there is often confusion and misleading use of some of those concepts. The misleading use of the concepts of perception and thinking is particularly serious and is discussed after the models of cognition are analyzed. Only Freud and Sullivan propose theories about consciousness/attention arousal. Ego analysts such as Rapaport elaborated on Freud's view of

the development of ego functions through a rationale for learning with awareness. Others explicitly use Freud's or Sullivan's theories, or use therapy methods that imply those theories.

Freud's topographic model introduced the ideas of unconscious processes (latent content) that could become manifest content in conscious thought through preconscious processes. Inwardly directed perception was the means by which unconscious (latent) content could be brought into awareness through preconscious processes. He said the "ego" resulted from modification of portions of the "id" by the direct influence of the external world through the operation of perception-consciousness, which is called learning in modern psychology. "Ego" functions, or "secondary process thought" perform conscious governing, organizing, and change functions through a mobile, manipulable energy of consciousness, called *hypercathexis*, which is Freud's term for selective attention. Therefore, one could make the unconscious conscious by directing selective attention or "hypercathexis" to it, and thereby gain conscious, intentional control over it and create or learn new patterns. People use a variety of "defensive" maneuvers to prevent attending to unconscious thoughts that would be very distressing if they became conscious.

Sullivan's key ideas are attention and inattention rather than conscious and unconscious. People are aware of what they attend to, so the contents of consciousness are current perceptions resulting from directing attention to inner or outer sensory sources, or to thought processes. Patterns may function outside awareness if people do not attend to them. To gain intentional control over and to modify dysfunctional habitual patterns, people must overcome habits of inattention so that they can become aware of the dysfunctional patterns.

All the procedural models studied, including contemporary BT imply that learning requires awareness. It follows that one criterion for adaptive, effective, self-organizing, and self-directing—or healthy—functioning is the capability for unrestricted awareness of all kinds of perceptions generated by the flow of a person's activity, thoughts, and contexts. HT substitutes the concept of "experience" for "perception" and represents this assumption with the phrase, openness to experience. Because learning requires awareness, and the contents of awareness are perceptions resulting from selective attention, all the procedural models use strategies and methods for guiding clients' attention to key aspects of their functioning and thoughts that need to be changed or learned. This process takes two forms. When the goal is to gain control over and modify unconscious bad habits, attention must be focused on those habits as they occur (PT; ISCT; BT; CT; EIT). When the goal is to learn a new, good habit, clients must focus attention on the content of the new habit while it is being performed by others—social modeling—and while they are performing the actions themselves, simulated or in vivo. (e.g., HT; BT; CT; CBST; BMHT; EIT). Some procedures aim at the subgoal of helping clients learn habits of attending to all sources of perceptions, such as the "experiencing" methods of HT.

Emotional Arousal: Comparative Framework Proposals

Like most current theories of emotions, our comparative framework assumes that humans begin life with a few inborn emotional patterns that are the result of evolutionary processes. These are prototypical patterns of biological, affective, and action components that evolved to regulate behavior in dealing with different kinds of adaptive issues. Each one provides affective experiences with evaluative qualities that perform regulatory functions. Awareness of the significance of such affective or emotional experiences is adaptively useful to people. Our comparative framework views cognition and emotion as essential partners in the motivation and regulation of behavior; one (cognition) is not "good" and the other (emotion) "bad." Although qualitatively different, both are simultaneously involved in the ongoing operation of the person.

Each emotional pattern is activated under relevant prototypical behavior episode conditions and facilitates prototypical actions, such as approach or avoidance; fight or flight. Initially, the inborn prototypical elicitors for each emotion are direct perceptions: loud, sudden sounds startle and frighten babies; affectionate caresses sooth and please them. Soon, however, learned anticipatory evaluative thoughts rapidly become the primary elicitors. Emotions are learnable in two senses: (1) They are activated by perceptions and anticipatory evaluative thoughts; through learning, almost any event can come to be interpreted by a person so as to activate an emotional pattern. As an example, people can learn to be frightened or sexually aroused by almost anything, including their own thoughts. (2) People can learn to inhibit some components of each pattern, or to blend components of two patterns. Emotions evolved to function as temporary augmentations of activity and consciousness/attention arousal processes, so they rapidly dissipate once the behavior episode they serve ends. This is true unless conditions persistently activate them, such as generalized, anticipatory evaluative thoughts. Persistent activation is biologically expensive, and so it may produce enduring changes in relevant biological steady-state parameters, such as blood pressure levels. Thus, habitual, persistent emotional activation is a key source of somatic symptoms in psychotherapy patients as well as a source of habits of inattention, thought, or action learned to control emotional states—the "defense mechanism."

Emotional Arousal: Therapy Theory Proposals

Historically, particularly in Western cultures, rationality (conscious cognitive control of functioning) was idealized, and irrationality (emotionality) was considered undesirable or animalistic. Socialization was aimed at cultivating rationality and inhibiting irrationality. Initial forms of psychotherapy—for example, Freud's psychoanalysis—implicitly adopted this cultural rationale: (The "id" is a "seething cauldron" of "passions" that dominates "unconscious, primary process thought" [irrationality], whereas "ego" involves conscious, logically organized, reality-oriented "secondary process thought" [rationality]. Psychopathology was linked to irrationality and emotionality. An undercurrent of this view may still exist in psychotherapy theories of psychopathology. Some, such as HT, consider this stress on rationality at the expense of emotionality to be "dehumanizing." They argue that emotions enrich human experience, using as an example the monotony of life as a flat line of affect with no variations of joy, sorrow, curiosity, fear, affection, anger, excitement, guilt, or sexual arousal.

Given the importance most psychotherapy approaches attribute to emotions in their models of psychopathology, their procedural models, and their discussions of specific cases, it is surprising that their theories have so little to say about this domain. Some (such as EIT—Constructivists) argue that distinctions between emotions and other kinds of responses are misguided. Others—CT and HT—acknowledge such distinctions, but stress the invariable linkages among emotions, thoughts, and actions. Often there is an implicit reliance on categories used in everyday language or in the discipline of psychology, (e.g., CT; BT; CBST; HT; BMHT). Some stress certain types of emotions. For example, Freud's concept of "signal anxiety" has evolved into a general fear-avoidance model.

The concept of affect is frequently used but with vague meaning. Clear distinctions are often not made between emotions and their conscious manifestations in affective experience (e.g., CT; HT; ISCT). Some distinguish between affects and emotions, but their differences and relationships remain undefined (e.g., CBST—Meichenbaum). The concept of feelings is often used, sometimes referring to affective experience and sometimes including cognition. Why emotions occur is often not theoretically explained. Some propose that cognitions—evaluative thoughts—can activate emotions; (e.g., BMHT; CT; HT; ISCT). Most assume that emotions influence thought and action, and some assume they can influence biological functioning (e.g., BMHT).

Sometimes, emotions are labeled *positive* or *negative* (e.g., CT). No criteria are explicitly stated for such classifications, although the usual implication is that positive is good and negative is bad. Examples imply that the designation *negative* refers to affective experiences people find aversive, detrimental to their welfare, destructive of social cohesion, or maladaptive for individuals and social groups. Some suggest that *positive* emotions facilitate behavior to produce, retain, or restore conditions that generate them, whereas *negative* ones facilitate behavior to interrupt, discontinue, or forestall conditions that produce them (e.g., ISCT).

Such dichotomizations of emotional states are so imprecise and laden with implicit value judgments that they need to be replaced with more precise models. Our comparative framework and most current theories of emotions construe each basic kind of emotion to be adaptively useful—that is, positive in that sense. For example, to be apprehensive and cautious in any situation where danger lurks is prudent; affection, guilt, and shame can facilitate cohesive group living. Empirical evidence suggests that intense emotions of any kind flood the system with arousal and disrupt coherent patterns of thought and action; they produce "irrational" behavior. Sometimes, the ways people learn for preventing or controlling such intense states prove to be dysfunctional in other ways; for example, phobic avoidance patterns can interfere with other aspects of living. It seems probable that quantitative rather than qualitative variations in emotional states contribute to dysfunctional development (see CT—Ellis for examples). Cultural values may also lead to a rejection of certain actions expressive of emotions, defining them as dysfunctional.

"Positive" emotions are typically given far less attention than "negative" ones, but the role of prosocial emotions of belongingness, such as affection and love, is increasingly stressed by some therapy theorists. For example, theoretical models of development and motivation stress interpersonal relationships and the constructive influence of affectionate, caring affiliative interpersonal patterns; (e.g., ISCT; HT; CBST; EIT). Moreover, most procedural models stress the value of such affective patterns in the creation and functioning of therapeutic relationships.

We agree with Greenberg and his associates (HT) who assert that psychotherapy theory has given insufficient theoretical attention to the very important emotional aspect of human function/dysfunction, and that this neglect has detracted from the creation of more precise and effective interventions. Drawing on current scientific literature, they propose a model of emotions similar to that of our comparative framework. They use the concept of emotional schemes to represent the complex habitual patterns of physiological, cognitive, and action components said to emerge from the learned modification of the primary emotional patterns that are innate in each person.

Greenberg and associates also distinguish between emotional patterns per se and the conscious experience of them—that is, feelings. They note that feelings are composed of information from multiple sources, including the direct perception of the nonvolitional physiological and sensory-motor aspects of the pattern, a semantically based emotional memory system, or meaning, and a verbally based language system. Their concept of emotional schemes, differing from the typical meaning of schemas, shows similarities to our concept of behavior episode schemas, particularly if one assumes that some kind of emotion is a component of all behavior episode schemas. However, their model fails to address the relationships between emotional components and cognition, language, and action. Our open system, comparative framework, allows a theorist to treat emotions as one significant component of complex functional patterns, rather than to consider them a separate organizational form.

PSYCHOLOGICAL COMPONENTS: INFORMATION PROCESSING AND COGNITIVE FUNCTIONS

Most basic forms of psychotherapy were created during the first two-thirds of the twentieth century when "mentalism" was held in disfavor in psychology. There was little theory and scant evidence about human cognition in the human sciences at the time. Even so, psychotherapists could not ignore the importance of cognition being manifested in client problems; thus, their ideas about these psychological functions were necessarily constructed from their clinical experience with clients. Their models of cognition predated and probably gave some impetus to the revolution in cognitive and brain sciences that has been occurring in the last third of this century. This intense interest has produced a massive amount of theory and evidence about these psychological functions, but few psychotherapists have updated their ideas using that growing base of knowledge.

Our comparative framework uses both clinical and scientific knowledge to represent humans as being self-organizing and self-constructing in two basic ways. First, they are biologically self-organizing and self-constructing. People seek and ingest material/energy-forms—food, water, oxygen—which their bodies take apart, reassemble, and use to construct, organize, maintain, repair, operate their biological structures, and eliminate undesirable forms. Second, humans are also psychologically and behaviorally self-organizing and self-constructing. They collect information/meaning-forms from sources within and without their bodies. They combine these or take them apart and reassemble them into useful forms. People can also imaginatively combine this information into new forms to represent objects, experiences, and meanings they have not yet experienced and that may not even exist. They then use these forms to direct, regulate, and control their functioning, to synchronize it with the functioning of other people through communicative exchanges, and to construct and operate social and cultural forms to facilitate group living.

Often, this information/meaning-based capability is called information processing and/or cognitive functions. Our comparative framework includes proposals to explain how information processing functions produce diverse information/meaning-based forms. These are then linked with remembering functions to perform governing functions, creating unified, adaptive patterns of activity in varying contexts.

PSYCHOLOGICAL COMPONENTS: PERCEPTION AND INFORMATION PROCESSING

The Comparative Framework Model

People have an astonishing creative adaptiveness. It stems from their capacity to organize their current behavior by combining their knowledge of current events with the fruits of their experience and their anticipations of probable or possible futures. Our comparative framework assumes that humans have inborn capabilities for monitoring the flow of events within and around them, and for constructing and using many types of information/meaning-based representations.

People are born with different kinds of sensory structures that can collect information from different kinds of material carriers—such as light and sound waves. They also collect information from intraperson sources, such as affective experiences. When attention is directed to any of these sources, the person becomes aware of the information being produced at that moment by that source. That awareness is a *perception* or *observation*. The behavior of neonates is controlled by perceptions, a phenomenon sometimes called *stimulus controlled behavior*. The information/meanings that perceptions can convey are limited because (1) they are fleeting, present for a moment in experience and then replaced as another stimulus occurs, and (2) they can provide information only about conditions with which the person currently has direct, immediate contact because sensory structures rely on material/energy carriers to obtain their information. Nevertheless, perceptions are adaptively very important because they are people's only direct source of information about reality—the nature and operation of their bodies and the world around them. Because perceptions are people's only direct source is the reason that scientists rely so heavily on observational data.

Evolutionary processes solved the limitations of direct perception by enabling humans to construct generalized cognitive representations of consistencies in content and propositional information found in sets of similar perceptions. Because these representations are generalized versions of perceptions and use the codes of the sensory domains that produce the perceptions—for example, the visual domain—we call them imagistic or first-order abstractions or concepts. Infants immediately begin constructing imagistic concepts, perhaps even before birth. Once they have created such perceptually based concepts, people can begin using them for information/

meaning-based self-construction, much like their bodies use food for biological self-construction. People can combine such concepts, or take them apart and reassemble the parts in new ways, thereby creating new concepts that are no longer directly related to perceptions. We call these *abstract* concepts because they are no longer represented in imagistic codes.

This process of combining/transforming existing cognitive representations to construct new information/meaning forms is called *thinking* or *ideation*. It is continuous, leading to increasingly high levels of abstraction representing imagined rather than observable phenomena. These meaning structures or cognitive representations include different kinds of knowledge: conceptual (what is it?), propositional (how does it work?), and procedural (how can it affect me and how can I influence it?). With meaning structures, people can free themselves from stimulus control and become increasingly self-controlled.

Perceptions provide the content of consciousness. Meaning structures cannot be directly perceived because they are not imagistically coded. As a result, thinking with cognitive abstractions occurs outside of awareness. How, then, can people consciously control their thinking or make others aware of their thoughts? Abstract meanings can be made accessible to awareness and susceptible to conscious control by being linked to some perceptible representative of them—by being recast in some iconic, analogue, or symbolic code. Language is a key tool in this process. It enables people to manipulate and control their thoughts consciously, analogous to the way a computer keyboard enables people to manipulate and control computer programs. However, words are not the same as the meanings they represent. To equate words with things is to commit the fallacy of reification; to equate words with thoughts is to lapse into the linguistic fallacy. People think not with words but with abstract meanings. If their words activate meanings in others different from those intended, miscommunication occurs. This proposition has obvious implications for verbal psychotherapy.

Once a person has constructed a repertoire of cognitive representations, these representations are used by the person to interpret the potential meaning and utility of new perceptions, a process that typically occurs at tacit or unconscious levels. Then, the way a person behaves in any behavior episode will reflect the way he or she combines information/meanings in perceptions and conceptions. Thus, people take account of current reality by interpreting perceptual information in relation to their personally constructed meanings, their cognitive representations. When discrepancies occur between perceptual and cognitive meanings, the person applies the principle of unitary functioning to restore coherent cognitive organization. This is done (1) by ignoring the perceptual information, or interpreting it to fit the existing meaning structure, called *assimilation*, or (2) by revising the meaning structure to accommodate the new perceptual information. Thus, meaning structures are dynamic and continually evolving, but perception is inevitably selective because it results from selective attention. People use their meaning structures to direct their attention—the feedforward processes—to selectively perceive information relevant to their current concerns. They can also use the same process to avoid perceiving information they may consider to be disruptive or distressing, thereby preserving their existing meaning patterns.

Proposals in Therapy Theories

All the theorists reviewed in this book explicitly assert or implicitly assume that humans have capabilities for creating cognitive representations and for using them to organize and guide their behavior; people are "meaning makers." The theorists differ greatly, however, in the extent to which they theorize about the nature of those capabilities. In general, they give more attention to describing the *kinds* of structures people create than to the *processes* through which the structures are created. The theorists generally distinguish between conscious and unconscious thought, but they seldom propose theories concerning the nature of consciousness, or unconsciousness, and they provide no criteria for determining why or when thinking is unconscious. Constructivist theorists EIT—Guidano; Mahoney; Neimeyer—view people as *meaning makers*. They describe abstract representations as taking account of, but going beyond the information available in perceptions. Their proposals and the schematic processing view of Greenberg et al. and other humanists, build on evidence from empirical research and are similar to the model of information processing in our comparative framework.

We found no theories about the nature of perception nor its relationship to meaning making or thinking. Most theorists use the term *perceive* to represent a form of interpretive or inferential thought (for example, "I 'perceived' that she was lonely") rather than to represent conscious manifestations of selective attention and sensory processes, as in our comparative framework. Frequently, the term *experience* is used to refer to the phenomena our framework, calls *perception*.

PT offers an elaborate theory about thinking processes. Freud proposed two types. *Primary process thought* operates at unconscious levels, ungoverned by rules of logic. It is unreflective, noncritical, value free, follows no orderly temporal sequence, typically uses imagistic rather than symbolic codes, and functions to gratify instinctual drives without regard for reality. Examples of subtypes are condensation and displacement. Magical thinking and dreaming are types of this form of thinking. *Secondary process thought* is consciously controlled and follows logical rules. It is rational, reflective, and self-monitored; it is anchored in reality; differentiated in terms of past, present, and future; it typically uses symbolically coded cognitions. It organizes and guides behavioral transactions with the environment. There are reports in current literature regarding *states of consciousness* of phenomena, similar to primary process thought PTs. Primary process forms seem to occur when the intentional organizing influence of consciousness/attention arousal is at a low amplitude. This occurs, for example, in rapid eye movement (REM) sleep states when dreaming takes place, and in some kinds of meditative and stimulus deprivation states, when meanings are represented with iconic and analogue rather than symbolic codes.

Other theorists propose ideas about some information/meaning-based processes that correspond to parts of our comparative framework, but they do not propose a general theory. Constructivists, (for example, Mahoney and Guidano) describe people as meaning-making agents who use meanings to guide their actions. However, they do not clearly define *meaning* although Mahoney discusses possibilities; they do not propose a theory about how meanings are constructed or explain their relationship to perception and action. They specify two levels of knowing. The verbally explicit level involves conscious processes that mediate transactions with environments. The tacit or unconscious level provides the structure for the explicit level through "deep structures;" these are basic assumptions, causal theories, and tacit rules of abstraction and inference that operate outside awareness. The constructivists agree that unconscious processes are a normal part of everyday functioning.

When people think, they are manipulating and organizing meanings. It is critical that they distinguish between words and the meanings or thoughts to which they are related, (EIT—Wachtel). Kanfer (EIT) distinguishes between automatic information processing that operates outside awareness and consciously controlled information processing. People use multiple information processing strategies that operate automatically at unconscious levels. It is a mistake to equate inner speech with thought; thought is something other than simply "talking to oneself," although inner speech is one aspect of thinking. Language is a learned tool for the conscious regulation of thought, emotion, and behavior; through the use of words acquired in the course of socialization, people can consciously organize and regulate their patterns of functioning and their interpersonal relationships (CBST—Meichenbaum). The thinking of clients and therapists may differ markedly because of their language differences, (CBST—Goldstein). Good interpersonal relationships rely on mutual, compassionate understanding of one another's personal meanings, obtained through honest, clear communication of them through verbal and gestural language, (CBST—Guerney).

The concept of schema involves not only content, but also a "program of rules" that are typically tacit and function outside of awareness. Although the content and rules remain largely unconscious, some portions, labeled automatic thoughts, are said to be products of them and more accessible to consciousness (CT—Beck). Complex cognitive patterns are hierarchically organized, with higher ones serving as overarching organizations for more specific ones that function in a more context-specific manner, and they operate outside of awareness. (HT—Wexler & Rice; Greenberg et al.). People's lives involve a sequence of choices, and the vast proportion of mental activity underlying those choices operates outside of awareness (ISCT—Mitchell).

Their ideas about psychopathology often involve faulty modes of information processing, discussed further in Chapter 16. Some describe the variety of errors in thinking that clients display. Many use PT's types of defense mechanisms. Others specify types of cognitive distortions, such as dichotomous thinking, overgeneralization, and nonsequitur reasoning (CT—Beck); the use of denials or distortions (HT—Bohart); and introjection and retroflection (HT—Yontef). Ellis's (CT) lists of irrational beliefs could be viewed as faulty habits of information processing. Greenberg et al. (HT) group all information processing dysfunctions into six major types.

Some do not directly address information/meaning-based self-construction. (e.g., BMHT). Typically, distinctions between conscious and unconscious information processing, and between words and thoughts are not clearly defined or explained. Almost none of the theorists address these questions: How does one know it is unconscious? How does unconscious content become conscious, and vice versa? BT theorists seem to assume that thought is covert speech, that it occurs in linguistic codes. This idea implies that changing what people say produces changes in what they think. Some cognitive therapists refer to thoughts as internalized statements or self-statements (e.g., Ellis) or self-talk (e.g., Maultsby). Phenomenologists (e.g., HT) often assert that what clients say should be accepted at face value, a statement that seems to imply that what clients say is the same as what they think.

PSYCHOLOGICAL GOVERNING FUNCTIONS: DIRECTION, CONTROL, REGULATION, AND REMEMBERING

Most psychotherapy theorists agree that habitual patterns of psychological functioning are the principal means by which people govern the content, organization, and modification of their patterns of activity. This leads to several key questions: What is the nature of these governing functions? How can they be analyzed and understood? What are the most useful ways of categorizing them in terms of their content and their operations? Ideas about the nature of information/meaning-based self-constructing processes were just discussed. Here, ways in which those processes operate to govern specific patterns of activity are considered. Our comparative framework derives four types of governing functions from an open systems model: (1) directive, (2) control, (3) regulation, and (4) remembering. Directive, control, and regulation functions use previously constructed patterns or meanings to organize, guide, and alter activity in behavior episodes. Remembering selectively reconstructs the learned patterns useful to those functions in a current episode.

Remembering Processes: Comparative Framework and Therapy Proposals
Our comparative framework asserts that over time, a person constructs a large repertoire of functional patterns; cognitive representations or meanings, as defined in the contents of abstractly coded information/meaning forms; and behavior episode schemas as prototypical biological, psychological, behavioral, and contextually linked patterns. Only a few of all of those constructions are potentially relevant and useful in any specific behavior episode. The process by which specific representations are reactivated for current use is called remembering. The commonly used metaphor for this process is a filing system, in which cognitive representations are stored as memories. Remembering involves a search of the "files," using retrieval cues to find "memories" relevant to the task at hand.

Contemporary theory and research on remembering reject that metaphor and replace it with a reconstruction metaphor. Memories aren't stored anywhere, any more than the note a tuning fork emits when properly struck is stored in the tuning fork. Reconstructing a motoric act, such as driving a car, is illustrative. The act isn't stored in the brain or muscles but is created by selective activation of an appropriate psychomotor pattern. The nature of the action pattern will vary depending on current conditions—such as kind of car or traffic conditions. Similarly, reconstructing a memory involves using selective attention to activate a neural pattern to fit current conditions. The goals, context, and state of a person in an ongoing behavior episode provide the information/meaning cues that selectively activate a reconstruction of relevant patterns, based on earlier learning. The content of the recreated patterns may include all aspects of a person—that is, a behavior episode schema—or some more limited content, such as an idea or emotion. Different conditions will facilitate the reconstruction of different kinds of patterns. Because no two behavior episodes are ever identical, the nature of the reconstructed patterns will never be identical either. Because they are reconstructions, memories can never duplicate the experiences from which they were originally constructed; they are not an iconic representation of events, like a photograph. Thus, thinking is a proactive process in which a person combines selective perceiving and selective remembering to construct patterns relevant to current behavior episode conditions.

Psychotherapy proposals about remembering processes have attracted considerable public attention in recent years as some therapists have asserted that clients can remember previously "repressed memories"—such as long-forgotten "memories" of sexual abuse as a child. It was Freud's painful conclusion that patients' childhood sexual memories were usually fiction rather than fact that led to basic changes in his theory. Research now reveals that conditions under which memories are reported, such as conditions created by a therapist, can lead some people to reconstruct erroneous memories. This observation illustrates the need for therapists to establish a more precise understanding of the nature of the remembering process.

All therapy procedures involve remembering processes. For example, clients are expected to remember their appointment schedules, therapists' instructions about the rules of therapy, and what happened from one therapy session to the next. Some methods prompt clients to remember and describe past behavior episodes, or serve to activate relevant "transference," "vicious cycles," "schemas," "interpersonal circles," or other habitual "structures." Modeling methods assume that clients will remember and be able to use what they observe. All theorists assume that it is memories of the feedback information they get when they try different patterns of functioning that influence clients to change. Clients' inability or unwillingness to remember certain things is considered "resistance" or a "defense" by some theorists, (e.g., PT).

Most of these theorists do not propose theories of remembering to guide the use and understanding of either their own or their clients' remembering processes. Some do describe remembering in relation to cognitive functioning in terms similar to our comparative framework. (e.g., HT—Greenberg et al.; EIT—Mahoney; Guidano). However, the terms *memory* and *remembering* are seldom included in the subject indexes of books about psychotherapy. Often, remembering is mentioned in the narrow sense of some conscious cognitive reconstruction representing a specific past event. Even so, many theorists do not restrict processes of remembering to conscious content; memories may be "explicit" or "tacit," "conscious" or "unconscious." (e.g., PT; HT; CT; ISCT; EIT).

If awareness is not a defining attribute of phenomena called memories, by what criteria can memories be differentiated from other kinds of phenomena? All theorists recognize that previously learned patterns of functioning of any kind can become reactivated or recreated to operate in a current behavior episode, even though a person may be unaware of their operation. This appears to be an implicit definition of remembering, though typically not designated as such. An exception is Freud's (PT) concept of "repetition," and Mahoney does in the context of a "motor theory of mind." Within a broad definition such as this, conscious reconstruction of prior events or previously learned patterns would be an important subtype, as awareness of a pattern is considered a prerequisite for learning or relearning of that pattern.

Some theorists (e.g., HT) differentiate subtypes of conscious symbolic reconstructions in terms of content: episodic, semantic, general, and autobiographical memories. Theorists who assume that information/meanings are organized as coherent stories consider conscious symbolic reconstructions to be narrative inventions (e.g., EIT—Goncalves and Meichenbaum). Most describe remembering as a dynamic, reconstructive process. Memories must be understood as current patterns of functioning, even though they are intended to represent past events, (HT—Bohart; Bugental; Yontef). Memories are continually being "remodeled" or "retranscribed" with additional experience, (ISCT—Modell; EIT—Mahoney). Because it is the nature of current patterns of functioning that is deemed important, regardless of their origins in the past, some theorists do not seem to consider a concept of memory essential (e.g., BT, EIT—Lazarus). Nevertheless, their treatment methods often rely on remembering processes, as in the construction of "hierarchies" of eliciting conditions in systematic desensitization and reciprocal inhibition, and in the use of "covert" (imaginal) "rehearsal" techniques. Some do not seem to differentiate remembering from cognitive processes in general, (e.g., CBST). Yet all information processing terms are not considered synonyms—for example, remembering, imagining, and hallucinating all refer to types of cognitive constructions with somewhat different properties.

Directive Function: Comparative Framework and Therapy Proposals
Our comparative framework proposals derive the concept of a directive function in humans by analogy from the engineering control system function that specifies a "reference signal" or a "state" of specific variables to be produced or maintained. The assumption that self-direction is an inborn aspect of human functioning is supported by a large, growing body of theory and empirical evidence in developmental psychology, particularly infant development. Human behavior is inherently proactive, future oriented, and predictive; it is anticipatory, intentional, or purposive, aimed at creating states deemed desirable and avoiding those deemed undesirable.

Because behavior always occurs in the present, the only way it can be future oriented is for a person to imagine a future state—typically called purposes, intentions, objectives, or goals—and use that idea to organize a pattern of functioning to produce or avoid that state. For conceptual clarity, our comparative framework calls such ideas *goals*. The ability to construct ideas about things, events, or personal states and how they function when they do not presently exist enables people to engage in anticipation and foresight and to direct their behavior in relation to anticipated futures rather than remaining limited to reactions to present events. People are not simply reactive organisms; they function proactively and view themselves as "agent" or "cause" that can anticipate a variety of possible futures, select those they consider desirable, and organize their functioning to bring them about.

Goals are constructed or learned, like all other information/meaning-based representations. They may be self-created or adopted from others; idiosyncratic—personal—or shared—social. Personal goals organize a person's functioning; social goals help synchronize the functioning of a group of people. Once learned, goals may become habitual and operate outside of awareness like any other construct or functional pattern. What distinguishes goals from other cognitive representations? They specify a state called goal content, that a person desires—the goal value or valence—and that the person believes he or she, can create—the goal commitment. Any content can function as a goal: an affective state, a problem solution, a skill, an intimate relationship. This is so as long as the goal is valued and considered potentially attainable. The intensity with which a person pursues a goal is a function of its value and commitment aspects. Goals exert their directive influence when goal content provides feedforward signals that selectively influence remembrance content that serves control and regulatory functioning.

Goals can vary on several dimensions, such as simple to complex, short to longer term. They can also vary in terms of their value to the person and his or her commitment to the goal. Goals may conflict, requiring prioritizing. A person's goals typically become organized in hierarchical groupings, and any particular behavior episode is often guided by more than one goal. Some serve as subgoals to facilitate the achieving of more complex or longer term goals. Combinations of goals usually provide stronger motivational patterns than single goals. People construct and pursue many goals in the course of a lifetime. Goals and their interrelationships elaborate and change as people's experience, knowledge, values, and commitments change, and as their social and cultural contexts change. The first step in trying to understand people's functioning is to identify the personal goals guiding their activity in relevant behavior episodes.

Our analyses indicate that all contemporary psychotherapy approaches agree with our comparative framework that people are primarily proactive entities, and that human behavior is inherently purposive in operation. Thus, people are innately purposive, "equipped with goals, purposes, and desires" (CT—Ellis). Humans' biological base is inherently purposive, directed toward "maximizing pleasure and minimizing pain" (CT—Beck). People are proactive, innately self-directing, goal directed in orientation, purposive in operation, and governed by representations of desirable future states, (HT). Humans are proactive, seeking preferred states and consequences through effective relationships with their contexts; they operate as a goal-directed system. The prototypic organization of both motor and social behavior is goal directed; people function as "goal-seekers" (CBST). The proactive, anticipatory mode of operation of the human system is basic to its overall functioning, and the person as a system is intentional, goal directed, and purposive in orientation, (EIT—Guidano; Mahoney). The self-regulatory system of the person is goal directed, (EIT—Kanfer). People's intentions guide their patterns of functioning to produce the consequences they desire (EIT—Wachtel).

One might suppose there would be some exceptions, as the initial forms of both PT and BT used a reactive organism model. However, in each of these approaches, treatment goals were specified; this implies the operation of some kind of directive process or function. For example, Freud's (PT) dictum, "where id was, ego should be, "implies facilitating patients' capability for conscious self-control as a treatment goal. Likewise, BT models stressed the need for patient-therapist agreement on treatment goals and noted that successful treatment requires implementing a shared action plan, (e.g., BT—Wolpe). Contemporary versions of PT and BT explicitly use concepts indicative of some type of directive function. For example, Greenspan (PT) asserts that children begin experiencing themselves as a cause, creating a basis for the emergence of self-directed functioning, and Hartmann's (PT) ego psychology describes most human behavior as intentionally directed toward consciously selected consequences. Bandura's recent social cognitive learning model, to which many BT theorists subscribe, represents people as proactive, being guided by representations of preferred states and consequences.

However, to name a set of processes does not account for how they operate. One needs a theory with which to do this, and theories about self-direction are characteristically missing from psychotherapy writings and teaching. For example, discussions of goal content do not address the great diversity of goals humans pursue. Often these therapists subsume the heterogeneity of goal content under content-free categories, such as "actualizing one's potential" or "self-actualization," (e.g., HT) or group goals under very broad, abstract categories, such as "freedom," "autonomy," or "innovation" and "creation" (HT—James). Some stress social goal content, such as approval, acceptance, affection, encouragement, compassion, and support from significant others (e.g., ISCT, CBST). Behavior therapists connote a similar view in referring to the therapist as "a powerful social reinforcer." There is little discussion of how or why goals develop and change, why people pursue different goals, why some goals are pursued with more intense effort than others, why people sometimes do not pursue a thing they really desire, how multiple goals may be related, how people reconcile discrepancies among goals, and whether goals must be represented in awareness to influence behavior.

Control Function: Comparative Framework and Therapy Proposals

Our comparative framework proposals derive from the analogous engineering control system function and from relevant theory and evidence in multiple disciplines. This is the "how to accomplish the goal" or "problem-solving" function of human cognition. People combine perceptual information about current conditions with conceptual, propositional, and procedural knowledge relevant to achieving their goals, enabling them to formulate and implement activity likely to produce the consequences specified by the goal content. This aspect of cognition is the one most extensively studied by psychologists, under such topics as intelligence, problem solving, planning, decision making, practical or social judgment, and coordination of actions. Our comparative framework partitions control functions into three interrelated, iterative phases: (1) problem formulation, (2) problem solving/plan formulation, and (3) plan execution.

Problem formulation involves identifying the nature of the discrepancy that exists between current states and the preferred state specified by the goal, and the facilitating and constraining conditions within which a solution must be formulated such as time, cost, or skills required. The content of this formulation limits the remembering process to a subset of one's repertoire of constructs that meet those criteria, thereby restricting the solutions that may be considered. In *problem solving/plan formulation*, people construct and consider options for achieving the goal within the constraints of the problem formulation. They select an approach—decision making—using processes such as alternative, consequential, and means-end thinking. People construct or learn heuristics for dealing with recurring types of problems efficiently. To do so involves using habitual strategies of thinking that have been effective in the past and appear relevant to the current task. Like all habits, problem-solving heuristics may function outside the person's awareness and may lead him or her to jump to conclusions before adequately formulating and considering other alternatives. The plan selected provides feedforward signals that set in motion and coordinate activity aimed at producing the desired consequences, a sequence called *plan execution*.

Describing problem solving in terms of phases has some utility as long as the phases are not presumed to occur in lock-step, linear fashion. They function as an integrated, iterative process. For example, while formulating a plan, a person discovers new options if he or she reframes the problem. In psychotherapy, clients' initial framing of their problems may be a barrier to their formulating effective solutions. Reframing may bring to clients' awareness knowledge or ideas they had not considered earlier ("I never thought of it that way before"). A rearrangement of ideas often results in insight that may lead to reframing the problem to be solved. Outcomes of plan execution may lead to problem reframing or revision of the client's plan for gaining the goal.

The theoretical proposals made about these control functions vary from explicit to implied among the various schools of therapy. In case descriptions, most theorists include comments about clients weighing alternatives, choosing a course of action, or reaching decisions about what they want to do or how to proceed. The CBST family is the most explicit in using theoretical models of problem solving to design skill training procedures. Meichenbaum describes the way effective problem-solving strategies operate to select and organize perceptions, memories, and ideas; these are then used as the base for imagining potential courses of action to solve problems or produce desired outcomes. Problem-solving skills underlie the use of all other skills, because they are tools for making "judicious decisions" about how to behave in any situation; training can help clients become proficient in identifying problems, gathering relevant information, considering alternatives, and evaluating potential consequences and outcomes, (Goldstein). People must be able to use problem solving to flexibly and creatively construct plans for achieving goals, and to implement these plans with skillful interpersonal actions. These theorists believe people accomplish this by using expectations, and imaginatively taking the role of others. (Gambrill, Trower). Collaborative problem solving is a key to resolving interpersonal conflicts; it involves subskills, such as searching for solutions that serve all parties' interests rather than settling for simple compromise, and preparing in advance for possible difficulties. (Guerney).

Theorists of other schools provide for some aspects of control functions but often without defining their nature or operation. Descriptions of expectations are similar to consequential thinking. Clients are seen to operate in terms of consequences they expect to occur (ISCT) or in terms of social role expectations, (EIT—Beutler) or relate to psychotherapy in terms of their expectations of therapeutic assistance (EIT—Goldfried; Weinberger). Some use the concept of "choice" in a way that implies other aspects of problem solving in addition to decision making. People control their own lives, not only by the ways they interpret events, but also by the ways they choose to pursue their purposes and deal with their life circumstances (CT—Ellis). The HT family stresses humans' ability to make choices, and the implications of this choice-making ability for personal freedom and responsibility. People are always in a position of choice, of whether to act or not, even though they cannot foresee all that will ensue (Bugental). People's choices are guided by their awareness of present and possible future states rather than by past events, and they implement their goals by using their cognitive capabilities to make choices, solve problems, weigh alternatives, and form and execute plans of action (Tageson). In the Gestalt experience cycle, clients scan themselves and/or the environment to determine what possibilities, options, or choices are available to meet a need; then they choose an option and implement it (Korb et al.) Gestalt therapy facilitates clients' problem-solving capabilities by helping them to acquire problem-solving tools (Yontef).

Early forms of BT implied the feedforward influence of control functions with concepts like *cue* and *discriminative stimuli,* as these enable people to anticipate rather than just react to reinforcing and punishing consequences. Contemporary BT gives greater emphasis to control functions, with its reliance on social learning theory (e.g., Bandura). Descriptions of ego functions include problem-solving capabilities (PT), as do descriptions of the operation of "self," "object" and "selfobject" cognitions, and "interpersonal circles" (ISCT).

Regulatory Functions: Comparative Framework and Therapy Proposals
The Comparative framework proposes combining the reactive, negative feedback dynamics and proactive, feedforward regulatory dynamics of control systems with concepts like moral reasoning, attitudes, values or valuing, and self- or performance regulation, appraisal, or evaluation described by scholars and clinicians. Regulation is based on a comparison of different states, for example, a current state with other possible states, or current and potential interpersonal relationships. Comparisons require evaluative criteria or rules about what is considered desirable, or good, and undesirable, or bad. These evaluative rules are often called values or standards. Shared values or standards regulate the functioning of social groups. Qualitatively different states may be compared—such as being married versus being a nun. Also, a state may exist to differing degrees, so evaluative comparisons often require judgments of relative value; these could include setting priorities among goals or personal states, or evaluating progress toward goals.

Humans use two kinds of evaluative, regulatory processes: affective and cognitive. The quality of people's affective experience—whether they experience pain or fear or love—partly governs whether they will seek to reproduce or avoid it on some later occasion. In the first few months of life, affective experience exerts the strongest regulatory influence. Behavior is also regulated by comparison rules involving cognitive evaluations, such as the criteria for being a so-called good or bad boy or girl. These are human constructions that may be created from affective experiences, cognitions, or both. People learn personal evaluative rules in the course of socialization by parental, religious, or peer groups; people construct their own individual rules based on what they privately feel, experience, think, or believe. The evaluative rules a person constructs may sometimes conflict: for example, a behavior or belief may "feel right" but be judged socially wrong. Therefore, regulatory processes must also operate to set priorities and resolve conflicts among multiple evaluative rules. Cultures differ in the extent to which they value cognitive or rational regulation as opposed to affective or irrational regulation.

At any place and time, the goals people pursue result from the way they prioritize their goals at that moment; this prioritizing is called *goal evaluation.* The initial conditions of a behavior episode—its guiding goals, the person's biological and affective state, and context conditions—selectively activate relevant evaluative regulatory rules through a remembering process. As problem solving about "how to do it" proceeds in a specific behavior episode, a person imagines alternate scenarios, he or she thinks or simulates different behavior episodes and evaluates their relative merits: feasibility, likely effectiveness, social and ethical acceptability. This process is called *means evaluation.* As people begin implementing a plan, they continuously evaluate its effectiveness to guide its execution and modification if necessary to ensure success: this judging process is called *performance evaluation.* In familiar behaviors, people are generally not aware that they are doing this evaluation.

Regulatory processes can function in both anticipatory and reactive ways; for example, cognitive problem solving involves comparing and evaluating anticipated possibilities rather than actualities. Anticipatory thoughts can come to activate emotional states, such as fear, anger, and sexual excitement. A key form of anticipatory regulation involves making evaluative judgments about one's capabilities and how contexts may respond to one's efforts, called *personal agency beliefs and evaluations.* Anticipatory regulation is more efficient than trial-and-error selection of effective behaviors, but it may also be erroneous and produce self-defeating, dysfunctional behavior. For example, it may keep people from pursuing goals they could achieve, or it may produce emotional states that disrupt other aspects of their lives (see Chapter 16 for discussion).

Proposals found among the psychotherapy theorists reveal virtual unanimity about the key role of these evaluative regulatory processes, despite differences in the terminology the theorists employ. People operate as a self-regulatory system, guided by a hierarchy of values, rendering them self-monitoring, self-evaluative, and self-reinforcing (EIT—Kanfer). Based on feedback from repeated instances of similar information-action-consequences episodes, habitual cyclical patterns develop (EIT—Wachtel). People continually monitor their performances and decide how to behave based on feedback they obtain regarding outcomes of their efforts (CBST—Argyle; Trower). People are innately capable of making immediate, direct evaluations, termed *organismic* (Rogers) and *internal* (Perls) valuing processes (HT). The beliefs that clients hold can be empirically tested in terms of their correspondence with empirical evidence and their utility in attaining personal or collective goals (CT—Beck; Ellis). People construct and retain models and representations on the basis of their judged coherence and viability (EIT—Mahoney; Neimeyer). The use of evaluative feedback to clients constitutes an important set of methods for helping them alter their guiding schemas or improve their performance (e.g., HT—Korb, Yontef, CBST—Goldstein; Guerney). Biofeedback enables clients to evaluate perceptible indicators of their own current biological states and to learn consciously to regulate those states (BMHT).

Most theorists stress the influence of anticipatory evaluative regulation as well. A person's choices are guided by values and the valuing of consequences (HT—Bugental). The system or person operates so as to regulate and control not only its outputs, but also its inputs, by means of feedback and feedforward processes (EIT—Mahoney). For many clients, the implementation of effective skills and the accomplishment of important tasks requires explicit training in values clarification, prioritization, and methods of value resolution (CBST—Goldstein). People's innate self-regulatory capabilities use internal standards and judgments about their self-efficacy and outcome expectations (BT, CBST—Bandura). They use primary appraisals, anticipatory evaluations of the probable impact of events on them, and secondary appraisals, evaluations of their capability for coping, often called personal agency or self-efficacy beliefs (CBST—Meichenbaum). Reliance on clear, explicit, and doable goals, combined with effective problem-solving procedures, will yield positive self-concepts and positive self-esteem (CBST—Argyle, Trower). A beneficial side-effect of the use of biofeedback treatment is an increase in clients' sense of personal efficacy (BMHT). Choices are guided by values and valuing of consequences; evaluation of one's acts and attributes results in construction of self-efficacy beliefs (HT—Bugental). Positive self-efficacy, also termed a sense of agency or ableness, emerges from effective coping with tasks and contexts (HT—Bohart).

Even approaches with their initial roots in a reactive organism model stress evaluative regulatory processes. The concept of super ego (PT) includes self-observation, standard setting, and adherence to ideals and moral standards. Ego analysts elaborated super ego functions to include special types of evaluative thoughts capable of eliciting emotional reactions (PT—Hartmann). Despite their initial aversion to so-called mentalistic theorizing, a number of original concepts within BT connote an evaluative regulatory function; among these are *positive* and *negative reinforcement,* and *punishment.* Constructing "gradients" of exposure as part of desensitization treatment strategies implies the use of anticipatory evaluation regarding the sets of events likely to produce different degrees of distress. The reliance of contemporary BT on social learning theory leads them to place importance on clients' anticipatory evaluations that they can do what the treatment requires—self-efficacy evaluations—and that the treatment will work—positive context beliefs. Some also assert that the cultivation of clients' self-control and self-regulating capabilities is a desirable treatment goal.

PSYCHOLOGICAL COMPONENTS: COMMENTARY

Between 1963, when we published *Systems of Psychotherapy,* and 1997, scholars in psychology and the brain sciences have caught up with therapists' long-standing emphasis on the importance of consciousness and attention, emotions, and cognitive functions in human life. These phenomena are now mainstream topics of scientific inquiry. A large and growing body of relevant knowledge has become available. During much of this century, therapists legitimately complained that science offered little knowledge directly relevant to psychotherapy practice, primarily because of its commitment to mechanistic, antimentalistic models. That complaint is no longer valid, but few contemporary therapy approaches utilize that new knowledge. Most continue to rely on ideas created before scientists rediscovered the significance of mind, emotions, and consciousness. Now, psychotherapy needs to catch up with science.

A few theorists, such as Mahoney, and Greenberg and associates, are trying to bring the relevance of that burgeoning literature to the attention of psychotherapists. Careful examination of this growing body of knowledge for clinically useful ideas and findings would appear to be one important avenue toward improving psychotherapy. Efforts by members of the CBST family to apply the basic literature on problem-solving processes, and Goldstein's leadership in abstracting clinically useful generalizations from the social psychological literature illustrate the potential value of such efforts. Attempts to synthesize knowledge in the human sciences to produce clinically relevant models of psychological functioning may be found in Ford (1987, 1994), and M. Ford (1992).

The Need for Theoretical Precision

In our judgment, there is a general problem that pervades most therapy theorizing. We discuss it here because psychological functions are the ones emphasized by most therapies, so the majority of theorists' concepts refer to psychological phenomena. In general, these theorists show a serious lack of definitional precision in specifying, and being consistent in the use of, the meanings of their key concepts. Critics have characterized therapy theory as a Tower of Babel, and with some justification. The problem is manifested in several ways. The same theorist may use the same term with different meanings at different junctures in his or her writing. Even when a theorist tries to define a concept precisely, "conceptual drift" in meaning is common because "followers" do not exercise care in adhering to the original definitions. (Freud complained about this.) The followers also fail to clarify how they have changed the meanings of terms and why. Variations in the use of the concept of transference illustrates this problem. Additionally, the same term may be used by different theorists, but with different meanings. This practice produces confusion for trainees and therapists who are likely to assume the meanings to be the same because the terms are the same. We have struggled with such conceptual imprecision as we have tried to accurately identify or infer and clearly summarize the intended meanings of these therapy theorists. We encourage readers, in the spirit of a cooperative effort to improve psychotherapy theory and practice, to do their own analyses and to try to identify and correct any errors of interpretation we may have made.

Two examples illustrate the problem. The first involves concepts about psychological processes by which people collect and interpret information—such as *perceiving, observing, experiencing, thinking,* and *meaning making*—and products produced with those processes—such as *perceptions, observations, experiences, thoughts, constructs,* and *meanings.* What are the phenomena to which these terms refer and how are they related? For example, do the terms *perception, observation,* and *experience* refer to the same or different phenomena? How are perceptions or experiences related to constructs or meanings? These theorists cannot answer such questions precisely because they have not clearly defined the concepts. A second example is the term *self* used in many variants: self-concept, selfobject, self-efficacy, self-esteem, self-construct, selfhood, and self-organizing. To what kinds of phenomena does the term *self* refer? Does it refer to all of a person's constructs, or only those with self-referent content? Are all self-referent thoughts interrelated? At one extreme, some seem to use the term *self* to refer to a person's entire repertoire of functional patterns and their interrelationships (e.g., Guidano). At another extreme, the term seems to refer to specific kinds of self-evaluative thoughts that may differ from one kind of situation to another (e.g., Bandura's concept of self-efficacy). Some theorists talk as if there is only one such pattern—that is, a self—while others argue that there are multiple patterns or selves.

Some (such as Freud) deliberately avoid defining terms, arguing that to do so constrains sound theory development. Others reject existing concepts as unsound without adequately documenting their reasons, and without clearly defining alternatives; some constructivists fall into this category. Some stress the integrated wholeness of behavior, neglecting to specify the nature of the parts that are integrated into a whole or the form of organization to which *integrated* refers. This is true of some HT theorists. Some theorists seem to believe that conceptual precision is best left to each client/therapist pair. In our judgment, these arguments are not persuasive. Criteria for the construction of satisfactory concepts are well-known. Thus, they should be cast in denotative language that specifies the relevant phenomena; they should be open to consensual use, yield reliable judgments about the occurrence of the phenomena, demonstrate minimal overlap with other concepts, and have utility in the theoretical model of which they are a part. The field of psychotherapy cannot hope to advance until its concepts become fashioned in accordance with these criteria.

BEHAVIORAL AND ENVIRONMENTAL COMPONENTS

Our comparative framework proposals are based on an open systems model. It asserts that people exist, maintain themselves, and develop through continual transactions with their environments. Three kinds of transactional functions are specified: (1) information collection, (2) communicative acts, and 0w(3) instrumental acts. Environmental phenomena are grouped into four categories: (1) natural, (2) designed, (3) interpersonal, and (4) sociocultural.

Environments

We found little theorizing or consensus about how to represent the role of environments in people's functioning. Despite general agreement that the person-in-context is the preferred unit of reference for psychotherapy, there are large differences in the ways in which contexts are thought to be influential, and the degree to which they are included in the various therapies' theoretical models. One of our four comparative framework categories, interpersonal contexts, is emphasized in all procedural models; they all stress the motivational importance of the client/therapist interpersonal relationship, and many stress its role as a setting for new learning.

Several different ways of conceptualizing contextual influences are used by these theorists, depending on their answers to some general questions. Is it useful to construe contexts as phenomena separate from, but related to, the functioning of people? If so, should one develop a taxonomy of concepts to represent kinds of contexts of significance to human functioning, and propositions representing how person and context factors are related? If not, are there more useful ways of representing the effects of environments on people?

One answer has been to adopt the principle, often attributed to the philosopher Epictetus, that people are not moved by things, but rather by the views they take of them. Thus, some therapists propose that the influence of contexts is not direct but is mediated by psychological processes. Accordingly, separate conceptual units representing contexts are not needed; rather they are represented in terms of their psychological impact with concepts like "experience," "interpretation," "evaluation," or "meaning" (e.g., HT; ICST—analysts; EIT—constructivists). A second answer, used by a few, acknowledges the operation of both person and context factors, but attempts to combine them in analytic units that represent the unitary functioning of a person-in-context. An example is the concept of "interpersonal circles" (ISCT—Kiesler).

A majority of these theorists adopt the answer (as does our comparative framework) that it is useful to distinguish between person and context factors, and to propose the ways they influence one another. This group categorizes contexts in two ways. One focuses not on the content of contexts but on their functional relationships with behavior. For example, concepts are used that identify contextual events in terms of whether they occur before or after some behavior—that is, whether they are stimuli or consequences: whether they influence the recurrence of some behavior or whether they produce certain states—that is, whether they are reinforcers/punishers or stressors. (e.g., BT; BMHT). In principle, any kind of event can come to function as a stimulus, consequence, reinforcer, punishment, or stressor, so all kinds of environments are potentially relevant and no taxonomy of kinds of contexts is proposed.

A second approach is to distinguish among different kinds of contexts considered especially significant for human development and dysfunction. Thus, some theorists stress the role of different kinds of *interpersonal relationships*. For example, interpersonal relationships are the only kind of context included in Lazarus's (EIT) BASIC I.D. Significant others are (e.g., ISCT—Kiesler), and significant interpersonal events such as social pressures, divorce, or the death of a loved one (e.g., CT) refer to interpersonal contexts. The CBST family emphasizes the importance of skills for effectively relating to spouses, children, friends, co-workers, and peer groups. Some stress the importance of familial contexts, particularly in early development, with certain kinds of family dynamics considered precursers to the development of psychopathology. (e.g., PT; ISCT—Fairbairn; Klein; Kohut; Winnicott). Some cite the importance of families as sources of both support and stress. (e.g., CT; EIT—Beutler, Prochaska, & DiClemente; Wachtel). Sometimes, very broad categories of contexts are mentioned, such as life events (CT), "alpha variables" (EIT—Kanfer) or environmental opportunities and resources, such as job opportunities (CT; EIT—Beutler).

Clearly, the analysis of contextual factors has been given far less attention than person factors by these theorists. The exception is the extensive and valuable literature specifying different facets of therapy relationships and how they influence clients. Given their shared emphasis on a person-in-context unit, the theorists' neglect of environments in their theories is a gap in contemporary therapy theory that needs to be addressed.

Transactional Functions: Communicative and Instrumental Actions
Information collection functions were discussed earlier in the section on psychological processes. Concepts related to communicative and instrumental actions are considered here. As a general rule, most approaches refer to a category of functions typically termed actions or behavior, but in only brief and superficial ways. We were surprised to see how rarely either actions or behaviors were actually defined. No taxonomies of, or theoretical models about, the ways people transact with their contexts are proposed, despite the theorists' endorsement of a person-in-context view.

Given the emphasis on the importance of interpersonal contexts among these theorists, it is not surprising that they stress the role of *communicative behavior,* as the primary means by which people relate to and influence one another. Because language and speech are the key tools for interpersonal communication, some suggest that knowledge of those symbolic processes is relevant to effective psychotherapy (e.g., CBST—Meichenbaum; ISCT—Kiesler). Others, (e.g., BT) elide distinctions between language (overt responses) and thought (covert responses). BT stresses the relationship of verbal or language behavior to covert responses, such as thoughts. Kiesler's (ISCT) view of the relation of language to thought or meanings is similar to our comparative framework.

CBST theorists give extensive, detailed attention to identifying specific communicative skills that can facilitate desired interpersonal relationships, and to designing training programs to help people become proficient in those skills. They view both verbal and gestural communicative acts as ways people convey personal meanings to, and seek to influence, one another. Each person must understand the other well enough to phrase his or her communications so as to have the desired impact. This task requires sensitivity to and knowledge about personal and sociocultural patterns. Because people differ in their sociocultural and linguistic backgrounds, personal experiences, and beliefs, they may differ in the ways they interpret and react to the same communicative act. Recognizing the need for this knowledge, CBST therapists have designed their training programs to teach skills for understanding other people and their communications, and skills for constructing communicative acts that will produce desired results. Proposals for psychotherapies designed for clients with different sociocultural backgrounds—such as women, and racial, ethnic, and religious subcultures—also speak to these issues.

Commentary

People cannot function apart from their contexts, so the nature and organization of those contexts make a major difference in their behavior. People are innately social entities; they live their lives embedded in sociocultural contexts, and derive most of their joys, sorrows, satisfactions, stresses, and distress from them. Knowledge of such environments and the ways people engage with them would seem to be crucial for the effective conduct of psychotherapy. Extensive, potentially relevant knowledge is available from social psychology, sociology, and anthropology. Psychotherapy theorists would do well to search these areas for potential applications. Communicative processes and transactions are central in both psychotherapy and daily life. Therefore, existing knowledge in the language and communication sciences and professions might yield valuable information for the development of explicit models to guide psychotherapists' work. The fruits of one effort to do this may be found in Ford (1987, 1994).

Although people regularly use the concept of *motivation,* and a sizable and growing body of knowledge about motivation has developed in psychological science, there is scant discussion of the topic in contemporary psychotherapy theory. Psychotherapists must deal daily with the question of why people behave as they do, so they might find useful some of the ideas and information available in contemporary literature on motivation. M. Ford (1992) has summarized much of the evidence and has provided a comparative summary of contemporary theories of motivation, together with an integrative model that combines personal goals, emotions, and personal agency beliefs. Psychotherapists might find his motivational systems theory model useful.

CHAPTER 16

Propositional Models: Organization, Change, and Development

A CONCEPTUAL MODEL defines the *what* of a theory—that is, the kinds of phenomena it considers important. Propositions define the *why* or dynamics—the ways phenomena interact to produce stability, variation, and change of pattern. Design criteria for the comparative framework summarized in Chapter 2 identified three questions that therapists' propositional models should address: How do the phenomena specified in their conceptual model relate to, or interact with, one another to create and maintain the stability of functional patterns—that is, how are they organized? By what dynamics are variation and change produced? How do functional and dysfunctional patterns develop over time—for example, with people's maturation, and experience? This chapter uses a set of principles that represent a consensus in the human developmental sciences, synthesized with the prototypical dynamics of complex, open, nonlinear systems models, to compare and analyze the ways therapy theorists deal with these major issues.

DYNAMICS OF ORGANIZATIONAL CONSISTENCY AND STABILITY

Our comparative framework proposes three basic principles: (1) unitary functioning, (2) self-organizing, and (3) stability maintaining, to represent the properties of organization that enable a person, to maintain consistency as a being while continually in the process of becoming.

Unitary Functioning

Comparative Framework Proposal

A person is an organization of specialized biological, psychological, and behavioral component structures, functions, and patterns operating in contexts that are also organizations composed of diverse components. Each person, his or her context, and the components of each are in continuous flux, involved in a never-ending process of variation and change. However, adaptive effectiveness and life itself require unitary functioning: A person must engage in harmoniously organized transactions with his or her contexts. Because of this demand, humans evolved so that all their parts are functionally interdependent, operating in facilitating and constraining relationships with one another so that an individual can function as a unified whole in coherent transactional relationships with his or her contexts. This does not mean that all the psychological/behavioral patterns a person constructs or learns must be interrelated in one grand, unified organization, as proposed by some (e.g., EIT—Guidano). People construct generalized patterns to serve different purposes in different contexts—that is, behavior episode schemas—each of which must manifest unitary functioning. Different combinations of purposes and contexts activate different schemas, and because only one schema can operate to organize a person's functioning in any behavior episode, all of a person's schemas need not be harmonized; they only need to be segregated. For example, incompatible beliefs may be segregated in logic-tight compartments. Multiple personality phenomena illustrate segregated organizations of different groups of functional patterns or behavior episode schemas.

Therapy Theory Proposals

All the theorists reviewed assume that human functioning is organized in patterns of various kinds. Early versions of PT (Freud) and BT manifest the analytic and reductionist views typical of nineteenth- and early-twentieth-century scientific thinking that prevailed when they were created. Basic elements and relationships among them were identified; for example, instincts were linked to intrapsychic structures (PT—Freud), or responses and stimuli were linked in antecedent–behavior–consequent patterns (BT). Once formed, the patterns were thought to function as units, but person-level unitary functioning was not proposed. In contrast, early versions of HT (e.g., Rogers) stressed humans' innate "self-actualizing" or "formative" tendency.

Assumptions about organization among contemporary theories are more similar to our comparative framework, although biological aspects are only implied in some discussions of unitary functioning. Elaborations of psychoanalysis by ego analysts characterize people as operating to create coherent organization of their many and often contradictory representations of themselves; also included in this organization are people's relationships with their contexts, embracing others and their culture, or reality. The purpose is to produce effective functioning and a sense of psychological continuity and consistency. (PT—Hartmann; Erikson). BT now utilizes Bandura's version of social learning theory, which proposes a prototypical organization similar to our comparative framework. Some propose more integrative units than the traditional stimulus-response chains. (BT—Rachlin; Hallam; O'Leary & Wilson).

CBST theorists (e.g. Goldstein; Guerney) endorse Bandura's proposition of mutual causation in which environmental, psychological, and behavioral factors operate as interacting determinants of one another. Meichenbaum (CBST) asserts that all aspects of a person are dynamically interrelated so that the person can function in a unified way. Similar views are held by the cognitive therapists, who see people acting as relatively stable organizations of interlocking patterns of cognitive, memory, affective, motivational, and action functions (Beck). Mutual causality exists among psychological, emotional, and behavioral functions (Freeman). Hard and fast distinctions cannot be drawn among emotions, thoughts, and actions as they invariably include elements of one another, and emotions are interwoven with biological, cognitive, and behavioral patterns (Ellis). With a slightly different slant, the humanists also see people functioning as organized wholes; it is their use of current experience in forming their interpretations and actions that enable unified functioning (Yontef, Korb). Each person's individualized and unique psychological organization enables him or her to function as a unit; people create complex cognitive patterns (schemas) that operate as units outside their awareness; activation of any part activates the whole pattern (Greenberg).

Several theorists espouse propositions that are essentially the same as our comparative framework principle of unitary functioning. People operate as integrated biopsychosocial units in a context, and both illness and health are influenced by the reciprocal nature of the relations among biological, psychological, behavioral, social, and environmental factors (BMHT). People can be understood in terms of seven discrete, interactive modalities of functioning, or kinds of biological, psychological, and behavioral events that operate in patterns of reciprocal influence to produce unified patterns. (EIT—Lazarus). Human behavior is organized in complex patterns of interrelated levels of functioning involving psychological, behavioral, situational, and interpersonal/social components (EIT—Prochaska & DiClemente). A complex systems model can be used to represent the dynamic but unified nature of humans' biopsychosocial functioning in contexts (EIT—Kanfer; CBST—Gambrill; Trower). Mind and body are inseparable; people are best understood as somatopsychic entities (EIT—Mahoney). Maintaining "internal coherence" in their "self-construct" is the basic self-organizing invariant (EIT—Guidano). All aspects of a person are organized in patterns of "cyclical dynamics" that involve "circular causality" in relation to contexts (EIT—Wachtel). ISCT theorists assume inborn processes for producing unified functioning; from the start, the ego seeks unified functioning (Fairbairn); there is an innate need and striving for organization (Bacal), or a tendency to produce cohesion, harmony, and preservation of the self (Suttie) and an integrated or whole person (Winnicott).

In sum, the evidence suggests that implicit consensus exists among contemporary therapy theorists concerning a proposition of unitary functioning. They differ primarily in the aspects of humans that their theories emphasize. Most are silent about how the constructs or multiple patterns a person learns are interrelated. The meanings some give to concepts like personality, self-concept, or self-construct imply that all patterns must be linked in unified forms (e.g., HT; EIT—constructivists). Others (e.g., BT; CBST) imply that different patterns function autonomously and that integration of all patterns is not necessary. Therapy theory and practice could benefit from careful theoretical and empirical examination of these alternate views.

SELF-ORGANIZING

Comparative Framework Proposals
If unified functioning is an essential attribute of humans, there must be processes that produce and maintain it. Traditionally, natural science has assumed that order exists throughout the universe. An emerging view is that order in natural phenomena results from self-organizing processes. The most recent theory of the universe is that it is a product of self-organization, not fixed natural laws; a world that has made itself (Smolin, 1997). Our comparative framework assumes that living systems are inherently self-organizing; from cells to societies, they function to create and maintain coherent organization within themselves, and between themselves and their contexts, despite being bombarded and disrupted by continually varying conditions within and around them. Unlike machines that are created by an outside entity that constructs parts and links them together, life begins as an organized state in the form of a single fertilized cell, and organization is maintained

throughout life despite massive and diverse changes that occur in the person and his or her contexts. Organizational changes always result from differentiation, elaboration, or reorganization of existing organized states through the operation of people's own dynamics, and their environmental transactions. From an evolutionary view, self-organizing processes are essential. Deficiencies in self-organizing processes, or insufficient or defective organization, are hazardous and distressing. They threaten survival and reproductive success. When organizational disruptions occur, self-organizing processes recreate organization to preserve life and some degree of adaptiveness. Diverse organizational forms may result—serial, parallel, cyclical, and hierarchical—that may differ in their utility for different conditions of living.

Therapy Theory Proposals

Therapy theories have always stressed the organized nature of human functioning, and ideas similar to self-organization are manifest in much contemporary theorizing by psychotherapists. Theorists differ, however, about the aspects of humans that demonstrate self-organizing processes and the best ways to represent the kinds of organization that result.

For example, initial forms of PT and BT indicated that psychological/behavioral organization exists. However, these therapists assumed that the organization resulted from the operation of automatic and mechanistic processes—instincts, stimuli, and reinforcers—that shaped people from without and within, independent of their conscious control. People were assumed to be reactive organisms. Freud initially assumed that a defining characteristic of the id was its lack of organization and that "mental structures" (the ego) evolved in reaction to id influences to produce some coherent psychological organization. Different patterns of functioning were said to develop in a built-in, orderly, and universal maturational sequence (PT—Freud; Erikson). Behaviorists assumed that complex behavior patterns resulted from automatic linkages of discrete stimuli and responses through conditions of contiguity and reinforcement.

Developments in ego psychology, however, emphasize psychological functions that provide humans with a capacity for organizing their own experience and behavior. These elaborations of PT portray infants as organized entities with inherent "ego functions" (such as sensory-perceptual, sensory-motor, and cognitive capabilities) that operate in an "average expectable environment" to create habitual, adaptive functional patterns in relation to "reality" (PT—Hartmann). These capabilities are said to appear early in life and to increase with the maturation of the central nervous system. As a result, the complexity of organization of which the infant and later the child is capable emerges in phases (PT—Greenspan). Moreover, PT's procedural model implies a self-organizing proposition, in which strategies and methods rely on patients' self-organizing capabilities. These capabilities allow the patient to identify his or her dysfunctional patterns through free associations. Then, by using the therapists' interpretations, the client can revise these patterns and restore coherent functional organization.

A self-organizing proposition is made more explicit in some other psychotherapy theory families. HT theorists propose that people are innately self-organizing; there is an inherent tendency toward consistency (Adler) or organization (Rogers). People are innately self-organizing and impose coherent organization on their continuously varying flow of moment-to-moment experience (Bugental). ISCT theorists assert that people have an innate need and striving for organization (Bacal). They function to organize psychological elements to fit together and produce cohesion, harmony, and preservation of the self (Suttie), and an integration of the entire person (Winnicott). There is a universal "master motive" to develop self-satisfying, coherently organized goals, values, skills, and patterns of living that are accepted, valued, and socially confirmed by one's relational matrix (Stern). People have a pervasive tendency to preserve the continuity, connections, and familiarity of their personal world—external and internal (Mitchell). EIT theorists assume that people seek to impose order on their experience (Wachtel). Their fundamental self-organizing processes continually structure and revise the flow of experience to generate a coherent self-construct and a sense of self-identity (Guidano). The constructivist therapists rely on self-organizing, open systems rationales, a view that allows for an open-ended process of human development (Mahoney). Other theorists speak of self-construction capabilities that subsume self-organizing processes.

Many of these theorists discuss self-organizing processes only in relation to psychological and behavioral functions. This limitation may stem from their implicit assumption that the organized characteristics of the human body may be taken as a given, and that it is the organization of other aspects of the person that need to be explained. However, this view ignores the mutual influences among biological and other functions that are considered important in our comparative framework.

STABILITY MAINTENANCE

What are the dynamics by which self-organizing processes maintain unitary functioning?

Comparative Framework Proposal

The survival and adaptive effectiveness of a living system depend on its ability to function in organized ways, but everything within and surrounding it undergoes continual, never-ending, and often unpredictable variation and change. The system must engage in continual self-organizing activity to maintain its unitary functioning and to restore coherent organization whenever it is disrupted. Processes that protect and maintain existing states are thus understood to be both natural and essential for living systems; they are a key to a person's continuity of existence.

The issue of maintaining stability is typically encountered in the psychotherapy literature in the context of a classic question: How can one account for the persistence of psychological and behavior patterns that appear to be inappropriate, unwanted, ineffective, self-defeating, and productive of unhappiness and misery? The answer from our comparative framework is that such patterns persist because they retain some functional utility, both for producing some desired consequences and for defending existing patterns from disruption so as to preserve some form of unified functioning. Of course, the same pattern that is functional with respect to the maintenance/restoration of one steady state may be simultaneously dysfunctional with respect to another desired state. However, maintaining unified functioning is typically accorded a higher priority than achieving other goals, so stability-maintaining processes can simultaneously yield both functional and dysfunctional results.

The comparative framework proposes two basic ways by which humans' self-organizing processes may maintain unified functioning of existing steady states. Both of these rely on negative feedback, deviation-reducing dynamics characteristic of control systems. The first way involves the use of feedforward or anticipatory processes. By imagining, a person may anticipate the occurrence of events that would disrupt an existing habitual state—that is, produce a deviation from a preferred state. He or she could then behave in ways to forestall, prevent or minimize the occurrence of such imagined, disruptive conditions. Fear-avoidance patterns and pursuit of a healthy lifestyle to forestall illness illustrate this anticipatory strategy. Anticipatory prevention is not always feasible, however, and a person may have to deal with real rather than imagined potential disruptions. Therefore, the second strategy involves the operation of negative feedback dynamics to eliminate actual disruptions. This *reactive correction* is accomplished through activity calculated to overcome the disruption and restore the previous state. Its purpose is to reduce the discrepancy between the current disrupted state and the habitual preferred state. Once a pattern of anticipatory prevention or reactive correction proves effective through frequent and repeated use, it can become habitual and operate automatically in future similar conditions without a person attending to its occurrence. Its operation becomes unconscious.

Therapy Proposals

We found substantial agreement among therapy theorists with the comparative framework's proposition regarding stability maintenance. Freud's (PT) ideas about resistance and defense mechanisms anticipated modern control systems' negative feedback stability-maintaining processes. They appear in various forms in many contemporary therapy theories. He proposed that humans have inborn functions that operate to maintain their level of arousal within a preferred range of variation. He called this the principle of constancy. The occurrence of some unconscious wish or unbearable idea that would threaten one's welfare if it became conscious and acted on activates distressing emotions, such as fear, guilt, shame, or anger. Distressing affective states signal the existence of such a threat, which he termed *signal anxiety*. Different strategies of thought, interpretation, or action, called *defense mechanisms*, become mobilized to reduce the threat of unbearable ideas entering awareness. This strategy reduces the distressing emotions to tolerable levels. Freud's defense mechanisms are analogous to our framework's stability-maintaining processes; some are anticipatory prevention methods and others are reactive correction methods. He focused on their operation in managing dysfunctional conditions, whereas in our comparative framework, they are considered operative in both functional and dysfunctional arrangements.

Freud's descriptions of defense mechanisms—repression, projection, displacement, denial, undoing—have been refined and elaborated, first by his daughter, Anna, and later by many others. Standard listings are routinely used—for example, in personality and personal adjustment theory, abnormal psychology, social work, and psychiatry. In addition, the psychophysiological patterns that make up aversive affective states have become more carefully specified and some additional ones have been added; these include depressive states, stress reactions, states of frustration and exasperation, conflict-induced tension states, and exhaustion or fatigue states.

The basic elements of this view are still discernible within the PT, ISCT, HT, CT and CBST therapy families. They are expressed in somewhat different terms from one to the next, or with greater emphasis on certain aspects as opposed to others. For example, people are said to have innate tendencies to avoid conscious anxiety because of its disorganizing effects, by such means as selective inattention, response substitution, splitting, denial, or distortion (ISCT; HT; EIT—Wachtel). People are organized to find ways to prevent and minimize uncomfortable or noxious subjective experiences, such as pain, gastric discomfort, fear, fatigue, and anger; they have protective patterns that are activated when they feel threatened, criticized, misunderstood, or rejected (CBST—Goldstein; Guerney; Meichenbaum).

Some theorists' proposals are directly comparable to our comparative framework propositions, including the view that stability maintenance is of central importance to the survival and adaptive effectiveness of each person and is not confined solely to the management of dysfunctional states. For example, several theorists explicitly use a control system model as the basis for their approach (CBST—Gambrill; Trower; EIT—Kanfer). Constructivist models consider such processes essential for protecting the coherence, integrity, and viability of people's self-constructs, self-perceptions, and self-evaluations in the face of continually changing conditions. Otherwise, they would be incapable of proper functioning and would lose their very sense of reality. Therefore, one should expect people to exercise vigorous efforts to resist disruptions of, and changes in, their habitual guiding ideas. People function not only to create but also to protect coherently organized patterns of functioning (CT—Goldfried). The patterns a person has constructed over the years (such as a self-world construct system) can prevent excessive stress and provide for some satisfaction; tendencies to resist and defend against change tend to predominate (HT—Bugental).

Some theorists imply propositions about stability maintenance in their discussions of the selective effects of habitual guiding beliefs or schemas operating through feedforward processes. For example, when people face a new behavior episode, they use previously constructed schemas to select and interpret information about current events in ways they consider relevant to guiding their choice of actions (EIT—Wachtel). A person's schemas lead them to encode and retrieve schema-consistent information more readily than information that would require their modification (CT—Goldfried). People prejudicially view or experience events in the light of their expectations or biased beliefs (CT—Ellis). The use of one's schemas results in a "confirmatory bias" because they filter out disconfirming information, resulting in the occurrence of self-fulfilling prophecies (CBST—Meichenbaum; CT—Beck; Freeman).

A few suggest the proposition that habits vary in strength because of conditions of learning, and the stronger the habit, the harder it is to change. Both rational and irrational beliefs tend to be "strongly held," and vigorous efforts are required to change them (CT—Ellis). When an existing pattern is a strong habit, it functions as a "closed system" operating to resist modification and to remain the same (ISCT—Fairbairn). Habit strength is not defined, and criteria for identifying variations in strength are not provided. Therapy examples imply a relationship between habit strength and related emotional states.

DYNAMICS OF VARIABILITY AND CHANGE

How can a person know when something has changed? Propositions distinguishing between variability and change are needed. A psychotherapist's basic task is to help people change, so propositions about how change occurs are also needed. Our analysis of therapy theorists' proposals are organized under three types of propositions included in our comparative framework: self-construction, incremental change, and transformational change.

DIFFERENCES, VARIABILITY, AND CHANGE

People never behave precisely the same way, even in similar behavior episodes. Their functioning always differs in some ways, but that does not necessarily mean they have changed.

Comparative Framework Proposals

Our framework uses an explicit rationale to define change (see Ford & Lerner, 1992, for details). It starts with the concept of difference. Sensory-perceptual capabilities enable people to compare things and to perceive differences in kind (qualitative) or amount (quantitative) among them. Two types of comparisons are possible: (1) One thing may be compared with another. When people are compared, the results are called interindividual differences. (2) A thing may be compared with itself on different occasions. The results of this comparison are called intraindividual differences. Inferences about variability and change are based on intraindividual differences, that is, the same attributes of the same client must be compared across occasions. The more occasions on which comparisons are made, the larger will be the sample of differences on which inferences about variability and change can be based. The concept of variability means that a thing displays differences on different occasions; when it does not, mathematicians call it a constant.

The kind of stability displayed by living systems, such as humans, involves variability; the value of any human attribute continually varies but in a consistent pattern within limits. This kind of stability is called a steady state. Some differences detected from one occasion to another in the value of an attribute, such as body temperature, simply reflect normal, steady-state variability. What, then, are the properties of differences that indicate the occurrence of a change? There are two: (1) There must be a set of differences that exceed normal steady-state boundaries for the attributes of interest. (Note that such comparisons require explicit knowledge of relevant normal steady-state boundaries.) (2) Those differences must endure over time and occasions. These differences may vary with respect to their duration. Some disappear after a period of time; for example, a broken arm heals. These are temporary changes. Others persist over extended periods of time; for example, a child learns to talk. These are enduring changes. Psychotherapy clients seek enduring changes.

Therapy Theory Proposals

Evaluation of client progress and of the effectiveness of any psychotherapy approach requires distinguishing between stready-state variations and temporary or enduring changes. None of these therapy theorists, however, deal with this issue in their propositional models, nor do they propose criteria to guide such judgments. Most rely on client judgment. If the client says a change has occurred, the therapist assumes that this is so. Therapists whose procedural models espouse any form of diagnosis early in therapy implicitly seek to establish steady-state descriptions of dysfunctional patterns to be changed; these can be used as a reference point for later comparisons. If clients are to make the comparisons, they must understand what is to be compared. Therapists assert that collaboration between client and therapist in defining the patterns to be changed helps serve that purpose. Some evidence suggests that in-therapy changes alone tend to be only temporary. Therapists whose procedural models include strategies and methods for facilitating transfer and maintenance of changes from therapy to daily life believe that such strategies are necessary to ensure enduring changes.

SELF-CONSTRUCTION

Self-construction is a key means by which people's self-organization is maintained as conditions and personal goals and values change.

Comparative Framework Proposals

The framework proposition asserts that individual development results from the operation of inborn processes that create and maintain life itself. No one else can change a person; only a person can change himself or herself. There are two forms of self-construction, but both operate with essentially the same kinds of dynamics. Biological self-construction involves the ingestion of needed material-energy forms and elimination of the unneeded parts. The usable forms are disassembled and reassembled to construct, elaborate, modify, integrate, maintain, and repair biological structures. Another use is to make possible and fuel all biological and other functions. Psychological and behavioral self-construction involves collecting information, and organizing, disassembling, and reassembling this information in different ways. The purpose is to construct, elaborate, modify, integrate, maintain, and repair personal information/meaning forms and psychological and behavioral patterns. The viability of these patterns is tested through transactions with contexts.

Self-construction possibilities are not unlimited, however. They are facilitated and constrained by the contexts, resources, genetic histories, and current personal biological, psychological, and behavioral states available to the person. It is possible to influence people's development by altering their facilitating and constraining conditions with different contexts, resources, and information/meaning forms, but how a person uses those new conditions cannot be controlled. Alternate developmental pathways are possible within any set of conditions. The two kinds of self-construction are interdependent; neither can exist without the other. Biological processes make psychological/behavioral functions possible, but do not control the content of the patterns constructed. However, it is through psychological and behavioral functioning that material/energy forms needed for biological self-construction are obtained and damaging forms are avoided.

Therapy Proposals

Most contemporary psychotherapy theorists use a similar type of proposition. Freud (PT) initially assumed that all thought and behavior is driven by biologically based instincts or drives, with ego and superego structures reactively seeking to establish order and control over their operation. Later PT theorists emphasized the proactive and autonomous aspects of ego-functioning that characterize contemporary psychoanalysis. They stressed initiation and elaboration of flexible instrumental behavior by means of conscious, intentional, thoughtful planning and action. For example, these theorists claim that infants, exercising their innate capabilities, construct habitual patterns of interaction with their contexts, creating simple mental representations and then using them to organize intentional behavior. Children proceed to construct increasingly complex cognitive/emotional/behavioral patterns and emerge with adult personalities that undergo modification and change throughout life (PT—Hartmann). People organize and form mental images and symbols into representational/structural configurations (PT—Greenspan). It is the synthetic functions of the ego that enable people to pursue lifelong efforts to create a coherent organization of their varied representations of themselves (PT—Erikson). People construct dysfunctional as well as functional beliefs (PT—Weiss).

An emphasis on humans' self-constructing capabilities appears in virtually all other psychotherapy theories. For example, through the use of their innate symbolizing capabilities, people process and transform transient experiences into internal models that function as rules to guide the construction of useful patterns of behavior; they form cognitive representations of future desired events, and by observing the differential outcomes of their actions, they eventually construct representations of new behavior patterns and the appropriate circumstances for their use (BT—Bandura). People create coherent patterns of organization. Once constructed, these patterns tend to become habitual and automatized, and hence not ordinarily a part of the contents of consciousness (CT—Ellis). Some of these patterns, however, may have been initially acquired in tacit and nonverbal form and never made consciously explicit (CT—Beck).

People have innate abilities to create psychological representations using both their inner and outer experiences. These habitual representations of self, ego, objects, and interpersonal relationships are constructed from, and are not mere copies of, people's perceptions or experiences of themselves and their interactions with others; their ideas result from the processing and refashioning of experiences, which they then use to create psychological and behavioral patterns. People are a self-causing system, (ISCT—Klein; Kohut; Pine; Winnicott). Humans are innately self-constructing, continually engaged in the creation of patterns from their flow of experience. Their continually varying experience activates an inherent tendency to create order, stability, and coherence within that variability to which some kind of meaning can be attached. People's conception of reality emerges from the meanings they construct from their experiences and intuitions; every encounter is a dynamic, constructive process and never simply an elicitation of routinized habits (HT—Bohart; Bugental; Korb; Yontef).

Clients' capabilities enable them to change themselves (EIT—Prochaska & DiClemente). Each person constructs his or her own unique patterns of functioning (EIT—Lazarus). People have the capacity to direct and regulate their own functioning and thereby influence both themselves and their environments (EIT—Kanfer). People seek to create a coherent view of self and self-esteem (EIT—Wachtel). People function as self-organizing and self-constructing living systems; they are literally constructive (form giving) in operation. The constructs they develop operate to create coherent organization and generalized meaning out of the flow of transient experience and serve to organize their behavior. They are representational models of the world. People co-construct their representations of the world, and all forms of knowledge are ultimately social constructions because knowledge is culturally mediated, interwoven with social action, and constructed in relation to shared collective goals and sustained by social processes. Nonetheless, all individuals demonstrate their own idiosyncratic ways of organizing and assembling their knowledge and self-constructs (EIT—Guidano; Mahoney; Neimeyer).

Incremental Change
Organized patterns of functioning are essential for survival and adaptive effectiveness, but no pattern can serve indefinitely. Things and people change; events and circumstances never remain the same; different opportunities and constraints are continually presenting themselves. When changing conditions do not fit a person's existing patterns, the patterns are no longer effective. When changes generate states that are unpleasant, noxious, or aversive, and stability-maintaining processes are inadequate to deal with them, some accommodation must be made. The person must also change to remain adaptive and still maintain unified functioning. This can be accomplished when changes occur in incremental fashion.

Comparative Framework Proposals
Our comparative framework includes seven propositions about incremental change processes. (See Chapter 5 and Ford, 1987, 1994, for more detail.)

1. *Change always starts with what exists.* As described earlier, human change and development does not occur by adding on new parts. Rather, it results from revision, differentiation, elaboration, and reorganization of existing patterns through self-organizing, self-constructing, unitary functioning dynamics, illustrated by embryonic development of a human fetus.

2. *Enduring changes in people's habitual psychological/behavioral patterns are accomplished through changes in their guiding generalized representations (behavior episode schemas).* Psychotherapy seeks to change habitual patterns. Instances of functional or dysfunctional behavior in specific situations (behavior episodes) are organized and guided by previously learned generalized representations (called behavior episode schemas in our framework). They occur within possibilities and constraints provided by current contexts. Thus, to cause enduring changes in behavior in specific behavior episodes requires changing the guiding pattern, the behavior episode schema. But patterns of functioning—the schemas—do not exist except when they are operating in a specific behavior episode.

3. *The pattern to be changed must be occurring in a current behavior episode to be susceptible to change.*

4. *The person must attend to and be aware of the pattern as it is presently oc-curring, and of possible changes that may make it more functional or dys-functional.* Learning does not occur outside of awareness. People are aware of what they attend to.

5. *The pattern to be changed—the behavior episode schema—must be disrupted by the behavior episode conditions under which it is currently operating.* In-cremental change occurs through negative and positive feedback dy-namics that are activated when a discrepancy exists between current and preferred states, real or imagined. Disruption of operating pat-terns, the schema, creates such discrepancies. Negative and positive feedback processes operate to produce incremental change, under the conscious guidance of the person's governing functions and selective attention, so as to eliminate disruptions and to produce desired states.

6. *The means by which the disruption can be removed, or the discrepancy be-tween the existing and desired state can be reduced, must be limited to chang-ing some aspect of the old pattern—the schema—rather than returning to the old pattern.* Change will not occur if feedback dynamics function as stability-maintaining processes to restore the disrupted state. A key way to prevent that is for people to commit themselves to achieving a different state, thereby defining the old pattern as discrepant from a preferred state. Then, a person typically uses more diverse ideas and information to formulate, consider, and try other ways of achieving desired results. He or she selects for further use those that seem to pro-duce desired consequences.

7. *For a temporary try to become an enduring change in a pattern, it must yield outcomes that the person evaluates as serving his or her guiding goals and val-ues in real-life behavior episodes. This action is called selection by conse-quences.* Temporary changes will not endure unless they work. This judgment must result from a person's own regulatory or evaluative processes. The criterion is whether the discrepancy is sufficiently re-duced between what the person wants and what the person is getting, from the person's point of view. It usually takes several tries for an in-dividual to become convinced that a change has enduring utility.

Therapy Proposals

Given the basic importance of change processes to psychotherapy, it was sur-prising to discover how few contemporary theories of psychotherapy include clear, explicit propositions concerning the processes of change. Discussions of change are often phrased in terms of outcomes desired rather than processes for producing such outcomes. The BT family is the exception as it uses formal propositions derived from psychological learning theory. For those who describe life as a process (e.g., HT), change is assumed to be an inherent part of daily living, so explanations of change seem unnecessary. We found a few explicit propositions made by others. Several adopt the propositions of assimilation (fitting new experiences into existing patterns, similar to stability-maintaining processes) and accommodation (changing existing patterns to fit new experiences, similar to incremental change processes), adopting them from other theorists, such as Piaget. However, they do not explicitly apply them in their procedural models. Many propositions described in our analyses were inferred from their discussions of their procedural models, which are analyzed in Chapter 17, so only a brief discussion of them is included here.

Most imply but only a few explicitly state (e.g., BT; ISCT), that *change starts with what exists,* that it involves differentiation, elaboration, revision, or reorganization of existing patterns. There is broad agreement that *patterns are susceptible to change only while they are occurring.* For example, the humanists focus on the here and now and the what and how of conscious experience. A patient's illness is not simply an event in the past, but a present-day force. Only through their real, immediate here-and-now conscious experience will clients be able to establish a link between their intellective insights and their ongoing behavior, so that it makes sense to them, (PT). Clients' childhood-based and pathological interpersonal beliefs and patterns must become active in relation to their analyst if the beliefs are to be modified, (ISCT). Therapeutic situations must be created in which old habits occur and can be modified, and/or in which new habits can occur and be practiced (BT; CT; CBST; BMHT; EIT).

All theorists agree that *enduring behavior changes require changes in clients' guiding habitual representations,* called behavior episode schemas in our comparative framework. There is disagreement over the nature of the representations, however. For example, Freud (PT) stressed alteration of "intrapsychic oedipal conflicts"; contemporary PT broadens that view to modifying dysfunctional information/meaning-based patterns termed *psychic structures.* ISCT focuses on modifying psychic structures of "self," "selfobject," or "self-other" relations or "maladaptive transaction cycles," that govern clients' interpersonal behavior. Contemporary BT assumes that habitual patterns involve some form of internal or mental representation, that it is the "knowledge" of relationships among events in the conditioning experience rather than the direct strengthening of a response that accounts for learning (Dickinson). People construct and use models of predictive and causal contingencies among events to guide their behavior (Bandura). Changes in schemas, belief systems, or cognitive/affective/behavioral schemes are prerequisites for changes in behavior (CT—Beck; Ellis; Greenberg). Psychological patterns such as gestalts; meanings or meaning patterns; self-world construct systems, models, or schemas, that function not only to organize experience but also to coordinate a person's behavior are the focus of change (HT). The content and organization of skillful performance includes guiding cognitive representations of the nature of the skill and of behavior-consequence relationships (CBST). BMHT trains people in habits of conscious, cognitive regulation of biological functions and healthy lifestyles. Construct systems, self-constructs, self-narratives, or assumptive beliefs linked in hierarchical systems are the focus of change (EIT).

Psychotherapy theory might be advanced significantly by an intensive evaluation of these alternate ways of construing the guiding patterns to be changed. Our analyses suggest that the phenomena considered important are not as diverse as the concept labels used to represent them might suggest.

Theorists unanimously agree that *learning requires clients' attention to, and awareness of, the patterns to be changed.* For example, making the unconscious conscious by attending to patterns while they are functioning is a fundamental principle in psychoanalysis (PT; ISCT). Clients must become aware of their dysfunctional cognitive patterns and must focus their attention on aspects that need to be changed for cognitive restructuring to occur, (CT). Attention to and awareness of predictive and causal contingencies, such as cues and reinforcers, is a key ingredient in changing old habits and learning new ones (BT). Clients' attending to and becoming aware of the nature of their experiences is the key to positive self-development (HT). Change requires attention to, awareness of, and serial processing of information (EIT—Kanfer). Selective attention to relevant variables within and around oneself and conscious regulation of one's thought processes make intentional change possible (CBST—Trower). To learn a new pattern or change an existing one requires the client to direct attention to its content and organization, and to the conscious formulation and practice of preferred patterns in relevant contexts (CBST).

The proposition that the *initiation of change requires a disruption of the person's habitual patterns of functioning* is generally endorsed by all theorists. Kiesler (ISCT) states that the "essential therapeutic task" is to "disrupt" the patient's vicious circle of self-defeating actions. Wachtel (EIT) says "almost all the interventions described" represent efforts "to disrupt the vicious circles" in which the patient is caught. Kanfer (EIT) says "guide clients" through a process that "disrupts their ineffective or self-defeating automatic processing patterns." Others state it in different ways. Therapeutic interpretations disrupt patients' habitual patterns of resistance and defense against the operation of unconscious wishes and unbearable ideas and the underlying intrapsychic structures (PT). ISCT analysts combine interpretation with modeling of "good" parental functioning to disrupt childhood-based, faulty interpersonal beliefs. As clients fully attend to the flow of their experience and relate it to their existing desires, beliefs, and patterns of action, they will discover discrepancies, thereby disrupting their own habitual patterns of functioning (HT). For cognitive restructuring and behavior change to occur, clients must encounter discrepant information or experiences that perturb the organizational coherence of their schemas or beliefs (CT). Therapeutic behavior episodes create predictive and causal contingencies—cues and reinforcers—that contradict those in the pattern to be changed (BT). Trainees must realize they cannot produce consequences they want with the beliefs and social and communicative skills that they have (CBST). New information provides "a new light" that exposes "the darkness of old thinking" (EIT—Beitman).

As part of their procedural models, most of these theorists discuss *how self-organizing and self-constructing activity resulting from disruptions might be selectively channeled* toward one kind of change or another. Except for learning theory-based proposals, they give little theoretical attention to this issue. Behavior therapists and others who use their assumptions propose that cues—predictors of the possible occurrence of desired and undesired consequences—and reinforcing contingencies or desired consequences exert a selective influence on the nature of the changes that will occur. Behavior change can thus be channeled through careful arrangements of cues and reinforcers such as those used in token economies.

Most psychotherapy procedural models imply two other propositions. One is that clients' own goals, values, and beliefs about their capabilities and contexts exert a selective influence that will lead them toward useful changes. Therapists need only to facilitate that self-discovery process and to avoid biasing it by introducing their own ideas. For example, the process of discovery through conscious attention to their ongoing experience is said to augment clients' experiential awareness and to facilitate symbolization of new aspects of experience not previously in focal awareness. When these new elements are added and accepted, clients become capable of forging new ways of synthesizing old and new experiences. They learn to bring conflicting aspects of their lives into harmonious wholes, to extract and construct new meanings, and to reorganize their ongoing experiences in more productive and adaptive ways (HT).

The second proposition is that change can be channeled through processes of social modeling. Therapists may verbally propose or demonstrate different ways of functioning that clients may reject or try to use (e.g., PT; ISCT; BT; CT; CBST; BMHT; EIT). Proposals are manifested in various forms of verbal interventions, and all the theories analyzed use some types of such interventions. Some verbal interventions are intended to constrain stability-maintaining processes, such as pointing out and interpreting resistance or defensive maneuvers, so that they don't obstruct change. Others are intended to facilitate alternate ways of functioning. For example, certain interventions may provide information that can selectively influence how clients think about their concerns. Some therapists may make comments that selectively direct clients' attention toward one set of possibilities rather than others. Other therapists may make interpretive, explanatory, or constructive statements aimed at helping clients interrelate diverse strands of their experience, beliefs, and behaviors; intended to help clients form a meaningful, integral whole. It often involves something of historical significance in the client's life and its connection to his or her current patterns of functioning. Some therapists may provide generalized rationales. These may be used to show the relation of childhood learning to current behavior; how learning processes work; how self-constructs or narratives, schemas, beliefs, or vicious circles provide integrative frameworks for what a person thinks and does; how self-awareness provides the basis for self-development; how body and mind influence one another. Clients may then reject these suggestions, or "incorporate," "introject," "internalize," or "assimilate" them into their own frameworks, or "accommodate" to them by changing their frameworks and using them to guide future activity.

Proposals can also be made by way of demonstration. (e.g., BT; CT; CBST; EIT—Kanfer) Several model the use of problem-solving strategies and tactics, and suggest that clients practice using these strategies on current problems. Some (e.g. CBST) may demonstrate instrumental skills, such as how to communicate clearly with a spouse, which clients may then try to copy.

Most of these therapists appear to use combinations of self-discovery, social modeling, and contingency management, though they differ greatly in which of these they emphasize. Some seem to use this formula: Facilitate self-discovery when possible; suggest and explain if necessary. Others appear to consider self-discovery, by itself, too slow and inefficient a process for psychotherapy and rely much more heavily on integrative explanation and demonstration. Because of the power of selection by consequences, some theorists consider it more efficient to include contingency management in their approach to help ensure that when clients or trainees try a preferred pattern, they will experience success or a reinforcing consequence. Some, (e.g., EIT—Mahoney) see the process as "dialectical," with new patterns emerging out of contrasting meaning patterns. In this process, client and therapist collaborate as "co-constructionists."

All seem to agree that producing enduring changes in clients' real-life functional patterns is an important objective, but only a few offer specific propositions about that issue. Some (e.g., PT; ICST; HT) may assist clients to identify, evaluate, and choose among possible courses of action, but seem to assume that generalization of changes to and maintenance in real life will occur automatically, so special attention to this process is unnecessary. Note, however, that in these approaches, validation of the effectiveness of treatment and decisions to terminate tend to be governed by the extent to which clients have become able to negotiate their daily affairs without the burdens imposed by their earlier anxieties and inhibitions (PT), to implement within-session changes on a reliable and enduring basis (ICST), or to make choices and follow them with appropriate actions (HT).

Others assume that some therapy strategies are necessary to facilitate generalization and maintenance. For example, contemporary BTs propose that theorists' clients will learn both respondent conditioning—which generates cognitive models serving a feedforward function in organizing behavior in anticipation of consequences ("type A")—and instrumental conditioning—which results from consequences ("type B")—only if these conditions prove to be functional or have some kind of adaptive value. By observing the outcomes of their actions, people can construct cognitive representations of relationships between their behavior and contexts. They tend to select successful actions and to eliminate ineffective ones (BT—Bandura). Changes in existing patterns requires creating both the content and organization of preferred alternatives, and their practice in relevant contexts (CBST—Guerney), so as to discover that use of more adaptive patterns is rewarding (CBST—Meichenbaum). People learn skills when feedback about the consequences of their use indicates that a skill fulfills their goals in keeping with their values, (i.e., that they "work," are "reinforced," or "rewarded" CBST—Gambrill; Trower). "Cognitive restructuring" must be accompanied by enactment in the real world of the reorganized beliefs, where production of desired consequences serves to validate their utility and to promote their more frequent use; homework assignments may be needed to accomplish this (CT—Beck; Ellis). Although changes in psychological patterns ordinarily lead to changes in actions in real-life settings, clients may need help in experimenting with new behavior outside therapy, making sure that it remains consistent with their core identity constructs (EIT—Neimeyer). The process is cyclical, with new behavior producing different consequences and feedback. This leads to new insights, which promote more new behavior (EIT—Kanfer; Wachtel). From basic scientific literature, Goldstein (CBST) derives guiding principles that encompass others' proposals; these principles are summarized in Chapter 17.

TRANSFORMATIONAL CHANGE

The rapid growth of the study of nonlinear dynamics in complex systems (e.g., chaos and complexity theory) reveals that systems may function in consistent patterns of variability until they reach certain critical states; these states are sometimes called bifurcation points. The systems then suddenly transform themselves into a different consistent pattern rather than pursuing a gradual, step-by-step process of incremental change. Our comparative framework calls this process *transformational change.*

Comparative Framework Proposals

When disruptions of the existing pattern are small enough that they can be overcome with limited changes in some aspect of the total pattern, stability-maintaining and incremental change processes are sufficient to restore unitary functioning and maintain functional viability. Sometimes, however, disruptions produce so much instability in an existing state that limited change cannot overcome it, for example, under the influence of positive feedback processes. Then, the only way to restore a unified pattern is to reorganize the entire pattern into a different steady-state form—to introduce transformational change. This kind of change process can be observed at periodic stages of embryonic development, such as transformation from the blastula to the gastrula phase. These periods of disorganization between one state and another are times of both danger and opportunity. They are dangerous because the system is more vulnerable then: For example, spontaneous abortions most frequently occur during embryonic transitions from one state to another. They are periods of opportunity because they lead to different developmental pathways that open up new possibilities, both good and bad. In between such transformations, embryonic development occurs by incremental change through differentiation and elaboration of existing patterns.

Something similar may occur with information/meaning-based psychological/behavioral patterns. Prolonged physical and psychological stress may push a person to critical levels of instability and tenuous functional organization. Then, events that would ordinarily produce minor perturbations may push the person "over the edge" into a severe state of disorganization, such as a panic attack or psychotic break. Such states cannot be tolerated for extended periods of time, so a reorganization into some new steady state will occur to reduce the stress and instability. Different forms of reorganization are always possible, and which will evolve is unpredictable. When a person is at such a critical level or has entered a severe state of disorganization, often called a crisis, change is more readily achieved than when the person has reorganized into a new steady state. That is the underlying rationale for crisis interventions. However, the process of disruption-disorganization-transformational reorganization may also produce desirable outcomes. For example, after struggling with a set of unconnected ideas for a period of time, a person may suddenly experience a reorganization of those ideas into a coherent pattern, often called insight or an "aha" experience.

Therapy Proposals

In general, the therapy theorists reviewed did not consider this kind of change process in either their propositional or procedural models. We found a few scattered references to it. Thus, one theorist noted that stress may overwhelm adaptive ego functioning (PT—Mishne). Others observed that severe stress may disrupt some biological states (BMHT). Some seem to consider disorder and disequilibrium to be natural processes, with transformations moving in the direction of higher order and more viable forms of organization. (e.g. some EIT). Perhaps these theorists consider transformational change a specialized topic deserving separate treatment rather than inclusion as a part of a general therapy model. We did not examine the specialized literature about crisis states, such as suicidal states or crisis intervention. However, such crisis states sometimes occur during or are precipitated by psychotherapy; therefore, we believe that psychotherapy theories should encompass such transformational change conditions.

PROPOSITIONS ABOUT THE CONTENT, ORGANIZATION, AND DYNAMICS OF DEVELOPMENT

In our comparative framework, stability-maintaining and change-producing dynamics operate continuously through time and varying conditions to produce elaborations of each person's biological, psychological, and behavioral characteristics and capabilities in relation to different kinds of contexts and purposes. Typically this is called development. Material/energy-based processes produce biological structural and functional changes. Information/meaning-based processes produce changes in both psychological/behavioral patterns—usually called personality, social, or skill development—and in component functions, such as cognitive, emotional, motoric, or speech development. Because biological and psychological/behavioral processes are mutually influential, a change of pattern in one may produce changes in the other.

THE NEED FOR THEORIES OF FUNCTIONAL (NORMAL) AND DYSFUNCTIONAL (PATHOLOGICAL) DEVELOPMENT

Some developmental outcomes are called functional or normal and are considered desirable; others are called dysfunctional or pathological and are considered undesirable. People enter therapy because they have some patterns they judge to be undesirable that they have been unable to change on their own. Psychotherapy should be understood as an intervention in ongoing developmental processes that were occurring before the person entered therapy and that will continue after the person leaves. Therapy is aimed at helping a person alter unwanted or dysfunctional behavior and to construct preferred or functional developmental outcomes and pathways.

The two are related because judging something to be dysfunctional involves comparing it with criteria for what is functional. Therefore, theoretical frameworks are needed that define both normal or functional and pathological or dysfunctional development. They must also offer a way for therapists and clients to distinguish between the two. Understanding the content and dynamics of dysfunctions is essential for creating intervention strategies to help clients change them to functional patterns. Therapists continually face choices about which patterns of clients should be the focus of interventions, and which should be affirmed. The absence of satisfactory theories for this purpose can undermine the best of intentions and hours of conscientious effort.

Our comparative framework is essentially a model of the content, organization, and dynamics of development in general. It does not provide a specific model of psychopathology. It does not present different kinds of dysfunctional patterns or indicate how psychotherapy should be conducted; it is not a theory of psychotherapy. However, its propositions about basic stability-maintaining and change-producing dynamics provide a general theoretical frame for discussing the dynamics by which both functional and dysfunctional change and development can occur.

ASSUMPTIONS ABOUT THE NATURE AND DYNAMICS OF FUNCTIONAL OR NORMAL DEVELOPMENT

The concepts of function, process, dynamics, and development were discussed in Chapter 4. They are briefly reviewed next to frame our analyses of therapy theory proposals.

MODELS OF FUNCTIONAL OR NORMAL DEVELOPMENT

Comparative Framework Assumptions

A process that generates a consequence it is designed to produce is called a *function*. For example, the function of skeletal muscles is to exert physical forces to produce and constrain physical movement. Our comparative framework specifies a set of functions of which all humans are capable; for example, they all experience directive and regulatory cognitions, remembering, emotions, and communication. Unified person-level patterns require that all component functions operate in harmonious interaction. Therefore, a person is considered to be functionally effective when the following conditions are in place: the person can perform all basic human functions; each function is in good working order and is occurring within satisfactory boundaries of variability; all functions are appropriately organized in relation to one another and to the contexts in which they are occurring so as to serve the person's purposes. Developmental processes produce patterns, or behavior episode schemas, that are functionally effective for certain purposes in certain kinds of contexts or behavior episodes. The same pattern may be functionally effective for some episodes and not others; as an example, leaving one's doors unlocked may be safe in some places and unsafe in others. The same pattern may work for some people and not others. e.g. some people enjoy seafood; for others it produces serious allergic reactions. One pattern may be effective at one time of life and not others; for example, childish behaviors may be functional when a person is 4 years of age and dysfunctional when he or she is 34.

Historically, four prototypic metamodels of human development have been influential: mechanistic, contextual, organismic, and developmental systems developmental contextualism (see Chapter 1 and Ford & Lerner, 1992, for descriptions). Our comparative framework uses the developmental systems model. It represents development as a creative process of self-construction, fueled by the myriad of continual and varying intraperson and person-context transactions that make up the ongoing process of living. These transactions take place within the constraints and possibilities of people's biological characteristics, their environments, and their current states that are products of their developmental/learning history, which change through processes of living. As examples, a person may become blind or may move from a rural to a city context.

Individual differences in personal characteristics—genes, neurochemistry, gender—provide starting points and provide constraints and possibilities, but there are no inborn "potentialities" to be "actualized." Because development is an ongoing creative process, earlier development may constrain and facilitate but does not determine later development. People can compensate for constraints and create possibilities in many ways. Developmental possibilities continually change as a function of changes in person and context characteristics at different points in time. As a consequence, multiple developmental pathways are possible for any person. The respective merits of these pathways will vary, depending on the purposes and values they serve in relation to the person's life contexts, so developmental pathways are not predetermined. Development is open-ended and somewhat unpredictable, and it can continue throughout life.

This metamodel leads to an emphasis on people's current patterns of functioning and adaptations to their present contexts as well as on the possibilities inherent in the combination of the two. The model implies that interventions should focus on people's current patterns and dynamics so as to promote their optimal functioning in relation to their personal aspirations, and within their current biological and contextual constraints that they cannot, or choose not to, change. Examining clients' developmental history may sometimes be a useful tool for understanding their current functional patterns, but not always. For example, a therapist may be able to understand and facilitate changes in a phobic pattern based solely on understanding of the current contexts and dynamics of the pattern's occurrence. Moreover, because future possibilities are not fully determined by prior conditions and current patterns, interventions can focus on facilitating new possibilities so as to expand the array of developmental pathways a person might pursue.

Therapy Theorists' Assumptions

Organismic and mechanistic models of development guided initial therapy theories. In retrospect, it is not surprising that Freud's initial PT used an organismic model consistent with the prevailing views of the time. In this biocentric organismic metamodel, there is a biologically determined course of development characteristic of humans, and an inborn developmental progression that each person traverses. The metamodel proposes that development occurs in a sequence of stages; prototypic properties are associated with each stage and the prototypic end point is called maturity. Each person may be expected to follow the same general developmental pathway and attain his or her full potentialities or maturity, unless conditions prevent the natural developments from taking place, or cause deviation from the expected course. Events at one stage are precursors or causes of later ones: What happens to the child will govern what takes place later on. Freud's version is a psychosexual developmental theory that assumes a series of stages: oral-receptive, oral-sadistic, anal-retentive, anal-sadistic, phallic, latency, and maturity or adulthood. His theory involves propositions of stage fixation and stage regression and emphasizes the shaping of adult personality by earlier developments in infancy and childhood. Freud attempted to construct explanations for the development of different kinds of psychopathology linked to his stage theory of development.

Initial versions of learning theory-based BT used a mechanistic, reactive organism model of development. People's functional patterns were assumed to be automatically shaped by "contingencies" and "reinforcers" in the contexts in which they behaved. So no normative patterns of development are to be expected unless a culture provides normative contingencies and reinforcers for all people in it—for example, age-graded contexts, roles, and responsibilities.

With growing evidence about the inadequacies of organismic and mechanistic developmental models, contemporary psychotherapy theories appear to have moved away from them and toward a developmental systems meta-model. Elaborations of PT by ego analysts, and modifications by self and object relations theorists, (ISCT), emphasize the plasticity of human development afforded by processes of learning. While continuing to acknowledge some maturational influences, they now view learning as the primary source of developmental change, enabling people to create and organize increasingly complex patterns of adaptation to the varying contexts they encounter throughout their lives.

For PT, self-organization and self-construction occur through various ego operations, such as anticipating, synthesizing, integrating, coordinating, centralizing, organizing, and directing functions (e.g., Hartmann; Erikson). For ISCT analysts, children are said to learn to regulate their own functioning and to gradually achieve self-regulated, mutual interdependence with others (e.g., Fairbairn). Some theorists continue to see developmental stages as useful and share the proposal that later phases of development are governed by infancy and childhood experiences. Progression through successive stages, however, is characterized in terms of successive learnings (e.g., Fairbairn; Greenspan). For example, Erikson (PT) assumes that everyone must cope with an orderly and universal set of maturational tasks, but everyone resolves them differently because each person's physical, social, and cultural contexts will affect that person uniquely in terms of what he or she is able to learn.

Most contemporary theorists agree that the functional patterns people habitually use at any time were previously learned because of their functional utility for some purposes in some contexts; that is, because of their adaptive value (BT) or viability (EIT—constructivists), or because they facilitate a satisfactory person-context fit (CBST). Because human development is considered a continual, interactive, and mutually influencing process between people and their contexts throughout their life course, old patterns may change and new ones emerge. Therefore, clients' current modes of functioning within their current life contexts must be the focus; the here-and-now aspects of their lives provide the basis for change (BT; BMHT; CT; CBST; HT; EIT).

Inquiry into the historical sources of clients' difficulties is not essential, though placing events within a historical context may sometimes help a therapist to understand the dynamics of clients' current functioning. However, reconstruction of prior events with any degree of certitude is not possible. Clients' memories are always constructions that are influenced by current events and the remembering process. There is also the possibility that a person's guiding representations have become functionally autonomous from their historical antecedents (ISCT). Finally, the developmental pathways that a person has been following can always be significantly altered by new experiences. It is for this reason that psychotherapeutic interventions can have utility.

CRITERIA FOR IDENTIFYING FUNCTIONAL DEVELOPMENT

Many of the theorists reviewed recognize the need for criteria with which to differentiate functional from dysfunctional forms of development within this more flexible model.

Comparative Framework Proposals

For centuries, health was defined as the absence of illness, similar to defining peace as the absence of war. For example, medicine traditionally focused on identifying different kinds of illness, injury, or disease, and on ways of overcoming them. Our comparative framework conceives of these as different forms of material/energy disruptions of normal or functional biological steady states. During the twentieth century, people have realized that facilitating a state of health involves more than alleviating biological disruptions, just as creating peace involves more than the cessation of conflict. Overcoming biological disruptions is a necessary but not sufficient condition for attaining health. The promotion of health requires additional criteria for deciding what characteristics and capabilities should be facilitated.

Our comparative framework defines health as functional effectiveness. Healthy people, and their components, develop to produce and maintain desired states and outcomes. In all complex, open systems composed of multiple components and functions operating in relation to multiple goals, coherent organization of all components must exist to ensure effective operation of the system as a whole. Variations in the performance of each function are inevitable, but they occur within steady-state boundaries or parameters that differ among functions, from occasion to occasion, and from one system to the next. There is a range of variation that is optimal for every function. There is a wider range within which variability is permissible—that is, within which other functions can accommodate to produce or retain functional effectiveness for the entire system. Variability that exceeds this permissible range jeopardizes the functional effectiveness of the system as a whole. No system, or system function, can be considered in isolation from the contexts within which it is operating; any function may be appropriate in some behavior episodes and not others. For example, self-generated visual images are appropriate in dreams, but as hallucinations they are dysfunctional in waking life; killing someone in a military battle or self-defense is acceptable, but not in daily life.

Therefore, identifying whether a system's functioning is appropriate and effective requires knowledge of the degree to which (1) component functions are available and operative, (2) the functions are suitably interrelated so they facilitate one another's effective operation in achieving system purposes, (3) the system effectively interrelates with its contexts, and (4) the system operates within acceptable ranges of variability. Because humans consciously monitor their own functioning, another criterion is important for them: (5) Appropriate, effective functioning is signaled by affective and cognitive evaluations or experiences of well-being and goal accomplishment, including social acceptance.

These criteria can be used by a person or a psychotherapist to evaluate functional effectiveness. A person's behavior cannot be termed functional or dysfunctional except in the context of specific behavior episodes. Behavior is considered appropriately organized and functionally effective for a given episode when the following conditions are occurring:

1. Biological states are supportive.
2. Attention is adequately deployed.
3. Requisite kinds and levels of physical activation and emotional arousal are mobilized.
4. Cognitive directive functions provide realistic and doable immediate and longer term goals to pursue.
5. Cognitive control functions operate to anticipate and devise, appraise, choose, initiate, and coordinate means for achieving the guiding goals.
6. Transactional functions provide all requisite information collection and motoric and communicative actions needed for successful implementation of those means.
7. Cognitive and affective regulatory functions enable determinations of the extent to which desired outcomes and states are being achieved or corrective actions are needed.

8. Achieving goals results from transactions with responsive environments, and as most require social transactions, facilitative social relationships and adherence to prevailing constraints of the relevant natural, designed, social, and cultural contexts are needed.

Because behavior episodes are organized and guided by previously learned generalized approaches—behavior episode schemas—deficiencies in any of these component functions or their interrelationships in a behavior episode imply comparable deficiencies in the guiding schema.

Therefore, effective behavior occurs when a biologically capable, motivated, person, guided by selectively collected, constructed, organized, and accurately interpreted relevant information, knowledge, and ideas, produces skillful transactions with a responsive environment (see M. Ford, 1992, for detailed discussion).

Therapy Proposals
None of the theories analyzed explicitly proposes a theory of, or criteria for identifying normal or functional development. Some, (e.g. PT) seem to view health as the absence of illness, focusing primarily on remediation of dysfunctional patterns. HT and CT discuss attributes of optimal functioning, recognizing their relevance for differentiating between clients' functional and dysfunctional patterns and for formulating therapy goals. Most provide some scattered, unsystematic discussion of these important issues, and their ideas about desirable attributes can be inferred from their discussions of therapy goals (e.g., ISCT; CBST; BMHT; EIT). Collectively, their explicit and implied ideas encompass most of the factors in our comparative framework. Some deal with person-level functioning and others with component-level criteria.

Adaptation is one criterion proposed. It is called viability by Mahoney (EIT). Adaptation refers to the extent to which the patterns contribute to achieving goals (see Guerney, CBST), especially people's survival and maintenance (see Beck, CT and Neimeyer, EIT). Effective behavior denotes individual competence in obtaining valued consequences, (CBST). This can include suitable patterns of exercise, eating and sleeping, and avoidance of addictive substances. (BMHT).

Adjustment is an implied criterion in discussions about the extent to which arousal is successfully maintained within preferred ranges of variability. Thus, effective behavior is characterized by internal equilibration (CBST), minimal emotional distress (CT), minimal states of aversive emotions (e.g., BT; ICST—Kiesler; most EIT), fear reduction (BT), and the regulation of tension and stress within tolerable levels (ICST; BMHT).

Integrative behavioral organization is a criterion most discuss or imply. The need for integration of psychological functioning has been particularly emphasized. Effective behavior depends on psychological coherence (BMHT); on smoothly interacting psychological structures (ISCT); on integrated schemas or patterns of beliefs (CT); on internally coherent constructs suitably integrated with other components of the person (Niemeyer—EIT); on coherently organized personal narratives (EIT—Constructivists); or on orderly patterns of thoughts and goal-directed behavior (BT—Bandura). The integration of consciousness/attention functions with other functions is often stressed. Conscious selective attention ensures intentional control (HT; CBST), and enables people to engage in conscious, deliberate self-direction, self-regulation, self-construction and effective decision making (HT; CT; EIT—Kanfer; Wachtel). The components of a person's BASIC I.D. must fit together (EIT—Lazarus). A sign of integrated functioning is an absence of intrapsychic conflict, and the presence of conscious, realistically oriented organization and control of one's affect, thought, and action (PT).

Integrated person-in-context organization is a criterion some emphasize. Effective functioning requires synchronous relations with opportunities and demands of contexts or "external equilibration," especially the maintenance of socially acceptable interpersonal relations in conformity with cultural mores (CBST). Effective people are emotionally interdependent with others (ISCT—Fairbairn), establish and maintain comfortable, conjunctive and complementary (ISCT—Kiesler), cooperative, allocentric, mutually trustful and empathic (CBST), relationships and act with enlightened self-interest in the pursuit of social (collective) interests (CT—Ellis).

Versatility in the kinds of alternate behavior patterns a person can generate and use and the ease with which these patterns can become mobilized is a criterion suggested by some theorists. Effective functioning is indicated by both flexibility and creativity. Illustrative proposals include a repertoire of flexible coping skills, and the availability of flexible, creative constructs with sound plans (CBST), the recognition that one's constructions constitute hypotheses to be subjected to empirical test (CT), the creative imagining of alternative solutions and the flexible capacity to accept change (HT), a commitment to creative pursuits (CT—Ellis), or the exploration of creatively different styles of living (ISCT—Winnicott; EIT—Mahoney).

Effective functioning of component processes is a criterion implied in many discussions. For example, effective cognitive directive functions require clear, appropriate, and appropriately organized goals, together with an explicit awareness of them (CBST; EIT—Kanfer). Effective cognitive problem solving and control functions help people select relevant information; these functions help individuals select and organize perceptions, memories, and ideas to devise alternative solutions and plans, set problem priorities, make decisions, and coordinate actions for goal attainment (CT; CBST; EIT). Effective information collection functioning involves continuing "contact" with oneself and one's surroundings, remaining open to new experience and to the ongoing data from all levels of oneself (HT), effective self-monitoring (EIT—Kanfer), selective attention to relevant cognitive, affective, behavioral and environmental events and information (CBST), observations that correspond to the properties of the real world (CT), and careful and accurate observations of communications, feelings and actions of oneself and others (CBST—Guerney).

Effective communicative and instrumental actions require a large and varied repertoire of skills and competencies. These include adaptive, empathic, expressive, discussion, and negotiation skills; accurate, sensitive communication; and multiple coping skills (CBST; BMHT). When regulatory functions are operating effectively, actions and emotions are continuously being monitored (CBST; HT; EIT), and the differential outcomes of one's actions are noted (BT; CT; CBST; EIT), particularly the feedback one receives from social transactions (CBST; ISCT). The validity of one's beliefs (hypotheses) and constructs remains open to evaluation and testing, and ineffective cognitive constructions are questioned and subjected to change (CT; HT; BT; EIT). Favorable evaluation of one's characteristics and capabilities generate a sense of self-efficacy (BT; CT; HT; CBST; BMHT; EIT), and enable the person to feel special, unique and affirmed by others, that life is worth living, and that they can regulate their own self-esteem (ISCT).

There is a large, sophisticated literature about both formative and summative evaluation in other fields, such as education, program planning and evaluation, that is relevant to setting criteria for effective functioning. Those ideas might be usefully applied to psychotherapy.

ASSUMPTIONS ABOUT THE NATURE AND DYNAMICS OF DYSFUNCTIONAL DEVELOPMENT

The concept of dysfunction and its relationship to functional development was discussed in Chapter 4. It is briefly reviewed here to frame our analyses of therapy theory proposals.

MODELS OF DYSFUNCTIONAL OR PATHOLOGICAL DEVELOPMENT

Comparative Framework Proposals
Dysfunctional or pathological states or patterns develop through the same processes as do functional patterns, so they are a version of functional states

in general, rather than representing qualitatively different developmental dynamics and outcomes; they are a subtype of functional states. This idea differs from the tradition of sharply distinguishing between the content and dynamics of the "natural" and "unnatural," the "normal" and "abnormal." What people now label dysfunctional or pathological patterns are simply alternative developmental outcomes with properties judged to be unacceptable, inappropriate, or unwanted in some contexts on the basis of some criteria. Those judgments may change with time and cultural contexts. For example, people who display what are now called psychotic patterns once were honored in some cultures as having a unique and valued relationship with "the gods."

Dysfunctional patterns develop and persist because they are functional in serving some of a person's purposes in some contexts. They differ from other functional patterns in that their operation interferes with, detracts from, or is incompatible with accomplishing additional functions or purposes. Such patterns impede the maintenance of unified, dynamic organization within the pattern and between it and the person's contexts; they are accompanied by "pathos," or suffering, in the form of distressing anticipations, evaluations, and experiences. Because dysfunction is defined as a deviation from what is functional, or normal, therapists' ideas about the nature of dysfunctional patterns will differ as their theories of normal human development differ. The differences will reflect whether the theorists adopt a mechanistic, organismic, contextualist, or developmental systems model of development.

Our comparative framework represents a person as a unified organization of interrelated components (see Figure 3.2). Dysfunction-producing disruptions or changes can theoretically occur in any of those components; something can go amiss with respect to every single function of which a person is capable. For example, some neurochemical process may go awry; one may lose a limb; one's personal goals, beliefs, or self-evaluations may conflict; one's problem-solving and decision-making capabilities may erode; one may lose control of remembering ability or emotions. Sensory-perceptual, communicative, or movement capabilities may become disrupted; contexts may change and distort previously functional habits. However, dysfunctional changes cannot occur in isolation, as all components are interrelated; a dysfunctional change in one component will generate changes in other components. For example, changes in pituitary functioning may produce changes in hormonal functioning; changes in anticipatory evaluative thoughts may produce changes in emotional states. A dysfunctional change in any component will lead to reconfiguration in the person's pattern of functioning; the general process may be described as functional organization ➤ disruption ➤ disorganization ➤ reorganization into a revised, attenuated, or elaborated functional pattern.

Because change processes occur over a period of time, therapists' interventions always take place at some juncture in the developmental course of a dysfunctional condition. Therefore, therapists who are dealing with dysfunctional changes must have some knowledge of their course over time because the strategy and methods that can be effectively used will be governed to some degree by the extent to which the condition has progressed—its severity, chronicity, and complexity. Intervention early in a dysfunctional pattern's development can produce desired changes more easily and quickly than when it has become chronic—a highly practiced habit. If it is chronic, it must first be disrupted to become susceptible to change, and that disruption may be difficult to achieve.

As examples, interventions must be adapted to the stage at which a condition of alcohol or drug addition has progressed; the highly elaborated features of chronic paranoid conditions present different challenges from those in which delusional formation has recently begun. The course of development of a dysfunctional condition is revealed in answers to questions such as these: When did it begin? How long has it been going on? How has it changed since it first began? Is it continuing to change or get worse? The developmental content and pathway of a dysfunctional condition will display some idiosyncratic properties for each person, because each of us has a different biological and personal history and context of development. It is also possible, however, that some properties of the condition are prototypic for all people for at least some kinds of dysfunctional conditions. That is the basic idea behind the diagnostic typologies of the *DSM-IV* (APA, 1994). Where prototypic developmental properties have been demonstrated to exist, they can provide a context for a clearer understanding of a person's idiosyncratic pattern.

Therapy Theory Proposals
Our analysis of therapists' ideas about normal development reveals that their theories are unclear but seem to have moved toward a developmental systems model. Theorists' ideas about dysfunctional development, although often sketchy and unsystematically presented, are compatible with that theoretical trend. All discuss the dynamic operation of dysfunctions, particularly in what causes dysfunctional patterns to develop. The view that one theory of symptom development is as "true" as any other, so therapists should follow their personal preference in choosing a model of dysfunction (EIT—Beutler), is a distinctly minority opinion. Most consider the choice of a model of dysfunction to be of considerable importance. Different causal patterns have been proposed by different theorists. Eight receiving considerable attention are summarized here: somatogenic, trauma, anxiety-reduction, stress-reduction, deprivation, deficit, conflict, and learning models. The reader may find it in-

teresting to infer the assumptions about normal development that each model implies.

A *somatogenic model* proposes that at least some dysfunctions are the direct result of deviations from normal patterns in biological components, such as genetic vulnerabilities, changes in neurochemical or metabolic functions, a different constitutional makeup, or adventitious injury or disease leading to impaired psychological or behavioral capabilities. Several theorists mention this model (e.g., BMHT; CBST; CT; EIT) they do not, however, proceed to formulate specific propositions about dysfunctional biopsychobehavioral relationships.

The *trauma model,* as created by Breuer and Freud (PT), proposes that specific events that generate intensely aversive emotional states have a disorganizing effect. This disorganization directly produces maladaptive psychobehavioral patterns, evidenced subsequently in a lack of conscious recall of the distressing events and in indirect symptoms (e.g. EIT—Beitman). Two current uses of this model are illustrative: (1) the proposal that childhood sexual abuse traumatizes the child and leads to dysfunctional adult psychological/behavioral patterns; (2) the syndrome termed posttraumatic stress disorder. An assumption of this model is that only one or very few traumatic experiences can produce a dysfunctional pattern, thus implying a proposition comparable to the idea of transformational change in our comparative framework. The other models assume that a fairly lengthy series of experiences is usually necessary, implying a proposition analogous to the idea of incremental change in our framework.

The *anxiety-reduction* or *fear-avoidance model* proposed by Freud (PT) later in his career and elaborated by Dollard and Miller (1950) is used by a considerable number of therapists. It could be considered an elaboration of the basic idea underlying the trauma model. Anxiety (fear) and its anticipation are said to be inherently aversive. Dysfunctions are characterized as various patterns of avoidance designed to forestall, minimize, or otherwise prevent its recurrence. Avoidance patterns help reduce anxiety but they do nothing to assist the person in acquiring needed adaptive skills, to properly frame and resolve problems, to achieve significant goals in life, and so on (e.g., PT; BT—Wolpe; EIT—Wachtel). When avoidance patterns occur, anxiety is probably operating in some form. The therapist's task is to identify the antecedents, the kinds of behavior episodes that activate it, and the responses that function to prevent or reduce its intensity. Therapy involves disrupting the linkage between the eliciting behavior episodes and the occurrence of the fear so that the avoidance responses can be replaced with more adaptive and satisfying behaviors. An example of the current use of this model is in the treatment of phobias using exposure strategies and methods.

The *stress-reduction model* can be considered an elaborated version of the anxiety-reduction model. Some assume that intense and prolonged stress can overwhelm effective cognitive self-regulation and self-control, or "adaptive ego functioning" (PT—ego psychology) such stress can lead to construction of dysfunctional patterns. Others assume that ineffective coping with intense and prolonged stress leads to cumulative and persistence states of arousal and erosion of people's adaptive capabilities, thus making them vulnerable to disease processes or disruptions of biological functions (e.g., BMHT). This model is frequently used in current behavioral medicine treatments—for example, controlling hypertension.

The *deprivation model* typically assumes that certain conditions must be available in the person's environment for normal functional development to occur. For example, consistent and positive parental love and support are generally necessary to the satisfaction of the person's inherent need for affection and security. When these conditions are absent, the unsatisfied needs persist and dominate the person's life (e.g., ISCT—Winnicott). Persistent frustration or thwarting of relevant need-satisfaction sequences is said to result in various dysfunctional consequences, such as feelings of rejection, inadequacy, insecurity, or self-criticality. These consequences can account for recurrent dysfunctional patterns discernible in later life. A reconstruction of the circumstances surrounding the person's early developmental experiences is needed to identify the bases of the contemporary difficulties. Object relations therapies typically use this model.

The *deficit model* assumes that dysfunctional patterns result from various kinds of functional deficiencies, such as incompetent and ineffective behavior (e.g., CBST), inadequacies in existing beliefs, rationales and cognitive structures that misguide their functioning (e.g., CBST; CT; ISCT; EIT), or ego deficits, impaired capacities for internalization or reality testing, and insufficient drive modulation (e.g., PT—ego psychology). Often, skills and capabilities needed for effective and satisfying living in socially acceptable ways are simply not in the person's repertoire, presumably because they have not had occasion to acquire them, and often because they have adopted the prevailing pattern within their familial and social contexts (e.g., CBST). Such social modeling can also lead to the practice of cultural patterns (e.g., diet) that cultivate illness (e.g., BMHT). Current use of this model is illustrated by assertiveness training.

The *conflict model*, initially proposed by Freud (PT) assumes that the presence of conflicting, incompatible, and often unconscious psychological components—often called intrapsychic conflict—leads to the construction of dysfunctional patterns. Notable among these is the psychoanalysts' view that represents dysfunction as the product of nuclear conflicts. These occur between instinctively based wishes that are opposed by ego and/or superego constraints. The symptoms constitute compromise-formations for dealing with such conflicts. Others construe conflict to be central to dysfunctional development but describe the content differently. For example, there are deeply conflicted dynamics, or conflicting dualities, within the person's core interpersonal schemas (e.g., some EIT), competing skill patterns (CBST), or various kinds of incongruities and conflicts within the person's psychological organizations (HT) or among their schemas or beliefs (CT).

The *learning model* assumes that all but inborn functional patterns are the product of learning processes, whether they are judged to be functional or dysfunctional; people are equally capable of learning effective/ineffective, appropriate/inappropriate patterns of functioning. For example, capacities to think "rationally" or "crookedly" exist in everyone (CT—Ellis). All people seek to maintain their stability in the face of continually changing conditions, even if to do so requires misperceptions or inattention to feedback (HT). Fear, like other patterns of response, can become linked to diverse objects, people, or even a person's inner experiences. Learning can produce dysfunctions in any person component as well as in complex patterns, such as the schemas or beliefs people have acquired (CT), their self and world constructs (HT), their personal narratives (EIT—constructivists), or their interpersonal schemas (ISCT—Kiesler).

To understand people's dysfunctional patterns, a therapist does not need to know their developmental histories. Instead, he or she can identify those patterns and understand their dynamics by analyzing the recurrent episodes occurring in the clients' current lives that are causing them difficulty, appraising how they deal with these patterns, and observing what habits of attention, thought, feeling, or action seem to be causing difficulties, including both things that are present and those that are missing. Such analyses yield an understanding of current eliciting conditions for dysfunctional patterns, the nature of the patterns themselves, and the consequences they generate for the person. That understanding serves to guide therapy interventions.

Most contemporary psychotherapy theorists seem to subscribe to the learning model, compatible with the trend in their thinking toward something like a developmental systems model of normal or functional development. All other models except for the somatogenic model can be encompassed within the learning model; that is, trauma, anxiety, stress, deprivation, deficit, or conflict origins of dysfunction can all be learned.

Most psychoanalysts (PT; ISCT) now agree that dysfunctional patterns are learned, but many retain the idea of stages of development typical of an organismic model and link it to the development of dysfunctional patterns. Theorists who espouse a stage model propose that different developmental conditions, occurring at different stages of development, produce different kinds of deficits, distortions, or defects—for example, through developmental "fixation" or "arrest". They also claim that difficulties in a later stage may lead to "regression" in patterns used in an earlier stage. To determine the stage at which developmental disruption occurred for a client, therapists must understand the stage sequences, the prototypic patterns for each, the kinds of events that may interfere with successful transition from each stage to the next, and the adult form of patterns typically associated with fixated, arrested, or regressed states. They must also assume that they can obtain accurate knowledge about clients' early development through the clients' retrospective reconstruction of their developmental history. Analysts assume that to change dysfunctional patterns, they must reconstruct and modify in analytic sessions the kinds of developmental conditions patients experienced in the stage at which development was disrupted. This process allows patients to renew their developmental progress and to traverse the necessary stages successfully.

THE PERSISTENCE OF DYSFUNCTIONAL PATTERNS

The ordinary person is inclined to express impatience or even disgust when disturbed friends or relatives persist in behaving in apparently senseless or futile or self-defeating ways. Clients themselves often consider much about their thoughts and actions to be eminently reasonable, but they also complain that they continue to fail in achieving their purposes despite their best efforts to do otherwise. A model of dysfunctional development must be able to account for why and how dysfunctional patterns persist and remain immune to the usual processes of change despite their continually generating unwanted outcomes. This accounting is necessary because therapy interventions will have to deal with those stability-maintaining habits.

Comparative Framework Proposals

Propositions about the dynamics of organizational consistency and stability were discussed at the beginning of this chapter. Within a learning model, the same propositions apply to stability maintenance of dysfunctional patterns. In summary, patterns persist because they serve some personal goals by generating some desired consequences: they display functional utility. Moreover, many habitual patterns serve multiple goals simultaneously, so they are multiply determined; the more desired consequences a pattern produces, the harder it is to change. Patterns are termed dysfunctional when some of their guiding goals are not well served, when they interfere with achieving valued goals, and when they produce unwanted effects or consequences. From this perspective, psychotherapy is partly a matter of enabling clients to construct more suitable and effective means of accomplishing their goals without producing unwanted side effects.

Like many functional patterns, the clients' dysfunctional ones have a long history of use that has resulted in their becoming "automated." This means that they are typically performed without the client's conscious forethought, control, or regulation. Thus, people are normally unaware of some aspects of what they are doing, why they are doing it, and what the resulting consequences are. One of the problem-producing characteristics of dysfunctional patterns is that some aspects of their stability-maintaining dynamics serve to avoid distress for the person and to maintain unitary functioning by ensuring that the person remains unaware of dysfunctional aspects. When patterns function in tacit, unconscious fashion, they are less susceptible to change because learning does not occur without awareness of the pattern's current operation. Dysfunctional patterns persist because they have some functional utility for the people performing them; although these patterns produce some experiences and consequences the performers dislike, the people manage to remain unaware of how or why these behaviors happen.

Therapy Theory Proposals

Most therapy theorists agree that dysfunctional patterns persist primarily because they have some functional utility, though theorists differ in the ways they describe that utility. Thus, some (PT) assume that symptoms persist because they constitute compromise solutions that facilitate the person's stability both by reducing the level of distressing affect (primary gain), and by providing partial gratification of forbidden impulses (secondary gain). Pathological patterns persist because they serve a function; they are ways of trying to preserve some social connectedness through real or fantasied relationships, inadequate though they may be (ISCT). Dysfunctional patterns represent self-protective strategies designed to prevent retraumatization; the behaviors succeed in mitigating, controlling, or eliminating the disastrous effects of anxiety, even though they deny the person the opportunity to learn alternate, potentially more effective ways of behaving (ISCT).

Other theorists assume that dysfunctional patterns result from faulty learning, and persist because they produce consequences the person values, even though unwanted outcomes may also occur that make the behavior appear dysfunctional to others (BT). Behavior is selected, organized, and maintained by cognized future outcomes so the person can retain coherence and direction, despite the occurrence of dissuading immediate effects (BT—Bandura). Faulty habits are maintained because they have some functional utility in producing short-term desired consequences, even though they generate unhealthy long-term effects (BMHT). Irrational beliefs and inaccurate cognitive schemas continue to be maintained because they demonstrate some functional utility (CT). Dysfunctional processes are discernible whenever people focus on protecting their being rather than participating in the processes of becoming; this occurs when people assign priority to stability maintenance over pursuit of personal goals, or adaptation to changing circumstances. People impose an order on their experience and vigorously seek to defend a coherent view of themselves that affords self-respect and self-esteem (HT). Dysfunctions constitute measures that control anxiety, even though they produce further problems in the long term (EIT—Wachtel). The natural tendencies of living systems to maintain their own coherence and organization lead them to resist changes in general (EIT—Guidano; Mahoney).

There is considerable agreement with the idea that the persistence of dysfunctional patterns is facilitated by their automatic operation, outside the person's focal awareness, though some do not include it among their proposals (e.g., BT; BMHT). A few endorse Freud's (PT) initial proposal that people's unconscious nature characterizes all dysfunctional patterns. Repression is proposed to be an automatic stability-maintaining function serving to prevent instinctually based processes from entering awareness. Moreover, the processes governing the operation of dysfunctional patterns become disguised, neutralized, and transformed through reality-focused secondary process thought, such as defense mechanisms.

Some, (e.g., CT—Beck; Ellis) are critical of that formulation. They propose the term *unconscious* be used to refer to all aspects of people's functions that remain tacit and unstated, and hence not part of their current experiential awareness. Large portions of dysfunctional patterns are assumed never to have been consciously recognized and labeled, so they function outside of awareness and are relatively immune from processes of change. Examples of these are the content and rules of underlying schemas (CT—Beck), or psychological aspects of habitual patterns (EIT—Wachtel).

Some cite the progressive nature of unconscious processes, proposing that they tend to compound the person's problems by producing consequences that contribute to development of additional dysfunction—similar to positive feedback processes in our comparative framework. Thus, failure to attend to and symbolize their ongoing behavior and experience, serves to compromise the people's ability to achieve sufficient satisfaction for their personal goals and to adapt effectively to changing circumstances. Therefore, they persist in no-longer-appropriate patterns of functioning, which lead to inevitable feelings of stress, helplessness, and inadequacy. (e.g., HT). A few theorists point to processes of automatization as the reason people are not aware of some of their patterns of functioning. Thus, the persistence of dysfunctional processes is said to be frequently due to their automatic occurrence outside awareness, (e.g., EIT—Beitman, Kanfer). The repeated practice of functional patterns leads to their becoming automatic and to persist in the form of "mindless scripts" due to absence of the person's attention to, and conscious formulation of, their content and organization (e.g., CBST—Meichenbaum).

CRITERIA FOR IDENTIFYING FORMS OF DYSFUNCTIONAL DEVELOPMENT

The problem confronting clients and their therapists is of the following form. A client has one or more patterns that she finds distressing and undesirable (State A). She would like to change them to some preferred form (State B), although she may not be clear about what that is. Because clients have been unable to produce such changes with their own means and resources, some additional means must be added to their own capabilities. They expect psychotherapy to provide those supplemental means. Therefore, psychotherapy's tasks are to identify the characteristics of States A and B, to determine ways in which A can be changed to B, and to help clients effectively implement the necessary means to produce that result. Conceptually, it is a sequential process; in practice, it is usually an iterative process. States A and B may have to be periodically redefined and means for addressing them altered or elaborated as therapy proceeds.

Often, clear specification of States A and B is not an easy task. Dysfunctional processes do not occur singly or in isolation from one another. Because functions are interrelated, a dysfunction in one aspect is likely to affect other aspects as well. Moreover, people attempt to compensate for dysfunctional deviations with other functional modifications. Therefore, clients' dysfunctional patterns are typically composed of some aspects that are a *direct result* of the dysfunction—for example, fear-based physiological changes—and others that reflect *compensatory efforts,* such as "defense mechanisms". Compensatory changes may produce additional dysfunctional problems, called a positive feedback process in our comparative framework. An example would be a withdrawal pattern to control fear that may disrupt a person's work or interpersonal relations. A faulty specification of State A can lead to misguided intervention efforts; the therapist might focus only on compensatory aspects of the dysfunctional pattern. An adequate theory of psychopathology or dysfunction will provide criteria to enable a precise and explicit specification of the major characteristics of State A.

Comparative Framework Proposals
Criteria for normal development were reviewed earlier. A pattern may become dysfunctional to the extent that any of its aspects detract from, interfere

with, or are incompatible with effective, normal functioning. A dysfunction occurs when some conditions disrupt a functional pattern in some way, thus producing some kind of disorganization in it. A person's functioning occurs in a continual, varying stream of activity that is organized in internally coherent chunks or units called behavior episodes. Dysfunctional patterns can be observed only during the enactment of some kind of behavior episode—for example, remembering past interpersonal episodes, enacting behavior episodes with a therapist, initiating episodes assigned by a therapist, or performing behavior episodes prompted by assessment procedures, such as the Rorschach technique. Thus, identification of dysfunctional patterns by clients and therapists occurs through the observation and analysis of specific behavior episodes and may focus on faulty functioning at both the person-in-context and component levels of analysis.

At the person-in-context level, a person's functioning is *maladaptive* if its relationship to environmental conditions jeopardizes the person's health, welfare, safety, or survival. It is *maladjustive* if it fails to produce harmonious organization among parts of the pattern, as in maintaining the person's level of arousal within preferred ranges for that pattern. The functioning is *ineffective* if it proves to be inadequate, insufficient, or inept in producing intended consequences, or *inefficient* if the accomplishment of the desired goals requires an excessive amount of resource expenditure. Functioning is *irrelevant* when demonstrating no pertinence to the goals or contexts with which it is connected. It is *inappropriate* when it is inadequately related to the contexts within which it occurs. Functioning is *illegal* if it is discrepant from patterns defined as acceptable by laws, and *nonconformist* if legal but not in accord with behavioral norms and expectations established and preferred within the person's reference groups. A person may be conformist in some groups and nonconformist in others.

At component levels, a function may be *absent*—for example, a person may be blind. The function may be potentially available but *inactivated* so that it does not occur as needed; an example is the inactivation of memory in amnesia. A function may be available but *impaired* in operation, occurring in some partial or limited form; in this case it could be diminished in latency, duration, rate, quality, value, or amplitude. When components are available, but inadequately or inappropriately interrelated, in either simultaneous or sequential forms, a pattern is termed *poorly integrated.* For example, two or more incompatible components may be simultaneously activated, but they cannot occur simultaneously; this condition is referred to as conflict. A function may be "running free," operating autonomously from regulation by other components; these could be uncontrolled thoughts intruding into ongoing activities. The clinical psychology, psychiatric, medical, and social work literatures describe a large variety of faulty interrelationships (see Table 4.3 for more examples).

Therapy Theory Proposals

None of the theories analyzed provide criteria for identifying forms of dysfunctional patterns in a clear, explicit, and systematic way, even those whose procedural models stress the importance of idiographic diagnosis. Some, (e.g., BT) provide essentially no criteria for making such decisions, except for a client's assertion that a pattern is unwanted. A few recognize the need for multiple criteria (BMHT; CT; EIT). In general, however, one of two conditions prevails: The criteria that a theorist uses remain implicit and unstated; the dysfunction would be whatever in the therapist's judgment seems to make a client miserable or interferes with effective functioning. Alternately, reliance is placed on the criteria the clients use; whatever they identify as unsatisfactory becomes the focus of change. A few theorists appear to use criteria provided by standard diagnostic classifications, such as the *DSM-IV* (APA, 1994).

Most theorists speak to this issue, but in fragmented and unsystematic ways, often in the context of discussing their procedural models or describing specific cases. Several used the criterion of maladaptation. For example, dysfunctions include patterns that fail to promote the person's maintenance, survival, and further adaptive development (e.g., CT; HT), fail the test of viability (EIT—Mahoney), or erode the person's health and place their life or welfare in jeopardy (BMHT). Several use a maladjustment criterion, stressing "negative" affective states. For example, dysfunction exists when there is an impaired ability to maintain anxiety and distress within manageable limits (EIT—Beutler); when behavior is unduly intense (ISCT—Kiesler), generates excessive states of negative affect or tension (EIT—Lazarus), results in inappropriate or excessive emotionality, discomfort, suffering or fear (CT—Beck; EIT—Beutler), or leads to the occurrence of acute or chronic patterns of intense stress, (e.g., intense or noxious subjective experiences such as pain, fear, fatigue or anger) (BMHT).

Ineffectiveness is perhaps the most frequently cited criterion. For example, patterns are dysfunctional when they fail to produce desired outcomes (CT—Beck), or alleviate or prevent stress (BMHT); or they were learned in a context where they had some utility but are currently used in inappropriate ways and contexts (EIT—Kanfer; ISCT). The self-defeating characteristics of dysfunctional patterns (e.g. vicious circles or cycles) is often cited (e.g. EIT—Wachtel; Lazarus; ISCT—Kiesler). Faulty integration is another frequently cited criterion, illustrated by a lack of coherence among a person's constructs or within their personal narrative (EIT—constructivists); the presence of incongruities in the person's psychological patterns (HT); or the presence of "conflictual dynamics" in a person's patterns of functioning (e.g., PT; EIT—Beutler).

Inappropriate connections between people's functioning and their life contexts are sometimes mentioned, particularly within social/interpersonal contexts, as evidence of dysfunction. For example, patterns are judged dysfunctional when they have become overgeneralized and repeated across a range of situations and contexts (e.g., CT—Beck; Ellis; EIT—Beutler), when they lead to intra- and interpersonal effects that are socially unacceptable, or generate deleterious social effects, or are inconsistent with social consensus (e.g., ISCT—Kiesler; CBST; EIT).

Often, more attention is given to dysfunctional attributes of specific components or their relationships than to other personal characteristics. For example, CT provides lists of kinds of faulty contents and organization of clients' cognitive patterns; some are accompanied by definitions such as dichotomous thinking and overgeneralization. For HT, it is the organization of components rather than their content that produces dysfunction: for example, incongruence between current experience and one's felt sense of oneself, or one's self-concept.

COMMENTARY

There seems to be a general tendency to reduce explanations of the development of dysfunctional patterns to a single form of dysfunction; examples are Freud's attribution of diverse dysfunctional patterns to one kind of intrapsychic conflict, the oedipal complex, and other analysts' attempts to consider faulty parent-child relations to be the source of most dysfunctional patterns, or efforts by some to represent all dysfunctional patterns in terms of an anxiety-reduction or fear-avoidance model. Moreover, criteria are often presented through the use of examples rather than as formal definitions. Rules to govern the application of criteria identifying dysfunction are routinely absent—as when intrusive thoughts, high levels of emotion, or forgetting are indicative of psychopathology, and when they are not. If the primary purpose of psychotherapy is to alter or replace dysfunctional patterns, a lack of clarity about what patterns are dysfunctional and how to identify their occurrence is a serious theoretical weakness.

The proclivity to reduce explanations of dysfunction to a single form is a serious deficiency in the field of psychotherapy; examples of this single-cause tendency are proposing dysfunction to be a result of instinctually-based wishes, faulty cognitions, or guiding schemas of various kinds; inappropriate self-representations; inadequately attended to and organized experience; faulty actions; or troublesome contexts. Extensive empirical evidence supports the view that dysfunctions may develop in multiple ways under multiple influences. Similar dysfunctional patterns may develop within different developmental conditions, and different dysfunctional patterns may develop within similar conditions. Our comparative framework suggests that person-level dysfunctional patterns may originate within any component function or combinations of functions (see Table 3.2). Each of the forms proposed by different therapy theorists may help account for some dysfunctional patterns, and doubtless others are yet to be proposed. This issue is of significance for the design of a therapist's procedural model because the kinds of intervention strategies and methods that may be most effective may differ depending on the form and dynamics of the dysfunctional pattern and the stage of its development. A great deal more attention needs to be given to this aspect of psychotherapy theory.

CHAPTER 17

Procedural Models: Psychotherapy Strategies and Methods

PSYCHOTHERAPY IS ONE form of intervention into human affairs; there are many others such as surgery, medication, teaching, preaching, and imprisonment. The term *intervention* means to enter between two points in time, or two circumstances; to facilitate or constrain an action; or to maintain or alter a condition. Interventions may be described in terms of strategies and related tactics or methods. A *psychotherapy strategy* is an arrangement of conditions, methods, and activities, implemented over an extended period of time and aimed at producing some kind of enduring change in clients. Different strategies may be needed for producing different kinds of changes. *Tactics* or *methods* are specific procedures for implementing strategies.

STABLE STRATEGIES AND FLEXIBLE METHODS

Different methods can implement the same strategy, so different therapists may use different methods directed toward similar outcomes. The effectiveness of different methods for the same strategy may vary depending on the idiosyncratic content and organization of clients' problems; their life circumstances and personal history; their personal attributes, such as age; their contexts, such as socioeconomic status; the therapist's knowledge and skills; and the simultaneous pursuit of other strategies—psychological and behavioral. For example, clients with strong habits and skills of verbal communication and introspection may benefit from traditional verbal dialogue strategies, whereas clients whose socialization has stressed action, rather than communication and introspection, may benefit more from strategies of modeling and behavioral practice (CBST—Goldstein). If multiple goals are pursued, as is often the case, combinations of strategies and methods may be required.

The need to match specific methods to clients' idiosyncratic patterns is a key reason for flexibility of methods in implementing stable strategies; this diversity illustrates what is often called the "art" of psychotherapy. It may also help to explain why therapy theorists often only specify therapy strategies, rely on the "good judgment," "intelligence," and "tact" of the therapist for choice of methods (PT—Freud) and argue against the "tyranny of technique" (EIT—Guidano). A rationale of stable strategy–flexible method is implicit in proposals for methodological eclecticism.

Unfortunately, some therapists neglect to specify their tactics because of a conviction that flexibility of methods is desirable, and fear that others will convert suggested methods into fixed rules and dogma—a problem that Freud experienced. However, the number of ways a strategy can be implemented are finite, and the effectiveness of any method for a particular strategy can be empirically examined, though that may be a complex issue. For example, some methods may serve one strategy but contradict another; thus, the same method may be effective with one combination of strategies and ineffective, or perhaps even detrimental, with another. Alternatively, a strategy may be effective in one phase of therapy but not another—for example, introductory versus transfer of change phases. Some therapists suggest that the same method may have different meanings and impacts depending on the theoretical framework within which it is used (Safran & Messer, 1997). In any case, the utility of any strategy can be evaluated only indirectly by assessing the effectiveness of the methods used to implement it. Therefore, it is critical that therapists be explicit about both their strategies and the methods used to implement them.

Our analyses reveal that most therapists do not distinguish clearly between strategies and methods, and do not state explicitly that multiple methods may be used effectively to implement essentially the same strategy. Many discuss interventions in terms of strategies—creating understanding, establishing an empathic relationship, or interpreting resistance—without specifying the methods for implementing them. This lack of specificity is a serious barrier to efforts to compare the utility of different approaches, because the actual conduct of therapy occurs at the tactical or method level. BT, CBST and BMHT approaches have sought to be more explicit about the link between method and strategy, making evaluative research about their approaches more feasible and fruitful. The recent trend toward formulating explicit strategy/method therapy protocols, or treatment manuals, for specific dysfunctions seeks to remedy this historic vagueness in psychotherapy procedural models.

PROCEDURAL MODELS IMPLEMENT MODELS OF DYSFUNCTIONAL AND NORMAL DEVELOPMENT

The way that a problem is framed influences the choice of solutions, so different models of psychopathology and normal development should lead to different procedural models. Based on our analyses in Chapter 16, we conclude that therapists rely on two models of normal development: (1) unfolding of inborn potentials (called organismic models in developmental psychology), and (2) learning or constructing functional patterns for different purposes and contexts (developmental systems/contextualism models). Their theories of dysfunction can be grouped into three broad types, depending on the source to which they attribute the client's dysfunctional development: (1) illness or faulty habits, (2) developmental arrest or delay, or (3) deficit or incompetence. The types may be combined. For example, Freud (PT) combined illness and developmental arrest.

Illness or Faulty Habits and Organismic Development

The model based on illness or faulty habits assumes that there is a psychological cause for any dysfunctional behavior pattern. The remedy is to remove the cause and the dysfunction will disappear, a treatment that is analogous to curing a physical illness by eliminating the causal infectious agent. Eliminating or resolving intrapsychic conflicts (PT—Freud), "desensitizing" distressing fear patterns (BT—Wolpe), or altering dysfunctional personal narratives (EIT—some constructivists) illustrate strategies serving this model of dysfunction. The illness or faulty habits model is typically coupled with an organismic model of normal development. The underlying assumption for this link is that once the cause of dysfunction is removed, inborn developmental processes will automatically produce more satisfactory patterns. Therefore, procedural models typically focus on "eliminating the negative" and give less attention to "cultivating the positive."

Developmental Arrest or Delay and Organismic Development

The developmental arrest or delay model assumes that normal development unfolds in a sequence of prototypical, functional patterns guided by inborn processes. Dysfunction results when conditions of living—such as inadequate parenting during infancy and childhood—obstruct those inborn processes; as a result, a person gets stuck in patterns of functioning that are relevant to earlier stages of development but dysfunctional in later stages. The remedy is to help clients become "unstuck" by removing the obstructing conditions and thereby freeing the inborn developmental processes. Removing the barriers allows the person to continue growing and to develop normal patterns of functioning prototypical for different stages of development. For example, by altering faulty "object relations" or "selfobject" psychological patterns, the "aborted or defective self" will "mobilize its striving" to complete its development thereby helping "a frightened infant inside grow up" (ISCT—self psychology and object relations psychoanalysis). The focus of therapy is to "free" clients' "self-actualizing" or "intrinsic" processes of "optimal functioning," so that the operation of those processes can produce normal, self-satisfying self development (HT).

DEVELOPMENTAL DEFICITS AND LEARNING OR CONSTRUCTING FUNCTIONAL PATTERNS

The developmental deficits model assumes that people function in faulty ways because they have not learned skills essential for effective functioning in important life contexts. Adaptive deficits can produce social rejection or isolation, negative self-evaluations, and distressing affects, thereby leading to various forms of "mental disorder." The remedy is to eliminate the functional deficits by helping people learn effective skills relevant to their personal objectives, contexts, and concerns. Helping clients learn specific cognitive, motivational, communicative, and social skills and how to combine them into complex, flexible patterns will enable clients to produce preferred outcomes and to generate a more positive view of themselves and of their contexts. The focus is on stressing the positive rather than removing the negative (CBST).

PREFERRED DEVELOPMENTAL PATHWAYS AND PROCESSES

Regardless of their differences in theory and terminology, the theorists evidence broad consensus that therapy should help people become capable of constructing their own developmental pathways, using inborn capabilities for being self-organizing, self-constructing, self-directing, and self-regulating. A number of theorists state this as a given without providing theoretical justification. Some anchor it to metaphysical assumptions about the uniqueness and value of each person. Most of the procedural models discussed here state that a goal of therapy is to "free" and "enhance" people's self-development capabilities so that the individuals no longer need a therapist to help them chart their course and deal with their problems of living. Therapists choose strategies and methods in the belief that they contribute to that outcome. For some, this is the key therapy goal and they reject any strategies and methods they believe contradict it (e.g. HT). Others believe that methods facilitating client self-direction can be cultivated in combination with more directive therapeutic strategies and methods. There is no longer any significant reliance on mechanistic models of human nature in contemporary models of psychotherapy. Self-government is stressed, and the influence of environments is viewed as mediated by those self-governing processes. A frequently repeated dictum is that therapists can't change clients; they can only help clients change themselves.

UNITARY FUNCTIONING AND SYSTEM CHANGE

Our comparative framework asserts that all behavior patterns are organizations of component functions. Therefore, the content of all a client's behavior patterns, whether functional or dysfunctional, includes all aspects of that person organized to operate as a unit, integrated by the prototypical dynamics of an open, living system. Because of this unitary functioning, a change in one component of a pattern is likely to affect the pattern as a whole (see Figure 3.2).

For example, altering what people pay attention to (consciousness/attention arousal) can alter how they think, feel, and act, and lead to different consequences. Altering the way people act (transactional functions) can produce different consequences and the changed feedback can alter how they think and feel. Altering how they feel (emotional arousal functions) can influence how they think and act, which can lead to different outcomes. Altering people's goals or evaluative thoughts (directive and regulatory cognitive functions) can alter what they attend to, how they feel and act, and the consequences they produce. Altering the heuristics they use to plan and organize their actions (cognitive control functions) can change what they do, the results they get, and how they think and feel. Altering neurochemical balances (biological functions) can alter mood, which can change how people think and act, and the consequences of these actions. Altering context can produce different consequences for people's actions, which can alter thoughts, emotions, what they will try to do, and how they will try to do it.

Therapy Strategies May Differ in the Component Functions Targeted for Change

Because component functions are interrelated, psychotherapists can target changes in different aspects of a client's functioning, using various strategies, and yet produce similar system changes. This variability may be one reason that research evaluating the efficacy of different approaches typically finds that therapy is better than no therapy but finds few differences among approaches. It is also possible that the efficiency with which change is facilitated and the correlated changes or side effects that occur are functions of which component is targeted and the type of pattern to be changed or learned. For example, Prochaska and DiClemente (EIT) suggest that the appropriate focus may differ with different kinds of problems and in different therapy phases. Their *key level* strategy assumes that certain kinds of patterns are most easily changed by targeting one component that plays a central role in the dysfunctional pattern, an example is treating phobias by desensitizing the fear component. A *shifting levels* strategy focuses on one component and then another, when the sequencing of changes appears useful; here the therapist would first reduce anxiety, then change thoughts. Their *maximum impact* strategy focuses on multiple components to increase the rate and scope of change. In this strategy, the therapist would treat depressions by simultaneously targeting changes in neurochemical, interpersonal, and anticipatory evaluative thought components of the depressive pattern.

The therapy families we analyzed emphasize different person components. Some of these therapists stress altering cognitions and assume that changes in other components will follow (PT; ISCT; CT; EIT some constructivists). Some focus on combinations of affective and cognitive change (HT). There seems to be an increasing tendency to use a multicomponent focus, in which changes in other components are seen as means to facilitate desired changes in actions such as social relations, or biological states like blood pressure or drug addiction (BT; CBST; BMHT; EIT).

PHASES OF THERAPY AND SETS OF STRATEGIES AND METHODS

The theorists implicitly share the general view that there are interrelated subsets of therapy goals, and that there are strategies and methods relevant to each subset. Broadly speaking, achieving each subset of goals is dependent on prior achievement of other subsets, so some theorists arrange these groupings in a temporal sequence and call them *phases* or *stages of psychotherapy*. Even so, all recognize therapy to be an iterative process that moves back and forth among these subsets of goals as necessary; as an example, problem definition is typically an early goal, but reframing the problem periodically may be necessary and useful.

For example, Kanfer (EIT) developed these seven phases: structuring roles and creating a therapeutic alliance; developing a commitment for change; performing the behavioral analysis; negotiating treatment objectives and methods; implementing treatment and maintaining motivation; monitoring and evaluating progress; and providing for maintenance, generalization and termination of treatment. Prochaska and DiClemente (EIT) list five phases: precontemplation, contemplation, preparation, action, and maintenance. CBST's groupings are introduction or conceptualization, skill training, and generalization and maintenance. We discuss all their proposals about strategies and tactics in five groupings: (1) strategies of preparing clients for therapy: defining therapy contexts and processes; (2) strategies of social influence: creating and maintaining a therapeutic relationship; (3) strategies of awareness and understanding: identifying and activating patterns to be altered; (4) strategies of change: learning to control or alter relevant patterns; and (5) strategies of perpetuating change: transfer to and maintenance in daily life.

STRATEGIES FOR PREPARING CLIENTS FOR THERAPY: DEFINING THERAPY CONTEXTS AND PROCESSES

Theorists agree that psychotherapy requires a major investment of time, effort, and resources by both clients and therapists, so a decision to initiate therapy should not be made lightly. First, therapists must decide that psychotherapy is an appropriate intervention for the client's presenting problems, and theorists differ in the content and explicitness of the criteria for that judgment. Next, several decisions about what Beutler and Clarkin (EIT) call the *context of treatment* must be made. What should be the treatment setting (e.g., inpatient, outpatient)? The answer involves preliminary judgments about the nature, severity, and acuteness of the presenting problems. What treatment modes (e.g., psychosocial, medical, combinations) and formats (e.g., individual, family, group, or combination therapies) may be of most value? Is the therapist's approach best for this client, or should the client be referred to another therapist whose approach may be of potentially greater value for this person? What should be the treatment intensity (e.g., frequency and duration of sessions; length of therapy)? These must be collaborative decisions, and will require exchanges of information between client and therapist—about the client's availability and ability to pay; about the nature of the therapy proposed and what it would require of the client. These are preliminary decisions that can be altered later if conditions warrant change.

The Therapy Alliance

Theorists generally agree that before therapy begins clients should have a clear understanding and agreement about procedural arrangements, such as fees and payment schedules, and interview schedules, general therapy goals, and client and therapist roles and responsibilities. These understandings are often called the *therapy contract* (e.g., PT), *global task agreement* (HT) and the *therapy (working) alliance* by most others. Some rules may not be enunciated unless events during therapy require them—such as rules about gifts. Arrangements should be compatible with the larger cultural milieu; this means that therapists should observe relevant customs and holidays. When the "rules of the game" are made explicit in the beginning, and clients' understanding of them is assured, clients' deviations from those rules during therapy may provide meaningful information about their current states and motivation, if such deviations are assumed to be motivated rather than unintentional (e.g., PT; ISCT).

Client and Therapist Goal Alignment

Our comparative framework asserts that clear goals are important because they exert an organizing influence on the rest of a person's behavior (see Figure 3.2). *Goal alignment* is essential for collaborative efforts among people. When efforts are directed at different goals, therapist and client will be working at cross purposes; their efforts will be inefficient, unproductive, and likely to yield misunderstanding and mistrust. There are two broad types of therapy goals: solving current problems or changing personality structures, often called *outcome goals* (illustrated by BE goals), and learning general strategies and methods for future problem solving, often called *process goals* (illustrated by goals of HT and CBST—Guerney). Clients often initially focus on symptom relief. Some therapists prefer a focus on symptom causes; others view the symptoms—the dysfunctional pattern—as the problem to be addressed. Goal alignment involves discussion and negotiation. All theorists agree that the goals sought may be refined, elaborated, and changed as therapy proceeds.

Some approaches distinguish between general and specific goals. Some assume that general goals are the same for all clients: to overcome unbearable ideas (PT), to alter faulty object relations or selfobject patterns or maladaptive transaction cycles (ISCT), to change dysfunctional habits (BT), to alter irrational beliefs or dysfunctional schemas (CT), to change core interpersonal schemas, BASIC I.D.s, vicious cycles or dysfunctional narratives (EIT), to facilitate operation of self-actualization processes (HT), or teach needed social and communicative skills (CBST). The specific content and organization of each client's patterns will differ, even though the general form of the problem is the same. Specific goals represent each client's unique personal patterns, and clients must be relied upon to identify them.

Teaching a Schema for How to Be a Client

Most of these theorists recommend providing clear instructions to clients before therapy begins about the rationale for the kind of therapy to be provided, and about client and therapist roles and responsibilities. Discussing explicit rules about how to behave can reassure clients that they are capable of doing what is expected; this discussion can also serve as a form of skill training for clients about how to perform their roles. In our comparative framework, such instruction is aimed at creating an initial client schema for guiding clients' functioning in therapy behavior episodes. If that is not done, clients resort to using an interpersonal schema they have already learned, such as the schema they use with their medical doctor or religious adviser. These schemas may be inappropriate to the psychotherapeutic task.

The content of the instruction is designed to teach behavior episode schemas that reflect differences among approaches in therapists' theoretical and procedural models. For example, clients may be taught the "fundamental rule" of free association and the necessity of "complete honesty;" (PT; ISCT—psychoanalytic forms). The idea that people are "self-changers," and the value of "openness to experience" for that process may be explained (HT). The dynamics of the learning process, and how that will be used in designing therapeutic learning episodes may be stressed (BT). The role of irrational beliefs or faulty schemas in creating clients' problems, and the importance of being candid about one self, trusting the therapist, and being open to therapists' information, advice, and suggestions may be discussed (CT). The role of interpersonal and communicative skills in social relations, and the way clients will be helped to learn new skills may be explained (CBST).

The initial schema that clients are taught will exert selective influences on what they do, on how they interpret their problems and behavior, and on what their expectations and interpretations are for therapists' behavior. Some (e.g., EIT—constructivists) argue that therapy clients need some rationale for understanding and organizing their experiences, beliefs, and actions, and that there is no objectively correct rationale. Any rationale, whether it is psychoanalytic, humanistic, cognitive, behavioral, or constructivist, may do as long as it "works" for the client. Others, (e.g., PT; ISCT; BT; CT—Ellis) assume that their theoretical model does provide the correct rationale. The therapist's style in defining the context and preparing the client for therapy is a key first step in constructing a therapeutic relationship.

Strategies of Social Influence: Creating and Maintaining a Therapeutic Relationship

Freud (PT) considered the psychotherapeutic relationship to be of basic importance because it performs two important functions, which he called *natural positive transference* and pathological *negative and erotic transference*. He described natural positive transference as creating and maintaining clients' motivation for participating in and enduring the therapy process until the process itself yields consequences that are themselves rewarding and motivating. Our analyses reveal that all contemporary therapy theorists agree with Freud about this motivational function, but use different terms—such as "real relationship," "therapeutic alliance," and "authentic relationship."

Freud (PT) described pathological transference as clients' inappropriate transferral to analysts of their childhood interpersonal habits related to their parents. When this happens, the analyst can observe and try to change those childhood-based habits while they are presently occurring in real-life behavior episodes of the therapy relationship. We found that many contemporary theories use other versions of this general idea—that the therapy relationship provides real-life interpersonal behavior episodes through which relearning or new learning of habitual interpersonal patterns can occur. Both the motivational and learning functions of psychotherapeutic relationships are analyzed.

Strategies for Using the Psychotherapy Relationship to Motivate Clients

Therapy is a daunting experience and task. For a person to admit that he or she needs such help is often experienced as an admission of personal failure, incompetence, and loss of personal control of his or her life. The process of revealing private thoughts, feelings, and past actions about which a person feels ashamed or guilty is embarrassing. The process may activate distressing thoughts and affective states. Becoming aware of and admitting that cherished and self-protective habits are dysfunctional and should be changed is threatening and distressing. Not knowing what to do instead may create a sense of helplessness and fear. Changing those habits is demanding work and may often be discouraging until payoffs begin to appear. These are among the reasons that therapy clients have been unable to resolve their concerns on their own. The motivational nature of a positive psychotherapeutic relationship is considered by all therapists to be the key reason clients are able to enter, persist in, and endure psychotherapy. It provides "the soil" that enables techniques to "take root" (EIT—Lazarus). It provides a "holding environment" while patients resolve their problems (ISCT—psychoanalysts). Extensive empirical evidence indicates that a positive therapeutic alliance is the strongest predictor of therapeutic outcomes (Binder & Strupp, 1997). Some theorists describe the relationship as one of social influence, and draw propositions and evidence from social psychology about processes of social influence. Clients' motivation and therapists' social influence appear to be two sides of the same coin. What are those properties?

Our comparative framework uses the integrative motivational systems theory (M. Ford, 1992) as a model of motivational processes. The concept of motivation represents the combined functioning of directive and regulatory processes: Every pattern of motivation combines some kind of emotion, personal goals, and personal agency beliefs. These three components must function as a "team" for effective motivation to exist. If they conflict, motivation is ineffective.

Our framework defines *personal goals* as cognitive representations of potential future conditions the person considers desirable; they give selective direction to behavior. The framework identifies a limited number of different kinds of *emotions*, each of which facilitates a prototypical pattern of action. Some—curiosity, interest, hope, affection, love, sexual excitement—prototypically lead to exploratory, approach, or affiliative behaviors. Some—anger, resentment, disgust—lead to competitive, rejecting, or aggressive behaviors. Some—fear, embarrassment, guilt, shame, depression—lead to withdrawal or avoidance behaviors. There are two kinds of *personal agency beliefs: Capability beliefs* are the clients' assumptions about their competence to pursue a particular goal; *context beliefs* are assumptions about the extent to which they believe the context will support or be responsive to their efforts. People typically won't pursue a goal, despite its desirability, unless (1) they consider the emotions in that motivational pattern to be positive—they won't try if they are too embarrassed, frightened, or resentful; (2) they think they are capable of pursuing the goal; and (3) they believe that if they try, the context will be responsive.

All theorists describe the motivational properties of psychotherapeutic relationships in terms similar to those in our comparative framework. Their emphasis on clarity and agreement about the goals of therapy was discussed earlier. They stress positive emotions as the second element. Their models of dysfunctional behavior typically propose that negative emotions, such as anger, guilt, or fear, play a key role. Controlling those emotions, particularly fear or anxiety, is considered a prerequisite to changing dysfunctional patterns, and a positive psychotherapeutic relationship is the primary strategy for accomplishing that process subgoal.

Because positive and negative emotions cannot occur simultaneously, activating positive emotions in the relationship inhibits negative emotions and the avoidance and antagonistic behaviors they activate (ISCT; HT; BT; CT; CBST; EIT). The presence of positive emotions increases clients' "openness" and "willingness to explore" their experiences, (HT); facilitates "willingness to try new behaviors" (BT); reduces chances of "resistance" and "noncompliance" (PT; ISCT; CT); increases therapists' "prosocial potency" as a "model" and "reinforcer" (CBST); increases therapists' "social influence" (EIT—Beutler; Lazarus); makes clients feel "safe" (all); increases their "trust" that therapists will not hurt them and will try to be helpful, and facilitates learning (all). Therapists cultivate positive emotions and inhibit negative ones in many ways, described by various theorists as being honest, neutral, nonevaluative, empathically communicative, warm, caring, calm, and genuine; by avoiding actions that make clients feel threatened, misunderstood, rejected, criticized, and inadequate. Guerney's (CBST) explicit strategies and tactics for effective interpersonal communication are useful tools for therapists-in-training to learn.

The third motivational component, capability and context personal agency beliefs, are implied in their descriptions. Positive capability beliefs are cultivated when therapists are nonevaluative, display respect and unconditional positive regard and acceptance, are collaborative and nonmanipulative rather than authoritarian, and listen attentively and take concerns seriously. Clients' belief in their capability is increased by therapists' minimizing the impression that they seek to impose their own ideas and values, by explicitly expressing confidence in clients' ability to succeed in therapy, and by providing explicit training in skills clients can use. Cultivation of positive context beliefs appears in statements like these: Clients must have faith in their therapist; competent performance elicits confidence in the therapist's expertise; therapists' demonstrations of skill in explaining therapy and preparing clients for it, in accurately understanding their concerns and clearly communicating that understanding to them, and in conducting therapy sessions cultivates belief in the therapist's expertise and confidence that therapy will be helpful and not hurtful.

Creation of a motivating relationship begins with the first contact—and perhaps before, based on therapists' public reputation; it continues throughout therapy. The first sessions are critical, as first impressions shape the client's initial behavior episode schema, but therapy's ups and downs require continual maintenance and strengthening of this motivating relationship. Recurrent ruptures in the relationship inevitably occur, typically as a function of client-therapist transactions involving covert or overt hostile sentiments and behavior. Evidence indicates that most therapists have great difficulty dealing with this "negative therapeutic process," which is a major obstacle to effective treatment (Binder & Strupp, 1997).

Psychotherapy is an intense, intimate, two-person system involving both clients' and therapists' motivations. Several theorists warn that therapists must guard against evolvement of a relationship that is too personal; this can result when the therapist is too sympathetic, caring, supportive, or affectionate, and when he or she uses the relationship to serve personal needs—a phenomenon called countertransference by psychoanalysts. Open discussion of recurrent, thematic relationship issues, called metacommunication, appears to be the most effective way of overcoming relationship ruptures (Kiesler, 1996), but training therapists to do this effectively is very difficult (Binder & Strupp, 1997). Even so, effective psychotherapy requires more than the comforting support of a good "friendship," or a "caring relationship" (EIT—Beutler).

Using the Therapy Relationship for Learning Episodes
Theorists propose two ways in which the therapy relationship provides interpersonal behavior episodes through which clients can learn or alter functional patterns. One way assumes that clients may be using dysfunctional interpersonal habits learned earlier in life to relate to their therapist, thereby making those faulty habits accessible to change in therapy episodes. Some use the concept of transference (PT; ISCT—psychoanalysts; IET—Wachtel). However, most reject Freud's (PT) instinctually based formulation and broaden the meaning to refer to all kinds of learned interpersonal habits, such as "object relations" or "selfobject" patterns. Others use different terminology but with similar meaning. For example, clients' "prototaxic distortions" or "maladaptive transaction cycles" (ISCT—Sullivan; Kiesler), or "core interpersonal schemas" or "vicious cycles" (EIT—Beitman; Wachtel) may become manifest in therapy sessions, and thereby become available for modification.

The second way the therapy relationship can provide interpersonal opportunities for learning functional patterns relies on the rationale of social modeling. Clients are assumed to learn better patterns of functioning by observing and imitating functional patterns the therapist consistently uses with them. For example, analysts provide patients a model of "good parental functioning" so that the patient can experience the analyst as a "primary object" and can relearn better "object relations" or "selfobject" patterns, (ISCT—psychoanalysts); clients "assimilate" or "introject" therapists' modes of functioning (HT); the therapist teaches and models the preferred empirically-based "analytic" or "problem solving" strategy to enable clients to learn to use it (CT); therapists model a process of behavioral analysis and modification that clients can emulate in their daily lives (BT); "trainers" model social skills in their relations with "trainees" (CBST).

Strategies of Awareness and Understanding: Identifying Patterns to Be Altered

Selective Attention: Awareness and Conscious Control of Functional Patterns
Our comparative framework proposes that feedback signals provide the contents of consciousness that enable people to monitor and regulate their functioning intentionally. Feedforward signals enable people to proactively organize their functioning in anticipation of what may occur and what they want to occur. Selective attention is assumed to be the psychological process by which feedback and feedforward signals are identified and organized.

All these theorists agree that to be aware of and to consciously control all aspects of one's functional patterns whenever needed is a cornerstone of psychological health, behavioral effectiveness, and new learning. Explicitly or implicitly, they consider the avenue to awareness and conscious control of habitual patterns to be focusing attention on the patterns as they are taking place; they concur that a pattern can be altered only while it is occurring. Thus, all therapists have strategies and methods to help clients activate relevant patterns during therapy so that clients can become aware of them; by examining these patterns with a therapist, clients can come to understand their nature and operation: (e.g., "where id was, ego should be," PT—Freud); clients should shift from "automatic processing" to "consciously controlled processing" (EIT—Kanfer).

These theorists propose a diversity of methods for selectively influencing the direction of clients' attention during therapy sessions. Some focus attention on a part of their current dialogue using various methods: restatement of content, reflection of feeling, noting gestural events such as body posture, asking questions, (e.g. "What were you feeling when you said that?"), noting gaps in or topics not included in the current dialogue, summarizing an understanding of what the client has been saying, and sharing their subjective reactions to the current dialogue. Some therapists selectively focus on remembering or anticipating events, such as asking the client to recall past behavior episodes with significant others (e.g., "What happens when . . . ?"), or asking the client to imagine future events (e.g., "What do you think would happen if . . . ?"). Some focus on predictive or causal contingencies between certain events, such as different parts of clients' own patterns (e.g., "Have you noticed that when you talk about . . . you typically feel . . . ?"), or their actions and the reactions of others (e.g., "It seems that when you . . . they usually respond by . . ."). Some focus on underlying themes or meanings with explanatory or interpretive statements (e.g., "You seem to love and hate your mother at the same time, and this results in contradictory and confusing feelings and actions"). Therapists' conceptual and propositional models and therapeutic goals differ in what they consider important; therefore, therapists differ in where they choose to direct clients' attention and how they choose to do it.

Attention cannot be focused on something, however, unless that something is occurring, and psychotherapy targets only some parts of a person's behavioral repertoire. Strategies and tactics are needed for identifying and agreeing about the relevant patterns to which attention should be directed. The theorists we analyzed propose two broad types of strategies and methods for identifying dysfunctional patterns. We call these *functional analysis* and *therapy process* strategies. As our analysis indicates that their theories of functional and dysfunctional development are fragmented and incomplete, and identification of dysfunctional patterns implicitly relies on assumptions about functional and dysfunctional development, it is not surprising to find that their proposals about how to identify clients' dysfunctional patterns tend to be equally sketchy.

Functional Analysis Strategies
The purpose of functional analysis is to enable clients and their therapists to explicitly identify and reach agreement about the dysfunctional patterns to be changed or the new patterns needed, so that efforts to alter or learn them can be targeted efficiently.

Two types of functional analyses are proposed: normative diagnosis and idiographic diagnosis. The version borrowed from physicians we call *normative diagnosis*. Its rationale is based on two assumptions: (1) Different kinds of problems result from different causes; removing the cause will eliminate the problem. (2) There is a set of symptoms—events clients can observe and report about themselves—and signs—events physicians can observe through clinical examination and test procedures—that manifest each kind of problem; this set is called a *syndrome*. By identifying the syndrome, a therapist can infer the etiology and prescribe appropriate treatment. This normative approach is currently applied in psychotherapy through a tool called the *Diagnostic and Statistical Manual of Mental Disorders* (APA, 1994), which is an agreed-on classification system, created primarily by psychiatrists, for syndrome descriptions of diverse psychological/behavioral disorders.

A syndrome is a normative description of a set of characteristics a group of patients have been observed to share. No person's pattern exactly matches the prototypic descriptions because people differ somewhat in the symptoms and signs different antecedents will produce. To decide that a patient's condition is an example of one of the diagnostic categories, a patient must be judged to have many, but need not have all, of the normative indicators defining that category. It is a *polythetic* classification system. Each syndrome includes signs and symptoms that also appear in other syndromes, so any patient's pattern may partially match several syndromes. Thus, individual differences in the ways "illnesses" are manifested, and the possibility that there may be multiple problems and causes operating simultaneously makes reliable diagnosis difficult. We call this a *normative diagnosis* because it involves matching a patient's specific pattern to a prototypical pattern or norm.

None of the theorists analyzed relies primarily on the use of normative diagnoses. A few consider it useful for identifying the "general form of the problem domain" and for providing "clues" about the nature of clients' problems (e.g., CT—Beck). Many consider it of no value, and use what we call *idiographic diagnosis;* they call it *functional* or *behavioral analysis* (BT; CT; CBST; ISCT—Kiesler; EIT [except constructivists]). This idiographic approach seeks to identify precisely the unique content and organization of clients' dysfunctional patterns, where and when they occur, and their dynamics, i.e. what activates and maintains them, such as their maladaptive transaction cycles (ISCT—Kiesler), irrational beliefs (CT—Ellis), faulty schemas (CT—Beck), vicious cycles (EIT—Wachtel), BASIC I.D. (EIT—Lazarus), skill deficits (CBST), or dysfunctional behavior patterns (BT). Some give the product of their functional analysis a name, e.g. modality profile (EIT—Lazarus); S-O-R-K-C formula (EIT—Kanfer); A(ntecedent)—B(ehavior)—C(onsequence) pattern (CT—Ellis)

All treat this analysis as a multimethod, collaborative task. They rely heavily on clients' therapy interview reports, supplemented by additional methods that may be helpful, such as checklists, questionnaires, self-monitoring procedures, personal journals, direct observation, and reports from others. A number of therapists have created assessment tools that fit their specific approach (e.g., CT—Beck; Ellis; EIT—Lazarus). Some provide detailed guidelines for the process (e.g., EIT—Kanfer & Schefft). The general strategy is to examine multiple kinds of information, representing multiple behavior episodes, for recurrent themes or patterns. Their belief is that with a shared view of the patterns to be altered or changed, client and therapist can work together most efficiently and effectively. While most propose that a functional analysis should be accomplished in the initial therapy sessions, they recognize that it may need to be altered or elaborated as therapy proceeds.

Therapy Process Strategies

The subset of theorists who use therapy process strategies do not consider diagnosis or functional analysis essential to treatment for at least four reasons. Some assert that traditional diagnostic categories are so general and vague as to be useless in understanding and helping individual clients; people are unique and cannot be "pigeonholed." Others consider diagnosis unnecessary because the problem is already known: Their theories assert that the general underlying nature of clients' difficulties is the same for all, though the day-to-day manifestations are unique to each person. For example, they have unbearable intrapsychic oedipal conflicts (PT), faulty object relations or selfobject constructs (ISCT—analysts), inadequate core structures or narratives (EIT—constructivists), or maladaptive processes of living (HT). If all clients demonstrate the same problem, no diagnosis is needed; if all clients are to receive the same treatment, no prescription is required. For some, a primary focus of therapy is not on specific dysfunctional patterns but on facilitating innate self-organizing and self-constructing processes that the person can then use to solve his or her own problems (HT; ISCT—analysts; EIT—constructivists). Some reject diagnosis on philosophical grounds, saying it treats humans as "objects" rather than as unique, self-directing persons (HT).

The ultimate goal of process oriented therapies is for clients to become self-directing and self-regulating so they can pilot their own ship on the sea of life with confidence and competence. The process by which therapy is conducted is believed to play a key role in cultivating those capabilities, so it should be one of self-exploration and self-discovery by the client, with therapists assisting in the process by providing a "holding environment" (ISCT—analysts), or serving as "collaborators" or "co-constructionists" (HT; EIT—constructivists). The focus is on clients' subjective experiences, the way clients interpret these experiences, or the meanings they attribute to them.

Achieving an understanding of clients' subjective states requires therapists to project themselves into the inner life of the client, a condition called *empathic understanding*. Therapists also enrich their knowledge of the client with their observations of their own subjective reactions resulting from their transactions with the client. By openly communicating their subjective interpretations, client and therapist can reach a shared understanding of the client's patterns, a phenomenon sometimes called intersubjectivity—an understanding formed at the interface of "reciprocally interacting" worlds of experience (EIT—constructivists; HT; ISCT—analysts). Specific problems are identified and addressed as a natural part of the client's becoming more effectively self-constructing, self-directing, and self-regulating. A diagnostic attitude conflicts with the goal of putting clients in charge and of understanding the dynamics of their subjective patterns because it encourages a dependent relationship on an "expert" and an "objective" rather than a "subjective" perspective.

The Limitations of Normative Diagnosis

Why do all these theorists reject or minimize the utility of a normative diagnostic strategy? We suggest two possible reasons. They do not believe the implicit mechanistic metaphysical model underlying it corresponds with the nature of humans as they observe them. For example, traditional normative diagnosis is based on a typological rationale. It implicitly assumes that if different people display a similar functional pattern or syndrome, it must have developed from similar antecedents; similar patterns follow similar developmental pathways—etiologies and prognoses—even though the *DSM* manuals deny that they use that assumption. Where that assumption holds, traditional diagnostic strategies can be very useful.

Most theories we examined assume that learning is the basis of clients' difficulties as well as the development of new patterns, and that learning is primarily a self-constructing rather than a reactive process. Theoretically, this assumption implies that people may construct different patterns from similar experiences, and similar patterns from different experiences. For example, contemporary behavioral genetics teaches that even when there may be a genetic vulnerability to some type of dysfunction—such as alcoholism—the developmental influence of that genetic characteristic will vary with the context in which the gene's influence operates; not everyone with a genetic vulnerability for alcoholism will develop that pattern. There is much scientific evidence about learning and developmental processes indicating that people do arrive at similar developmental outcomes though they start from different backgrounds and follow different developmental pathways. Also, they may arrive at different outcomes though they have similar starting points.

Therefore, it may be an error to assume that when clients have similar dysfunctional patterns the causes are the same and require the same treatment. The way any learning experience, such as a behavior episode, may affect a person will be a function of that person's state at the moment, and of the nature of his or her self-constructing, self-organizing, self-directing, and self-regulating habits at the time. It follows that to design learning experiences that will be effective for any person requires knowledge of the person's current states, patterns, and dynamics. These can vary between people, and for the same person from one occasion to the next. This may be the principle reason why most of these theorists rely primarily on their detailed understanding of each client to guide their treatment decisions.

A second reason, suggested by a clinician-scholar who has studied diagnostic issues extensively over a 50-year career, is that the typological approach used in the *DSM* diagnostic categories does not fit the phenomena of concern. Available evidence makes it doubtful that there are many genuine "types, taxa, or disease entities" in psychopathology (Meehl, 1997).

Utility in Combining Normative and Idiographic Diagnosis
But, here as elsewhere, we believe that an either-or stance is self-defeating. Combining these two should be possible and of value. People display both differences and similarities, and knowledge of both can be useful. Although individual differences are extensive, similarities also exist. Therefore, although a great diversity of dysfunctional patterns is possible, there is not an infinite number. All developmental possibilities are constrained by a shared evolutionary history that has produced a shared basic group of structures, functions, and patterns of organization, and their development occurs in a shared terrestrial and social environment.

For example, in terms of learning outcomes, there is extensive evidence that people with similar heritage, who develop in similar subcultures, use the same language, and perhaps have the same biological limitations or defects, are likely to construct some similarities in functional patterns; their social values; styles of communication, grooming, and diet; self-appraisals; depressive states will probably be similar. That premise underlies recent efforts to tailor psychotherapy to subpopulations whose members are thought to share similar experiences, perspectives, and problems; (examples are feminist therapies and therapies for groups sharing racial or ethnic backgrounds, as well as treatment for phobias, depression, or panic attacks).

So, normative representations of different kinds of protypical dysfunctional patterns may have some value if they have demonstrated utility in representing important subgroups of prototypical patterns, and if they can help guide the design of relevant interventions and learning experiences. Meehl (1997) suggests that this may require a different diagnostic model—a shift from a typological to a dimensional model. We suggest that an important starting point is to create a clear theory of normal, functional development as a reference frame, such as our comparative framework. Such a theory would help ensure that no significant aspect of a person would be overlooked by a therapist trying to understand the person's dysfunctional patterns. The theory would provide information about the multiple parts of the person toward which interventions might be directed. One of the strengths of the field of medicine is that physicians have a shared anatomical and physiological model of normal or functional human biological organization and development. Their diagnoses of biological dysfunctions—diseases, injury—refer to the aspects of that model that are not functioning normally.

Even so, normative understanding of the prototypical form of a type of dysfunctional pattern must be supplemented with idiographic understanding of the specific content and organization of each client's pattern; for example, phobias may be similar in form (i.e., a powerful fear avoidance pattern), but their eliciting conditions and specific kind of avoidance pattern may differ. As with any classification system, the viability and utility of diagnostic categories should be subject to empirical test. Until validated, classification systems should be used with caution because they hold the danger of stereotyping people and therefore of mistreating them.

In terms of learning processes, there is no evidence that the way people learn is unique to each person, even though what they learn may be. Therefore, assuming psychotherapy to be primarily a learning-based process and that learning always starts with what exists, it may be possible to construct normative learning arrangements for people who start with similar dynamic patterns and seek similar changes. Thus, idiographic diagnosis or functional analysis of the content and dynamics of clients' patterns might be used as a base for identifying some types of patterns for which normative learning conditions might be designed and evaluated. For example, functional analyses might reveal differences in depressive patterns for which different treatments or treatment combinations are warranted—such as environmental interventions like social support and photo therapy for some forms; social skill training for others; psychotherapy focused on cognitive changes for a third group; or medication and counseling for still others.

Developmental Origins Versus Current Dynamics

There is one basic difference among these theorists about the kinds of phenomena that should be subject to examination. Some (e.g., PT; ISCT—analysts; EIT—Guidano) assume that it is essential for clients to become aware of the developmental pathway that led to their current dysfunctional states, especially the influence of early childhood experiences. These therapists focus much of the remembering process on the clients' becoming aware of and understanding childhood developmental experiences, especially with parents; therapists' interpretive comments about current behavior are phrased in terms of that developmental view—for example, transference phenomena.

Others (e.g., HT; BT; CT; CBST; BMHT; most EIT) assert that therapy should focus on the current content and dynamics of such patterns. Change can occur without an understanding of the developmental origins of dysfunctional patterns. Therefore, these therapists focus attention on the nature of current experiences, on current life behavior episodes, and on the current functional utility that maintains clients' dysfunctional patterns. Discussion of developmental conditions is considered useful only if it helps clients understand the current content and dynamics of their dysfunctional patterns. Some therapists argue that "dwelling on the past" may function as an avoidance pattern for clients, keeping them from facing and dealing with the present.

It would be interesting to learn whether psychoanalysts could achieve equally satisfactory outcomes by interpreting transference phenomena primarily in terms of their current functional utility instead of early parent-child relationships, or whether the results achieved by others would be enhanced with the use of developmental explanations. The propositions about change processes in our comparative framework lead to the prediction that a focus on current dynamics and contexts would be the more efficient and effective strategy, and that historical developmental analyses would be useful only when they facilitate an understanding of here-and-now functioning.

STRATEGIES OF AWARENESS AND UNDERSTANDING: ACTIVATING RELEVANT PATTERNS

People cannot become aware of and understand something unless they can observe it, and they can observe it only when it is occurring. All these theorists we have examined propose strategies for activating relevant patterns to serve these objectives. In essence, there appear to be several versions of one broad strategy, with related tactics. The overall strategy is to activate a specific behavior episode in which the client participates in a way that is likely to manifest a relevant functional pattern. Terms like *exposure* and *transference* refer to this general process. We group the proposed strategies into five categories: Remembered or imagined behavior episodes, role-playing behavior episodes, socially modeled behavior episodes, therapist relationship behavior episodes, and real-life behavior episodes.

Remembered or Imagined Behavior Episodes

Relevant patterns are usually activated initially in verbal psychotherapy through remembered or imagined behavior episodes. Clients describe their concerns, and episodes of daily life that manifest those concerns (remembered episodes), or what they believe may happen in the future (imagined episodes). Therapists assume that in a facilitating therapeutic relationship, conscious, detailed discussion of a significant behavior episode will tend to re-activate all aspects of the pattern of functioning that occurred in that episode—what clients thought, said, and felt, and how they reacted to others.

One strategy, *free association* (PT), simply asks the client to report and dis-cuss honestly everything that comes to mind. The assumption is that all be-havior is organized and motivated, and that unconscious conflicts or trou-blesome interpersonal habits will gradually and spontaneously become activated and manifested both in the content of clients' statements and in the way clients relate to the analyst during therapy sessions. Relevant remem-bered or imagined behavior episodes—and dreams are a form of imagined episodes—will arise without prompting from the therapist. Directly asking for such episodes is not considered fruitful because "repression" and "defenses" obstruct the client's becoming aware of them. Analysts typically use direct questions sparingly, but use indication or notation (selectively drawing at-tention to something said or done) to facilitate client awareness of relevant as-sociations.

A second strategy is described as a shared process of search and self-discovery. Here the clients control the content and pace, but therapists col-laborate as "participant observers" to facilitate the clients' complete experi-encing and awareness. The strategy is called *targeted free association* (ISCT—analysts) and *dialogue* (HT). Unlike free association, this strategy uses the therapists to facilitate more complete activation of the person's experi-ences in relevant remembered or imagined behavior episodes. The therapists make responses that selectively direct clients' attention to aspects of their cur-rent statements, actions, or experiences. Illustrative methods are empathic re-flections ("You feel distressed"), exploratory questions ("Why do you suppose you feel that way?"), self-disclosure of clients' impacts ("As you described that situation I felt . . ."), and empathic confirmation to facilitate fuller ex-pression and understanding of forbidden experiences.

In a third strategy, therapists ask clients to describe relevant behavior episodes and may facilitate activation and awareness of the total pattern with methods such as probes, questions, reflections, and comments (BT; CT; CBST; EIT). Specific types of behavior episodes may be targeted. Therapists can fa-cilitate full and accurate recall by clients by teaching them self-monitoring skills and asking them to keep a record or diary of relevant behavior episodes that occur or that they remember between sessions. An example would be an episode in which the client began to experience a panic state. The therapist is seeking as detailed a description as possible so that therapist and client can understand the nature of the pattern, the behavior episode conditions that elicit it, and the consequences that follow.

Theorists agree that an intellectualized reconstruction is insufficient. For clients to reexperience an episode as they describe it is desirable, a form of remembering Freud called "repetition." Several types of *phenomenal experimentation,* (HT—Gestalt; Experiential) may be used to activate more fully all the ways a client experiences an episode. *Evocative and systematic evocative unfolding* encourages clients to reconstruct and reexperience an episode in detail. Phenomenal focusing asks clients to describe a behavior episode as if it were occurring at that moment. Imagining a frightening episode is one procedure for trying to desensitize a phobia (BT—Wolpe). Experiential focusing directs attention to subjective experiences occurring during a behavioral episode. Awareness of the prototypical pattern underlying similar episodes, such as the conditions that activate the fear pattern provides the basis for patient-therapist collaborative design and implementation of behavior episode experiences to alter the pattern.

Role-Playing Behavior Episodes
Sometimes simply describing a behavior episode is not sufficient to reactivate all parts of the pattern. Role playing an episode may help the client become more fully aware of and understand all aspects of the experience. For example, the *two-chair dialogue or enactment* or the *empty chair dialogue* both require the client to portray an imaginary interpersonal behavior episode by pretending he or she is one person and then the other in the interaction (HT). *Expressive exercises* involve "acting out" an emotional episode with some object. Client and therapist may role play an episode together, or a third party may be present to help with a role play. This method may be used to activate old patterns as well as new ones.

Socially Modeled Behavior Episodes
In the social modeling strategy, clients vicariously experience a behavior episode by watching someone else perform it. Discussion helps them become aware of and understand all facets of the experience. This strategy may be used with remembered, imagined, and role-playing behavior episodes (CBST).

Therapist Relationship Behavior Episodes
Therapy sessions are composed of a series of intimate, interpersonal behavior episodes. Patients have a long history of functioning in many other intimate interpersonal episodes, and for many patients, such real-life episodes are the source of their dysfunctional patterns. Thus, clients usually use previously learned, habitual, interpersonal behavior episode schemas to carry out their client-therapist interpersonal episodes. The psychoanalytic concept of

transference represents these as "as if" performances—that is, the patient behaves toward the analyst as if the therapist were the patient's parent. The
strategies of free association and neutrality are designed to keep the analyst
from actually behaving like such significant others in the patient's life, so
when the patient acts that way, it must be the result of his or her intrapsychic
conflicts rather than something the therapist has said or done. Thus, patients
activate in a current behavior episode a parent-child behavior pattern constructed early in life, creating conditions under which they might be able to
become aware of and understand that dysfunctional pattern.

Other theorists reject Freud's concept of transference as too narrow a view
of this significant process. They argue that the client-therapist relationship is
a real interpersonal relationship and that clients' therapy session behaviors
are a function of that real transaction. That is, the client's current goals, states,
and actions are in transaction with what the therapist says and does—a
person-in-context functional unit (ISCT; CT; EIT). Clients' interpersonal
habits function to have desired impacts on and to elicit desired responses
from others; therefore, therapists can understand clients' patterns by observing the clients' behavior and their own reactions in their interpersonal
transactions (e.g., ISCT—Kiesler). Thus, "transference reactions" aren't "as
if" performances, but are displays of clients' habitual ways of dealing with
interpersonal behavior episodes in their current lives. Clients use their habitual patterns to try to relate to the therapist, displaying their maladaptive
transaction cycles, vicious circles, dysfunctional schemas, BASIC I.D.s or irrational beliefs as they do so.

Thus, there is broad agreement among these theorists that therapy often involves two interrelated streams of behavior episodes—"a play within a play."
For example, while clients are talking about their concerns and describing
past or potential behavior episodes with significant others in their lives, they
are simultaneously behaving with a significant other—their therapist. Therapists must be alert to the fact that such simultaneous behavior episodes can
activate client functional patterns in a therapy session.

Therapists use various types of denotative, explanatory, or interpretive
communications to direct clients' attention to and to help clients understand
what they are doing and to see relationships among parts of the pattern, the
functions it is intended to serve, and the ways it is dysfunctional.

Real-Life Behavior Episodes

The most powerful circumstances for activating dysfunctional or potential
new patterns are those within which clients live their daily lives. The most
powerful elicitors are those real-life circumstances for which functional pat-

terns were constructed, and the most powerful modifying influences are the natural, real-life consequences of clients' actions. Some approaches use this real-life type of behavior episodes (e.g., BT; CT; CBST; BMHT; EIT). Sometimes, the therapist may accompany and observe a client as he or she performs a behavior episode in a real-life setting. However, direct participation by therapists is often not feasible. For this reason, the more frequently used strategy is called *homework*. Clients are instructed and sometimes trained with role-play behavior episodes to expose themselves to a particular kind of episode in a relevant real-life setting. They are taught to observe carefully and perhaps record what happens, including their thoughts and feelings, and to discuss these later with their therapist. This strategy is a powerful way to help clients become aware of and understand the nature of specific person-in-context functional patterns.

STRATEGIES OF CHANGE: LEARNING TO CONTROL OR ALTER RELEVANT PATTERNS

Generally, the theorists agree that awareness and understanding of faulty patterns, their origins, and how they influence current functioning (often called insight) is a necessary but not sufficient condition for change. If the process stops there, all clients have learned is a different way of thinking and talking about their concerns. This is the result when therapists focus on explaining clients' patterns to them at a time and in a way that doesn't stimulate change. All therapists agree, however, that therapeutic communication can create conditions for change. What, then, are those conditions?

Our Comparative Framework's Theory of Change Processes
Unitary functioning is essential if people are to exist, develop, and effectively transact with their contexts. Disruption of a functional pattern while it is occurring activates change processes to eliminate discrepancies produced by the disruption. Then, human's inherent self-organizing and self-constructing processes operate through negative and positive feedback and feedforward dynamics to restore unitary functioning.

People deal with disruptions in two ways. In the first, negative feedback-based *stability-maintaining processes* operate to overcome or prevent the disruption, thereby restoring or maintaining the original pattern. *Defense mechanisms* and *avoidance behaviors* are different ways people learn to maintain their stability; examples are by physically avoiding conditions that produce disrupting feedback signals, or ignoring or reinterpreting the disrupting feedback. Because humans are open systems, their functioning is continuously disrupted by transactions with their contexts, so stability-maintaining processes are essential for personal unity and continuity in a variable environment.

If maintaining stability were their only way of dealing with disruptions, people could never learn new adaptive patterns. Therefore, the second way people can deal with disruptions of existing patterns is through *incremental or transformational change processes* that help to restore unitary functioning. This restoration occurs when stability-maintaining processes are prevented from or are ineffective in overcoming the disruption and restoring the habitual steady-state pattern. When biological patterns are disrupted, the change process is called development, growth, or healing. When psychological/behavioral patterns are disrupted, the correction process is typically called learning.

What causes disruptions? *Primary disruptions* are caused when feedback signals are generated by current functioning in a specific context. For example, when a therapist conveys the message that a client is a respected, valued, competent person, this message can disrupt habits of negative self-evaluation and expectations of persistent failure. Paying attention to the causal links between their actions and those of others can disrupt clients' irrational beliefs or faulty interpersonal schemas. *Secondary disruptions* result when disrupting feedback leads to change in a component of a pattern; this could be a change in guiding goals, regulatory values, or physical capabilities. The change then disrupts habitual relationships among components of the pattern. For example, new values may make old action patterns unacceptable; a physical disability may leave a person unable to perform old action patterns; revised goals could require revised implementing strategies; a new skill might lead to altered self-efficacy beliefs; a change in context could require revision of activity patterns.

Disruption itself does not determine what kinds of changes may result. The change processes activated by disruptions always function to create organized patterns that restore unitary functioning; but there is no single way this can be done, so the outcome is unpredictable. The kinds of facilitating and constraining conditions operating in the ongoing behavior episode at the time of the disruption will determine whether the old pattern is maintained or an altered pattern is constructed. These conditions also determine the nature of any alterations that occur. For example, emotional states of fear, anger, or interest; anticipatory cognitions of hope or failure; or threatening or supportive environmental conditions facilitate and constrain different kinds of possibilities. Therefore, the kinds of changes that may occur can be influenced by shaping the behavior episode conditions operative when a disruption occurs. An example is behavior episode conditions that constrain fear and facilitate interest and hope as a means of altering a phobia.

Change processes always operate through specific behavior episodes. When people begin a new episode, previously learned prototypical patterns or schemas for functioning in that type of episode are activated to guide their functioning. In that sense, humans are creatures of habit. Those behavior episode schemas persist because they have some functional value for clients, even though they may be dysfunctional in some respects. Because the schemas are habitual, people are typically unaware at the time of their specific properties; they will, however, be aware of specific events that occur during the behavior episode if they attend to the event. If that schema, produces intended and desired consequences in that behavior episode, the habit works, the episode ends, and another begins. If unintended and unwanted consequences occur, however, these produce feedback signals that disrupt the guiding schema. Effective, well-adjusted people are then able to direct their attention to their guiding schema and relevant behavior episode conditions. They can become aware of and understand the functional pattern and the ways it is going awry in that context, and try changes they think may work. That is the way incremental change typically occurs.

The basic problem that brings people to psychotherapy is that they do not effectively use those self-constructing incremental change processes. Some of their significant habitual behavior episode schemas persistently produce disruptive undesired consequences and subjective distress, but the clients have been unable to resolve those disruptions satisfactorily. Instead, they protect the dysfunctional schemas with powerful stability-maintaining processes. They are unaware of the dysfunctional properties of their guiding behavior episode schemas and of the ways they persistently protect these schemas from change. These people only know they are ineffective, unhappy, and distressed, but they don't know why.

In our comparative framework, the key to conscious understanding and change lies in the nature of the feedback signals a person generates and pays attention to. Feedback signals representing current events and consequences of behavior are generated by direct selective perceptions of intraperson and person-in-context events. Feedback signals may also be generated by imagined or simulated behavior episodes, and that is a key part of what is called cognitive problem solving. Therefore, the key to facilitating people's conscious understanding of their functioning and to influencing changes in that functioning lies in affecting the content of the feedback signals available to people and to which they attend. That facilitation is accomplished in psychotherapy by the ways therapists act toward and communicate with their clients. Of course, clients influence therapists by the same means.

It follows that effective psychotherapy must (1) help clients become aware of and understand their dysfunctional behavior episode schemas, (2) disrupt the schemas while they are occurring in relevant behavior episodes, (3) provide facilitating and constraining conditions that channel change processes toward constructing more effective schemas, and (4) provide conditions that help clients make their altered or new schemas operate automatically as habits in real-life situations. Strategies and tactics for (1) were considered earlier; therapists' proposals about the others are considered next.

A Strategy for Disrupting Dysfunctional Patterns

The therapy theorists examined assume that disrupting an ongoing pattern in a current behavior episode creates conditions for change. Three methods are proposed to implement a disruption strategy. In all of these, the therapist or client must be aware of the content and dynamics of the dysfunctional pattern so that one or the other can guide recognition of conditions that are disruptive and the discrepancies these disruptions produce in the dysfunctional pattern. The first type assumes that clients must disrupt their own patterns by discovering discrepancies between how the pattern works and what the clients want (e.g., HT). Therapists using this method assume that when clients become fully aware and accepting of all aspects of their experience they will recognize unwanted discrepancies. Thus, the methods used are the same as those for facilitating awareness and understanding. All therapist comments are made in a "nonauthoritative manner" as "suggestions" or "possibilities" rather than "instructions" or "truths."

The second type includes comments, explanations, or interpretations made by the therapist to provide information and suggest meanings or feedback signals that contradict some aspect of the dysfunctional pattern. (PT; ISCT; CT; EIT—except constructivists). These signals may take many forms, but generally they focus on relationships among components of a pattern. They may be descriptive ("You say you believe this, but then you do that"; "Your words say . . . , but your body language and voice intonations convey . . . ."). They may be in question form ("How do you reconcile this with that?"). They may be explanatory, representing hypotheses about how the dysfunctional pattern operates to produce consequences the person does not want and to prevent consequences he or she does want, such as eliciting rejection and avoidance rather than acceptance and affection from a significant other). The signals may be direct disputations and confrontations ("Your mustabatory beliefs are irrational and self-defeating"). Evidence from clients' behavior may be summarized to increase the credibility of therapists' statements. Although different theorists propose different methods, there seems to be little evidence that one method is inherently better than any other. In general, the theorists suggest that methods be selected to fit the nature of the problem, the kinds of observational data available as evidence, clients' and therapists' characteristics and relationships, and the nature of therapy goals.

The third type of disruption strategy is effective when the pattern to be disrupted is being used to transact with the therapist—for example, transference—or is functioning in a learning behavior episode designed by the therapist—such as a controlled exposure. Every functional pattern or behavior episode schema is learned because it functions, within certain contingencies, to produce valued consequences. Therefore, it can be disrupted when it occurs by providing in the behavior episode predictive and causal contingencies and consequences that do not match those of the guiding behavior episode schema, thereby generating disruptive feedback signals. Kiesler (ISCT) calls these "noncomplementary" responses and metacommunications. In BT it is called "contingency management" using differential "cues" and "reinforcers"—predictive and causal contingencies and consequences. By "playing out" their faulty interpersonal pattern in their therapy relationship, clients can discover that it doesn't "end" the way their faulty pattern predicts (EIT—Beitman).

The three types of disruption strategies are often used in combination. For example, a therapist might start with guided self-discovery, and then use interpretation and contingency management methods to add credibility and to help the client experience the disruption more fully. There is broad agreement among therapists that this disruption must be a slow and cautious process. Premature, unskilled, or insensitive use of disruption strategies may simply activate and strengthen the stability-maintaining processes that perpetuate the dysfunctional pattern, thereby making therapeutic progress more difficult for the client. The accuracy of the therapist's interpretations, his or her phrasing, the extent of the phenomena encompassed, the frequency, and the necessity of linking the interpretations to real, here-and-now experience all influence their impact on patients.

Strategies for Channeling Change: Facilitating and Constraining Conditions
For humans, as complex systems, states of disorganization are unacceptable. Once organization becomes disrupted, people will do something to restore coherent organization, but different reorganizations are possible. There is no guarantee that a more adaptive state will emerge. People can get "worse" as well as "better." By providing selected facilitating and constraining conditions, therapists can influence the reorganization process toward states considered more desirable. To be effective, though, the interventions must be introduced when the disruption occurs, and during the resulting period of disorganization, which may last for a period of time. If the intervener waits until reorganization has occurred, obtaining the desired changes becomes much more difficult because the new pattern will now have to be disrupted

before change becomes possible. The change processes are the same for all disruptions but are more dramatically evident for extreme disruptions. For example, a severely distressed person may fall apart so to speak and reorganize into a dissociative state in order to control high level distress. Changing such dissociative patterns can be very difficult, but interventions at the point of disorganization—such as hospitalization, sedation, intense psychotherapy—can prevent a dysfunctional reorganization and facilitate an alternate resolution of the distress. That is the rationale underlying *crisis intervention*. Skillful therapists are careful to avoid creating disrupting conditions that provoke such crises.

These theorists agree that clients must become aware of the discrepancies in their functional pattern that results from the disrupting conditions, and they must consciously commit themselves to eliminating the discrepancies by learning a more functional pattern. The motivational and social influence aspects of the psychotherapy relationships are crucial at this point, and therapists may use their relationship-building methods to ensure adequate motivation. Disruption is distressing. The task of changing oneself can be threatening, so clients may "back off." To move forward, clients must be sufficiently confident that the effort is worthwhile, that they can do it, and that the therapist can be counted on to help them through the process. Notice the inclusion of all three components of motivation: goal commitment, supporting emotions, and positive personal agency beliefs.

Once the commitment is made, the issue becomes "What should I do?" The client is then in a problem-solving mode. In periods of transition after old patterns are disrupted, people will consider a greater diversity of possibilities than when they are in steady states, even if those steady states are dysfunctional. Four strategies are proposed by these theorists, ranging from "let the client do it" to prescriptive approaches.

Therapists who stress a process goal of helping clients become more effective "self-changers" (e.g. HT) explicitly avoid strategies and methods to influence the specific nature of the changes sought. Rather, they apply essentially the same strategies and methods used to facilitate client self-awareness and self-understanding to problem solving-content: They encourage clients to generate their own possibilities, to evaluate possibilities using their own criteria that result from the expanded self-understanding therapy has brought them, and to choose the ones they will try to implement. This strategy implicitly assumes that clients have the knowledge to identify and evaluate relevant potential courses of action and the skills to implement them, or that they will find the knowledge and learn the necessary skills.

Other strategies assume that enactive learning is necessary for clients to construct more satisfying alternative patterns. That means that clients can alter their dysfunctional patterns or learn new patterns only while they are performing them under behavior episode conditions that constrain less desirable and facilitate more desirable forms. Therapists using these strategies differ in the kinds of behavior episodes they use for this purpose and the kinds of facilitating and constraining conditions the episodes provide.

One group uses behavior episodes occurring in the therapy relationship as their change context. They assume that dysfunctional interpersonal patterns are the problem, and that clients will use those patterns to guide their interpersonal transactions with their therapists (e.g., PT; ISCT). They use two strategies to facilitate change. The first is interpretation, which they use to point out to the clients the inappropriateness of using those transferred patterns with the therapist, thereby pointing clients toward "more mature" possibilities. The second strategy is modeling. The therapists model alternate styles of interpersonal patterns in their actual relationship with clients; they avoid the behaviors of those people from whom the clients learned their dysfunctional patterns so as not to reinforce clients' transferred patterns. Such therapists emphasize that intellectual understanding is insufficient; it must be linked to "real experience" because it is only through his own experience and mishaps that a person learns "sense" (PT—Freud). Therefore, therapists should make interpretations only at points of "affective urgency" when anxiety is occurring during clients' transference relationship with the analysts (PT). Clients evaluate the utility of an interpretation in explaining their immediate experience and in guiding future experience, so the interpretation should be made when convincing examples of transference are occurring (ISCT). Once clients are aware of the dysfunctional nature of their transference patterns, they begin to consider alternatives and to try them in the safety of the therapy relationship. As they become more comfortable with using an alternate pattern with the analyst, analysts assume the clients will try that pattern outside therapy and discuss the results in therapy sessions.

The group that relies on idiographic diagnosis explicitly creates behavior episodes with facilitating and constraining conditions specific to the dynamics of each patient's dysfunctional patterns and aimed at altering these patterns in desired ways (e.g., BT; CT). These methods are typically called exposure strategies, of which systematic desensitization is an early example (BT—Wolpe). They use all the types of behavior episodes described earlier under activating strategies, but they include agreement with the client about alternate patterns to be learned, and predictive and causal contingencies to facilitate that learning. One such contingency is the rewarding social influence the therapist provides through positive feedback about clients' effort and progress. Clients may discover new behavior patterns through self-discovery (CT—Beck); they may also find new patterns by doing what the therapist tells them to do (CT—Ellis). Cognitive therapists often facilitate clients' cognitive restructuring by using such methods as cognitive rehearsal and imagery techniques, role playing, and modeling in the safety of therapy sessions before they encourage clients to try these behaviors in the real world. Desired changes may be facilitated by relaxation and imagery methods to control clients' emotions, graded exposure to a relevant range of contexts, encouragement, explanations, and skill training (EIT—Wachtel).

Some therapists use a prescriptive approach (CBST; BMHT). Once clients commit themselves to the need to learn alternate patterns, this group defines in detail preferred alternate patterns that have demonstrated utility for the kinds of daily life situations that clients must deal with, and the therapists provide a series of carefully designed and sequenced training episodes to teach those patterns, typically called skills. Trainers "prosocial potency" as "models" and "reinforcers" is a key contingency in influencing learning. Specific methods are used to provide feedback to trainees about their learning progress. An important motivator is the satisfaction trainees feel as they learn to perform the skills successfully and discover the utility of these skills in dealing with social situations important to the trainees.

All the theorists agree that learning altered or new patterns is a lengthy process. Pathological habits are particularly hard to change because they have some utility, even though they are dysfunctional for other purposes. Therefore, one interpretation is insufficient, no matter how accurate, and many repeated episodes are necessary to produce the desired learning, called *working through.* Observational learning can produce a preliminary understanding about how to perform a skill—a behavior episode schema—but only enactive practice can link the schema to actual performance skill (CBST). So, repeated practice of an altered or new pattern is proposed as essential for consolidating the learning and active use of such patterns.

Practice, however, is useful only if it produces feedback signals that facilitate progress in learning the new pattern and confirm its effectiveness in producing desired consequences. Thus, part of the art of psychotherapy is to ensure that the "right" feedback occurs at the "right" time. Some, (e.g., CBST) may even try to influence or select real-life contexts that are highly likely to provide the right feedback conditions. Guerney's (CBST) methods for training husbands and wives to communicate with each other in ways that facilitate their marital relationship illustrates this method. These training methods are illustrative of the importance of right feedback–right time conditions. Different theorists emphasize practice in different kinds and combinations of be-havior episodes—such as imagined episodes, role-play episodes, or behavior episodes that simulate real-life situations. Some use transactional behavior episodes—such as transference episodes—with therapists as well as real-life behavior episodes. Throughout this process of learning and practice, the mo-tivating function of a positive client-therapist relationship plays a crucial role in facilitating clients' persistence of effort, particularly when difficulties and setbacks occur.

STRATEGIES FOR PERPETUATING CHANGES: GENERALIZATION TO AND MAINTENANCE IN DAILY LIFE

Generalization refers to the use of patterns learned in therapy in real-life be-havior episodes. *Maintenance* means persistence in the use of those patterns after therapy terminates. Some approaches do not propose specific strategies and methods for facilitating generalization and maintenance; instead, thera-pists assume that clients will naturally begin to apply changes they learn dur-ing therapy sessions in their daily life (e.g., PT; ISCT; HT). The clients of such therapists may report and discuss with the therapist efforts they have made to apply their new understandings in real-life episodes, and such discussions may facilitate generalization. Some propose that occasional follow-up ses-sions are useful in facilitating maintenance.

Other therapists point to the evidence that in-session changes often do not generalize to or persist in clients' real-life behavior episodes (e.g., BT; CT; CBST; some EIT). They propose strategies and methods for facilitating both generalization and maintenance. Goldstein (CBST) has created strategies and methods, based on basic principles for facilitating generalization and maintenance abstracted from learning and social psychology theory and re-search, that encompass those proposed by all the other therapists. To facil-itate generalization, he proposes teaching clients basic principles to help ensure cognitively mediated transfer, having clients overlearn to increase the availability of responses, encouraging practice in varied types of be-havior episodes, using identical elements in practice and in real-life behav-ior episodes, and practicing sequential modification. Ways of facilitating maintenance are thinning and delay of reinforcement, fading of prompts, preparing clients for occasional failure in their real-life contexts, follow-up booster sessions after termination, using reinforcers during training like those operative in the daily environment, programming for reinforcement by significant others in the daily environment, and recruiting supportive models.

EVALUATING CLIENT PROGRESS DURING THERAPY, AND THERAPY TERMINATION

The purpose of psychotherapy is to help people change, but only some changes are judged desirable—that represent progress. Evaluation of change requires a comparison of clients' *initial dysfunctional patterns* when they entered therapy with their *current pattern* at the time of evaluation. At the start of therapy, the two are the same. If the two become different, change has occurred. Evaluation of progress requires criteria for judging whether that change is desirable. The criteria should be the therapeutic goals or outcomes on which client and therapist have agreed; these should be formulated as a description of the *preferred pattern*. A decision that therapy has been completed relies on comparisons of the dysfunctional, current, and preferred patterns. Effective psychotherapy is occurring when it increases the difference between clients' initial dysfunctional pattern and their current pattern and (2) it decreases the difference between their current and preferred patterns (that is, the change is in the desired direction). In evaluating clients' progress, it is important to realize that clients can get "worse" as well as "better."

The adage that you can't compare apples with oranges is applicable to the issue of evaluation. For example, comparing clients' *interpersonal style* at the beginning of therapy with their *employment status* at therapy termination would be an inappropriate basis for judging therapeutic benefit; the content compared should be the same: Interpersonal or employment patterns should be compared with themselves on different occasions. It is not practical to try to create descriptions of patterns that define the status of every biological, psychological, behavioral and contextual aspect of the patterns. Therefore, descriptions of dysfunctional, current and preferred patterns must be selective, limited to those variables considered salient, significant, and pertinent to the purposes at hand—evaluation. For example, a client and therapist might be interested in changes in distressing emotions but not changes in client's eating habits. For every dysfunctional pattern targeted for change, there should be a comparable preferred pattern (therapy goal) so that legitimate comparisons can be made. If additional dysfunctional patterns become targeted as therapy proceeds, then additional preferred patterns or therapy goals must also be formulated. The variables considered important and relevant for inclusion in descriptions of dysfunctional and preferred patterns may differ because of differences in therapists' guiding theories. For example, some therapists (e.g., PT; EIT—constructivists) will emphasize extensive personality change; some (e.g., CT; HT) will stress psychological change; and some (e.g., BT; CBST) will focus on behavioral change.

Carefully prepared descriptions of initial dysfunctional patterns and preferred patterns to be sought are sometimes called case formulations. A case formulation organizes extensive and often contradictory information about a client to help guide choice, use and timing of intervention strategies and tactics (Ellis, 1997).

The usefulness of evaluative comparisons will depend on the clarity of the pattern descriptions. If the description of a dysfunctional pattern is vague or absent, comparing it with a later version of that same pattern to evaluate change will be difficult or impossible. Similarly, if the description of the preferred pattern or therapy goals is vague, absent, or different in type from the dysfunctional description, comparisons relevant to evaluation of progress will be difficult or impossible. Without a clear specification of the patterns to be compared, clients and therapists are free to attribute any change, including serendipitous ones, to the effects of therapy. Evaluating progress during therapy and making therapy termination decisions are typically considered related and to be collaborative actions, with clients playing the leading role because only they have direct knowledge of their psychological functioning and behavioral effectiveness outside therapy. Because clients are expected to play a key role in evaluating their progress and deciding when to end therapy, they as well as the therapist must understand clearly the descriptions of the dysfunctional and preferred patterns and the strategies and methods for evaluating change and progress. There is consensus among therapy theorists that agreement about therapeutic goals is an important part of the therapeutic alliance, but few are explicit about the form in which therapy goals—preferred pattern descriptions—should be stated. Examples are used, but they are usually vague and generalized. They seldom include context components. For example, a typical description would be "reduce anxiety" rather than the context-specific "reduce the frequency and intensity of anxiety when involved in a sexual encounter with spouse." The theorists also agree that therapists make moment-to-moment and session-to-session decisions about strategies and tactics, based on how therapy is progressing. This decision-making pattern implies the use of multiple judgments about relationships among dysfunctional, current, and preferred patterns.

These theorists differ, however, in their willingness to be explicit about the dysfunctional pattern. Those who advocate a functional analytic strategy seek patient-therapist agreement about an explicit description of dysfunctional patterns whose content they expect to be unique for each patient (idiographic diagnosis). A few assert that the form of an initial state description—a normative diagnosis—may be similar for different clients, as with phobic patterns; the contents, however, will be unique. A few (e.g., CS—Beck; BT—Wolpe) propose that the *general form* of the dysfunctional description may be similar for different clients (like a normative diagnosis), but that the specific *content* will be unique for each client. Some specify a general form for describing the clients' dysfunctional patterns—such as the BASIC I.D. (EIT—Lazarus) or an A-B-C analysis (CT—Ellis). Even so, these therapists often do not link that dysfunctional description to the form used for their description of preferred patterns or therapy goals. The explicitness of the dysfunctional and preferred state pattern, however, facilitates evaluative judgments. For example, Wolpe (BT) might describe a preferred pattern as a decline in the fear experienced and avoidance behaviors displayed in phobic situations representative of the dysfunctional pattern he is trying to change. CBST therapists might specify increased proficiency in performing the skills being taught. Both these are descriptions of preferred patterns that can be explicitly observed by clients and therapists.

Those advocating a *therapy process strategy* explicitly reject both idiographic and normative diagnoses. However, they assert the importance of therapy goals, a position implying that there is a state that is unsatisfactory to the client. Because they emphasize cultivating client self-direction and self-construction, they imply that each client's initial state is somehow inadequate. Evaluating progress would be facilitated if these therapists helped clients explicitly formulate both the dysfunctional pattern description ("What don't you like about your current state?") and the preferred pattern description ("How would you like to be?") in terms of the "processes of living" variables they stress, as a framework for evaluative judgments.

Some theorists (e.g., PT; EIT—Guidano) advocate "personality reorganization" and suggest that the form of that reorganization will emerge only as therapy proceeds. Therefore, they cannot specify in advance the nature of the preferred pattern—the reorganized personality. They consider initial dysfunctional states to be symptomatic of an underlying dysfunctional personality, so a focus on eliminating symptoms is not considered useful. How, then, can clients judge whether they are making progress toward or have achieved that goal? These therapists' answer seems to be, "They will know." If there are symptoms that manifest an "underlying dysfunctional personality," then there should be other characteristics that manifest an "underlying functional personality." Therefore, these theorists should at least be able to formulate descriptions of the dysfunctional and preferred patterns manifesting the dysfunctional and reorganized personality structures.

Few theorists propose any special strategies or methods for evaluating therapy progress. Client and therapist judgments, unverified by others or by independent evidence, typically provide the basis for decisions. Explicit and systematic criteria for making those judgments are not provided. It is implied that agreed-on goals provide the criteria. To evaluate progress, client and therapist rely on anecdotal evidence resulting from observations of in-therapy functioning, including clients' reports about their daily lives. Observations by others outside therapy and of other clients in group therapy may also be used. Some therapists suggest that a routine element of therapy sessions should be an evaluative discussion of client progress, at least in relation to therapy sub-goals, such as effectiveness in homework assignments (e.g., CT—Beck). Follow-up sessions after termination are also a method used to discuss client reports about persistence and elaboration in the use of new patterns. PT and ISCT therapists consider making termination decisions a valuable part of therapy. They provide patient-therapist behavior episodes, such as those deal-ing with separation anxiety, that patients can use to understand more fully some aspects of the ways they relate to others.

When therapists evaluate the usefulness of different approaches to psy-chotherapy, they must rely on data about the value of these different ap-proaches for specific types of clients. Therefore, deficiencies in methods for evaluating the progress of individuals within therapy will render evaluative comparisons between different approaches to therapy.

STRATEGIES FOR EVALUATING THE APPROACH

Accountability requirements are increasing for psychotherapy as a part of more general changes in health care delivery systems, such as managed care and third-party payment for treatment. This accountability takes two forms. The first requires evidence that the approach selected for use with particular clients for their particular problem has documented utility for that kind of problem, sometimes called *efficacy evaluation*. The second type of account-ability requires evidence that the client benefited from the approach used, sometimes called *effectiveness evaluation* or *clinical utility* (Shapiro, 1996). There is concern that strategies and methods used in the past for evaluating the ef-ficacy and effectiveness of an approach may not be adequate to meet in-creasingly strict accountability demands.

Two Types of Strategies

Broadly speaking, two strategies for evaluating therapy approaches, each with related methods, have been used in the past. One, initiated by Freud, is a strategy on which various forms of psychoanalysis have relied. It uses an in-ductive scientific approach. Clinical observations by therapists of their own clients provide the database both for building theoretical and procedural models and for evaluating them. This strategy involves the construction of generalizations based on many observations of each patient, so a primary criterion seems to be internal consistency within a set of observations. This type of evaluation is similar to what might be called, in current research design terms, a single-subject design using qualitative data. It includes no safeguards to ensure the reliability or representativeness of the observations; for example, selective perception, interpretation, and remembering by clients or therapists may be producing biased data. Also, there is no way to evaluate the validity of the generalizations formed. As a result, there is little evidence of verified reliability and validity with which to evaluate their theoretical and procedural models. It would be possible to create a much more rigorous version of this strategy, but that has not yet been done by psychoanalysts (but, see Edelson, 1988, for relevant suggestions). Some contemporary psychoanalysts acknowledge the deficiencies in their traditional evaluative strategies. One acknowledges that they have sorely neglected developing a real "methodology of evidence" (PT—Compton); another observes that there is no agreed-on method for reporting clinical material in order to make different reports comparable (PT—Boesky).

A second strategy for evaluating therapy approaches relies on the use of standard methods of empirical inquiry employed in the human sciences, particularly psychology (e.g., BT; CT; CBST; BMHT; EIT; HT). It follows two general patterns. One form involves identifying relevant theory and research in the human sciences and then using it to help create theoretical and procedural models for psychotherapy. The soundness of the resulting theories and procedures is validated, in part, by the soundness of this scientific base. Behavior therapy (BT) was initially created in this way, but others have also made rigorous use of this form (see CBST—Goldstein). A second form uses traditional empirical research designs to collect and analyze data from the actual conduct of psychotherapy. Psychotherapists with a background in psychology have been its primary proponents.

An extensive body of empirical evidence continues to be generated, along with many critiques of the adequacy of the research designs and measures used and of the data produced (e.g., Dawes, 1994; Freedheim, 1992). Carl Rogers (HT) pioneered this second form, but most contemporary HT therapists do not follow his example. Rogers focused primarily on specifying and evaluating the efficacy of the strategies and methods of his particular approach. Other researchers have focused on comparing the efficacy of different approaches, such as client-centered and behavior therapy. As psychotherapy research evolved, the use of empirical research designs and methods has become more sophisticated. In recent years the focus has been shifting toward evaluating and comparing different strategies and methods for dealing with specific kinds of problems, such as depression, phobias, and panic attacks.

Deficiencies in Research Strategies

Two basic issues about traditional research strategies are often discussed. One is that the lack of specificity in psychotherapy procedural models is a serious impediment. Without clear specifications of therapy strategies and methods, it is difficult to evaluate the connection of strategies and methods to changes produced or to compare the efficacy of different strategies and methods. The recent development of manuals outlining specific treatments seeks to remedy this weakness, but others criticize this approach as deficient in external validity (e.g., Garfield, 1996; Havik & Vandenbos, 1996). Some criticize it as not capturing the importance of therapists' personal characteristics and variability, or relationship factors. Those are not criticisms of the idea of making treatments explicit but of the adequacy with which the idea has been implemented in contemporary efforts to be more specific in describing treatments. It would be useful if a common format for therapy manuals could be agreed on to help ensure their comprehensiveness and to facilitate comparisons. One possible format could be one analogous to the topical format used for comparing procedural models in this chapter.

Without clear definition of the aspects of people targeted for change, it is difficult to construct reliable and valid ways of observing and measuring those variables and to evaluate changes and how they were produced. This is true even if clients' observations are the data collection methods of choice. Clients need a clear idea of what to look for (e.g. different types of "experience"), and how to label it so it can be shared with others. For example, if clients call a sensation "anxiety," does that have the same meaning as if they called it "fear"? This kind of specificity involves content typically termed *diagnosis* and *therapy goals* or *outcomes*. These are two sides of the same coin. *Diagnosis* (normative or idiographic) seeks to identify the dysfunctional patterns to be changed. *Therapy goals* or *outcomes* identify the preferred patterns sought to replace the dysfunctional ones. One limitation of past psychotherapy research is that it examines only intended outcomes; it seldom assesses unintended ones, or side effects.

The second issue related to research is the adequacy of the research strategies themselves (e.g., Meehl, 1997). Some theorists argue that traditional research designs and data analytic models are based on inadequate metaphysical and epistemological assumptions. Some argue that alternate strategies and methods must be created to fit what they believe are sounder assumptions (e.g., EIT—constructivists). They typically make a few illustrative suggestions—such as the potential utility of hermeneutic strategies—but have yet to fully construct and demonstrate the utility of alternatives. Our comparative framework supports and seeks to justify the use of pluralistic metaphysical and epistemological perspectives.

Limitations of space, time, and competence make it impossible for us to summarize and analyze existing empirical evidence of the efficacy and effectiveness of the approaches analyzed, or the pros and cons revealed in debates about research design issues, so we close with a few personal opinions regarding processes of evaluation and validation of approaches.

EVALUATION AS AN ESSENTIAL ELEMENT OF PSYCHOTHERAPY

The difficulty of the very complicated problem of evaluation leads some to declare it an intractable dilemma and an impossible task. We share Meehl's (1997) view:

> The vast experimental literature on human error agrees with history of medicine, folklore, and superstition in discrediting knowledge claims based solely on anecdotal impressions. Since clinical experience consists of anecdotal impressions by practitioners, it is unavoidably a mixture of truths, half-truths, and falsehoods. The scientific method is the only known way to distinguish these, and it is both unscholarly and unethical for psychologists who deal with other persons' health, careers, money, freedom, and even life itself to pretend that clinical experience suffices and that quantitative research on diagnostic and therapeutic procedures is not needed. . . . [The issue] is simply one of distinguishing knowledge claims that bring reliable credentials and others that do not. (p. 91)

There now exists a sizable and growing body of empirical and anecdotal evidence that psychotherapy can be helpful to many people for many types of problems, so its continued use is warranted, despite gaps in its supporting knowledge base. However, interventions can do harm as well as good. The welfare and rights of clients must be protected from those who would exploit them for personal gain as well as from those whose intentions are good but who accept no responsibility for documenting the effects of their efforts. Licensure is one method of protection that has been adopted, but the utility of licensure rests upon criteria of competence. These, in turn, rest on a body of knowledge about the utility of different strategies and methods for different purposes and on ways of judging professional expertise in their use.

A significant start toward constructing such a body of knowledge about psychotherapy interventions has been made during the past half century, and those who have helped create that base should be honored. However, they are among the first to acknowledge its inadequacies. The proliferation of purportedly different psychotherapies during the past third of a century, with limited evidence that they truly are different in practice or utility, attests to the inadequacy of our knowledge base. Improvements in ways of judging professional expertise and of training for it can occur only when the nature of the expertise itself has been defined and verified.

Professional responsibility requires that psychotherapists persist in the effort to expand their knowledge base, no matter how difficult the task. Society will increasingly demand it, as illustrated by current changes in health care delivery systems in the United States. If psychotherapists do not move aggressively to meet growing accountability requirements, government agencies, corporate health care delivery systems, third-party payers, lawyers, and judges are likely to discipline or discredit practitioners of psychotherapy. Careful evaluation of psychotherapy approaches must be done, though progress is likely to be slow and decades of research will be required to achieve major results.

NECESSITY FOR COLLABORATION BETWEEN PSYCHOTHERAPY PRACTITIONERS AND RESEARCHERS

But psychotherapy practitioners cannot wait for a more adequate knowledge base to try to serve the troubled people seeking their help. Critics and researchers must accept the truism that, because of gaps in the verified knowledge base, health and human services practitioners often have to go beyond established knowledge to try to help clients. Their interventions are guided by their theories and clinical experience when they do so. There is a positive side to these creative efforts, and that is the discovery of new treatment possibilities and variations worthy of more rigorous evaluation. However, professional practice is demanding: personally, professionally, administratively, and economically. It leaves limited time and energy for conducting or keeping abreast of evaluative research. A more explicit and closer collaboration between psychotherapy researchers and practitioners could be of value to both (Borkovec, 1997). A recent special section in *Psychological Science* provides several examples of efforts to link psychotherapy development and psychological science (Onken & Blaine, 1997). We suggest three possibilities that might facilitate closer collaboration; others can undoubtedly think of more.

Relevant organizations could sponsor regular meetings at which psychotherapy researchers would provide practitioners updates on advances in empirical knowledge about different treatments for different kinds of problems. Practitioners would provide researchers updates on hypotheses they have generated in their clinical practice that may be worthy of more rigorous evaluation, and on their experiences in trying to apply findings from previous research. These sessions should be designed so that practitioners could use them to meet continuing professional education requirements. It would be desirable for those requirements to include evidence that practitioners have kept abreast of relevant empirical evidence. This step could bring these two streams of efforts closer together, help increase the external validity of psychotherapy research, and stimulate the creativity of practitioners and their efforts to evaluate their own work.

A second possibility is that psychotherapy researchers might collaborate with practitioners in designing formats for use in process and outcome evaluation with individual clients. These could include computer programs for categorizing and analyzing the resulting information with regard to the progress of each client. Such computer advances could have several advantages. They could help practitioners more efficiently and effectively evaluate and improve their interventions. They could provide therapists with a database for documenting the effectiveness of their interventions to potential clients, health care delivery systems, and third-party payers. They could provide a basis for preparing presentations and publications of clinical reports so others could profit from practitioners' work. They could provide a database for evaluative research collaborations among practitioners, and between practitioners and researchers, both to evaluate specific approaches and to compare different approaches. The Practice Research Network established by the Pennsylvania Psychological Association with the help of pilot funds from the American Psychological Association illustrates such a strategy.

Psychotherapy practitioners have little time to conduct library searches for information and evidence that might be helpful to them in treating specific kinds of client problems, or to read the massive flow of journal articles and books that might be relevant—including this one. In a third possibility, psychotherapy practitioners and researchers might collaborate in creating a computer-based, continually updated information system, relevant to their daily practice, available through the Internet or some other more limited delivery system. Its organization and content would need to be created in a form that is useful and efficient for the needs of typical practitioner settings—such as the latest evidence on treating panic states. A record of the use of such an information system would provide a database for studying the frequency and geographic distribution of particular kinds of dysfunctions and the treatment approaches being considered for potential use.

RESEARCH AND EVALUATION STRATEGIES AND METHODS

It might be useful to step back from debates about the relative merits of different research designs, data collection methods, and data analysis models and reexamine our problem definition. Reframing problems often leads to additional and alternate ideas about how to deal with them. Next, we briefly discuss a few ideas to try to stimulate our readers' thinking.

The biggest problem may be conceptual rather than methodological. Much research to date has implicitly assumed that psychotherapy approaches are specified clearly enough that we can assume each practitioner's use of an approach is comparable to every other's use of it. Investigators have infrequently sought to document the actual nature of the therapy given. In recent years, increasing doubt has been expressed about the validity of that assumption, and researchers have taken steps to document the treatment used.

Most theorists acknowledge that there is considerable variability in practice by those who purport to use their therapy model. There is a little evidence that as effective therapists become more experienced, they become more alike in what they actually do in therapy, regardless of their theoretical differences. Our comparative analyses reported in this book suggest that more rapid progress in evaluating psychotherapy approaches could result from a more precise and explicit formulation of conceptual, propositional, and procedural models. Careful evaluation of how something works and how well it works is not possible without clear definition of what *it* is. Some of the best psychotherapy research programs (e.g., the Vanderbilt studies) try to address this issue (Strupp, 1993).

Thus, one reframing of the problem is that the field needs to "polish" its existing models of psychotherapy into more clearly defined forms. We need precise, explicit definitions of concepts and propositions, and clear specification of intervention strategies and the methods by which they are implemented. With greater clarity, psychotherapy research designs that are appropriate to the nature of those models can be selected or created. Research designs and data-analytic models are simply formal tools to help answer questions in ways others can replicate, as a supplement to our informal, everyday problem-solving practices of observation and inference. No one can decide which tool fits a task until the task itself is defined; a hammer is not suitable for every job.

Perhaps the focus should shift to different kinds or forms of questions. Psychotherapy has developed as different therapists have proposed and promoted different "models," "systems," or "schools" of therapy. The kinds of questions psychotherapy research has addressed have been largely formulated in relation to those "schools." For example, "Is humanist therapy effective?" or "Is behavior therapy more effective than traditional psychoanalysis, or than a control group?" Or, in more specific forms, "Is cognitive therapy more effective than behavior therapy in alleviating depression?" "For which kinds of problems is cognitive therapy, or humanist therapy, or cognitive-behavioral/skill training therapy most effective?"

Shapiro (1996) suggests:

> The assumption that treatment methods as currently defined are prime determinants of change is remarkably resilient in the face of largely disconfirmatory evidence. . . . there is no reason to believe that partitioning intervention strategies by "brand names" carves nature at the joints. Rather, it is by delineation of change principles, and using a wide range of methodologies appropriate to specific research questions, that we will find out how psychotherapies help people change. Evidence that even well-researched methods achieve their effects via the mechanisms posited by their instigators is not overwhelmingly strong. (p. 257)

For example, our analyses of procedural models in Chapter 17 is organized around change principles rather than schools of psychotherapy.

Wilson (1996) has noted that "identifying effective treatments for specific problems, using the best scientific research available, is arguably the best way to improve on this unsatisfactory state of affairs. It has worked well for some disorders, and it is reasonable to assume that it might for others" (p. 243). Barlow (1996) has observed, "The question 'Do drugs work?' or 'Do psychosocial interventions work?' without further specification of type of drug or psychological intervention, or the disorder that provides the context for the intervention, is simply not relevant to those constructing clinical practice guidelines." (p. 239).

Perhaps reformulation of the dependent variables used to evaluate effectiveness should be considered. Almost all the therapy theorists we analyzed consider normative diagnosis as represented by *DSM-IV* (APA, 1994) to be useless for planning and conducting psychotherapy. Moreover, many of them argue that labeling a client with one of those categories can result in a form of stereotyping that can significantly bias treatment. One wonders whether so many talented and experienced people can be wrong. However, these diagnostic categories seem to have become the key criteria for evaluating therapy effectiveness—for example, which approach is most effective with depressive conditions, posttraumatic stress disorders, obsessive-compulsive disorders, panic disorders, different kinds of phobias, or different combinations of disorders (called comorbidity)?

What's wrong with these traditional categories? The comments of several theorists are informative: "Problems of reliability and validity remain, patients given the same diagnosis are not necessarily identical and even identified treatments do not produce identical or similar results" (Garfield, 1996, p. 219). "Many relevant target disorders or problems, such as relational problems, are not included in *DSM-IV*. . . . The next iteration should reflect . . . more emphasis on dimensional approaches" (Barlow, 1996, p. 239). "It is generally agreed that there is heterogeneity across individuals within diagnostic categories. . . . We need to move beyond this level of categorization to more refined matches of treatments with particular problems in individual patients. . . . successful matching will require empirically established decision rules" (Wilson, 1996, p. 242). Despite the "consensus assessment that psychotherapy, as a generic process, is effective . . . there are still differences in effectiveness, both within and between therapists (and between patients). One of the sources of these differences is undoubtedly a technique/disorder-specific effect, which can be best operationalized and made most obvious with highly targeted symptoms" (Havik & Vandenbos, 1996, p. 266).

The problem is that society uses the tools available to deal with its problems. *DSM-IV* (APA, 1994) is the only credible tool available for representing differences in people's psychopathology. Therefore, it is the one managed care companies and psychotherapy researchers are using. If psychotherapists find this way of representing clients' dysfunctional patterns unsatisfactory, then they need to create a credible alternative; criticizing the existing scheme won't change anything. Creating a new categorization system would be a daunting task, but if all of these theorists are right, it may be necessary.

Perhaps the research designs and data-analytic models being used don't fit the nature of the phenomena. Another potential reframing results from considering the implications of the consensus we found about the kind of metamodel (ontological and cosmological assumptions) these theorists now believe most appropriately represents human nature. For example, none currently espouse a mechanistic metaphysical model, yet most of the research designs and data-analytic models that have been used to evaluate psychotherapy reflect such a model. The assumption in most experimental designs and in analysis of variance statistical models is of a constant, additive effect of an independent variable on a dependent variable.

A typical application in psychotherapy research of such designs is to identify samples of patients who have received different forms of psychotherapy—including placebo therapies and no-therapy wait lists—and to compare the samples on variables thought to be relevant to all (e.g., Was anxiety or depression reduced?). In more sophisticated versions, efforts are made to identify patients or clients who have similar problems and then to randomly assign them to different treatment conditions, as a way of controlling for some other sources of variability. The basic form of data analysis is to compare means of different samples. The underlying rationale is that everyone will react the same way on the average to the same treatment. That is a property of mechanistic models; their dynamics are linear.

Contemporary psychotherapy theorists, however, share a different meta-model of human nature. They assume that people are complex, open systems that exist and develop only in transaction with contexts. All people construct their own developmental pathway and functional patterns, within variable and changing facilitating and constraining conditions provided by their bodies and contexts. Borkovec (1997) summarizes this view:

> Human beings, however, are nonlinear, dynamic systems involving processes like attention, thought, imagery, memory, emotion, physiology, and behavior, all constantly interacting in response to changing interpersonal and noninterpersonal environments and based on developmental and biological history. . . . Cognition affects and is affected by emotion; behavior influences cognition and emotion, even as it is influenced by them; reactions of others define how we view ourselves even within our noninterpersonal environments; and all of these events are best viewed (and investigated) as moment-to-moment process over time. Understanding human behavior and experience will necessarily involve an integrated view of all relevant human systems, so every area of psychology has an essential contribution to make. The same can therefore be said for understanding psychopathology and therapeutic change mechanisms. (p. 145)

A reductionistic strategy for understanding how people work is therefore inappropriate. People cannot be disaggregated into their parts, the nature and functioning of each part understood separately, and the understanding of those parts added together to provide an understanding of the whole. The parts have to be understood in the context of the whole, and the whole and the parts are mutually influential. Therefore, the units of analysis should represent patterns—such as behavior episodes and behavior episode schemas—rather than just different kinds of responses.

One implication for research designs is that researchers cannot assume that the same intervention will have the same effect for all clients, even if they have similar problems. People do not react; they transact. They interpret and use the experiences generated by interventions, through the operation of their self-organizing and self-constructing dynamics, to serve their purposes. The same intervention may have different effects on different people, or on the same person when he or she is operating within different functional states— for example, when feeling frightened or loving. Warm, caring relationship-building strategies and methods may ease the fears of one client and increase them for another. One cannot evaluate therapy approaches by comparing the means of a selected variable for samples of patients. Some other forms of research design are needed that fit this kind of metaphysical model. Borkevec (1997) asserts that traditional therapy comparison designs have limited theoretical and practical value, and suggests three other possibilities that he calls dismantling, constructive, and parametric designs.

This alternate metaphysical model has been emerging in many fields of science (see Capra, 1975) and applications in the human sciences by Robertson and Camlea, 1995, and Port and VanGelder, 1995, not surprisingly, this same problem has surfaced and is being addressed in other fields—such as the study of adult development and aging; motor development and functioning—by sophisticated methodologists like John Nesselroade (e.g., Nesselroade & Featherman, 1997). Methodologists are creating and evaluating alternate research designs and data-analytic models appropriate to this newer metaphysical view. Psychotherapy scholars might follow that literature for research methods they could find useful.

One model that we think has considerable merit is called a *replicated, single-subject design*. It fits psychotherapists' assumptions about the uniqueness of each person and the emphasis on idiographic diagnosis, because it treats each person as a separate formal study, as a single-subject design. Samples are defined in terms of the number and kinds of occasions such as therapy sessions, or behavior episodes within therapy sessions on which one person is observed or measured rather than in terms of a certain number and kind of people. Data analysis focuses on identifying intraindividual patterns of consistency and variability rather than on average differences among groups of people (interindividual similarities and differences). The result of such a study is a detailed understanding of the content and dynamics of the functional patterns of a single person. In effect, that is what psychotherapists do every day in their clinical practice. What does the term *replicated* mean in this context? It means to repeat a single-subject design with another person, and another and another. Then, different people can be compared (interindividual comparisons) in terms of their intraindividual patterns of consistency and variability. In this way, groups of people with similar intraindividual patterns can be identified. Such common patterns can then be used to examine the differential effects of interventions, thereby building nomothetic knowledge from a solid idiographic knowledge base. Results from this form of research design are more easily generalizable to clinical practice. Two leading psychotherapy researchers, Binder and Strupp (1997), recently recommended this basic form of research design for the future, and a psychoanalyst (Edelson, 1988) proposes a version described as a rigorous form of case study.

Quantitative measures of selected variables can be used in such analyses, just as they can in traditional group designs. However, psychotherapists are typically interested in *patterns* of functioning, and it is usually difficult to create and measure a quantitative indicator of such patterns. This problem is not unique to psychotherapists; it appears in other fields as well, such as developmental psychology, sociology, and nursing. That has led to efforts by a diversity of scholars to create ways of representing such patterns in descriptive rather than quantitative terms, and to create data-analytic models relevant to such representations. These are typically called qualitative methods; in traditional measurement theory terms they can be considered a nominal level of measurement. The practice and development of psychotherapy has relied primarily on qualitative methods, and a sizable body of knowledge about strategies and methods for constructing qualitative representations of patterns of functioning have resulted from that history of clinical experience. It is a relatively short step to transform that knowledge and skill into forms useful for sophisticated replicated, single-subject research designs.

Actually, this kind of research design has been around for along time. Psychologists will recognize it as the one used in the construction and testing of theories of learning; Skinner used it to build his operant psychology. Its major influence on the design of behavior modification strategies and methods was due, in part, to its focus on the dynamics of individual organisms. Its limitation was that Skinner interpreted the data obtained with the design within a mechanistic rationale. Those familiar with the strategy by which syndromes of infectious diseases were constructed will also recognize it. A physician would identify a pattern of signs and symptoms in one patient, note its similarity to the pattern of another patient, and publish a paper describing the pattern and the treatment that was used. Other physicians would identify a similar pattern in some of their patients and report their findings and treatments. Gradually the accumulation of a sufficient number of cases that were similar would allow researchers to document the existence of such a syndrome. Then, more formal research might be used to try to understand what was causing it and which treatments were most effective.

Psychotherapists are already accustomed to thinking in terms of individual cases. They have developed clinical strategies and methods for the intensive study of the patterns of individual persons, and for the representation of those patterns in qualitative terms, as a routine part of their diagnostic and treatment approaches. It would be a relatively short step to transform those ways of thinking and those strategies and methods into formal replicated, single-subject research designs. If psychotherapists could agree on a format for a single-subject design—such as a shared way of formatting qualitative data—then different therapists could prepare analyses of some of their clients, and their analyses could be used for studying a variety of issues.

The data-analytic models used in the past can also be used in single-subject analyses, but these may not be the most appropriate for the complex, nonlinear dynamics characteristic of living systems. Binder and Strupp (1997) "believe that the most productive research strategies will use multidimensional process analyses with statistical strategies that manage time-dependent sequences of interacting variables [and] that integrate quantitative and qualitative data, in order to give vivid clinical meaning to patterns of data" (p. 135). A variety of potentially useful tools already exist, such as multivariate time served dynamic factor analysis, taxometric methods, and structural P technique—and it may be necessary to seek the help of sophisticated statisticians to develop new approaches, such as variants of graph theory or path analyses (see Hoyle, 1997; Meehl, 1997; Nesselroade & Featherman, 1997; Nesselroade & Ford, 1987; Nesselroade & Molenaar, in Press; Nesselroade & McArdle, 1986) for examples of data analytic strategies and models psychotherapy researchers may find useful).

One potential benefit from such designs is that studies can be conducted with fewer clients, thereby reducing the cost and increasing the feasibility of good research. Quite possibly, the yield will also be greater. We may discover that solid, useful results accrue faster when they are built on a lot of knowledge and understanding about each person in a small set of clients, than on a little knowledge about a larger number of people. In traditional research designs, it is possible to measure and analyze only a few variables on a few occasions in a single study.

We should behave as we ask our clients to do. One psychotherapy strategy is to create conditions in which clients will relinquish their tight grip on their habitual patterns, so as to free their imagination to explore alternatives. We suggest that psychotherapists apply the same strategy to themselves so as to permit the exploration of for improving both evaluation of progress in individual cases and evaluation of the comparative efficacy of therapy approaches. Psychotherapy research must not only address inadequacies in the use of traditional research designs, but also inadequacies in the designs themselves.

Epilogue

OUR CAREERS AS psychologists and psychotherapists have spanned the last half of the twentieth century, so we have lived through much of the development of the field of psychotherapy. The summaries and comparative analyses of contemporary models of psychotherapy reported in this book involved our reading thousands of books, chapters, reviews, research reports, professional articles, and media reports about the field, just as we did when we wrote the original *Systems of Psychotherapy* published by Wiley over a third of a century ago. Over the years, we have discussed many of these issues with hundreds of colleagues and doctoral students. These combined experiences have provided a degree of familiarity with the field that we are emboldened to make a few comments about past and potential future developments.

HISTORICAL PERSPECTIVE
AN ASTONISHING SUCCESS STORY

If one takes the long view, the development in just 100 years of the diverse array of psychotherapeutic treatments now available to the public is an astonishing accomplishment. Corresponding changes in sociocultural attitudes are equally astonishing. Until nearly mid-twentieth century, public attitudes toward psychological dysfunctions tended to regard them as shameful conditions to be hidden from public view. Moreover, the public was skeptical of the motives of those who sought to provide psychotherapy as reflecting prurient interests in the problems of others, or indicating that therapists themselves were problem laden. The public also doubted the utility of psychotherapy. In the last 50 years, public attitudes have been turned upside down. Psychotherapy is now a respected and desired form of treatment for psychological/behavioral problems. It is now common for people to assume they are apt to need some counseling or psychotherapy at some time during their life. When Americans decide they have a general need, they expect that need to be filled and relevant services to be available. This is manifested in public and governmental acceptance of psychological problems as a health issue, and the inclusion of their treatment in health benefit packages. Such a sweeping cultural change in such a short span of time is a tribute to those who have developed the field in both theory and practice.

THREE STREAMS OF PSYCHOTHERAPY DEVELOPMENT

Psychotherapy Models. We discern three very broad streams of activity that have shaped the development of psychotherapy over the past 100 years. The first is the creation of different schools, systems, or models of psychotherapy, each aimed at providing a comprehensive approach for the treatment of a broad spectrum of human psychological and behavioral difficulties. Such diversity has led to the successive appearance of one approach after another, with each promoted as a different and yet more powerful way of correcting human problems, each attracting a number of advocates and being applied with unabashed confidence to an increasingly broad range of human problems. Only a small minority of these psychotherapy models, and only parts of them, have been subjected to thorough scientific verification. At its present stage of development, the field has accumulated hundreds of such models, differing from one another to some largely unknown degree. Proliferation has occurred; it has had creative value. Most, if not all, psychotherapy strategies and methods available today were created in that process. Most psychotherapy research has been focused on efforts to evaluate, compare, and elaborate these schools. However, what we have acquired is an aggregate, a mass, a collection of disparate approaches only loosely associated with one another, rather than a progressively accumulated and systematically organized body of knowledge and know-how.

Differential Psychotherapies. A second stream of activity, that has gained increasing momentum in recent years, is defined in terms of dysfunctional states. It focuses on trying to understand the interrelated dynamics of different kinds of problems (e.g., anorexia; depressions; panic states; addictions), for different people (e.g., men; women; minorities), in different phases of life (e.g., children; adolescents; elderly), living in different conditions (e.g., families; institutions), and on creating intervention strategies and methods for helping people deal with specific sets of problems.

This general approach, focus on creating and validating treatments for different kinds of problems, has a long and successful history in the field of medicine, where it has been directed toward biologically based problems, referred to by physicians as differential diagnosis and differential treatment. This stream has also produced a variety of brief psychotherapies. This set of activities has likewise been productive, although it is not completely unrelated to the first stream, because typically it uses theoretical and procedural models created by the different schools of psychotherapy.

Psychotherapy Integration. A third stream focused on psychotherapy integration has emerged as a function of the abundant results achieved through the activity of both the comprehensive psychotherapy model and differential approaches. It assumes that the great diversity of approaches created cannot be entirely different and that there must be some basic similarities in theoretical and procedural proposals underlying their surface diversity. It seeks to identify and create a synthesis of those underlying similarities at both theoretical and procedural levels.

CONTEXTUAL INFLUENCES

The patterns of development that any field follows are influenced by the contexts within which it functions. Psychotherapy's developmental course in the past, present, and times yet to come, is facilitated and constrained by multiple factors in its environments. The first phase of development involved the creation of multiple versions of Freud's psychoanalytic approach and served private clients on a fee-for-service basis. Then, psychologists' interest and involvement in psychotherapy grew, which brought an empirical science orientation to the field. The legitimization of clinical psychologists and others as psychotherapists who could function independently of psychiatric supervision fueled great growth in the diversity of psychotherapy theory and methods, and growth in the number, diversity, and settings of clients served. For example, three-fourths of the clinical psychologists surveyed in a recent study were involved in full- or part-time private, fee-for-service clinical practice (Norcross, Karg, & Prochaska, 1997). All these events have culminated in public acceptance of psychotherapy as a form of health care.

Currently, the large changes taking place in the economics and delivery of health care are having an enormous impact on the development and day-to-day practice of psychotherapy. Public expectations have led to the designation of psychological treatments as forms of health care to which all persons in need should have ready access, with costs defrayed by group-based insurance plans. Managed health care organizations, traditionally designed to provide insurance coverage for medical problems, are responding to consumer demand by cautious expansion of coverage into the spheres of mental health. In doing so, they have exerted steady pressure on psychotherapists to conform to the managerial procedures found feasible in meeting the costs of medical treatment. Thus, to be reimbursed for providing services to a person enrolled in the insurance plan, psychotherapists are being required to meet certain criteria, such as (1) clearly defining clients' problems in a classification system acceptable to the insurance plan, (2) using procedures judged consistent with contemporary standards and of demonstrated utility for each kind of problem, and (3) accepting reimbursement for procedures used rather than for the amount of time spent (e.g. number of therapy sessions). These developments have been disruptive to the customary practices of many psychotherapists, but it must be recognized that it is a consumer-driven process embedded in society's beliefs, traditions, and expectations about the delivery of health care.

OPTIONS FOR FUTURE DEVELOPMENT

Prepare to Function in Managed Care Delivery Systems. Insurance-based health care is not prepared to pay for multiyear psychotherapy, aimed at major personality change. Some amount of private, fee-for-service will doubtless continue, unfettered by health insurance and managed care requirements, because there will be some people willing to pay for it from their own resources. That has been the traditional market for psychoanalysts. There are already signs that this market segment is shrinking, and that trend is apt to continue. In the future, most psychotherapists will have to function within a market-driven, insurance-financed, managed care-controlled delivery system. That assumption leads us to four suggestions.

Focus on Improving Existing Models, and Integrating Similar Models. Psychotherapists should abandon the tradition of continually creating new systems or models of psychotherapy. The field is saturated with hundreds of purportedly different approaches. The primary focus now should be on validating and improving what already exists, and on trying to identify and create a synthesis of underlying theoretical and procedural similarities, at least within families of similar approaches. As a corollary, research programs aimed at comparing models should no longer be pursued in an effort to determine which is the best. There is sufficient evidence that (1) all have some utility, but it isn't clear why, or for which purposes; and (2) the view that any one of the current models can serve all needs can no longer be maintained.

Focus on Targeted Approaches for Specific Conditions. Given the insurance-based, managed care context in which most psychotherapy will be provided, psychotherapists should focus primarily on designing and validating precisely defined treatments for specific kinds of conditions, for people of different ages. Many such efforts are already under way, illustrated by a diversity of research centers for specific conditions, a flow of publications about treatments for specific conditions, the generation of treatment guidelines, and identification of empirically validated treatments for specific conditions. Effective implementation of this targeted strategy, however, requires both theoretical and procedural precision. This approach has several requirements: (1) clear and unambiguous definitions of types of dysfunctional patterns on which treatment is focused; (2) specification of client and contextual factors that help maintain or facilitate change in each pattern; (3) explicit and precise descriptions of the outcomes, or alternate functional states, sought; (4) specification of interventions intended to help clients transform their dysfunctional state to the preferred state and which can be safely and reliably implemented within the constraints that prevail; and (5) identification of evidence by which treatment effectiveness can be assessed, and specification of means for collecting such evidence.

The hundreds of existing psychotherapy models can serve as a resource from which specific methodologies may be drawn, tailored to the particular requirements of a given treatment task. In fact, many existing models were originally created for specific dysfunctional patterns (e.g., Beck first created his cognitive therapy as a way of treating depressive states). Drawing on existing models to create targeted treatments may be considered a form of psychotherapy integration. The development of sound targeted approaches requires a valid way of defining the "targets." Such definitions must rely on sound models of normal and dysfunctional development.

A Shared Theory of Normal, Prototypical Human Development is Needed. In a fundamental sense, all pathological or dysfunctional human states are defined as deviations from what are considered normal, prototypic, or healthy states, and all interventions are aimed at eliminating or compensating for dysfunctional states by restoring or creating normal states. Therefore, all diagnosis and treatment in both medicine and psychotherapy is at least implicitly anchored to conceptual and propositional models of normal, prototypic, or healthy development.

One of the strengths of the field of medicine is that it has an explicit, agreed-on model of normal, prototypic, healthy human biological development and functioning that integrates the knowledge of human biology created over the centuries. It is an integrated, multilevel model specifying the nature, functioning, and interrelationships of cells, tissues, organs, organ systems, and functional patterns as they operate to create unified functioning at the person level. That shared model makes possible the cumulative integration of new knowledge about any aspect of biological functioning with existing knowledge, so that the model is continually evolving. It also facilitates integration of knowledge about biological dysfunctions and medical interventions. Diagnosis of any medical condition basically refers to deviations from that model at some level and in some of its aspects. Medical treatments— pharmacological or surgical—are based on assumptions about how normal bodily functioning will respond to such interventions. Sarbin (1997) argues that the psychiatric diagnostic manuals (DSMs) reflect hidden theoretical assumptions about normal psychological and behavioral development and functioning that are inappropriate and unsound, and their application is leading to a "medicalization" of all human misery.

Advances in psychotherapy's effectiveness in specifying different types of dysfunctional patterns for which psychotherapy is an appropriate treatment and in designing and validating effective interventions for each type, are severely limited by the lack of a shared model of normal, prototypic, healthy psychological and behavioral development. The field would benefit from a major effort to create such a model. Although our analyses identified some disagreements among theorists, we found a considerable core of agreement about many ingredients that such a model should include. Our comparative framework reflects our efforts to create such a model and might be one useful starting point for such an effort. There are other possibilities as well.

A shared theory of dysfunctional development and a way of specifying types of dysfunctions that result is needed. Most psychotherapy theorists we studied criticize the standard psychiatric classification system for psychological/behavioral dysfunctional patterns (e.g., *DSM-IV*) as inadequate or inappropriate for representing and understanding their clients' dysfunctional patterns.

Sarbin (1997) summarized inadequacies of the DSM approach and argues that it should be "jettisoned." He contends that both the reliability and validity of that classification system are grossly inadequate; the implicit theoretical rationale on which it is based is unsound in light of current knowledge; and its use leads to seriously misleading social policies and practices.

A recent issue of *Clinical Psychology: Science and Practice* examines the current lack of agreement about a definition of psychopathology (Bergner, et. al, 1997).

A targeted approach requires a theory of psychopathology and some classification system of dysfunctional patterns. Therefore, if the existing system of classification is considered unsatisfactory, a major effort is needed to create an alternative one that health insurance and managed care leaders find credible and useful. Economic pressures demand increasing levels of productivity, defined as maximal benefits with least resource expenditure. The pressures on psychotherapy are to find treatment procedures with hi-effect, lo-cost characteristics. Of course, dysfunctional conditions differ in complexity and therefore will require differing amounts of time and effort to resolve. This is true in medicine as well: It is simpler to treat a cyst in a woman's breast than breast cancer. To meet the economic pressure for brief and effective treatments the field of psychotherapy needs to create a credible and acceptable rationale for justifying treatments of varying lengths. Such a rationale might start with the assumption that dysfunctional conditions for which psychotherapy is the appropriate treatment are primarily products of learning and must be changed through a learning process. There is an extensive literature about factors influencing learning that might be brought to bear; an example is that habits of long standing that produce multiple desired outcomes in addition to dysfunctional ones, such as addictions, are difficult to change.

Focus on integration of procedural models. Our analyses reveal that most approaches already borrow intervention strategies and tactics from one another, so a form of assimilative integration of interventions within existing models is already occurring. There is considerable agreement that although interventions were created within particular theoretical rationales, they may have broader significance than envisioned by that rationale. This process of procedural integration has been largely informal so far; the field might find value in addressing procedural integration more formally and systematically. Relevant professional organizations might collaborate in systematically collating all forms of intervention strategies and methods independent of the therapy models that spawned them, and in collecting and organizing evidence about the kinds of dysfunctional conditions for which they appear to have demonstrated utility. This collaboration could provide a valuable resource for practitioners seeking to design and evaluate targeted interventions. Chapter 17 illustrates one classification system for intervention strategies that might be used for this purpose. Undoubtedly other and better ones can be developed.

Some theorists have argued that the creation of integrated models of normal and dysfunctional development, and of psychotherapy strategies is not possible. We reject that view—difficult, perhaps, but not impossible. The first efforts will be far from perfect, but, one cannot improve if one doesn't begin. To cite an African saying: "How do you eat an elephant? One little bite at a time."

References

Abend, S. M. (Ed). (1990a). The psychoanalytic process. *The Psychoanalytic Quarterly, 59,* 527–781.

Abend, S. M. (1990b). The psychoanalytic process: Motives and obstacles in the search for clarification. *The Psychoanalytic Quarterly, 59,* 532–549.

Abrams, S. (1987). The psychoanalytic process: A schematic model. *International Journal of Psychoanalysis, 68,* 441–452.

Abramson, L. Y., Alloy, L. B., & Metalsky, G. I. (1988). The cognitive diathesis-stress theories of depression: Toward an adequate evaluation of the theories' validities. In L. B. Alloy (Ed.), *Cognitive processes in depression* (pp. 3–30). New York: Guilford.

Ader, R. (Ed.). (1981). *Psychoneuroimmunology.* New York: Academic Press.

Ader, R., & Cohen, N. (1993). Psychoneuroimmunology: Conditioning and stress. *Annual Review of Psychology, 44,* 53–85.

Adler, A. (1924). *The practice and theory of individual psychology.* New York: Harcourt Brace.

Adler, N., & Matthews, K. (1994). Health psychology: Why do some people get sick and some stay well. *Annual Review of Psychology, 45,* 229–259.

Allport, G. W. (1955). *Becoming: Basic considerations for a psychology of personality.* New Haven, CT: Yale University Press.

Allport, G. W. (1961). *Patterns and growth in personality.* New York: Holt, Rinehart, and Winston.

American Psychiatric Association. (1994). *Diagnostic and statistical manual of mental disorders* (4th ed.). Washington, DC: Author.

Anchin, J. C. & Kiesler, D. J. (1982). *Handbook of interpersonal psychotherapy.* Elmsford, NY: Pergamon

Anderson, W. (1974). Personal growth and client-centered therapy: An information-processing view. In D. A. Waxler & L. N. Rice (Eds.), *Innovations in client-centered therapy* (pp. 21–48). New York: Wiley.

Andreas, C., & Andreas, S. (1987). *Change your mind and keep the change.* Moab, UT: Real People Press.

Andrews, J. (1991). Interpersonal challenge: The second integrative relationship factor. *Journal of Psychotherapy Integration, 1,* 267–288.

Andrews, J. D. W. (1991). *The active self in psychotherapy: An integration of therapeutic styles.* New York: Gardner.

Anokhin, P. K. (1969). Cybernetics and the integrative activity of the brain. In M. Cole and I. Maltzman (Eds) *A Handbook of contemporary soviet psychology,* 830–856 NY: Basic Books

Antonovsky, A. (1979). *Health, stress and coping.* San Francisco: Jossey-Bass.

Antonovsky, A. (1984). The sense of coherence as a determinant of health. In J. D. Matarazzo, S. M. Weiss, J. A. Herd, N. E. Miller, & S. M. Weiss (Eds.), *Behavioral health: A handbook of health enhancement and disease prevention* (pp. 114–129). New York: Wiley.

Araki, S. (Ed.). (1992). *Behavioral medicine: An integrated biobehavioral approach to health and illness.* Amsterdam: Elsevier.

Arbib, M. A. (1989). *The metaphorical brain 2. Neural networks and beyond.* New York: Wiley.

Arbib, M. A., & Hesse, M. B. (1986). *The construction of reality.* Cambridge: Cambridge University Press.

Argyle, M. (1967). *The psychology of interpersonal behavior.* London: Penguin.

Argyle, M., Furnham, A., & Graham, J. A. (1981). *Social situations.* Cambridge: Cambridge University Press.

Arkowitz, H. (1989). The role of theory in psychotherapy integration. *Journal of Integrative and Eclectic Psychotherapy, 8,* 8–16.

Arkowitz, H. (1992). Integrative theories of therapy. In D. K. Freedheim (Ed.), *History of psychotherapy: A century of change* (pp. 261–304). Washington, DC: American Psychological Association.

Arkowitz, H. (1995). Common factors or processes of change in psychotherapy? *Clinical Psychology: Science and Practice, 2,* 93–100.

Arlow, J. A., & Brenner, C. (1988). The future of psychoanalysis. *Psychoanalytic Quarterly, 57,* 1–13.

Arnkoff, D. B., & Glass, C. R. (1982). Clinical cognitive constructs: Examination, evaluation, and elaboration. In P. C. Kendall (Ed.), *Advances in cognitive-behavioral research and therapy* (Vol. 1, pp. 2–35). New York: Academic Press.

Arnkoff, D. B., & Glass, C. R. (1992). Cognitive therapy and psychotherapy integration. In D. K. Freedheim (Ed.), *History of psychotherapy: A century of change* (pp. 657–694). Washington, DC: American Psychological Association.

Assagioli, R. (1965). *Psychosynthesis.* New York: Viking Press.

Assagioli, R. (1973). *The act of will.* New York: Viking Press.

Auchin, J. C., & Kiesler, D. J. (1982). *Handbook of interpersonal psychotherapy.* New York: Pergamon Press.

Authier, J., Gustafson, K., Guerney, B., & Kasdorf, J. (1975). The psychological practitioner as a teacher: A theoretical-historical and practical review. *Counseling Psychologist, 5,* 31–50.

Bacal, H. (1985). Optimal responsiveness and the therapeutic process. In A. Goldberg (Ed.), *Progress in self psychology* (pp. 202–226). New York: Guilford.

Bacal, H. A. (1990). The elements of a corrective self-object experience. *Psychoanalytic Inquiry, 10,* 347–372.

Bacal, H. A., & Newman, H. M. (1990). *Theories of object relations: Bridges to self-psychology.* New York: Columbia University Press.

Bachrach, H., Galatzer-Levy, R., Skolnikoff, A., & Waldron, S. (1991). On the efficacy of psychoanalysis. *Journal of the American Psychoanalytic Association, 39,* 871–916.

Bacon-Greenberg, K. (1986). Winnicott: The man and his theory. [Review of the book *In search of the real: The origins and originality of D. W. Winnicott and in one's bones: The clinical genius of Winnicott.*] *Contemporary Psychology, 41,* 383–385.

Bakan, D. (1966). *The duality of human existence: Isolation and communism in western man.* Boston: Beacon Press.

Balint, M. (1965). *Primary love and psycho-analytic technique.* London: Tavistock.

Balint, M. (1968). *The basic fault.* London: Tavistock.

Bandler, R. (1985). *Using your brain for a change.* Moab, UT: Real People Press.

Bandura, A. (1969). *Principles of behavior modification.* New York: Holt, Rinehart, and Winston.

Bandura, A. (1977). *Social learning theory.* Englewood Cliffs, NJ: Prentice-Hall.

Bandura, A. (1986). *Social foundations of thought and action: A social-cognitive analysis.* Englewood Cliffs, NJ: Prentice-Hall.

Barker, R. (1968). *Ecological psychology: Concepts and methods for studying the environment of human behavior.* Stanford, CA: Stanford University Press.

Barlow, D. H. (1996). The effectiveness of psychotherapy: Science and policy. *Clinical Psychology: Science and Practice, 3,* 236–240.

Barrett, C. (1997). APA workgroup provides input for changes to International Diagnostic Classification System. *Practitioner, 10,* 9.

Beck, A. T. (1961). A systematic investigation of depression. *Comprehensive Psychiatry, 2,* 162–170.

Beck, A. T. (1963). Thinking and depression. *Archives of General Psychiatry, 9,* 324–333.

Beck, A. T. (1967). *Depression: Clinical, experimental and theoretical aspects.* New York: Harper & Row.

Beck, A. T. (1976). *Cognitive therapy and the emotional disorder.* New York: International Universities Press.

Beck, A. T. (1987). Cognitive therapy. In J. T. Zeig (Ed.), *The evolution of psychotherapy* (pp. 55–66). New York: Brunner/Mazel.

Beck, A. T. (1993). Cognitive therapy: Past, present, and future. *Journal of the Consulting Clinical Psychologist, 62,* 194–198.

Beck, A. T. (1995). Cognitive therapy: Past, present, and future. In M. J. Mahoney (Ed.), *Cognitive and constructive psychotherapies: Theory, research, and practice* (pp. 29–40). New York: Springer.

Beck, A. T., Emery, G., & Greenberg, R. L. (1985). *Anxiety disorders and phobias: A cognitive perspective.* New York: Basic Books.

Beck, A. T., Freeman, A., & Associates (1990). *Cognitive therapy of personality disorders.* New York: Guilford.

Beck, A. T., & Hurvich, M. (1959). Psychological correlates of depression. *Psychosomatic Medicine, 21,* 50–55.

Beck, A. T., Rush, J., Shaw, B., & Emery, G. (1979). *Cognitive therapy of depression.* New York: Guilford.

Beck, A. T., & Ward, C. H. (1961). Dreams of depressed patients: Characteristic themes in manifest content. *Archives of General Psychiatry, 5,* 462–467.

Beck, A. T., & Weishaar, M. (1989). Cognitive therapy. In A. Freeman, K. M. Simon, L. E. Bentler, & H. Arkowtiz (Eds.), *Comprehensive handbook of cognitive therapy* (pp. 325–349). New York: Plenum.

Beckman, E. E. (1990). Psychotherapy of depression at the crossroads: Directions for the 1990's. *Clinical Psychology Review, 10,* 207–228.

Beer, S. (1964). *Cybernetics and Management.* NY: Wiley

Beitman, B. D. (1987). *The structure of individual psychotherapy.* New York: Guilford.

Beitman, B. D. (1992). Integration through fundamental similarities and useful differences among the schools. In J. C. Norcross & M. R. Goldfried (Eds.), *Handbook of psychotherapy integration* (pp. 202–230). New York: Basic Books.

Beitman, B. D., Goldfried, M. R., & Norcross, J. C. (1989). The movement toward integrating the psychotherapies: An overview. *American Journal of Psychiatry, 146,* 138–147.

Beitman, B. D., Hall, M. J., & Woodward, B. (1992). Integrating pharmacotherapy and psychotherapy. In J. C. Norcross & M. R. Goldfried (Eds.), *Handbook of psychotherapy integration* (pp. 533–560). New York: Basic Books.

Bellack, A. S., & Hersen, M. (Eds.). (1985). *Dictionary of behavior therapy technique*. New York: Pergamon Press.

Bellack, A. S., Hersen, M., & Kazdin, A. E. (Eds.). (1990). *International handbook of behavior modification and therapy* (2nd ed.). New York: Plenum.

Bellack, A. S., Mueser, K. T., Gingerich, S. and Agresta, J. (Eds.). (1997). *Social skills training for schizophrenia.* NY: Guilford.

Bellak, L. (1993). *Psychoanalysis as a Science.* Needham Heights, MA: Allyn & Bacon.

Belloc, N. B., & Breslow, L. (1972). Relationships of physical health status and health practices. *Preventive Medicine, 1,* 409–421.

Benjamin, J. (1992). Recognition and destruction. An outline of intersubjectivity. In N. J. Skolnick & S. C. Warshaw (Eds.), *Relational perspectives in psychoanalysis* (pp. 43–60). Hillsdale, NJ: The Analytic Press.

Benjamin, L. S. (1993). *Diagnosis and treatment of personality disorders: A structural approach.* New York: Guilford.

Benson, H. (1975). *The relaxation response.* New York: William Morrow.

Benson, H. (1984). The relaxation response and stress. In J. D. Matarazzo, S. M. Weiss, J. A. Herd, N. E. Miller and S. M. Weiss (Eds.). *Behavioral Health. A Handbook of Health Enhancement and Disease Prevention.* NY: Wiley

Bergin, C. A. C. (1987). Prosocial development of toddlers: The patterning of mother-infant interactions. In M. E. Ford & D. H. Ford (Eds.), *Humans as self-constructing living systems: Putting the framework to work* (pp. 121–143). Hillsdale, NJ: Lawrence Erlbaum

Bergner, R. M. et. al. (1997). A set of papers about difficulties in defining psychopathology and discussion of alternate definitions. *Clinical Psychology: Science and Practice, 4,* 285–287.

Berne, E. (1961). *Transactional analysis in psychotherapy.* NY: Grove

Bernstein, N. (1967). *The coordination and regulation of movements.* London: Pergamon Press.

Beutler, L. E. (1983). *Eclectic psychotherapy: A systematic approach.* New York: Pergamon Press.

Beutler, L. E. (1986). Systematic eclectic psychotherapy. In J. C. Norcross (Ed.), *Handbook of eclectic psychotherapy* (pp. 94–131). New York: Brunner/Mazel.

Beutler, L. E. (1995). Common factors and specific effects. *Clinical Psychology: Science and Practice, 2,* 79–82.

Beutler, L. E., & Clarkin, J. (1990). *Differential treatment selection: Toward targeted therapeutic interventions.* New York: Brunner/Mazel.

Beutler, L. E., & Consoli, A. J. (1992). Systematic eclectic psychotherapy. In J. C. Norcross & M. R. Goldfried (Eds.), *Handbook of psychotherapy integration* (pp. 264–299). New York: Basic Books.

Beutler, L. E., Mohr, D. C., Grawe, K., Engle, D., & MacDonald, R. (1991). Looking for different treatment effects: Cross-cultural predictors of differential therapeutic efficacy. *Journal of Psychotherapy Integration, 1,* 121–141.

Bevan, W. (1991). A tour inside the onion. *American Psychologist, 46,* 475–483.

Binder, J. L., & Strupp, H. H. (1997). Negative process: A recurrently discovered and underestimated facet of therapeutic process and outcome in the individual psychotherapy of adults. *Clinical Psychology: Science and Practice, 4,* 121–139.

Bingham, W. V. (1953). Psychology as a science, as a technology, and as a profession. *American Psychologist, 8,* 115–118.

Binswanger, L. (1963). *Being in the world* (J. Needleman, Trans.). New York: Basic Books. (Original work published 1951).

Blanck, G., & Blanck, R. (1974). *Ego psychology: Theory and practice.* New York: Columbia University Press.

Blanck, G., & Blanck, R. (1979). *Ego psychology II: Psychoanalytic developmental psychology.* New York: Columbia University Press.

Blackmore, W. R. (1981). Human software. *Behavior Research Methods and Instrumentation, 13,* 553–570.

Boesky, D. (1990). The psychoanalytic process and its components. *The Psychoanalytic Quarterly, 59,* 550–584.

Bohart, A. C. (1995). The person-centered psychotherapies. In A. S. Gurman & S. B. Merser (Eds.), *Essential psychotherapies: Theory and practice* (pp. 85–187). New York: Guilford.

Borkovec, T. D. (1997). On the need for a basic science approach to psychotherapy research. *Psychological Science, 8,* 145–147.

Borysenko, J. (1984). Stress, coping, and the immune system. In J. D. Matarazzo, S. M. Weiss, J. A. Herd, & N. E. Miller (Eds.), *Behavioral health. A handbook of health enhancement and disease prevention* (pp. 248–274). New York: Wiley.

Boss, M. (1963). *Psychoanalysis and daseinanalysis* (L. B. Lefebre, Trans.). New York: Basic Books. (Original work published 1957)

Bower, G. H. (1993). The fragmentation of psychology. *American Psychologist, 48,* 905–907.

Bowlby, J. (1969). *Attachment and loss: Vol. 1. Attachment.* New York: Basic Books.

Bowlby, J. (1982). *Attachment and loss: Vol 1. Attachment* (2nd ed.). New York: Basic Books.

Bozarth, J. D. (1984). Beyond reflection: Emergent modes of empathy. In R. F. Levant & J. M. Shlieu (Eds.), *Client-centered therapy and the person-centered ap-*

proach: New directions in theory, research, and practice (pp. 59–75). New York: Praeger.

Bozarth, J. D. (1990). The essence of client-centered therapy. In G. Lictaer, J. Rombants, & R. Van Balen (Eds.), *Client-centered and experiential psychotherapy in the nineties* (pp. 59–64). Leuven, Belgium: Leuven University Press.

Brady, J. P., Davison, G. C., DeWald, P. A., Egan, G., Fadiman, J., Frank, J. D., Gill, M. M., Hoffman, I., Kempler, W., Lazarus, A. A., Raimy, V., Rotter, J. B., & Strupp, H. H. (1980). Some views on effective principles of psychotherapy. *Cognitive Therapy and Research, 4,* 269–306.

Breslow, L., & Engstrom, J. E. (1980). Persistence of health habits and their relationship to mortality. *Preventive Medicine, 9,* 469–483.

Brigham, J. A., & Dengerink, H. A. (1983). Self-management of health-related behaviors. In J. E. Carr & H. A. Dengerink (Eds.), *Behavioral science in the practice of medicine* (pp. 201–223). New York: Elsevier Biomedical.

Brim, O. G., Jr., & Kagan, J. (Eds.). (1980). *Constancy and change in human development.* Cambridge, MA: Harvard University Press.

Brodley, B. T., (1988). Responses to person-centered versus client-centered? *Renaissance, 5,* 1–12.

Brodley, B. T. (1993). Response to Patterson's "Winds of change for client-centered counseling." *Journal of Humanistic Education and Development, 31,* 139–143.

Bronfenbrenner, U. (1979). *The ecology of human development.* Cambridge, MA: Harvard University Press.

Broskowski, A. (1971). Clinical psychology: A research and development model. *Professional Psychologist, 2,* 235–242.

Bruner, J. S. (1982). The nature of adult-infant transaction. In M. Van Cranach & R. Harŕe (Eds.), *The analysis of action* (pp. 313–327). Cambridge: Cambridge University Press.

Bruner, J. (1990). *Acts of meaning.* Cambridge, MA: Harvard University Press.

Buber, M. (1957). *I and thou.* New York: Charles Scribner's Sons.

Buck, R. (1984). *The Communication of Emotion.* NY: Guilford.

Bugental, J. F. T. (Ed.). (1967). *Challenges of humanistic psychology.* New York: McGraw-Hill.

Bugental, J. F. T. (1978). *Psychotherapy and process: The fundamentals of an existential-humanistic approach.* Reading, MA: Addison-Wesley.

Bugental, J. F. T. (1981). *The search for authenticity.* New York: Irvington.

Bugental, J. F. T. (1986). Existential-humanistic psychotherapy. In I. L. Kutash & A. Wolf (Eds.), *Psychotherapist's casebook: Theory and technique in the practice of modern therapies* (pp. 222–236). Northvale, NJ: Aronson.

Bugental, J. F. T. (1987). *The art of the psychotherapist.* NY: Norton.

Bugental, J. F. T. (1993). Existential-humanistic psychotherapy. In I. L. Kurtash & A. Wolf (Eds.) *Psychotherapists casebook: Theory and technique in the practice of modern therapies* (pp 222–236). Northvale, NJ: Aronson.

Bugental, J. F. T., & McBeath, B. (1995). Depth existential therapy: Evolution since World War II. In B. Bongar & L. E. Bentler (Eds.), *Comprehensive textbook of psychotherapy: Theory and practice* (pp. 111–122). New York: Oxford University Press.

Bugental, J. F. T., & Sterling, M. M. (1995). Existential-humanistic psychotherapy: New perspectives. In A. S. Gurman & S. B. Messer (Eds.), *Essential psychotherapies: Theory and practice* (pp. 226–260). New York: Guilford.

Bugliarello, G., & Doner, D. B. (Eds.). (1979). *The history and philosophy of technology.* Urbana: University of Illinois Press.

Buhler, C. (1959). Theoretical observations about life's basic tendencies. *American Journal of Psychotherapy, 13,* 561–581.

Buhler, C. (1964). The human course of life and its goal aspects. *Journal of Humanistic Psychology, 4,* 1–18.

Caddy, G. R., & Byrne, D. G. (Eds.). (1992). *Behavioral medicine. International perspectives* (Vol. 2). Norwood, NJ: Ablex Publishing Corp.

Cambel, A. B. (1993). *Applied chaos theory. A paradigm for complexity.* San Diego, CA: Academic Press.

Cameron, N. (1947). *Psychology and the behavior disorders.* Boston: Houghton-Mifflin.

Capaldi, E. J., & Proctor, R. W. (1994). Contextualism: Is the act in context the adequate metaphor for scientific psychology? *Psychological Bulletin and Review, 1,* 239–249.

Capra, F. (1975). *The tao of physics.* New York: Bantam Books.

Carlson, C. R., & Bernstein, D. A. (1995). Relaxation skills training: Abbreviated progressive relaxation. In W. O'Donohue & L. Krasher (Eds.), *Handbook of psychological skills training. Clinical techniques and applications* (pp. 20–35). Boston: Allyn & Bacon.

Carlson, J. G., & Seifert, A. R. (Eds.). (1991). *International perspectives on self-regulation and health.* New York: Plenum.

Carmody, T. P., & Matarazzo, J. D. (1991). Health psychology. In M. Hersen, A. E. Kazdin, & A. E. Bellack (Eds.), *The clinical psychology handbook* (2nd ed., pp. 695–723). New York: Pergamon Press.

Carr, J. E., & Dengerink, H. A. (Eds.). (1983). *Behavioral science and the practice of medicine.* New York: Elsevier Biomedical.

Carr, J. E., Funabiki, D., & Dengerink, H. A. (1983). Behavioral medicine: Basic concepts and clinical applications. In J. E. Carr & H. A. Dengerink (Eds.), *Behavioral science and the practice of medicine* (pp. 185–199). New York: Elsevier Biomedical.

Carson, R. C. (1969). *Interaction concepts of personality.* Chicago: Aldine.

Carson, R. C. (1991). The social-interactional viewpoint. In M. Hersen, A. E. Kazdin, & A. S. Bellack (Eds.), *The clinical psychology handbook* (2nd ed., pp. 185–199). New York: Pergamon Press.

Cartledge, G., & Milburn, J. F. (1985). *Teaching social skills to children and youth* (3rd ed.). Boston: Allyn & Bacon.

Carver, C. S. (1979). A cybernetic model of self-attention processes. *Journal of Personality and Social Psychology, 37,* 1251–1281.

Carver, C. S., & Scheier, M. F. (1984). A control-theory approach to behavior and some implications for social skills training. In P. Trower (Ed.), *Radical approaches to social skills training* (pp. 92–106). London: Croom Helm.

Cashdan, S. (1988). *Object relations therapy: Using the relationship.* New York: Norton.

Cautela, J. R. (1967). Covert sensitization. *Psychological Reports, 20,* 459–468.

Cautela, J. R., & Kastenbaum, R. A. (1967). Reinforcement survey schedule for use in therapy, training, and research. *Psychological Reports, 20,* 1115–1130.

Cautela, J. R., & Kearney, A. J. (1990). Covert conditioning. In J. K. Zeig & W. M. Munion (Eds.), *What is psychotherapy: Contemporary perspectives* (pp. 130–134). San Francisco: Jossey-Bass.

Chestnut, H. (1967). *Systems engineering methods.* New York: Wiley.

Chrzanowski, G. (1982). Interpersonal formulations of psychotherapy: A contemporary model. In J. C. Anchin & D. J. Kiesler (Eds.), *Handbook of interpersonal psychotherapy* (pp. 25–45). New York: Pergamon Press.

Churchman, C. W. (1968). *The systems approach.* New York: Delacorte Press.

Cohen, S., & Herbert, T. B. (1996). Health psychology: Psychological factors and physical disease from the perspective of human psychoneuroimmunology. *Annual Review of Psychology, 47,* 113–142.

Comtom, A. (1990). Psychoanalytic process. *The Psychoanalytic Quarterly, 59,* 588–596.

Conger, J. C., & Conger, A. J. (1982). Components of heterosocial competence. In J. P. Curran & P. M. Monti (Eds.), *Social skills training. A practical handbook for assessment and treatment* (pp. 313–347). New York: Guilford.

Consumer Reports. (1995). Mental health. Does therapy help? *60,* pp. 734–739. Yonkers, NY: Consumer Union.

Cooper, A. M. (1987). Changes in psychoanalytic ideas: Transference interpretation. *Journal of the American Psychoanalytic Association, 35,* 77–98.

Cooper, A. (1991). Creating a scientific psychoanalysis? A man with a mission. *Contemporary Psychology, 36,* 441–442.

Coyne, J. C. (1976). Depression and the response of others. *Journal of Abnormal Psychology, 85,* 186–193.

Coyne, J. C. (1990). Interpersonal processes in depression. In G. I. Keitner (Ed.), *Depression and families: Impact and treatment* (pp. 31–53). Washington, DC: American Psychiatric Press.

Craig, E. (1986). Sanctuary and presence: An existential view of the therapist's contribution. *The Humanistic Psychologist, 1,* 22–28.

Cramer, P. (1991). *The development of defense mechanisms. Theory, research, and assessment.* New York: Springer-Verlag.

Curran, J. P. (1985). Social competency training. In H. J. Marlowe & R. G. Weinberg (Eds.), *Competence development* (pp. 50–82). Springfield, IL: Charles C. Thomas.

Curran, J. P., & Monti, P. M. (Eds.). (1982). *Social skills training. A practical handbook for assessment and treatment.* New York: Guilford.

Cushman, P. (1992). Psychotherapy to 1992: A historically situated interpretation. In D. K. Freedheim (Ed.), *History of psychotherapy: A century of change* (pp. 21–64). Washington, DC: American Psychological Association.

Davar, B. V., & Bhat, P. R. (1995). *Psychoanalysis as a human science—beyond foundationalism.* Thousand Oaks, CA: Sage.

Davidson, R. J., & Schwartz, G. E. (1976). The psychology of relaxation and related states: A multiprocess theory. In D. I. Mostofsky (Ed.), *Behavior control and modification of physiological activity* (pp. 102–117). Englewood Cliffs, NJ: Prentice-Hall.

Davies, D., Banfield, T., & Sheehan, R. (1976). *The humane technologist.* New York: Oxford University Press.

Davis, R. (1974). Technology as a deterrent to dehumanization (editorial). *Science, 185.*

Davison, W. T., Pray, M., & Bristol, C. (1990). Mutative interpretation and close process monitoring in a study of psychoanalytic process. *The Psychoanalytic Quarterly, 59,* 600–629.

Dawes, R. M. (1994). *House of cards: Psychology and psychotherapy built on myth.* New York: Free Press.

Deese, J. (1996). Contextualism: Truth in advertising. *The General Psychologist, 32,* 56–61.

Delprato, D. J. (1995). Interbehavioral psychology: Critical, systematic, and integrative approach to clinical services. In W. O'Donohue & L. Krasher (Eds.), *Theories of behavior therapy. Exploring behavior change* (pp. 609–636). Washington, DC: American Psychological Association.

deRivera, J. (1977). *A Structural Theory of Emotions*. NY: International Universities Press.

Deutsch, K. W. (1951). Mechanism, organism, and society. *Philosophy of Science, 18*, 230–252.

Dickinson, A. (1987). Animal conditioning and learning theory. In H. J. Eysenck & I. Martin (Eds.), *Theoretical foundations of behavior therapy* (pp. 57–80). New York: Plenum.

DiGiuseppe, R. (1986). The implication of the philosophy of science for rational-emotive theory and therapy. *Psychotherapy, 23*, 634–639.

DiGiuseppe, R., McGowan, L., Simon, K. S., & Gardner, F. (1990). A comparative outcome study of four cognitive therapies in the treatment of social anxiety. *Journal of Rational-Emotive and Cognitive-Behavioral Therapy, 8*, 129–146.

DiZumilla, T. J., & Goldfried, M. R. (1971). Problem-solving and behavior modification. *Journal of Abnormal Psychology, 78*, 107–126.

Dobson, K. S. (1988a). *Handbook of cognitive-behavioral therapies*. New York: Guilford.

Dobson, K. S. (1988b). The present and future of the cognitive-behavioral therapies. In K. S. Dobson (Ed.), *Handbook of cognitive-behavioral therapies* (pp. 387–414). New York: Guilford.

Dobson, K. S. (1989). A meta-analysis of the efficacy of cognitive therapy for depression. *Journal of Consulting and Clinical Psychology, 57*, 414–419.

Dobson, K. S., & Block, L. (1988). Historical and philosophical basis of the cognitive-behavioral therapies. In K. S. Dobson (Ed.), *Handbook of cognitive-behavioral therapies* (pp. 3–38). New York: Guilford.

Dobson, K. S., & Shaw, B. F. (1995). Cognitive therapies in practice. In B. Bongar & L. E. Bentler (Eds.), *Comprehensive textbook of psychotherapy: Theory and practice* (pp. 159–172). New York: Oxford University Press.

Dollard, J., & Miller, N. E. (1950). *Personality and psychotherapy: An analysis in terms of learning, thinking, and culture*. New York: McGraw-Hill.

Dorpat, T. L., & Miller, M. L. (1992). *Clinical interaction and the analysis of meaning. A new psychoanalytic theory*. Hillsdale, NJ: The Analytic Press.

Dryden, W. (1987). *Counseling individuals: The relational-emotive approach*. London: Taylor and Francis.

Dryden, W., & Ellis, A. (1988). Rational-emotive therapy. In K. S. Dobson (Ed.), *Handbook of cognitive-behavioral therapies* (pp. 214–272). New York: Guilford.

Eagle, M. N., & Wolitzky, D. L. (1992). Psychoanalytic theories of psychotherapy. In D. K. Freedheim (Ed.), *History of psychotherapy: A century of change* (pp. 109–158). Washington, DC: American Psychological Association.

Edelman, G. M. (1989). *The remembered present. A biological theory of consciousness.* New York: Basic Books.

Edelson, M. (1988). *Psychoanalysis: A theory in crisis.* Chicago: University of Chicago Press.

Eells, T. D. (Ed.). (1997). *Handbook of psychotherapy case formulation.* NY: Guilford.

Efran, J. S., & Fauber, R. L. (1985). Radical constructivism: Questions and answers. In R. A. Neimeyer & M. J. Mahoney (Eds.), *Constructivism in psychotherapy* (pp. 275–304). Washington, DC: American Psychological Association.

Eifert, G. H. (1987). Language conditioning: Clinical issues and applications in behavior therapy. In H. J. Eysenck & I. Martin (Eds.), *Theoretical foundations of behavior therapy* (pp. 167–193). New York: Plenum.

Einstein, A., & Infold, L. (1938). *The evolution of physics.* New York: Simon and Schuster.

Eisenthal, S. (1992). Recognition of and response to counter-transference: Psychoanalytic and interpersonal communication approaches. In J. S. Rutan (Ed.), *Psychotherapy for the 1990s* (pp. 139–165). New York: Guilford.

Eissler, K. R. (1953). The effect of structure of the ego on psychoanalytic technique. *Journal of the American Psychoanalytic Association, 1,* 104–143.

Ekman, P. (Ed.). (1982). *Emotion in the human face* (2nd ed.). Cambridge University Press.

Ekman, P. & Davidson, R. J. (Eds.). (1994). *The nature of emotions,* NY: Oxford University Press.

Elkin, I., Shea, M. T., Watkins, J. T., Imber, S. D., Sotsky, S. M., Collins, J. F., Glass, D. R., Pilkonis, P. A., Leber, W. R., Docherty, J. P., Fiester, S. J., & Parloff, M. B. (1989). National Institute of Mental Health treatment of depression collaborative research program: General effectiveness of treatments. *Archives of General Psychiatry, 46,* 971–982.

Ellenberger, H. F. (1970). *The discovery of the unconscious: The history and evolution of dynamic psychiatry.* New York: Basic Books.

Elliott, R., & Greenberg, L. S. (1995). Experiential therapy in practice: The process-experiential approach. In B. Bongar & L. E. Beutler (Eds.), *Comprehensive textbook of psychotherapy: Theory and practice* (pp. 123–139). New York: Oxford University Press.

Ellis, A. (1957). Outcome of employing three techniques of psychotherapy. *Journal of Clinical Psychology, 13,* 344–350.

Ellis, A. (1962). *Reason and emotion in psychotherapy.* New York: Stuart.

Ellis, A. (1970). Rational-emotive therapy. In L. Hersher (Ed.), *Four psychotherapies* (pp. 47–83). New York: Appleton-Century-Crofts.

Ellis, A. (1971). *Growth through reason.* North Hollywood, CA: Wilshire.

Ellis, A. (1977a). The basic clinical theory of rational-emotive therapy. In A. Ellis & R. Grieger (Ed.), *Handbook of rational-emotive therapy* (Vol. 1, pp. 1–32). New York: Springer.

Ellis, A. (1977b). Rational-emotive therapy: Research data that supports the clinical and personality hypotheses of RET and other modes of cognitive-behavior therapy. *The Counseling Psychologist, 7,* 2–43.

Ellis, A. (1979). The practice of rational-emotive therapy. In A. Ellis & J. M. Whitely (Eds.), *Theoretical and empirical foundations of rational-emotive therapy* (pp. 61–100). Monterey, CA: Brooks/Cole.

Ellis, A. (1980). Rational-emotive therapy and cognitive-behavior therapy: Similarities and differences. *Cognitive Therapy and Research, 4,* 325–340.

Ellis, A. (1985). Expanding the ABCs of rational-emotive therapy. In M. J. Mahoney & A. Freeman (Eds.), *Cognition and psychotherapy* (pp. 313–323). New York: Plenum.

Ellis, A. (1986). Rational-emotive therapy. In I. L. Kutash & A. Wolf (Eds.), *Psychotherapist's casebook* (pp. 277–287). San Francisco: Jossey-Bass.

Ellis, A., & Bernard, M. E. (Eds.). (1983). *Rational-emotive approaches to the problems of childhood.* New York: Plenum.

Ellis, A., & Bernard, M. E. (Eds.) (1985). *Clinical applications of rational-emotive therapy.* NY: Plenum.

Ellis, A., & Dryden, W. (1987). *The practice of rational emotive therapy.* New York: Springer.

Ellis, A., & Greiger, R. (Eds.). (1977). *Handbook of rational-emotive therapy.* New York: Plenum.

Ellis, A., & Harper, R. A. (1975). *A new guide to rational living.* North Hollywood, CA: Wilshire.

Ellis, A., McInerney, J. F., DiGuisippe, R., & Yeager, R. J. (1988). *Rational-emotive therapy with alcoholics and substance abusers.* Boston: Allyn & Bacon.

Ellis, A., Sichel, J. L., Yeager, R. J., DiMattia, D. J., & DiGuisippe, R. (1989). *Rational-emotive couples therapy.* New York: Pergamon Press.

Erickson, M. H. (1980). *The collected papers of Milton H. Erickson* (Vols. 1–4). New York: Irvington.

Erickson, M. H., & Rossi, E. (1979). *Hypnotherapy: An exploratory casebook.* New York: Irvington.

Erikson, E. H. (1946). Ego development and historical change. *The Psychoanalytic Study of the Child, 2,* 359–396.

Erikson, E. H. (1950). *Childhood and society.* New York: Norton.

Erikson, E. H. (1956). The problem of ego identity. *Journal of the American Psychoanalytic Association, 4,* 56–121.

Erikson, E. H. (1963). *Childhood and society* (2nd ed.). New York: Norton.

Erikson, E. H. (1968). *Identity, youth and crisis*. New York: Norton.

Erikson, E. H. (1975). *Life history and the historical movement*. New York: Norton.

Erwin, E. (1978). *Behavior therapy: Scientific, philosophical and moral foundations*. New York: Cambridge University Press.

Etchegoyen, R. H. (1991). *The fundamentals of psychoanalytic technique*. London: H. Karmac (Books).

Eysenck, H. J. (1952). The effects of psychotherapy: An evaluation. *Journal of Consulting Psychology, 16,* 319–324.

Eysenck, H. J. (1957). *The dynamics of anxiety and hysteria*. London: Routledge and Kegan Paul.

Eysenck, H. J. (1959). Learning theory and behavior therapy. *The Journal of Mental Science, 105,* 61–75.

Eysenck, H. (1969). *The effects of psychotherapy*. New York: Science House.

Eysenck, H. J. (1985). Incubation theory of fear/anxiety. In S. Reiss & R. R. Bootzin (Eds.), *Theoretical issues in behavior therapy* (pp. 83–105). Orlando, FL: Academic Press.

Eysenck, H. J. (1987a). Behavior therapy. In H. J. Eysenck & I. Martin (Eds.), *Theoretical foundations of behavior therapy* (pp. 3–29). New York: Plenum.

Eysenck, H. J. (1987b). The role of heredity, environment, and "preparedness" in the genesis of neurosis. In H. J. Eysenck & I. Martin (Eds.), *Theoretical foundations of behavior therapy* (pp. 379–402). New York: Plenum.

Eysenck, H. J. (1988). Psychotherapy to behavior therapy: A paradigm shift. In D. B. Fishman, F. Rotgers, & C. M. Franks (Eds.), *Paradigms in behavior therapy: Present and promise* (pp. 45–76). New York: Springer.

Fagan, J., & Shepherd, I. L. (Eds.). (1970). *Gestalt therapy now*. Palo Alto, CA: Science and Behaviour Books.

Fairbairn, W. R. D. (1952). *An object relations theory of the personality*. New York: Basic Books.

Feixas, G. (1995). Personal constructs in systemic practice. In R. A. Neimeyer & M. J. Mahoney (Eds.), *Constructivism in psychotherapy* (pp. 305–338). Washington, DC: American Psychological Association.

Fenichel, O. (1945). *The psychoanalytic theory of neurosis*. New York: Norton and Co.

Fiedler, F. E. (1950a). The concept of the ideal therapeutic relationship. *Journal of Consulting Psychology, 14,* 239–245.

Fiedler, F. E. (1950b). Comparisons of therapeutic relationships in psychoanalytic, nondirective, and Adlerian therapy. *Journal of Consulting Psychology, 14,* 436–445.

Fine, R. (1979). *A history of psychoanalysis.* New York: Columbia University Press.

Fine, S., & Fine, E. (1990). Four psychoanalytic perspectives: A study of differences in interpretive interventions. *Journal of the American Psychoanalytic Association, 38,* 107–141.

Finn, T., DiGuiseppe, R., & Culver, C. (1991). The effectiveness of rational-emotive therapy in the reduction of muscle contraction headaches. *Journal of Cognitive Psychotherapy: An International Quarterly, 5,* 93–103.

Fischer, C. T. (1991). Phenomenological-existential psychotherapy. In M. Heisen, A. E. Kazdin, & A. S. Bellack (Eds.), *The clinical psychology handbook* (2nd ed., pp. 534–550). New York: Pergamon Press.

Fischer, J. (1995). Uniformity myths in electic and integrative psychotherapy. *Journal of Psychotherapy Integration, 5,* 41–56.

Fischer, W. (1978). *Theories of anxiety.* New York: Harper & Row.

Fishman, D. B., & Franks, C. M. (1992). Evolution and differentiation within behavior therapy: A theoretical and epistemological review. In D. K. Freedheim (Ed.), *History of psychotherapy: A century of change* (pp. 159–196). Washington, DC: American Psychological Association.

Fishman, D. B., Rotgers, F., & Franks, C. M. (Eds.). (1988a). *Paradigms in behavior therapy: Present and promise.* New York: Springer.

Fishman, D. B. Rotgers, F., & Franks, C. M. (1988b). Paradigms in wonderland: Fundamental issues in behavior therapy. In D. B. Fishman, F. Rotgers, & C. M. Franks (Eds.), *Paradigms in behavior therapy: Present and promise* (pp. 7–19). New York: Springer.

Fishman, S. T., & Lubetkin, B. S. (1983). Office practice of behavior therapy. In M. Hersen (Ed.), *Outpatient behavior therapy: A clinical guide* (pp. 21–41). New York: Grune and Stratton.

Flexner, A. (1910). *Medical education in the United States and Canada. A report to the Carnegie Foundation for the Advancement of Teaching.* Boston: Updyke.

Ford, D. H. (1987). *Humans as self-constructing living systems. A developmental perspective on behavior, personality, and health.* New York: Erlbaum.

Ford, D. H. (1994). *Humans as self-constructing living systems. A developmental perspective on behavior, personality, and health* (2nd ed.). State College, PA: IDEALS, Inc.

Ford, D. H., & Lerner, R. M. (1992). *Developmental systems theory. An integrative approach.* Newbury Park, CA: Sage.

Ford, D. H., & Urban, H. B. (1963). *Systems of psychotherapy: A comparative study.* New York: Wiley.

Ford, M. E. (1985). The concept of competence: Themes and variations. In

H. J. Marlowe & R. G. Weinberg (Eds.), *Competence development* (pp. 3–49). Springfield, IL: Charles C. Thomas.

Ford, M. E. (1987). Processes contributing to adolescent social competence. In M. Ford & D. Ford (Eds.). *Humans as self-constructing living systems: Putting the framework to work* (pp. 199–233). Hillsdale, NJ: Erlbaum.

Ford, M. (1992). *Motivating humans: Goals, emotions, and personal agency beliefs.* Newbury Park, CA: Sage.

Ford, M. E., & Ford, D. H. (1987). *Humans as self-constructing living systems: Putting the framework to work.* Hillsdale, NJ: Erlbaum.

Ford, M. E., & Nichols, C. W. (1991). Using goal assessments to identify motivational patterns and facilitate behavioral regulation and achieveement. In M. L. Maehr & P. R. Patrick (Eds.), *Advances in motivation and achievement* (Vol. 7, pp. 51–84). Greenwich, CT: JAI.

Ford, M. E., & Nichols, C. W. (1992). *Manual: Assessment of personal goals.* Palo Alto, CA: Consulting Psychologist Press.

Forgas, J. (1979). *Social episodes: The study of interaction routines.* (European Monographs in Social Psychology No. 17). London: Academic Press.

Fosshage, J. L. (1992). The self and its vicissitudes. In J. J. Sholnick & S. C. Warshaw (Eds.), *Relational perspectives in psychoanalysis* (pp. 21–42). Hillsdale, NJ: The Analytic Press.

Frank, J. D. (1961). *Persuasion and healing.* Baltimore: Johns Hopkins Press.

Frank, J. D. (1977). Nature and functions of belief systems: Humanism and transcendental religion. *American Psychologist, 32,* 555–559.

Frank, J. D. (1982). Psychotherapy integration: An historical perspective. In J. H. Harvey & M. M. Parks (Eds.). *The master lecture series, Vol. 1, psychotherapy research and behavior change* (pp 73–122). Washington, DC: American Psychological Association.

Frankl, V. E. (1962). *Man's search for meaning: An introduction to logotherapy.* Boston: Beacon Press.

Frankl, V. E. (1967). *Psychotherapy and existentialism.* NY: Washington Square Press.

Frankl, V. E. (1969). *The will to meaning.* New York: World Publishing Co.

Frankl, V. E. (1975). *The unconscious god.* NY: Simon & Schuster.

Franks, C. M. (1984). On conceptual and technical integrity in psychoanalysis and behavior therapy: Two fundamentally incompatible systems. In H. Arkowitz & S. B. Messer (Eds.), *Psychoanalytic therapy and behavior therapy: Is integration possible?* (pp. 223–247). New York: Plenum.

Franks, C. M., & Barbrack, C. R. (1983). Behavior therapy with adults: An integrative perspective. In M. Hersen, A. E. Kazdin, & A. S. Bellack (Eds.), *The clinical psychology handbook* (pp. 507–524). New York: Pergamon Press.

Franks, C. M., & Barbrack, C. R. (1991). Behavior therapy with adults: An integrative perspective for the nineties. In M. Hersen, A. E. Kazdin, & A. S. Bellack (Eds.), *The clinical psychology handbook* (2nd ed., pp. 559–566). New York: Pergamon Press.

Franks, C. M., & Rosenbaum, M. (1983). Behavior therapy: Overview and personal reflections. In M. Rosenbaum, C. M. Franks, & Y. Jaffe (Eds.), *Perspectives on behavior therapy in the eighties* (pp. 3–16). New York: Springer.

Franks, C. M., & Wilson, G. T. (1975). *Annual review of behavior therapy: Theory and practice* (Vol. 3). New York: Brunner/Mazel.

Freedheim, D. K. (Ed.). (1992). *History of psychotherapy: A century of change.* Washington, DC: American Psychological Association.

Freedman, M. B., Leasy, T. F., Ossorio, A. G., & Coffey, H. S. (1951). The interpersonal dimensions of personality. *Journal of Personality, 20,* 143–161.

Freeman, A. (1987). Cognitive therapy: An overview. In A. Freeman & V. Greenwood (Eds.), *Cognitive therapy: Applications in psychiatric and medical settings* (pp. 19–35). New York: Human Sciences Press.

Freeman, A., & Leaf, R. (1989). Cognitive therapy of personality disorders. In A. Freeman, K. M. Simon, L. E. Bentler, & H. Arkowitz (Eds.), *Comprehensive handbook of cognitive therapy* (pp. 403–434). New York: Plenum.

Freeman, A., & Simon, K. M. (1989). Cognitive therapy of anxiety. In A. Freeman, K. M. Simon, L. E. Bentler, & H. Arkowitz (Eds.), *Comprehensive handbook of cognitive therapy* (pp. 347–366). New York: Plenum.

Freeman, A., Pretzer, J., Fleming, B., & Simon, K. M. (1990). *Clinical applications of cognitive therapy.* New York: Plenum.

Freeman, A., Simon, K. M., Bentler, L. E., & Arkowitz, H. (Eds.) (1989). *Comprehensive handbook of cognitive therapy.* New York: Plenum.

Freimuth, M. (1992). Is the best always preferred? *American Psychologist, 5,* 673–674.

French, T. M. (1933). Interrelationships between psychoanalysis and the experimental work of Pavlov. *American Journal of Psychiatry, 89,* 1165–1203.

Freud, A. (1936). *The ego and the mechanisms of defense.* New York: International Universities Press.

Freud, S. (1940). On the theory of hysterical attacks (with J. Brewer). In J. Strachey (Ed.), *The standard edition of the complete psychological works of Sigmund Freud* (Vol. 1, pp. 151–154). London: Hogarth Press. (Original work published 1892).

Freud, S. (1953a). The interpretation of dreams. In J. Strachey (Ed.), *The standard edition of the complete psychological works of Sigmund Freud* (Vol. 5, pp. 339–627). London: Hogarth Press. (Original work published 1900)

Freud, S. (1953b). Three essays on the theory of sexuality. In J. Strachey (Ed.), *The standard edition of the complete psychological works of Sigmund Freud* (Vol. 7, pp. 125–245). London: Hogarth Press. (Original work published 1905)

Freud, S. (1954a). *The origins of psychoanalysis: Letters to Fliess.* New York: Basic Books. (Original work published 1895)

Freud, S. (1954b). *The origins of psychoanalysis. Letters to Wilhelm Fliess; drafts and notes.* M. Bonaparte, A. Freud, & E. Kris (Eds.). New York: Basic Books. (Original work published 1887–1902)

Freud, S. (1955a). Beyond the pleasure principles. In J. Strachey (Ed.), *The standard edition of the complete psychological works of Sigmund Freud* (Vol. 18, pp. 7–64). London: Hogarth Press. (Original work published 1920)

Freud, S. (1955b). A child is being beaten: A contribution to the origins of sexual perversions. In J. Strachey (Ed.), *The standard edition of the complete psychological works of Sigmund Freud* (Vol. 17, pp. 177–204). London: Hogarth Press. (Original work published 1919)

Freud, S. (1957a). Instincts and their vicissitudes. In J. Strachey (Ed.), *The standard edition of the complete psychological works of Sigmund Freud* (Vol. 14, pp. 117–140). London: Hogarth Press. (Original work published 1915)

Freud, S. (1957b). On the history of the psychoanalytic movement. In J. Strachey (Ed.), *The standard edition of the complete psychological works of Sigmund Freud* (Vol. 14, pp. 2–66). London: Hogarth Press. (Original work published 1914)

Freud, S. (1957c). On narcissism: An introduction. In J. Strachey (Ed.), *The standard edition of the complete psychological works of Sigmund Freud* (Vol. 14, pp. 73–102). London: Hogarth Press. (Original work published 1914)

Freud, S. (1957d). The unconscious. In J. Strachey (Ed.), *The standard edition of the complete psychological works of Sigmund Freud* (Vol. 14, pp. 166–215). London: Hogarth Press. (Original work published 1915)

Freud, S. (1958a). The dynamics of transference. In J. Strachey (Ed.), *The standard edition of the complete psychological works of Sigmund Freud* (Vol. 12, pp. 97–108). London: Hogarth Press. (Original work published 1912)

Freud, S. (1958b). Formulations on the two principles of mental functioning. In J. Strachey (Ed.), *The standard edition of the complete psychological works of Sigmund Freud* (Vol. 12, pp. 89–96). London: Hogarth Press. (Original work published 1911)

Freud, S. (1958c). Observations on transference-love (further recommendations on the technique of psycho-analysis III). In J. Strachey (Ed.), *The standard edition of the complete psychological works of Sigmund Freud* (Vol. 12, pp. 157–171). London: Hogarth Press. (Original work published 1915)

Freud, S. (1958d). On beginning the treatment (further recommendations on the technique of psycho-analysis). In J. Strachey (Ed.), *The standard edition of the complete psychological works of Sigmund Freud* (Vol. 12, pp. 121–144). London: Hogarth Press. (Original work published 1913)

Freud, S. (1958e). Recommendations to physicians practicing psychoanalysis. In J. Strachey (Ed.), *The standard edition of the complete psychological works of Sigmund Freud* (Vol. 12, pp. 109–120). London: Hogarth Press. (Original work published 1912)

Freud, S. (1958f). Remembering, repeating and working through (further recommendations on the technique of psycho-analysis II). In J. Strachey (Ed.), *The standard edition of the complete psychological works of Sigmund Freud* (Vol. 12, pp. 145–156). London: Hogarth Press. (Original work published 1914)

Freud, S. (1958g). Three contributions to the psychology of love. In J. Strachey (Ed.), *The standard edition of the complete psychological works of Sigmund Freud* (Vol. 7, pp. 246–259). London: Hogarth Press. (Original work published 1910)

Freud, S. (1959). Inhibitions, symptoms and anxiety. In J. Strachey (Ed.), *The standard edition of the complete psychological works of Sigmund Freud* (Vol. 20, pp. 80–114). London: Hogarth Press. (Original work published 1926)

Freud, S. (1961a). Civilization and its discontents. In J. Strachey (Ed.), *The standard edition of the complete psychological works of Sigmund Freud* (Vol. 21, pp. 59–145). London: Hogarth Press. (Original work published 1930)

Freud, S. (1961b). The ego and the id. In J. Strachey (Ed.), *The standard edition of the complete psychological works of Sigmund Freud* (Vol. 18, pp. 12–66). London: Hogarth Press. (Original work published 1923)

Freud, S. (1961c). Group psychology and the analysis of the ego. In J. Strachey (Ed.), *The standard edition of the complete psychological works of Sigmund Freud* (Vol. 18, pp. 65–143). London: Hogarth Press. (Original work published 1921)

Freud, S. (1961d). The loss of reality in neurosis and psychosis. In J. Strachey (Ed.), *The standard edition of the complete psychological works of Sigmund Freud* (Vol. 19, pp. 183–187). London: Hogarth Press. (Original work published 1924)

Freud, S. (1961e). Neurosis and psychosis. In J. Strachey (Ed.), *The standard edition of the complete psychological works of Sigmund Freud* (Vol. 19, pp. 149–153). London: Hogarth Press. (Original work published 1924)

Freud, S. (1963) Introductory lectures on psycho-analysis. In J. Strachey (Ed.), *The standard edition of the complete psychological works of Sigmund Freud* (Vol.

15, pp. 1–240; Vol. 15, pp. 241–496). London: Hogarth Press. (Original work published 1916–1917)

Freud, S. (1964a). Analysis terminable and interminable. In J. Strachey (Ed.), *The standard edition of the complete psychological works of Sigmund Freud* (Vol. 23, pp. 216–253). London: Hogarth Press. (Original work published 1957)

Freud, S. (1964b). New introductory lectures in psychoanalysis. In J. Strachey (Ed.), *The standard edition of the complete psychological works of Sigmund Freud* (Vol. 22, pp. 5–182). London: Hogarth Press. (Original work published 1933)

Freud, S. (1964c). An outline of psychoanalysis. In J. Strachey (Ed.), *The standard edition of the complete psychological works of Sigmund Freud* (Vol. 23, pp. 141–207). London: Hogarth Press. (Original work published 1940)

Freud, S. (1966). Project for a scientific psychology. In J. Strachey (Ed.), *The standard edition of the complete psychological works of Sigmund Freud* (Vol. 1, pp. 295–391). London: Hogarth Press. (Original work published 1895).

Freud, S., & Brewer, J. (1957). *Studies in hysteria.* New York: Basic Books. (Original work published 1895)

Fromm, E. (1969). *Escape from freedom* (2nd ed.). New York: Avon.

Gabbard, G. O. (1994). *Psychodynamic psychiatry in clinical practice. The DSM-IV edition.* Washington, DC: American Psychiatric Press, Inc.

Gallistel, C. R. (1980). *The organization of action: A new synthesis.* Hillsdale, N.J.: Erlbaum.

Gambrill, E. (1977). *Behavior modification: Handbook of assessment, intervention, and evaluation.* San Francisco: Jossey-Bass.

Gambrill, E. (1984). Social skills training. In D. Larsen (Ed.), *Teaching psychological skills. Models for giving psychology away* (pp. 104–130). Monterey, CA: Brooks/Cole.

Gambrill, E. (1985). Social skills training with the elderly. In L. L'Abate & M. A. Milan (Eds.), *Handbook of social skills training and research* (pp. 326–357). New York: Wiley.

Gambrill, E. (1986). Social skills training with the elderly. In C. Hollin & P. Trower (Eds.), *Handbook of social skills training* (Vol. 1, pp. 211–238). New York: Pergamon Press.

Gambrill, E. (1995a). Helping shy, socially anxious, and lonely adults: A skill-based contextual approach. In W. O'Donohue & L. Krasher (Eds.), *Handbook of psychological skills training. Clinical techniques and applications* (pp. 247–286). Boston: Allyn & Bacon.

Gambrill, E. (1995b). Assertion skills training. In W. O'Donohue & L. Krasner

(Eds.), *Handbook of psychological skills training: Clinical techniques and applications* (pp. 81–118). Boston: Allyn & Bacon.

Garcia, E. J. (1977). Working on the E in RET. In J. L. Wolfe & E. Brand (Eds.), *Twenty years of rational therapy* (pp. 72–87). New York: Institute for Rational-Emotive Therapy.

Garfield, S. L. (1980). *Psychotherapy: An eclectic approach.* New York: Wiley.

Garfield, S. L. (1992). Eclectic psychotherapy: A common factors approach. In J. C. Norcross & M. R. Goldfried (Eds.), *Handbook of psychotherapy integration* (pp. 169–201). New York: Basic Books.

Garfield, S. L. (1996). Some problems associated with "validated" forms of psychotherapy. *Clinical Psychology: Science and Practice, 3,* 218–229.

Garfield, S. L., & Bergin, A. E. (1994). Introduction and historical review. In A. E. Bergin & S. L. Garfield (Eds.), *Handbook for psychotherapy and behavior change* (4th ed., pp. 3–8). New York: Wiley.

Gelhorn, E., & Loofbourrow, G. N. (1963). *Emotions and emotional disorders: A neurophysiological study.* New York: Harper & Row.

Gendlin, E. T. (1962). *Experiencing and the creation of meaning.* New York: Free Press.

Gendlin, E. T. (1964). A theory of personality change. In P. Worchel & D. Byrnes (Eds.), *Personality change* (pp. 129–174). New York: Wiley.

Gendlin, E. T. (1969). Focusing. *Psychotherapy: Theory, research and practice, 6,* p. 4–5.

Gendlin, E. T. (1973). Experiential psychotherapy. In R. Corsini (Ed.), *Current psychotherapies* (pp. 317–352). Itasca, IL: F. E. Peacock.

Gendlin, E. T. (1978). *Focusing.* New York: Everest House.

Gendlin, E. T. (1981). *Focusing* (2nd ed.). New York: Bantam Books.

Gendlin, E. T. (1996). *Focusing-oriented psychotherapy: A manual of the experiential method.* New York: Guilford.

Ghent, E. (1992). Foreword. In N. J. Skolnick & S. C. Warshaw (Eds.), *Relational perspectives in psychoanalysis* (pp. xiii–xxii). Hillsdale, NJ: The Analytic Press.

Gibbs, J. C. (1979). The meaning of ecologically oriented inquiry in contemporary psychology. *American Psychology, 34,* 127–140.

Gibbs, J. C., Potter, G. B., & Goldstein, A. P. (1995). *The EQUIP program: Teaching youth to think and act responsibly through a peer-helping approach.* Champaign, IL: Research Press.

Giblin, P., Sprenkle, D. H., & Seehan, R. (1985). Enrichment outcome research: A meta-analysis of premarital, marital, and family intervention. *Marital and Family Therapy, 11,* 257–271.

Gilbert, P., & Trower, P. (1990). The evolution and manifestation of social anxiety. In W. R. Crozier (Ed.), *Shyness, embarrassment: Perspectives from social psychology* (pp. 144–177). New York: Plenum.

Gill, M. M. (1954). Psychoanalysis and exploratory psychotherapy. *Journal of the American Psychoanalytic Association, 2*, 771–797.

Gill, M. (1982). Analysis of transference, Vol. 1: Theory and technique. *Psychological Issues*, Monograph 53. New York: International Universities Press.

Gill, M. M. (1983). The interpersonal paradigm and the degree of the therapist's involvement. *Contemporary Psychoanalysis, 19*, 200–237.

Gill, M. M. (1984). Psychoanalytic, psychodynamic, cognitive behavior, and behavior therapies compared. In H. Arkowitz & S. B. Messer (Eds.), *Psychoanalytic therapy and behavior therapy: Is integration possible?* (pp. 179–187). New York: Plenum.

Glass, C. R., & Arnkoff, D. B. (1992). Behavior therapy. In D. K. Freedheim (Ed.), *History of psychotherapy: A century of change* (pp. 587–628). Washington, DC: American Psychological Association.

Gleick, J. (1987). *Chaos: Making a new science.* New York: Viking.

Gold, J. R. (1996). *Key concepts in psychotherapy integration.* New York: Plenum.

Golden, W. L., & Dryden, W. (1986). Cognitive-behavioral therapies: Commonalities, divergences and future developments. In W. Dryden & W. L. Golden (Eds.), *Cognitive-behavioral approaches to psychotherapy* (pp. 356–378). London: Harper & Row.

Goldfried, M. R. (1980). Toward the delineation of therapeutic change principles. *American Psychologist, 35*, 991–999.

Goldfried, M. R. (1991). Research issues in psychotherapy integration. *Journal of Psychotherapy Integration, 1*, 5–25.

Goldfried, M. R. (1995). *From cognitive-behavior therapy to psychotherapy integration.* New York: Springer.

Goldfried, M. R. & Newman (1986). Psychotherapy integration: An historical perspective. In J. C. Norcross (Ed.) *Handbook of eclectic psychotherapy* (pp. 25–61). NY: Bruner-Mazel.

Goldfried, M. R., & Robins, C. (1983). Self-schemas, cognitive bias, and the processing of learning experiences. In C. C. Kendall (Ed.), *Advances in cognitive-behavioral research and therapy* (Vol. 2, pp. 221–247). New York: Academic Press.

Goldfried, M. R., & Safran, J. D. (1986). Future directions in psychotherapy integration. In J. C. Norcross (Ed.), *Handbook of eclectic psychotherapy* (pp. 463–483). New York: Brunner/Mazel.

Goldiamond, I., & Dyrud, J. E. (1968). Some applications and implications of behavior analysis for psychotherapy. In J. M. Shlien (Ed.), *Research in psychotherapy* (pp. 54–89). Washington, DC: American Psychological Association.

Goldsmith, J. B., & McFall, R. M. (1975). Development and evaluation of an interpersonal skill-training program for psychiatric inpatients. *Journal of Abnormal Psychology, 84,* 51–58.

Goldstein, A. P. (1973). *Structured learning therapy. Toward a psychotherapy for the poor.* New York: Academic Press.

Goldstein, A. P. (1981). *Psychological skill training: The structured learning technique.* New York: Pergamon Press.

Goldstein, A. P. (1988). *The prepare curriculum: Teaching prosocial competencies.* Champaign, IL: Research Press.

Goldstein, A. P. (1990). Generating transfer: Toward a technology of transfer and maintenance enhancement. In D. R. Snyder & D. Forsyth (Eds.), *Handbook of clinical-social psychology* (pp. 31–33). New York: Pergamon Press.

Goldstein, A. P. (1991). *Delinquent gangs: A psychological perspective.* Champaign, IL: Research Press.

Goldstein, A. P. (1995). Coordinated multitargeted skills training: The promotion of generalization-enhancement. In W. O'Dononue & L. Krasner (Eds.), *Handbook of psychological skills training, clinical techniques, and applications* (pp. 383–400). Boston: Allyn & Bacon.

Goldstein, A. P., Gershaw, N. J., & Sprafkin, R. P. (1985). Structured learning: Research and practice in psychological skill treatment. In L. L'Abate & M. Milan (Eds.), *Handbook of social skills training and research* (pp. 284–302). New York: Wiley.

Goldstein, A. P., & Glick, B. (1987). *Aggression replacement training. A comprehensive intervention for aggressive youth.* Champaign, IL: Research Press.

Goldstein, A. P., Heller, K. H., & Sechrest, L. B. (1966). *Psychotherapy and the psychology of behavior change.* New York: Wiley.

Goldstein, A. P., & Huff, C. R. (Eds.). (1993). *The gang intervention handbook.* Champaign, IL: Research Press.

Goldstein, A. P., & Kanfer, F. H. (Eds.). (1979). *Maximizing treatment gains, transfer enhancement in psychotherapy.* New York: Academic Press.

Goldstein, A. P., Keller, H., & Erne, D. (1985). *Changing the abusive parent.* Champaign, IL: Research Press.

Goldstein, A. P., & Michaels, G. Y. (1985). *Empathy: Development, training and consequences.* Hillsdale, NJ: Erlbaum.

Goldstein, A. P., Monti, P. J., Sardino, T. J., & Green, D. J. (1979). *Police crises intervention.* New York: Pergamon Press.

Goldstein, A. P., Reagles, K. W., & Amann, L. L. (1990). *Refusal skills. Preventing drug use in adolescents.* Champaign, IL: Research Press.

Goldstein, A. P., Sprafkin, R. P., & Gershaw, N. J. (1976). *Skill training for community living: Applying structured learning therapy.* New York: Pergamon Press.

Goldstein, K. (1939). *The organism: A holistic approach derived from pathological data in man.* New York: American Book.

Goncalves, O. F. (1995). Cognitive narrative psychotherapy: The humanistic construction of alternative meanings. In M. J. Mahoney (Ed.), *Cognitive and constructive psychotherapies: Theory, research and practice* (pp. 139–162). New York: Springer.

Graham, J. A., Argyle, M., & Furnham, A. (1980). The goal structure of situations. *European Journal of Social Psychology, 10,* 345–366.

Greenberg, J. R., & Mitchell, S. A. (1983). *Object relations in psychoanalytic theory.* Cambridge, MA: Harvard University Press.

Greenberg, L. S., Rice, L. N., & Elliott, R. (1993). *Facilitating emotional change: The moment-by-moment process.* New York: Guilford Press.

Greenberg, L. S., & Safran, J. D. (1987). *Emotion in psychotherapy: Affect, cognition, and the process of change.* New York: Guilford Press.

Greenberg, L. S., & Safran, J. D. (1989). Emotion in psychotherapy. *American Psychologist, 44,* 19–29.

Greenson, R. R. (1965). The working alliance and the transference neurosis. *Psychoanalytic Quarterly, 34,* 155–181.

Greenson, R. R. (1967). *The technique and practice of psychoanalysis* (Vol. 1). New York: International Universities Press.

Greenspan, S. I. (1989). *The development of the ego. Implications for personality theory, psychopathology, and the psychotherapeutic process.* Madison, CT: International Universities Press.

Grotstein, J. S. (1996). A rich tapestry of psychoanalytic sources. A review of the fundamentals of psychoanalytic technique by R. H. Etchegoyen. *Contemporary Psychology, 41,* 273–274.

Grotstein, J. S., & Rinsley, D. B. (Eds.). (1994). *Fairbairn and the origins of object relations.* New York: Guilford.

Grünbaum, A. (1984). *The foundations of psychoanalysis: A philosophical critique.* Berkeley: University of California Press.

Guerney, B. G., Jr. (1977). *Relationship enhancement.* San Francisco: Jossey-Bass.

Guerney, B. G., Jr. (1984). Relationship enhancement therapy and training. In D. Larson (Ed.), *Teaching psychological skills* (pp. 171–206). Monterey, CA: Brooks/Cole.

Guerney, B. G., Jr., Brock, G., & Coufal, J. (1986). Integrating marital therapy and enrichment: The relationship enhancement approach. In N. S. Jacobson

& A. S. Gurman (Eds.), *Clinical handbook of marital therapy* (pp. 151–172). New York: Guilford.

Guerney, B. G., Jr., Vogelsong, E., & Coufal, J. (1983). Relationship enhancement versus traditional treatment: Follow-up and booster effects. In D. H. Olson & B. C. Miller (Eds.), *Family studies review yearbook* (Vol. I, pp. 738–756). Beverly Hills, CA: Sage.

Guerney, L. F. (1984). Play therapy in counseling settings. In T. Yawkey, & R. Pellegrini (Eds.), *Child's play: Developmental and applied* (pp. 290–316). Hillsdale, NJ: Erlbaum.

Guerney, L., & Guerney, B. G., Jr. (1985). The relationship enhancement family of family therapies. In L. L'Abate & M. A. Milan (Eds.), *Handbook of social skills training and research* (pp. 506–524). New York: Wiley.

Guidano, V. F. (1984). A constructivist outline of cognition processes. In M. A. Reda & M. J. Mahoney (Eds.), *Cognitive psychotherapies: Recent developments in theory, research and practice* (pp. 31–45). Cambridge, MA: Ballinger.

Guidano, V. F. (1987). *Complexity of the self.* New York: Guilford.

Guidano, V. F. (1988). A systems, process-oriented approach to cognitive therapy. In K. S. Dobson (Ed.), *Handbook of cognitive-behavioral therapies* (pp. 307–356). New York: Guilford.

Guidano, V. F. (1991). *The self as process.* New York: Guilford.

Guidano, V. F., & Liotti, G. (1983). *Cognitive processes and emotional disorders: A structural approach to psychotherapy.* New York: Guilford.

Guidano, V. F., & Liotti, G. (1985). A constructivist foundation for cognitive therapy. In M. J. Mahoney & A. Freeman (Eds.), *Cognition and psychotherapy* (pp. 101–142). New York: Plenum.

Guntrip, H. (1961). *Personality structure and human interaction: The developing synthesis of psychodynamic theory.* New York: International Universities Press.

Guntrip, P. (1969). *Schizoid phenomena, object relations and the self.* New York: International Universities Press.

Haaga, D. A. F., & Davison, G. C. (1991). Cognitive change methods. In F. H. Kanfer & A. P. Goldstein (Eds.), *Helping people change: A textbook of methods* (4th ed., pp. 248–304). New York: Pergamon Press.

Hallam, R. S. (1987). Prospects for theoretical progress in behavior therapy. In H. J. Eysenck & I. Martin (Eds.), *Theoretical progress in behavior therapy* (pp. 315–329). New York: Plenum.

Hall, N. R. S., & Kvarnes, R. (1991). Behavioral interventions and disease, possible mechanisms. In J. G. Carlson & A. R. Seifert (Eds.), *International perspectives on self-regulation and health* (pp. 183–195). New York: Plenum.

Harter, S. L. (1995). Clinical mythology and borderline processes. In R. A. Neimeyer & M. J. Mahoney (Eds.), *Constructivism in psychotherapy* (pp. 371–383). Washington, DC: American Psychological Association.

Hartmann, H. (1958). *Ego psychology and the problem of adaptation.* New York: International Universities Press.

Hartmann, H., Kris, E., & Lowenstein, R. M. (1946). Comments on the formation of psychic structure. *The Psychoanalytic Study of the Child, 2,* 11–38.

Hartmann, H., & Lowenstein, R. M. (1962). Notes on the superego. *The Psychoanalytic Study of the Child, 17,* 42–81.

Havik, D. E., & Vandenbos, G. R. (1996). Limitations of manualized psychotherapy for everyday clinical practice. *Clinical Psychology: Science and Practice, 3,* 264–267.

Hayek, F. A. (1952). *The sensory order.* Chicago: University of Chicago Press.

Haynes, S. N. (1992). *Models of causality in psychopathology. Toward dynamic, synthetic and nonlinear models of behavior disorder.* New York: MacMillan.

Hebb, D. O. (1949). *The organization of behavior.* New York: Wiley.

Heidessen, M. (1962). *Being and time* (J. Macquarrie & E. S. Robinson, Trans.). New York: Harper & Row. (Original work published 1949)

Hersen, M., & Last, C. G. (1985). *Behavior therapy casebook.* New York: Springer.

Hess, W. R. (1957). *Functional organization of the diencephelon.* New York: Grune and Stratton.

Hilgard, E. R. (1948). *Theories of learning.* New York: Appleton-Century-Crofts.

Hillenberg, B., & Collins, F. (1982). A procedural analysis and review of relaxation training research. *Behavior Research and Therapy, 20,* 251–260.

Hoffman, I. Z. (1983). The patient as interpreter of the analyst's experience. *Contemporary Psychoanalysis, 19,* 389–422.

Hollin, C. R., & Trower, P. (Eds.). (1986). *Handbook of social skills training. Vol 2. Clinical applications and new directions.* New York: Pergamon Press.

Hollon, S. D., & Beck, A. T. (1994). Cognitive and cognitive behavioral therapies. In A. E. Bergin & S. L. Garfield (Eds.), *Handbook of psychotherapy and behavior change* (4th ed., pp. 428–466). New York: Wiley.

Holt, R. R. (1989). *Freud reappraised. A fresh look at psychoanalytic theory.* New York: Guilford.

Holyoak, K. J., & Spellman, B. A. (1993). Thinking. *Annual Review of Psychology, 44,* 265–315.

Horney, K. (1939). *New ways in psychoanalysis.* New York: Norton.

Horowitz, M. J. (1988). *Introduction to psychodynamics: A new synthesis.* New York: Basic Books.

Horowitz, M. J. (1991). New theory for psychotherapy integration. *Journal of psychotherapy integration, 1,* 85–102.

Horton, D. L., & Mills, C. B. (1984). Human learning and memory. *Annual Review of Psychology, 35,* 361–394.

Hoyle, R. H. (Ed.) (1997). *Statistical strategies for small sample research.* Thousand Oaks, CA: Sage

Hussal, E. (1977). *Phenomenological psychology* (J. Scanlon, Trans.). The Hague: Nijhoff. (Originally published 1925)

Izard, C. E. (1991) *The Psychology of Emotions.* NY: Plenum

Jackson, H. (Ed.). (1994). *Using self-psychology in psychotherapy.* Northvale, NJ: Aronson.

James, M. (1995). Transactional analysis. In A. S. Gorman & S. B. Messer (Eds.) *Essential Psychotherapies: Theory and Practice.* (pp. 304–332). NY: Guilford Press.

Jantsch, E. (1980). *The self-organizing universe.* Oxford: Pergamon Press.

Jensen, J. P., Bergin, A. E., & Greaves, D. W. (1990). The meaning of eclecticism: New survey and analysis of components. *Professional Psychology: Research and Practice, 21,* 124–130.

Jessor, R. (1984). Adolescent development and behavior health. In J. D. Matarozzo, S. M. Weiss, J. A. Herd, N. E. Miller, & S. M. Weiss (Eds.), *Behavioral health. A handbook for health enhancement and disease prevention* (pp. 69–90). New York: Wiley.

Johnson, M. K., & Hasher, L. (1987). Human learning and memory. *Annual Review of Psychology, 38,* 631–668.

Johnston, M., Weinman, J., & Marteau, T. M. (1991). Health psychology in hospital settings. In A. A. Kaptein, H. M. van der Ploeg, B. Garssen, P. J. G. Schreurs, & R. Beunderman (Eds.), *Behavioural medicine. Psychological treatment of somatic disorders* (pp. 15–32). New York: Wiley.

Jones, E. (1953, 1955, 1957). *The life and work of Sigmund Freud* (Vols. 1–3). New York: Basic Books.

Jones, H. S. (1956). The application of conditioning and learning techniques to the treatment of a psychiatric patient. *Journal of Abnormal and Social Psychology, 52,* 414–420.

Kagan, J. (1989). Temperamental contributions to social behavior. *American Psychologist, 44,* 668–674.

Kamin, L. J. (1969). Selective association and conditioning. In N. J. MacKintosh & W. K. Honig (Eds.), *Fundamental issues in associative learning* (pp. 42–64). Halifax, NS: Dalhousie University Press.

Kanfer, F. H. (1968). Verbal conditioning: A review of its current status. In T. R. Dixon & D. L. Horton (Eds.), *Verbal behavior and general behavior theory* (pp. 245–290). Englewood Cliffs, NJ: Prentice-Hall.

Kanfer, F. H. (1971). The maintenance of behavior by self-generated stimuli and reinforcement. In A. Jacob & L. B. Saobs (Eds.), *The psychology of private events* (pp. 39–57). San Diego, CA: Academic Press.

Kanfer, F. H. (1977). The many faces of self-control, or behavior modification changes its focus. In R. B. Stuart (Ed.), *Behavioral self-management* (pp. 1–48). New York: Brunner/Mazel.

Kanfer, F. H., & Gaelick-Buys, L. (1991). Self-management methods. In F. H. Kanfer & A. P. Goldstein (Eds.), *Helping people change* (4th ed., pp. 305–360). New York: Pergamon Press.

Kanfer, F. H., & Goldstein, A. P. (Eds.). (1975). *Helping people change. A textbook of methods.* New York: Pergamon Press.

Kanfer, F. H., & Goldstein, A. P. (Eds.). (1986). *Helping people change: A textbook of methods.* (rev. 3rd ed.) NY: Pergamon Press.

Kanfer, F. H., & Goldstein, A. P. (Eds.). (1991). *Helping people change. A textbook of methods* (4th ed.). New York: Pergamon Press.

Kanfer, F. H., & Grimm, L. G. (1977). Behavioral analysis: Selecting target behaviors in the interview. *Behavior Modification, 1,* 7–28.

Kanfer, F. H. & Grimm, L. G. (1980). Managing clinical change: A process model of therapy. *Behavior Therapy, 4,* 419–444.

Kanfer, F. H., & Karoly, P. (1972). Self-control: A behavioristic excursion into the lion's den. *Behavior Therapy, 3,* 348–416.

Kanfer, F. H., & Phillips, J. S. (1970). *Learning foundations of behavior therapy.* New York: Wiley.

Kanfer, F. H., & Schefft, B. K. (1988). *Guiding the process of therapeutic change.* Champaign, IL: Research Press.

Kantor, J. R. (1941). Current trends in psychological theory. *Psychological Bulletin, 38,* 29–65.

Kaptein, A. A., van der Ploeg, H. M., Garssen, B., Schreurs, P. J. G., & Beunderman, R. (Eds.). (1990). *Behavioral medicine: Behavioral treatment of somatic disorders.* New York: Wiley.

Karasu, T. B. (1986). The specificity versus non-specificity dilemma: Toward identifying therapeutic change agents. *American Journal of Psychiatry, 143,* 687–695.

Karoly, P. (1991). Self-management in health-care and illness prevention. In C. R. Snyder & D. R. Forsyth (Eds.), *Handbook of social and clinical psychology: The health perspective* (pp. 579–606). New York: Pergamon Press.

Karoly, P. (1993). Self-regulatory mechanisms. In L. W. Porter & M. R. Rosensweig (Eds.), *Annual review of psychology* (Vol. 44, pp. 23–51). Palo Alto, CA: Annual Reviews, Inc.

Karoly, P. (1995). Self-control theory. In W. O'Donohue & L. Krasner (Eds.), *Theories of behavior therapy: Exploring behavior change* (pp. 259–286). Washington, DC: American Psychological Association.

Katon, W., & Dengerink, H. A. (1983). Somatization in primary health care. In J. E. Carr & H. A. Dengerink (Eds.), *Behavioral science in the practice of medicine* (pp. 145–132). New York: Elsevier Biomedical.

Kazdin, A. E. (1978a). *History of behavior modification: Experimental foundations of contemporary research.* Baltimore: University Park Press.

Kazdin, A. E. (1978b). Behavior therapy: Evolution and expansion. *The Counseling Psychologist, 7,* 34–37.

Kazdin, A. E. (1989). *Behavior modification in applied settings* (4th ed.). Pacific Grove, CA: Brooks/Cole.

Kazdin, A. E. (1996). Combined and multimodal treatments in child and adolescent psychotherapy: Issues, challenges, and research directions. *Clinical Psychology: Science and Practice, 3,* 69–100.

Kelley, M. J. (1987). Hormones and clinical anxiety. An imbalanced neuro-modulation of attention. In H. J. Eysenck & I. Martin (Eds.), *Theoretical foundations of behavior therapy* (pp. 403–432). New York: Plenum.

Kelly, G. A. (1955). *The psychology of personal constructs* (Vols. 1–2). New York: Norton.

Kelly, G. A. (1969). *Clinical psychology and personality: The selected papers of George Kelly* (B. Maher, Ed.). New York: Wiley.

Kelso, J. A. S. (1995). *Dynamic patterns: The self-organization of brain and behavior.* Cambridge, MA: MIT Press.

Kendall, P. C., & Bacon, S. F. (1988). Cognitive behavior therapy. In D. B. Fishman, F. Rotgers, & C. M. Franks (Eds.), *Paradigms in behavior therapy: Present and promise* (pp. 141–167). New York: Springer.

Kendall, P. C., & Bemis, K. M. (1983). Thought and action in psychotherapy: The cognitive-behavioral approaches. In M. Hersen, A. E. Kazdin, & A. S. Bellack (Eds.), *The clinical psychology handbook* (pp. 565–592). New York: Pergamon Press.

Kendall, P. C., & Hollon, S. D. (1979). *Cognitive-behavioral interventions: Theory, research and procedures.* New York: Academic Press.

Kendall, P. C., & Turk, D. C. (1984). Cognitive-behavioral strategies and health enhancement. In J. D. Matarazzo, S. M. Weiss, J. A. Herd, N. E. Miller, & S. M. Weiss (Eds.), *Behavioral health: A handbook of health enhancement and disease prevention* (pp. 393–405). New York: Wiley.

Kendall, P. C., Vitousek, K. B., & Kane, M. (1991). Thought and action in psychotherapy: Cognitive-behavioral approaches. In M. Hersen, A. E. Kazdin, & A. S. Bellack (Eds.), *The clinical psychology handbook* (2nd ed, pp. 596–626). Elmsford, NY: Pergamon Press.

Kernberg, O. (1982). Self, ego, affects and drives. *Journal of the American Psychoanalytic Association, 30,* 893–917.

Kiesler, D. J. (1988). *Therapeutic metacommunication: Therapist impact disclosure as feedback in psychotherapy.* Palo Alto, CA: Consulting Psychologist Press.

Kiesler, D. J. (1996). *Contemporary interpersonal theory and research. Personality, psychopathology, and psychotherapy.* New York: Wiley.

King, M. E., & Citrenbaum, C. M. (1993). *Existential hypnotherapy.* New York: Guilford.

King, M. E., Golden, C. J., King, M., & Citrenbaum, C. (1989). *The courage to recover.* Littleton, MA: Copley Press.

Klein, M. (1932). *The psychoanalysis of children. The writings of Melanie Klein.* London: Hogarth Press.

Klein, M. H., Dittmann, A. T., Parloff, M. B., & Gill, M. M. (1969). Behavior therapy: Observations and reflections. *Journal of Counseling and Clinical Psychology, 33,* 259–266.

Kluckhohn, C., & Murray, H. A. (1967). *Personality in nature, society and culture* (2nd ed.). New York: Knopf.

Kobasa, S. C. (1982). The hardy personality: Toward a social psychology of stress and health. In G. S. Sanders & J. Suls (Eds.), *Social psychology of health and illness* (pp. 3–32). Hillsdale, NJ: Erlbaum.

Koch, S. (1959). Epilogue. In S. Koch (Ed.), *Psychology: A study of a science* (Vol. III, pp. 729–788). New York: McGraw-Hill.

Koch, S. (1993). "Psychology" or "the psychological studies"? *American Psychologist, 48,* 902–904.

Koestenbaum, P. (1978). *The new image of the person: The theory and practice of clinical philosophy.* Westport, CT: Greenwood Press.

Koestler, A. (1978). *Janus.* New York: Random House.

Kohut, H. (1977). *The restoration of the self.* New York: International Universities Press.

Kohut, H. (1984). *How Does Analysis Cure?* Chicago: University of Chicago Press.

Kohut, H. (1991). *The search for the self. Collected papers of Heinz Kohut.* P. H. Orstein (Ed.). Madison, CT: International Universities Press.

Korb, M. P., Gorrell, J., & Van De Riet, V. (1989). *Gestalt therapy: Practice and theory* (2nd ed.). New York: Pergamon Press.

Kozlowski, L. T. (1989). Reduction of tobacco health hazards in continuing users: Individual behavioral and public health approaches. *Journal of Substance Abuse, 1,* 345–357.

Krasner, L. (1971). Behavior therapy. *Annual Review of Psychology, 22,* 483–532.

Krasner, L. (1988). Paradigm lost: On a historical/sociological/economic perspective. In D. B. Fishman, F. Rotgers, & C. M. Franks (Eds.), *Paradigms in behavior therapy: Present and promise* (pp. 23–44). New York: Springer.

Kris, E. (1951). On preconscious mental processes. In D. Rapaport (Ed.), *Organization and pathology of thought* (pp. 474–493). New York: Columbia University Press.

Kubie, L. S. (1934). Relation of the conditioned reflex to psychoanalytic techniques. *Archives of Neurology and Psychiatry, 32,* 1137–1142.

Kuo, Z. Y. (1967). *The dynamics of behavior development.* New York: Random House.

LaBarba, R. C. (1984). Prenatal and neonatal influences on behavioral health development. In J. D. Matarazzo, S. M. Weiss, J. A. Herd, & N. E. Miller (Eds.), *Behavioral health. A handbook of health enhancement and disease prevention* (pp. 41–55). New York: Wiley.

L'Abate, L., & Milan, M. A. (Eds.). (1985). *Handbook of social skills training and research.* New York: Wiley.

Laing, R. D. (1969). *The divided self.* NY: Pantheon.

Lambert, M. J. (1992). Psychotherapy outcome research: Implications for integrative and eclectic therapists. In J. C. Norcross & M. R. Goldfried (Eds.), *Handbook of psychotherapy integration* (pp. 94–129). New York: Basic Books.

Lambert, M. J., & Bergin, A. E. (1994). The effectiveness of psychotherapy. In A. E. Bergin & S. L. Garfield (Eds.), *Handbook of psychotherapy and behavior change* (4th ed., pp. 143–189). New York: Wiley.

Lanyon, R. I. (1971). Mental health technology. *American Psychologist, 12,* 1071–1076.

Lanyon, R. I., & Broskowski, A. (1969). An engineering model for clinical psychology. *Clinical Psychologist, 22,* 140–141.

Larson, D. (Ed.). (1984). *Teaching psychological skills. Models for giving psychology away.* Monterey, CA: Brooks/Cole.

Lazarus, A. A. (1967). In support of technical eclecticism. *Psychological Reports, 21,* 415–416.

Lazarus, A. A. (1969). Broad-spectrum behavior therapy. *AABT Newsletter, 4,* 5–6.

Lazarus, A. A. (1971). *Behavior therapy and beyond.* New York: McGraw-Hill.

Lazarus, A. A. (1973). Multimodal behavior therapy: Treating the basic ID. *Journal of Nervous and Mental Disease, 156,* 404–411.

Lazarus, A. A. (1976). *Multimodal behavior therapy.* New York: Springer.

Lazarus, A. A. (1981). *The practice of multimodal therapy.* New York: McGraw-Hill.

Lazarus, A. A. (Ed.). (1985). *Casebook of multimodal therapy.* New York: Guilford.

Lazarus, A. A. (1986). Multimodal therapy. In J. C. Norcross (Ed.), *Handbook of eclectic psychotherapy* (pp. 65–93). New York: Brunner/Mazel.

Lazarus, A. A. (1989). *The practice of multimodal therapy.* Baltimore: Johns Hopkins University Press.

Lazarus, A. A. (1990). Multimodal therapy. In J. K. Zeig & W. M. Munion (Eds.), *What is psychotherapy? Contemporary perspectives* (pp. 221–225). San Francisco: Jossey-Bass.

Lazarus, A. A. (1992). Multimodal therapy: Technical electicism with minimal integration. In J. C. Norcross & M. R. Goldfried (Eds.), *Handbook of psychotherapy integration* (pp. 231–263). New York: Basic Books.

Lazarus, A. A. (1995a). Different types of eclecticism and integration: Let's be aware of the dangers. *Journal of Psychotherapy Integration, 5,* 27–40.

Lazarus, A. A. (1995b). Integration and clinical verisimilitude. *Clinical Psychology: Science and Practice, 2,* 399–402.

Lazarus, A. A. (1996). The utility and futility of combining treatments in psychotherapy. *Clinical Psychology: Science and Practice, 3,* 59–68.

Lazarus, A. A., & Davison, G. S. (1971). Clinical innovation in research and practice. In A. E. Bergin & S. L. Garfield (Eds.), *Handbook of psychotherapy and behavior change* (pp. 196–216). New York: Wiley.

Lazarus, R. S. (1966). *Psychological stress and the coping process.* New York: McGraw-Hill.

Lazarus, R. S. (1991). *Emotion and adaptation.* New York: Oxford University Press.

Lazarus, R. S., & Folkman, S. (1984). *Stress, appraisal and coping.* New York: Springer.

Lazarus, R. S., & Launier, R. (1978). Stress-related transactions between person and environment. In L. A. Pervin & M. Lewis (Eds.), *Internal and external determinants of behaviors* (pp. 287–327). New York: Plenum.

Leary, T. (1957). *Interpersonal diagnosis of personality.* New York: Ronald.

Lehman, A. K., & Salovey, P. (1990). An introduction to cognitive-behavior therapy. In R. A. Wells & V. J. Gianatti (Eds.), *Handbook of the brief psychotherapies* (pp. 239–260). New York: Plenum.

Leo, J. (1997). *U. S. News and World Reports, 123,* 2D.

Levine, F. J. (1995). Out from behind the couch: Interviews with leading psychoanalysts. *Contemporary Psychology, 40,* 302–303.

Levis, D. J. (1985). Implosive therapy: A comprehensive extension of conditioning theory of fear/anxiety to psychopathology. In S. Reiss & R. R. Bootzin (Eds.), *Theoretical issues in behavior therapy* (pp. 49–80). Orlando, FL: Academic Press.

Lewin, K. (1931). The conflict between Aristotelean and Galilean models of thought in contemporary psychology. *Journal of General Psychology, 5,* 141–177.

Lewin, K. (1951). *Field theory in social science.* New York: Harper.

Lewin, R. (1992). *Complexity. Life at the edge of chaos.* New York: Macmillan.

Lietaer, G. (1991). *The authenticity of the therapist: Congruence and transparency.* Paper presented at the 2nd International Conference on Client-Centered and Experiential Psychotherapy, Stirling, Scotland.

Locke, E. A. & Latham, G. P. (1990). *A theory of goal setting and task performance.* Englewood Cliffs, NJ: Prentice-Hall

Loewald, H. W. (1960). On the therapeutic action of psychoanalysis. *International Journal of Psychoanalysis, 41,* 16–33.

Lowenstein, R. M. (1953). *Drives, affects and behaviors.* New York: International Universities Press.

Lowenstein, R. (1966). Heinz Hartmann-psychology of the ego. In F. Alexander, S. Eisenstein, & M. Grotjahn (Eds.), *Psychoanalytic pioneers* (pp. 469–483). New York: Basic Books.

Luborsky, L. (1996). *The symptom-context method: Symptoms as opportunities in psychotherapy.* Washington, DC: American Psychological Association.

Luborsky, L., Singer, G., & Luborsky, L. (1975). Comparative studies of psychotherapies. Is it true that everyone has one and that all must have prizes? *Archives of General Psychiatry, 32,* 995–1008.

Luthe, W. (Ed.). (1969). *Autogenic therapy* (Vols. 1–5). New York: Grune and Stratton.

Lyddon, W. J. (1995). Forms and facets of constructivist psychology. In R. A. Neimeyer & M. J. Mahoney (Eds.), *Constructivism in psychotherapy* (pp. 69–92). Washington, DC: American Psychological Association.

MacIntosh, N. J. (1984). *Conditioning and associative learning.* Oxford, England: Clarendon Press.

Macmillan, M. (1991). *Freud evaluated: The completed arc.* Amsterdam: North-Holland.

Mahoney, M. J. (1974). *Cognition and behavior modification.* Cambridge, MA: Ballinger.

Mahoney, M. J. (1977a). Reflections on the cognitive-learning trend in psychotherapy. *American Psychologist, 32,* 5–13.

Mahoney, M. J. (1977b). A critical analysis of rational-emotive theory and therapy. *The Counseling Psychologist, 7,* 44–46.

Mahoney, M. J. (1977c). Personal science. In A. Ellis & R. Grieger (Eds.) *Handbook of rational psychotherapy* (pp. 352–366). NY: Springer

Mahoney, M. J. (1980). Psychotherapy and the structure of personal revolution. In M. H. Mahoney (Ed.), *Psychotherapy process* (pp. 157–180). New York: Plenum.

Mahoney, M. J. (1985). Psychotherapy and human change processes. In M. J. Mahoney & A. Freeman (Eds.), *Cognition and psychotherapy* (pp. 3–48). New York: Plenum.

Mahoney, M. J. (1988). The cognitive sciences and psychotherapy: Patterns in a developing relationship. In K. S. Dobson (Ed.), *Handbook of cognitive-behavioral therapies* (pp. 357–386). New York: Guilford.

Mahoney, M. J. (1990). Developmental cognitive therapy. In J. K. Zeig & W. M. Munion (Eds.), *What is psychotherapy?/Contemporary perspectives* (pp. 164–168). San Francisco: Jossey-Bass.

Mahoney, M. J. (1991). *Human change processes: The scientific foundations of psychotherapy.* New York: Basic Books.

Mahoney, M. J. (1995). Theoretical developments in the cognitive psychotherapies. In M. J. Mahoney (Ed.), *Cognitive and constructive psychotherapies: Theory, research, and practice* (pp. 3–19). New York: Springer.

Mahoney, M. J. (1996). Constructivism and the study of complex self-organization. *Constructive Change, 1,* 3–8.

Mahoney, M. J., & Arnkoff, D. (1978). Cognitive and self-control therapies. In S. Garfield & A. E. Bergin (Eds.), *Handbook of psychotherapy and behavior change* (pp. 689–722). New York: Wiley.

Mahoney, M. J., & Kazdin, A. E. (1979). Cognitive behavior modification: Misconceptions and premature evaluations. *Psychological Bulletin, 86,* 1044–1049.

Mahoney, M. J., Kazdin, A. E., & Lesswing, N. J. (1974). Behavior modification: Delusion or deliverance? In C. M. Franks & G. T. Wilson (Eds.), *Annual review of behavior therapy* (Vol. 2, pp. 11–40). New York: Brunner/Mazel.

Mahoney, M. J., Miller, H. M., & Arciero, G. (1995). Constructive metatheory and the nature of mental representation. In M. J. Mahoney (Ed.), *Cognitive and constructive psychotherapies: Theory, research and practice* (pp. 103–120). New York: Springer.

Mahrer, A. R. (1983). *Experiential psychotherapy: Basic practices.* New York: Brunner/Mazel.

Mahrer, A. R. (1989). *How to do experiential psychotherapy: A manual for practitioners.* Ottawa: University of Ottawa Press.

Markus, H. (1977). Self-schemata and processing information about the self. *Journal of Personality and Social Psychology, 35,* 63–78.

Marlowe, H. J., Jr. (1985). Competence: A social intelligence perspective. In H. J. Marlowe & R. G. Weinberg (Eds.), *Competence development* (pp. 50–82). Springfield, IL: Charles C. Thomas.

Marlowe, H. J., Jr., & Weinberg, R. G. (Eds.). (1985). *Competence development.* Springfield, IL: Charles C. Thomas.

Marshall, W. L. (1985). Aversive conditioning. In A. S. Bellack & M. Hersen (Eds.), *Dictionary of behavior therapy techniques* (pp. 15–21). New York: Pergamon Press.

Marsh, E. J., & Hunsley, J. (1990). Behavioral assessment. A contemporary approach. In A. S. Bellack, M. Hersen, & A. E. Kazdin (Eds.), *International handbook of behavior modification and therapy* (2nd ed., pp. 87–106). New York: Plenum.

Martin, I., & Levey, A. B. (1987). Knowledge, action, and control. In H. J. Eysenck & I. Martin (Eds.), *Theoretical foundations of behavior therapy* (pp. 133–152). New York: Plenum.

Martin, P. R. (Ed.). (1991). *Handbook of behavior therapy and psychological science: An integrative approach.* New York: Pergamon Press.

Mash, E. J., & Terdal, L. G. (1988). *Behavioral assessment of childhood disorders* (2nd ed.). New York: Guilford.

Maslow, A. H. (1954). *Motivation and personality.* New York: Harper & Row.

Maslow, A. H. (1968). *Toward a psychology of being* (2nd ed.). Princeton, NJ: Van Nostrand.

Maslow, A. H. (1970). *Motivation and personality* (rev. ed.). New York: Harper & Row.

Matarazzo, J. D. (1984a). Behavioral health: A 1990 challenge for the health sciences professions. In J. D. Matarazzo, S. M. Weiss, J. A. Herd, N. E. Miller, & S. M. Weiss (Eds.), *Behavioral health. A handbook of health enhancement and disease prevention* (pp. 3–40). New York: Wiley.

Matarazzo, J. D. (1984b). Behavioral immunogens and pathogens in health and illness. In B. L. Hammonds & C. J. Scheires (Eds.), *Psychology and health: The master lecture series* (Vol. 3, pp. 9–43). Washington, DC: American Psychological Association.

Matarazzo, J. D., Weiss, S. M., Herd, J. A., Miller, N. E., & Weiss, S. M. (Eds.). (1984). *Behavioral health.* New York: Wiley.

Maturana, H. R. (1975). The organization of the living: A theory of the living organization. *International Journal of Man-Medicine Studies, 7,* 313–332.

Maultsby, M. C., Jr. (1984). *Rational behavior therapy*. Englewood Cliffs, NJ: Prentice-Hall.

May, R. (Ed.). (1961). *Existential psychology*. New York: Random House.

May, R. (1969). *Love and will*. New York: Dell.

May, R. (1981). *Freedom and destiny*. New York: Norton.

May, R. (1989). *The art of counseling* (rev. ed.). New York: Gardner Press.

May, R., Angel, E., & Ellenberger, M. F. (Eds.). (1958). *Existence: A new dimension in psychiatry and psychology*. New York: Basic Books.

McClelland, D.C. (1961). *The Achieving Society*. Princeton, NJ: Van Nostrand.

McDougall, W. (1933). *The Energies of Men*. NY: Scribners.

McFall, R. M. (1982). A review and reformulation of the concept of social skills. *Behavioral Assessment, 4*, 1–33.

McFall, R. M., Treat, T. A., & Viken, R. J. (1997). Contributions of cognitive theory to new behavioral treatments. *Psychological Science, 8*, 174–180.

McGinnis, E., & Goldstein, A. P. (1990). *Skill training in early childhood*. Champaign, IL: Research Press.

McGuigan, F. S. (1978). *Experimental psychology: A methodological approach*. Englewood Cliffs, NJ: Prentice-Hall.

McLemore, C. W., & Hart, P. P. (1982). Relational psychotherapy: The clinical facilitation of intimacy. In J. C. Anchin & J. D. Kiesler (Eds.), *Handbook of interpersonal psychotherapy* (pp. 227–247). Elmsford, NY: Pergamon Press.

Meehl, P. E. (1997). Credentialed persons, credentialed knowledge. *Clinical Psychology: Science and Practice, 4*, 91–98.

Meichenbaum, D. (1973). Cognitive factors in behavior modification: Modifying what clients say to themselves. In C. M. Franks & G. T. Wilson (Eds.), *Annual review of behavior therapy, theory, and practice* (pp. 416–431). New York: Brunner/Mazel.

Meichenbaum, D. (1974). *Cognitive behavior modification*. Morristown, NJ: General Learning Press.

Meichenbaum, D. (1977). *Cognitive behavioral modification: An integrative approach*. New York: Plenum.

Meichenbaum, D. (1985). *Stress innoculation training*. Boston: Allyn & Bacon.

Meichenbaum, D. (1986). Cognitive behavior modification. In F. H. Kanfer & A. P. Goldstein (Eds.), *Helping people change* (3rd ed., pp. 346–380). New York: Pergamon Press.

Meichenbaum, D. (1995). Changing conceptions of cognitive behavior modification: Retrospect and prospect. In M. J. Mahoney (Ed.), *Cognitive and constructive psychotherapies: Theory, research, and practice* (pp. 20–26). New York: Springer.

Meichenbaum, D., Butler, L., & Gruson, L. (1981). Toward a conceptual model of social competence. In J. D. Wine & M. D. Smye (Eds.), *Social competence* (pp. 37–53). New York: Guilford.

Meichenbaum, D., & Gilmore, J. (1984). The nature of unconscious processes: A cognitive-behavioral perspective. In K. Bowers & D. Meichenbaum (Eds.), *The unconscious reconsidered* (pp. 273–298). New York: Wiley.

Menninger, K. A., Mayman, M., & Pruyser, P. W. (1963). *The vital balance: The life process in mental health and illness.* New York: Viking Press.

Messer, S. (1992). A critical examination of belief structures in integrative and eclectic psychotherapy. In J. C. Norcross & M. R. Goldfried (Eds.), *Handbook of psychotherapy integration* (pp. 130–168). New York: Basic Books.

Messer, S. B., & Winokur, M. (1984). Ways of knowing and visions of reality in psychoanalytic therapy and behavior therapy. In H. Arkowitz & S. B. Messer (Eds.), *Psychoanalytic therapy and behavior therapy: Is integration possible?* (pp. 63–100). New York: Plenum.

Miller, G. A. (1970). Assessment of psychotechnology. *American Psychologist, 25,* 991–1001.

Miller, G. A., Galanter, E., & Pribram, K. H. (1960). *Plans and the structure of behavior.* New York: Holt, Rinehart, and Winston.

Miller, J. G. (1978). *Living systems.* New York: McGraw-Hill.

Miller, N. E. (1983). Behavioral medicine: Symbiosis between laboratory and clinic. *Annual Review of Psychology, 34,* 1–31.

Miller, N. E., & Dollard, J. (1941). *Social learning and imitation.* New Haven, CT: Yale University Press.

Milsum, J. H. (Ed.). (1968). *Positive Feedback* Oxford: Pergamon Press.

Mishne, J. M. (1993). *The evolution and application of clinical theory. Perspectives from four psychologies.* New York: The Free Press.

Mitchell, S. A. (1988). *Relational concepts in psychoanalysis. An integration.* Cambridge, MA: Harvard University Press.

Mitchell, S. A. (1992). True selves, false selves, and the ambiguity of authenticity. In N. J. Skolnick & S. C. Warshaw (Eds.), *Relational perspectives in psychoanalysis* (pp. 1–20). Hillsdale, NJ: The Analytic Press.

Mitchell, S. A. (1994). The origin and nature of the "object" in the theories of Klein and Fairbairn. In J. S. Grotstein & D. B. Rinsley (Eds.), *Fairbairn and the origin of object relations* (pp. 66–87). New York: Guilford.

Modell, A. H. (1985). Object relations theory. In A. Rothstein (Ed.), *Models of the mind: Their relationship to clinical work* (pp. 85–100). New York: International Universities Press.

Modell, A. H. (1990). *Other times, other realities. Toward a theory of psychoanalytic treatment.* Cambridge, MA: Harvard University Press.

Moustakas, C. (1986). Being in, being for, and being with. *The Humanistic Psychologist, 14,* 100–104.

Mowrer, O. H. (1950). *Learning theory and personality dynamics.* New York: Arnold.

Mueser, K. T., & Liberman, R. P. (1995). Behavior therapy in practice. In B. Bon Gar & L. E. Beutler (Eds.), *Comprehensive textbook of psychotherapy. Theory and practice* (pp. 89–110). New York: Oxford University Press.

Murray, H. A. (1938). *Explorations in Personality.* NY: Oxford University Press.

Murray, H. A. (1951). Some basic psychological assumptions and conceptions. *Dialectica, 5,* 266–292.

Murray, H. A. (1954). Toward a classification of interaction. In J. Parsons & E. A. Shils (Eds.), *Toward a general theory of action* (pp. 3–29). Cambridge, MA: Harvard University Press.

Murray, H. A. (1959). Preparations for the scaffold of a comprehensive system. In S. Koch (Ed.), *Psychology: A study of science* (Vol. 3, pp. 7–54). New York: McGraw-Hill.

Murray, H. A., & Kluckhohn, C. (1956). Outline of a conception of personality. In C. Kluckhohn, H. A. Murray, & M. Schneider (Eds.), *Personality in nature, society and culture* (2nd ed., pp. 47–79). Hillsdale, NJ: Erlbaum.

Neimeyer, R. A. (1987). An orientation to personal construct therapy. In R. A. Neimeyer & C. J. Neimeyer (Eds.), *Personal construct therapy casebook* (pp. 3–19). New York: Springer.

Neimeyer, R. A. (1990). Personal construct theory. In J. K. Zeig & W. M. Munion (Eds.), *What is psychotherapy? Contemporary perspectives* (pp. 159–164). San Francisco: Jossey-Bass.

Neimeyer, R. A. (1993a). An appraisal of constructivist psychotherapies. *Journal of Consulting and Clinical Psychology, 61,* 221–234.

Neimeyer, R. A. (1993b). Constructivist psychotherapy. In K. T. Kuehlwein & H. Rosen (Eds.), *Cognitive therapies in action* (pp. 268–300). San Francisco: Jossey-Bass.

Neimeyer, R. A. (1995a). An appraisal of constructivist psychotherapies. In M. J. Mahoney (Ed.), *Cognitive and constructive psychotherapies: Theory, research, and practice* (pp. 163–194). New York: Springer.

Neimeyer, R. A. (1995b). Constructivist psychotherapies: Features, foundations, and future directions. In R. A. Neimeyer & M. J. Mahoney (Eds.), *Constructivism in psychotherapy* (pp. 11–38). Washington, DC: American Psychological Association.

Neimeyer, R. A., & Mahoney, M. J. (Eds.). (1995). *Constructivism in psychotherapy.* Washington, DC: American Psychological Association.

Neisser, U. (1967). *Cognitive psychology.* New York: Appleton-Century Crofts.

Nesselroade, J. R., & Featherman, D. L. (1997). Establishing a reference frame against which to chart age-related changes. In M. A. Harvey (Ed.) *Conceptual and methodological issues in the study of aging and social change.* (pp. 191–205) Thousand Oaks, CA: Sage.

Nesselroade, J. R., & Ford, D. H. (1987). Methodological considerations in modeling living systems. In M. E. Ford & D. H. Ford (Eds.), *Humans as self-constructing living systems. Putting the framework to work* (pp. 47–80). Hillsdale, NJ: Erlbaum.

Nesselroade, J. R., & McArdle, J. (1986). Multivariate causal modeling in alcohol research. *Social Biology, 32,* 272–296.

Nesselroade, J. R. & Molenaar, P. C. M. (in press). Pooling logged covariance structures based on short, multivariate time series for dynamic factor analysis. In R. H. Hoyle (Ed.) *Statistical strategies for small sample research.* Thousand Oaks, CA: Sage.

Nevid, J. S., Lavi, B., & Primavera, L. H. (1986). Cluster analysis training orientations in clinical psychology. *Professional Psychology: Research and Practice, 17,* 367–370.

Newell, K. M. (1991). Motor skill acquisition. *Annual Review of Psychology, 42,* 213–237.

Newman, R. (1993). Debate on guidelines: Quality vs. autonomy. *American Psychological Association Monitor, 24,* 22.

Nichols, C. W. (1991). *Manual: Assessment of care goals.* Palto Alto, CA: Consulting Psychologist Press.

Norcross, J. C. (1990). Eclectic-integrative psychotherapy. In J. K. Zeig & W. M. Munion (Eds.), *What is psychotherapy? Contemporary perspectives* (pp. 218–243). San Francisco: Jossey-Bass.

Norcross, J. C., & Goldfried, M. R. (1992). *Handbook of psychotherapy integration.* New York: Basic Books.

Norcross, J. C., Karg, R. S., & Prochaska, J. O. (1997). Clinical psychologists in the 1990s: Part I. *The Clinical Psychologist, 50,* 4–9.

Norcross, J. C., & Newman, C. F. (1992). Psychotherapy integration: Setting the context. In J. C. Norcross & M. R. Goldfried (Eds.), *Handbook of psychotherapy integration* (pp. 3–45). New York: Basic Books.

Norcross, J. C., Prochaska, J. O., & Gallagher, K. M. (1989). Clinical psychologists in the 1980s: II. Theory, research and practice. *The Clinical Psychologist, 42,* 45–52.

Novaco, R. W. (1995). Clinical problems of anger and its assessment and regulation through a stress coping skills approach. In W. O'Donohue & L. Krasner (Eds.), *Handbook of psychological skills training. Clinical techniques and applications* (pp. 20–35). Boston: Allyn & Bacon.

O'Connor, K. P. (1987). A response process model of behavior. In H. J. Eysenck & I. Martin (Eds.), *Theoretical foundations of behavior therapy* (pp. 353–378). New York: Plenum.

O'Donohue, W., & Krasner, L. (Eds.). (1995a). *Handbook of psychological skills training: Clinical techniques and applications.* Boston: Allyn & Bacon.

O'Donohue, W., & Krasner, L. (1995b). Theories of behavior therapy and scientific progress. In W. O'Donohue & L. Krasner (Eds.), *Theories of behavior therapy. Exploring behavior change* (pp. 695–706). Washington, DC: American Psychological Association.

O'Donohue, W., & Krasner, L. (1995c). *Theories of behavior therapy. Exploring behavior change.* Washington, DC: American Psychological Association.

Ogden, T. H. (1994). The concept of internal object relations. In J. S. Grotstein & D. B. Rinsley (Eds.), *Fairbairn and the origins of object relations* (pp. 88–111). New York: Guilford.

O'Leary, K. D., & Wilson, G. T. (1987). *Behavior therapy: Application and outcome* (2nd ed.). Englewood Cliffs, NJ: Prentice-Hall.

Onken, L. S., & Blaine, J. D. (1997). Behavior therapy development and psychological science: Reinforcing the bond. *Psychological Science, 8,* 143–144.

Orlinsky, D. E., & Howard, K. J. (1986). Process and outcome in psychotherapy. In S. L. Garfield & A. E. Bergin (Eds.), *Handbook of psychotherapy and behavior change* (3rd ed., pp. 311–381). New York: Wiley.

Omer, H., & Alon, N. (1996). *Constructing therapeutic narratives.* Northvale, NJ: Aronson.

Overton, W. F., & Reese, H. W. (1973). Models of development: Methodological implications. In J. R. Nesselroade & H. W. Reese (Eds.), *Life-span developmental psychology: Methodological issues* (pp. 65–86). New York: Academic.

Pattishall, E. G., Jr. (1989). The development of behavioral medicine: Historical models. *Annals of Behavioral Medicine, 11,* 43–48.

Pauli, W. (1994). *Writings on physics and philosophy.* New York: Springer-Verlag.

Pepper, S. (1942). *World hypotheses.* Berkeley, CA: University of California Press.

Pepper, S. C. (1972). Systems philosophy as a world hypothesis. *Philosophy and Phenomenological Research, 32,* 548–553.

Perls, F. (1969). *Gestalt therapy verbatim.* New York: Bantam Books.

Perls, F. (1973). *The Gestalt approach and eyewitness to therapy.* Palo Alto, CA: Science and Behavior Books.

Perls, F., Hefferline, R., & Goodman, P. (1951). *Gestalt therapy.* New York: Julian Press.

Pervin, L. A. (1960). Existentialism, psychology and psychotherapy. *American Psychologist, 15,* 305–309.

Pervin, L. A. (1991). Self-regulation and the problem of volition. In M. L. Maehr & P. R. Pintrich (Eds.), *Advances in motivation and achievement* (Vol. 7, pp. 1–20). Greenwich, CT: JAI.

Petrinovich, L. (1979). Probabilistic functionalism: A conception of research method. *American Psychologist, 34,* 373–390.

Phillips, E. L. (1985). Social skills: History and prospects. In L. L'Abate & M. A. Milan (Eds.), *Handbook of social skills training and research* (pp. 3–21). New York: Wiley.

Piaget, J. (1970). *Psychology and epidemiology: Towards a theory of knowledge.* New York: Viking.

Pierce, T. W. (1995). Skills training in stress management. In W. O'Donohue & L. Krasner (Eds.), *Handbook of psychological skills training: Clinical techniques and applications* (pp. 306–319). Boston: Allyn & Bacon.

Pine, F. (1990). *Drive, ego, object and self. A synthesis for clinical work.* New York: Basic Books.

Plomin, R. (1986). *Genetics, development, and psychology.* Hillsdale, NJ: Lawrence Erlbaum.

Plutchik, R. (1980). Emotion: A Psychoevolutionary synthesis. NY: Harper and Row.

Polster, E., & Polster, M. (1973). *Gestalt theory integrated.* New York: Brunner/Mazel.

Pool, R. (1989). Is it healthy to be chaotic? *Science, 243,* 604–607.

Popper, K. R. (1957). *The poverty of historicism.* Boston: Beacon Press.

Popper, K. R. (1963). *Conjectures and refutations.* London: Routledge and Kegan Paul.

Popper, K. R. (Ed.). (1972). *Objective knowledge: An evolutionary approach.* London: Oxford University Press.

Port, R. F. & van Gelder, T. (Eds.) (1995). *Mind as motion: Elaborations in the dynamics of cognition.* Cambridge, MA: MIT Press

Powers, W. T. (1972) *Behavior: The control of perception.* Chicago: Aldine Publishing Co.

Premack, D. (1965). Reinforcement theory. In D. Levine (Ed.), *Nebraska symposium on motivation* (pp. 123–188). Lincoln: Nebraska University Press.

Pribram, K. H. (1986). The cognitive revolution and mind/brain issues. *American Psychologist, 41*, 507–520.

Prigogine, I., & Stengers, I. (1984). *Order out of chaos.* New York: Bantam Books.

Prochaska, J. O. (1984). *Systems of psychotherapy: A transtheoretical analysis* (2nd ed.). Homewood, IL: Dorsey.

Prochaska, J. O., & DiClemente, C. C. (1986). The transtheoretical approach. In J. C. Norcross (Ed.), *Handbook of eclectic psychotherapy* (pp. 163–200). New York: Brunner/Mazel.

Prochaska, J. O., & DiClemente, C. (1984). *The transtheoretical approach: Crossing the traditional boundaries of therapy.* Homewood, IL: Dow-Jones-Irwin.

Prochaska, J. O., & DiClemente, C. C. (1992). The transtheoretical approach. In J. C. Norcross & M. R. Goldfried (Eds.), *Handbook of psychotherapy integration* (pp. 300–334). New York: Basic Books.

Prochaska, J. O., Rossi, J. S., & Wilcox, N. J. (1991). Change processes and psychotherapy outcome in integrative case research. *Journal of Psychotherapy Integration, 1*, 103–120.

Prokasy, W. F. (1965). Classical eyelid conditioning. Experimental operations, task demands, and response shaping. In W. F. Prokasy (Ed.), *Classical conditioning.* New York: Appleton-Century-Crofts.

Rachlin, H. (1988). Molar behaviorism. In D. B. Fishman, F. Rotgers, & C. M. Franks (Eds.), *Paradigms in behavior therapy. Present and promise* (pp. 77–105). New York: Springer.

Rachman, S. J., & Wilson, G. T. (1971). *The effects of psychological therapy.* Oxford: Pergamon Press.

Rank, O. (1945). *Will therapy and truth and reality.* New York: Alfred Knopf.

Rapaport, D. (1951). *The organization and pathology of thought.* New York: Columbia University Press.

Razran, G. (1939). A quantitative study of meaning by a conditioned salivary technique. *Science, 90*, 89–90.

Reese, H. W., & Overton, W. F. (1970). Models of development and theories of development. In L. R. Goulet & P. B. Baltes (Eds.), *Life span developmental psychology: Research and theory* (pp. 115–145). New York: Academic Press.

Reiss, S., & Bootzin, R. R. (Eds.). (1985). *Theoretical issues in behavior therapy.* Orlando, FL: Academic Press.

Reiss, S., & McNally, R. J. (1985). Expectancy model of fear. In S. Reiss & R. R. Bootzin (Eds.), *Theoretical issues in behavior therapy* (pp. 107–122). Orlando, FL: Academic Press.

Rescorla, R. A., & Wagner, A. R. (1972). A theory of Pavlovian conditioning:

Variations in the effectiveness of reinforcement and nonreinforcement. In A. H. Black & W. F. Prokasy (Eds.), *Classical conditioning II: Current research and theory* (pp. 64–99). New York: Appleton-Century-Crofts.

Rice, L. N., & Greenberg, L. S. (1990). Fundamental dimensions in experiential therapy: New directions in research. In G. Lietaer, J. Rombauts, & R. Van Balen (Eds.), *Client-centered and experiential psychotherapy in the nineties* (pp. 397–414). Leuven, Belgium: Leuven University Press.

Rice, L. N., & Greenberg, L. S. (1992). Humanist approaches to psychotherapy. In D. K. Freedheim (Ed.), *History of psychotherapy: A century of change* (pp. 197–224). Washington, DC: American Psychological Association.

Rimm, D. C., & Cunningham, H. M. (1985). Behavior therapy. In S. J. Lynn & J. P. Garske (Eds.), *Contemporary psychotherapies: Models and methods* (pp. 88–100). Columbus, OH: Charles E. Merrill.

Robbins, M. (1994). A Fairbairnian object relations perspective on self-psychology. In J. S. Grotstein & D. B. Rinsley (Eds.), *Fairbairn and the origins of object relations* (pp. 502–518). New York: Guilford.

Roberts, M. C., Maddux, J. E., & Wright, L. (1984). Developmental perspectives in behavioral health. In J. D. Matarazzo, S. M. Weiss, J. A. Herd, N. E. Miller, & S. M. Weiss (Eds.), *Behavioral health. A handbook of health enhancement and disease prevention* (pp. 56–68). New York: Wiley.

Robertson, R. & Combs, A. (Eds.). (1995). *Chaos theory in psychology and the life sciences.* Mahwah, NJ: Lawrence Erlbaum.

Robins, C. J., & Hayes, A. M. (1995). An appraisal of cognitive therapy. In M. J. Mahoney (Ed.), *Cognitive and constructive psychotherapies: Theory, research, and practice* (pp. 41–66). New York: Springer.

Rodin, J., & Salovey, P. (1989). Health psychology. *Annual Review of Psychology, 40,* 533–579.

Roediger, H. L. III (1980) Memory metaphors in cognitive psychology. *Memory and Cognition, 8,* 231–246.

Rogers, C. R. (1942). *Counseling and psychotherapy.* Boston: Houghton Mifflin.

Rogers, C. (1947). The organization of personality. *American Psychologist, 2,* 358–369.

Rogers, C. R. (1951). *Client-centered therapy.* Boston: Houghton Mifflin.

Rogers, C. R. (1957). The necessary and sufficient conditions of therapeutic personality changes. *Journal of Consulting and Clinical Psychology, 21,* 95–103.

Rogers, C. R. (1958). A process conception of psychotherapy. *American Psychologist, 13,* 142–149.

Rogers, C. R. (1959). A theory of therapy, personality and interpersonal relationships, as developed in the client-centered framework. In S. Koch (Ed.),

Psychology: A study of science; formulations of the person and the social context (pp. 184–256). New York: McGraw-Hill.

Rogers, C. R. (1961). *On becoming a person.* Boston: Houghton Mifflin.

Rogers, C. R. (1980). *A way of being.* Boston: Houghton Mifflin.

Rogers, C. R. (1985). Toward a more human science of the person. *Journal of Humanistic Psychology, 25,* 7–24.

Rogers, C. R. (1993). Client-centered therapy. In I. L. Kintash & A. Wolf (Eds.), *Psychotherapist's casebook* (pp. 197–208). Northvale, NJ: Aronson.

Rogers, C. R., & Dymond, R. F. (Eds.). (1954). *Psychotherapy and personality change.* Chicago: University of Chicago Press.

Rogers, C. R., & Skinner, B. F. (1956). Some issues concerning the control of human behavior. *Science, 124,* 1057–1066.

Rosen, H. (1993). Developing themes in the field of cognitive therapy. In K. T. Kuehlwein & H. Rosen (Eds.), *Cognitive therapies in action: Evolving innovative practice* (pp. 403–434). San Francisco: Jossey-Bass.

Rosenzweig, S. (1936). Some implicit common factors in diverse methods in psychotherapy. *American Journal of Orthopsychiatry, 6,* 412–415.

Ross, E. R., Baker, S. B., & Guerney, B. G., Jr. (1985). Effectiveness of relationship enhancement therapy versus therapist's preferred therapy. *American Journal of Family Therapy, 13,* 11–21.

Rubenstein, B. B. (1967). Explanation and mere description: A metascientific examination of certain aspects of the psychoanalytic theory of motivation. *Psychological Issues, 5* (Monograph No. 18119), 20–77.

Rubenstein, B. B. (1975). On the clinical psychoanalytic theory and its role in the inference and confirmation of particular clinical hypotheses. *Psychoanalysis and Contemporary Science, 4,* 3–57.

Rubenstein, B. B. (1976). On the possibility of a strictly clinical psychoanalytic theory: An essay on the philosophy of psychoanalysis. *Psychological Issues, 9* (Monograph No. 36), 229–364.

Ruitenbeck, H. N. (1962). *Psychoanalytic and existential philosophy.* NY: Dutton.

Safran, J. D. (1984a). Assessing the cognitive-interpersonal cycle. *Cognitive Therapy and Research, 8,* 333–348.

Safran, J. D. (1984b). Some implications of Sullivan's interpersonal theory for cognitive therapy. In M. Reda & M. Mahoney (Eds.), *Cognitive psychotherapies: Recent developments in theory, research, and practice* (pp. 223–250). Cambridge, MA: Ballinger.

Safran, J. D. (1988). *A refinement of cognitive behavioral theory and practice in light of interpersonal theory.* Toronto: Clarke Institute of Psychiatry.

Safran, J. D., & Greenberg, L. S. (1991). *Emotion, psychotherapy and change.* New York: Guilford.

Safran, J. D., & Messer, S. B. (1997). Psychotherapy integration: A postmodern critique. *Clinical Psychology: Science and Practice, 4,* 140–152.

Safran, J. D., & Segal, Z. V. (1990). *Interpersonal process in cognitive therapy.* New York: Basic Books.

Salter, A. (1949). *Conditional reflex therapy.* New York: Creative Age Press.

Sarafino, E. P. (1994). *Health psychology. Biopsychosocial interactions* (2nd ed.). New York: Wiley.

Sarbin, T. R. (1997). On the futility of psychiatric diagnostic manuals (DSMs) and the return of personal agency. *Applied and preventive psychology, 6,* 233–243.

Sartre, J. P. (1947). *Existentialism.* New York: Philosophical Library.

Schaap, C., Bennun, I., Schindler, L., & Hoogduin, K. (1993). *The therapeutic relationship in behavioral psychotherapy.* New York: Wiley.

Scarr, S. (1985). Constructing psychology: Making facts and fables for our times. *American Psychologist, 40,* 499–512.

Scarr, S. (1987). Personality and experience: Individual encounters with the world. In J. Aronoff, A. I. Robin, & R. A. Zucker (Eds.), *The emergence of personality* (pp. 49–78). New York: Springer.

Schact, T. E. (1984). The varieties of integrative experience. In H. Arkowitz & S. B. Messer (Eds.), *Psychoanalytic therapy and behavior therapy: Is integration possible?* (pp. 107–132). New York: Plenum.

Schafer, R. (1976). *A new language for psychoanalysis.* New Haven: Yale University Press.

Scharff, D. E. (1992). *Refinding the object and reclaiming the self.* Northvale, NJ: Aronson.

Scharff, J. S. (1992). *Projective and introjective. Identification and the use of the therapist's self.* Northvale, NJ: Aronson.

Schlundt, D. G., & McFall, R. M. (1985). New directions in the selection of social competence and social skills. In L. L'Abate & M. A. Milan (Eds.), *Handbook of social skills training and research* (pp. 22–49). New York: Wiley.

Schofield, W. (1964). *Psychotherapy, the purchase of friendship.* Englewood Cliffs, NJ: Prentice-Hall.

Schroots, J. J. F. (1988). On growing, formative change, and aging. In J. E. Birren & V. L. Bengston (Eds.), *Emergent theories of aging* (pp. 299–329). New York: Springer.

Schunk, D. H., & Carbonari, J. P. (1984). Self-efficacy models. In J. D. Matarazzo, S. M. Weiss, J. A. Herd, N. E. Miller, & S. M. Weiss (Eds.), *Behavioral health. A handbook of health enhancement and disease prevention* (pp. 230–247). New York: Wiley.

Schwartz, G. E. (1984). Biofeedback as a paradigm for health enhancement and disease prevention: A systems perspective. In J. D. Matarazzo, S. M. Weiss, J. A. Herd, N. E. Miller, & S. M. Weiss (Eds.), *Behavioral health. A handbook of health enhancement and disease prevention* (pp. 308–325). New York: Wiley.

Schwartz, G. E. (1988). From behavior therapy to cognitive behavior therapy to systems therapy: Toward an integrative health science. In D. B. Fishman, F. Rotgers, & C. M. Franks (Eds.), *Paradigms in behavior therapy: Present and promise* (pp. 294–322). New York: Springer.

Schwartz, G. E. (1991). The data are always friendly: A systems approach to psychotherapy integration. *Journal of Psychotherapy Integration, 1,* 55–69.

Schwartz, M. S., & Associates (1995). *Biofeedback. A practitioner's guide* (2nd ed.). New York: Guilford.

Sears, R. R. (1944). Experimental analysis of psychoanalytic phenomena. In J. McV. Hunt (Ed.), *Personality and the behavior disorders* (pp. 306–332). New York: Ronald Press.

Segal, Z. V., & Shaw, B. F. (1986). Cognition in depression: A reappraisal of Coyne and Gotlib's critique. *Cognitive Therapy and Research, 10,* 671–693.

Selye, H. (1976). *The stress of life* (rev. ed.). New York: McGraw-Hill.

Shafer, R. (1981). Narration in the psychoanalytic dialogue. In W. J. Mitchel (Ed.), *On narrative* (pp. 212–253). Chicago: University of Chicago Press.

Shaffer, J. B. P. (1978). *Humanistic psychology.* Englewood Cliffs, NJ: Prentice-Hall.

Shanon, B. (1987). On the place of representation in cognition. In D. N. Perkins, J. Lockhead, & J. Bishop (Eds.), *Thinking: The second international conference* (pp. 33–49). Hillsdale, NJ: Erlbaum.

Shapiro, D. A. (1996). "Validated" treatments and evidence-based psychological services. *Clinical Psychology: Science and Practice, 3,* 256–259.

Shapiro, M. B. (1964). Behavior therapy. In *Proceedings of a conference: Principles of treatments of psychosomatic disorders* (pp. 47–56). London: Pergamon Press.

Shlien, J. M., & Levant, R. F. (1984). Introduction. In R. F. Levant & J. M. Shlien (Eds.), *Client-centered therapy and the person-centered approach: New directions in theory, research and practice* (pp. 1–16). New York: Praeger.

Shoben, E. J. (1949). Psychotherapy as a problem in learning theory. *Psychological Bulletin, 46,* 366–392.

Simkin, J. S., Simkin, A. N., Brien, L., & Sheldon, C. (1993). Gestalt therapy. In I. L. Kutash & A. Wolf (Eds.), *Psychotherapist's casebook* (pp. 209–221). Northvale, NJ: Aronson.

Simon, H. A. (1992). What is an "explanation" of behavior? *Psychological Science, 3,* 150–161.

Simons, R. C. (1990). Our analytic heritage: Ideals and idealizations. *Journal of the American Psychoanalytic Association, 38,* 5–38.

Skinner, B. F. (1981). Selection by consequences. *Science, 213,* 501–504.

Skolnick, N. J., & Warshaw, S. C. (Eds.). (1992). *Relational perspectives in psychoanalysis.* Hillsdale, NJ: The Analytic Press.

Slife, B. B., & Williams, R. N. (1997). Toward a theoretical psychology. *American Psychologist, 52,* 117–129.

Smith, D. (1982). Trends in counseling and psychology. *American Psychologist, 37,* 802–809.

Smith, L. B., & Thelen, E. (Eds.). (1993). *A dynamic systems approach to development: Applications.* Cambridge, MA: MIT Press.

Smolin, L. (1997). *The life of the cosmos.* New York: Oxford University Press.

Snyder, C. R. (1996). Construing more workable realities and revising our personal stories. *Journal of Contemporary Psychology, 41,* 658–659.

Snyder, C. R., & Forsyth, D. R. (Eds.). (1991). *Handbook of social and clinical psychology: The health perspective.* New York: Pergamon Press.

Sorenson, R. C., Gorsuch, R. L., & Mintz, J. (1985). Moving targets: Patients' changing complaints during psychotherapy. *Journal of Consulting and Clinical Psychology, 53,* 49–54.

Spence, D. (1984). *Narrative truth and historical truth: Meaning and interpretation in psychoanalysis.* New York: Norton.

Spence, S., & Shepherd, G. (Eds.). (1983). *Developments in social skills training.* New York: Academic Press.

Spitzer, R. L. (1997). *Clinical Psychology: Science and Practice, 4,* 259–291

Spivak, G., & Shure, M. B. (1974). *Social adjustment of young children. A cognitive approach to solving real-life problems.* San Francisco: Jossey-Bass.

Sprafkin, R. P., Gershaw, N. J., & Goldstein, A. P. (1993). *Social skills for mental health.* Boston: Allyn & Bacon.

Squire, L. R., Knowlton, B., & Musen, G. (1993). The structure of organization of memory. *Annual Review of Psychology, 44,* 453–495.

Staats, A. W. (1991). Unified positivism and unification psychology: Fad or new field. *American Psychologist, 46,* 913–920.

Staw, B. M., Sandelands, L. E., & Dutton, J. E. (1981). Threat-rigidity effects on organizational behavior: A multilevel analysis. *Administrative Science Quarterly, 26,* 501–524.

Steger, J. C. (1983). Biofeedback and psychophysiological disorders. In J. E. Carr & H. A. Dengerink (Eds.), *Behavioral science in the practice of medicine* (pp. 263–282). New York: Elsevier Biomedical.

Stelmach, G. E. & Requin, J. (Eds.) (1980) *Tutorials in Motor Behavior.* Amsterdam: North Holland

Stern, D. (1985). *The interpersonal world of the infant.* New York: Basic Books.

Stolorow, R. D., Atwood, G. E., & Brandchafts, B. (Eds.). (1994). *The intersubjective perspective.* Northvale, NJ: Aronson.

Stone, L. (1984). *Transference and its context.* New York: Aronson.

Strachey, J. (1934). The nature of the therapeutic action of psycho-analysis. *International Journal of Psycho-Analysis, 15,* 127–159. (Reprinted in *International Journal of Psycho-Analysis, 50,* 275–292, 1969)

Strachey, J. (Ed.). (1953–1974). *The standard edition of the complete psychological works of Sigmund Freud.* London: Hogarth Press.

Stricker, G., & Gold, J. R. (Eds.). (1993). *Comprehensive handbook of psychotherapy integration.* New York: Plenum.

Stricker, G., & Gold, J. R. (1996). Psychotherapy integration: An assimilative psychodynamic approach. *Clinical Psychology: Science and Practice, 3,* 47–58.

Strickland, B. R. (1984). Levels of health enhancement: Individual attributes. In J. D. Matarazzo, J. A. Herd, N. E. Miller, & S. M. Weiss (Eds.), *Behavioral health. A handbook of health enhancement and disease prevention* (pp. 101–113). New York: Wiley.

Strupp, H. H. (1982). Foreword. In J. C. Anchin & D. J. Kiesler (Eds.), *Handbook of interpersonal psychotherapy* (pp. ix–xi). New York: Pergamon Press.

Strupp, H. H. (1993). The Vanderbilt Psychotherapy Studies: Synopsis. *Journal of Consulting and Clinical Psychology, 61,* 431–433.

Strupp, H. H. (1995). The psychotherapist's skills revisited. *Clinical Psychology: Science and Practice, 2,* 70–74.

Strupp, H. H., & Binder, J. L. (1984). *Psychotherapy in a new key. A guide to time-limited dynamic psychotherapy.* New York: Basic Books.

Suinn, R. M., & Richardson, F. (1971). Anxiety management training: A non-specific behavior therapy program for anxiety control. *Behavior Therapy, 2,* 498–510.

Sullivan, H. S. (1953a). *The interpersonal theory of psychiatry.* New York: Norton.

Sullivan, H. S. (1953b). *Conceptions of modern psychiatry.* New York: Norton.

Sullivan, H. S. (1954). *The psychiatric interview.* New York: Norton.

Sulloway, F. J. (1979). *Freud, biologist of the mind: Beyond the psychoanalytic legend.* New York: Basic Books.

Suttie, I. D. (1935). *The origins of love and hate.* London: Kegan Paul, Trench, Trubney.

Swenson, C. H. Jr. (1973). *Introduction to interpersonal relations.* Glenview, IL: Scott, Foresman.

Tageson, W. C. (1982). *Humanistic psychology: A synthesis.* Homewood, IL: Dorsey Press.

Thelan, E., & Smith, L. B. (1994). *A dynamic systems approach to the development of cognition and action.* Cambridge, MA: MIT Press.

Thompson, J. B. (Ed.). (1981). *Psychoanalysis and the human sciences.* Cambridge, MA: Cambridge University Press.

Thompson, M. G. (1994). *The truth about Freud's technique. The encounter with the real.* New York: New York University Press.

Thoresen, C. E. (1973). Behavioral humanism. In C. E. Thoreson (Ed.), *Behavior modification in education* (pp. 221–238). Chicago, IL: University of Chicago Press.

Thoresen, C. E. (1984). Overview. In J. D. Matarazzo, J. A. Herd, N. E. Miller, & S. M. Weiss (Eds.), *Behavioral health. A handbook of health enhancement and disease prevention* (pp. 297–307). New York: Wiley.

Timberlake, W. (1995). Reconceptualizing reinforcement: A causal system approach to reinforcement and behavior change. In W. O'Donohue & L. Krasner (Eds.), *Theories of behavior therapy: Exploring behavior change* (pp. 59–96). Washington, DC: American Psychological Association.

Toffler, A. (1984). Foreword. Science and change. In I. Prigogine & I. Stengers (Eds.), *Order out of chaos* (pp. xi–xxvi). New York: Bantam Books.

Tolman, E. C. (1932). *Purposive behavior in animals and men.* New York: Appleton-Century.

Trower, P. (1982). Toward a generative model of social skills: A critique and synthesis. In J. P. Durran & P. M. Monti (Eds.), *Social skills training* (pp. 397–427). New York: Guilford.

Trower, P. (1984). A radical critique and reformulation: From organism to agent. In P. Trower (Ed.), *Radical approaches to social skills training* (pp. 129–141). London: Croon Helen.

Trower, P. (1986). Social skills training and social anxiety. In H. R. Hollin & P. Trower (Eds.), *Handbook of social skills training, Vol. 2. Clinical applications and new directions* (pp. 39–66). New York: Pergamon.

Trower, P. (1995). Adult social skills: State of the art and future directions. In W. O'Donohue & L. Krasner (Eds.), *Handbook of psychological skills training: Clinical techniques and applications* (pp. 54–80). Boston: Allyn and Bacon.

Trower, P., Bryant, B., & Argyle, M. (1978). *Social skills and mental health.* Pittsburgh: University of Pittsburgh Press.

Turk, D. C., & Rudy, T. E. (1995). Strategies and tactics in the treatment of persistent pain patients. In W. O'Donohue & L. Krasner (Eds.), *Handbook of psy-*

chological skills training: Clinical techniques and applications (pp. 339–362). Boston: Allyn and Bacon.

Turkat, I. D., & Feuerstein, M. (1978). Behavior modification and the public misconception. *American Psychologist, 33,* 194.

Turner, S. M., Calhoun, K. S., & Adams, H. E. (Eds.). (1992). *Handbook of clinical behavior therapy* (2nd ed.). New York: Wiley.

Ullmann, L. P., & Krasner, L. (1965). *Case studies in behavior modification.* New York: Holt, Rinehart and Winston.

Upper, D., & Cautela, J. R. (Eds.). (1979). *Covert conditioning.* New York: Pergamon.

Urban, H. B. (1978). The concept of development from a systems perspective. In P. B. Battes (Ed.), *Life-span development and behavior,* Vol. 1, NY: Academic Press.

Urban, H. B. (1981). Improving counseling through research: The need for an engineering as opposed to a scientific strategy. *Children and Youth Services Review, 3,* 373–390.

Urban, H. B. (1987). Dysfunctional systems: Understanding pathology. In M. E. Ford, & D. H. Ford (Eds.), *Humans as self-constructing living systems: Putting the framework to work* (pp. 313–346). Hillsdale, NJ: Erlbaum.

Urban, H. B. (1991). Humanist, phenomenological and existential approaches. In M. Hersen, A. E. Kazdin, & A. S. Ballack (Eds.), *The clinical psychology handbook* (2nd ed., pp. 200–222). New York: Pergamon.

Vahinger, H. (1924). *The philosophy of "as if."* Berlin: Reuther and Reichard.

Vaillant, G. E. (1993). *The wisdom of the ego.* Cambridge, MA: Harvard University Press.

Vallis, T. M. (1991). Theoretical and conceptual bases of cognitive therapy. In T. M. Vallis, J. L. Howes, & P. C. Miller (Eds.), *The challenge of cognitive therapy: Applications to non-traditional populations* (pp. 3–24). New York: Plenum.

Vanaerschot, G. (1990). The process of empathy: Holding and letting go. In G. Lietaer, J. Rombants, & R. Van Balen (Eds.), *Client-centered and experiential psychotherapies in the nineties* (pp. 269–294). Leuven, Belgium: Leuven University Press.

Vandenbos, G. R., Cummings, N. A., & Deleon, P. H. (1992). A century of psychotherapy: Economic and environmental influences. In D. K. Freedheim (Ed.), *History of psychotherapy: A century of change* (pp. 65–102). Washington, DC: American Psychological Association.

Van Dusen, W. (1960). Existential analytic psychotherapy. *American Journal of Psychoanalysis, 20,* 310–322.

Viken, R. J., & McFall, R. M. (1994). Paradox lost: Implications of contemporary reinforcement theory for behavior therapy. *Current Directions in Psychological Science, 3,* 121–125.

Von Bertalanffy, L. (1968). *General Systems Theory.* NY: George Braziller

Von Foerster, H. & Zoff, G. W. (Eds.) (1962). *Principles of Self-Organization.* NY: Pergamon Press.

Von Glaserfeld, E. (1984). An introduction to radical constructivism. In P. Watzlawich (Ed.), *The invented reality* (pp. 18–40). New York: Norton.

Wachtel, E. F., & Wachtel, P. L. (1986). *Family dynamics in individual psychotherapy.* New York: Guilford.

Wachtel, P. L. (1977). *Psychoanalysis and behavior therapy: Toward an integration.* New York: Basic Books.

Wachtel, P. L. (1982). (Ed.). *Resistance.* New York: Plenum.

Wachtel, P. L. (1987). *Action and insight.* New York: Guilford.

Wachtel, P. L. (1993). *Therapeutic communication: Principles and effective practice.* New York: Guilford.

Wachtel, P. L., & McKinney, M. (1992). Cyclical dynamics and integrative psychodynamic therapy. In J. Norcross & M. R. Goldfried (Eds.), *Handbook of integrative psychotherapy* (pp. 335–370). New York: Basic Books.

Walen, S. R., DiGiuseppe, R., & Wessler, R. L. (1980). *A practitioner's guide to rational-emotive therapy.* New York: Oxford University Press.

Wallace, C. J. (1982). The social skills training project of the mental health clinical research center for the study of schizophrenia. In J. P. Curran & P. M. Monti (Eds.), *Social skills training: A practical handbook for assessment and treatment* (pp. 57–89). New York: Guilford.

Wakefield, J. C. (1992a). The concept of mental disorder: On the boundary between psychological facts and social values. *American Psychologist, 47,* 373–388.

Wakefield, J. C. (1992b). Disorder as harmful dysfunction: A conceptional Critique of DSM-III-R's definition of mental disorder, *Psychological Review, 99,* 232–247.

Walen, S. R., DiGiuseppe, R., & Wessler, R. L. (1980). *A practitioner's guide to rational-emotive therapy.* New York: Oxford University Press.

Wallace, C. J. (1982). The social skills training project of the mental health clinical research center for the study of schizophrenia. In J. P. Curran & P. M. Monti (Eds.), *Social skills training: A practical handbook for assessment and treatment* (pp. 57–89). New York: Guilford.

Wallerstein, R. S. (1990). Psychoanalysis: The common ground. *International Journal of Psycho-Analysis, 71,* 3–20.

Wandersman, A., Popper, P. J., & Ricks, D. F. (Eds.). (1976). *Humanism and behaviorism: Dialogue and growth.* Elmsford, NY: Pergamon Press.

Warnock, M. (1970). *Existentialism.* London: Oxford University Press.

Wartofsky, M. W. (1979). *Models: Representation and scientific understanding.* Dordrecht, Holland: D. Reidel Publishing Co.

Waterhouse, G., & Strupp, H. (1984). The patient-therapist relationship: Research from a psychodynamic perspective. *Clinical Psychology Review, 4,* 77–92.

Waters, D. B., & Lawrence, E. C. (1993). *Competency, courage and change. An approach to family therapy.* Dunmore, PA: Norton.

Watzlawick, T. (1984). *The invented reality.* New York: Norton.

Weaver, W. (1948). Science and complexity. *American Scientist, 36,* 536–544.

Weimer, W. B. (1977). *Notes on the methodology of scientific research.* Hillsdale, N.J.: Erlbaum.

Weimer, W. B. (1979). A conceptual framework for cognitive psychology: Motor theories of the mind. In R. Shaw & J. Bransford (Eds.), *Perceiving, acting and knowing* (pp. 267–311). Hillsdale, NJ: Erlbaum.

Weimer, W. B. (1982). Hayek's approach to the problems of complex phenomena: An introduction to the theoretical psychology of the sensory order. In W. B. Weimer & D. S. Palermo (Eds.), *Cognition and the symbolic processes* (Vol. 2, pp. 267–311). Hillsdale, NJ: Erlbaum.

Weinberger, J. (1995) Commonfactors aren't so common: the common factors dilemma. *Clinical Psychology: Science and Practice, 2,* 45–69.

Weinshel, E. M. (1990). How wide is the widening scope of psychoanalysis and how solid is its structural model? Some concerns and observations. *Journal of the American Psychoanalytic Association, 38,* 275–296.

Weiss, J., & Sampson, H. (1986). *The psychoanalytic process. Theory, clinical observations and empirical research.* New York: Guilford.

Weiss, P. A. (1971) The basic concept of hierarchic systems. In P. A. Weiss (Ed.) *Hierarchically Organized Systems in Theory and Practice.* NY: Hafner Publishing Co.

Weiss, S. M. (1992). Behavioral medicine and international health: Opportunity and challenge. In S. Araki (Ed.), *Behavioral medicine: An integrated biobehavioral approach to health and illness* (pp. 3–16). Amsterdam: Elsevier.

Welford, A. T. (1966). The ergonomics approach to social behavior. *Ergonomics, 9,* 357–369.

Welford, A. T. (1980). The concept of skill and its application to social performance. In W. T. Singleton, P. Spurgeon, & R. B. Stammers (Eds.), *The analysis of social skill* (pp. 11–22). London: Plenum.

Wessler, R. A., & Wessler, R. L. (1980). *The principles and practice of rational-emotive therapy.* San Francisco: Jossey-Bass.

Wexler, D. A., & Rice, L. N. (Eds.). (1974). *Innovations in client-centered therapy.* New York: Wiley.

Whitaker, C. A. & Malone, T. P. (1953). *The roots of psychotherapy.* NY: Blakiston

White, P. A. (1990). Ideas about causation in philosophy and psychology. *Psychological Bulletin, 108,* 3–18.

Wicker, A. W. (1979). Ecological Psychology. Some recent and prospective developments. *American Psychologist, 34,* 755–765.

Wiener, N. (1948). Cybernetics: *Control and communication in the animal and the machine.* NY: Wiley.

Wiggins, J. S. (Ed.). (1996). *The five factor model of personality: Theoretical perspectives.* New York: Guilford.

Wilson, G. T. (1980). Toward specifying the "nonspecific" factors in behavior therapy: Social learning analysis. In M. J. Mahoney (Ed.), *Psychotherapy process* (pp. 283–307). New York: Plenum.

Wilson, G. T. (1996). Empirically validated treatments: Reality and resistance. *Clinical Psychology: Science and Practice, 3,* 241–244.

Wilson, F. E., & Evans, I. M. (1983). The reliability of target behavior selection in behavioral assessment. *Behavioral Assessment, 5,* 15–32.

Wilson, G. T., & O'Leary, K. D. (1980). *Principles of behavior therapy.* Englewood Cliffs, NJ: Prentice-Hall.

Winell, M. (1987). Personal goals: The key to self-direction in adulthood. In M. E. Ford & D. H. Ford (Eds.), *Humans as self-constructing living systems: Putting the framework to work* (pp. 261–287). Hillsdale, NJ: Erlbaum.

Winnicott, D. W. (1958). *D. W. Winnicott, collected papers.* London: Tavistock.

Winnicott, D. W. (1965a). *The maturational process and the facilitating environment.* London: Hogarth Press.

Winnicott, D. W. (1965b). *The family and individual development.* London: Tavistock.

Winnicott, D. W. (1971). *Playing and reality.* Middlesex, England: Penguin.

Wolf, E. S. (1990). Foreword. In H. A. Bacal & H. M. Newman (Eds.), *Theories of object relations: Bridges to self-psychology* (pp. ix–xii). New York: Columbia University Press.

Wolpe, J. (1952). Objective psychotherapy of the neuroses. *South African Medical Journal, 26,* 825.

Wolpe, J. (1953). Learning theory and "abnormal fixations." *Psychological Review, 60,* 111.

Wolpe, J. (1958). *Psychotherapy by reciprocal inhibition.* Stanford, CA: Stanford University Press.

Wolpe, J. (1981). Behavior therapy versus psychoanalysis: Therapeutic and social implications. *American Psychologist, 36,* 159–164.

Wolpe, J. (1990). *The practice of behavior therapy* (4th ed.). Elmsford, NY: Pergamon Press.

Wolpe, J. (1995). Reciprocal inhibition: Major agent of behavior change. In W. O'Donohue & L. Krasner (Eds.), *Exploring behavior change* (pp. 23–57). Washington, DC: American Psychological Association.

Wolstein, B. (1992). Some historical aspects of contemporary pluralistic psychoanalysis. In N. J. Skolnick & S. C. Warshaw (Eds.), *Relational perspectives in psychoanalysis* (pp. 313–331). Hillsdale, NJ: The Analytic Press.

Womack, W. M., Vitaliano, P. P., & Maiuro, R. D. (1983). The relation of stress to illness and health. In J. E. Carr & H. A. Dengerink (Eds.), *Behavioral science in the practice of medicine* (pp. 227–248). New York: Elsevier Biomedical.

Woods, A. M., & Birren, J. E. (1984). Late adulthood and aging. In J. D. Matarazzo, S. M. Weiss, J. A. Herd, N. E. Miller, & S. M. Weiss (Eds.), *Behavioral health: A handbook of health enhancement and disease prevention* (pp. 91–100). New York: Wiley.

Yalom, I. (1981). *Existential psychotherapy.* New York: Basic Books.

Yankelovich, D., & Barrett, W. (1970). *Ego and instinct: The psychoanalytic view of human nature—revised.* New York: Random House.

Yates, F. E. (1988). The dynamics of aging and time: How physical action implies social action. In J. E. Birren & V. L. Bengston (Eds.), *Emergent theories of aging* (pp. 90–117). New York: Springer.

Yontef, G. M. (1969). *A review of the practice of Gestalt therapy.* Los Angeles: Trident Books.

Yontef, G. M. (1995). Gestalt therapy. In A. S. Gurman & S. B. Messer (Eds.), *Essential psychotherapies: Theory and practice* (pp. 261–303). New York: Guilford.

Young, H. S. (1977). Counseling strategies with working class adolescents. In J. L. Wolfe & E. Brand (Eds.), *Twenty years of rational therapy* (pp. 187–202). New York: Institute for Rational-Emotive Therapy.

Young, K. (1952). *Personality and problems of adjustment.* New York: Appleton-Century-Crofts.

Zeanah, C. H., Anders, T. F., Seifer, R., & Stern, D. N. (1989). Implications of research on infant development for psychodynamic theory and practice. *Journal of the American Academy of Child and Adolescent Psychiatry, 28,* 657–668.

Zeleny, M. (Ed.). (1981). *Autopoiesis: A theory of living organization.* New York: Elsevier.

Zimring, F. M., & Raskin, N. J. (1992). Carl Rogers and client/person centered therapy. In D. K. Freedheim (Ed.), *History of psychotherapy: A century of change* (pp. 629–656). Washington, DC: American Psychological Association.

Zook, A., & Walton, J. M. (1989). Theoretical orientations and work settings of clinical and counseling psychologists: A current perspective. *Professional Psychology: Research and Practice, 20,* 23–31.

Zukav, G. (1979). *The dancing Wu Li Masters. An overview of the new physics.* New York: Bantam Books.

Author Index

Subject Index

This index is designed to help find information about (1) specific therapy approaches, (2) specific concepts and propositions, and (3) the comparative framework for analyzing psychotherapies and the living systems ideas that underly it.